Encyclopedia of
Latino Popular Culture

Encyclopedia of Latino Popular Culture

Volume II

M–Z

Cordelia Chávez Candelaria
Executive Editor

Arturo J. Aldama
Co-Specialist Editor

Peter J. García
Co-Specialist Editor

Alma Alvarez-Smith
Managing Editor

GREENWOOD PRESS
WESTPORT, CONNECTICUT • LONDON

Library of Congress Cataloging-in-Publication Data

Encyclopedia of Latino popular culture [two volumes] / edited by Cordelia Chávez
    Candelaria, Peter J. García, and Arturo J. Aldama ; Alma Alvarez-Smith, assistant editor.
        p. cm.
    Includes bibliographical references and index.
        ISBN 0–313–32215–5 (set : alk. paper) — ISBN 0–313–33210–X (v. 1 : alk. paper) —
    ISBN 0–313–33211–8 (v. 2 : alk. paper)
        1. Hispanic Americans—Social life and customs—Encyclopedias. 2. Hispanic
    Americans—Intellectual life—Encyclopedias. 3. Hispanic Americans and mass
    media—Encyclopedias. 4. Hispanic American arts—Encyclopedias. 5. Popular
    culture—United States—Encyclopedias. 6. United States—Civilization—Hispanic
    influences—Encyclopedias. 7. United States—Ethnic relations—Encyclopedias. I.
    Candelaria, Cordelia. II. García, Peter J. III. Aldama, Arturo J., 1964–
    E184.S75E59 2004
    305.868'073'03–dc22   2004047454

British Library Cataloguing in Publication Data is available.

Library of Congress Catalog Card Number: 2004047454
ISBN: 0–313-32215–5 (set)
        0-313-33210–X (vol. I)
        0-313-33211–8 (vol. II)

First published in 2004

Greenwood Press, 88 Post Road West, Westport, CT 06881
An imprint of Greenwood Publishing Group, Inc.
www.greenwood.com

Printed in the United States of America

The paper used in this book complies with the
Permanent Paper Standard issued by the National
Information Standards Organization (Z39.48–1984).

10 9 8 7 6 5 4 3 2 1

Advisory Board

Contents

Alphabetical List of Entries

Entries by Subject

Entries of People by Field of Endeavor

Entries of People by Country of Origin or Heritage

Encyclopedia of
Latino Popular Culture

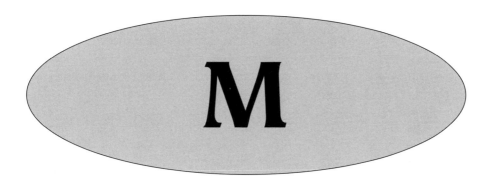

Machito (1912–1984). Afro-Cuban jazz pioneer Frank Grillo, better known as "Machito," made a lasting impact on the growth of Latin music in the United States and Latin America. Born on February 16, 1912, in Tampa, Florida, Machito was raised in Cuba and grew up listening to and playing with Cuba's leading musicians, while his father managed a restaurant. After gaining experience by performing at places such as the Havana Montmartre Club, he returned to the United States in 1937 and became one of the most influential orchestra leaders in the Latin music movement in New York during the 1940s. As he assembled his own band in 1940 called Machito and His Afro-Cubans, he collaborated with fellow Cuban musician Mario *Bauzá to form a musical ensemble in a style reminiscent of the big band period. Machito also performed with other orchestra leaders such as Xavier *Cugat, and he hired drummers such as Tito *Puente to play in his band. Machito and His Afro-Cubans were known for musical compositions such as "Tanga," which became one of Machito's signature pieces and is also considered the first Afro-Cuban jazz song.

Machito's major contribution to Latin music lay in his talent for fusing various musical styles and genres from the United States and Cuba into what later would be termed Afro-Cuban jazz. He took Afro-Cuban dance forms such as the *rumba and guaracha and combined them with big band jazz, bebop, and other dance forms popular at the time in New York City. In 1957, Machito and Bauzá returned to Havana to participate in the Fifty Years of Cuban Music festival. They received a welcoming reception as national icons. Since Machito was familiar with the musical talents of Duke Ellington, Charlie Parker, and Dizzy Gillespie in Spanish Harlem, he became an innovator in mixing both African American and Afro-Cuban musical styles into what later would give rise to the modern genres of *salsa and *Latin jazz. Machito's mixed Cuban heritage led him to experiment with music and culture in a way that transcended conventional boundaries.

In many ways, Machito's band was instrumental in providing younger jazz musicians with a solid background in musical experimentation. Although the popularity of the *mambo craze in dance and music began to wane at the end of the 1950s, Machito continued to tour both the United States and abroad. In 1982 Machito won a Grammy Award for Best Latin Album for *Machito and His Salsa Big Band*. He died on April 15, 1984, in London, England. His selected discography includes *Mucho Macho: Machito and His Afro-Cuban Salseros* (1948), *Machito and His Afro-Cubans* (1948), *Tanga* (1949), *Afro Cubop* (1949), *Afro-Cuban Jazz Suite* (1950), *Latin Soul Plus Jazz* (1957), *Kenya: Afro-Cuban Jazz* (1957), *Machito at the Crescendo (Live)* (1960), *World's Greatest Latin Band* (1960), *Afro-Cuban Jazz Moods* (1975), and *Live at the North Sea* (1982).

Further Reading

Machito: A Latin Jazz Legacy. Videocassette. Produced and directed by Carlos Ortiz. New York: First Run/Icarus Films, 1987.

Yanow, Scott. *Afro-Cuban Jazz*. San Francisco, CA: Miller Freeman, 2000.

Juanita Heredia

Magazines and Broadsides. *See* Newspapers and Periodicals.

Magic Realism. The phrase "magic realism" describes a literary style that is associated with an impressive body of mostly Latin American fiction writers, including several Nobel Prize laureates, whose work gained both critical acclaim and international popularity in the 1960s and later decades of the twentieth century. Identified in Spanish as *lo real marvilloso*, literally translated as "the fantastic or marvelous reality," the style combines naturalistic realism with elements of fantasy and supernatural motifs seen in such successful movie titles as *Kiss of the Spider Woman* (1985) and *Like Water for Chocolate* (1993), for example; and in the writings of Colombian novelist Gabriel García Márquez, recipient of the 1982 Nobel Prize for Literature, and Guatemalan writer of fiction and poetry Miguel Angel Asturias, winner of the Nobel Prize for Literature in 1967. One measure of the continuing pop culture impact in 2004 of the literature of magic realism is Oprah Winfrey's selection of García Márquez's modern classic *One Hundred Years of Solitude* (1967, original title: *Cien años de soledad*) as one of her 2004 book recommendations to her tens of millions of television viewers. Other examples of the style's impact in the United States are apparent in the novels *Bless Me, Última* (1972) and *Caramelo or puro cuento* (Caramel or Pure Fiction, 2003) by Mexican American writers Rudolfo *Anaya and Sandra *Cisneros, respectively, as well as the *Chicano-produced and-directed movie *El

Norte (1983). The distinguishing characteristics of *lo real marvilloso* in literature include a concern with mirroring the dynamic and contradictory fragments of experience as part of one vast present reality—whether material and publicly visible or interior and private as in spaces of the psyche, the spirit, the imaginary, and even of ghosts and the afterlife. Writers of magic realism also seek to capture the common beliefs, grassroots customs, and unique imaginaries of people and cultures in their local settings as their everyday lives are affected by and collide with the policies and politics of governments and the powerful elites that run them. Another distinctive feature of magic realism is its reflexivity; that is, its self-conscious use of language and literary form to call attention to the very act and craft of fiction–making itself.

The 1960s literary explosion of Latin American magic realists came to be called "the Boom" in the media and among literary critics and scholars and eventually led to a worldwide revitalization of interest in the diverse arts and popular cultures of all the Americas. Interestingly, many Boom writers, like García Márquez and Mexican novelist Carlos Fuentes, credit such U.S. American writers as Herman Melville, Walt Whitman, and especially William Faulkner as the primary literary influences for their own innovative combination of romance and realism in the treatment of conquest, colonialism, slavery, gender, and *race and ethnicity in the Americas. Although the fantastic or marvelous qualities of *lo real marvilloso* and the Boom renaissance have been the focus of much of the North American and other English-language discussions of the style, Spanish-language readers and critics often tend to emphasize the way the "magic" elements mask and subvert hard-edged satires that expose the greed, corruption, violence, and oppressive tactics of many government and political institutions. García Márquez's celebrated *One Hundred Years of Solitude* (1967), for example, explores both the oddities and cruelties that resulted from the collusion of corrupt Colombian politicians and military leaders with corrupt American government and multinational corporate officials. Similarly, in his fiction and commentary Ariel Dorfman, Chilean author of more than sixty books including *Hard Rain* (1973, original title: *Moros en la costa*) and *How to Read Donald Duck: Imperialist Ideology in the Disney Comic* (1991, original title: *Para leer al Pato Donald*), uses humor and experimental techniques to subvert the sham of political repression. At the same time Dorfman's self-reflexive narratives expose how art, entertainment, and literature are themselves distorted by the sociopolitical power structures that they parody. Effectively integrating gender, dimensioned portrayals of women, and feminist concerns into their work are such powerful representations as the novels *The House of the Spirits* (1982, original title: *La casa de los espíritus*) by Chile's Isabel Allende; *The Apple in the Dark* (1967, original title: *Amaçã no escuro* [1957]) by Brazil's Clarice Lispector; and *Hasta no verte, Jesús mío* (1961, Here's to You, Jesusa! [2001]) by México's Elena Poniatowska. Their many decades of literary achievements have helped introduce North American and worldwide readers to the amazing stories of the inner lives and public political histories of ordinary people in their respective Latin American homelands. Their celebrated work presents an approach to magic realism that captures the challenges, paradoxes, and chaos ensuing from European colonialism in contact with the multiple realities of the indigenous, now colonized, populations of the Americas, including the forced African immigrants brought to the Western Hemisphere as slaves. Part of the "magic" of the genre's storytelling technique is how the indigenous peoples, cultures, and places of the colonized—that is, the empire talking back—create(d) triumphs out of tribulations. This aspect lies at the heart of Argentina's Manuel Puig's stunning novel about the intertwined psychopolitical impact of political tyranny, homophobia, and pop culture, *El beso de la mujer araña* (1976, *Kiss of the Spider Woman), and México's Carlos Fuentes's now-classic examination of the intersection of machismo and politics in *The Death of Artemio Cruz* (1964, original title: *La muerte de Artemio Cruz* [1962]). Fuentes exploits even further the possibilities of *lo real marvilloso* in many other novels, including one adapted to the motion picture screen, *The Old Gringo* (1985, original title: *Gringo viejo*), that graphically shows the interlocking of the living past in the immediacy of the present Latin American psyche.

Literary scholars trace the historical roots of magic realism to the early work of Argentine Jorge Luis Borges (1899–1986), internationally praised writer, literary scholar, and cultural critic. His first poems and stories, *Ficciones*, published in the late 1930s and 1940s, his experimental detective tales, *Seis problemas para Don Isidro Parodi* (1942, Six Problems for Don Isidro Parody), and his numerous other writings (e.g., *El Aleph* [The Aleph], 1949; *Laberintos* [Labyrinths], 1977; *Biblioteca de Babel* [The Library of Babel], 2000; etc.) initiated a new narrative style that combined the satirical wit of his native Spanish language and Argentine insight with the humor and grotesquerie of twentieth-century pop culture to expose the sociopolitical problems of his country and to attack literary and linguistic conventions as part of the same system of repressive societal traditions. Borges, who since infancy was completely bilingual in Spanish and English, innovated a prose style ("Borgesian") that played with the rules of grammar and the tradition of strict literary form in ways that transformed reading into a game of decoding, much in the experimental style of Edgar Allan Poe's extraordinary tales of ratiocination, forerunner to pop culture's detective fiction. Another precursor to *lo real marvilloso* was the Guatemalan Miguel Angel Asturias (1899–1974), winner of the 1967 Nobel Prize for Literature, for his experiments in poetry and prose fiction. His unflinching depiction of tyranny in the novel *El señor presidente* (1948, The President) helped open the portal to free political expression through literature in his country and throughout Latin America. Similarly influential was Mexican writer Agustín Yáñez for his modernist experimentation with narration in the manner of James Joyce. His exploration of the complex roots of his country's revolution of 1910, the novel *Al filo del agua* (1947, The Edge of the Storm) has become a classic in the merging of reportorial realism with innovative narrative techniques. Also included in this avant-garde trajectory were two other of Borges's Argentine countrymen, Eduardo Mallea and Julio Cortázar. Mallea wrote two important novels of unvarnished social realism, *La bahía de silencio* (1940, The Bay of Silence) and *Todo verdor perecerá* (1941, All Green Shall Perish), among others.

Scholars usually place Cortázar in inventiveness and stylistic originality as among the chief innovators of the new Latin American literature and aesthetic sensibility. Cortázar's much-heralded *Rayuela* (1963, translated internationally with the English title *Hopscotch*) is written in a self-reflexive style of nonsequential interlocking fragments that require active engagement and participation by each reader. This author-reader-text interaction produces a transparent and utterly unique result with each reading, thereby undermining such traditional literary assumptions as story, plot, narration, and even original authorship. In this way Cortázar and *Hopscotch* especially challenged the entire structure of fiction by blurring boundaries of craft and construction.

These and many other bold Latin American literary and artistic forebears helped advance the reading sophistication of audiences, as well as helped to open publishing houses to new and, importantly, to innovative *bilingual* literary forms. Out of this vibrant literary history of vanguard experimentation came the next literary generation and Boom writers mentioned above, as well as many other accomplished writers in Latin America. Writers like the Cuban Alejo Carpentier, the Peruvians Mario Vargas Llosa and José María Arguedas, the Brazilians João Guimarães Rosa and Jorge Amado, and the Mexican Juan Rulfo deepened the texture of magic realism and emphasized the Latin *and* Latina/o literary power of the Western Hemisphere. They joined Cubans Guillermo Cabrera Infante and Reinaldo Arenas, the Puerto Rican Luis Rafael Sánchez, and Chile's José Donoso in exposing the harsh effects of political and military tyranny on individuals and ordinary families through the use of stylistic and linguistic experiments every bit as bold as the social revolutions their writings espoused. Writers from other parts of the globe also are associated with the style as, for instance, the expatriate Filipino writer Ninotchka Rosca whose fiction mingles supernatural elements to represent the collision of disparate cultures and languages in her homeland. The novels of Italo Calvino of Italy and Salman Rushdie of Iran also reflect magic realistic aspects in their portrayals of the psychological and spiritual lives hidden within the ethnic colonial's material history and social reality. Several of 1993 Nobel laureate U.S. American writer Toni Morrison's fictions, particularly her novel *Beloved* (1987), exemplify *lo real marvilloso*. Considered alongside the other Nobel recipients from the Americas, this fact underscores the compelling convergence of popular culture, creative imagination, and high literary tradition that define magic realism.

Further Reading

Aldama, Frederick Luis. *Postethnic Narrative Criticism: Magicorealism in Oscar "Zeta" Acosta, Ana Castillo, Julie Dash, Hanif Kureishi, and Salman Rushdie.* Austin: University of Texas Press, 2003.

Angulo, Maria-Elena. *Magic Realism: Social Context and Discourse.* New York: Garland, 1995.

Brogan, Jacqueline V., and Cordelia Candelaria, eds. *Women Poets of the Americas: Toward a Panamerican Gathering.* Notre Dame, IN: University of Notre Dame Press, 1999.

Durix, Jean-Pierre. *Mimesis, Genres, and Post-Colonial Discourse: Deconstructing Magic Realism.* New York: St. Martin's Press, 1998.

Shapiro, Michael J., and Hayward R. Alker, eds. *Challenging Boundaries: Global Flows, Territorial Identities.* Minneapolis: University of Minnesota Press, 1996.

Walter, Roland. *Magical Realism in Contemporary Chicano Fiction: Ron Arias, The Road to Tamazunchale (1975), Orlando Romero, Nambe-Year One (1976), Miguel Mendez M., The Dream of Santa Maria de las Piedras (1989).* Frankfurt am Main: Vervuert Verlag, 1993.

Williams, Raymond L. *The Twentieth-Century Spanish American Novel.* Austin: University of Texas Press, 2003.

Zamora, Lois Parkinson, and Wendy B. Faris, eds. *Magical Rrealism: Theory, History, Community.* Durham, NC: Duke University Press, 1995.

Cordelia Chávez Candelaria

MALDEF. The Mexican American Legal Defense and Education Fund (MALDEF) is the leading Latino litigation organization, responsible for more than 90 percent of the litigation affecting Mexican Americans in the United States. MALDEF concentrates its efforts in the areas of employment, education, *immigration, political access, language, public resource, and equity issues and never has a shortage of cases pending. Through Constitution-based litigation, the nonprofit organization has established fairer systems to elect officials, hire and promote employees, and educate children.

MALDEF was established in 1968 in San Antonio, Texas, through the efforts of a Texas civil rights attorney named Pete Tijerina. After meeting in New York with Ford Foundation representatives, Tijerina was granted $2.2 million, with the agreement that it would be spent over five years, it would cover a five-state area including Arizona, Texas, California, New Mexico, and Colorado, and $250,000 would be used for scholarships for Chicano law students. Tijerina was appointed as the first executive director, and with the help of Jack Greenberg, director of the National Association for the Advancement of Colored People (NAACP) Legal Defense Fund (LDF), MALDEF was created and modeled after the NAACP LDF. The organization took on the mandate to assist Hispanics in using legal means to secure their rights and to perpetuate assistance in the future. MALDEF focused efforts on providing educational assistance and leadership development for Mexican Americans.

MALDEF's goals are to foster sound public policies, laws, and programs that safeguard the rights of Latinos and expand their opportunities to participate fully in society and to make positive contributions toward its well-being. These goals are achieved through a number of programs and initiatives including increasing the number of Chicano students pursuing law careers by awarding higher education scholarships in law and communications; leadership development programs that train and empower mid-career professionals to take on policymaking roles and serve on boards and commissions at the local, state, and national levels; and parent leadership programs that provide parents with skills and knowledge to remove bureaucratic barriers and advocate for a better education for their children.

Originally created to focus attention on deficits in the southwest, MALDEF has grown and is now headquartered in Los Angeles, California, maintaining regional offices in Atlanta, San Antonio, Chicago, and Washington, D.C. It is guided by a thirty-five-member board of directors made up of community leaders from private and public sectors, government, and law firms.

Further Reading

http://www.maldef.org.

Alma Alvarez-Smith

Malinche, La. *See* La Malinche.

Mambo. The mambo is a musical genre originally from Cuba whose immense popularity in the United States began in the 1950s and led to the development of a unique dance style. The origins of the mambo are difficult to ascertain and highly debated among music researchers and investigators. While there is little doubt of the genre being of Afro-Cuban origin, different sources and individuals trace it to either Bantu or Yoruba groups that were forcibly relocated from Africa to Cuba during the colonial period. The lineage rests largely on etymological evidence that suggests that the word *mambo* was at one point used in reference to the musical practices associated with various Congolese religious cults that had taken up residence in Cuba. While this genealogy is quite possible, the scarce information regarding these Afro-Cuban religious practices in centuries past makes it impossible to determine whether these had specific musical stylistic elements in common with the genre that begins to take shape during the first part of the twentieth century in Cuba.

The first contemporary reference is generally attributed to a **danzón* (country dance) composition titled "Mambo," written in 1939 by cellist Orestes López. López and his brother, bassist/arranger Israel "Cachao"

López, were members of the group Orquesta Arcaño y Sus Maravillas, led by the celebrated flautist Antonio Arcaño. The coda or ending of the composition in question featured repeated melodic and harmonic *ostinatos* (short repeated melodic and rhythmic patterns) that were used as means of cueing solos from the various members of the band, a practice that appears to have become common with subsequent danzón compositions. This innovation, however, was already a feature of some variations of the Cuban *son, most specifically the *son montuno* style. Within the context of the *montuno*, whose accompaniment is also characterized by a variety of rhythmic, melodic, and harmonic ostinatos known as *tumbaos* (Cuban rhythms), the mambo referred to an instrumental passage in which all melodic instruments would play a particular melody or lick in unison. Blind *tres* player, bandleader, and arranger, Arsenio Rodríguez, is largely credited for these innovations. While at times these mambo sections consisted of precomposed musical material, it was also common for a number of performers and bandleaders without formal musical training to make them up on the spot and then quietly sing them to the other band members, just before cueing the start of the section. This latter performance practice technique allowed some notable bandleaders, such as Dámaso *Pérez Prado, to follow successful careers as arrangers and composers. Throughout the 1940s the mambo began to take shape as an independent musical genre, and instrumental mambolike compositions began to appear not only in Cuba but also in México and the United States. From a broad perspective, these early compositions featured instrumental writing with tight counterpoint where trumpet, trombone, and saxophone sections alternated contrasting roles such as playing melodies, providing ostinato accompaniments, or rhythmically and harmonically punctuating the overall musical texture.

The first individual to coin the word *mambo* as a formal genre with which to identify a particular composition was Pérez Prado. Having started out as a movie theater organ player, Prado began his experimentations with mambo as early as 1942 while he was still playing piano for the Orquesta Casino de la Playa. In 1948, seeking more success and recognition than he was getting in Cuba, Prado started his own band and moved to México, where he recorded a number of mambos mainly for RCA in Mexico City. These recordings were meant for the Latin American and U.S. Latino markets, but some of his mambos quickly crossed over and sparked what would become the mambo craze of the 1950s. Among his most celebrated hits were "Mambo No. 5," "Mambo No. 8," "Mambo No. 9," "Mambo No. 10," "Caballo Negro" (Black Horse), "Qué Rico el Mambo" (How Rich Is the Mambo), "María Cristina," "Cerezo rosa" (Cherry Pink and Apple Blossom White), "Skokian," and "Patricia." The "discovery" of Prado by American bandleader Sonny Burke during a trip to México also led to the quick emergence of a number of American groups that imitated Prado's mambo style, and in the opinion of many critics, this led to the quick commercialization of the genre. In fact, to many Americans not previously familiar with the Latin music world in the United States, Pérez Prado's relatively sparse arrangements, with its moderate tempos, saxophone ostinatos, bright staccato (short) punctuation by the brass, and his trademark "grunts" during instrumental breaks, became the characteristics by which mambos would be defined in the commercial arena. At the same time, Prado was an influential figure to a number of musicians that performed in his band throughout the years, most notably among them Beny Moré, Johnny *Pacheco, and Mongo Santamaría.

Pérez Prado was by no means the single force behind the development and dissemination of mambo in the United States. Other big bandleaders were Stan Kenton, Xavier *Cugat, José Curbello, Al Levy (Alfredito), Tito *Puente, Tito *Rodríguez, and *Machito. These last three bandleaders became particularly influential after 1952 when the Palladium Dance Hall adopted an all-mambo policy and featured their three bands almost exclusively. All these bands featured full Afro-Cuban rhythm sections and traditional Cuban structural elements such as the *son montuno*. At the same time, these bandleaders featured stronger jazz influences in their arrangements such as the use of swing and dense harmonic voicings in the brass and woodwinds. The popularity of the Palladium not only with Latinos but also with African American, Jewish, and Italian residents of New York City led to the development of a dance style that was a synthesis of Cuban casino style–dancing—*rumba, the lindy, and the jitterbug—as fast, dynamic, and agile as the music that accompanied it. The popularity of the mambo among New Yorkers peaked in 1954 as venues like the Apollo and the Savoy instituted mambo nights, and smaller local clubs would shut down and reopen as locales featuring Latin music. Nationally, a number of recording artists also jumped on the mambo bandwagon, most notably Nat "King" Cole, Ella Fitzgerald, Earl Bostic, Peggy Lee, Rosemary Clooney, Sophie Tucker, Ruth Brown, and exotica queen Yma Sumac.

In the late 1950s, mambo began to decrease in popularity, something that is often attributed to the advent of the *cha cha cha, a dance genre that had emerged from the Cuba *charanga* bands and whose slower tempos, catchy melodies, and relatively simpler choreography seem to have overshadowed the mambo. Another factor was the rise of rock and roll, which seems to have diverted the attention of the American public away from Latin music. Nevertheless, the mambo as a dance form managed to find a space within the professional ballroom dancing arena. Throughout the 1990s there was a partial revival of the mambo, largely led by the release of three albums under the direction of Cuban-born Mario *Bauzá, former lead trumpeter and brother-in-law to the famed Machito. Despite the success of these recordings and their featuring a virtual who's who of contemporary Latin jazz, Bauzá's sudden death in 1993 seems to have cut this renaissance short. Nevertheless, a number of other artists continue to pay tribute to the mambo from time to time, something that is particularly apparent in some of the recent work of Óscar d'León, of the Orquesta de la Luz, and perhaps most explicitly on Jesús Alemañy's album titled *Cubanismo* (1996).

Further Reading

Roberts, John Storm. *The Latin Tinge: The Impact of Latin Music on the United States*. 2nd ed. New York: Oxford University Press, 1999.

Javier F. León

Mambo Kings. Featuring original music and appearances by famous Latin musicians such as Tito *Puente and Celia *Cruz, this 1992 *film adaptation of Oscar *Hijuelos's Pulitzer Prize–winning novel *Mambo Kings Play Songs of Love* (1989) follows the rise and fall of two brothers, César (Armand Assante) and Nestor (Antonio Banderas) Castillo. Told from a sepia-tinged perspective—the events occurring from 1952 to 1955—it is the impassioned story of two Cuban émigré musicians coming into their own as they climb ladders from small-time Havana nightclubs to New York's grand music halls and a spot on the *I Love Lucy* show with Desi *Arnaz. César's resistance to "selling out"—his stubborn refusal to sign with a ruthless mobster promoter (played by Roscoe Lee Brown)—leads to their eventual demise.

Although director Arne Glimcher does little to present his characters—especially César—as satirical representations of Latino machismo, a theme in which author Hijuelos excels, he does bring to the screen Hijuelos's richly lyrical sense of the *mambo musicians in their struggles with forces of assimilation and a deep sense of loss of homeland, as well as their status as émigrés and parvenus within this story of rags to riches to rags. Mambo, *cha cha cha, and *rumba are the powerful percussive beats played by Puente and Cruz that accompany the emotional roller coaster and final defeat of the musician brothers.

Further Reading

Hijuelos, Oscar. *Mambo Kings Play Songs of Love*. New York: HarperCollins, 2003. http://www.spiritualityhealth.com/newsh/items/moviereview/item_6292.html.

Luis Aldama

Maná. Maná is an award-winning Latin rock/fusion band whose worldwide audience includes fans in the United States, Latin America, Europe, and Japan. Maná consists of four musicians who banded together in Guadalajara, México, in the 1970s. At the time, they performed under the name of Sombrero Verde (Green Hat) and were mainly known for their Spanish interpretations of legendary rock groups such as Led Zeppelin, the Beatles, and the Rolling Stones. Although membership in the band has changed over the years, the current members are Fernando (Fher) Olvera on vocals, Alex González on drums, Sergio Vallín on guitar, and Juan Calleros on bass.

They recorded their first album as Maná in 1987, adopting more Latin rhythms in their musical repertoire. Considered one of Latin rock's most popular bands, Maná has blended rhythms and lyrics from its Mexican roots to express universal concerns such as love, social justice, and the search for freedom. Over time, Maná has moved from a national stage in México to an international one by appealing to younger audiences worldwide. In 1992, Maná began its global odyssey by recording the album *¿Dónde jugarán los niños?* (Where Will the Children Play?) in a studio in Los Angeles. Doing so expanded Maná's public to the United States as well as to the rest of Latin America. In the 1990s, Maná experimented with various musical genres including rock, reggae, and ballads, forging a style of its own. After the release of the album *Sueños líquidos* (Liquid Dreams) in 1997, which won a Grammy Award for Best Latin Rock/Alternative Performance (1998), the band became more attuned to Afro-Cuban rhythms and created a fusion rock-reggae genre for the 1999 *Maná MTV Unplugged* album. This album led to a Latin Grammy Award for Best Pop Band in 2000. In its recent tours of the United States, Maná has had sold-out performances in over thirty cities.

Maná has also collaborated with other noted Latina and Latino musicians. The legendary Carlos *Santana invited the members of this vanguard fusion group to perform for his Grammy Award–winning album *Supernatural* (1999), for which Maná wrote the award-winning song "Corazón espinado" (Pierced Heart). In 2002, Maná reciprocated by inviting Santana and another prominent figure in Latin music, Rubén *Blades, to join the band members in the production of their latest work, *Revolución de amor* (Love Revolution), which garnered two Latin Grammy Awards for Best Rock Album (2003) and Best Engineered album (2003). In 1995, Maná became involved in environmental causes and founded Selva Negra (Black Jungle), a nonprofit organization responsible for protecting land and vegetation along México's Pacific coast. Maná's selected discography includes *Maná* (1987), *¿Dónde jugarán los niños?* (1992), *Falta amor* (1992), *Maná en vivo* (1994), *Cuando los ángeles lloran* (1995), *Sueños liquídos* (1997), *Maná MTV Unplugged* (1999), *Todo Maná* (1999–2000), *Grandes Maná* (2001), and *Revolución de amor* (2002).

Further Reading

Martínez, Rubén. "Corazón del Rocanrol." In his *The Other Side: Notes from the New L.A., Mexico City, and Beyond*. New York: Vintage Press, 1992.

Juanita Heredia

MANA. MANA, a National Latina Organization, was originally founded by Mexican American women in 1974 under the name of the Mexican-

American Women's National Association. Its original purpose was to provide a voice for Mexican American women in all walks of life through empowerment. In 1994, the organization changed its name to better reflect the growing diversity represented in their membership, which now includes Latinas of Mexican, Puerto Rican, Dominican, Cuban, Central American, South American, and Spanish descent.

MANA is a nonprofit advocacy group whose mission is to empower Latinas through leadership development, community service, and advocacy. MANA is a national community of Latinas actively working to create a better quality of life for Hispanics. At the core of MANA's programs—whether they are to develop leadership skills, encourage community activism, or promote sharing culture and heritage—is a belief that through education Latinas can be stronger and more empowered to stand up and be heard. One such program is called AvanZamos, which focuses on leadership development for adult Latinas through national conferences and local workshops. Hermanitas is a program designed to help keep young Latinas in school and focused on attaining higher academic goals. Activities in this program include summer institutes, mentoring programs, and a Girl Scout partnership. Support for these programs comes from members, corporations, foundations, and government grants.

In 1990, MANA established what would become an annual recognition of achievement by Latinas and those who are leaders in their field. The awards are given in seven categories: arts, business, communication, community service, leadership, science, and sports. Among the past recipients of the annual awards are a U.S. surgeon general, a Pulitzer Prize winner, and a bestselling author. Some of the past recipients are Congresswoman Ileana *Ros-Lehtinen (1990), Congresswoman Nydia *Velásquez (1993), Tish Hinojosa (1995), Congresswoman Loretta *Sánchez (1999), Peggy Baca (2000), entrepreneur Linda *Alvarado, and television announcer Elizabeth *Vargas (2001).

MANA has a national office in Washington, D.C., with local chapters and university chapters throughout the United States. It is governed by a fifteen-member board of directors and regularly publishes the *MANA Newsletter* and the *ProActivista Bulletin* with information of importance to Latinas and the Hispanic community.

Further Reading

http://www.hermana.org.

Alma Alvarez-Smith

"Mañanitas, Las." *See* "Las Mañanitas."

'Manitos. The Spanish words for brother, *hermano*, and for sister, *hermana*, are often used to describe native *nuevo mejicanos*, that is, New Mexicans of Mexican origin. The diminutive familiar form of the word is *'manito* (masculine form) and *'manita* (feminine form), and both are commonly used to identify Chicanas and *Chicanos born in New Mexico. A large number of *'manitos* can trace their *family roots to the first Spanish expeditions north from Mexico City and Vera Cruz in the early sixteenth and seventeenth centuries. These explorations established the first European settlements in North America—many of which have been continuously inhabited since their founding—decades before Plymouth Rock. The descendants of Spaniards, American Indians, and their hybrid (i.e., mestizos) thus consider themselves the earliest "Americans" after the indigenous peoples. A minority of *'manitos* describe themselves as "Hispanos" in recognition of their long generational lineage, as well as of the archaic Spanish-language forms still used by many speakers of New Mexican *español*. For these and related reasons, many twenty-first century *'manito/a* individuals, families, and communities in America's *barrios and borderlands assert that "we didn't cross the border, the border crossed us," in reference both to current antiimmigrant scapegoating, to history, and to the signing of the *Treaty of Guadalupe Hidalgo in 1848. The treaty ceded México's vast northern territories to the United States and transformed the nationality of thousands of actually rooted Mexicans in the Southwest.

One of the most well-known, contemporary bestselling Chicano writers, *Rudolfo Anaya, writes of *'manito* culture in New Mexico. Before him, the writings of historian and cultural memoirist Fray Angélico Chávez (1890–1900), of scholar poet Sabine Ulibarrí (1919–   ), some of the work of an English writer associated with Taos, D.H. Lawrence (1885–1930), and the artwork of American painter Georgia O'Keeffe (1887–1986), associated with Abiquiu, also are credited with memorializing aspects of the *'manito* experience and homeland. In the late twentieth century, other noteworthy *'manita/o* New Mexicans include writers Denise *Chávez, Demetria *Martínez, and Nash Candelaria; scholar writers Erlinda González Berry, Cordelia Chávez Candelaria, Enrique Lamadrid, and Arturo Madrid; documentary filmmaker Paul D. *Espinosa; artists Edward González, Pedro Roméro, and others.

Further Reading

Anaya, Rudolfo A., and Simon Ortiz, eds. *A Ceremony of Brotherhood*. Albuquerque, NM: Academia Press, 1981.

González-T., César A., ed. *Rudolfo A. Anaya: Focus on Criticism*. La Jolla, CA: Lalo Press, 1990.

Márquez, Teresa, Director. *100 Years of Literature in New Mexico: A Literary Discussion with Rudolfo Anaya, John Nichols, and Simon Ortiz*. Moderator: Gabriel Meléndez. Albuquerque: Center of Southwest Research, University of New Mexico, 2001. Videorecording.

Ann Aguirre

MAOF. *See* Mexican American Opportunity Foundation.

MAPA. The Mexican American Political Association, also known as MAPA, was established in Fresno, California, in 1960 with the purpose of getting Mexican Americans elected to office and giving the Latino community a political voice. This nonpartisan organization, dedicated to the constitutional and democratic principle of political freedom and representation, continues to work for the social, economic, cultural, and civic betterment of the Latino community. MAPA operates on the firm belief that to move Latino issues to the top of the public policy agenda there must be more Latinos in office. To claim a place in the political arena, Latinos must take a stand on public issues and be heard; this can be done only by penetrating the political system.

The goals and objectives of MAPA are to create political power through the education and participation of the Latino community in the art of politics; to mobilize political power in amending or replacing those laws and regulations that hinder full participation of Latinos in the political process, to enforce those laws that enhance that participation; and to assist the Latino community in all areas of concern, including, but not limited to, *immigration, education, health, housing, *police-community relations, employment opportunities, agriculture, economic development and aid, and nurturing and development of the *family (*la familia*).

The organization strives to achieve these goals and objectives through MAPA's action plan, which includes recruitment of Latino/a candidates, training, fund-raising, lobbying and testifying on legislative issues, monitoring the judicial selection process, supporting qualified Latinos for office, and developing voter registration and education programs for the Latino community. With a state national headquarters office in Los Angeles, MAPA maintains the majority of the organization chapters in the state of California, although new chapters have also emerged in Arizona, Texas, Nevada, and Oklahoma.

Further Reading

http://www.mapa.org.

Alma Alvarez-Smith

Maquiladora. In standard Spanish, *maquiladora* means a certified or bonded assembly plant. In everyday speech, particularly among bilingual Latina and Latino Americans, *maquiladora* is often used to refer to a worker in the plant or factory and is sometimes abbreviated as "*maquila*." *Maquiladoras* are part of the *globalization outsourcing and offshore development of corporations and industries whose home bases are in the United States and other developed nations. Located in the *barrios and borderlands of the United States and elsewhere, *maquiladoras* are important in any consideration of popular culture because of their impact on the people they affect and, by extension, on the surrounding communities. Like other effects of globalization, new Latina/o pop culture forms have been created and existing products and practices altered by the presence of these foreign-based plants capitalizing on the impoverished status and environments of the host countries.

Numerous manufacturing facilities owned and controlled by American and other major powers have been located throughout México, Latin America, and Asia, primarily to take advantage of the cheap labor and other manufacturing costs, which is the principal incentive for outsourcing. Among the business interests with extensive *maquiladora* investments are automotive, clothing, electronic, medical, packaging, and a variety of other manufacturing and assembly industries. Those policymakers who favor this type of outsourcing promote the practice as a way of helping Third World societies through corporate investment and business development. Opponents believe that the practice may have short-term economic benefits but ultimately results in long-term negative impacts such as displaced families, unchecked urban growth, increase in crime, and loss of jobs in the home base country.

Recent examples of the *maquila* impact on society include the movies *Traffic* (2000), *Amores Perros* (2002), and *Real Women Have Curves* (2002). The *maquiladora* outsourcing has led to international distribution of Latina/o art, music, food, and related forms and practices. As well, the harmful effects of *maquiladoras* have led to the formation of new grassroots and community-based groups. Among these are the Puebla Worker Assistance Centre (CAT) in México, the Canadian Maquila Solidarity Network (MSN), and many others.

Further Reading

Pérez Sáinz, Juan Pablo. *From the Finca to the Maquila: Labor and Capitalist Development in Central America.* Boulder, CO: Westview Press, 1999.

Stromberg, Per. *The Mexican Maquila Industry and the Environment: An Overview of the Issues.* Mexico City: Naciones Unidas CEPAL/ECLAC: Sede Subregional de la CEPAL en México, 2002.

Tiano, Susan. *Patriarchy on the Line: Labor, Gender, and Ideology in the Mexican Maquila Industry.* Philadelphia, PA: Temple University Press, 1994.

Cordelia Chávez Candelaria

Mariachi. Mariachi is one of several regional music ensembles of México heard throughout the United States. In the early twentieth century, mariachi ensembles moved from the villages of Jalisco and nearby states to the major cities of Guadalajara and Ciudad de México (Mexico City), and by the middle of the century mariachi was regarded as *the* Mexican music ensemble. In the last quarter of the century, mariachi influence expanded outside Mexican borders, becoming an ensemble of the world and a symbol of mestizo culture. This entry examines the name; history, including the role of women; instrumentation; genres performed and venues; costume and image;

role of professional, university, and other amateur ensembles; and impact of mariachi conferences and festivals, especially in the United States.

The word *mariachi* can refer to the ensemble, a performer within the group (also called *mariachero*), or a musical style, and is even sometimes used as a derogatory appellation. While no one knows for sure the derivation of the term, the two most prominent theories are most likely untrue: based on the French word *mariage* (marriage) or as a corruption of the name of a local Virgin, "María H." The former has been proven false with the finding of a letter from Padre Cosme Santa Anna in 1852 containing the term *mariachi* nearly a decade prior to the French domination of México in the 1860s; the latter appears unlikely, as there is no real proof. More likely is the possibility that the name comes from an indigenous term for the platform used by dancers who were accompanied by mariachis or the tree from which the wood for the platform came—commonly called the *cirimo* tree (*Tilia mexicana*)—or even the name of a very small village (from Spanish census records) now long forgotten.

Likewise the exact date and development of the mariachi ensemble is also uncertain. Mariachi mythology credits two villages in Jalisco as the birthplace(s), Cocula and Tecolotlán, but mariachi is really a "regional" music belonging to the area of Jalisco, Colima, Nayarit, and Michoacán. Early mariachis often called themselves *cuartetos* (quartets) and appended the name of their local village or area, such as the Cuarteto Coculense (Quartet from Cocula), first recorded in 1908. Early instrumentation varied considerably (often depending upon what instruments and performers were available), but two distinct quartets had developed by the late nineteenth century: (1) from Cocula, two violins, a *vihuela*, and a *guitarrón* (*see* Musical Instruments), and (2) from Tecolotlán, harp, two violins, and a *guitarra de golpe* (a small Mexican guitar). Photographs from the early twentieth century show a wide variety of instrumentation including clarinet, flute, and valve trombone.

The Mexican Revolution at the beginning of the twentieth century began a new era of nationalism and indirectly resulted in the movement of mariachi from the rural areas or semirural regions to the cities. In 1920 Mariachi Coculense de Cirilo Marmolejo was brought to Mexico City by Luis *Rodríguez to perform for important politicians, friends of General Álvaro Obregón. Unlike previous groups such as El Cuarteto Coculense de Justo Villa, who played for President Porfirio Díaz (of México) in 1905 and again in 1907, Cirilo and his mariachi remained in Mexico City. They are credited with several "firsts": the first mariachi stage show in Teatro Iris, the first mariachi in a sound film (*Santa*, 1931), and the first to make "electric" recordings. They also played in the Salón Tenampa, the first mariachi bar adjacent to Plaza Garibaldi. Other mariachis were also subsidized by patrons, for example, Mariachi Vargas de Tecalitlán, by the Mexico City Police Department, and Mariachi Tapatío, by Eusebio Acosta Velazco, owner of Autobuses de Occidente.

With the development of mariachis performing for the cinema, radio, and recordings, a standardization of instrumentation and costume soon developed. This instrumentation included violins, *vihuela*, and *guitarrón*. Between 1929 and 1931 a single trumpet was added to some ensembles (Miguel Martínez became the first permanent trumpet player for Mariachi Vargas in 1941), but it wasn't until the 1950s that pairs of trumpets became popular. The late twentieth century witnessed a renewed use of two earlier instruments: the *arpa* (harp) and *guitarra de golpe* (Mexican guitar). Flutes were often used especially in recordings of *huapangos* (son huasteco; see *Son*), and French horns, flugelhorns, and accordions were often used when recording *canciones *rancheras* (ranch songs) or *polcas* (polkas). Although mariachi has long been considered a *macho* (male) ensemble, the first Mexican female group was organized by Carlota Noriega and named Mariachi las Coronelas in the mid-1940s, while Mariachi Las Estrellas de México was directed by Lupita Morales in the 1960s, and Mariachi Las Perlitas Tapatías of Guadalajara was formed in 1989. By the end of the century there were more than a dozen all-female ensembles and many more groups that included one woman or more. Teresa Cuevas is credited with forming the first all-female mariachi in the United States, Mariachi Estrella in 1977, and José Hernández founded Mariachi Reyna de Los Ángeles in 1994.

The *traje *charro* (Mexican gentleman rancher's suit) was first worn by mariachis coming to Mexico City to perform for the political aristocrats. Some credit Cirilo Marmolejo's group for the costume that was later adopted as picturesque in early *cines* (cinemas) and has since become the standard mariachi dress. Early mariachis usually wore the typical peasant dress of their region. The *cine* also made many early mariachis and singers famous, among them Jorge Negrete, Javier Solís, Pedro Infante, Lucha Reyes, Lola Beltrán, Lucha Villa, and more recently, Vicente Fernández.

Mariachis perform most of the same genres and many of the same pieces played by other Mexican regional ensembles: *son*, *huapango*, *canción ranchera*, *polca*, *bolero*, *marcha*, *chotis*, *cumbia*, *paso doble*, *vals*, and others. Most mariachis have extremely large repertories of traditional songs, numbering in the hundreds, and are expected to play by memory any song requested by their listeners. Although considered "folk" music, most of the repertory has been composed within the last 150 years by notable composers such as Agustín Lara, Tomás Méndez Sosa, Cuco Sánchez, Pepe Guizar, Juan Zaizar, José Alfredo *Jiménez, and the famous team of Silvestre Vargas with Rubén Fuentes, and today Juan Gabriel. By the mid-twentieth century mariachis were also playing *música clásica* (classical music arrangements) and *música internacional* (music from other Latin American countries as well as jazz and popular music). Well-known classical compositions include "Poeta y campesino" (Suppe's Poet and Peasant Overture), "Las bodas de Luis Alonso" (the intermezzo to a *zarzuela* [Spanish operetta or musical comedy] by Jerónimo Giménez), and *Carmen* (based on the Prelude to the opera by

Bizet), as well as the typical wedding marches. Early-twentieth-century Mexican composers such as José Pablo Moncayo García and Blas Galindo incorporated mariachi into their classical compositions. In 1944 the classically trained arranger Rubén Fuentes joined Mariachi Vargas de Tecalitlán and has become the best-known arranger of mariachi-style music in México.

Today Plaza Garibaldi near the center of Mexico City is considered the home of mariachis, where mariachi musicians congregate in the plaza, waiting for patrons and tourists to audition them and invite them to perform. The plaza is surrounded by cantinas and stores where various mariachi accoutrements can be purchased: *trajes* (suits), *gala* (the silver decorations on the suit), *moños* (bow ties), *cinturones* (belts), and recordings. Mariachis play for all types of occasions such as *bodas* (*weddings), *cumpleaños* (birthdays), *aniversarios* (anniversaries), saint's days, *misas* (masses), concerts, and any other type of fiesta (party). They perform in *cantinas*, homes, churches, and today in concert halls (*see* Holidays and Fiestas).

Since the urbanization of mariachis, there has been a parallel development of professional mariachis along with the hundreds of "folk" mariachis existing in the villages of México. Mariachi Vargas de Tecalitlán has been considered the premier Mexican mariachi for nearly a century. Mariachi México de Pepe Villa is well known, especially for their performances of *polcas*; Mariachi América de Jesús Rodríguez de Hijar is known for his contemporary mariachi arrangements, and the recently formed Mariachi Sonidos de América recorded an excellent CD within weeks of their formation in 2001. In the United States the three most prominent professional mariachis are Los Camperos de Nati Cano, Mariachi Sol de México de José Hernández, and Mariachi Cobre. The first two are based in California; Camperos established the first dinner show club for mariachis in the United States in the mid-1960s at La Fonda Restaurant, and Cobre performs at Epcot Center in Florida. In 1987 Linda *Ronstadt performed mariachi style at the Tucson International Mariachi Conference and recorded *Canciones de mi Padre* (Songs of My Father), effectively bringing mariachi music to a wider audience, thus expanding its pop culture appeal.

In nearly every city in México and most cities in the United States one will find working mariachis. These groups perform *al talón* (for hire), usually performing songs as requested. With the spread of the popularity of mariachi in the last quarter of the twentieth century, ensembles were formed at universities. Some exist as part of *ethnomusicology or ethnic studies programs, others as extracurricular activities. In 1961 the first university-based mariachi, Mariachi Uclatlán, was formed at the University of California at Los Angeles (today known as Mariachi UCLA), followed by Mariachi Internacional of Texas A&M University, Laredo, Texas, and UTPA Mariachi of the University of Texas Pan American. In 1984 the Arizona State University Mariachi Program (Mariachi Diablos del Sol and Mariachi A.S.U.) was established. Texas A&M and Arizona State University were the first to offer scholarships for university students. Most other college groups are extracurricular organizations including the groups at Arizona's South Mountain Community College, the University of Arizona, and Pima College. Mariachi Cardenal was formed at Stanford University in 1994 and is among the most active of extracurricular groups. Today many other universities and colleges have mariachi ensembles. The growth of university mariachis was precipitated by the development of student mariachis at the elementary, middle, and high school levels. One of the first such groups was Los Changuitos Feos (The Ugly Monkeys), a community youth mariachi formed in Tucson in 1963, but the surge in school mariachis must be attributed to the growth of school ensembles, especially in the Texas school systems.

Belle San Miguel Ortiz, a music educator from San Antonio, Texas, began a public school mariachi program in 1966. Today there are hundreds of mariachis in Texas, New Mexico, Arizona, and California schools. By 1979 San Miguel Ortiz realized that there were over 500 student mariachis who needed the guidance of professionals; therefore, she organized the first International Mariachi Conference in San Antonio and asked Mariachi Vargas de Tecalitlán to be the instructors. From the start the San Antonio conference emphasized education and included competitions for various grade levels. Her success was reflected in the dozens of other cities that began to host mariachi conferences. The Tucson International Mariachi Conference, begun in 1983, is now the largest. Today one can find conferences nearly year-round in cities such as Albuquerque, Las Cruces, Las Vegas, and San Jose. In New York the Mariachi Association of New York has recently opened the Mariachi Academy of New York.

Although customarily considered an oral tradition, all of the mariachi conferences now use Western music notation to help the fledgling musicians learn the songs. In 1994 the primer Encuentro del Mariachi (First Mariachi Conference) in México was held in Guadalajara as the educational techniques of the United States moved back to the *patria* (fatherland). Other cities such as Phoenix (Mariachi Christmas Festival), Hollywood Bowl (Mariachi USA Festival), Las Vegas, and Denver have chosen to host mariachi concerts with two or three major groups performing but without instructional classes. Once considered only regional music of central-western México, today the *pasión* (passion), the *alma* (soul), and the *corazón* (heart) of mariachi belong to the whole world but most especially to México and to Latinas and Latinos in the United States.

Further Reading

Hermes, Rafael. *Origen e Historias del Mariachi*. Mexico City: Editorial Katun, 1983.

Jáquez, Candida. "Meeting La Cantante through Verse, Song, and Performance." In *Chicana Traditions: Continuity and Change*, edited by Norma Cantú and Olga Nájera-Ramírez. Chicago: University of Chicago Press, 2002.

Sheehy, Daniel. "Mexican Mariachi Music: Made in the U.S.A." In *Musics of Multicultural America: A Study of Twelve Musical Communities*, edited by Kip Lornell and Anne Rasmussen. Belmont, CA: Wadsworth Publishing, 1999.

Sheehy, Daniel. "Popular Mexican Musical Traditions: The Mariachi of West Mexico and the Conjunto Jarocho of Veracruz." In *Music and Cultures of Latin America: Regional Traditions*, edited by John Shecter. Belmont, CA: Wadsworth Publishing, 1999.

J. Richard Haefer

Mariachi, El. *See El Mariachi.*

Mariachi Cobre. Mariachi Cobre (Mariachi Copper) is one of the three top professional *mariachi ensembles in the United States. Based in Arizona, the "Copper State," they currently perform Tuesdays through Saturdays at the Mexican Pavillion of the Epcot Center in Orlando, Florida. One of their trademarks is the performance of traditional mariachi repertory, only occasionally presenting *popurrís* (potpourris) and modern stage arrangements.

Randy and brother Steve Carrillo, together with Mack Ruiz and Frank Grijalva, formed the group in 1971. The first three had been members of Mariachi Los Changuitos Feos de Tucson (Tucson's Ugly Little Monkeys), a youth mariachi begun in 1964 by Father Charles Rourke at the Catholic Youth Center of All Saints Parish. Mack's older brother was one of the founding members of Los Changuitos. Once they developed their mariachi talents with Los Changuitos, they decided to expand and form a professional mariachi in Tucson.

In 1981, after having gained recognition well beyond Tucson and Arizona, they initiated the start of the now well-known Tucson International Mariachi Conference. The following year they began their performances at the Epcot Center. They have performed with most of the major mariachis of the United States and México and have accompanied such renowned singers as Lucha Villa, Lola Beltran, Anna Gabriel, Linda *Ronstadt, Julio *Iglesias, José Luis Rodríguez, and many others.

Of the present twelve members of the mariachi—six *violines* (violins), two *trompetas* (trumpets), *guitarrón* (bass guitar), *vihuela* (five-stringed harmony/rhythm guitar), *guitarra* (guitar), and *guitarra de golpe* (small "struck" guitar)—ten hail from Tucson, and the others are originally from México. Nearly all have attended university-level classes, and several possess bachelor degrees. While most of them have many and varied music interests, all agree that the study of classical music is important in the development of modern mariachi performance.

In addition to their performances in Florida, members of Mariachi Cobre regularly serve as instructors at mariachi conferences throughout the United States. Mack Ruiz and Roberto Martinez, with degrees in education, organize these professionally run classes, while Steve Carrillo and Frank Grijalva provide the music arrangements. For the last several years, Mariachi Cobre has also been involved with presenting concerts for mariachi and orchestra and have performed with major orchestras in several states including the Boston Pops Orchestra.

Further Reading

http://www.mariachi-cobre.com.

J. Richard Haefer

Marielitos. The term *Marielitos* refers to over 120,000 Cubans who were boat-lifted from the port of Mariel, Cuba, to Florida in 1980. The Marielitos were for the most part men, many of whom had family members in the United States and a small percentage were men the Cuban government considered undesirable. The group included prison convicts, mental health patients, and homosexuals, and were the first emigrants from Cuba denied refugee status by the U.S. government. Arriving during a period of economic recession, the newcomers were viewed by the U.S. State Department as economic burdens rather than victims of political oppression. Although internal correspondence referred to the immigrants as "refugees," officially and publicly the Carter administration labeled the Cubans "entrants." In contrast to earlier waves of Cuban migration of affluent Spanish descent or active opposition to Fidel *Castro, the Marielitos were younger (averaging about thirty years of age) and more racially diverse; they also had less formal education, falling in the bottom quartile of professional skills, and many were socialists.

The media stigmatized the Marielitos as criminals and troublemakers who were forced on the United States by Castro's government, making it difficult for them to find sponsors. Cubans already established in the United States, who are normally a tightly knit community and lobby group, responded to the new arrivals by distancing themselves from them, fearing that their "model immigrant" image would be tarnished. The plight of the Marielitos and their stigma in the United States have been a subject of documentaries, such as *Against Wind and Tide: A Cuban Odyssey* (1981) and *Los Marielitos* (1983), and have been further popularized in such commercial features as *Scarface* (1983) starring Al Pacino, and *The Perez Family* (1995), both of which have been highly criticized for their stereotypical depictions of the Marielitos as criminal and lazy. The Marielito boat lift was also discussed in the memoirs of famed gay Cuban exile writer and playwright Reinaldo Arenas, whose deathbed memoirs *Before the Night Falls* (1993) were made into a feature film by Julian Schnabel in 2000.

Further Reading

García, María Cristina. *Havana USA: Cuban Exiles and Cuban Americans in South Florida 1959–1994.* Berkeley: University of California Press, 1996.

Más allá del mar. Produced and directed by Lisandro Peréz-Rey. Miami: Florida International University, 2002. Videocassette.

http://www.lanic.utexas.edu/la/cb/cuba/asce/cuba5/FILE26.PDF.

Leonora Anzaldúa Burke

Marín, Cheech (1946–   ). Richard Anthony Marín was born to Elsa and
Oscar Marín, a Los Angeles Police Department police officer, on July 13,
1946, in Los Angeles, California. A third-generation Mexican American, he
earned the nickname "Cheech" because of his love of *chicharrones*, a snack
of spicy, fried pork skins, also known as cracklings. Marín pursued a Bachelor of Arts degree in English at California State University at Northridge
during the 1960s. He is best known as Cheech of the comedy duo Cheech
and Chong, who satirized *stereotypes about Mexican Americans, Chinese
Americans, and the hippies of the 1960s drug culture.

Marín met Tommy Chong, his future partner-in-comedy, when he moved
to Vancouver, British Columbia, in 1968 to escape the draft during the Vietnam War. The two comedians became involved in improvisational theater
while perfecting their act and soon were appearing at nightclubs in Canada
and California before eventually opening for major rock and roll concerts.
By the early 1970s they were recording comedy albums and won a Grammy
for Best Comedy Record for their 1973 comedy album *Los Cochinos* (The
Dirty Ones). By the late 1970s, the pair had graduated into film, making
their hit comedy *Up in Smoke* (1978), which was so successful that it
spawned five subsequent film projects cowritten by and starring the comedic
duo: *Cheech and Chong's Next Movie* (1980), *Cheech and Chong's Nice
Dreams* (1981), *Cheech and Chong's Still Smokin'* (1983), and *Cheech and
Chong's The Corsican Brothers* (1984). Before they broke up in 1985,
Cheech and Chong also appeared in *It Came from Hollywood* (1982), *Yell-
owbeard* (1983), and *After Hours* (1985).

In 1987, Marín wrote, directed, and starred in *Born in East L.A.*, a
movie, based on an earlier music video parody done by Marín, about a Mexican American wrongfully deported by the Immigration and Naturalization
Service (INS) to Tijuana, México. Other film credits include *Echo Park*
(1986), *Charlie Barnett's Terms of Enrollment* (1986), *Fatal Beauty* (1987),
Ghostbusters II (1989), *Rude Awakening* (1989), *Troop Beverly Hills*
(1989), *The Shrimp on the Barbie* (1990), *Far Out Man* (1990), *A Million
to Juan* (1994), *Desperado* (1995), *From Dusk Till Dawn* (1996), *The Great
White Hype* (1996), *Tin Cup* (1996), *Paulie: A Parrot's Tale* (1998), *Nuttiest
Nutcracker* (1999), *Picking Up the Pieces* (2000), *Luminarias* (2000), *Spy
Kids* (2000), *Spy Kids 2* (2002), *The Late Henry Moss* (2002), and *Masked
and Anonymous* (2002).

Marín's first major regular television role was in the television sitcom *The
Golden Palace* (1992–1993), in which he played Mexican chef Chuy Castil-
los. He went on to play opposite Don Johnson in the television drama *Nash
Bridges* (1996–2001). Other television appearances include *La Pastorela*
(1991), *Ring of the Musketeers* (1992), *The Cisco Kid* (1994), *The Court-
yard* (1995), *Latino Laugh Festival* (1996), and the series *Resurrection
Blvd.* (2000). Beginning in January 2004, Marín began appearing as a regular on *Judging Amy*. Marín has been involved in many entertainment pro-

Cheech Marín. *Courtesy of Photofest.*

ductions designed for children, including vocal portrayals in animated films such as *Oliver and Company* (1988), *Ferngully: The Last Rainforest* (1992), *The Lion King* (1994), the television series *Santo Bugito* (1995), *It's Tough to Be a Bug* (2000), and *Pinocchio* (2002).

Besides his career in entertainment, Marín is also a benefactor and volunteer for a number of different Hispanic charities and a collector of *Chicano art. In 1999, he developed a line of hot sauces for two restaurant chains—The House of Blues and Joe's Crab Shack—to donate a portion of the profits to Latino charities. His private collection of Chicano art has been displayed in the Smithsonian and other national galleries and is currently on tour as "Chicano Visions: American Painters on the Verge," accompanied by a multimedia, interactive exhibit titled "Chicano Now: American Expressions," organized in collaboration with Marín. This collection is the subject of his book titled *Chicano Visions: American Painters on the Verge* (2002), in which he argues that Chicano art is the most recent school in American art.

Further Reading

Marín, Cheech. *Chicano Visions: American Painters on the Verge.* Boston, MA: Bulfinch Press, 2002.

Menard, Valeri. *Cheech Marín: A Real-Life Reader Biography.* Bear, DE: Mitchell Lane Publishers, 2001.

Lynn Marie Houston

Marín, Richard Anthony. *See* Marín, Cheech.

Marquez, Thomas J. (1945–   ). One of the first Mexican Americans to achieve extraordinary business and commercial success, Thomas J. Marquez became a multimillionaire for his work and partnership with Texas entrepreneur and former presidential candidate H. Ross Perot. Marquez's business success in the information technology industry was capped in 1976 when he contributed $10 million to the University of Notre Dame to establish the Aurora and Thomas Marquez Chair in Information Theory and Computer Technology. Named to honor his parents, the prestigious chair and endowed professorship was one of the first of its kind in the world.

The son of tenth-generation New Mexico and Colorado *families, Marquez grew up in the Pine River valley of southern Colorado, where his father, Tom Marquez, formerly a New Mexico farmer, became a highly prosperous cattle trader and wool buyer. His mother, Aurora Candelaria Marquez, was an active community volunteer and served on the Colorado Civil Rights Commission in the early 1970s. Both parents were explicitly bilingual, bicultural Mexican Americans with strong ties to their native states of origin. Marquez and his siblings attended St. Columba's Catholic Schools in Durango, Colorado.

After graduating from the University of Notre Dame in 1959 with a degree in business and mathematics, Marquez worked for IBM Corporation before joining Perot in Dallas, Texas, to build Electronic Data Systems, one of the first global computerized information systems companies. He and Perot innovated data-processing methods for speed and convenience and were aggressive in selling their vanguard methods to federal and other publicly funded contractors. As his business successes grew, Marquez became increasingly active in state, national, and international drug prevention programs, as well as vigorously involved with his college alma mater. He has served on the University of Notre Dame's Advisory Council for the Mendoza College of Business since 1972. He and his wife Carolyn are the parents of four children.

Cordelia Chávez Candelaria

Martí, José (1853–1895). One of Cuba's most famous writers and martyrs, José Martí is considered by many Latin Americans to be the symbolic father of Caribbean literature. He is renowned for his powerful poems on political liberty as well as for his essays on political and economic justice as indispensable to individual and collective freedom. In the United States, Martí may be best known as the composer of the verses to the populist song "Guantanamera," which became one of the anthems of the antiwar movements of the 1960s and 1970s along with "We Shall Overcome" and "De Colores" (Of Colors). As an essayist and poet, he is credited for bringing simplicity and transparent lyricism into the poetry of the Americas as a means of bridging the hemisphere's differences of language, *race, class, and educational level. He is also celebrated for introducing the concept of negritude (i.e., Afrocentric blackness in aesthetics and the dark shadows of psychological and political reality) into language, verse, music, and art. His tireless work on behalf of Cuban independence from Spain, as well as his activism for political and economic freedom throughout Latin America, made him a people's hero during his lifetime and led to his death on the battlefield and martyrdom at the age of forty-two.

José Julián Martí y Pérez was born in Havana on January 28, 1853, where he attended school. As a teenager he published poems in local newspapers, and when he was sixteen, he even founded a newspaper, *La patria libre* (The Free Homeland), in the capital to express the revolutionary sentiments that were gaining strength in the 1860s and 1870s. He openly joined Cuba's revolutionary movement in 1868, describing himself as a true patriot of the *patria*. His politics landed him in prison and then deportation to Spain in 1871. The exile provided him an opportunity to further his formal education, and at the University of Záragoza he eventually earned both a master's in jurisprudence and a law degree in 1874. Throughout his Spanish college years he continued writing and publishing on revolutionary politics, as well as traveling in France before returning to the Western Hemisphere and in 1878 finally returning to Cuba.

His return to his homeland was short-lived, however, due to his ongoing political activism. As a result, in 1879 the Cuban authorities again punished Martí by expelling him once again to Spain. Eager to return to his own world and interests, he soon left to France, where he found easier escape first to New York City and then in 1881 to Caracas, Venezuela. That same year he established another independence periodical, the *Revista Venezolana* (Venezuelan Review), a paper that vigorously defended the rights of the people against government and military tyranny. The intense politics of democracy of the *Revista Venezolana* enraged the country's dictator president, and Martí again was forced to escape to New York to protect his life.

Cuba's near obsession with the nature of *cubanidad* (Cuban identity) to a large extent enters the literatures and popular cultures of the Americas through Martí's poetry and his essays, arguably his most important achievement as a writer. During his North American exile he maintained an active publishing schedule including the penning of a regularly syndicated feature in the Argentine periodical *La nación* (The Nation), which contributed to his fame throughout Latin America. His essays address diverse topics on the history and evolution of the cultures of the Americas, and they are acclaimed for their attempt to synthesize the defining "Americanness" of the hemisphere in such essays as "Nuestra América" (Our America, 1881), "Emerson" (1882), "Whitman" (1887), "Bolívar" (1893), and his translation of Helen Hunt Jackson's *Ramona (1929). Considered innovative at the time, Martí's style of prose was personal, subject based, simple in its diction and syntax, and intended to reach broad audiences. Like Ernest Hemingway's prose in English, Martí's technique is still praised as an exemplar of good writing in Spanish.

Martí's poetry also is still read. It is marked by profound feeling, earnest beliefs about democracy, and keen insight into human nature—all captured in the poignant verses of "Guantanamera." His major collection, *Versos libres* (Free Verses), was published in 1913 and contains poems written through 1882. Others of his work in English translation include *Inside the Monster: Writings on the United States and American Imperialism* (1975); *Our America: Writings on Latin America and the Cuban Struggle for Independence* (1978); and *On Education* (1979).

Despite his exile in New York, the political party he cofounded in Cuba, the Partido Revolucionario Cubano (Cuban Revolutionary Party), elected Martí to head the group in 1892, and he accepted. From his New York base, he made preparations for takeover of his country's opposition groups and to lead Cubans in a decisive overthrow of its foreign government. The year 1895 was the revolutionary's fateful year. He embarked to the *Antilles in January with fellow Cuban revolutionaries and landed in Santo Domingo, where they moved quickly to implement their plans. Their invasion of Spanish-controlled Cuba began in April, and Martí was killed on the battlefield on May 19, 1895, in Dos Ríos, an eastern province marked by flat plains. His death preceded by a scant seven years his lifelong desire for Cuban independence.

Further Reading

Foner, Philip Sheldon. *The Spanish-Cuban-American War and the Birth of American Imperialism, 1895–1902.* New York: Monthly Review Press, 1972.

Martí, José. *Major Poems: A Bilingual Edition.* Translated by Elinor Randall. Edited with an introduction by Philip S. Foner. New York: Holmes & Meier Publishers, 1982.

Cordelia Chávez Candelaria

Martin, Ricky (1971–   ). Born in San Juan, Puerto Rico, on December 24, 1971, Enrique Martín Morales is more popularly known by the stage name Ricky Martin. In 1984, at the age of twelve, Martin began his five-year membership with the all-boy Latino group *Menudo. Following his departure from the group, Martin recorded solo albums including *Ricky Martin* (1991) and *Me Amaras* (You Will Love Me, 1993), while maintaining an acting career in Mexican soap operas, earning a Heraldo (Herald), an award similar

Ricky Martin poses with his awards during the *Billboard* Latino Awards 2004 in Miami, April 29, 2004. *By permission of the artist and* L.A. Weekly.

to an Emmy. In 1994, Martin began work on the popular soap opera *General Hospital*, playing Puerto Rican bartender-turned-singer Miguel Morez. After leaving *General Hospital*, Martin appeared on Broadway in *Les Miserables*.

In 1995, Martin released the album *A Medio Vivir* (Live Half a Life), followed by *Vuelve* (Come Back, 1998), featuring the song "La Copa de la Vida" (Cup of Life), which became a number-one single in thirty countries. Martin was selected to sing this song as the official song for soccer's 1998 World Cup, making his presence known worldwide. However, it was during the 41st Annual Grammy Awards show when Martin performed the song and received an award for Best Latin Pop Performance for the album *Vuelve* that he garnered the attention of mainstream audiences in the United States. In 1999, Martin also received two *Billboard* Latin Music Awards for Album of the Year, *Vuelve*, and Hot Latin Track of the Year, "Vuelve." His self-titled English-language album released in 1999 debuted at number one on the *Billboard* 200 album charts and sold 15 million copies worldwide. The song "Livin' *La Vida Loca*" from that album became a number-one single in five international markets, while the album itself became number one in ten international markets. Martin was named Male Artist of the Year and Male Hot 100 Singles Artist of the Year at the 10th Annual Billboard Music Awards, while "Livin' *La Vida Loca*" was awarded Latin Pop Track of the Year at the 7th Annual Billboard Latin Music Awards. Martin followed this success with another English-language album, *Sound Loaded* (2000), and two Spanish collections, *La Historia* (The History, 2001) and *Colleción de Oro* (Gold Collections, 2002). In 2000, at the 2nd Annual Latin Grammy Awards, Martin received an award for Best Music Video for "She Bangs" (Spanish), a single from *Sound Loaded*.

Aside from industry-endorsed awards such as the Grammy and *Billboard* awards, Martin has received extensive recognition from the popular media. These include being named one of *People Magazine*'s 50 Most Beautiful People in the World, Entertainer of the Year by Entertainment Weekly, Male Entertainer of the Year from the American Latino Media Arts Awards, and recipient of multiple MTV Video Music awards including Best Dance Video and Pop Video for "Livin' *La Vida Loca*." Martin's performance at the 41st Annual Grammy Awards and the success of his self-titled English-language album are popularly credited for beginning what was termed in the popular press as "The Latin Explosion," which impacted the fame of other artists like Jennifer *López (*On the 6*, 1999) and *Shakira (*Laundry Service*, 2001), as well as more established artists like Marc *Anthony (*Marc Anthony*, 1999) and Enrique *Iglesias (*Enrique Iglesias*, 1999), into the fold of English-language pop music.

Further Reading

www.rickymartinmanagement.com.

Bernadette Calafell

Martínez, Demetria (1960–   ). Award-winning Chicana writer of novels and poetry, Demetria Martínez is also a professional journalist whose first novel, *Mother Tongue* (1994), grew out of her work as a columnist for the *Albuquerque Journal* and the *National Catholic Reporter*. Born and reared in Albuquerque, New Mexico, where she graduated from Albuquerque High School, Martínez moved to New Jersey to enter Princeton University to pursue policy studies in the Woodrow Wilson School of Public and International Affairs. She earned her Bachelor of Arts degree in public policy in 1982 and returned to Albuquerque, where she joined the Sagrada Art School and began writing poetry. Published in a volume titled *Turning* (1987), this early body of poetry was part of what propelled Martínez's career as a professional writer.

Winner of the 1994 Western States Book Award for Fiction, *Mother Tongue* was first published by the Bilingual Review Press in 1994 and reissued by Ballantine in 1996. The novel is drawn in part from Martínez's journalistic coverage of the Sanctuary Movement, working for peace and social justice reforms in El Salvador during the 1980s, as well as from a 1987–1988 federal indictment issued against her. The indictment charged her with smuggling two refugee women into the United States when, in her reporter's role, she accompanied a Lutheran minister to cover his efforts to provide safe haven to persecuted Salvadoran refugees entering the country under the protection of Sanctuary supporters in New Mexico. The prosecution used Martínez's poem "Nativity, for Two Salvadoran Women" as evidence, garnering international attention to issues such as the right of a journalist to cover refugee activities, even if deemed illegal for foreign policy expedience, and the constitutional right not to have political and religious beliefs used against witnesses in court. Celebrated by peace activists, her 1989 acquittal also was considered a major First Amendment victory, and it gave Martínez positive public attention. Along with its critical and popular acclaim, *Mother Tongue* has been adopted for use in university courses and was chosen for the 1995 Chautauqua Literary and Scientific Circle reading list—a 117-year-old tradition of the Chautauqua Institute in New York. In March 2001, the author discussed her novel at the first international colloquium on testimonial literature in Latin America held in San Salvador.

Martínez's poetry and fiction have appeared as well in over a dozen anthologies including *Wachale! Poetry and Prose about Growing Up Latino in America* (2001), *Floricanto Si: A Collection of Latina Poetry* (1998), and *Power Lines: A Decade of Poetry from Chicago's Guild Complex* (1999). Two books of her poetry, *The Devil's Workshop* (2002) and *Breathing between the Lines* (1997), were published by the University of Arizona Press, and her work appears on the online magazine, *Voices from the Gaps: Women Writers of Color*. She is compiling her first collection of essays, *Just What Exactly Is Olive Skin*, in 2004. Martínez serves on the board of directors for the twenty-five-year-old Curbstone Publishing Company known for its publication of the literatures of social change produced by Latin American, North American, and Vietnamese writers. A frequent reader and lecturer, Martínez has appeared at the Smithsonian Institution twice, as well as at churches, synagogues, high schools, and a variety of grassroots organizations, advocating for the goals of peace and justice, universal literacy, and immigrant rights.

A visiting assistant professor at Arizona State University in Tempe for the 1998–1999 academic year, Martínez taught workshops for creative writing graduate students titled "Writer as Witness." The workshops examined the role of the writer as a political intellectual, a vision that girds her own craft. She has also been a writer-in-residence at Duke University's Center for Documentary Studies, worked with African American elementary school students on a writing project about Mexican immigration, and participated in a curriculum development workshop on photography and literacy.

Further Reading

"Contemporary Authors Online." *The Gale Group*. http://www.galegroup.com.
"US Latina Poets." http://www.edtech.csupomona.ed.u/students/juana/poets.html.
http://demetriamartinez.tripod.com/bio/index.html.

BJ Manríquez

Matachines. *Matachines* is a popular pantomime and ritual drama performed throughout the Southwest by *Chicano and Indian people during
*holidays and fiestas, or feast days. Based on a medieval Spanish mystery
play, it was first introduced to México and later diffused to Texas, New Mexico, and Arizona, and depicts the conversion of Montezuma by the Spaniards.
The term *matachines* refers to the dance troupe consisting of twelve
danzantes (dancers), which are believed to represent the twelve apostles or
tribes of Israel. As performers, their identity and gender are masked, and
today both males and females dance together. Their individual personalities
remain anonymous, and likewise their own personal reasons for participation are kept secret. *Danzantes* wear a bright costume decorated with long
ribbons, a cape, and a *cupil* (elaborate headdress similar to a bishop's miter).
In sixteenth-century Europe a *matachín* was a masked entertainer who performed with a sword. Today, they no longer use swords but perform with
three-pronged *palmas* (palm fronds) and maracas (gourd rattles), which are
played in time as part of the musical ensemble. They are accompanied by violin and guitar among the participants in New Mexico and Arizona, by guitar and accordion in Texas, and by Native American percussion and chanting
among some of the Indian groups throughout New Mexico. *La Malinche
is also a central figure in the *Matachines*. The innocent young Malinche is
associated with the Virgin Mary, the monarca with Montezuma or "someone with power." Their pairing and face-to-face interaction (of dancers and
characters) is a constant of the dance. Like the *danzantes*, but unlike the
abuelos (clowns contributing comic relief) and the *toro* (bull representing evil
and wanderlust), they are serious, conventional figures with no charter for
improvisation or interaction with the audience.

Further Reading

Rodríguez, Sylvia. *The Matachines Dance: Ritual Symbolism and Interethnic Rela-
    tions in the Upper Rio Grande Valley*. Albuquerque: University of New Mex-
    ico Press, 1996.
Romero, Brenda. "The Matachines Music and Dance in San Juan Pueblo and Al-
    calde, New Mexico: Context and Meanings." Ph.D. dissertation, University
    of California, Los Angeles, 1993.

Peter J. García

Matos, Luis Palés (1898–1959). One of Puerto Rico's most distinguished
and influential writers, Luis Palés Matos was a lyric poet who is credited
with reintroducing African motifs and ideology into Puerto Rican poetry. In

so doing his work raised consciousness to the importance of the African heritage and négritude to Latin American culture. He also is noted for creating a new genre of Latin American literature called Afro-Antillian poetry and for cofounding two literary movements, Diepalismo and Negrismo. His literary influence extends beyond Puerto Rico and into the Greater Antilles region of Panama, Colombia, Ecuador, Uruguay, and Venezuela. One measure of his importance is that his books *Tuntun de pasa y grifería* (Drumbeats of Kink and Blackness; Biblioteca de Autores Puertorriqueños, 1937) and *Poesia 1915–56* (Ediciones de la Universidad de Puerto Rico, 1957) are still available in the twenty-first century.

Palés Matos was born on March 20, 1898, in Guayama, Puerto Rico, a predominantly black village, and was reared in a literate household. His parents were educated, and his father, Vicente Palés Anés, his brothers, Vicente and Gustavo Palés Matos, and his mother, Consuelo Matos Vicil, were all significant poets. For example, his father and brothers were poet laureates of Puerto Rico. A voracious reader as a child, Palés Matos began writing poems when he was thirteen, and he self-published his first collection of poems when he was seventeen. To support himself he worked at many jobs including as a journalist, secretary, bookkeeper, civil servant, and teacher. In 1918, Palés Matos married Natividad Suliveres, and he was devastated by her death shortly after the birth of their son. His second collection of poems, *El palacio en sombras 1919–20* (The Darkened Palace), expresses his sorrow over her loss.

Palés Matos did not gain much attention for his poetry until 1921, when he moved to San Juan and began publishing his work in magazines. Connected with other writers and artists, he joined Jose T. de Diego Padró to cofound an avant-garde, postmodernist literary movement called Diepalismo. The name derived from a blending of their two names, and the style emphasized the musicality of language through onomatopoeia. In 1926 *La Democracia* published "Pueblo Negro" (Black Town), which gave rise to the influential and Negrismo movement that merged concern for *race and ethnicity, *folklore, and African words into the Spanish verse of Puerto Rico, evoking the language and life of West Indian blacks and musical African rhythms. The poem was from a manuscript that was never published called *Canciones de la vida media* (Mid-life Songs). Finally in 1937, Palés Matos's collection of Negrismo poems, *Tuntun de pasa y grifería*, were published to general acclaim, including an award from the Institute of Puerto Rican Literature. *Tuntun de pasa y grifería* earned him a place with Afro-Cuban poet Nicolas Guillén as the founders of the Negrismo literary movement that preceded the Latin American Boom of the late twentieth century. The book also drew criticism from some who believe that Palés Matos, who was not black, was exploiting Africanism. After *Tuntun de pasa y grifería*, he concentrated more on Afro-Antillian poetry that did not focus on black themes as heavily. Until the time of his death in 1959, he served as lecturer to the Faculty of Humanities of the University of Puerto Rico. He died in Santurce, Puerto Rico, of a heart attack.

Further Reading

Academy of American Poets. "Luis Palés Matos." http: //www.poets.org/poets/poets. cfm?prmID=656.

Enguidanos, Miguel. *La poesia de Luis Palés Matos*. Río Piedras: Editorial de la Universidad de Puerto Rico, 1962.

Julie Amparano García

MEChA. The Movimiento Estudiantil Chicano de Aztlán, commonly known as MEChA, sometimes punctuated as M.E.Ch.A., was a direct outgrowth of the international student movements and anti–Vietnam War coalitions of the 1960s. Formed in 1968, the group's name translates as the Chicano Student Movement of [the people's symbolic homeland of] *Aztlán. Many prominent Mexican-American advocates, political figures, scholars, and other leaders of the late twentieth century and early years of the twenty-first century were first initiated into public service and advocacy for social justice through their college involvement in MEChA in the 1970s, 1980s, and 1990s. During the 2003 recall campaign against California Governor Gray Davis, however, one such leader, Lieutenant Governor Cruz Bustamante, was viciously attacked by Republican Party opponents as a "racist separatist" because of his MEChA membership as a young man. Current and former MEChistas (MEChA members) immediately came to Bustamante's and the organization's defense by pointing out that the group was formed to promote the empowerment of *Chicanos through education, a mission that continues in 2004 through a solid record of retention efforts to build an educated foundation of Latinas and Latinos to meet society's need for teachers, professors, lawyers, and other trained specialists prepared to serve all sectors of society, including America's bilingual, bicultural peoples.

Historically, MEChA grew out of two important documents developed during the early stages of the *Chicano Movement, the 1967 El Plan Espiritual de Aztlán (Spiritual Plan of Aztlán) and the 1968 El Plan de Santa Barbara (the Santa Barbara Plan). Both documents are part of a long tradition in American history of proclamations for mutual aid, independence, and self-determination such as the pre-1620 Iroquois League of Confederation, the 1776 Declaration of Independence, the 1848 Seneca Falls Declaration of Women's Independence, and others. The 1967 Plan Espiritual de Aztlán proclaimed an identity of mestizo solidarity through pride in being, in the words of the Plan, a "bronze people with a bronze culture," and rhetorically declared that "Aztlán belongs to those who plant the seeds, water the fields, and gather the crops." Continuing the tradition of rallying rhetoric, the brief Plan Espiritual de Aztlán concludes by declaring "the independence of our mestizo nation," a declaration that many Chicana/o activists interpreted as a call for grassroots activism and mestizo solidarity for self-determination in the face of the nation's historic policies of racial segregation and white superiority.

The much longer 1968 Plan de Santa Barbara was written by many of the same persons involved in composing the first manifesto to provide more in-depth background and specific details for the compilation of a proactive agenda for positive social change. Because the 1968 Plan de Santa Barbara served as one of the foundations of the Chicano Movement, it, too, like the 1967 Plan, is fundamental to the MEChA mission and philosophy. In summary, the 1968 Santa Barbara proclamation asserted that Chicanos were descendants of the indigenous people of Aztlán and therefore part of a bronze nation with identifiable cultural values and a desire to achieve liberation from racism and government policies of double standards as a means of strengthening the Chicano and Chicana community.

Out of these principles of community advocacy and rallying cries to soli-

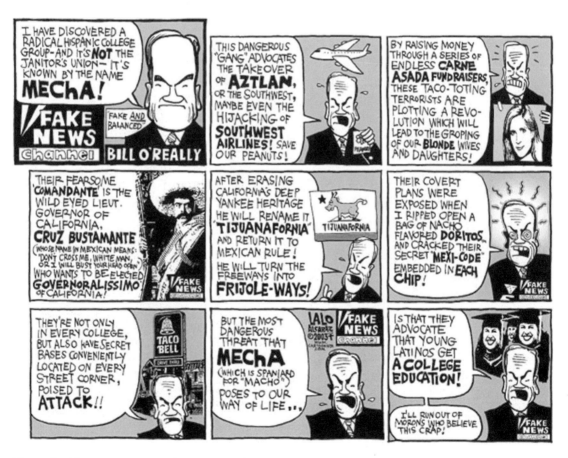

This Lalo Alcaraz cartoon on the 2003 California gubenatorial recall election satirizes right-wing attacks on Lieutenant Governor Cruz Bustamante for his college student participation in MEChA, a campus group promoting empowerment through education. *Courtesy of Lalo Alvarez. Originally published in* LA Weekly.

darity, MEChA was formed to address the educational plight of Chicana and Chicano students whose needs and best interests were, to quote the organization's statement of philosophy, "ignored by insensitive administrators." The group's philosophy included raising consciousness to the school "push-out rates" of Chicano and Chicana students, a failure that "force[s] many Chicanos and Chicanas to a life of poverty." Another key concern of the organization is the "government . . . campaign" to "assimilate our Gente [i.e., people or community] by labeling us 'Hispanic,'" a term viewed as an attempt "to anglicize and deny our indigenous heritage by ignoring our unique socioeconomic and historical aspect of our Gente." The continuing unfair and exclusionary policies and politics of the United States led MEChA "to affirm our philosophy of liberation (i.e., educational, socioeconomic, and political empowerment) for our Chicano and Chicana nation." These principles and their offshoots and updatings to meet the gender and political needs of the times constitute the historical basis for the organization.

In practice, MEChA as a student organization on university and college campuses, and more recently at high school and presecondary levels, has been visionary in leading the call for culturally complete and nonracist curricula at every level of education. Specifically this has led to Chicana/o studies integration of and into the classroom curriculum and research agendas, as well as the production of research-based material about Mexican America. MEChistas also participate in many service, civic, and consciousness-raising programs like fund-raising for Latina and Latino scholarships, symposia, arts, and culture programming. In this way, the organization joins with other community-based groups intent on ending the cultural tyranny caused by institutional discrimination and historical racism. As the preamble to the national MEChA constitution states, "Chicano and Chicana students of Aztlán must take upon themselves the responsibilities to promote Chicanismo within the community . . . for the self-determination of the Chicano people for the purpose of liberating Aztlán."

Further Reading

Drury, Jennifer. "M.E.Ch.A." Term Paper for CCS 300, Arizona State University, 2002.

"MEChA National Webpages." http://www.panam.edu/orgs/mecha/nat.html.

Valle, Maria Eva. "MEChA and the Transformation of Chicano Student Activism: Generational Change, Conflict, and Continuity." Ph.D. dissertation, University of California, San Diego, 1996.

Cordelia Chávez Candelaria

Menudo. Also called *mondongo* in many Latin American countries and by many Latinas and Latinos in the United States, *menudo* is the Mexican name given to a hearty tripe stew that is touted as a sure cure for a hangover. *Menudo* is prepared in an *olla* (earthen pot) or other large container filled with water, diced beef or sometimes pork tripe, other edible innards, some-times *posole* (hominy), and spices (usually garlic, onion, oregano, cumin, *chili, and salt). The ingredients are simmered for hours, and particularly in New Mexico cuisine, the tripe is combined with an equal amount of posole and, depending on the family recipe, other meats. Often served with a *salsa cruda* (uncooked salsa) and fresh *tortillas and/or *sopaipillas* (*see* *Food and Cookery), *menudo* is treated with the endearing respect of a genuine Mexican/Chicano soul food staple, even as it is recognized as one popular culture item that probably will not cross over into mass acceptance—except, of course, for the pop music sensation *Menudo.

Further Reading

De'Angeli, Alicia Gironella, and Jorge De'Angeli. *El gran libro de la cocina mexi-cana.* Mexico City: Ediciones Larousse, 1980.

Gilbert, Fabiola Cabeza de Baca. *We Fed Them Cactus.* Albuquerque: University of New Mexico Press, 1954.

Cordelia Chávez Candelaria

Menudo. Formed in 1977 in Puerto Rico, Menudo was one of the most internationally successful Latino teenage boy pop groups who recorded their songs in Spanish, English, Portuguese, Italian, and even Tagalog to cater to the Philipino market. Composed of teenage boys, Menudo appeared in weekly TV shows throughout Spanish-language television in Latin America and the United States. In 1983, a couple of performances in México broke records for the largest audience attendance ever, and as a result Menudo is listed in the *Guinness Book of World Records*. In the United States, they sold out Madison Square Garden for four shows in two days.

Two of Menudo's biggest hits were released in 1984: "Quiero Ser" (I Wanna Be) and "Subete a mi moto" (Get into My Car). Their 1984 album *Reaching Out* included several of the group's most popular English-version songs. A few of Menudo's ex-associates have tried to make it on their own; however, the only ones who truly have achieved successful solo careers are Marc *Anthony and Ricky *Martin. Martin performed with Menudo beginning in 1984, at the age of twelve, and is featured in their 1986 album *Can't Get Enough* in the song "No one Can Love You More." Menudo recorded and released close to fifty albums, including several recompilations and re-releases, as well as a 1998 Christmas CD, *Feliz Navidad*, which contained the popular hit "Chili Navideño" (Christmas Chili). Menudo renamed itself MDO in the late 1990s, and the members are now older than sixteen and no longer exclusively native Puerto Ricans. Some of their more recent popular songs include "Ay Amor" (There Is Love) from their 1997 debut MDO album and "Baila la *Rumba" (Dance the Rumba) from their album *Un Poco Mas* (A Little More), released in 1999.

Further Reading

http://www.mdo4ever.tripod.com.
http://www.musicopucitorico.com/en/menudo.html

Robert Chew

Merengue. Merengue, a dance music in 2/4 time from the Dominican Republic, has risen from its origins as a rural, regionally specific art form to become a symbol of national identity and an object of pride for Dominicans everywhere. Dating to the 1840s, its roots run throughout the Caribbean, and its history is interwoven with that of the Dominican Republic itself. Antecedent forms include musical styles as diverse as the Puerto Rican *danza, the Afro-Antillean *kalenda*, and the Cuban *upa habanera*. Another form of the same rhythm evolved simultaneously in the French-speaking western part of the island (now Haiti) and came to be known as *mereng*; Colombia and Venezuela also developed their own merengue variants. Today Dominicans play three main styles of merengue: *orquesta*, or big band merengue; merengue *típico* or *perico ripiao*, traditional accordion-based merengue; and the guitar-based merengue played by *bachata* groups. Regional variants like *pri-prí* (merengue *palo echao*), merengue *de atabales*, and merengue *redondo* are seldom, heard in the United States.

Perico ripiao or merengue *típico* is the oldest style still commonly performed. Originating from a rural northern valley region near Santiago called the Cibao, it is also referred to as merengue *cibaeño*. Older groups used chordophones including guitar, *tres*, or *cuatro*; idiophones including *güira*, a metal scraper; and membranophones like the two-headed *tambora* drum. Bass instruments called marimbas were used occasionally. Marimbas are direct descendants of African *mbiras* (thumb pianos), which are wooden-sounding boxes with five to eight metal keys. The combination of ethnic sounds and instruments reflects the region's tricultural heritage heard in the musical combinations of European guitar or, later, accordion; African marimba and *tambora*; and the *güira*, which may have originated from the extinct native Taíno culture.

The *güira* remains significant in merengue as it has from the beginning despite major changes in the ensemble. One important development occurred when Germans migrated to the island during the 1870s, bringing their accordions, music, and dancing. Accordions became popular among native musicians throughout the early twentieth century. Francisco (Ñico) Lora was an early composer of merengue, and his works are still played today. Accordions eventually replaced the original *tres* and *cuatro* as the principal instruments in the *típico* ensemble. Today, two-row diatonic button accordions are preferred by most *típico* musicians but the Hohner remains the most popular instrument of choice, while one-row Hohners are also played. Today the *tambora* is typically played with one stick in the right hand and the flat palm of the left hand. According to legend, a turn-of-the-century musician dropped his left-hand stick during an important performance but kept going. Other drummers heard the new *tambora* sound and liked it—hence, a new musical style emerged.

Merengue music has always been used primarily for dancing. Its simple two-beat basic step is easy to learn, a major reason both for its great popularity at present and for its rapid adoption during the colonial period (it quickly replaced earlier fads like the *tumba*). Early written accounts described the dance as indecent and in poor taste because of the close partner hold and pronounced hip movements. One peculiar variant wherein one leg is dragged after the other with a down-and-up hip motion is said to have developed as a result of a general who was lame in one leg. In order not to offend him, other partygoers began dancing with a limp as well. Originally executed mainly with side-to-side movement, the partners seldom separating, merengue dancers may now also do complicated turn patterns (*figuras* or *floreos*).

Early merengue *típico* was considered disreputable not only for the dance's lascivious reputation but for other reasons as well. *Perico ripiao* literally means "ripped parrot," and lore has it that it was a name of a bordello where merengue was performed. With suggestive choreography and occasionally political lyrics, attempts often were made by moralists to both censor the music and ban the dance with little success. Merengue *cibao* was heard well into the twentieth century but took its place among several popular dances including *mangulina*, *carabiné*, polka, *guarapo*, and *zarambo*.

The United States backed Dominican Republic dictator Rafael Trujillo from 1930 to 1961. Trujillo realized the powerful significance afforded by merengue music, and he recognized its popular appeal, especially among poor rural voters. Trujillo is credited with promoting merengue over other dances, an effort that eventually transformed it into a nationalist musical symbol. Merengue's audience continued to grow and even crossed class lines. Accordionists Lora and Toño Abreu were invited to accompany Trujillo during his political campaigns, which helped further popularize the unique regional style of *perico ripiao* throughout the nation. Once elected, Trujillo had numerous merengues composed in his honor and eventually brought the music to the middle class. The music was heard on radios and performed in respectable ballrooms. Trujillo encouraged bandleaders like Luis Alberti, who helped adapt merengue to the standard big band sound popular in the United States. The accordion was replaced with a large brass section and eventually led to the stylistic differences between urban merengue *de orquesta* and rural *perico ripiao*, that remain today.

Trujillo was assassinated in 1961, but the two musical styles developed along separate but parallel directions. *Típico* musician Tatico Henríquez is hailed as the godfather of modern *perico ripiao* because he updated his ensemble's sound during the 1960s. Musicians replaced the marimba with electric bass and added saxophones to harmonize with the accordion.

Throughout the 1990s the "standard" instrumentation was complemented by the addition of percussion including a bass drum, played with a foot pedal by the *güirero*. Younger bandleaders also added congas and keyboards to the sound, attempting to close stylistic gaps between *típico* and *orquesta* in order to increase their listening audience.

Orquestas have experienced more change in style than in instrumentation. In the 1960s, Johnny Ventura's Combo Show took the country by storm with a slimmer lineup of just two to five brass instruments, choreographed staging, and musical influences from *salsa. In the 1970s, Wilfrido Vargas sped up the tempo and incorporated influences from disco and rock. In the 1980s and 1990s, Juan Luis Guerra further internationalized the music through collaborations with African guitarists, experimenting with both *bachata* and indigenous Caribbean music. He also explored Dominican roots music with *típico* accordionist Francisco Ulloa.

Today, both merengue *orquestas* and *típico* combos play a number of different rhythms, often within the same song. Merengue *derecho*, or straight-ahead merengue, is the kind of fast-paced merengue Americans are most used to hearing. *Pambiche*, or merengue *apambichao*, developed during the American occupation of the Dominican Republic (1916–1924) and takes its name from the "Palm Beach" fabric worn by American soldiers. Its tempo is usually slower than merengue *derecho*, and it can be recognized by the double-slap rhythm on the *tambora*. *Guinchao* is a third rhythm that is a combination of the other two. *Típico* groups may still occasionally play a *mangulina* or a *guaracha*. The former is a dance in 6/8 time; the latter is a clave-based style in 4/4 originally from Cuba. The once-common *paseo*, a slow introduction during which couples would promenade around the dance floor, has nearly disappeared.

Most merengue *típico* artists continue to play the traditional repertoire of songs by Tatico Henríquez, Ñico Lora, el Ciego de Nagua, and others, though in their own, unique style. Some groups also create new compositions either in the rustic style of classic *típico* or in tight, sectional arrangements. *Orquestas*, on the other hand, perform primarily original rather than traditional songs; the remaking (*fusilamiento*) of hits from other genres like *bachata*, Mexican *mariachi, Colombian *vallenato*, and American pop music is also common. Both *típico* groups and *orquestas* have been obliged to add more *mambo, the part of the song where melody instruments (sax, trumpet, or accordion) unite to play catchy, syncopated riffs, or *jaleos*, which help motivate and stimulate dancers. However, in most merengue *típico* groups the emphasis is still on improvisation, while *orquestas* emphasize written arrangements.

In the United States, the Dominican community is a highly transnational bicultural one. Many Dominicans actively maintain economic, social, and familial ties in both countries, traveling back and forth frequently and blurring international and intercultural boundaries in the process. Musicians are no exception, since many perform and record both in the United States and in Santo Domingo—one factor contributing to the wide variety of styles present in merengue today. Some have introduced rhythms from other types of music like salsa or *bachata*; others have experimented with more versatile instruments, as *típico* musician Rafaelito Román did with the chromatic button accordion. New York–born Dominican groups, like the crossover success Fulanito, are playing with novel combinations of *perico ripiao* and *hip-hop, overlaying traditional accordion melodies with rap vocals. Fulanito originated during the colonial period among African slaves kidnapped from the Fulani nation who were brought to the Spanish colonies in the Spanish Caribbean. Regarded as great merchants, Fulanitos brought their economic talents and eventually gained respect throughout the Caribbean.

Much has been made of the fact that merengue is enjoying unprecedented popularity in the United States and abroad, often surpassing even *salsa. However, such statements do not take into account the differing status of the various styles of merengue. *Orquesta* merengue rivals the popularity of salsa on New York City radio; however, guitar merengue does better, no doubt due to its association with *bachata*. Merengue *típico* gets little airplay, most likely due to its perception as rural and unsophisticated and also the payola system governing Latin radio in general. In addition, the different styles occupy different market niches. *Orquesta* tends to attract a younger, urban crowd and appeals equally to Dominicans and non-Dominicans. *Típico* is supported mainly by recent immigrants and older Dominicans who enjoy its nostalgia-inducing powers. Although some young *típico* musicians like El Prodigio are attracting crossover listeners, it remains to be seen whether they can overcome class stigma and achieve the same economic success as their *orquesta* counterparts.

Further Reading

Clark, Donald, ed. *The Penguin Encyclopedia of Popular Music.* 2nd ed. New York: Penguin Books, 1998.

Roberts, John Storm. *The Latin Tinge: The Impact of Latin American Music on the United States.* 2nd ed. New York: Oxford University Press, 1999.

Sydney Hutchinson

Mestizaje. *Mestizaje* is the Spanish word for racial mixture. In the Latin American context, it refers specifically to the hybrid mixture of Spanish, Native American, and African heritage that has constituted Latina and Latino cultural and anthropological identity since the colonial period. Interracial mixture is fundamental to the human species because of (trans)migration and trade networks from the earliest recorded history, as well as because of the need for exogamy (breeding outside one's blood group). For these and other reasons associated with differences between genetic inheritance, recessive genes, and physical appearance, many anthropologists reject the very concept of *race as an accurate trait for human grouping. *Mestizaje* was central to Spanish methods of colonization because most of the first Spaniards who came to the "New World" were men, many of whom married and/or took native concubines (often by force) and produced children and *families to populate the new Spanish colony. The Spanish crown and the Catholic Church initially endorsed marriage with Native American women as a way to facilitate "hispanicization" of the native populations. Marriage to women of noble native families also enabled land acquisition. The introduction of African slaves added additional racial elements to Latin American *mestizaje*. In popular *folklore, the first mestizo is often ascribed to the sons of *La Malinche and Hernán Cortés. More likely, the first mestizos were the offspring of some of the men (e.g., Gonzalo Guerrero) left behind by Christopher *Columbus on his first voyage in 1492.

By its very hybrid nature of interlocking characteristics, *mestizaje* complicates the drawing of strict racial boundaries. Nevertheless, Spain, like other European nations, instituted a complex caste system in an attempt to differentiate between so-called pure Spaniards and "others" of diverse racial mixtures. Privilege and higher status were given to those who were born in Spain or to two Spanish-born parents, and conversely, lower social status was imposed on indigenous natives and African immigrants and their offspring, whether hybrid or "pure." Because of its elaborate classification by the amount of Indian and/or African blood quantity (half, quarter, eighth, sixteenth, etc.), the caste system was difficult to implement and had little impact on public perceptions of race, which were based more on individual appearance, context, profession, education, or class. The *castas* (genetic caste groupings) included mestizos, *mulatos*, *criollos*, and over four dozen other categories of racial mixing. Often the visual distinction between the mixed *castas* was slight, leading to some social fluidity for individuals whose racial appearance was ambiguous and whose classifications sometimes changed throughout their lives. It was even possible to buy certificates forging purity of blood, enabling mestizos with wealth to purchase higher status in the racial hierarchy. Despite this fluidity, racism persisted, and the nobility of the Spanish colonies were typically those with the least African or indigenous ancestry.

The term *mestizo* is still used to describe Latin Americans and Latinos throughout the Americas and thus refers to a broad range of genetic, cultural, historical, and chromatic identities. The makeup of *mestizaje* varies throughout Latin American nations and regions, based on their different racial histories, economies, patterns of development, and slavery: more Europeanized in Argentina, more predominantly indigenous in Guatemala, more Africanist in Cuba and Brazil (often described as "afro-*mestizaje*"). Though their colonial histories differ significantly, Latin American nations share a foundation of racial and cultural mixture.

In an effort to solidify national unity, *mestizaje* was embraced as a defining characteristic in Latin American nationalist movements. Both the *Cuban Revolution and the Mexican Revolution of the twentieth century were represented as movements of racially mixed peoples. Two of the most famous Latin American thinkers celebrated *mestizaje* as a quality that distinguished Latin America from more racially polarized regions (like South Africa and the United States) and that ideally could present a foundation for *fraternidad* (brotherhood) across races and nations. Cuban poet and revolutionary José *Martí declared in 1891 that there is no racial hatred in "nuestra América mestiza" (our mestiza America) because there are no races. In 1925, José Vasconcelos, at that time Mexican minister of education, idealized *mestizaje* as a blend of the genius and the bloods of all American peoples: a racial synthesis capable of universal vision and fraternity. Both Martí and Vasconcelos turned to *mestizaje* as a source of common ground within racially and culturally diverse nations, and their emphasis on unity overlooked existing racial hierarchies and conflicts.

In the United States, the addition of various Euro-American heritages has further transformed the *mestizaje* of U.S. Latinos and Latinas, creating cultural hybrids based on social experience and exposure (e.g., Nuyoricans or Puerto Ricans living in New York and *pochos* [Mexican Americans]). Many *Chicano nationalist movements disclaimed the "gringo invasion" of Mexican culture and embraced Vasconcelos's cosmic race. Two of the most important texts of this movement, *El Plan Espiritual de Aztlán* (1969) and Corky Gonzáles's poem *Soy Joaquín/I Am Joaquín* (1967), celebrate *la raza de bronce* (the bronze race) with indigenous heritage at its center. Amado Peña's 1974 silkscreen *Mestizo* captures the multiplicity, as well as the simultaneous harmony and contradiction, embedded within the term by superimposing three faces of three different shades facing in three different directions.

Feminists have critiqued the masculinist emphasis on brotherhood in Latin American and U.S. Latino articulations of *la raza* and revalued women's roles in bridging cultures. Many Latina feminists have turned to the semi-mythical original mothers of *mestizaje*, like La Malinche in México or Anayansi in Panama, native women given to the Spanish colonizers to serve as translators, guides, and, ultimately lovers. Mexican poet and thinker Octavio *Paz cites La Malinche as a source of shame for Mexicans, and the epithet "malinchista" refers to someone who betrays one's people. Contemporary feminists, however, argue that Malinche and Anayansi were themselves betrayed and that

Demonstrating the cultural hybridity of *mestizaje*, Corky D.C. Clapp, who is half Pawnee and half Mexican American, offers "The Lord's Prayer" in native sign language accompanied by Plains drums and rattles. *Courtesy of the Cordelia Candelaria Private Collection.*

they exercised their bicultural, bilingual agency to resist the indigenous empires that had enslaved them and to forge new, mestizo alliances. Chicana lesbian poet and theorist Gloria *Anzaldúa's influential 1987 writings on mestiza consciousness have contributed to a late-twentieth-century rethinking of *mestizaje* in academic studies (feminist studies, in particular). Anzaldúa theorizes that mestizos' juggling of multiple racial and cultural elements presents a model for negotiating differences, sustaining contradictions, and defying binary oppositions, adding a female mestiza and *jotería* (queer) consciousness to the concept.

Most of the best-known U.S. Latina/o authors (Chicano/as, Puerto Ricans, Cubano/as, Dominicans) address the ambiguity, fluidity, or internal contradictions of mestizo identity. In contemporary American popular culture, it has been celebrated along with other "new," or newly recognized, American mixtures. In the 1990s—with the advent of the movement for a multiracial census category, the craze surrounding golfer Tiger Woods's "Cablinasian" identification, the Latin explosion in American popular music, and demographic statistics foretelling "the browning of America"—*mestizaje* paralleled the complex, "spicy," and for some, threatening mix that has come to characterize American culture for the new millennium. The contemporary tension between embracing differences and fearing diversity, celebrating hybridity versus championing undiluted traditions, reflects the ambivalence that *mestizaje* has met throughout its history in the Americas.

Further Reading

Anzaldúa, Gloria. *Borderlands/La Frontera: The New Mestiza*. 2nd ed. San Francisco, CA: Aunt Lute Books, 1987.

Gonzáles, Rodolfo "Corky." *Soy Joaquín/I Am Joaquín. With a Chronology of People and Events in Mexican and Mexican American History*. Oakland, California: n.p., 1967; reprint New York: Bantam Books, 1972.

Martí, José. *Our America*. New York: Monthly Review Press, 1981.

McWilliams, Carey. *North from Mexico: The Spanish-Speaking People of the United States*. Westport, CT: Greenwood Press, 1968, 1990.

Paz, Octavio. *The Labyrinth of Solitude: Life and Thought in Mexico*. New York: Grove Press, 1961.

Sedillo López, Antoinette. *Historical Themes and Identity: Mestizaje and Labels*. New York: Garland Publishing, 1995.

Suzanne Bost

Mexican American Legal Defense and Education Fund. *See* MALDEF.

Mexican American Opportunity Foundation (MAOF).

The Mexican American Opportunity Foundation (MAOF) was established in 1963 with an $80,000 job development grant from the U.S. Department of Labor and has grown to be the largest Hispanic-serving nonprofit organization in the nation, with an annual budget of over $60 million. Serving several counties in California, MAOF has been providing training, child care, and senior citizen assistance for over forty years.

The mission of MAOF is to provide multipurpose educational and charitable assistance to the general public, with emphasis on *families at risk, senior citizens, and children. To that end, they provide computer training and on-the-job training in retail and offer job placement services to help Mexican Americans gain access to the workforce. MAOF provides child care services for low-income families while the parents are in training classes. Senior citizens enjoy a wide array of services from MAOF, including minor home repairs, legal assistance, Meals on Wheels food service, counseling services, transportation services, assistance with *immigration issues, and utility assistance.

Born in Arizona, MAOF founder Dionicio Morales grew up in an agricultural community in California, where he saw racism and prejudice. Tiring of mountains of research on Chicano issues and data that resulted in no action, he vowed to create an organization that would work to solve problems at the grassroots level and improve working conditions for Mexican Americans. Morales's hands-on approach and passion for helping others have made MAOF successful, enabling it to be named number one in the 2003 *Hispanic Business Magazine*'s list of Top 25 National Hispanic Non-Profits.

Further Reading

Russell, Joel. "Quiet Man with a Mission." *Hispanic Business Magazine* (May 2003): 20.

http://www.maof.org.

Alma Alvarez-Smith

Mexican American Political Association. *See* MAPA.

Mexican Museum. In 1975 Peter Rodríguez founded the Mexican Museum in San Francisco. It is one of the legacies of the *Chicano Movement, and its original mission was "to foster the exhibition, conservation, and dissemination of Mexican and Chicano art and culture for all peoples." In the 1990s, this mission was broadened to "reflect the soul and spirit of the arts and cultures of México and the Americas." The museum's history is divided into three stages: the rascuache period (Mission District), the developmental phase (Fort Mason Art Center near the marina), and the expansion and Latino era (Civic Center). While located on the waterfront the museum experienced major growth, focusing on staff development, exhibition, publication, and preservation. This growth required larger facilities, and in 1991 the museum initiated a search for a downtown location with construction slated for 2004. Designed by Ricardo Legorreta, the new facility allows the museum to fully implement its mission, of which the permanent collection is an important part. The five areas of its collection include Pre-Conquest, Colonial, Popular, Modern and Contemporary Mexican and Latino art, and Chicano art. Inclusive of thousands of years of Mexican history and culture within the Americas, it illustrates a neo-indigenist mythos for Chicanas/os and a bridge to other Latino populations. Programming for a broader public has been central to the museum since its early years. As a permanent arts institution, it continues to offers an alternative perspective.

Further Reading

http://www.mexicanmuseum.org.

Karen Mary Dávalos

Mexican-American Women's National Association. *See* MANA.

México Lindo. One of the cultural by-products of Latina and Latino *immigration to the United States has been the grassroots social networking among immigrants seeking friendship and support during the periods of adjustment to their new environments. The massive emigration from México into the United States that began in the 1890s and accelerated until the Great Depression produced just such a popular culture development that many historians and *folklore scholars identify as the *México Lindo* (Beautiful México) phenomenon. Described as an informal mutual identification among immigrants in *el México de Afuera* (expatriate México), the development sparked a cohesive nationalism in the United States that served as one foundation for later mutual support and advocacy organizations, that is, *mutualistas*.

As expatriates responded to civil rights abuses, segregation, police brutality, and lack of acceptance by mainstream society, the ideology of *México Lindo* attracted many adherents of all backgrounds. Its major components were:

1. Spanish-language preservation and respect for bilingualism;
2. Pride in *mestizaje* (Indian-Spanish hybridity);
3. Commemoration of the *fiestas patrias* (Mexican patriotic holidays like the 16 de Septiembre and *Cinco de Mayo) (*see* Holidays and Fiestas);
4. Education and reverence for patriotic heroes like Miguel Hidalgo y Costilla and Benito Juárez (*see* *History, Chicana/o and Mexican American);
5. The prevalence of Catholicism, particularly as manifested by the *Virgin of Guadalupe; and
6. An ambivalence toward the United States due to the country's history of racial prejudice, institutional discrimination, segregation, and Caucasian-dominant power structure.

These components varied in importance and focus from area to area, and certain towns and cities emphasized particular concerns over others. Although *México Lindo* was a popular, bottom-up ideology, it took hold and spread widely through the support of expatriate newspaper publishers, who provided an infrastructure by which the sentiment, based on an evolving homeland patriotism, could spread even to Mexican Americans with weak immediate ties to *la patria* (the homeland). Publishers and other members of the educated immigrant class maintained close relations with each other across the country and with the Mexican consular service that strove to maintain immigrant loyalty to whichever political faction controlled México during this era.

The *México Lindo* identity came earlier to communities like Tucson and San Antonio, where immigration first appeared on a large scale in the late nineteenth century. By the 1920s, communities with large numbers of recently arrived immigrants promoted the *México Lindo* ideology more forcefully. In Chicago during the 1920s, immigrants from Jalisco or Guanajuato encountered *paisanos* (compatriots) who had themselves only recently arrived and lacked the political influence or urban survival skills needed in the second largest city in the United States. Mexican immigrants to Illinois had to adjust to bone-chilling winters (a painful contrast to the warmer latitudes of Central México) schools, neighborhoods, and a justice system far different from anything they had known. The *México Lindo* mutual support system resulted in an efficient and often rapid coalescing that proved essential to recreating a safe and welcoming ethnic space in the *barrios and borderlands of what often felt like strange and dangerous terrain.

Further Reading

Castro, Rafaela G. *Chicano Folklore: A Guide to the Folktales, Traditions, Rituals and Religious Practices of Mexican-Americans.* New York: Oxford University Press, 2001.

Rosales, Arturo. *Testimonio: A Documentary History of the Mexican American Struggle for Civil Rights.* Houston, TX: Arte Público Press, 2000.

F. Arturo Rosales

Mi Familia/My Family. Director Gregory *Nava's *Mi Familia/My Family* (1995) is a major tribute to the genesis of Mexican immigrant communities in the twentieth century. It seeks to embed the Chicano experience of *immigration in the same history of other immigrant *family experiences that make up the fabric of American culture. Nava follows an immigrant family from México over three generations during the 1920s, 1950s, and 1980s and recreates the saga of the Sánchez family from their beginning as a humble couple, José and María, to a much more complicated one as their children all take distinctive paths in their lives. The children—Paco (Edward James *Olmos), Irene (Lupe *Ontiveros), Toni (Constance Marie), Memo (Enrique Castillo), Chucho (Esai *Morales), and Jimmy (Jimmy *Smits)—individually form the intricate portions of the story. *Mi Familia* shares a family's journey through changes and obstacles to make their dreams come true. Throughout the film's progression and through the help of the narrator, Paco, the children begin demonstrating and developing their personal strength and determination to carve out their own identities and to find themselves within American society.

Mi Familia is divided into three sections within which various parts of the family's story are shared. In the first part, Nava illustrates the struggles of starting a new life in the 1920s. Young José (Jacob Vargas) begins his search for his dream when he leaves México for a small village in the United States called Los Angeles. José begins his journey believing it will take a week to reach Los Angeles, but as we later learn, José walked for a year before meeting his relative, El Californio (Leon Singer). José finds work as a gardener in the Anglo neighborhoods on the other side of the bridge where he meets María (Jennifer *Lopez), who is working as a nanny. The story begins with the parents, José and María, and their struggles as members of the working class and as American citizens who nevertheless face deportation. Nava illustrates María's strength and determination to return to her family after her deportation while pregnant with their third child. She returns to her family and continues the life she had already started.

In the second section of the film, which takes place in the 1950s, Nava illustrates the roads to be taken by each child. Images of Irene's wedding and celebration are shadowed by the *gang hostility that exists within Chucho's world, which is set aside temporarily for the purpose of rejoicing in the family's celebration. Paco wishes to be a writer; Toni, a nun; Memo wants to go to law school; Chucho simply lives a street life; and Jimmy, the baby of the family, spends most of his life dealing with the trauma of watching his brother Chucho shot by the *police.

The third section of the film takes place during the 1980s. After returning from South America, Toni's level of political involvement increases to the point of getting Jimmy, now a young man, to marry a woman from El Salvador to avoid her deportation and possible death. In adjusting to his new marriage while still holding on to the pain of seeing his brother murdered, Jimmy learns that he shares many painful experiences with his new wife. In the last images of the film, the family gathers together and shows how a painful past of struggles and hardships can make a family stronger by sharing their experiences together.

Mi Familia offers a glimpse at the formation of an immigrant family with roots in México as well as California. Nava successfully combines all the joys of the family through humor as well as through the pain of losing one's dreams and hopes. The film is full of experiences familiar to many immigrant families—a child following the expected tradition to make the family proud, those lost between two cultures fighting to become dominant in a changing society, and the child who wants nothing to do with the past and who goes so far as to change his or her name for benefit of English speakers. This film illustrates its relevance to the struggles still faced today by many families starting their new life in a world that continuously changes without acknowledging the conflicting traditions.

Mi Familia/My Family was produced by Francis Ford Coppola and distributed by New Line Cinema. The cast also includes Eduardo Lopez Rojas, Jenny Gago, and Elpidia *Carrillo.

Further Reading

Keller, Gary D. *A Biographical Handbook of Hispanics and United States Film.* Tempe, AZ: Bilingual Press, 1997.

Silvia D. Mora

Mi Vida Loca. The movie *Mi Vida Loca* (My Crazy Life, 1994) looks at the conditions of poverty, racism, *police harassment, and sexism and their effects on the lives of Chicanas in the Echo Park area of Los Angeles. A group of young girls struggle for self-identity and the safety of belonging to a group; they form and join *gangs based on the *Pachuco-era philosophies of *La Vida Loca (The Crazy Life). In the best case, this lifestyle engenders ethnic pride, pride in one's neighborhood, and a large network of support. Unfortunately, with the onset of the drug economies as an alternative to economic survival, these gangs involve themselves in aspects of the drug distribution chain as dealers and brokers to members in, and especially outside, their communities.

In *Mi Vida Loca*, writer and director Allison Anders gives cinematic attention to the working-class Latinas she encountered when she lived in Echo Park and presents several stories about how two best friends since childhood—one newly arrived from México ("Sad Girl," played by Angel Aviles) and the other a U.S.-born Chicana ("Mousie," played by Seidy López)—almost destroy each other when they become teenage mothers by the same teenage homeboy (Jacob Vargas). Once they realize that no man is worth fighting over, much less killing each other for, they, along with their other homegirls (played by actual members of the Echo Park community), decide to enact their own autonomy. As Latinas they decide to become less dependent on the homeboys of the *barrio, to not base their self-esteem on male validation, to run their own businesses, and to administer their own personal and community affairs. Although this is one of the few feature *films that focuses on the struggles that working-class Latinas face, the film has received mixed reaction in the Latino community for its *stereotypes of Latinas as teenage mothers and welfare dependents who are violent and involved in the drug trade.

Produced by Daniel Hassid and Carl-Jan Colpaert and distributed by Sony Pictures Classics, *Mi Vida Loca* also features Magali Alvarado, Jesse Borrego, Salma *Hayek, and Julian Reyes.

Further Reading

Brown, Monica. *Gang Nation: Delinquent Citizens in Puerto Rican, Chicano and Chicana Narratives.* Minneapolis: University of Minnesota Press, 2002.

Fregoso, Rosa Linda. *Mexicana Encounters: The Making of Social Identities on the Borderlands.* Berkeley: University of California Press, 2003.

Erin M. Fitzgibbons-Rascón

Miguel, Luis (1970–   ). Singer Luis Miguel has become known as one of Latin America's top artists whose high-quality studio productions and dynamic live performances have contributed to his growing fan base, especially among Latinas/os in the United States. His most avid admirers have given him the nickname "Micky." He is acclaimed for his Spanish-language romantic pop ballads but has demonstrated equal grace and facility with *mariachi classics.

He was born Luis Miguel Gallegos in Puerto Rico on April 19, 1970, and raised in México. Between 1982 and 1984, Miguel recorded four albums including *Un Sol* (One Son), *Directo al Corazón* (Straight to the Heart), *Decídete* (Decide), and *Palabra de Honor* (Word of Honor). During this time he began touring internationally and made his film debut in *Ya Nunca Mas* (Never Again, 1984). He won his first Grammy Award in 1985 at age fifteen. During the same year he won two other prestigious awards: the Antorcha de Plata at the Chilean Viña del Mar Festival and second prize at the Italian San Remo Song Festival.

In 1986 Miguel released his fifth studio album, *Soy Como Quiero Ser* (I Am as I Want to Be), for which he received five platinum and eight gold records. This marked the start of his collaboration with producer/composer Juan Calderón. His sixth album, *Un Hombre Busca una Mujer* (A Man Seeks a Woman), was released in 1988. This album yielded a single, "La Incondicional" (The Unconditional), that stayed at the top of the Latin charts for a record-breaking span of seven months. A total of seven singles from this album reached the top of *Billboard*'s Latin charts.

Miguel's album *20 Años* (20 Years) was released in 1990 and sold 600,000 copies in its first week. Six singles from the album entered the Mexican Top 100 simultaneously, and the album was followed by a Latin American and U.S. tour that was unprecedented in success. The year 1990 also brought him Spain's "European Excellence" award. Additionally, Miguel became the first Latin artist to win the "Best-Selling Artist" award at the World Music Awards in Monaco. He also succeeded once again at the Viña del Mar festival, this time winning two Antorcha de Plata awards.

In 1991 his eighth album, *Romance*, was released, selling 7 million copies worldwide and earning over seventy platinum awards. This album, the first in a series of three *bolero albums, won him the status of first Spanish-speaking artist to win gold records in the United States, Brazil, and Taiwan. Miguel also won two awards for the album at Venezuela's Ronda awards. Additionally, he won an award for Best Artist from a Non-English-Speaking Country at the Korean International Music Awards and Trofeo Ace in Argentina. *Romance* also yielded many awards into 1992, including three *Billboard* awards: Best Latin Artist, Best Album, and Best Spanish-Singing Artist. He won the Chilean Laurel de Oro award for Best Album of the Year.

In 1992 Miguel was the only Latin artist invited to contribute to the album *Barcelona Gold*, recorded for the Olympics. He was also the only Latin artist asked to participate in the Seville Expo '92 closing ceremony. He won Best International Video at the MTV Awards for America during the same year. Miguel also gave a benefit concert to raise funds for the Children's Museum in México in 1992.

He released his ninth studio album, *Aries*, in 1993, which yielded forty platinum as well as six gold records and resulted in his second Grammy Award for Best Latin Pop Album. He also won prestigious Lo Nuestro awards for Pop Artist of the Year and Best Pop Album. For the same album, he again won *Billboard* awards for Best Male Artist of the Year and Best Album of the Year. In 1993, Miguel became the first Latin singer to completely sell out Madison Square Garden in New York and the first Latin artist to achieve four consecutive sellouts at Los Angeles's Universal Amphitheater.

He released *Segundo Romance* (Second Romance) in 1994, an album that won three *Billboard* awards and earned fifty platinum records. With this album he became the first foreign artist recording in his own language to sell 2 million copies of two albums, *Romance* and *Segundo Romance*, for which he was recognized by the Recording Industry Artists of America. These high-selling albums also made him the only Latino artist to have two Spanish-language albums achieve platinum status. The same year he played sixteen consecutive concerts at Mexico City's National Auditorium and was ranked third in having sold the most tickets for consecutive concerts at a single venue.

In 1995 he won his third Grammy Award as well as winning Monaco's World Music Award for Best Selling Latin Artist of the Year. During this year he released the live album *El Concierto* (The Concert), recorded during his 1994's tour. It included not only his greatest hits but also his versions of some mariachi classics including **rancheras* by José Alfredo *Jiménez. He also released the album *Musipistas* during this year. He again won the Lo Nuestro award for Best Latin Artist of the Year.

In 1996, Miguel recorded "Sueña" for Disney's *Hunchback of Notre Dame* sound track. The film *Speechless* (1994) also included a song recorded by Miguel. He released the album *Nada es Igual* (Nothing Is Like It), which earned thirty platinum records. Within a week, its first single went to number one on all Spanish-language stations in the United States as well as on all playlists in México, Central America, South America, and Spain. Also in 1996, Miguel was given a star on Hollywood's Walk of Fame. During the same year he became the highest paid Latin artist to perform in Las Vegas and was invited to perform at Caesar's Palace for its thirtieth anniversary celebration.

In 1997 Miguel produced and released *Romances*, the third in his series of three bolero albums. The advent of this album made history by being the first Spanish-language record ever to debut at number fourteen on the *Billboard* Top 200. He was honored in Spain with two awards for Best Latin Artist of the Year at the Primer Amigo and Primer Ondas awards. He was also recognized by *Pollstar Magazine* during his subsequent tour as the only Latin artist ever to be recognized as having been on their top twenty list for most tickets sold for consecutive concerts at one venue.

He won his fourth Grammy for Best Pop Performance in 1998. He also won two *Billboard* awards and once again the World Music Award for Best Selling Latin Artist that year. The same year he co-starred in the film *Fiebre de Amor* (Fever of Love). His music also appeared on the movie's sound track.

In 1999 Miguel released *Amarte Es un Placer* (Loving You Is a Pleasure). He received four platinum and four gold records for this album in 2000. He again surpassed his record, playing twenty-one consecutive shows at the National Auditorium in Mexico City during his 1999–2000 tour. The William Morris Agency recognized the tour as the highest-grossing concert tour ever performed by a Spanish-speaking artist. In 2000, Miguel won three Grammys at the first Latin Grammy Awards. In the same year he released *Vivo* (Alive), a live album including more mariachi songs previously unrecorded by Miguel. The video release of *Vivo* was the first Spanish concert video ever released in PAL, NTSC, and DVD formats.

In 2001, Miguel again won *Billboard*'s Best Male Artist Pop Album of the Year, this time for *Vivo*. He was nominated for a Latin Grammy that year as well. His new album *Mis Romances* (My Romances) was released in November, and its first single was selected as the main title for the Mexican soap opera *El Manantial*. In 2002 he won *Billboard*'s Best Male Artist Pop Album of the Year for *Mis Romances*.

Miguel's music received nominations for the 2003 Latin Grammy Awards for Record of the Year with a track from his latest album *Mis Boleros Favoritos* (My Favorite Boleros) and for his producer, Bebu Silvetti, as Producer of the Year for the work he did on the song "Hasta Que Vuelvas" (Until You Return).

Miguel's impact as a Latin American artist is extensive. He has been a pioneer of Latin popular music, winning countless awards and selling record-breaking numbers of albums throughout much of the world. Although there were indications that Miguel would record an English-language album, he has not but has instead continued to be extremely successful with Spanish-language music.

Further Reading

Cobo, Leila. "Luis Miguel's No-Show Disappoints." *Billboard* (March 2001): 54–56.

http://www.delafont.com/music_acts/luis-miguel.htm.

http://www.lacasadeluismiguel.com.

http://www.love-that-luis.com/newsarch2003/2003-01jan-july.html.

http://www.terra.com/specials/latingrammy/luis_miguel.html.

Christina Burbano-Jeffrey

Milagro Beanfield War, The. Directed by Robert Redford and produced by Redford and Moctêzuma Esparza, *The Milagro Beanfield War* (1988) was adapted from John Nichols' novel of the same title. The *film is a classic of *Chicano-themed cinema that dramatizes the heated debate over land and water rights in the small town of Milagros in northern New Mexico, one of the oldest continuously lived in areas of the *barrios and borderlands. When Joe Mondragón (Chick Vennera), the main character, kicks in an irrigation gate one day, he begins a series of events that bring the entire town into conflict with nearby land developers who are building a golf resort. This film examines the traditions of the Chicano community and the socioeconomic changes that have led many to leave for jobs in bigger cities. Joe plants beans in his father's dry field and waters them illegally, causing controversy over the water rights issue, which rich white developers and politicians are scheming to cover up. From Ruby (Sonia *Braga), a woman who owns a local garage and organizes a town meeting, to Amarante (Carlos Riquelme), the town's eldest citizen who stirs up violence when he takes his *pistola* to the local bar one day, everyone gets involved. The plot shows how Spanish-Indian-Mexican culture clashes with the modern-day white land encroachments that threaten to destroy the community and its economic base. The film culminates with a manhunt for Joe; the townspeople finally gather to pick the beans together, making a statement about the need for solidarity to fight corporate capitalism. The film's complex cast of characters makes it clear that there are no easy answers even among the townspeople but that Hispanic traditions are alive and well in New Mexico. The cast also includes Rubén *Blades, Julie Carmen, Richard Bradford, Freddy *Fender, Christopher Walken, John Heard, Melanie Griffith, and Daniel Stern. Distributed by Universal Pictures, *The Milagro Beanfield War* won an Oscar for Best Score in 1988.

Further Reading

Keller, Gary D. *A Biographical Handbook of Hispanics and United States Film.* Tempe, AZ: Bilingual Press, 1997.

Cheryl Greene

Minoso, Minnie (1922–   ). Often described in the early years of his professional baseball career as the Cuban Babe Ruth, Minnie Minoso was the first black player to wear a White Sox uniform when he joined the Chicago club in 1951. The Hall of Famer's actual debut in the white major leagues occurred in 1949, two years after Jackie Robinson's watershed integration of the *sport. Some sports studies specialists describe Minoso as a Latino Robinson because he was the first player to gain prominence as a Latino player in the majors. Hitting a home run in his first at bat for the White Sox in a game against the champion New York Yankees, Minoso was named Rookie of the Year by the influential trade paper *The Sporting News.* In 1951 he also led both leagues in stolen bases, a feat he repeated in 1954. The left fielder and power hitter tied for stolen base leader in the American League

(AL) in 1956. In 1954 he led the AL in triples and in doubles in 1957. His statistics and consistency as a player made him an admired player by his peers and fans, who called him the "Cuban Comet," and also helped open up opportunities for other Latinos in the still largely segregated game and society.

Minnie Saturnino Orestes Arriéta Armas was born on November 29, 1922, in Havana, Cuba, where he grew up playing sandlot ball. Even as a boy, he was energetic and resourceful in getting on base, often taking a body hit from fastball pitches to earn a walk. Later in the majors, over sixteen seasons he set the American League record of getting on base by being hit 189 times. Although he helped inaugurate the "Go-Go" White Sox, he was traded to the Cleveland Indians in 1957 and thus missed Chicago's 1959 winning of the AL pennant. Owner Bill Veeck awarded Minoso an honorary championship ring anyway. Retraded to the White Sox in 1960, he led the AL with 184 hits and was second to Roger Maris in runs batted in. That year he batted over .300 for the eighth and final time.

Besides Chicago and Cleveland, he also briefly played for the St. Louis Cardinals and Washington Senators before retiring in 1964 after completing seventeen seasons of play. Twelve years later when Veeck regained ownership of the White Sox, Minoso was invited out of retirement to serve as Chicago's designated hitter. From 1976 to 1978 he was hired to coach the White Sox, and in 1980 he became the second major leaguer in history to play five decades in the big leagues when he was again activated to pinch hit for Chicago. Hugely popular, his number, 9, was retired in 1983, and he was kept on the payroll as goodwill ambassador for the team and the city. Amazingly, Minoso played one more professional game again in 1993 when he was asked to don a minor league uniform for an independent Florida club. Voted into the Major League Hall of Fame in 1990, Minoso personifies the Latino best and brightest of professional sport talent.

Further Reading

The Baseball Encyclopedia: The Complete and Official Record of Major League Baseball. 10th ed. New York: Macmillan, 1996.

Regalado, Samuel. *Viva baseball! Latin Major Leaguers and Their Special Hunger.* Urbana: University of Illinois Press, 1998.

http://www.baseballlibrary.com/baseballlibrary/ballplayers/M/Minoso_Minnie.stm.

http://www.thehistorymakers.com/biography/biography.asp?bioindex=338&category=sportsMakers.

Cordelia Chávez Candelaria

Miranda, Carmen (1909–1955). With her exaggerated accent, actress and singer Carmen Miranda became one of the most iconic and enduring images of Latin America to emerge from Hollywood before World War II. María de Carmo Miranda Da Cunha was born on February 9, 1909, in Marco de Canavezes, Portugal, and she immigrated with her parents at the age of three months to Río de Janeiro, Brazil. Although she is a familiar cultural referent worldwide, she appeared in a surprisingly small number of films (twenty-one total, fourteen in the United States). She achieved fame in her adopted country of Brazil through her records and radio performances. During this period, she adopted her well-known costume with the fruit hat and bare midriff that in many ways caricaturized the dress worn by the Afro-Brazilian Bahia food merchants. Her first film appearance was in the Brazilian documentary

Carmen Miranda in *The Gang's All Here. Courtesy of Photofest.*

A Voz do Carnaval (A Voice of the Carnival, 1933), followed by acting roles in *Alo Alo Brasil* (Alo Alo Brazil, 1935) and *Estudantes* (Students, 1935), which cemented her screen stardom in Brazil. In 1939 Miranda arrived in New York with much fanfare and armed with only twenty words of English. The language difference resulted in her being characterized as idiotic and cartoonish in the American press. However, performances in New York and especially in *The Streets of Paris* on Broadway won her devoted fans in the United States. She soon was signed by Twentieth Century–Fox and given major supporting roles in films like *Down Argentine Way* (1941, in which she sings her signature song "South American Way"), *That Night in Rio* (1941), *Weekend in Havana* (1941), and *The Gang's All Here* (1943). In the latter film, Miranda sang "The Lady in the Tutti-Frutti Hat" in a Busby Berkeley number that included phallic bananas protruding from Miranda's hat. The image was so scandalous and offensive that the film was banned in Brazil. During her Hollywood period, Brazilians became disenchanted with Miranda, believing she had become assimilated to American life. Although she was the highest-paid performer in the United States during the 1940s, she was trapped in her role as the "Brazilian Bombshell." She attempted to extend her acting talents in such films as *Copacabana* (1947), in which she played dual roles opposite Groucho Marx, and *If I'm Lucky* (1946), where she played an Irish American character, Margaret O'Toole. The public, though, would not accept Miranda in any other role. In 1954, she returned to Brazil, and while singing her hit song "Boneca de Pixe" (Tar Doll) to an adoring crowd, she collapsed. She returned to Los Angeles in 1955 for an appearance on the *Jimmy Durante Show*, where she fell during a dance number on the show, not realizing that she had suffered a heart attack. She died the following day, August 5, 1955, at the age of forty-five.

Further Reading

Gil-Montero, Martha. *The Brazilian Bombshell: The Biography of Carmen Miranda.* New York: Donald Fine, 1989.

William Orchard

Mission, The. This 1986 British feature *film directed by Roland Joffé, with original music score by Ennio Morricone, chronicles the enslavement, exploitation, and extermination of Guaraní Indians in the middle of the seventeenth century by the Spanish and the Portuguese, and defense by Jesuit missionaries, in the Amazonian area where Brazil, Argentina, and Paraguay meet. The cast includes Robert De Niro (in the role of Rodrigo Mendoza), Jeremy Irons (in the role of Father Gabriel), as well as Ray McAnally, Aidan Quinn, Cherie Lunghi, Liam Neeson, and Ronald Pickup.

Each scene, each shot, is beautiful and interesting, and the locations are spectacular (the Iguazú waterfall and the jungle). Father Gabriel is entirely devoted to the task of converting the natives and building with them the mission San Carlos, but he is willing to surrender them to the forces of destruction and slavery spearheaded by the European soldiers without any resistance. The recent convert and former mercenary and slave trader Rodrigo Mendoza believes it is his duty to fight the invaders and oppressors that have come to burn the mission and kill all its inhabitants. At the end, both options prove to be equally ineffective, and both characters are killed. In the last instance, the brutality of the soldiers and their masters is the brutality of nascent capitalism, accompanied and supported by the Catholic Church as an institution.

This film brings together a host of talented and acclaimed artists. Robert De Niro won an Academy Award for Best Supporting Actor in 1974 and another for Best Actor in 1980; Jeremy Irons won the Best Actor Oscar in 1990; Ennio Morricone has never won an Oscar, but he has composed scores for films that every moviegoer immediately recognizes (the scores for Sergio Leone's *The Good, the Bad and the Ugly* [1967] and *Once Upon a time in America* [1984], for instance), and his scores for *The Mission* and for *The Untouchables* (1987) were nominated for Oscars; Chris Menges has won the Academy Award for cinematography twice (in 1984 for *The Killing Fields* and in 1986 for *The Mission*); playwright and screenwriter Robert Bolt was thrice nominated for Academy Awards for *Lawrence of Arabia* (1962), *Doctor Zhivago* (1965), and *A Man for All Seasons* (1966), winning it for the last two; and Roland Joffé, who directed *The Mission*, had an acclaimed feature debut with *The Killing Fields*, which won the Golden Palm at the Cannes Film Festival.

Further Reading

http://www.imdb.com/title/tt0091530/.
http://www.movie-gazette.com/cinereviews/281.
http://www.suntimes.com/ebert/ebert_reviews/1986/11/117159.html.

Luis Aldama

Mixed Blessings: New Art in a Multicultural America. Written by art historian Lucy R. Lippard and published in 1990, this is the first "art" book to discuss cross-cultural visual art productions by Latino, Native, African, and Asian Americans. Lippard includes a vast array of reproductions of artwork that range from large murals to performance pieces. The book discusses the history of art by calling into question the canon of Western art that has ignored the work by artists of other cultural traditions. Lippard includes quotes from the various artists, activists, and scholars and asks important questions about the meaning of art and its political purpose for ethnic Americans. She divides the book into chapters that explore Latino, Native, African African, and Asian American experiences and address cultural *stereotypes. The book presents works that encompass the themes of diaspora, *family, identity, and the politics of representation. Bringing visual evidence to bear on the history of oppression in America, this book stresses the need for including multicultural visual art in museums, galleries, and educational institutions, as well as the importance of public and community art projects to dispel the Eurocentrism of the dominant culture.

Further Reading

Lippard, Lucy R. *Mixed Blessings: New Art in a Multicultural America.* New York: Pantheon, 1990.

Cheryl Greene

Molcajete. One of the most commonplace and basic utensils of Mexican *food and cookery, the *molcajete* refers to a simple stone mortar and pestle. The most traditional types are made of volcanic rock with the bowl or tub area (i.e., the mortar or *cajete*) for grinding and pounding curved up from three short legs, and the separate pestle (called *mano*) made of the same stone material. The small kitchen *molcajete* is used to pound and ground spices, chile, and other herbs, while the larger ones are used to grind grain. Still very commonly seen throughout México and Central America, even in the age of blenders and electronic food processors, the *molcajetes* date to the pre-Columbian era and indigenous cooking. The word itself is close to its

The *molcajete*, a common utensil for grinding spices in Mexican and Caribbean cuisines, is made of volcanic stone and wears down with years of usage. *Photo by Emmanuel Sánchez Carballo.*

Aztec or Náhuátl roots: *molli*, referring to salsa, and *caxitl*, referring to bowl, combined to form *molcajete*. Today expert cooks still rely on the volcanic rock *molcajete* for preparation of traditional dishes like *chocolate mejicano* (Mexican cocoa), *mole*, *atole* (blue corn meal porridge), and many others.

Further Reading

De'Angeli, Alicia Gironella, and Jorge De'Angeli. *El gran libro de la cocina mexicana*. Mexico City: Ediciones Larousse, 1980.

Gilbert, Fabiola Cabeza de Baca. *We Fed Them Cactus*. Albuquerque: University of New Mexico Press, 1954.

Santamaría, Francisco J. *Diccionario de Mejicanismos*. Mexico City: Porrúa, 2000.

Gabriella Sánchez and Cordelia Chávez Candelaria

Molotov. *See Rock en Español.*

Montalbán, Ricardo (1920–   ). Ricardo Gonzalo Pedro Montalbán y Merino, a Latino icon in *film and television, was born on November 25, 1920, in Mexico City, México, and moved to Los Angeles as a schoolboy. While

Ricardo Montalbán serenades local girls during the filming of *Sombrero* in México. *Courtesy of Photofest.*

attending high school, he participated in school plays, in which he demonstrated talent and commitment. He relocated to New York around 1940 and performed small roles in several Broadway productions, including a role opposite Tallulah Bankhead. In 1941 he returned to México, where he acted in thirteen Spanish-language films and earned an Ariel nomination (the equivalent of the Oscar) before he was recruited in 1945 by MGM as a "Latin Lover" type. His first Hollywood film was opposite Esther Williams in *Fiesta*. He signed a ten-year contract and was cast in numerous roles over the years, playing many characters of different ethnic or national backgrounds.

Montalbán has enjoyed a successful movie-acting career spanning five decades. Some of his films include *Neptune's Daughter* (1949), *Right Cross* (1950), *The Queen of Babylon* (1956), *Cheyenne Autumn* (1964), *Sweet Charity* (1969), *Sol Madrid* (1968), *Escape from the Planet of the Apes* (1971), *Conquest of the Planet of the Apes* (1972), and *Star Trek II: The Wrath of Khan* (1982).

His television credits include segments of *The Loretta Young Show* (1959), *Colombo* (1976), *Wonder Woman* (1974), *Combat* (1965), and *Wagon Train* (1958). His most memorable television role was that of Mr. Rourke on the hit show *Fantasy Island* (1978–1984), which ran for seven years. After *Fantasy Island*, Montalbán played a Greek tycoon on *The Colbys* (1987). He won an Emmy Award in 1979 for his role as Chief Satangkai in the miniseries *How the West Was Won*. In addition to his acting career, Montalbán is dedicated to promoting Latina/o performing arts. In 1970 he founded a nonprofit organization called Nosotros (meaning "we" or "us") to protest the way Spanish surnamed actors were typecast and treated in the industry. The scope of the organization grew to include improving the image of Latinas/os in Hollywood films and improving conditions for Latina/o actors.

Further Reading

Axford, Roger W. *Spanish-Speaking Heroes*. Midland, MI: Pendell Publishing, 1973.

Alma Alvarez-Smith

Montez, María (1917–1951). María África Antonia Gracia Vidal de Santa Silos was a popular figure in cinema, referred to as "The Queen of Technicolor" and as "The Caribbean Cyclone," monikers that suggest both the kinds of *films in which she was featured and the larger-than-life star persona she cultivated. Montez was born on June 6, 1917, in Barahona, Dominican Republic, where her father was the Spanish consul. After a brief stint as a model in New York City, she changed her name from María Gracia to María Montez (after the dancer Lola Montez, whom her father greatly admired), and she signed with Universal Studios. Universal capitalized on her striking looks and pronounced accent by casting her in a number of exotic and escapist films beginning with a small part in *The Invisible Woman* (1940). Montez started acting at the relatively late age of twenty-eight and never pursued professional training for her craft. Although critics often deride her thespian skills, she remained a popular figure through World War II. She received positive notices for her performance opposite Carmen *Miranda and Don Ameche in *That Night in Rio* (1941). Her performances in *Arabian Nights* (1942), *White Savage* (1943), and *Ali Baba and the Forty Thieves* (1944)—each of which was filmed in luscious Technicolor—earned her the "Queen of Technicolor" nickname and cemented her stardom. After the war, the appetite for such escapist films waned. Montez left the United States with her French actor husband and appeared in only a handful of European films before her very early death in 1951 in Paris, France.

Further Reading

Keller, Gary D. *A Biographical Handbook of Hispanics and United States Film.* Tempe, AZ: Bilingual Press, 1997.

William Orchard

Mora, Pat (1942–   ). A recipient of numerous awards, Pat Mora is a well-known Chicana writer from the Texas border region. In 1983, the National Association for *Chicano Studies presented her with its Creative Writing Award; she received the 1984 New America: Women Artists and Writers of the Southwest poetry award, and the *El Paso Herald-Post* named her to its Writers Hall of Fame in 1988. Mora also received Southwest Book Awards from the Border Regional Library for two collections of her poetry, *Chants* (1985) and *Borders* (1987). She and her illustrator Raúl Colón received the third annual Tomás Rivera Mexican American Children's Book Award for *Tomás and the Library Lady* in 1997 for bringing honor to Mexican American people, culture, and history through the celebration of the Mexican and Chicana/o traditions of literature and the arts, values that lie at the center of Mora's creative vision.

Born in El Paso, Texas, on January 19, 1942, to Raúl Antonio Mora, an optician and business owner, and Estela Delgado Mora, a homemaker, Mora attended Saint Patrick's grade school and Loreto Academy, a high school for girls, both run by the Roman Catholic Sisters of Loreto. She received her Bachelor of Arts in 1963 from Texas Western College (now the University of Texas at El Paso [UTEP]) and began teaching English and Spanish at the elementary and high school levels. Returning to UTEP for a master's degree in 1967, she became a part-time instructor in English and communication at El Paso Community College, a position she held for seven years. In 1981, Mora was appointed assistant to the vice president of academic affairs at UTEP and also published her first poem. Her work was published in the bilingual *Revista Chicano-Riqueña Kikiriki/Children's Literature Anthology* (1981) and *Tun-Ta-Ca-Tun* (1983), both edited by Sylvia Cavazos Peña. Her first book, *Chants*, a collection of poetry, was published in 1984, and her second, *Borders*, appeared in 1986. That same year she received a Kellogg

Fellowship to study national and international issues of cultural conservation. In 1988, Mora was named director of the UTEP Museum and assistant to the university president.

Mora decided to become a full-time writer and speaker in 1989 and left El Paso for Cincinnati, Ohio, when her husband, an expert on Mayan culture, took a position to teach anthropology at the University of Cincinnati. In 1991 *Communion* was published by Arte Público Press, a work of poetry that features Mora's reflections on her travels to Cuba, India, Pakistan, and New York City. Two years later, Mora produced a memoir about her father after his death, *House of Houses* (1997), which, like her other books, features her family extensively. In 1992 she produced *A Birthday Basket for Tía* (1992), her first picture book for children, which featured her aunt, Ignacia Delgado (Tía). Considered among Mora's best works, *A Birthday Basket for Tía* follows a young female narrator in search of the perfect gift for her great-aunt Tía's ninetieth birthday party. This book, *Pablo's Tree* (1994), *The Rainbow Tulip* (1999), and *Tomás and the Library Lady* (1997) are children's books that combine three of Mora's prevalent themes: the joy of reading, the special quality of intergenerational relationships, and the healthy beauty of bilingual, bicultural identity. Two more books for juvenile audiences, *Confetti: Poems for Children* (1995), a collection of narrative poems in free verse for primary graders, and *My Own True Name: New and Selected Poems for Young Adults, 1984–1999* (2001), a collection composed of sixty poems from her adult books and several new poems, and *Love to Mama: A Tribute to Mothers* (2002), an anthology, constitute the highlights of Mora's literary work.

Her other titles address several subjects and themes that appear in her children's books, such as Mexican American culture, nature (especially the desert) and the importance of family. She often features Chicanas and Chicanos who have good relationships with adults, and they often revolve around celebrations, such as parties and *holidays, filled with *food and music. Mora promotes the importance of cultural heritage, proposing that young Chicanas/os can assimilate to the majority society while retaining their cultural identity. She stresses the support of family and friends, self-reliance, and the joys of literacy. Favoring a spare, evocative prose style filled with detailed descriptions and concrete imagery, she employs basic Spanish phrases in both English and Spanish to convey her themes. Many educators consider her poems "1910" and "Illegal Alien" classics, and Mora is acclaimed for introducing all children to Latino culture in a joyful and entertaining manner.

Mora served as a consultant for the W.K. Kellogg Foundation and as a member of the advisory committee for their national fellowship program. She also served as a consultant on the youth exchange program between the United States and México. In 1997 Mora lobbied successfully to establish a national day to celebrate childhood and bilingual literacy. Called El Día de los Niños/El Día de los Libros (*see* Día del Niño), the day is part of National Poetry Month. Mora has become a popular speaker and guest presenter at gatherings of teachers and education professionals. She often speaks at schools, universities, and conferences about such subjects as diversity, heritage, creative writing, cultural conservation, and multicultural education.

Further Reading

Ikas, Karen Rosa. *Chicano Ways: Conversations with Ten Chicana Writers*. Reno: University of Nevada Press, 2001.

Lomelí, Francisco A., and Carl R. Shirley, eds. *Chicano Writers: Third Series*. Vol. 209 of *Dictionary of Literary Biography*. Detroit, MI: Gale Group, 1992.

Morad, Deborah J., ed. *Children's Literature Review*. Vol. 58. Detroit, MI: Gale Group, 2000.

BJ Manríquez

Moraga, Cherríe (1952–   ). Playwright, poet, essayist, and editor/publisher, Cherríe Moraga is a major voice in Chicana and Latina letters, and her remarkable literary influence has crossed cultural and national borders since the 1980s. Her landmark coedited anthology *This Bridge Called My Back: Writings by Radical Women of Color* (1981) and her own personal narrative *Loving in the War Years: Lo que nunca pasó por sus labios* (1983) jettisoned Moraga into continuing national importance.

Moraga was born in Whittier, California, on September 25, 1952. The daughter of a Chicana mother, Elvira Moraga, and an Anglo father, Joseph Lawrence, Moraga's dual ethnicity and her lesbian sexual orientation are central to her work. Speaking as a Chicana lesbian, Moraga breaks traditional silences surrounding sexuality, lesbianism, the reality of sexism and homophobia in *Chicano culture, and the persistence of racism and classism in mainstream feminism. Moraga writes toward social transformation, bringing disenfranchised voices, especially Chicana lesbian voices, out of silence. Moraga attended a private college in Hollywood and earned her B.A. in 1974. She taught high school for three years before moving to San Francisco, where she earned an M.A. from San Francisco State in 1980. While working on her graduate degree, Moraga compiled with Gloria *Anzaldúa the groundbreaking *This Bridge Called My Back: Writings by Radical Women of Color*, a work advancing a feminism that recognizes the voices and diversity of women of color. Reprinted in 1983, *This Bridge Called My Back* was awarded the Before Columbus Foundation American Book Award in 1986. Including writing of multiple genres by women of diverse ethnicities, educational backgrounds, sexual orientations, and social class backgrounds, *This Bridge Called My Back* illustrates the intersections of oppressions women of color experience and continues to be read widely as both an illustration of these experiences and a model for solidarity among women of color. With Chicana feminist Ana *Castillo, Moraga edited the 1988 Spanish edition of *This Bridge Called My Back* (Esta puente, mi espalda: Voces de mujeres tercermundistas en los Estados Unidos). Also, as a response to the difficulty of finding a willing publisher for *This Bridge Called My Back*, Moraga and black feminist Barbara Smith cofounded Kitchen Table: Women of Color Press.

This Bridge Called My Back was soon followed by *Loving in the War Years: Lo que nunca pasó por sus labios* (1983), which was republished in a second and expanded edition in 2000. Perhaps Moraga's most widely read work and the first published book by an openly lesbian Chicana, this work is largely fueled by her autobiographical negotiation of *race, culture, and sexuality. Within the multigenre collage of poetry, personal narrative, and essay of *Loving in the War Years*, Moraga articulates the conflicts of being biracial, female, and lesbian in both Chicano culture and mainstream society. Because she experienced the dominant society's privileging of light skin and literacy in English, Moraga's lesbianism is what ultimately allows her to reidentify with Chicana experiences of racism, sexism, and classism, yet paradoxically her lesbianism, as subversion of traditional gender roles, is the facet of self that most alienates her from Chicano culture. Moraga considers *Loving in the War Years* a coming home, a reclamation of the parts of herself she was encouraged to deny—her Chicana self, her Spanish-speaking self, her lesbian self.

Moraga's work as author and editor has been rich and diverse. Recognizing the absence of lesbian voices and Latina voices in dialogue, Moraga worked with Alma Gómez and Mariana Romo-Carmona to publish *Cuentos: Stories by Latinas* (1983) and with Norma Alarcón and Ana Castillo to publish *The Sexuality of Latinas* (1993). In *The Last Generation: Prose and Poetry* (1993), Moraga combines poetry and prose, Spanish and English, speaks as Chicana lesbian, artist, and activist to argue toward a transformation of social consciousness, a reconceptualizing of sexuality, nationalism, art, race, and gender. When at age forty Moraga decided to become a mother, she documented her pregnancy and the challenge of the premature birth of her son in *Waiting in the Wings* (1997). Written in English and Spanish, *Waiting in the Wings* examines the social and spiritual effects of lesbian motherhood intimately.

As the premier Chicana playwright in the United States, Moraga's aims remain consistent with her work as poet, essayist, and editor as she centers issues of *gender, ethnicity, and sexuality. Her early plays include *La Extranjera* (The Stranger, 1985), *Giving Up the Ghost: Teatro in Two Acts* (1986), and *Shadow of a Man* (1988), winner of the 1990 Fund for New American Plays Award. Set in California's Central Valley and chronicling the struggle of Mexican migrant laborers who survive on minimal wages and experience the environmental hazard of pesticide exposure, the title play of Moraga's collection *Heroes and Saints & Other Plays* (1994) was awarded the 1992 Will Glickman Prize for Best Play as well as the Dramalogue, the

PEN West, and the Critics Circle awards. Moraga received the Fund for New American Plays Award from the Kennedy Center for the Performing Arts for her play *Watsonville: Some Place Not Here*, published with *Circle in the Dirt: El Pueblo de East Palo Alto* (2002). Developed through interviews conducted with residents in the two towns of Watsonville and East Palo Alto, these plays confront the changing California landscape of the 1990s, as anti-immigrant, antiyouth, and English only. Moraga's most recent work *The Hungry Woman: The Mexican Medea* (2002) is a recasting of the myths of Medea and *La Llorona at the end of the millennium. Depicting a woman gone mad, torn between her longing for another woman and for the Indian nation that is denied her, Moraga explores not only the embattled position of the Chicano population in the United States but the ways in which Chicanos turn against each other through sexism and homophobia. *The Hungry Woman* is published alongside *Heart of the Earth*, an allegorical and feminist revisioning of the Quiché Maya *Popul Vuh* story. Additionally, in an afterword to this publication, Moraga comments on nationhood, indigenism, queer sexuality, and gender formation. Moraga's plays challenge audiences to reexamine and reconceptualize conflicts of culture and passion. Moraga is currently an artist-in-residence at Stanford University.

Further Reading

Yarbro-Bejarano, Yvonne. *Wounded Heart: Writing on Cherríe Moraga*. Austin: University of Texas Press, 2001.

R. Joyce Zamora Lausch

Morales, Dionicio. *See* Mexican American Opportunity Foundation (MAOF).

Morales, Esai (1962–). Esai Manuel Morales, born to a single mother of Puerto Rican descent in Brooklyn, New York, on October 1, 1962, is an award-winning *film, television, and stage actor. His most prominent recent success is in his prime-time role as Lieutenant Tony Rodriguez in the Emmy Award–winning television series *NYPD Blue*. Morales attended New York's High School of Performing Arts in the Manhattan *theater district with a stage debut in *El Hermano* as part of the Ensemble Studio Theatre followed by *The Tempest* alongside Raúl *Julia while still a student. The quality of Morales's roles expanded as well as did his recognition, evidenced in his being awarded the Los Angeles Drama Critics Circle Award for his performance in *Tamer of Horses* (pre-1983).

Morales made his debut on film in *Bad Boys* (1983) with Sean Penn, a movie illustrating youth violence and the effect of being in and out of prison. His next film was *La Bamba* (1987) as musician Ritchie *Valens's half brother Bob. While making films, Morales also made an appearance in the award-winning TV movie depicting the activism and assassination of the advocate Chico Mendes, *The Burning Season* (1994). Working alongside

Edward James *Olmos and Jimmy *Smits, Morales's next major film was Gregory *Nava's film *Mi Familia* (1995) as Chucho, the troubled son caught in the difficulties of being a *gang member. In *The Disappearance of García Lorca* (1997), Morales played the role of a journalist looking for answers behind the mysterious death of García Lorca. Other television performances include his role in *Resurrection Blvd.* (2000) and *American Family* (2002).

In an effort to advance his dream of increasing the number and substance of roles for Latinas/os in the entertainment industry, Morales joined actors Smits and Sonia *Braga and Washington, D.C., attorney Felix Sánchez in establishing the National Hispanic Foundation for the Arts (NHFA) in 1997. NHFA goals include offering graduate scholarships to colleges and universities and expanding career opportunities in the field of performing arts. Aside from working to promote Latinos in entertainment, Morales participates as a founding board member of Earth Communications Office (ECO) to increase the awareness of important environmental issues. When not participating in entertainment and environmental advocacy issues, Morales works on advancing important health issues by participating in the Health Education AIDS Liaison (HEAL) organization.

Further Reading

http://www.nypdblue.org/actors/morales.html.
http://www.puertorico-herald.org/issues/2001/vol5n23/ProfMorales-en.shtml.
http://www.wchs8.com/abc/nypdblue/esaimorales.shtml.

Silvia D. Mora

Moreira, Airto. *See* Airto.

Moreno, Arturo (c. 1947–   ). In May 2003, Arturo Moreno became the first Latino to own controlling interest in an American professional *sports team when he purchased the Anaheim Angels baseball team for $183.5 million. His purchase of the 2002 World Series Champions elevated him to position five on the *Sports Illustrated* "101 Most Influential Minorities in Sports" list, following athletes Magic Johnson, Tiger Woods, Serena Williams, and Michael Jordan. In 2002, with a net worth of almost a billion dollars, Moreno was ranked number 246 in *Forbes Magazine*'s "Four hundred wealthiest people in America."

A fourth-generation Mexican American, Moreno was born and raised in Tucson, Arizona, where his parents ran a Spanish-language newspaper. One of eleven children, he grew up watching baseball spring training in Arizona, which gave him the opportunity to watch some of the greatest players of all time and intensified his love for the game. Moreno, who prefers to be called "Arte," did a tour of duty in the U.S. Army from 1966 to 1968 and is a Vietnam veteran. He graduated from the University of Arizona in 1973 with a Bachelor of Arts degree in marketing and took an entry-level position in the billboard industry, which he parlayed into a multimillion-dollar business.

In 1999, Moreno and partner William Levine sold Outdoor Systems Billboard Corporation to Infinity Broadcasting Company for $8.7 billion in stock.

In 1986, he and seventeen other investors bought the Salt Lake City Trappers, a minor league rookie team, and he has stakes in the Phoenix Suns basketball team. He was one of the original limited partners in the Arizona Diamondbacks baseball team in the 1990s, although in 2001, when he sought to buy controlling interest in the team, he was bought out by other investors in what is best described as a hostile takeover. With his purchase in 2003, Moreno became the third owner of the Anaheim Angels, following the Disney Corporation and the original owner, Gene Autry.

Moreno splits his time between Phoenix, Arizona, and La Jolla, California, where he lives with his wife Carole and their three children. He is described as a cordial, down-to-earth guy who enjoys coaching his son's teams in flag football, basketball, and baseball and is very proud to be a Mexican American.

Further Reading

Flores, Angelique. "Flying with the Angels." *Hispanic Magazine*, July–August 2003. http://www.hispaniconline.com/magazine/2003/july_aug/Business.

Neiman, David. "Angels' New Owner Looks Right at Home: Moreno Brings Personal Touch to His Job." *Washington Post*, May 27, 2003, DJ.

Alma Alvarez-Smith

Moreno, Rita (1931–   ). Rita Moreno was born Rosa María Alverio on December 31, 1931, in Humacao, Puerto Rico. Actress, singer, and dancer, Moreno is the first person and only Latina to win all of the four major entertainment awards: the Oscar, the Grammy, the Emmy, and the Tony. The only other performers who have since won all these awards are Audrey Hepburn, Sir John Gielgud, and Helen Hayes. After coming with her mother to New York at the age of five, Moreno began dance lessons with Paco Cansino, Rita *Hayworth's uncle. She was soon performing professionally and, billed as "Rosita Cosío," landed a role on Broadway in Harry Kleiner's *Skydrift*. Through the 1940s, Moreno sang and danced in nightclubs across the United States and Canada. Hollywood also called on her talents to dub the voices of such young stars as Elizabeth Taylor and Margaret O'Brien for *films to be distributed in Spanish-speaking countries. She made her film debut in *So Young, So Bad* (1950), in which she played a juvenile delinquent in a reform school.

She was soon contracted to MGM, which demanded that she shorten her name from "Rosita Moreno" to "Rita Moreno" (Moreno was her stepfather's surname). After several small roles in MGM films, she was dropped by the studio and had to find work alone, often playing stereotypical "Latin Spitfire" roles or portraying exotic foreigners. During this period, her most notable role was as Zelda Zanders in the musical *Singing in the Rain* (1952).

Rita Moreno. *Courtesy of Photofest.*

In 1954, her movie fortunes changed after she appeared on the cover of *Life* magazine and obtained a contract with Twentieth Century–Fox. In 1956, she starred as the Burmese slave Tuptim in the classic *The King and I*, in which she sang several Rodgers and Hammerstein songs and performed dances choreographed by Jerome Robbins, who would later choreograph *West Side Story*. Robbins recommended Moreno to Leonard Bernstein for the lead role of María, but she was unable to perform the role on Broadway due to other film commitments. Robbins, along with Robert Wise, directed the film version of *West Side Story*, casting Moreno in the supporting role of Anita, for which she won an Academy Award for Best Supporting Actress. *West Side Story* represented a zenith in Moreno's film career, although she continues to be seen in such recent films as *Piñero* (2001) and had small roles in films such as *Carnal Knowledge* (1971). Through the 1970s, she achieved wide acclaim in *theater. Among the major roles she played are Lola in *Damn Yankees*, Annie Sullivan in *The Miracle Worker*, Adelaide in *Guys and Dolls*, and Serafina in *The Rose Tattoo*. In 1975, she received a Tony for her portrayal of the chanteuse Googie Gómez in Terence McNally's *The Ritz*. During the same period and up to the present, Moreno has appeared in recurring roles in a number of television series, including *The Electric Company, B.L. Stryker, The Cosby Mysteries, Oz, *Resurrection Blvd.*, and most recently, *American Family.* Guest appearances on *The Rockford Files* and *The Mup-*

pet Show earned Moreno Emmy Awards, and her cast recording for *The Electric Company* earned her a Grammy Award.

Further Reading

"Moreno, Rita." *Current Biography* 46 (1985): 299–302.

William Orchard

Moreno Reyes, Mario. *See* Cantinflas.

Movimiento Estudiantil Chicano de Aztlán. *See* MEChA.

Mujeres Muralistas. The Mujeres Muralistas (Women Muralists, 1971–1976) was the first all-female muralist group formed in the United States. This collective of very well regarded artists in their own right, came together with the purpose of creating positive, uplifting, and gender-conscious murals of the Latina/o experience in the Latino community in California, especially the Mission *barrio of San Francisco. The group began when Graciela Carrillo (born in Los Angeles, California), Consuelo Méndez (born in Venezuela), and Patricia Rodríguez (born in Texas) met at the San Francisco Art Institute in 1970–1971. In 1971, Rodríguez was asked to do a mural at the James Town Community Center for children in San Francisco's Latino Mission District. Rodríguez, in addition to enlisting the other artists to collaborate on the mural, recruited Irene Pérez, who was a graphic art student at the San Francisco Academy of Art to work with them on their first mural. This was the core group. As they were offered more commissions and rapidly became highly publicized Latina artists, they inspired and attracted other aspiring Latina artists to come and work with them. The most prominent are Éster Hernández, who was an art student at University of California at Berkeley, Miriam Olivo, Ruth Rodríguez, and Susan Cervántez.

The immediate significance of the Mujeres Muralistas was their open challenge to do murals in public and outdoors, erecting scaffolding and doing the physical labor that is necessary to do large paintings in a busy neighborhood. Although male *Chicano artists supported their work, the Mujeres Muralisas often were subjected to harassment by men passing the women's work site. *Panamérica* or *Latinoamérica* (1974) and *Para El Mercado* (1979) are two of their best-known works. In *Panamérica*, images of women from different Latin American cultures in typical dress are in conversation within a distinct geographic setting. As a model of collaborative art work in *Panamérica*, each artist with her distinctive visual style was responsible for her own specific section; and they worked on integrating the distinct sections into a whole series of images that capture the historical richness of ancient civilizations in the Americas, the centrality of maize in ancient and contemporary Latina/o societies, and the enduring struggle of indigenous and mestiza/o peoples, especially women and children. In *Para El Mercado* women are shown growing *food, taking it to market, cooking and selling the food, and enjoying each other's company; and at the end of this panoramic view of one day, two women are seen going home, walking into the evening with their cargo on their heads. The lush colors and design of this work illustrate how women participate in the economic life of the community.

The Mujeres Muralistas have collaborated on a variety of other important murals in the San Francisco area, in Chicano park in barrio Logan San Diego with the collaboration of Yolanda M. *López, and in Los Angeles. These pioneering women artists created a space for Chicana/Latina artists in a field where men dominated the field and defined the content of Chicano Murals (*see* Chicano Mural Movement). Mujeres Muralistas, who did not call themselves feminist at the time and were critiqued by many because the content of their work was not perceived as "political," expanded the concept of what Chicano art is by activating Latinas' lives as part of the visual culture of Chicano art. They have inspired a wide variety of Latina artists and are the first and most enduring collective of Latina artists committed to the transformative power of public art for the Latina/o community. They were awarded the Lifetime Achievement Award by the San Francisco Precita Eyes mural organization in 2001.

Further Reading

http://www.eltecolote.org/0501/arts.html#mural.
http://www.precitaeyes.org/Insitespage%202.html.

Yolanda M. López

Museums. From the late 1960s to the 1980s, Latinos and other ethnic populations in the United States created institutions to interpret, exhibit, and promote the art and culture of their particular communities. Cultural centers, artists' collectives, and arts institutions emerged out of and/or participated in the civil rights movements, women's movements, Third World student movements, and nation-specific independence movements (such as the Puerto Rican Independence Movement) that flourished throughout the United States and the Caribbean. Reflecting their origins, each of these arts organizations tended to focus on the representation of one specific culture—for example, Chicana/o, Puerto Rican, or Cuban. They did so because they envisioned themselves as community-based institutions with commitments both to their immediate geographic setting and to their places of origin. The social and political upheavals of the concurrent civil rights and independence movements have dramatically shaped the Latino museums that were founded during the later decades of the twentieth century and those that are emerging in the twenty-first century.

Latino museums have interconnected goals of promoting art and social activism. Their practices and programs echo a social and political struggle for self-determination, liberation, and racial equality. The institutions are, therefore, more than simply places of cultural exhibition and production. The artistic goals of Latino museums are inseparable from social, educational, and political goals. Educational programs—such as school tours; bilingual instructional materials; the exhibition and interpretation of art and material culture; and the preservation of ceremonial objects, family photographs, and creative work—contribute to the restoration of collective memory among Latinas and Latinos in the United States and beyond. The effort to preserve heritage and culture necessarily overlaps with the drive for political empowerment. As a gathering place for activists, cultural centers and museums are central to grassroots organizing and dialogue. By promoting a cultural identity as well as political self-determination, the Latino arts organizations function as advocates for their communities, at times becoming directly involved in community development, political action, and protest.

In San Antonio, Texas, the physical presence of the Guadalupe Cultural Arts Center helped to reestablish Mexican and Chicana/o economic and cultural authority in the neighborhood by spawning other Mexican- and *Chicano-focused organizations and businesses. The Avenida Guadalupe Association, an economic development group that assists Chicano businesses, renovated a marketplace across from the Center and provided the necessary infrastructure to raise the standard of living for an impoverished neighborhood. In Chicago's Mexican community of Pilsen, the Mexican Fine Arts Center Museum generated and renewed development initiatives such as the Regeneration Project, which builds housing and facilitates loans to low-income residents, and educational programs for at-risk youth such as the Yollocalli Youth Museum and Radio Arte (WRTE 90.5 FM). Thus, Latino museums—a legacy of the civil rights movements of the 1960s and 1970s—are providing a foundation for continued social change in Latino communities.

From the start, a few institutions, such as the Mexican Museum (c. 1975) in San Francisco, the Mexican Fine Arts Center Museum (c. 1982) in Chicago, and El Museo del Barrio (Museum of the Neighborhood, c. 1969) in New York City, undertook the primary functions of a museum: the collection, exhibition, interpretation, and preservation of art, history, and culture. These were both philosophical choices and economic decisions. Latino arts institutions and artists' collectives perform a museum's function in that they establish an archive of Latino art and culture through regular exhibitions and workshops to produce creative works. "Latino museum" refers to a range of arts institutions that has produced, collected, interpreted, and exhibited Latino visual arts and cultures and thus has functioned as a museum.

The effort to restore collective memory, transform *stereotypes, and legitimize the embodied knowledge of Latinos diverges from the ideological function, origins, and practices of the public museum. Latino museums focus on subjects that tend to be ignored by public museums and public debates. Latino *centros* (centers), artists' groups, and institutions counterbalance the influence of mainstream America by bringing into public space the lives, arts, and cultures of a specific population or sets of populations that have little authority in the United States. The creation of a Latino presence is an important role of these museums and museumlike organizations.

Since its inception in 1968, Inquilinos Boricuas en Acción (IBA), a Puerto Rican community-based cultural and service center in Boston's South End, has reflected a mandate of social responsibility and artistic representation. Among the services that IBA provides are bilingual child care, a credit union, housing management, and economic development programs. IBA also hosts the annual Festival Betances (a cultural event in honor of Puerto Rican patriot Ramón Emeterio Betances), art exhibitions, performing arts shows, cultural instruction classes, and traditional and popular music concerts for the residents of Villa Victoria and its Boston neighbors. The Jorge Hernández Cultural Center, IBA's arts component, is an architectural and political achievement in itself. Originally built in 1898, the German Gothic-style structure was formerly the All Saints Lutheran Church. The reconstructed performing arts space is a registered South End Historical Landmark. Like other Latino arts institutions that have reached their fourth decade, IBA has expanded its constituency and programs with a clearer commitment to low-income residents of Boston.

Continuous *immigration from Latin America to the United States has influenced programs at Latino museums, particularly those relating to educational initiatives and funding. While Latino museums generally continue to serve as sanctuaries from the dominant society, a global and panethnic sensibility emerged in the 1990s. The mission and goals of some of the arts organizations, such as INTAR Gallery in New York City (c. 1978) and the Mission Cultural Center (c. 1975) in San Francisco, focus on a diverse Latino population by recognizing multiple languages, histories, national origins, and immigration patterns. In contrast, the new panethnic organizations were founded on the premise of Latino diversity and continuity across cultural boundaries and geopolitical borders. The National Hispanic Cultural Center (c. 1997) in Albuquerque, New Mexico, and El Museo de las Américas (Museum of the Americas, c. 1991) in Denver, Colorado, are designed to foster understanding of and appreciation for the achievements of Latinas and Latinos in the Americas. The Mexican Museum and El Museo del Barrio changed their mission during the late 1990s to include all Latinos and Latin Americans. Puerto Rican activists, artists, and cultural workers resisted the new direction of El Museo. In the case of the Mexican Museum, the more pan-Latina/o direction was generated from within its staff and governing body and not contested. Both organizations seek new types of funding opportunities that inspire the new mission. Activists and scholars are documenting a trend showing that panethnic programming favors non-U.S. Latinos at the expense of U.S. Latinos.

Both public and private foundations have influenced this and other trends in Latino museums. The Ford Foundation, the Smithsonian Institution, and the National Endowment for the Arts have supported initiatives to professionalize Latina/o museum workers. Since the mid-1980s, museum administrators and staff have been offered workshops on training and development, conservation, collections, entrepreneurship, and marketing. While economic autonomy is a goal of Latina/o arts organizations and training to enhance or generate revenue is welcome, the public and private funding opportunities for so-called professional Latino museums are uneven. In the 1980s and early 1990s, Latino museums found support from corporate sponsors, municipal and state agencies, as well as private foundations. Chicano scholars, such as Tomás Ybarra-Frausto at the Rockefeller Foundation, are recognized for channeling funds to Latino museums at strategic moments. However, the general pattern among other private and public sources for funding is less clear.

A 1994 report called *Willful Neglect: The Smithsonian Institution and U.S. Latinos* catalyzed the need for the Smithsonian, the largest conglomerate of museums in the United States, to examine and incorporate the U.S. Latino experience into its programs. The Smithsonian Center for Latino Initiatives was formed in 1998 with Refugio Rochín as the founding director. Since its inception, the Center has sponsored a large number of exhibitions, fellowships, and training seminars, along with giving general support for the diffusion of Latino culture and history in the United States.

Latina/o museum workers collaborate with other arts organizations to create their own advocacy organizations, such as the National Association for Latino Arts and Culture (NALAC). These joint efforts aim to provide government and private support for the arts, technical assistance in program and organizational development, and other services across the country. Such efforts help to sustain a pan-Latino sensibility in museums.

Latino museums range from emergent to established institutions, from panethnic to culturally specific companies, from multimillion-dollar arts organizations to store-front arts centers, and from accredited museums to self-fashioned temporary exhibition spaces. This diversity conveys both the position of Latinas/os in the United States and various strategies for community self-determination.

Further Reading

Ríos-Bustamante, Antonio Jose, and Christine Marin. *Latinos in Museums: A Heritage Reclaimed*. Malabar, FL: Krieger, 1998.

Smithsonian Institution Task Force on Latino Issues. *Willful Neglect: The Smithsonian Institution and U.S. Latinos*. Washington, DC: Smithsonian Institution, 1994.

Karen Mary Dávalos

Musicians, Cuban American. Fleeing political upheaval in their home country, many Cuban-born musicians have enriched North American popular music. In 1933, Cuban-born actor, musician, and television producer Desi *Arnaz fled to Miami with his father, following the revolution that toppled the regime of President Gerardo Machado. Within a year, the sixteen-year-old Arnaz joined a Cuban combo and was soon leading his own band. He came to the attention of the songwriting team of Richard Rodgers and Lorenz Hart, who cast him as the Latin male lead in *Too Many Girls*, a musical *film that brought Arnaz together with his future wife, Lucille Ball. In 1951 the two produced and starred in the television show *I Love Lucy*. Arnaz used his role as Ricky Ricardo, the fictional bandleader at New York's Tropicana Club, as an opportunity to showcase musical talent from Cuba.

Many jazz musicians who came to New York from Cuba during the 1940s and 1950s played with, or came under the tutelage of, the band Machito and the Afro-Cubans. The band, formed by Mario *Bauzá and Frank Grillo (*Machito) combined Afro-Cuban rhythms with the big band instrumentation that was popular in the United States. One of the most famous musicians to collaborate with Machito was *conguero* (conga player) Luciano Pozo y González (Chano *Pozo). Before coming to the United States in 1946, Pozo had played mostly for Afro-Cuban religious rituals. Bauzá recommended Pozo to African American bandleader Dizzy Gillespie when he expressed an interest in hiring conga players, making Pozo the first *conguero* to play with an American jazz band. Pozo and Gillespie collaborated on the composition of several jazz standards, most notably "Manteca," and their collaborations resulted in the introduction of Latin rhythms to American jazz.

During the time of Pozo and Gillespie's collaborations, Celia *Cruz was studying voice and theory at Cuba's Conservatory of Music. In the early 1950s Cruz and her *salsa-oriented orchestra, La Sonora Matancera, appeared in numerous Cuban-produced movies. Cruz and her orchestra routinely toured the United States and Latin America. The group defected to the United States in 1960 during a tour in México. Two years later, another popular female Cuban singer, La Lupe, immigrated to the United States. Born Victoria Guadalupe Yoli in Santiago, Cuba, La Lupe released two records in her home country. While living in New York she collaborated with Tito *Puente and fellow Cuban musician Mongo Santamaría before pursuing a career as a soloist. La Lupe is best remembered for electrifying performances in which she threw her shoes and jewelry at the audience, tore off her long black wig, and engaged in spiritual-like trances.

Dizzy Gillespie's interest in Cuban music, which continued throughout his career, took him to Cuba in 1977, where he met trumpet great Arturo *Sandoval. At the age of sixteen, the accomplished Sandoval held the first trumpet seat of the prestigious Orquesta Cubana de Música Moderna. He also performed with the Cuban band Irakere, which Gillespie helped introduce to U.S. audiences. The Gillespie-Sandoval friendship blossomed, and Gillespie included Sandoval and Cuban saxophonist Paquito d'Rivera in his United Nations Orchestra. D'Rivera defected to the U.S. embassy in Spain while on tour with Irakere in 1981. He continued to play saxophone and clarinet while also producing records. Sandoval defected to the United States in 1990 while touring with Gillespie. He continues to perform and record as a classical and jazz artist and was the inspiration for the HBO movie *For Love or Country: The Arturo Sandoval Story* (2000), directed by Joseph Sargent and starring Andy *García.

Within the realm of Latin pop, Gloria *Estefan and her husband Emilio and their band, the Miami Sound Machine, are credited with opening the door to numerous artists. Emilio, son of Lebanese immigrants, left Cuba in 1966 at the age of thirteen. Uncertain about their future after the *Cuban Revolution, Gloria's family fled to Miami when she was two years old. The Estefans' unique approach to pop lies in their experience as young immigrants listening to both American pop and Cuban music, such as that of Gloria's uncle, José Fajardo, a classical violinist and salsa flute player. The Estefans and their Miami Sound Machine drummer, Enrique (Kiki) García, channeled their bicultural experience into producing music that melded synthesizer pop with Afro-Cuban and African American rhythms. Their song "Conga" was the first single to enter the pop, dance, black, and Latin charts simultaneously. Jon *Secada cowrote half a dozen of the songs on Gloria Estefan's *Into the Light* (1991) album and joined her 1991 world tour as a backup singer with featured solos. Like the Estefans, Secada emigrated from Cuba to Miami at a young age. The multiplatinum singer, songwriter, and producer's pride in his African and Latino roots comes through in his music.

Cuban American artists have also had an influence in the world of *hip-hop music. Cuban-born Senen Reyes (Sen Dog) and Mexican Cuban Louis Freese (B-Real) are two members of the rap group Cypress Hill, whose stoned-funk style of blending rap with rock has garnered fans from the hip-hop and alternative rock communities. The band's second album, *Black Sunday* (1993), registered the highest first-week sales for a rap album up to that point and debuted at number one on *Billboard* charts.

Further Reading

Manuel, Peter, ed. *Essays on Cuban Music: North American and Cuban Perspectives*. Lanham, MD: University Press of America, 1991.

Moore, Robin. *Nationalizing Blackness: Afrocubanismo and Artistic Revolution in Havana, 1920–1940*. Pittsburgh: University of Pittsburgh Press, 1997.

Orovio, Helio. *Cuban Music from A to Z*. Durham, NC: Duke University Press, 2004.

Roy, Maya et al. *Cuban Music: From Son and Rumba to the Buena Vista Social Club and Timba Cubana*. New York: Markus Wiener, 2002.

Katynka Martínez

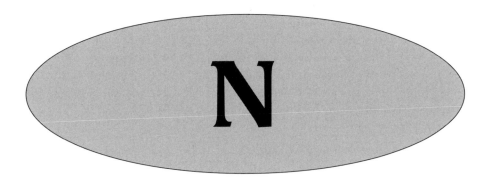

NACCS. The National Association for Chicano Studies (NACS) was established in 1972 during the *Chicano Movement to open a space in higher education where scholars, students, and other researchers interested in Mexican American history, culture, and politics could develop and advance knowledge. The founders who were interested in building political, cultural, and educational awareness within the Chicano community.

The organization's mission is threefold:

1. To advance the interests and needs of the Chicana and Chicano community;
2. To advance research in Chicana and Chicano studies; and
3. To advance the professional interest and needs of Chicana and Chicanos in the community.

The purpose of NACCS is to encourage and assist in the development of Chicana and Chicano studies, including the integration of Chicana and Chicano studies at all levels of education from kindergarten to college; recruitment and mentorship of Chicanas and Chicanos into all levels of academia; and facilitation of dialogue in the community.

After numerous name changes, the organization has settled on a name that reflects the goals and mission of its membership. When the organization was originally established, the membership was dedicated to research, so it was appropriately called the National Caucus for Chicano Social Scientists—a name it carried from 1972 until 1973. Having developed some structure and formality, the membership decided to change the name to the National Association of Chicano Social Scientists when they met in 1973. That name remained until 1976, when it was changed to the National Association for

Chicano Studies, encompassing a broader range of fields and occupations. In 1995, in a proactive move to be *gender inclusive, the second "C" was added and the name was changed to the National Association for Chicana and Chicano Studies. NACCS continues to be a strong network organization, having expanded its membership to include students and faculty throughout the United States and internationally. They hold an annual meeting to encourage and promote research and strengthen the sense of community through networking. Publications and written materials regarding the Chicana and Chicano community can be found on the NACCS Web site.

Further Reading

Montoya, Margaret E. "Mapping LatCrit's Intellectual and Ideological Foundations and Its Future Trajectories" [references NAC'C'S]. *Miami Law Review* 53.04 (July 1999): 1119–1142.

Alma Alvarez-Smith

Nacimiento. A *nacimiento*, from the Spanish word *nacer* (to be born), is a Christmas nativity scene. Recognized in the United States, México, the Caribbean, and Latin America, the practice of displaying a *nacimiento* began in 1224 when Saint Francis of Assisi introduced it to the church. The *nacimiento* is an important Christmas tradition, for it is a reenactment of the birth of Christ in the manger. Biblical figures include the infant Christ, Mary, Joseph, the Three Kings, and shepherds, and also added to the scene are animals, such as sheep, an ox, and a cow. *Nacimientos* are various sizes and can be placed indoors or outdoors.

Nacimientos traditionally are set up at the beginning of Las *Posadas on December 16 and stay up until the El Día de los Reyes Magos (Day of the Three Kings) on January 6, signaling Epiphany, when the Three Kings came bearing gifts for the infant Christ. The three gifts were gold, as it is given to kings; myrrh, as a prediction of death; and incense, as homage of divinity.

Further Reading

Hopkins, John Henry Jr. "We Three Kings." *The World of Royalty*. 2003. http://www.royalty.nu/history/religion/Magi.html.

Mónica Saldaña

Najera, Eduardo (1976–   ). In 2003, when Eduardo Najera signed a six-year, $24 million contract to play basketball with the National Basketball Association's (NBA) Dallas Mavericks, he was the only Mexican-born player in the league and described as the finest basketball player México had ever produced. With only three years of professional basketball experience Najera earns over $1 million annually on endorsements and is seen by U.S. and Latino marketers as the key to bridging the demographics.

Born in Chihuahua, México, Najera is one of seven children born to Servando Najera and Rosa Irene Pérez. He did not play basketball until he was fifteen years old, but he was a quick study, and by the age of seventeen, he was getting offers to play professionally. He opted to go to the University of Oklahoma on a scholarship and successfully completed his degree in 2000. That same year, he was selected as the draft's thirty-eighth pick by the Houston Rockets and was later traded to the Dallas Mavericks. Najera is only the second Mexican to play basketball for the NBA, following Horatio Lamas, who played for the Phoenix Suns in 1997. He is also only the second Mexican to be drafted by the league, following Manuel Rage, who was drafted by the Atlanta Hawks in 1970, although Rage never actually played in the NBA.

Eduardo Najera, forward for the Dallas Mavericks, is only the second Mexican to play in the NBA. *Courtesy of Ranelle Fowler.*

Najera is a spokesperson for Nike, Anheuser Busch Company, and American Movil S.A. He promotes the Hispanic Scholarship Fund and works with the NBA to provide over 5,000 scholarships for students at middle school, high school, and college levels. Understanding the basic principles of investing, Najera has diversified his interests by purchasing a restaurant and investing in real estate. He remains close to his family and hopes to eventually return to Chihuahua when he retires from the NBA to own and run a gym.

Further Reading

Ridgell, Patrick. "You Can't Keep a Good Man Down." *Latino Leaders* (December 2002): 40–45.

Alma Alvarez-Smith

NALEO. *See* National Association of Latino Elected and Appointed Officials.

Narcocorridos. *Corridos* are narrative ballads played by norteño groups, by *bandas*, by *tecnobandas*, or even just by individuals with guitars and are performed throughout the United States, México, and the Caribbean. The rhythm can be either a simple duple 2/4 *polca* or a simple triple 3/4 *vals*. *Narcocorridos* are a subdivision of this genre defined more by subject matter than by formal or stylistic features. They deal with the often-violent deeds of drug smugglers, or *narcos*, and they evolved in the drug-trafficking areas of northwest México, especially Sinaloa, and the U.S.-México border area. Most *narcocorridos* tell of true incidents culled from stories in the news, and many groups that compose and play *narcocorridos* are reportedly sponsored by a member of the Mexican mafia. Although *narcocorridos* seldom receive radio airplay, they are among the most popular form of *corrido* today.

Corridos telling of the daring feats of bandits and criminals date back at least a century, and smugglers became a favorite subject during the time of Prohibition. The *narco* theme can be dated to 1934 when *Tejano duo Gaytán y Cantú recorded "El Contrabandista" (The Smuggler), but the topic did not catch on and evolve into a distinct subgenre until 1972 when *Los Tigres del Norte recorded the famous ballad by Angel González titled "Contrabando y Traición" (Smuggling and Betrayal). Although the song is fictional rather than based on true events, it has served as the prototype for most *narcocorrido* composers since then. The singer introduces two protagonists by name, Emilio Varela and Camelia la Tejana; enumerates some of their exploits, including smuggling marijuana inside the tires of their car; and the song ends violently when Camelia kills Emilio in a jealous rage and escapes, never to be heard from again. As in most *narcocorridos*, the violent lyrics are set to an upbeat polka rhythm played on accordion—embellished with the addition of sound effects like gunfire. Los Tigres further established their supremacy in the genre through songs like "La Banda del Carro Rojo" (The Red Car Gang), a piece by top *corrido* composer Paulino Vargas that became so popular it was later made into a movie.

Possibly the single most influential figure in the history of *narcocorridos* was Rosalino "Chalino" Sánchez, who himself became a folk hero for many Mexican Americans. He immigrated from Sinaloa to Los Angeles in 1977, holding a series of menial jobs before he wrote his first *corrido* in 1984. This tale of the violent death of Chalino's brother in Tijuana gained the singer some notoriety, and he soon began to receive commissions to compose *corridos* about other Angelenos—many of whom also had come from Sinaloa, the center of México's drug trade. Though Chalino's *corridos* seldom explicitly discussed the drug trade, listeners familiar with Sinaloan culture implicitly understood its role. Chalino had a weak, raspy voice and an unpolished, countrified look and accent, but these factors, which would have seemed weaknesses to mainstream music labels, worked in his favor and helped to sell thousands of his self-produced recordings. Many Mexican Americans identified with his rural sound, humble presentation, and macho stance; Chalino seemed to be the "real thing," even wearing a pistol on stage at most of his performances. But his tough reputation and underworld connections eventually backfired; he was shot and killed after a May 1992 concert in Culiacán, Sinaloa, and his killers never were caught.

Chalino lives on through his music and his myth. His recordings continue to sell tens of thousands of copies per year, and many young performers of *narcocorridos* imitate Chalino's sound. The popularity of that sound may even have contributed to the 1990s *banda* craze, another Sinaloan musical style, and the attendant rage for the Western-style clothing Chalino wore. Commissioned *corridos* have since taken off in California and serve as a status symbol for the Sinaloan immigrants who pay for them. Over 100 *corridos* have been written about Chalino himself, and, like fans of another popular singer, some Chalino fans maintain that he is still alive after having faked his own death.

Since Chalino's death, *narcocorridos* have changed little musically but greatly in other areas. Some songwriters have become more explicitly violent, while others are using underworld slang to create a code that can only be broken by those already familiar with México's drug culture. One such *narcocorrido* is "Mis Tres Animales" (My Three Animals, 2000) by Los Tucanes de Tijuana. The "three animals" actually refer to heroin, marijuana, and cocaine, but because of its cryptic language, the song has been able to get more exposure than more explicit contemporary *narcocorridos*. While some singers continue to imitate Chalino's low-key tough-guy look, others have gone for over-the-top flashiness in the style of norteño stars. All types of ensembles from *tecnobandas* to norteño groups have been obliged to add *narcocrridos* to their repertoire because of the surging popularity of the style among youth.

For obvious reasons, many reporters and cultural critics have compared the Mexican American *narcocorrido* to African American gangsta rap. Indeed, some California-based *narcocorridistas* are now releasing English-language rap tracks on the same discs as their usual Spanish-language *polca norteña* fare, since many of these young singers grew up in Los Angeles listening to rap with their peers. In addition, both styles of music have stirred up discussion and controversy. In recent years, many Mexican states have initiated censorship of *narcocorridos* as a result of the urging of President Vicente Fox. Fox and other officials fear that songs glorifying drug traffickers and violent criminals will set a bad example for youth and encourage more violence. In 2002 the state legislatures of Chihuahua and Nuevo León passed radio bans on *narcocorridos*, while Baja California and Michoacán enacted voluntary bans. Those who oppose these restrictions argue that while drug culture is a big problem in northwest México and the border, any limitation on free speech is dangerous. The fact that many Mexican radio stations refused to play a Los Tigres del Norte *corrido*, "Crónica de un Cambio" (Chronicle of a Change), not because it was violent but because it was critical of President Fox, lends support to this argument.

Despite efforts to restrict their dissemination, *narcocorridos* are likely to continue to be recorded for some time both because of the economic support their singers receive from drug smugglers and because of their popularity among disenfranchised Mexicans and Mexican Americans. Many listeners identify with the songs' macho ethic and gritty portrayal of *valientes*, or brave men, seeing them as a continuation of the tradition of heroic *corridos* that go back to the time of the Mexican Revolution and heroes like Emiliano *Zapáta and Pancho *Villa at the turn of the last century. Sinaloans in particular may see *narcocorridos* as accurate reflections of daily life in their violent region; they may be more forgiving of the songs' protagonists, since many drug traffickers are very much involved in their communities. Los Tigres del Norte continues to be very popular, but many new acts have appeared on the scene to challenge its supremacy, including Los Tucanes de Tijuana, Grupo Exterminador, Jenni Rivera, Lupillo Rivera, Los Originales de San Juan, and El As de la Sierra.

Further Reading

Quiñones, Sam. *True Tales from Another Mexico*. Albuquerque: University of New Mexico Press, 2001.

Simonett, Helena. *Banda: Mexican Musical Life across Borders*. Middletown, CT: Wesleyan University Press, 2001.

Wald, Elijah. "Narcocorrido." http://www.elijahwald.com/corrido.html.

Wald, Elijah. *Narcocorrido: A Journey Into the Music of Drugs, Guns, and Guerillas*. New York: HarperCollins, 2001.

Sydney Hutchinson

National Association for Chicana and Chicano Studies. *See* NACCS.

National Association of Latino Elected and Appointed Officials (NALEO).

The National Association of Latino Elected and Appointed Officials (NALEO) is a nonprofit and nonpartisan organization dedicated to raising the level of Latino participation in public policy decision-making processes. NALEO provides issue analysis and dissemination, training and information exchanges, and advocacy at the national level.

Established in 1976, the organization now boasts over 6,000 elected and appointed officials of Latino descent in the United States. The group gathers annually for research and development planning on Latino empowerment issues and works throughout the year on organizing NALEO institutes that provide training for newly elected Latino officials.

NALEO also sponsors the National Association of Latino Elected and Appointed Officials Educational Fund, established in 1981 to develop and implement programs that promote the integration of Latino immigrants into American society. In addition, the Fund supports programs to develop Latino youth into future leaders and to conduct research on issues of importance to the Latino population.

Further Reading

http://www.naleo.org.

Alma Alvarez-Smith

National Council of La Raza (NCLR).

The National Council of La Raza (NCLR), a private, nonprofit group, is the largest national Latino advocacy and civil rights organization in the United States. Intent on eradicating poverty, discrimination, and barriers that impede the overall quality of life for Latinos, NCLR focuses efforts in four ways: a capacity-building initiative to support the Latino community-based organizations that facilitate needs locally; a focus on research and policy analysis for Latinos and Latino-related issues; an effort to support and conduct research on international projects that may impact Latinos; and a record of successful public outreach and information.

NCLR was established in 1968 in Phoenix, Arizona, by Julian Samora, a professor at Notre Dame; writer and activist Ernesto Galarza; businessman and social activist Herman Gallegos; and Macario Barrazas, a union and labor leader. Originally called the Southwest Council of La Raza, in 1972 the organization was renamed the National Council of La Raza and came to be recognized as a resource and information clearinghouse for *Chicano organizations, an emphasis that has expanded to Pan-Hispanic advocacy.

The mission of the organization is to improve opportunities for the nation's Hispanic population and help reduce poverty and discrimination in all communities. Their strategic plan, implemented in 1995, contains eight priority areas as follows: education, health, housing and community economic development, employment and antipoverty, civil rights and *immigration, leadership, media advocacy, and technology initiatives. Some of the initiatives implemented by NCLR to increase educational attainment include working with children at the head start or preschool level, encouraging financial and social support for students, and facilitating after-school and educational alternative programs. The organization serves as a lobbyist against cuts in funding for bilingual education, social policy advocacy work, and farmworkers education.

NCLR affiliates administer programs that target cardiovascular disease, diabetes, and breast and cervical cancers by providing health care outreach, collaboration with health care agencies, organization of research and conferences, and community education on these four curable diseases. To improve the quality of life in the Latino community, NCLR promotes programs to increase homeownership among low-income Latinos and to provide leadership development, technical assistance, and programs to improve economic development. In addition, NCLR facilitates programs to end unemployment and poverty conditions and help students find jobs after completing their education. In collaboration with AmeriCorps, NCLR assists individuals with literacy and job preparedness.

NCLR mobilizes the community by leadership development, media advocacy, and promotion of positive images in the media. The Hispanic Leadership Development and Support Initiative educates, funds, disseminates information, and trains Latino leaders, targeting seniors, community activists, women, and youth. The NCLR's media advocacy project encourages more Latina/o hires and positive portrayals in television.

The organization's policy think tank, the Policy Analysis Center, is politically nonpartisan and located in Washington, D.C. Enjoying a reputation for excellent research, the think tank addresses issues such as immigration, education, housing, poverty, civil rights, and foreign policy. The center is often called upon for expert testimony in these areas as well as on free trade, race relations, health policy, and tax reform. NCLR is headquartered in Washington, D.C., and has offices in thirty-nine states, the District of Columbia, and Puerto Rico. Under the capable leadership of Raul *Yzaguirre since 1974, the Board appointed attorney Janet Murguia to replace the retiring NCLR director in 2005.

Further Reading

http://www.nclr.org.

Alma Alvarez-Smith

National Hispanic Cultural Center of New Mexico. Situated on a sixteen-acre site in the traditionally Hispanic neighborhood called Barelas in Albuquerque, the National Hispanic Cultural Center of New Mexico (NHC-CNM) offers a wealth of cultural events that include the visual arts, drama, traditional and contemporary music, dance, literary arts, film, culinary arts, library research, lectures, storytelling, and other educational activities, as well as facilities such as an amphitheater, restaurants, broadcast and publication capabilities, gift shops, and studios featuring working artists. The mission of the NHCCNM "to preserve, interpret, and showcase Hispanic arts and lifeways" is accomplished through the many activities that take place in the Research and Literary Arts building and the Intel Technology and Visual Arts Complex, which house three large exhibition galleries, a technology classroom, and a 100-seat lecture hall, plus the Performing Arts Complex (home to a state-of-the-art proscenium theater, a film and video theater, and multimedia production facilities).

Originally operated as the New Mexico Hispanic Cultural Center, the center became funded, redefined, and renamed in 2000 as the National Hispanic Cultural Center of New Mexico, a division of the New Mexico Office of Cultural Affairs. In this capacity it is an agency of the State of New Mexico, but it works closely with the Hispanic Culture Foundation, an independent nonprofit 501 organization, which raises money for the center. The center receives the broad support of the New Mexico state legislature, the University of New Mexico, the National Park Services, the Department of Housing and Urban Development, the Albuquerque Hispano Chamber of Commerce, the Hispanic Culture Foundation, and other groups and individuals. Through an agreement with the Cervantes Institute of Spain, the Spanish-language teaching and Hispanic culture promoter, Instituto Cervantes, is located at the Albuquerque center.

Although the NHCCNM has focused on regional events and activities, there is a high expectation that it will serve its charter of service, outreach, and coverage of Hispanic cultures on a nationwide level. Educational ways and means include classes, seminars, lectures, school performances, youth-based projects, hands-on workshops, internships, and classroom materials.

Further Reading

http://www.nhccnm.org.

Luis Aldama

National Hispanic University. The National Hispanic University (NHU) is a private, independent institution that offers baccalaureate degrees in computer science, business administration, and liberal studies. It also offers a Multiple Subject Teaching Credential for K–8 teachers and a certificate program in Translation and Interpretation designed for health, legal, and business employees. Located in east San Jose, California, the NHU campus lies in the center of both a low-income Hispanic immigrant community as well as in Silicon Valley, one of the wealthiest postindustrial per capita income regions in the world. The university was established in 1981 to meet the higher education needs of Hispanics and other minorities, making it a potentially important contemporary influence on the rapidly growing numbers of twentieth- and twenty-first-century Latinas and Latinos in the United States. As such, the NHU is likely to have a significant effect on future Latina/o public domains including popular culture forms, practices, and values among the next generation of consumers.

The university holds national accreditation from the Accrediting Council of Independent Colleges and Schools and from the California Teacher Credentialing Commission. In addition, it has been awarded accreditation candidacy status from the Western Association of Colleges and Schools. In existence for over twenty years, NHU launched a $25 million capital campaign in 2000 to purchase an eleven-acre campus and to build a three-story state-of-the-art academic facility. The student enrollment approaches 1,000 students and consists of a demographic diversity of approximately 80 percent Hispanic, 10 percent Anglo, 4 percent Asian, 2 percent African American, and 4 percent members of other ethnic and racial identity groups. Slightly over 60 percent of the students are women. In terms of majors and disciplinary areas of study, approximately half of the students are enrolled in the postbaccalaureate teacher preparation program. At the undergraduate level the largest concentration of enrollments is in the liberal studies program. Computer science, Business Administration, and the Certificate Program in Translation and Interpretation are the next largest undergraduate programs in size. The NHU instructional staff comprises ten full-time faculty members and forty part-time instructors. To augment its resources the university maintains partnerships and articulation agreements with San Jose State University, San Jose City College, and the Evergreen Community College system.

Built around the motto made famous by labor leader César *Chávez, "Si Se Puede" (Yes, You Can Do It), NHU was founded by its first president, B. Roberto Cruz. As an at-risk student and potential dropout candidate from the low-income barrios of Corpus Christi, Texas, Cruz believes that receiving a football scholarship enabled him to finish high school and propelled him out of the poor barrio to college, making him a staunch advocate of higher education. He is a graduate of one of the nation's premier public institutions, the University of California at Berkeley, and he taught three years at the prestigious private Stanford University. Motivated by a strong belief that dramatic solutions must be developed to reverse the lack of higher educational achievement among Hispanics in America, he engaged in systematic study of historically black colleges and universities and of Jewish higher education institutions, principally Brandeis, Yeshiva, and Adelphi Universities in New York. His research found that although black colleges were enrolling only about 17 percent of the black college-eligible students at the time of his study (1979–1981), they were providing approximately 50 percent of the Bachelor of Arts degrees awarded to African American students in the United States. He also learned that the institutions he studied stressed high expectations of students and exemplary role models among the faculty and administration as a vehicle to accompany academics toward high-quality achievement in school and future career success.

In collaboration with East Side Union High School District, the university opened the Latino College Preparatory Academy (LCPA), a model charter high school for English-language learners (ELLs) in 2001. East Side Union High School District has the second largest enrollment of Hispanic high school students in California, next to the Los Angeles Unified School District. To address the great needs for scholastic success among recent immigrant Latinas and Latinos, the LCPA hopes to reverse the current retention challenge, which at the turn of the century produced a school dropout rate of between 45 and 65 percent before tenth-grade completion among immigrant students in California alone. The Latino College Preparatory Academy initially will serve 100 ninth-grade students who, as developing ELLs are unable to participate in the public high school preparatory curriculum. NHU will provide instruction in their native language while improving their academic English development as a means of ensuring that they meet college preparatory requirements and gain usable and applied proficiencies in English, Spanish, and computer literacy. According to the plan, 100 students were admitted into the ninth grade in 2001. As each cohort progresses and the students are promoted to the tenth, eleventh, and twelfth grades, by 2005 it is expected that 400 high school students will be attending the LCPA. Those successfully completing the high school requirements for graduation will be guaranteed enrollment into NHU.

Further Reading

Pérez, Monte E. "Developing Partnerships between Academic Affairs and Student Affairs in a Multicultural University: The National Hispanic University Model." Oxford Higher Education Roundtable, Oxford University, 2001.

Cordelia Chávez Candelaria

Nava, Gregory (1949–   ). A graduate of the University of California at Los Angeles (UCLA) School of Theater, Film, and Television, Gregory Nava is the founder of El Norte production company and one of the most widely recognized *Chicano *film director, writer, and producer. His artistic career has been dedicated to bringing to the wide screen aspects of the Chicano/Latino experience and identity that are not stereotypical. He has also made many films for television, such as the multicultural Showtime-produced *An American Family* (2002), starring Edward James *Olmos. After finishing film school, he made his directorial debut with *The Confessions of Amans* (1976), followed by *The End of August* (1982). However, it was his third film, *El Norte* (1983), that established his international reputation as a filmmaker and won him an Academy Award nomination for Best Screenplay. In it, he follows the lives of two Guatemalan Quiché siblings and vividly depicts their harsh experience crossing borders into the United States. The story is tragic but has many highly comical and touching moments. After directing *A Time of Destiny* (1988), a film about Italian American immigrants and generational divides that also ends in tragedy, he then turned to the exploration of the Chicana/o experience. This effort resulted in the epic chronicle of three generations of a Chicano *family living in East Los Angeles, the critically acclaimed film *Mi Familia/My Family* (1995), and in the biography of the crossover pop singer, the late *Selena (played by Jennifer *López), in the film *Selena* (1997).

Nava's work is characterized by a sense of journey, tragedy, and challenge to fate that takes place for the Latino community both literally and symbolically. While showing how the Latino presence and the struggles of the community actively reshape mainstream America, he makes complex otherwise simple and stereotypical Latino roles and themes. His work is to a large extent a celebration of stoic endurance, depicted with a curious mixture of harsh realism and nostalgic romanticizing. Nava has twice received the *ALMA Award for Outstanding Latino Director of a Feature Film (for *Selena* in 1997 and for *Why Do Fools Fall in Love* in 1998). He was nominated in 1985 for a Writers Guild of America Award and for an Oscar for the best screenplay for *El Norte* in 1983. A year earlier he had won the Grand Prix des Amériques for that same film. In 1995 he received the *National Council of La Raza Bravo Award and, at the San Sebastián International Festival, the OCIC (Organiçao Católica Internacional de Cinema) Award for *Mi Familia*/My Family.

Further Reading

Keller, Gary D. *A Biographical Handbook of Hispanics and United States Film.* Tempe, AZ: Bilingual Press, 1997.

Luis Aldama

NCLR. *See* National Council of La Raza (NCLR).

Newspapers and Periodicals. Mesoamerican writing systems have existed in the Americas for many, many years. The first book in the Americas was printed in Mexico City in 1539. The first newspaper in the Spanish colonies, *Gaceta de México y Noticias de Nueva España*, appeared in 1722. The U.S. Latino press was born in 1848 as an indirect result of the *Treaty of Guadalupe Hidalgo. Author and scholar América Rodriguez defines Latino journalism as "news that is purposefully and strategically created for United States residents of Latin American descent," which "denationalizes Latinos [as Latin Americans] as it renationalizes them as United States Hispanics." As such, Latino news mirrors, interprets, and perpetuates the community's ongoing acculturation. Samir Husni, a professor of magazine journalism at the University of Mississippi, has described Latino news readers in the United States as a community "that's still trying to keep their language, their heritage, but at the same time they want to know more about the country they're living in."

Rejecting the notion of mainstream news as solely white, Latino news constantly straddles the line between the U.S. and Latin American influences on its readers. The characteristics of Latino newspapers, magazines, and Internet-based news publications are shaped by the community's unique demographic composition. An estimated 40 percent of the U.S. Latino population was foreign born in 2002; Latin American immigrants accounted for more than half of the foreign-born population living in the United States that year with more than half of these immigrants arriving during the 1990s. In other words, like the dominant Anglo culture, Latin American culture is continuously shaping the U.S. Latino experience.

News of the Latino experience is published in English, Spanish, and bilingually in virtually every region of the United States. Some of the largest daily Spanish-language newspapers in the country include *La Opinión* in Los Angeles; *El Nuevo Herald* and *Diario Las Americas* in Miami; and *El Diario La Prensa* and *Hoy* in New York City. Some of the nation's largest Spanish-language weeklies include *La Raza* and *Exito!* in Chicago; *La Estrella* in Fort Worth, Texas; *Nuevo Mundo* in San José, California; *La Prensa* in San Antonio, Texas; *El Sol de Tejas* in Dallas, Texas; *Hispanos Unidos* and *La Prensa* in San Diego, California; and *La Voz* and *Prensa Hispana* in Phoenix, Arizona. These are but a few of an estimated 600-plus Spanish-language and bilingual newspapers printed in the United States in 2004, though some of these publications are short-lived or publish infrequently. In cities with substantial concentrations of Latinos, such as Houston, Dallas, Phoenix, and Los Angeles, readers can find as many as a half a dozen or more weekly or monthly Spanish-language publications whose circulations range from a few hundred a month to 50,000 or more.

Like English-language newspapers, Spanish-language publications in the United States emphasize local and regional news coverage. But unlike most of their English-language counterparts, these publications often have large international news sections. *El Nuevo Herald* and *Diario de las Americas*, for instance, provide extensive coverage of Latin America, especially Cuba, Puerto Rico, and the South American nations of Colombia, Venezuela, and Argentina. *La Opinion*, meanwhile, tends to highlight news about México, Central America, and other areas of Latin America. The importance of Latin American news coverage in these publications is a reflection of the familial, social, and economic ties that exist between Latino readers in the United States and their ancestral homelands or countries of origin.

In 2004, the National Association of Hispanic Publications, headquartered in Washington, D.C., had more than 200 members nationwide with a combined circulation of more than 10 million readers. From 1990 to 2000, the number of Latino newspapers grew from about 350 to 550, according to the National Hispanic Media Directory. During the same period, the number of Latino magazines grew from 177 to more than 350. Many of the publications targeting U.S. Latinos are owned by non-Latinos or affiliated with major news organizations. For instance, the publishers of the *Orlando Sentinel* launched the Spanish-language *El Sentinel* in 2001. Tribune Publishing owns *El Exito!* in Chicago, *La Opinión* in Los Angeles, and *Hoy* in New York.

People en Español is owned and operated by Time Inc. The Spanish-language version of *People* magazine focuses on popular culture, celebrity gossip and profiles, and human interest stories. In June 2002, *People en Español* reported a monthly circulation of 420,000, according to BPA International. *People en Español*'s publisher Lisa Quiroz told the *Christian Science Monitor* that the magazine industry began to understand the importance of the Spanish-language market in 1995. That year, *People* published its first "split cover"—two different covers for the same edition—featuring a cover story about the murder of *Tejano music star *Selena aimed at its West Coast readers. The Spanish-language version was launched in 1998.

Reader's Digest publishes *Selecciones*, which has a monthly circulation of over 325,000 in the United States. Like its English-language parent, *Selecciones* features stories on health and fitness, celebrities, human interest, and family life. The Spanish-language version was originally developed for *Reader's Digest*'s Latin American readers—the first edition was published in Cuba in the 1940s, ceasing operations there after the *Cuban Revolution. In recent years, however, Latino population growth has fueled a major expansion of *Selecciones'* operations in the United States. Advertising revenue for the publication increased more than 50 percent in 2002 over the previous year, and circulation was up 7.5 percent. The magazine had about 2.6 million readers in the United States and another 2 million in Latin America. In addition to *Reader's Digest*, dozens of other English-language magazines now publish Spanish-language editions, including *Vogue*, *Cosmopolitan*, and *Maxim*.

The Latino magazine industry also includes a growing number of English-language or bilingual magazines, including *Latina*, *Latina Style*, *Latin Girl*, *Urban Latino*, *Hispanic*, *Hispanic Business*, *Latin Beat*, and *El Andar*. Since 2002, *Latina*, *Hispanic*, and *Hispanic Business* each report monthly circulation of more than 200,000. *Latina* is a women's glamour and lifestyle magazine. *Hispanic* is a general-interest magazine featuring articles on human interest, politics, business, and entertainment. *Hispanic Business*, as its name implies, reports on Latino entrepreneurs and executives, Latino-owned corporations, and news impacting Latino workers, especially those involved in small business or corporations.

The Internet is the newest medium for printed news about Latinos. A study in 2000 by the Tomás Rivera Policy Institute of Latinos in Los Angeles, Houston, Miami, New York, and Chicago found that 63 percent of the respondents preferred English-language sites, 12 percent preferred Spanish-language sites, and 25 percent preferred bilingual sites. Yahoo.com and America Online were the most popular destinations for Latinos on the Internet in 2000, according to Cheskin Research, which tracks Internet usage.

For Spanish-language-dominant Internet users, Web sites operated by television giants Univisión (http://www.Univision.com) and Telemundo (http://www.Telemundo.com) and newspapers such as *El Nuevo Herald* (http://www.miami.com/mld/elnuevo) and *La Opinión* (http://laopinion.com) are among the most frequently visited. Other Web sites popular among Spanish-language-dominant Internet users include Yahoo En Español (http://www.espanol.yahoo.com), Terra.com, StarMedia.com, and Netmio.com. *Hispanic Magazine* (http://www.hispaniconline.com) and *Hispanic Business* magazine (http://www.hispanicbusiness.com) post original and wire service reports on their Web sites.

Latino news Web sites targeting a national audience but not affiliated with print or broadcast news outlets include AmericanLatino.net, Latinovote.com, and HispanicVista.com. AmericanLatino.net bills itself as a *Time* magazine for English-dominant Latinos on the Internet. Latinovote.com tracks Latino political news in English. HispanicVista features bilingual news and commentary with an emphasis on the West Coast.

Further Reading

Husni, Samir A. *Launch Your Own Magazine: A Guide for Succeeding in Today's Marketplace*. Nashville, TN.: Hamblett House; New York: Distributor, Oxbridge Communications, 1998.

Rodríguez, América. *Making Latino News: Race, Language, Class*. Thousand Oaks, CA: Sage Publications, 1999.

James E. García

Noloesca, Beatriz (1903–1979). Beatriz Escalona Pérez "La Chata" (button-nosed) Noloesca was a professional dramatic female actress during the Spanish-language *theater era (1920s–1940s) in the United States. As a Mexican American comedienne, her major contribution to theater was that of performing a variety of popular genres such as burlesque comedy, dramatic vignettes, comical vaudeville sketches, humorous songs, and traditional ballads. Noloesca's greatest contribution during the 1920s and 1930s Spanish-language theater era was creating the popular comic character "La Chata," which was based on two comedic characters: the Mexican national clown, *la peladita* (literally means peeled, naked, the naked one, or the underdog), and Mexican and Mexican American maids. *La peladita* was a streetwise, fast-talking, hardworking, industrious character who posed problems to the audience, poked fun at political scandals, and made remarks on punishment and treachery. Mexican and Mexican American maids were always the pun of Noloesca's jokes and buffoonery, and she poked fun at the relationship between the household servants and their employers. Dressed as a young maid, La Chata wore brightly floral or printed, ruffled cotton dresses with pigtails and huge bows, men's stocky shoes with striped socks or bizarre stockings, and preposterous makeup and exaggerated facial and bodily gestures. La Chata's savoir-faire exemplified a maid who was innocent, smart, quick-witted, strong-willed, sophisticated, affectionate, and full of grand demeanor and mannerisms.

Noloesca was born Beatriz Escalona Pérez in San Antonio, Texas, on August 20, 1903, to Mexican parents from Galeana, Nuevo León. Raised by her widowed mother, she spent most of her early childhood in Monterrey, Nuevo León. At the age of ten she sold bouquets, food, and coffee at a train station to passengers so that she could earn money to attend theater performances at the Teatro Independencia in Monterrey, México. After her family moved back to San Antonio, Texas, Noloesca at the age of thirteen continued to pursue her interest in theater, as she worked as an usher at the Teatro Zaragoza located in San Antonio's largest Mexican American community. Noloesca, at the age of seventeen, worked in the box office selling tickets for Teatro Nacional in San Antonio, at which time she met Cuban-born performer José Areu and his variety show company, Los Hermanos Areu. Areu invited Noloesca to travel with his company, and she made her debut performance at the age of eighteen at Teatro Colón in El Paso, Texas. Trained by Los Hermanos Areu company as an actress, dancer, singer, and comedienne, she later married Areu and had her first child, Belia. As Noloesca continued to perform with Los Hermanos Areu, she first took on the stage name of "Noloesca," refined her comedic sketches and dramatic roles, and built her reputation as a well-known musical comedy star throughout México and the Southwest.

In 1930 Noloesca's marriage to Areu ended, and so did her performances with Los Hermanos Areu. Noloesca formed her own company, Atracciones Noloesca, in Los Angeles, which she managed, and toured throughout the Southwest with her second husband, José de la Torre, her partner in comedy. After her first company went bankrupt during the Great Depression, Noloesca, in 1938, started her second company, Beatriz Noloesca 'La Chata' Compañía Mexicana, in San Antonio, Texas. She toured her musical song and dance variety shows and her comedy sketches throughout the United States and Cuba. Her company performed in large cities including San Antonio, Chicago, Tampa, and Havana and collaborated efforts with Teatro Hispano of New York City.

After having returned from touring throughout the United States, Noloesca ended her marriage with de la Torre and married her third husband, Rubén Escobedo, a well-known San Antonio musician. Noloesca continued to perform in her hometown of San Antonio, Texas, at local radio stations and benefit shows until 1975. In 1975, Noloesca was commemorated and recognized by the Mexican National Association of Actors in San Antonio, Texas, for her lengthy career in performance and her contribution to Spanish-language theater throughout the Southwest. Noloesca died in San Antonio, Texas, on April 4, 1979.

Further Reading

Arrizón, Alicia. *Latina Performance: Traversing the Stage.* Bloomington: Indiana University Press, 1999.

Kanellos, Nicolás. *A History of Hispanic Theatre in the United State: Origins to 1940.* Austin: University of Texas Press, 1990.

Ramírez, Elizabeth. *Chicanas/Latinas in American Theatre: A History of Performance.* Bloomington: Indiana University Press, 2000.

Cecilia Aragón

Norte, El. *See El Norte.*

Novena. *Novena* (from the Latin *novem*, nine) is a traditional nine-day private or public Catholic spiritual devotion usually performed to obtain special graces among Latinas/os under several circumstances. In the United States, because there are a large number of people of Mexican descent and growing numbers from South and Central America, it is sometimes difficult to distinguish these groups from one another regarding religious beliefs and customs. In matters of folk religion and spiritual practices, however, the dynamics of faith are similar for Mexican Americans and Latin Americans, at least in the Southwest.

The number nine indicates suffering and grief in Christian literature and also symbolizes the nine months of human pregnancy. The *novena* is recommended by the Catholic Church, but it is not a legitimate or official liturgy and hence is regarded as a folk, or popular tradition, meaning the transmission of Church teachings by alternative means other than inspired books and literature. As an expression of *religiosidad popular*, *piedad popular*, and *Catolicismo popular* (popular religion, piety, or devotion), the *novena* is regarded as a form of religiousity deeply rooted in traditional beliefs, customs, values, and practices of the common people and their faithful attitudes and expressions. It is regarded as a cherished folk expression throughout Latin America and the Caribbean and among Latinas/os in the United States. *Novenas* are classified according to types and include mourning, preparation, prayer, and indulgence, although this distinction is not exclusive. The most popular *novenas* among Latinas and Latinos in the United States are for mourning deceased family members, spouses, and friends. These may have originated during Roman times; however, by the Middle Ages *novenas* of preparation were offered during Advent and in preparation for various important feast days, especially in Spain and France.

Also during medieval times, the *novena* of prayer gained popularity among the masses during times of distress and need. Christians turned to popular saints, offering ritualized prayers to recover health or financial stability or survive some other calamity or crisis, particularly in France, Belgium, and the Lower Rhine. The *novena* of prayer was criticized by the Jansenists, members of a Catholic sect who regarded it as a pagan superstition rooted in pre-Christian rituals. By the fourteenth century, there was much canonical concern over the superstitious abuse of the *novena*, but it was not rejected. Today, the *novena* of prayer is a ritualized practice, which usually includes a petition.

During the nineteenth century the Church began to recommend *novenas* as concessions of indulgences. Alexander VII by the middle of the seventeenth century began granting indulgences for a *novena* in honor of St. Francis Xavier in Lisbon. Some of the earlist *novena* indulgences were granted in Rome. *Novenas* in preparation for the feast of St. Joseph were offered in the church of St. Ignatius. Franciscans also encouraged *novena* offerings for the feast of the Immaculate Conception with special indulgences. By the early nineteenth century various *novenas* offered indulgences on the part of the Church. Several *novenas* are intended as *novenas* of preparation for feasts such as the *Virgin of Guadalupe (December 12) or San Lorenzo (August 10), which are popular in the Southwest borderlands.

Indulgences are gained during any day throughout the *novena*, yet those who are ill or prevented from completing the ritual during the *novena* may still gain the indulgence by doing so as soon as possible. Private or public *novenas* may be made in public gatherings in the home, church, or *morada* (dwelling) or combined with various devotions such as the rosary or sacraments (confession or communion). Typically a partial indulgence is gained and a plenary indulgence is granted by the end of the entire *novena*. The indulgences gained from *novenas* contribute to an increase in confidence among the faithful believers in the obtained graces. Through praying *novenas* to the Virgin of Guadalupe, San Antonio de Padua, or other popular saint, faithful Latinas and Latinos seek and find help and relief. The history of *novenas* among Latinas/os in the United States is not yet written, but it is a major part of the veneration of the Virgin Mary and all the saints, of devotion to God, and especially of the spirit of prayer within the community. Much of the official literature of the Catholic Church on most matters of popular religion seems ambivalent at best.

Among Latinas/os in the United States the most popular *novena* devotion is probably to the Virgin of Guadalupe, which can be performed at any time of the year but usually the nine days prior to the official feast day on December 12. However, other novenas to El Santo Niño de Atocha (Holy Child of Atocha), San Antonio de Padua (Saint Anthony of Padua), Sagrada Corazón de Jesús y María (Sacred Heart of Jesus and Mary), and San Lorenzo (Saint Lawrence) are common, as is the *novena* of mourning for the deceased. Recitation of the rosary is central to the typical *novena* devotion, as are **alabanzas* (praises) and **alabados* (hymns), which are sung a capella by soloists or by groups. In its folk manifestation, the *novena de casa* usually takes place during one evening and may be held all night, in lieu of the official formal nine-day devotion. It is usually a neighborhood or extended-family gathering with food or coffee served, with some time for socializing.

Further Reading

"Novena." *Catholic Encyclopedia.* http//:newadvent.org/cathen/11141b.htm.

Peter J. García

Nuevo Teatro Pobre de América, El. Founded in 1963 by Pedro *Santaliz, El Nuevo Teatro Pobre de América (America's New Poor Theater) is a popular *theater troupe that performs on the streets in marginalized communities in Puerto Rico and in New York City. Until the 1980s El Nuevo Teatro Pobre de América traveled frequently between New York City and Puerto Rico performing plays focusing on the social and political issues of the lower and middle classes in Puerto Rico and in New York. El Nuevo Teatro Pobre's focus in the 1980s was the problem of domestic violence presented through such plays as *El castillo interior de Medea Camuñas* (The Interior Castle of Medea Camuñas, 1992), based on the Greek tragedy and myth of Medea. Founder Santaliz's interest was to express a radical position with respect to the subordinate and persecuted condition of women in society. Through the use of parody, humor, and the graphic aesthetics of violence, the group contributed a hard-edged Puertorriqueño perspective, which had been virtually invisible, to add to the feminist critique of patriarchy and institutional sexism. In this way El Nuevo Teatro Pobre responded to criticisms by Puerto Rican intellectuals of what they perceived as Puerto Rican and Latino docility with regard to domestic violence. Intense and satirical, the tragicomic themes of the plays explore such contemporary issues as drug and alcohol abuse, Latina/o unemployment, identity issues within the dominant culture, and political corruption.

Further Reading

Ramos-Perea, Roberto. *Perspectivas de la nueva dramatúrgia puertorriqueña: Ensayos sobre el nuevo drama nacional.* San Juan, Puerto Rico: Ateneo Puertorriqueño, 1986.

Rivera, Carlos Manuel. "El Esperpento Puertorriqueño: El Nuevo Teatro Pobre de América de Pedro Santaliz." Ph.D. dissertation, Arizona State University, 2000.

Carlos M. Rivera

Nuyorican Poets Café. The Nuyorican Poets Café has served as a venue for emerging Nuyorican (Puerto Rican) artists and writers in New York. The cafe was established on Manhattan's Lower East Side (or "Losaida" as it is called by its Spanish-speaking residents) with the help of the owner, Miguel *Algarín, a university professor, writer, and one of the leaders of the Nuyorican literary movement. The café is a writers' collective run by a board of directors that includes Algarín and other New York supporters of the arts and culture. *Nuyorican* is an informal term for Puerto Rican persons and culture more closely identified with New York City than with the island of Puerto Rico.

Emerging in the late 1950s, Nuyorican poetry developed as a voice and venue for the many Puerto Rican poets who had migrated to New York's *barrios and who felt alienated from the dominant poetry circles writing in English-only idioms. The first poets and playwrights who tried to publish their work and present poetry readings in the city during this era were rejected and remained unrecognized by other literary artists and followers. To combat the widespread racism and other societal biases that ostracized them and their work, the group formed an alternative literary circle that included Algarín, Américo Casiano, Sandra María Esteves, Felipe Luciano, Tato Laviera, Pedro Pietri, Miguel *Piñero, Louis Reyes Rivera, and others who collectively helped shape the future of Nuyorican writing. They produced a highly influential anthology of their writings titled *Nuyorican Poetry: An Anthology of Puerto Rican Words and Feelings* (1975), which in effect established the Nuyorican Poets Café.

A new generation of Nuyorican artists began to emerge by the late 1980s and mid-1990s, many of whom were exposed to the creative work of the original Nuyorican poets. Incorporating other forms of artistic expression, such as *hip-hop, into Nuyorican cultural production, the new generation were particularly instrumental in developing unique styles of oral presentation, notably the creation of poetry slams, which have grown in popularity throughout the United States. Among these important contemporary Nuyorican writers are Caridad de la Luz, Magda Martínez, Tony Medina, Sandra García Rivera, Héctor Luís Rivera, and Abraham Rodriguéz. They have produced a number of anthologies including *Aloud: Voices from the Nuyorican Poets Café* (1994), winner of a highly prestigious American Book Award, and *Action: The Nuyorican Poets Café Theater Festival* (1997). The cafe thus has become one of the premier stages for poets, writers, musicians, performance artists, and visual artists and also has been recognized for its commitment to providing a multicultural space for the artistic development of diverse members of the community. In 1993 the Nuyorican Poets Café was officially named a living treasure of New York City.

Further Reading

http://www.nuyorican.org.

Daniel Enríque Pérez

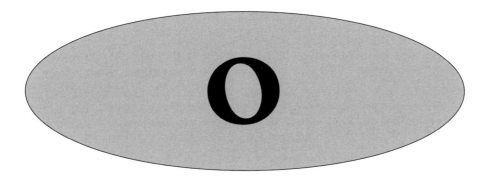

Obejas, Achy (1956–   ). A well-known *Cuban American writer, Achy Obejas is the versatile author of two novels, *Memory Mambo* (1996) and *Days of Awe* (2001), and a collection of short stories, *We Came All the Way from Cuba So You Could Dress Like This?* (1994). Obejas also wrote a sit-com pilot, *Aquí me quedo* (I'm Staying Here), aired in Chicago in 1985, which according to the *Chicago Sun-Times* was historic for being the first television show ever broadcast that was written by, for, and about Hispanics in the United States. She also worked as a news reporter for the *Chicago Tribune* from 1991 to 2002, writing as an arts critic and covering such current events in popular culture as the 1997 murder of haute couture designer Gianni Versace and the visit of Pope John Paul II to Cuba in 1998. For her sharply observed writing, Obejas has received several awards, including a highly coveted Pulitzer Prize in 2001 (shared with the *Chicago Tribune*'s investigative reporting team) for a series on air traffic irregularities and a Studs Terkel Award for Community and Neighborhood coverage in 1996. Her journalistic work has appeared in such topflight venues as *The Nation*, the *Village Voice*, *Vogue*, *Playboy*, and the *Los Angeles Times*.

Born in Havana on June 28, 1956, Obejas strongly identifes with her island Cuban roots. In Cuba, her father was a lawyer and her mother an educator. After the *Cuban Revolution and in opposition to Fidel *Castro, her parents left Cuba on a boat in 1963 with their daughter and son. The future writer and her brother grew up in a working-class neighborhood of Michigan City, Indiana, where both of her highly educated parents became Spanish-language teachers. After public schools, Obejas attended the Warren Wilson College in Swannanoa, North Carolina, where she earned a Master of Fine Arts degree in creative writing with a focus on fiction in 1993.

Although Obejas left Cuba as a small child, she has written that she identifies culturally as a Latina and Cuban American writer. Her frequent trips to the island have allowed her to maintain close ties with her native Cuban culture. The island, its people, and her past constitute important bilingual, bicultural elements of most of her published work. Besides Cuba, the city of Chicago also figures prominently in Obejas's writing as a diverse and multilayered urban space in which Latina and Latino cultures thrive in their vibrant interaction with one another and other ethnic communities. Her dramatic and entertaining short stories and novels often feature gay and lesbian characters who, far from being isolated or marginalized as social deviants, are represented as functioning, vibrant members of their nuclear and extended *families and the larger society. She is currently at work on two fiction books.

Further Reading

Araújo, Nara. "I Came All the Way from Cuba So I Could Speak Like This?: Cuban and Cubanamerican Literatures in the US." In *Comparing Postcolonial Literatures: Dislocations*, edited by Ashok Bery and Patricia Murray. New York: Palgrave Macmillan, 2000.

Harper, Jorjet. "Dancing to a Different Beat: An Interview with Achy Obejas." *Lambda Book Report: A Review of Contemporary Gay and Lesbian Literature* 5.3 (1996): 1, 6–7.

Obejas, Achy. *Days of Awe*. New York: Ballantine, 2001.

Obejas, Achy. "Writing and Responsibility." *Discourse* 21.3 (1999): 42–48.

Iraida H. López

Olmos, Edward James (1947–). Edward James Olmos, an award-winning actor, director, and producer of *films, was born on February 24, 1947, in East Los Angeles, California. His early years up to midteens, Olmos dedicated himself to baseball with the goal of becoming a professional baseball player and became the Golden State batting champion in California.

However, his interests changed as a teenager, and he became the lead singer, dancer, and pianist for a band called Pacific Ocean. After Olmos graduated from high school, he continued to devote his time to the band at night. During the day, Olmos attended East Los Angeles College, where he earned an associate's degree in sociology. Upon graduation, Olmos transferred to California State University, where he took drama classes to improve the performances of Pacific Ocean.

In 1978, Olmos landed a major acting role: El Pachuco, the narrator in the musical drama *Zoot Suit*, based on the Sleepy Lagoon Case and on the so-called *Zoot Suit riots in 1940s Los Angeles. *Zoot Suit* opened at the Mark Taper Forum and ran for a year due to overwhelming community support. Eventually, the play moved to Broadway, where Olmos was nominated for a Tony Award in 1979. The play was made into a feature film in 1981.

Olmos took on more acting roles in the early 1980s in movies such as *Blade

Runner and *Wolfen*. His next important role was that of Gregorio Cortez, a Mexican folk hero, in *The *Ballad of Gregorio Cortez*. Based on a true story, the film depicts the life of a Mexican farmer in San Antonio, Texas, who accidentally killed a sheriff in 1901. The historical Cortez was portrayed by the press as a thief and bandit. Research by scholar Amérigo Paredes found that Cortez was hunted, wrongly convicted, and imprisoned for twelve years as the result of a translator's mistake in Spanish, illustrating extreme racial prejudice in the U.S. judicial system. The film script has Olmos, as Cortez, speaking only Spanish to allow the viewer to understand the importance and difficulty that language difference plays in society.

In 1984, Olmos took on the role of Lieutenant Martin Castillo on the popular television series *Miami Vice*, which ran for five years. For this role,

Edward James Olmos. *Courtesy of Photofest.*

Olmos received an Emmy, a Golden Globe, and a People's Choice Award. In 1988 Olmos played the role of Jaime Escalante, an inspiring high school teacher, in the film *Stand and Deliver*, for which he earned an Academy Award nomination. Olmos directed and starred in *American Me* (1992), *The Burning Season* (1994), *Mi Familia* (1995), *Selena* (1997), *The Disappearance of Garcia Lorca* (1997), and *Zapatista* (1999). He also stars in the PBS television series *American Family* (2002–2005) about life in a Mexican American household in East Los Angeles. In April 1999, Olmos began to promote *Americanos: Latino Life in the United States*, a full-length documentary on U.S. Latina/o heritages, arts, and cultural practices, with an accompanying book, CD, and a traveling photo museum exhibit.

Olmos's long-standing commitment to community and humanitarian service is shown by the following leadership roles he plays: the U.S. Goodwill Ambassador for the United Nations Children's Fund (UNICEF), executive director for the Lives in Hazard Educational Project, and spokesperson for the Juvenile Diabetes Foundation. Olmos has received five honorary doctoral degrees from the University of Colorado, Whittier College, California State University in Fresno, Occidental College, and the American Film Institute.

Further Reading

Keller, Gary D. *A Biographical Handbook of Hispanics and United States Film.* Tempe, AZ: Bilingual Press, 1997.

Silvia D. Mora

Olvera Street. Olvera Street, formerly known as Wine Street (prior to 1877), is an active pedestrian social and commercial space located in El Pueblo de Los Ángeles Historic Monument. Olvera Street was renamed in 1877 in honor of the first county judge of Los Angeles, Agustín Olvera. The area surrounding El Pueblo, which includes the Plaza and the Plaza Catholic Church, Nuestra Señora La Reina de Los Angeles (often referred to collectively as La Placita), constitutes the oldest section of the city of Los Angeles, which was founded by the Spaniards in 1781. However, the present site including Olvera Street, the Plaza, and the Plaza Church was not actively developed until after Mexican independence from Spain in 1821. The area served as the center of the Mexican pueblo of Los Angeles following the completion of the Plaza Church in 1822 until the end of the war between the United States and México in 1848. By the 1870s, Olvera Street and the surrounding area had declined as American investment and settlement patterns established a new business district to the southwest. As a result, the area, often referred to as Sonoratown, became the primary social space for the town's segregated Mexican population. However, by the early 1900s, Italian, French, and Chinese immigrants had also established a presence in the area.

Olvera Street and the surrounding areas continued to fall into disrepair until the 1920s. After visiting Olvera Street in 1926, local resident Christine Sterling began a campaign to revitalize the area and to recreate the symbolic heart of Los Angeles as an idealized version of an early California village. At the center of Sterling's plan was a tourist attraction in the form of a Mexican marketplace that would occupy the length of Olvera Street itself. Sterling's work began as she successfully lobbied to save the Avila Adobe (c. 1818) from demolition. Soon after, Olvera Street was closed to through traffic and paved in brick. Olvera Street officially opened as a tourist destination and Mexican market on Easter Sunday, April 20, 1930. In the fall of 1932, David Alfaro Siqueiros unveiled a mural, *América Tropical*, which he had been commissioned to create on a wall overlooking Olvera Street. The mural proved to be controversial, as many people were offended by its antiimperialist/anti-American critique. Soon after its unveiling on October 9, 1932, the mural was whitewashed. In 1953, Olvera Street, the Plaza, and the Plaza Church were collectively designated as a state historic park. In 1992 control over the monument was given to the city of Los Angeles.

Olvera Street includes restaurants, shops, art galleries, and cultural facilities such as the Mexican Cultural Institute. Currently, Siqueiros's mural is undergoing a process of restoration, and there are ongoing debates concerning the representation of various immigrant groups on Olvera Street. The processes shaping Olvera Street in the present help to highlight the historic struggles over place and identity that have come to shape contemporary Los Angeles.

José Gamez

Ontiveros, Lupe (c. 1942–   ). Lupe Ontiveros is an enduring and iconic *film, television, and *theater actress whose roles have had an impact in the Chicana/o and Latina/o communities. Ontiveros, of Mexican American descent, was born in El Paso, Texas, and graduated from Texas Women's University with degrees in psychology and social work. For fifteen years, she worked as a social worker in East Los Angeles and Compton, raising her three sons and pursuing a career in acting simultaneously. She made her film debut playing the role of a prostitute in *The World's Greatest Lover* (1977). She is most associated with the role of a maid, having played it on a number of occasions in such films as *California Suite* (1978), *The Goonies* (1985), and *Universal Soldier* (1992). She has been featured in a number of key Latino films including *Zoot Suit* (1981), *El Norte* (1983), *Born in East L.A.* (1987), *Mi Familia/My Family* (1995), *Selena* (1997), and *Luminarias* (1999).

She received the National Board of Review's Best Supporting Actress Award for her portrayal of the Los Angeles theater manager Beverly Franco in Miguel Arteta's *Chuck and Buck* (2000). She won a special jury award at the Sundance Film Festival for her work in *Real Women Have Curves* (2002). Ontiveros has made guest appearances on such television shows as *Veronica's Closet*, *Caroline in the City*, and *Pasadena*. In homage to the maid roles that were her staple in her early acting years, Ontiveros narrated the yet-to-be-released documentary *Maid in America*, which examines the lives of Latina domestic workers in the United States. She is a favorite actress of independent film directors and in recent years has played substantial roles in such films as *Storytelling* (2001), *Passionada* (2002), and *Adaptation* (2002).

Further Reading

Keller, Gary D. *A Biographical Handbook of Hispanics and United States Film.* Tempe, AZ: Bilingual Press, 1997.

William Orchard

Operation Wetback. In the 1950s, after a decade of inviting thousands of Mexican workers into the United States to alleviate the labor shortage caused by World War II, the proliferation of Mexicans in the United States prompted a negative national reaction, which led the Immigration and Naturalization Service (INS) to launch "Operation Wetback," a quasimilitary operation meant to round up and deport undocumented workers and other immigrants back to México or other originating country.

The presence of Mexican workers in what is now known as the southwestern United States is nothing new, since they were part of the landscape long before the North American invasion in the mid-1800s. They openly and freely traveled back and forth to find work until 1924, when the Border Patrol was founded and the term *illegal alien* was introduced. Starting in 1942, when the *Bracero Program was launched, thousands of Mexican workers migrated to the United States on an annual basis, working in agricultural jobs and sometimes the railroad industry. The Bracero Program was a partnership between México and the United States, which benefited both countries, especially when many of the able-bodied men in the United States left to fight in World War II. By the time the war was over, and the men started returning home, the demand for cheap agricultural labor was greater than ever, but tensions began to mount between the two countries amidst accusations of discrimination and labor law violations. Concerns began surfacing about the uncontrolled *immigration population and the perception that undocumented workers were depressing wages and creating unwarranted employment competition.

Anti–immigration fears, fueled by the perceived costs of the rapidly growing immigrant population and compounded by xenophobia and the Cold War, gave birth to Operation Wetback in 1954. The code name is derived from the derogatory term *wetback*, or *mojado*, which literally translated means "wet." The pejorative word *mojado* is used to describe an individual who crosses the border illegally, because often the crossing entails physically getting across the Rio Grande River, which means the individual emerges, on the other side, wet. Led by INS Commissioner Joseph Swing, Operation Wetback was conducted in cooperation with state and city officials in California and Arizona and entailed roadblocks and cordoning off complete neighborhoods for the purpose of interrogating and ultimately deporting Mexicans thought to be in the United States illegally. Border Patrol from across the country descended on the southwestern states and, over the course of several months, arrested and repatriated over 1 million individuals to the interior areas of México. They were taken deep into México with the intention of making reentry more difficult. Many immigrants, learning of the ultimate destinations, chose to voluntarily return to México on their own. Although this was the first official INS-sanctioned repatriation, the act of criminalizing immigrant workers and repatriating them to México is known to have taken place as far back as the early 1900s.

Having achieved some of the program's goals, Operation Wetback was deemed an official success, but it was blemished. In their zealousness to round up illegal immigrants, the Border Patrol indiscriminately engaged in racial profiling, resulting in the deportation and harassment of U.S. citizens of Mexican or other Hispanic heritage. This experience of being mistaken for an illegal immigrant, deported to another country, and left to your own means to find your way back home is depicted in movies such as *Born in East L.A.* (1987) and *Mi Familia/My Family* (1995). Although Commissioner Swing was called on to explain some of the unlawful misconduct of citizens during Operation Wetback, the overwhelming public sentiment was that the Border Patrol had accomplished a service to the United States abated the possibility of any civil rights infractions.

In a case of history repeating itself, the Chandler, Arizona, *Police Department did not fare so well when they conducted a sweep to eradicate illegal immigrants from their city in 1997. According to the department, they were responding to citizen complaints about the ever-growing immigrant population when, over the course of five days in the summer of 1997, they arrested over 400 alleged illegal immigrants. Reminiscent of indiscriminating approaches taken in Operation Wetback, hundreds of people were racially profiled because of the color of their skin or preferred language, were detained, questioned, or mistreated. Lawsuits claiming discrimination and civil rights violations were filed and settled in favor of the harassed victims.

Further Reading

Calavita, Kitty. *Inside the State: The Bracero Program, Immigration, and the I.N.S.* New York: Routledge, 1992.

García, Juan Ramon. *Operation Wetback: The Mass Deportation of Mexican Undocumented Workers in 1954.* Westport, CT: Greenwood Press, 1980.

Gonzales, Manuel G. *Mexicanos: A History of Mexicans in the United States.* Bloomington: Indiana University Press, 1999.

http://www.farmworkers.org.

Alma Alvarez-Smith

Oso, Juan. Juan Oso (John Bear) is a character featured in folktales shared throughout Spain and the United States, particularly in the Southwest Borderlands, New Mexico, and California. As the story goes, Juan Oso is the son of a bear and a woman, usually a princess.

A popular version depicts a princess being kidnapped by a bear and giving birth to a son who is half bear and half human, Juan Osito (Little John Bear). Eventually, Juan Osito and the princess escape back to the palace, where Juan Osito grows up to be Juan Oso and leaves the palace to have adventures all across the land. Another version entangles a mother and her son with the bear. The bear kidnaps them and raises the boy as a bear. The half-wild Juan Oso and his mother escape the clutches of the bear, and although raised by a bear, Juan manages to become a refined and sensitive man.

The story of Juan Oso can be found in varied forms in *folklore, as demonstrated by Texas folklorist J. Frank Dobie in his 1935 novel *Tongues of the Monte*, New Mexican folklorist Aurelio Espinosa (1985) and his son José Manuel Espinosa (1937), and California folklorist Elaine Miller.

Further Reading

Dobie, J. Frank. *Puro Mexicano*. Denton: University of North Texas Press, 1980.

Espinosa, Aurelio M. *The Folklore of Spain in the American Southwest: Traditional Spanish Folk Literature in Northern New Mexico and Southern Colorado*. Edited by José Manuel Espinosa. Norman: University of Oklahoma Press, 1985.

Armando Quintero, Jr.

Ozomatli. Ozomatli—or Ozo, as its fans call it—is a popular band that was formed in Los Angeles, California, in the mid-1990s. The band is important both for the variety of its musical influences and for the strength of its social and political messages. The name Ozomatli comes from the Náhuatl name for the Aztec god of dance and passion. The Ozomatli is the monkey-like character in the lower left-hand corner of the Aztec calendar stone. The founding members of the band include Raúl "El Bully" Pacheco, Ulises Bella, Jiro Yamaguchi, Jose "Crunchy" Espinosa, Cut Chemist, Wil-Dog, William "Echo" Marrufo, Pablo Castorena, Justin "Niño" Porée, Asdru Sierra, and Chali 2na. Ozomatli may be regarded as a mixture of Latin and American musics, including *salsa, urban *hip-hop and rap, and even jazz. This variety makes for an interesting and entertaining Latina/o popular music with strong social and political messages. The band integrates various musical in-

Ozomatli combines salsa, urban rap/hip-hop, and jazz, for a unique, high-energy sound that consistently coaxes the audience out of their seats. *Courtesy of the Playboy Jazz Festival.*

struments from all over the globe. Although they sing in Spanish, their hip-hop numbers are in English.

The band got their start by playing the Los Angeles club circuit. In June 1998, the group released their first album titled simply *Ozomatli*. The group is proud of its multiethnic makeup and claims that its music is truly color-blind. Specifically, the band says their first album established them as a "poly-glot Black-Chicano-Cuban-Japanese-Jewish-Filipino crew, and as a band committed to social change and community building through the party plea-sure of musical collision." Ozo's most recent album was released in Septem-ber 2001 and is titled *Embrace the Chaos*.

Since the summer of 2001, Ozomatli has spent most of its time on the road. The group claims to have traveled throughout the United States more times than they can count. Their work has consisted of playing in everything from stadiums to political benefits to public high schools. The band has also traveled abroad to perform in Japan, Europe, Cuba, Australia, and México. Most notably, the band has performed with such established musicians as Carlos *Santana, *Los Lobos, Johnny *Pacheco, and Yomo Toro. The cur-rent members of Ozomatli are Raul Pacheco, lead vocals, guitar, and *bajo sexto*; Rene "Spinobi" Domínguez, turntables; Wil-Dog, funk, hip-hop, and Latin bass; José "Crunchy" Espinoza, alto sax and vocals; Anthony "Kanetic Source" Stout, rap and vocals; Ulises Bella, tenor sax; Asdru Sierra, trumpet and vocals; Andrew Mendoza, drums; Jiro Yamaguchi, *tablas*, bongos, and percussion; and Justin "Nino" Poree, congas and percussion.

Further Reading

http://entertainment.signonsandiego.com/profile/174863.
http://www.mtv.com/bands/az/ozomatli/bio.jhtml.
http://www.ozomatli.com.

Cristina K. Muñoz

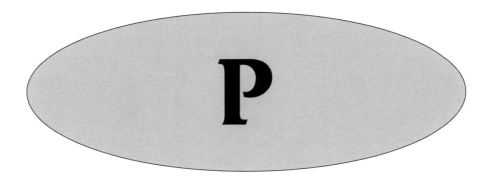

Pachanga. The *pachanga*, a fast, syncopated style of music, developed from Latino musical ensembles of the early 1960s called **charangas.* During the previous decade, musical groups began playing **cha cha cha* and other popular Cuban dances while introducing Latin rhythms such as the *pachanga.* Although the origins of the *pachanga*'s style have come into question, it seems to be Cuban, with a sound that can be described as a combination of both **merengue* and conga. Some sources cite Eduardo Davidson (1910–1994) as the creator of the *pachanga* rhythm in his 1959 recording of "La Pachanga," while others credit José Fajardo's (1919–2001) *charanga* as actually being the first to perform *pachanga.*

As its popularity grew on the East Coast, the *pachanga* became almost as much of a rage in Latin New York as the cha cha cha had been nationally. In fact, the *pachanga* surpassed the cha cha cha in the early 1960s as the most fashionable style of Latin music, especially among youth, even though it never reached the national popularity that it had enjoyed on the East Coast. Based on data presented in Farándula (show or theatre) NYC charts for 1960, Davidson's "La Pachanga" was the number-one single for seven months. The Afro-Cuban singer Rolando La Serie recorded with a brass and sax–led big band directed by Bebo Valdes on the LP *Sabor a Mi* (Flavor of Me). Some of the more popular artists who performed *pachangas* were Ray Báretto, Joe Arroyo, Grupe Niche, La Sonora Dinamita, Roberto Torres, Los Embajadores Vallentos, Los Titanes, and Diómedes Díaz.

The *pachanga*'s swift pace lends itself nicely to dancing, although it often requires a great deal of energy from the participant. Some critics claim that the *pachanga* may have lost some of its momentum because it proved to be too strenuous for the average dancer, yet it continues to enjoy some popularity within the *salsa dancing community today.

Further Reading

Roberts, John Storm. *The Latin Tinge: The Impact of Latin American Music on the United States.* 2nd ed. New York: Oxford University Press, 1999.

George Yáñez

Pacheco, Johnny (1935–   ). With a career as a flutist, percussionist, composer, bandleader, and producer that has lasted over forty years and accounted for collaborations with Latin musicians ranging both chronologically and stylistically from Dámaso *Pérez Prado to DLG (Dark Latin Groove), Johnny Pacheco has been an important figure in the popularity and development of musical genres including *charanga*, *pachanga*, and *salsa in the United States. Pacheco was born in Santiago de los Caballeros, Dominican Republic; his father, Rafael Azarías Pacheco, bandleader and clarinetist for the Orquesta Santa Cecilia, a famous *Latin jazz band, began Johnny's musical training at an early age. Pacheco's family moved to New York City when he was eleven, and he soon learned to play percussion, accordion, violin, saxophone, and clarinet. He attended Bronx Vocational High School, where he learned flute. He studied at the Juilliard School of Music as a percussionist and also received training as an engineer, a career path that he soon abandoned.

While still in high school, Pacheco began playing professionally, organizing a *mambo band, the Chuchulecos Boys (which featured Eddie *Palmieri on piano), playing accordion with *merengue bands, and later working as a percussionist with the Paul Whiteman Orchestra and a quartet he co-led with Palmieri. He also freelanced with other artists including Pérez Prado, Tito *Puente, and Xavier *Cugat. In 1958, he joined Charlie Palmieri's *conjunto* (a band featuring trumpets, guitars, and percussion that plays *son cubano* and is altogether distinct from Tex-Mex *conjunto*, which features accordion and *bajo sexto*, a twelve-string Spanish guitar), playing percussion. Later in the year, fueled by a New York performance by the well-known Cuban *charanga* (flute and violin orchestra specializing in Afro-Cuban music) group Orquesta Aragón, Pacheco switched to flute, and Palmieri hired four violinists. The group changed its name to Charanga Duboney, to reflect the change in style, and helped usher in a comeback of the *son cubano* genre.

After only eight months, Pacheco left that very influential group to form his own, the equally renowned Pacheco y su Charanga. The music they played, *pachanga*, a showier, up-tempo version of *charanga*, featuring two singers and the whole band dancing, became a new craze. The band signed with the newly formed Alegre Records and in 1961 released the album *Pacheco y su Charanga*, which sold over 100,000 copies in six months. During this time, the group toured internationally, becoming the first Latin band to headline the Apollo Theater in Harlem, and Pacheco recorded with the Alegre All-Stars, a jam session band made of the best musicians at the label. In 1963, he formed Pacheco y su Tumbao (one of the most traditional rhythms in Cuba), an Afro-Cuban *conjunto* group modeled on those of Arsenio Rodríguez (All Star Band) and La Sonora Matancera (literally the Sound of Matanzas, the name of a city in Cuba), who had both recently come to New York from Havana and recorded the classic album *Cañonazo* (Cannon Fire, 1964). This album was the first recorded for his own new record label, Fania Records, which he had cofounded in 1963 with Jerry Masucci, a lawyer who had developed an affinity for Cuban music while living on the island.

From very humble beginnings, with Pacheco and Masucci distributing records from the trunk of a car, Fania would go on to become the most influential record label in Latin music history, combining Cuban music with jazz elements and a young urban sensibility to recast it as salsa and achieving a virtual monopoly in the genre by the mid-1970s. Pacheco, as creative director, producer, and executive at Fania, played a significant role in shaping the new Latin sound and in promoting the rise of salsa. Ironically, while he was helping artists craft this innovative sound through his production, such as on the 1967 Willie *Colón and Héctor Lavoe landmark album, *El Malo* (The Bad One), on his own recordings he remained extremely faithful to the traditional Cuban *conjunto* sound. In the mid-1970s he lured Celia *Cruz to the label, collaborating with her on four albums—most notably, *Celia y Johnny* (1974), which went gold—and featuring her with the Fania All-Stars. Pacheco had formed the Fania All-Stars in 1968, taking a cue from his earlier experience at Alegre. Featuring the label's top musicians, the Fania All-Stars became something of a salsa supergroup and served as ambassadors for the music through their extensive touring, including concerts at New York's Cheetah Club and Yankee Stadium (these two concerts attained legendary status and were both later released as albums and films), tours throughout Latin America and Japan, and performances as part of the series of concerts leading up to performing at the 1974 Muhammed Ali–George Foreman fight, the "Rumble in the Jungle," staged in Kinshasa, Zaire.

Simultaneous to these endeavors, Pacheco made guest appearances on recordings by jazz and pop artists as diverse as McCoy Tyner, Quincy Jones, Stevie Wonder, and David Byrne, cowriting and producing three songs for the latter's scattershot foray into Latino rhythms, *Rei Momo* (King Momo, 1989). In the 1990s, he was featured on recordings by new-generation Latin music artists such as salsa fusionists DLG and rapper Mangú and continued to tour with his own band, Pacheco y su Tumbao Añejo (Pacheco and His Old Tumbao) into the twenty-first century. Now an elder statesman of Latin music, Pacheco has received several prestigious awards such as the Presidential Medal of Honor from his native Dominican Republic in 1996; the

National Academy of Arts and Sciences Governor's Award, also in 1996 (he was the first Latin music producer to receive the honor), and induction into the International Latin Music Hall of Fame in 1998.

Further Reading

"Johnny Pacheco: Biography." *SIMA, Inc.* http://www.johnnypacheco.com/biogra phy_pg.htm.

Steward, Sue. *¡Musica! Salsa, Rumba, Merengue, and More.* San Francisco, CA: Chronicle Books, 1999.

Yanow, Scott. *Afro-Cuban Jazz.* San Francisco, CA: Miller Freeman Books, 2000.

Ramón Versage

Pachucos. Pachucos (and, for women, pachucas) refers to male members of a Mexican American counterculture youth movement that emerged in the late 1930s and flourished in the early years of World War II through the 1950s. Some scholars trace the modern roots of the *Chicano Movement to *pachuquismo*: that is, the phenomenon associated with the *zoot suit that is characterized by a decidedly Chicano (as opposed to Mexican or other Latino) identity. The baggy zoot suit style was one of the major symbols of rebellion among Chicano boys and young men during the 1940s, particularly on the West Coast. The phenomenon eventually spread to others, including girls and young women who adopted an altered version featuring tight mini-skirts instead of the baggy trousers. Besides the dramatic style of dress, pachucos employed an interesting linguistic *cálo* (i.e., special dialect) that combined English, Spanish, and hip Afro-jazz and bebop terms. Some strands of pachuco *cálo* have been traced by language scholars to fifteenth-century Gypsy dialects in Spain. The hybrid idiom achieved the sought-after goal of making the pachuco in-group speech inaccessible to others, especially to their usually Spanish-speaking parents and to English-speaking authority figures.

The striking pachuco look and hip hybrid dialect intensified the young "zoot suiters'" sense of unique identity and solidarity during a period of social alienation when many felt like outcasts from both their American homeland and the Mexican *patria* (land of origin) of their parents and grandparents. Over time, these and other elements produced an identifiable subculture. However, many Mexican American youth did not participate or engage the trend fully, although in certain cities like Los Angeles the zoot suit and idiom attracted large numbers of adolescents. A majority of others donned the apparel but did not involve themselves deeply in the accompanying *la vida loca (crazy life) subculture. Characterized by social defiance and overtly hostile attitudes and poses, this form of *pachuquismo* is equated with such activities as a partying night life, marijuana smoking, involvement in *gangs, and occasionally other antisocial pathologies that include crime participation. Researchers estimate that these pachucos never totaled more than a tiny percentage of the Mexican American youth population (less than 3 percent by one estimate). However, due to their visible defiance and newspaper publicity about them, the pachuco movement has come to define the Chicano zoot suiter for the general public.

With the development of the Chicano Movement and literary and artistic offshoot known as the *Chicano Renaissance, the pachuco movement achieved iconic status in large measure because of the work of such writers as José Montoya, author of the classic poetic tribute to pachuco, *El Louie* (1969), and Luis *Valdez, founder of El *Teatro Campesino and director of the movie *Zoot Suit* (1981). Valdez adapted the film from his play of the same name, which he wrote to memorialize the historical and controversial event known as the Sleepy Lagoon case (*see* Zoot Suit entry). The drama's compelling story of the pachucos' persecution by police, sailors, press, judges, and the general public, coupled with its illuminating portrayal of the Chicano community's and liberal activists' efforts for social justice, has made Valdez's *Zoot Suit* a powerful documentary of one slice of life for American Latinos in the twentieth century.

At the start of the millennium, the zoot-suited pachuco is still romanticized by some as initiating the first modern counterculture youth movement based on the rights of individuals and minorities for social power. Others condemn *pachuquismo* as ushering in socially deviant and even pathological behaviors among Latino youth. Like the exciting dynamics of the Roaring Twenties, the historic realities and the iconic representations of pachucos and their era are too complex to reduce to the binary simplicity of only "good" or "bad." Research-based hindsight demonstrates that they drew attention to the struggle that immigrant children confront on a daily basis, and they did so with an empowered stance of *mestizaje* (indigenist/Spanish cultural hybridity) that borrowed from and amalgamated many sources with a fresh spirit that was ultimately quintessentially American.

Further Reading

Escobar, Edward. *Race, Police, and the Making of a Political Identity*. Berkeley: University of California Press, 1999.

Mazón, Mauricio. *The Zoot Suit Riots: The Psychology of Symbolic Annihilation*. Austin: University of Texas Press, 1984.

Villa, Rául. *Barrio-Logos: Space and Place in Urban Chicano Literature and Culture*. Austin: University of Texas Press, 2000.

Cordelia Chávez Candelaria

Padilla, Pilar (1972–   ). Pilar Padilla, born in Mexico City, is an accomplished stage, *film, and television actress in México. Padilla achieved international acclaim for her film debut as Maya in British director Ken Loach's *Bread and Roses* (2000). In that film, she plays a Mexican immigrant who crosses the border to live with her sister in Los Angeles, then works alongside her at an exploitative janitorial company. Maya ultimately works to improve worker conditions. Before her U.S. breakthrough, Padilla had significant stage and independent film experience in México. Padilla also starred alongside Salma *Hayek in the film adaptation of Julia Alvarez's *In The Time of Butterflies* (2001).

Arturo J. Aldama

Palmieri, Eddie (1936–   ). Eddie Palmieri is an influential *Latin jazz pianist, composer, and bandleader. He was born in Harlem, New York, in 1936 into a family who had immigrated to the United States from Puerto Rico. Palmieri started singing at a very young age, began playing the piano at the age of eight, and later learned to play the drums.

Palmieri has drawn upon a range of jazz piano styles, including those of artists such as Thelonious Monk, Herbie Hancock, and McCoy Tyner, which he has incorporated into Latin and non-Latin musical contexts. Percussionist Manny Oquendo introduced Palmieri to the rhythmical potential of Cuban music and influenced his music greatly. In 1955, Palmieri gained professional recognition by playing with Johnny Segui's orchestra, but he was dismissed for supposedly hitting the piano keys with too much force. Between 1958 and 1960 he played in Tito *Rodríguez's band, and in 1961, he formed his own band, Conjunto La Perfecta, which developed a distinctive sound featuring flute and two trombones. This replacement of trumpets with trombones was an unusual occurrence in Latin music and has become known as "trombanga."

Palmieri has recorded a substantial number of albums, dating from the 1960s to the 1990s. Following his band's split in 1968, Palmieri played with a variety of artists, including the trumpeter Alfredo "Chocolate" Armenteros, on the album *Champagne* (1968). This album contained elements of the musical style "boogaloo," which was a mix of rhythm and blues/Latin fusion. Palmieri never really embraced the boogaloo style of music, which he regarded as an inferior genre that had developed following the Cuban embargo. Some of Palmieri's music written during the 1960s is politically oriented. The album *Justicia* (Justice, 1969), released at the height of the civil rights movement, focused on the problem of economic and social deprivation in the United States.

In the 1970s, Palmieri experimented with a mix of rock, rhythm and blues, pop, and jazz styles. He was awarded his first Grammy in 1975 for the Latin album *Sun of Latin Music* and another Grammy the following year for *Unfinished Masterpiece*. His album *Macumba Voodoo* (1978) incorporated influences from the cultures of Brazil, Haiti, and Cuba.

Palmieri has made a lasting contribution to the history of American jazz, as evidenced by the 1988 placement of two of his recordings into a section of the National Museum of American History in the Smithsonian Institute in Washington, D.C. In 1995, Palmieri helped introduce a new category of Latin jazz to the National Academy of Recording Arts and Sciences, receiving nominations in this category in 1995 for his album *Palmas* and in 1996 for his album *Arete*. Palmieri continues to produce recordings that fuse a variety of musical influences and styles that contribute to the evolution of Latin jazz.

Further Reading

http://www.eddiepalmierimusic.com.

Helen Oakley

Pantoja, Antonia (1922–2002). Antonia Pantoja, recognized as one of Puerto Rico's most important activists and organizers, was the founder of *ASPIRA, an organization dedicated to investing in Latino youth. Her tireless commitment and work in Puerto Rico challenging barriers of poverty, increasing political involvement, and promoting economic development earned her the highest honor the nation bestows on a civilian, the Presidential Medal of Freedom, presented by President Bill Clinton in 1997.

Born in San Juan, Puerto Rico, in 1922, Pantoja studied at the University of Puerto Rico, where she received a Normal School Diploma (1942) before moving to New York in 1944. With a history of childhood poverty, she came to the United States with a passion and commitment to improving the community for herself, her neighbors, and other Puerto Ricans. She earned a Bachelor of Arts degree in 1952 from Hunter College, City University of New York, and in 1954 earned her master's in social work from Columbia University.

Operating on the philosophy that education is the way to develop youth, Pantoja founded ASPIRA in 1961, creating one of her greatest legacies. In 1970, she founded the Puerto Rican Research Resource Center in Washington, D.C. (dedicated to data collection and policy creation based on research) and the Universidad Boricua (a bilingual university), which she would later lead as chancellor, after earning her Ph.D. in 1973. Due to health issues, she moved to California in 1978 and became an associate professor in the School of Social Work at San Diego State University. While in San Diego, she founded and became president of the Graduate School for Community Development, where students gained skills and knowledge for grassroots problem solving and restoring their community.

Not satisfied with the status quo, when Pantoja identified a gap in the system, she forged ahead to fill it, as evidenced by her work in founding organizations, institutes, and associations. In 1985 she founded Producir, a community organization in Puerto Rico, to generate employment and other services; in 2001 she helped found the Latino Educational Media Center, to create media on the rich and diverse Latino experience; and in 2002, she founded Aspirante Alumni Fellowship, Inc., providing means for ASPIRA alumni to give back through networking, collaborating, and mentoring new generations of ASPIRA students.

A charter member of the New York Commission Intergroup Relations (one of the first multiracial task forces), Pantoja received numerous awards throughout her life, including honorary doctorates from the Universities of Connecticut, Massachusetts, and Puerto Rico. She will be remembered for her legendary role in the education and leadership development of youth and as founder of some of the longest-lasting Latino organizations and institutions. Pantoja died in 2002 at the age of eighty in Manhattan after a bout with cancer.

Further Reading

Pantoja, Antonia. *Memoir of a Visionary: Antonia Pantoja.* Houston, TX: Arte Público Press, 2002.

http://www.aspira.org/pantoja.htm.

http://www.aspira.org/PDF/Dr_Pantoja.pdf.

Alma Alvarez-Smith

Papel Picado. *Papel picado* (perforated paper) refers to the traditional Mexican craft of decorative cut paper, usually on thin colored tissue paper hung as banners for special occasions like birthdays, *weddings, baptisms, *holidays, *Día de los Muertos, Christmas, and other fiesta events. The punctured paper art is usually made by cutting the layers of tissue with sharp *fierritos* (small chisels) into lattice-work designs featuring images of human and animal figures, flowers, lettering, and other representations. Among the *papel picado* designs are skeletal figures (i.e., *calaveras*) engaged in everyday activities for Día de los Muertos altars and exhibits, etchings of the *Virgin of Guadalupe, Christmas symbols, and other festival themes. Often individual sheets of *papel picado* are strung together into festive, colorful banners hung aloft in attractive displays.

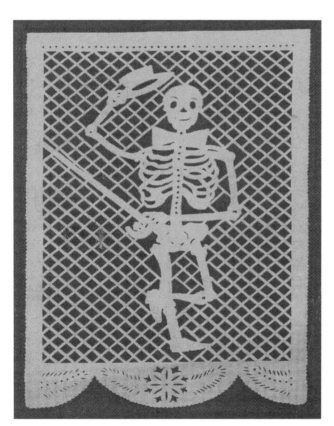

Publicity handbill for a Phoenix cultural event, made from reproduction of *papel picado* sheet crafted by an anonymous artisan. *Courtesy of the Cordelia Candelaria Private Collection.*

The production of *papel picado* art begins with a paper pattern used as a guide and placed upon up to fifty layers of tissue laid on top of a hard surface, usually a heavy lead sheet liner. The pattern is perforated with varying sizes of chisel points and a hammer. Traditional artisans still use paper, but increasingly *papel picado* is made of metallic and coated paper, as well as plastic sheets for outdoor presentation. In México the most famous source of *papel picado* is San Salvador Huixcolotla, Puebla. San Salvador paper art is used locally and exported to markets throughout México and abroad.

The historical record shows that cut paper crafts have enjoyed popularity in folk traditions worldwide since the Chinese invention of paper in A.D. 105 in Cathay. Long considered a humble art form, *papel picado* artisans often worked anonymously, and the fragile products of their work lack the lasting quality associated with other forms made of more durable media such as stone, metal, wood, and oils. Nevertheless, cut paper aesthetics circle the globe and include the Chinese *hua yang*, Japanese *kirigami* or *monkiri*, French *silhouettes*, German *Scherenschnitte*, and Polish *wycinanki*. Among the major artists who have worked with paper cutouts are Henri Matisse and Marcel Duchamp of France, Alexander Calder of the United States, and Frida *Kahlo of México.

Further Reading

Jablonski, Ramona. *The Paper Cut-Out Design Book*. Owing Mills, MD: Stemmer House Publishers, 1976.

"Papel Picado: The Art of Mexican Cut Paper." *North Texas Institute for Educators on the Visual Arts* 7.3 (Fall 1996). http://www.art.unt.edu/ntieva/news/vol_7/issue3/96falp11.htm.

Cordelia Chávez Candelaria

Pasíon, La. *See Penitentes.*

Pastor, Ed (1943–   ). Ed Pastor was the first *Chicano elected to represent the state of Arizona in the U.S. House of Representatives. Pastor's passion for public service is driven by his desire to give back to his community and his commitment to improving the lives of his constituents. In 1991, Pastor was elected to represent Arizona's Second Congressional District, which subsequently became District 4 in 2002, as a result of redistricting generated by the 2000 U.S. Census count. Pastor is thus a beneficiary of the expanding numbers of twentieth- and twenty-first-century Latina/o communities in the United States, as well as an important descendant of Latina and Latino historical political leaders of the past. He is a significant part of America's grassroots politics and popular culture with its accompanying media celebrity and public representation of Latina/o issues.

Pastor was the first of three children born to Enrique and Margarita Pastor in the small mining community of Claypool, Arizona. Born Edward López Pastor on June 28, 1943, Pastor grew up to be the first in his *family to pursue higher education, as he attended Arizona State University (ASU) and earned a Bachelor of Arts degree in chemistry in 1966, followed by a Juris Doctorate in 1974 from the ASU College of Law. One of the few members of the U.S. Congress with classroom teaching experience, the future congressman taught chemistry at North High School in Phoenix. His other work prior to the House of Representatives included three terms with the Maricopa County Board of Supervisors, a position he was elected to in 1976, working as a member of Arizona Governor Raúl Castro's staff in the 1980s and serving as deputy director of the community-based Guadalupe Organization Inc., an advocacy and service group.

In 1991 Pastor was chosen the Democratic nominee from Arizona's Second District and was successfully elected to become the first Hispanic in Arizona ever elected to the U.S. Congress. Since his election, Pastor has been an active member of the *Congressional Hispanic Caucus (CHC), serving a two-year term as the CHC chairman and also as secretary-treasurer of the caucus. In addition to participating in the CHC, the congressman has served on the Travel and Tourism Caucus, the Congressional Caucus for Women's Issues, and the Arts Caucus. Pastor's political career reflects numerous assignments and appointments, which have kept him actively engaged in representing his district. Some of his more current appointments include Democratic Chief Deputy Whip, Democratic Steering & Policy Committee, and the Democratic Leadership Advisory Committee. As a member of the House Appropriations Committee, Pastor serves on the Subcommittee on Energy and Water Development, the Subcommittee on Transportation, Treasury, Postal Service, and General Government, and the Subcommittee on District of Columbia. Some of the assignments that Pastor has held in the past include Education and Labor Committee, the Committee on Small Business, and the Subcommittee on Rural Development and Agriculture, just to name a few.

In addition to his many responsibilities as a congressman, Pastor serves on numerous boards for advocacy and civic organizations, such as Neighborhood Housing Services of America, *National Association of Latino Elected and Appointed Officials (NALEO), and the National Job Corps Alumni Association, and has historically been involved with Arizona community organizations such as *Chicanos por La Causa, Friendly House, and Valley of the Sun United Way.

The people of Arizona have honored the congressman by having a school named for him and his wife in 2000 when the Roosevelt School District #66 officially dedicated the Ed and Verma Pastor Elementary School in recognition of the Pastors' commitment and dedication to education. In addition, the city of Phoenix honored the congressman by christening the city's new transit center located at suburban South Mountain Village with his name in 2003.

Further Reading

http://www.edpastor.com.
http://www.house.gov/pastor.

Cristina K. Muñoz

Pastores, Los. *Los Pastores* (The Shepherds) is one of many religious medieval dramas brought from Spain to the New World by Franciscan missionaries in the sixteenth century. During the colonization of México, Catholic missionaries used folk plays like *Los Pastores* as one form of instruction to convert Indians to Christianity. The formal title is *El Coloquio de los Pastores*, which is translated in the vernacular as "The Mexican Shepherds' Play." The drama for *Los Pastores* was written in verse based on the New Testament and depicts the appearance of the angel of the Lord to the shepherds as they watched over their flocks to announce the birth of Jesus (Luke 2l:8–20). Pedagogical dramas were used as a teaching aid for instruction of the Indians and their mestizo descendants. However, in the seventeenth and eighteenth centuries, local cultural elements like language, music, colors, and Indian masks were woven into dramatizations of the Old and New Testament. As a result of the synthesis of European and indigenous cultural elements, a hybrid religious *theater in México developed, and new versions of religious dramas emerged. Church authorities viewed these dramas as profane forms of entertainment, banned them from the church grounds, and excluded them from official festivities. Communities continued to enact the dramas on their own without approval from the Church. Thus, folk drama was born, and *Los Pastores* became an important feature of Mexican folk traditions.

Although the basic structure of the shepherd's play remains constant, contemporary versions show a great variety in their use of language, humor, and comments on political and cultural issues. For example, in the Borderlands Theater of Tucson, Arizona, a comic version of *La Pastorela* presents Lucifer and his legions from hell parading in red high heels, and angels dressed as Batman or Robin. Another version drama depicts issues like the struggle between Mexican border crossers and the Border Patrol; shepherds are harassed by the devil in Border Patrol attire. In addition, in 1991, El *Teatro Campesino produced a video film of their production of *Los Pastores* titled *La Pastorela* for the PBS Great Performances series, which starred singer Linda *Ronstadt and comedian Paul *Rodríguez. Despite these comic dialogues and updated versions, the dramas serve to reinforce the biblical struggle between good and evil in the minds of children and adults.

In rural Chicano areas, communities come together on December 16 through December 24 to celebrate the Christmas holiday. *Los Pastores* plays are enacted by members of the community, and the traditional Christmas *foods like tamales, *pozole* (a type of corn soup), and *biscochitos* (a holiday cookie) are prepared for the festivities.

Further Reading

Flores, Richard. *Los Pastores: History and Performance in the Mexican Shephard's Play of South Texas*. Washington, DC: Smithsonian Institution Press, 1995.

Rose Marie Soto

Paz, Octavio (1914–1998). Born in Mexico City on March 31, 1914, Octavio Paz was arguably the most influential intellectual in México in the second half of the twentieth century, while Alfonso Reyes (1889–1959) was the intellectually dominant figure in the country during the first half of that century. Uncannily, both were intellectually precocious and rapidly became amazingly protean writers. They both were published writers in their teens; they both wrote essays on poetry, poets, poetics, literary theory, art, and history; they were both scrupulously precise and patient researchers as cultural historians; they both proposed social, historical, and psychological analyses of the Mexican people; they both wrote in a beautiful, clear, and rich prose, and they were both voracious readers; they both had the ambition of being remembered mostly for their poetry, though both of them will probably be read in the future essentially for their carefully crafted prose; they both translated into Spanish fundamental works of literature from many countries and many different epochs; and they both helped create important and long-lasting cultural institutions in México. The only big difference between them was that Reyes avoided politics his whole life, whereas Paz was always a political man.

In 1937 Paz traveled to Spain with his young wife, Elena Garro, who became an important novelist and from whom he was later divorced. Back in México, he participated in the creation of the magazine *Taller* (1938–1941) with the aim of publishing translations of important contemporary poets from all continents and giving a publishing outlet to young Mexican poets. The Guggenheim Fellowship he received in 1944 allowed him to obtain the firsthand knowledge of the United States that he later used in writing his most famous book, *The Labyrinth of Solitude*, published in 1951. In *Labyrinth of Solitude* Paz discusses the nihilism of Mexican self-identity and argues that "machismo" is a product of the Spanish conquest of México. He discusses the relationship between Spain's conquest of México's indigenous populations and what he regards as the pervasive sense among modern Mexicans that they are neither Indian nor Spaniard but subsist in a kind of intellectual, spiritual, and emotional solitude.

He joined México's diplomatic corps in 1941 and was appointed to countries such as France, Japan, Switzerland, and India. He served in this last country from 1962 to 1968, resigning in protest against the government's direct responsibility for the massacre of students and workers in the Three Cultures Plaza situated in the Tlatelolco borough, shortly before the opening of the Olympic Games in Mexico City. After teaching at Cambridge and Harvard from 1969 to 1972, Paz returned to México and founded the cultural magazine *Plural*, as a Sunday supplement to the then-prestigious daily *Excélsior*. When the Mexican government took over *Plural*, Paz immediately founded *Vuelta* (1976–1998), a literary, cultural, and political monthly. Several American universities awarded him honorary degrees, and he received some supremely prestigious awards, such as the Jerusalem Literature Prize and the (Mexican) Premio Nacional de Letras (both in 1977), the (Spanish) Cervantes Prize (in 1981), the German Booksellers Peace Prize (in 1984), the Oslo Poetry Prize (in 1985), the (Spanish) Menéndez Pelayo Prize (in 1987), and the Nobel Prize for Literature (in 1990).

Octavio Paz wrote extensively. His works translated into English include *Sun Stone* (1962), *Eagle or Sun?* (1970), *Configurations* (1971), *Renga: A Chain of Poems* (1972), *Early Poems: 1935–1955* (1973), *A Draft of Shadows and Other Poems* (1979), *The Monkey Grammarian* (1981), *Collected Poems* (1987), *The Labyrinth of Solitude* (1961), *Marcel Duchamp, or the Castle of Purity* (1970), *Claude Lévi-Strauss: An Introduction* (1970), *The Other Mexico: Critique of the Pyramid* (1972), *Alternating Current* (1973), *The Bow and the Lyre* (1973), *Children of the Mire: Poetry from Romanticism to the Avant-Garde* (1974), *Conjunctions and Disjunctions* (1974), *The Siren and the Seashell, and Other Essays on Poets and Poetry* (1976), *One Earth, Four or Five Worlds: Reflections on Contemporary History* (1985), *On Poets and Others* (1986), and *Convergences: Selected Essays on Art and Literature* (1987).

In addition to the profound impression the work made upon his compatriots, Paz's writings also helped shape generations of Latino thinkers and artists in the United States. His observations on the origins and manifestations of Mexican identity (and by extension that of Mexican Americans) have influenced *Chicano intellectuals for decades.

Further Reading

Fein, John. *Toward Octavio Paz: A Reading of His Major Poems, 1957–1976.* Lexington: University Press of Kentucky, 1986.

Paz, Octavio. *An Anthology of Mexican Poetry.* Translation by Samuel Beckett. Bloomington: Indiana University Press, 1958.

Phillips, Rachel. *The Poetic Modes of Octavio Paz.* London: Oxford University Press, 1972.

http://www.kirjasto.sci.fi/opaz.htm.

http://www.nobel.se/literature/laureates/1990/paz-bio.html.

Luis Aldama and James E. García

Peña, Elizabeth (1959–   ). Latina actress and director Elizabeth Peña has a career spanning several decades. Peña was born on September 23, 1959, in New Jersey to Margarita Estella Toirac and Mario Peña, a Cuban-born producer, director, and playwright. She was raised in Cuba until the age of eight, when the family came back to the United States and settled in New York. While growing up, Peña was influenced greatly by her parents, who ran the Latin American Theatre Ensemble. She graduated from the High School of Performing Arts in New York City and made her *film debut in *El Super* (1979). Some of her more notable movies include *Crossover Dreams* (1985), with Rubén *Blades; *Down and Out in Beverly Hills* (1986),

Elizabeth Peña. *Courtesy of Photofest.*

opposite Richard Dreyfus and Bette Midler; *La Bamba* (1987); *Jacob's Ladder* (1990); *Blue Steel* (1990); *Waterdance* (1992); *Lone Star* (1996); *Rush Hour* (1998); and *Tortilla Soup* (2001).

In addition to her movie credits, Peña has appeared in such television shows as *Tough Cookies* (1986), *I Married Dora* (1987), and *Shannon's Deal* (1990–1991). Peña's recent work was in the television drama series *Resurrection Blvd.* (2000–2002). Behind the camera, she has taken on the role of director and mentor to young Latina actresses.

Further Reading

Keller, Gary D. *A Biographical Handbook of Hispanics and United States Film.* Tempe, AZ: Bilingual Press, 1997.

Tardiff, Joseph C., and L. Mpho Mabunda, eds. *Dictionary of Hispanic Biography.* Detroit, MI: Gale Research, 1995.

Telgen, Diane, and Jim Kamp, eds. *Latinas! Women of Achievement.* Detroit, MI: Visible Ink Press, 1996.

Unterburger, Amy L., and Jane L. Delgado, eds. *Who's Who among Hispanic Americans 1994–1995.* Detroit, MI: Gale Research, 1994.

Alma Alvarez-Smith

Penitentes. Because of the extreme scarcity of clergy during the early Spanish colonial period in the southwestern United States, the local Hispano populations relied on their own social and religious organizations to provide spiritual sustenance and to see them through hard times. One important outgrowth of this was the emergence of the *penitentes* (penitents), grassroots groups of devoted believers who were sometimes called cults and sects by early ethnologists and other writers, mostly non-Hispanic outsiders. Examples of *penitente* practices and their secret chapels of worship called *moradas* still exist, particularly in Colorado, New Mexico, and Utah. They are significant to Latina and Latino popular cultures of the United States because they represent a strand of religious fundamentalism that is rooted in history and remains alive and active in the present moment. As such the *peni-*

tentes signify what many scholars describe as residual elements of traditional folk culture.

Within the local traditions of the Southwest, the *penitentes* were Hispanos who organized *cofradías* (confraternities or mutual aid societies) of *hermanos* (brothers) that in some regions occasionally included Pueblo and other American Indians. Called La Hermandad de Nuestro Padre Jesús Nazareno (Brotherhood of Our Father Jesus the Nazarene), since the 1860s the *penitente* religious observances adopted local indigenous features, and their practices came to include a high degree of religious mysticism, stern discipline, and physical suffering in reenactment of the Passion of Christ. Among their practices were self-mortification and occasionally even crucifixion during La Semana Santa (Holy Week). These beliefs are based on the medieval ideas perpetuated by followers of St. Bonaventure and of St. Francis of Assisi. Because the Catholic Church forbade these extreme religious observances as early as the thirteenth century, however, the *penitentes* were always sworn to secrecy. Perhaps for this reason, historical evidence of their presence in the Southwest dates only to the early nineteenth century. The Hermandad (Brotherhood) served the needs of many people by preserving faith in Jesus Christ and the Catholic Church and, importantly, by providing material aid to its members and pensions to their widows, among other services.

Ample scholarly evidence shows that both Spaniards and Moors practiced similar religious observances in Spain prior to the conquest of the Americas and continue even to the present day. Today the fundamental premise of what contemporary *penitentes* believe is that the nearest attainment of godliness on earth is through meditation on the sufferings of Christ and the Virgin Mary and, in some forms, in the reenactment of Christ's suffering. The songs connected with the *penitente* sects are laments called **alabados*. They describe the minute details of Christ's and Mary's suffering during the Passion, *la Pasión*, a term that refers to the last days of Christ's life, during which he was tried and suffered the tribulations of the Stations of the Cross and crucifixion. *Alabado* song style is typically call and response, with a leader singing the first part of a verse and a group responding with the remainder of the verse. There is no instrumental accompaniment except for the use of a drum (often a snare type) and whistle flute called the *pito*, played only in the interlude between verses. A *matraca* (ratchet noisemaker) often signals parts of the ceremony.

Elaborately carved wooden sculptures (*santos*) and paintings on wood (*retablos*) also accompany the *cofrados* in their worship, as visual reminders of Christ's suffering. Only the men practice self-mortification in this belief system that associates suffering with piety, and a passive female image permeates this worldview. Austerity is the rule, and the *morada* chapels are traditionally meagerly decorated except for religious images, often including a *carreta de muerk (death cart) ridden by a skeleton (usually known as Santa Sebastiana) as a reminder of human mortality. St. Jerome is the patron of the *penitentes*, and he is always visually represented holding a human skull. Because of the Church's prohibition of *penitente* worship, the *moradas* were purposely camouflaged as ordinary buildings and hidden from public view.

After 1848 and the *Treaty of Guadalupe Hidalgo, the *penitente* world-view encountered further hostility with the huge Euro-American population explosion into the Southwest during the westward expansion. The clash of cultures worsened in the latter half of the nineteenth century, culminating in the *penitentes* being condemned as a heretical sect by Bishop Jean Baptiste Lamy, thereby forcing the *hermanos* to even greater secrecy. More recently during the last half of the twentieth century, the Church began to recognize the important role the *penitentes* had played in preserving Catholicism in the Southwest, and some Church leaders softened their tone toward them. This was not enough to prevent the *cofradía* from declining in importance, however. One important factor in its decline was the liberalizing of customs surrounding the liturgy during the 1960s as a result of decrees by Vatican II.

Some scholars identify a contemporary revivalist spirit among Mexican Americans, pointing to *penitente* practices during Holy Week and some funeral observances, as well as to the involvement of greater numbers of young men in the *Hermandad*. The art of the woodcarver as *santero* (artisan who carves wooden statues of saints) is stronger than ever, and this art acknowledges rather than denies human suffering. *Penitentes* are found in most places that were colonized by Spain, including the Philippines. The tradition survives in some parts of Spain, where the brothers wear black hoods and capes. The Spanish counterpart of the *alabado* is the highly Moorish- and Gypsy-influenced *saeta*, which is also a lament.

Clearly, the *penitentes* represent the remarkable persistence and survival of southwestern Hispano and spiritual practices. When seen as a residual element of culture, we get a clearer picture of how deeply rooted some of the Latina/o cultures are in the United States. *Penitentes* are not exotic fossils from the past but continue to affect and influence the present indigenous Mexican, Chicana/o, and Latina/o cultures.

Further Reading

Gallegos, Phillip. Architect, personal communication, Denver, CO, 2003.

Gutiérrez, Ramón, A. *When Jesus Came, the Corn Mothers Went Away: Marriage, Sexuality, and Power in New Mexico, 1500–1846*. Stanford, CA: Stanford University Press, 1991.

Romero, Brenda. "The Matachines Music and Dance in San Juan Pueblo and Alcalde, New Mexico: Contexts and Meanings." Ph.D. dissertation, University of California, Los Angeles, 1993.

Steele, Thomas, and Rowena Rivera. *Penitente Self-Government: Brotherhoods and Councils, 1797–1947*. Santa Fe, NM: Ancient City Press, 1985.

Brenda Romero

Pérez, Rosie (1964–   ). Rosie Pérez, award-winning screen actress, was born in Brooklyn, New York, of Puerto Rican ancestry (Nuyorican) and began her career as a dancer on *Soul Train*. Her breakout *film role was the rapid-talking character Tina in Spike Lee's *Do the Right Thing* (1989). In 1991 and 1992 she played a similar character in the critically acclaimed *Night on Earth*, directed by Jim Jarmusch, and in the hit comedy *White Men Can't Jump*, but her breakthrough occurred in 1993 when she was showered with Best Supporting Actress awards (L.A. Film Critics, Boston, Chicago, Dallas Society of Film Critics, and Berlin's Outstanding Performance) and was nominated for an Oscar for her role as a plane-crash survivor in director Peter Weir's *Fearless* (1992). For Pérez, who struggled to make something of herself after surviving her teenage years in a group home, this proved to be a milestone. Since then, she has played alongside Nicolas Cage in *It Could Happen to You* (1994), and her more recent films include *Subway Stories* (1997), *A Brother's Kiss* (1997), *The 24 Hour Woman* (1999), *The Road to El Dorado* (2000), *King of the Jungle* (2001), *Riding in Cars with Boys* (2001), and *Human Nature* (2002). Despite coming from a working-class background, Pérez is one of the most recognized Latina actresses today.

Further Reading

Keller, Gary D. *A Biographical Handbook of Hispanics and United States Film.* Tempe, AZ: Bilingual Press, 1997.

Tardiff, Joseph C., and L. Mpho Mabunda, eds. *Dictionary of Hispanic Biography.* Detroit: Gale Research, 1995.

Telgen, Diane, and Jim Kamp, eds. *Latinas! Women of Achievement.* Detroit: Visible Ink Press, 1996.

Unterburger, Amy L., and Jane L. Delgado, eds. *Who's Who among Hispanic Americans 1994–1995.* Detroit: Gale Research, 1994.

Luis Aldama

Pérez Prado, Dámaso (1916–1989). Dámaso Pérez Prado, known as "The Mambo King," was an arranger, bandleader, composer, and pianist who was credited with promoting the musical genre of the *mambo. The origins of the mambo are Afro-Cuban, and it came to prominence in the 1950s, coinciding with a sense of postwar liberation. Pérez Prado was born in Matanzas, Cuba, in 1916, where he studied classical piano at the Principal School of Matanzas.

Pérez Prado started his career by playing in local clubs and cinemas. In 1942 he moved to Havana, where he played piano for various casino orchestras, which included the Orquesta del Cabaret Pennsylvania de la Playa de Mariano. He also played piano and composed arrangements for the famous Cuban band Orquesta Casino de la Playa, which was directed by Liduvino Pereira. In 1946, Pérez Prado started his own band, and in 1948 he moved to México, where he began to record for the RCA record label. In 1949 he made the hit records *Mambo No. 5* and *Qué Rico El Mambo*.

Pérez Prado provided a distinctive sound whose syncopated rhythms grew out of the music of Cuban pioneers of the mambo, such as Arsenio Rodríguez and Oreste López. The instrumentation used by Pérez Prado typically featured brass and saxaphone, sometimes organ, and his own characteristic vocal grunts. Pérez Prado experimented with a new, slower version of the mambo. He also interpreted the music as being in close touch with the elemental rhythms and sounds of the natural world.

In 1951, Pérez Prado made his first perfomance in the United States, and by 1954 the mambo craze had achieved the height of its popularity in his newly adopted homeland. Pérez Prado's songs "Cherry Pink and Apple Blossom White" (1955) and "Patricia" (1958) both reached number one on the U.S. charts. "Cherry Pink and Apple Blossom White" was used in the *film *Underwater* (1955) and his most famous song "Patricia" was used in the strip scene in the Italian director Federico Fellini's film *La Dolce Vita* (1960). In the 1960s Pérez Prado also had hits with other songs including "Patricia Twist," but by 1970 he had turned his attention away from the U.S. music scene to concentrate on writing and performing material in Latin American countries.

The music of Pérez Prado has had considerable influence upon later popular culture, both in the United States and on the international scene. In 1995, his hit song "Guaglione" reached the UK Top 10 due to its appearance on a television Guinness beer advertisement. In 1999, the singer Lou Bega paid a tribute to Pérez Prado when his reworking of the song "Mambo No. 5" reached the top of the charts all round the world. Pérez Prado died in Mexico City in 1989.

Further Reading

Unterberger, Richie. "Pérez Prado." *All Music Guide.* http://www.allmusic.com.
Walter, Aaron Clark, ed. *From Tejano to Tango: Latin American Popular Music.* New York: Routledge, 2002.

Helen Oakley

Periodicals. *See* Newspapers and Periodicals.

Pilón. A *pilón* generally refers to an added bonus or something extra that a merchant might give to a customer after a large purchase; such a reward is regarded as a common occurrence in the *tianguis* (Spanish farmers' markets) held in the Southwest United States, especially in cities like Santa Fe and Taos, New Mexico. One example of a *pilón* might be receiving a couple of extra mangos or apples when customers buy most or all of their fruit from one stand at a particular *tianguis*. This type of reward or bonus system is provided because the merchant knows that the customer could have purchased his or her fruit, *food, or other edible items at different stands at a lower price. The merchant generally wishes to reward the costumer's loyalty with the *pilón*.

Pilón can also refer to a brown sugar that is ground and molded into a conical shape; known as *azúcar de pilón* (*pilón* sugar), or *pilóncillo*, it can be mixed in with coffee or other types of foods. Coffee with *pilón*, properly known as *café de olla* (pot coffee), is coffee prepared in an *olla de barro* (pot made of clay), which gives it a distinct taste when accompanied with the *pilón*.

Further Reading

Gran Diccionario Enciclopedico Ilustrado. Vol 9. Mexico City: Reader's Digest México, 1979.

Mónica Saldaña

Piñatas. From the Spanish verb *apinar*, which means to cram, tie, or join together, piñatas are festively decorated papier-mâché or clay pot figures filled with toys and candies, confetti, or other types of party favors, used in popular celebrations such as birthdays, Christmas celebrations, and other fiestas or parties in México and in the United States, especially the Southwest borderlands. In Italy *pignattas* were colorful decorations hung from ceilings at masquerade balls, and piñatas are thought to be of Oriental origin due to the use of colorful crêpe paper. Piñatas probably originated in China and were brought to Sicily and Spain by Arabs and later to the New World during the Spanish conquests of México and the Southwest borderlands.

The piñata can be made into various shapes or figures including animals, cartoon characters, fruit, or other U.S. popular culture icons like Scooby Doo, Winnie the Pooh, or Mickey Mouse. Sizes vary, as do shapes and colors, and are now even popular among non-Latino groups in the United States including African Americans, Anglo-Americans, Native Americans, and even Asian Americans. In the Southwest and México, piñatas are traditionally part of birthday and Christmas Eve festivities, especially among the urban poor. Breaking the piñata is a popular game

Piñatas are filled with candy and treats for children's fiestas and holidays celebrations. *Photo by Emmanuel Sánchez Carballo*.

accompanied by a sing-song, nursery rhyme, or children's chant. The piñata is usually hung from a tree with a long rope that is lowered and raised by an adult while the child below is blindfolded and twirled around three times, handed a baseball bat, and led to the piñata by a guide. Most of the children are given a turn until the adult guide allows someone to break the piñata, and the rest of the participants dash to grab the falling candy and prizes.

Piñatas were first introduced to Christmas Eve Mass celebrations by Augustine priests during the seventeenth century, which later developed into Las *Posadas. During colonial times, the piñata was regarded as a symbol of evil, and the clay pot represented Satan or a demonic spirit, with the colorful decorations and inner treasure tempting humanity with the treats, sweets, toys, and prizes. The sweets and goodies were the simple carnal pleasures that tempted men and women, and the blindfolded child represented human innocence and faith blinded in combat with the evil spirit. The public destruction of the piñata symbolized the struggle of good versus evil and God's rewarding the faithful.

Further Reading

Castro, Rafaela G. *Chicano Folklore: A Guide to the Folktales, Traditions, Rituals and Religious Practices of Mexican-Americans.* New York: Oxford University Press, 2001.

Gallegos, Esperanza. "The Piñata-Making Tradition in Laredo." In *Hecho en Texas: Texas-Mexican Folk Arts and Crafts*, edited by Joe S. Graham. Denton: University of Texas Press, 1991.

Verti, Sebastian. *Tradiciones Mexicanas.* Mexico City: Editorial Diana, 1994.

Peter J. García

Piñero. The 2001 movie *Piñero* is a nonlinear narrative of the life of talented Puerto Rican playwright, poet, and actor Miguel *Piñero. The *film was directed and written by Leon Ichaso, produced by John Penotti, Fisher Stevens, and Tim Williams, and distributed by Miramax Films. Gaining literary prominence with his award-winning play *Short Eyes*, first performed at Joseph Papp's Public Theater in 1974, Piñero's poems and plays have been praised and widely anthologized, making him an icon in New York's Puerto Rican and Nuyorican community. This film offers an introduction to Piñero's art as well as provides the audience with a sense of his turbulent life that included drug use, crime and imprisonment, prostitution, and family upheaval. The movie begins with Piñero (portrayed by Benjamin *Bratt) reciting a poem in front of his fellow inmates at New York State's Sing Sing prison. Throughout the movie, Bratt evokes the power of Piñero's poetry through intensely exuberant performances. Award-winning stage and screen star Rita *Moreno plays Piñero's mother, giving a sensitive performance as a mother in agony over her son's dangerous life choices. Giancarlo Esposito plays Piñero's friend and university professor, Miguel *Algarín.

Algarín and Piñero cofounded the *Nuyorican Poets Café, which has fostered the writing of countless Puerto Rican and African American poets, actors, and spoken-word artists. Throughout the movie, Algarín plays the voice of reason to Piñero's self-destruction. In several scenes Algarín comes into conflict with Piñero but unfailingly comes to the poet's support even after Piñero steals Algarín's television set. Talisa *Soto and Mandy Patinkin perform the roles of Sugar, Piñero's love interest, and theatrical luminary Joseph Papp, respectively. Other actors include Michael Irby and Jaime Sánchez. Director Leon Ichaso chose to tell Piñero's story in both black and white and color, using a variety of techniques including slow motion and flashbacks. These techniques add to the tension of the story, which builds suspense and keeps the audience tense with wonderment in the face of Piñero's volatile spin from stardom and success to drugs, alcohol, and self-destructive behavior. Ichaso and director of photography Claudio Chea shot the streets of New York City and Piñero's Puerto Rican neighborhood to enhance the examination of both the working-class and hardcore underclass experience of black and Latina/o communities. In the same manner as movies such as *Fort Apache, the Bronx* (1981) and *New Jack City* (1991) focused on the dirt, dilapidated buildings, and squalid scenes of crime, drug use, and prostitution, *Piñero* similarly provides glimpses of Nuyorican home life, including religious, cultural, and educational institutions. The struggles of Puerto Rican women trying to maintain their families in the face of governmental neglect and poverty also receive sensitive and close-up attention.

Piñero does not shy away from the controversial aspects of its title subject's life, including homosexuality and the valorization of a working-class Puerto Rican identity. In one important scene of cultural symbolism, Piñero travels to Puerto Rico to meet with journalists and intellectuals, where he performs a riveting poem about his Nuyorican identity. When an audience member questions his Puerto Ricanness and scorns his lack of Spanish, use of slang, and valorization of street life, Piñero gives an extemporaneous speech that draws the audience in emotionally, thereby disclosing the poignant reality of his life and feelings, as well as reaffirms the genuineness of his *puertorriqueñidad* (Puerto Ricanness). The film does not apologize for Piñero's behavior, nor does it attempt to justify it through examinations of his relationship to his exploitive and absent father.

Although popular, especially to eastern urban audiences, some critics found *Piñero* flawed in its sensational and occasionally stereotypical depictions of Nuyorican working-class life. Other critics believed it succeeded in bringing Piñero's important and misunderstood talent to a larger public. The final scene depicting the poet's wake and funeral, attended by famous poets and friends, including Amiri Baraka and Algarín who recite Piñero's "A Lower Eastside Poem," in which he asks that his ashes be spread throughout the streets of the Lower East Side, powerfully captures the importance and impact of one of the Americas' most accomplished turn-of-the-millennium urban poets.

Further Reading

Algarín, Miguel, and Miguel Piñero, eds. *Nuyorican Poetry: An Anthology of Puerto Rican Words and Feelings*. New York: Morrow, 1975.

Piñero, Miguel. *Outrageous: One Act Plays*. Houston, TX: Arte Público Press, 1986.

Piñero, Miguel. *Short Eyes*. Produced by Lewis Harris; directed by Robert M. Young. New York: Wellspring Media, 2003. Videorecording.

Piñero, Miguel. *Short Eyes: A Play*. New York: Hill and Wang, 1975.

Louis "Pancho" McFarland and Cordelia Chávez Candelaria

Piñero, Miguel (1944–1988). Miguel Piñero, a poet, playwright, and actor, was described by *theater director Joseph Papp as the first Puerto Rican playwright to have a significant influence on the New York theater. His play *Short Eyes* won the New York Drama Critics Circle Award, an Obie, and a Tony nomination. With his longtime friend Miguel *Algarín, he cofounded the *Nuyorican Poets Café, providing a space for aspiring poets, artists, and performers to present their work.

Born in Gurabo, Puerto Rico, Piñero was the oldest of five children. His mother, a gifted storyteller with little formal education, wrote poetry and simple novels and always encouraged her son to write. In 1950, the family moved to Manhattan's Lower East Side, where he enjoyed reading and writing but struggled in school and was often expelled for his behavior. A product of institutional racism, inferior schooling, poverty, and police, family, and street violence, Piñero had a hard adolescence and young adulthood, which landed him in Rikers Island Prison. After his release from Rikers Island, Piñero joined activist groups and an antidrug Puerto Rican civil rights organization called the Young Lords party, which was modeled after the Black Panthers and other community mutual aid organizations.

In 1971, Piñero was arrested for burglarizing an apartment and was convicted and sentenced to five years in New York's Sing Sing penitentiary. It was during this prison stretch that Piñero turned to writing in earnest, producing poems, skits, and short plays. Encouraged by theater director Marvin Felix Camarillo, who met the aspiring writer while conducting theater workshops at the prison, Piñero wrote *Short Eyes*, the play that would eventually earn him a Tony nomination. *Short Eyes*, a play about an alleged child molester who ends up in a holding cell and is killed by his violent cellmates, only later found to be innocent, debuted at the Theatre of Riverside Church. Critics quickly took notice, comparing Piñero's work to Jean Genet, a French playwright and reformed thief. In March 1974, Joseph Papp produced *Short Eyes* at the Public Theatre, then at the Lincoln Center's Vivian Beaumont Theatre. While on parole, Piñero joined a street theater company of ex-offenders and in the ensuing years expressed himself as an actor and screenwriter. He wrote the screenplay for *Short Eyes* and other plays that continued to explore life on the streets, including *The Sun Always Shines for the Cool*, which premiered in 1978. Three years later, Piñero switched gears and

Miguel Piñero. *Courtesy of Photofest.*

premiered *A Midnight Moon at the Greasy Spoon*, a play about growing old, which received favorable reviews.

In 1973 and 1974, the Nuyorican Poets Café was started as a living room salon in Algarín's apartment and became a gathering place for Piñero and other pioneers of the Nuyorican poetry movement, such as Lucky Cienfuegos and Sandra María Esteves. In 1975, the two friends edited and published *Nuyorican Poetry: An Anthology of Puerto Rican Words and Feelings.*

In the late 1970s/early 1980s, Piñero moved to Los Angeles, where he continued to write plays but also turned to television. In addition to television appearances on *Miami Vice, Kojak,* and *Baretta,* he wrote episodes of *Baretta* and *Kojak* and appeared in motion pictures, including *Fort Apache, the Bronx* (1980), *Breathless, Exposed,* and *Deal of the Century* (all in

1983), and *The Pick-Up Artist* (1987). Piñero died of cirrhosis of the liver in 1988. A film about his life, **Piñero*, directed by Leon Ichaso, was released in 2001 and starred Benjamin *Bratt, Rita *Moreno, and Mandy Patinkin.

Further Reading

Jackson, Kenneth, Karen Markoe, and Arnold Markoe, eds. *The Scribner Encyclopedia of American Lives*. New York: Charles Scribner's Sons, 1998.

James E. García

Pinto Arte. Caló, the argot or slang spoken by *pachucos, *batos locos* (crazy dudes), and homeboys, identifies prison physically as *la pinta*. While *pinta* translates from standard Spanish as "spot," the English rendition has a dual meaning: (1) a place or location and (2) a visual marking. The word *pinto*, caló invocation for a male prison inmate, also has a double connotation in English: the act itself of painting or something or someone that has been painted. These word associations are particularly relevant when considered in the context of the most popular and prevalent art practiced in prison, namely, **tatuaje* (tattooing). It involves inscribing, painting, and/or "spotting" the body partially or wholly. Reviewed historically and globally, *tatuaje* is at once the *pinto*'s most conspicuous and persistent *arte* (art). This art matters especially because official census data estimates provided by the U.S. Department of Justice and reported in April 2003 by Human Rights Watch place the number of Hispanic/Latino inmates in U.S. prisons at an alarming near 400,000 men and women out of a staggering total prison and jail population in excess of 2 million.

Although tattooing is strictly prohibited within U.S. penitentiaries, the practice has continued unabated for generations, palpably challenging the very essence of the penal system: imposed systemic authority and control over all inmates. Don Ed Hardy, internationally noted San Francisco–based tattoo artist, believes that tattooing in prison is first and foremost an expression of freedom. Irrespective of the iconography and symbology underlying an individual tattooed image, all prison tattoos are essentially distinctive and discursive markers questioning and subverting authority, imbuing the wearer's body with her or his own unique sense of self-identification in a place ruled by anonymity and conformity. These outlaw(ed) images are worn and displayed as badges of honor, testimonials to a kind of rite of passage, or initiation from a life of relative freedom to one of absolute captivity. A tattoo's message may be quite matter-of-fact, as in the case of placasolike lettering—resembling stylized "Gothic" or Old English script appearing on *barrio murals—tattooed across an inmate's stomach, reading simply "PUERTORICO." Another *pinto* incarcerated in the State Penitentiary of New Mexico also underscores his captivity in geographical terms through a block letter tattoo emblazoned on his back, near shoulder height, reading "Santa Fe" (Holy Faith), a pun on both place and belief.

Seeking redemption, many *pintos* throughout the Southwest, and New Mexico in particular, transform their bodies into virtual religious altars or *ofrendas* (offerings). Their own human skin is turned into a canvas adorned with a pantheon of religious, talismanic icons. Thus inscribing their bodies, *pintos* are confessing, praying, and generally calling forth their faith through the *Virgin of Guadalupe and other Marian deities, Christ, angels, crosses, praying hands, thorns, roses, *el corazón sagrado* (sacred heart) and el Santo Niño de Atocha (Holy Child of Atocha), patron saint of prisoners, among other causes. If spiritual expression is an outlet helping release the *pinto*'s emotional pain, not surprisingly, what causes the hurt is addressed through secular imagery. Missed loved ones are remembered in idealized portrait likenesses. Depictions of guns, knives, gaming dice, hypodermic needles, and skulls symbolize the intrinsic violence and hedonism of *la vida loca y torcida* (the crazy and twisted life), one also chronicled on certain barrio murals lamenting fallen *gang members. Hourglasses, guard towers, barbed wire fences, and walls define the *pinto*'s life in what Richard Stratton, editor of *Prison Life*, calls the "breakdown lane of the joint." Markers or "tags" denoting one's gang affiliation, often acquired on the outside prior to imprisonment, might be understood as a bridge or link between the barrio and the *pinta*. Such tattoos usually betray the so-called hand-picked, crude method of tattooing accomplished with hand-held sewing needles. Inside prison, electric rotary machines—ingeniously fabricated out of stereocassette motors, sharpened guitar strings, and ink pens bound together with black electrical tape—apply black ink to create striking monochromatic images. The ink is obtained variously from a host of sources, including the ultra-thin pages common to Bibles. Color renderings are scarce, probably because they are more artistically complex, time-consuming, and expensive to produce.

Closely related to *tatuaje* is the art of drawing and painting on commercially available white cotton handkerchiefs. Called *paño arte* (cloth art) in the Albuquerque and Santa Fe areas of New Mexico, the generic designation of cloth is indeed more inclusive and telling than the mere label of *pañuelo* (standard Spanish reference for handkerchief). Inmates, after all, often hand tailor their own very large handkerchiefs—exceeding the traditional thirteen- to sixteen-inch-square commercial size and format—while at the same time commandeering bed sheet fragments and pillowcases for their *paño* craft. Interestingly, the tie-in with tattooing can be better appreciated in the argument advanced by Roland Barthes, the late-twentieth-century postmodernist French literary and social critic, for whom cloth is a "second skin" in relation to human or "first" skin. It bears mention that despite their ordinariness, handkerchiefs are highly personal items, carried close to one's person. Informed by a make do/do more-with-less aesthetic approach, *paño arte* is a wonderful embodiment of *rasquachismo*, a *Chicano sensibility articulated by Chicano cultural theoretician Tomás Ybarra-Frausto. Humble as this art form is, *paño arte* is arguably no less devout or therapeutic a practice for the *pinto* than tattooing. The New Testament's Book of Acts chronicles that St. Paul cured the sick with handkerchiefs he had touched (chapter 19, verse 12). Present-day Mormons and Pentecostals occasionally utilize "prayer handkerchiefs" in their services. Religious imagery appearing on *paños* is essentially identical to that already noted in *tatuaje*. That similarity extends even to the black-on-white compositions themselves, although color appears more frequently on the cloth pieces. That *pintos* are doing penance is strongly suggested in the juxtaposition on both skin and cloth of laughter and tears. The regretful sentiment "Laugh now, cry later" is conveyed through the depiction of raucous and tearful clowns or the classical masks of comedy and tragedy.

A notable difference between tattoos and handkerchiefs is the reach of their respective messages. Tattoos remain anchored to the *pinto*'s body, while many *paños* are mailed to *family in envelopes embellished to complement and reflect their precious contents. *Paños*, therefore, reinforce familial ties. A handkerchief turned valentine or birthday card or gift helps compensate, however little, for a husband's or father's absence. Like tattoos, *paños* thus function as containers of memories associated with life on the outside.

Unquestionably, *pinto arte* does involve other art forms beyond *paños* and *tatuaje*, but those are eclipsed by the prominence of these two more dominant and provocative practices. Only murals and easel-size paintings can sometimes compete for attention and popularity. Utilitarian objects made of woven paper (*tejido*), occasionally sewn with dental floss for greater durability, include boxes, frames, cup holders, baby shoes, purses, and jewelry articles. Leather belts, bracelets, wallets, and watchbands as well as miniature furniture and toys, including ships and windmills, constructed with popsicle sticks or toothpicks, number among the least-known products crafted behind stifling walls, razor wire, and cellblocks. In addition to those materials already cited, other *pinto art* materials or sources are both predictable as well as makeshift and unexpected in the *rasquachi* (or *rascuache*; *caló* term for "[economically or dirt] poor") vein: carbon and letter papers, glossy magazines, newspaper, desk blotters, old calendars, cigarette packages, hard lead and charcoal pencils, crayons, pastels, watercolors, coarse prison-issued toilet paper, soap, ceramic clay, pebbles and stones, window caulking, soft bread, socks, and T-shirts. Circumstances of incarceration and its attendant deprivation are dehumanizing but seem not to hamper the creativity and resourcefulness of *pinto* artists, echoing a broader theme about resilience and resistance within prisons and related institutions.

Further Reading

Govenar, Alan. "The Variable Context of Chicano Tattooing." In *Marks of Civilization: Artistic Transformations of the Human Body*, edited by Arnold Rubin. Los Angeles: Museum of Cultural History/UCLA, 1988.

Hall, Douglas K. *In Prison*. New York: Henry Holt, 1988.

Hall, Douglas K. *Prison Tattoos*. New York: St. Martin's Griffin, 1997.

Kornfeld, Phyllis. *Cellblock Visions: Prison Art in America*. Princeton, NJ: Princeton University Press, 1997.

Sorell, Víctor. "Illuminated Handkerchiefs and 'Body Altars': 'Outsider' Pinto Arte inside la Pinta." Unpublished essay.

Sorell, Víctor A. "Guadalupe's Emblematic Presence Endures in New Mexico: Investing the Body with the Virgin's Miraculous Image." In *Nuevomexicano Cultural Legacy: Forms, Agencies, and Discourse*, edited by Francisco Lomelí, V.A. Sorell, and Genaro M. Padilla. Albuquerque: University of New Mexico Press, 2002.

Ybarra-Frausto, Tomás. "Rasquachismo: A Chicano Sensibility." In *Chicano Art: Resistance and Affirmation, 1965–1985*, edited by Richard Griswold del Castillo, Teresa McKenna, and Yvonne Yarbro-Bejarano. Los Angeles, CA: Wight Art Gallery, UCLA, 1991.

Víctor Alejandro Sorell

Plena. Plena is a Puerto Rican song and dance genre created by the ethnically and culturally diverse working classes around the coastal city of Ponce in the early twentieth century and is an essential root in *salsa. Plena is characterized by the use of *panderetas*—hand-held frame drums that play syncopated, duple meter rhythms—and straightforwardly poignant topical lyrics in four- or six-line solo verses that alternate with choruses of similar length. First rising to popularity around the turn of the twentieth century, plena is a uniquely Puerto Rican blend of musical influences that were circulating around the Caribbean, most of which were already hybrid forms derived from Africa, the Americas, and Europe. Puerto Rico's traditional music from the conquest through the nineteenth century was not documented very well. For this reason, the musical precursors and early development of plena are uncertain. However, with the opening of Puerto Rico to settlement by non-Spanish nationals in the nineteenth century, laborers and slaves coming to work the sugar fields on Puerto Rico's coastal plains brought new sounds to the region that inspired plena's origination.

In particular, the English-speaking Afro-Caribbean immigrants to the coastal city of Ponce from the British Caribbean (such as St. Kitts, Nevis, Barbados, the Virgin Islands, and Jamaica) are attributed with sparking the emergence of the new plena style. The third largest island of the Caribbean, Puerto Rico has distinct cultural regions determined by the different geographic features and economic activities performed therein. The highlands were settled by poor peasant farmers of predominantly European ancestry who practiced subsistence agriculture and cattle ranching. In the 1850s, coffee and tobacco haciendas came to dominate the region, and peasants worked as sharecroppers or for wealthy large landowners. The popular music of this *jibaro* (white-skinned Puerto Rican farmer) culture was the *seis*, a music genre using sung poetry that is strongly related to Spanish folksong traditions from the Old World and is accompanied by guitar, *cuatro* (a guitarlike Puerto Rican adaptation), and güiro. In the coastal plains, sugar plantations concentrated around urban centers such as San Juan in the north and Ponce in the south. Large numbers of African slaves were brought to the island to work these plantations; likewise, emancipated slaves from other Caribbean countries migrated to these coastal areas in search of work. Consequently, the working classes in these regions today retain a strong Afro-Caribbean cultural heritage. The most popular music genres of the coastal working classes were the *bomba and plena—both of which contrast noticeably with the *jibaro* folk music of the highland.

The bomba was strongly associated with African heritage and especially with the slaves brought from the French Caribbean to work the sugar cane fields. Bomba was not widely accepted by Puerto Ricans of mixed ancestry; although they shared similar problems of economic hardship and discrimination with former slaves, they recognized a social stigma against African culture resulting from slavery and may not have felt a close affinity for bomba's musical style. Plena, however, proved to be a more broadly appealing mixture of Afro-Caribbean and Spanish folk musics and has been considered by some Puerto Rican music scholars as a truly "mulatto" synthesis. It is likely that most *pleneros*—plena performers—were originally *bomberos* who adapted their playing to the new styles they heard from the English-speaking migrants. Therefore, although plena was less overtly African in its social associations and musical style, it nevertheless is most often seen as an Afro-Puerto Rican genre. Traits resembling African music might include the use of melodies alternating between two- and three-note groupings over the accompanying two-beat pattern, the polyrhythmic approach of the *panderetas* (tambourines), the improvisation on the highest-pitched *pandereta* and of the solo vocalist, as well as certain vocal timbres and dance figures.

Ever more depressed economic conditions in the rural sector of Puerto Rico pushed many agricultural workers into urban centers where they collected in fringe areas of the cities, forming poorly serviced slums and shantytowns as early as the 1930s. Plena's popularity grew among Puerto Rico's working classes as migration to Puerto Rico's urban centers exploded between 1940 and 1960. Plena came to the U.S. mainland as Puerto Rican migrants sought work as semiskilled and unskilled laborers in cities such as Chicago, Boston, and Philadelphia but especially New York City—where Puerto Ricans settled largely in the black neighborhoods and ghettos of Harlem, the Bronx, or the Lower East Side. (By the 1980s, the Puerto Rican population in New York had grown to 1 million.) Social and economic conditions in the Puerto Rican *barrios, whether located in coastal cities of the island or in the United States, were very similar. Networks of family and friends helped to sustain people against economic uncertainty, racism, crime, and violence. In these conditions, plena served to spread news between the island and New York and helped Puerto Ricans maintain a shared cultural identity within the ever-circulating migrant communities.

It was in one of these rough barrios—neighborhoods—surrounding Ponce, named La Joya del Castillo, that the plena singer, prolific composer, and *pandereta* virtuoso Joselino "Bumbum" Oppenheimer formed the first group of *pleneros*. Legend has it that Bumbum composed plenas while laboring as a plowman; he then taught the young farmhands the choral responses so they could sing along. After working hours, he would share his new compositions in public gatherings in his neighborhood, accompanying himself on *panderata*, accordion, or güiros.

Plena spread in popularity to other barrios of southern Ponce, then to the coastal cities of Guayama and Mayagüez by about 1906. By the early 1920s, plena peaked in popularity in most regions of the island and had taken root in New York. The first recordings of plena were made around 1926. The recordings of singer/composer Manuel "El Canario" Jiménez (the Canary) were vital in bringing the plena sound from Puerto Rico and establishing its popularity among Puerto Ricans in the United States. With commercial recordings being marketed to broader international audiences, certain changes in the plena occurred that parallel innovations in Cuban *son*. Orchestra leader and trumpet virtuoso César Concepción adapted plena songs into a big band format, and by the 1930s dance bands were playing plenas in New York. Singer/composer Mon Rivera became popular for his new *la trabalengua*—a scatlike style of singing plenas. Rafael Cortijo—master conga drum player—joined forces with master improviser, vocalist Ismael "El Sonero Mayor" Rivera. These two professionals not only were top *pleneros* but were also major influences on commercial tropical music of the day. These commercial plenas were played not just in poor tenements of East Harlem but also by middle-class Puerto Ricans living on the Upper West Side.

While recordings and radio were of key importance in the dissemination of plena, and in securing its recognition even by the cultural elite, the commercialization of the plena caused simplification and burying of its *pandereta*'s rhythms under orchestral instrumentation and a gloss of pan-Latin percussion sounds as well as departure from its socially poignant lyrics in favor of more romantic topics. Between the 1950s and 1960s, there was a conscious effort by *pleneros* (like Mon Rivera, Cortijo, and Ismael Rivera) to return to plena's musical roots and its lyric's original concerns in the lives of the Puerto Rican working classes.

The original ensemble performing plena (like Joselito "Bumbum" Oppenheimer's) might have consisted of a solo vocalist, a chorus, *panderetas*, and güiro, with either a guitar or accordion accompaniment. The *pandereta* is a round frame drum, looking a lot like a tambourine but without jingles. Plena is characterized by the constant sounding of at least two *panderetas*, tuned to different pitches, the lowest pitch typically playing on every beat. The traditional plena used three *panderetas* tuned to lower, medium, and higher pitches (respectively, named *seguidor*, *puteador*, and *requinto*). The two higher-pitched *panderetas* play interlocking rhythm patterns around the lowest one's unvaryingly steady beat. Improvisation is expected and enjoyed, both in *panderetas* and in the texts. The *pandereta* player with the highest-pitch instrument would often improvise in addition to playing a fixed pattern. Plena instrumentation can vary widely from including only singers and a couple of *panderetas* in impromptu gatherings in public spaces in the barrio to being accompanied by full dance orchestras and Latin rhythm sections on recordings, in live concerts, or in dance halls. Plenas are written and sung also for funerals as well as for celebrations like Christmas.

Plena is often characterized as a "musical newspaper" covering any and all topics of interest, be it gossip, legend, national history, sports, current events, romantic love, domestic violence, politics, labor protests, or immigration. Beyond reporting, lyricists pride themselves on their clever commentary on the events, using witty yet straightforward language. The plena not only records labor protests of the past but has often been sung during workers' strikes where Puerto Ricans sought higher wages, benefits, or working conditions.

As countless variations in orchestration have occurred through the spread and commercialization of plena, two definitive features of its style have remained consistently recognizable since their establishment by the 1920s: (1) the characteristically heavy striking of a *pandereta* on every beat and (2) the topical character of its verses, always in short phrases grouped in four or six lines alternating with choral refrains. It seems that plena's versatility in both instrumentation and the topics of its poetry is largely responsible for its continued viability and recurrent appeal. Considering that the frequent overlaying of other Latin rhythms and varying instrumentations can obscure the sonic identity of the plena, the ability of its lyrics to adapt, as well as record historical events of a hundred years ago, is a primary reason that plena has remained a socially meaningful music to Puerto Rican working-class communities to the present day.

Plena has had little direct impact on commercial music markets in the United States. While recordings of plena have been available, if somewhat difficult to procure, from independent record shops and now from the Internet, they have never been aggressively marketed or promoted to wider audiences in the United States. But plena, nevertheless, holds an important place in U.S. popular music, not only due to its performers' influence upon and contributions to salsa but because its consumers are U.S. citizens. Since Puerto Rico was made a commonwealth of the United States (a colony) in 1952, Puerto Ricans have possessed all the rights and obligations of U.S. citizens (such as paying social security, receiving federal welfare, and serving in the armed forces). Plena must therefore be considered an extremely important genre of American music precisely because it is so important to this significant, albeit minority, sector of the American population.

Although since about 1972 salsa might have served urban Puerto Ricans as a symbol of nationalistic reconciliation between the predominantly mulatto plena, the more African bomba, and the more European *seis*, plena seems to be enjoying renewed popularity precisely because of its century-long history as an indigenously Puerto Rican folk tradition. Since the 1990s, both folkloric and contemporary plena ensembles have been appearing at a quick pace. Current groups marketing themselves as revivalists of Puerto Rican musical tradition include Gary Núñez and his band Plena Libre (Free Plena; formed in 1994), who just released their third recording, *Más Libre* (More Free), for the major label RykoLatino. The album *Más Libre* is far more international in its incorporation of pan-Latin styles in its plenas. Exceedingly competent and cosmopolitan, Plena Libre is obviously striving for a very wide and more sophisticated audience of Latin music fans. Certain art institutions and Puerto Rican families have been striving through all these years to promote plena's traditional musical sounds and function for Puerto Ricans. Notable are the efforts of the band, Los Pleneros de la 21 (The Pleneros of [Bus Stop] 21; formed in 1983 and performing a more traditional-sounding plena with topical lyrics), and City Lore's Roberta Singer in New York, who have conducted bomba and plena workshops with Puerto Rican children in el Barrio and the South Bronx. Notable efforts of folkloric preservation of plena in Puerto Rico include those of the musical groups, the Cepeda and Ayala families.

Further Reading

Duany, Jorge. "Popular Music in Puerto Rico: Toward an Anthropology of Salsa." In *Salsiology: Afro-Cuban Music and the Evolution of Salsa in New York City*, edited by Vernon Boggs. Westport, CT: Greenwood Press, 1992.

Flores, Juan. "Bumbum and the Beginnings of La Plena." In *Salsiology: Afro-Cuban Music and the Evolution of Salsa in New York City*, edited by Vernon Boggs. Westport, CT: Greenwood Press, 1992.

Plena Is Work, Plena Is Song. Produced and directed by Pedro A. Rivera and Susan Zeig. Distributed by the Cinema guild, n.d. 37 min. Documentary Film.

Quintero-Rivera, A.G. "Ponce, the Danza, and the National Question: Notes toward a Sociology of Puerto Rican Music." In *Salsiology: Afro-Cuban Music and the Evolution of Salsa in New York City*, edited by Vernon Boggs. Westport, CT: Greenwood Press, 1992.

Thompson, Donald. "Puerto Rico." In *New Grove Dictionary of Music and Musicians*, edited by Stanley Sadie. 2nd ed. New York: Grove's Dictionaries, 2001.

Vega Drouet, Héctor. "Puerto Rico." In *The Garland Encyclopedia of World Music*, edited by Dale Olsen and Daniel Sheehy. Vol. 2. New York: Garland, 1998.

Rebecca Sager

Plunkett, Jim (1947–   ). Mexican American Jim Plunkett gained his remarkable fame as an outstanding Stanford University quarterback who won the Heisman Trophy in 1970, a National Football League (NFL) Rookie of the Year in 1971, an NFL Comeback Player of the Year in 1980, and the Super Bowl's Most Valuable Player in 1981. He also quarterbacked the Super Bowl championship Oakland Raiders in 1984 as well. As a student at James Lick High School in San Jose, California, he excelled in football, wrestling, and baseball and earned a football scholarship to Stanford, where he enjoyed a stellar college career. In his senior season he led his team to the Pacific Athletic Conference title capped by a Rose Bowl victory in which he was named Player of the Game. His college career culminated with receipt of the Heisman, an annual award given to the best major college football player.

James William Plunkett was born on December 5, 1947, in Santa Clara, California, to Carmen Blea Plunkett and William Gutierrez Plunkett. Provided with a solid family and precollegiate public education, the future NFL star performed above average scholastically, which helped prepare him for his political science major in college. While at Stanford, besides starring on the football team, Plunkett also served as a volunteer peer counselor to Chicano youth in the San Francisco Bay area.

He was selected as the number-one pick by the Boston (soon to be New England) Patriots in the 1971 NFL draft and had an impressive rookie season. However, his four following seasons were injury plagued, and he was traded to the San Francisco 49ers in 1976. Cut by the 49ers in 1978, Plunkett reached the lowest point of his professional career. That same year he was signed by the Oakland Raiders, where he did not play at all for the rest of the season and played very little in 1979. However, in 1980 an injury to Dan Pastorini, the Raiders' starting quarterback, forced Plunkett into action as the backup quarterback, and he excelled to lead the Raiders to that season's Super Bowl title in January 1981. He continued as backup for several more years until a shoulder injury resulted in his retirement in 1987.

Further Reading

Neft, David, and Richard Cohen. *The Football Encyclopedia*. New York: St. Martin's Press, 1991.

Plunkett, Jim, and Dave Newhouse. *The Jim Plunkett Story*. New York: Arbor House, 1981.

Porter, David, ed. *Biographical Dictionary of American Sports: Football*. Westport, CT: Greenwood Press, 1987.

Clifford Candelaria

Police. Because of the crucial role they have played in shaping the lives of Latinos, relations with big city police are the subject matter in much Latina/o popular cultural expression. A dominant theme in almost all genres has been conflict and violence between police and Latinos. Most Latino authors and artists have tended to portray police as racist, exploitative, oppressive. Non-Latinos, with some notable exceptions, have tended to portray police as honorable and heroic and Latinos as criminals.

An early and persistent genre that addresses relations between Latinos and police is the *corrido* or ballad that is sung along the U.S.-México border. Nineteenth- and early-twentieth-century *corridos* focused on the depredations of rural law enforcement agencies such as the *Texas Rangers. Perhaps the best known is "El Corrido de Gregorio Cortez," which served as the basis for Américo Paredes's book *With a Pistol in His Hand* (1958) and the subsequent feature-length film *The *Ballad of Gregorio Cortez*. During the course of the twentieth century anonymous songwriters wrote various *corridos* that told stories of conflict between police and Mexican Americans. A notable example is "El Corrido de Juan Reyna," which told the story of how Reyna was unjustly imprisoned for killing a police officer in self-defense. More recently, *narcocorridos*, which glorify the exploits of violent drug traffickers usually at the expense of law enforcement agents, have become popular among Mexican Americans.

Popular literature has also addressed the issue with authors such as Piri *Thomas, in *Down These Mean Streets*, and Luis *Rodríguez, in *Always Running*, writing passionately about their encounters with police. Non-Latinos, such as James Elroy most notably in his novel *L.A. Confidential*, also write sympathetically about police brutality against Latinos. On the other hand, myriad early pulp fictions and more recent crime novels reinforce the *stereotype of Latinos as being *gang members or otherwise criminally inclined. This tendency is even more pronounced on film, either for television or the cinema. In the highly acclaimed police series *Hill Street Blues*, for example, the only Puerto Rican character is the leader of a street gang. Feature-length films, even those with a large Latino artistic presence, often strengthen negative stereotypes. An example is *Internal Affairs*, starring Andy *García, which tells the story of how Latino street gangs involved in the drug trade corrupt a white police detective. Occasionally, Hollywood films have portrayed Latino police officers in a generally positive light, with Perry López playing the role of the slightly corrupt but ultimately wise police detective Lou Escobar in the highly acclaimed 1974 film *Chinatown*, being a prominent example. For the most part, however, films and much popular fiction depict Latinos as being at odds with law enforcement.

The focus on conflict between Latinos and police in popular culture expressions reflects the historical experience. Throughout the twentieth century the relationship between Latinos and police has been fraught with suspicion and animosity. In the early part of the century, police and the Mexican community had, at best, ill-defined views of each other. Individual officers were sometimes brutal, playing out their own frustrations or racism, and Mexicans committed their fair share of crimes. There is no evidence, however, that police, as an institution, saw Mexicans as a particular crime problem or that Mexicans, as a community, found police any more troublesome than other aspects of American society.

Suspicion developed on both sides, however, as they came into conflict with one another in the first three decades of the century. Clashes occurred when police attempted to suppress expressions of the Mexican Revolution (1910–1921) from spilling over into the United States. Police harassment of Mexican revolutionary Ricardo Flores Magón and Texas law enforcement's violent response to the irredentist movement associated with the Plan de San Diego created long-lasting animosities. Police attempts to suppress Latino involvement in labor unions, either explicitly nationalist ones such as the Confederación de Unión Campesinos y Obreros Mexicanos or as part of predominantly white unions such as the steelworkers' union also created resentment. Finally, during this period, both Latino crime and police misconduct fueled mutual suspicions. Anecdotal evidence suggests that starting in the 1920s Latino juvenile crime became an area of increasing concern for urban police departments. At the same time, seemingly unrestrained instances of police misconduct, including excessive use of force, unwarranted arrest, unlawful searches, and discourteous conduct, fomented increasing discontent and public protest in Latino communities.

These tendencies came to a head in the 1940s when public fear over an alleged Mexican American crime wave created a crisis in Latino-police relations. The source of the fear was Latino youth's symbolic rebellion embodied by their wearing of the *zoot suit. Government leaders, including the police, the press, and the general public, mistook what is now recognized as classic youth rebellion for the inherent criminality of Latino youth. The notorious Ayres report circulated out of the Los Angeles County Sheriff's Department, for example, declared that Mexican Americans were biologically inclined toward violent crime. The resulting hysteria led to the infamous Sleepy Lagoon case and the June 1943 Zoot Suit Riots in Los Angeles.

As a result of the zoot suit hysteria and riots, police institutionalized the view that Latinos, in particular the youth, were either inherently or culturally inclined toward criminality. Patrol tactics in the *barrios became much more aggressive, with officers confronting, often violently, youths suspected of being gang members. At the same time, many Latinos came to view the police as an oppressive force in their community that must be controlled. These conflicting views have dominated relations between the two groups ever since and have found their way into cultural expressions.

The social and political movements of the 1960s and 1970s exacerbated the already tenuous relationship. Two factors contributed to the change. First, 1960s activists from the Young Lords in New York to the Brown Berets in Los Angeles went beyond petitions and lawsuits to militantly, and sometimes violently, confronting the institutions they defined as oppressive. Thus, when Latinos engaged in civil disobedience, they technically broke the law and came into conflict with police. Second, the heavy-handed and oppressive measures with which law enforcement often reacted to these protests led to a sense of outrage against the police and increased ethnic solidarity within the Latino community.

The postmovements era saw the continuation of patterns in Latino-police relations established earlier in the century. Police established special units to deal with Latino crime, in particular street gangs, while Latino organizations stood ready to protest police misconduct.

Further Reading

Escobar, Edward. *Race, Police, and the Making of a Political Identity*. Berkeley: University of California Press, 1999.

Haney López, Ian. *Racism on Trial: The Chicano Fight for Justice*. Cambridge, MA: Harvard University Press, 2003.

Edward Escobar

Portillo Trambley, Estela (1936–1998). Born in El Paso, Texas, on January 16, 1936, Estela Portillo Trambley was a playwright and fiction writer distinguished by her pioneering role as a successful feminist writer in Chicana and *Chicano literature. The first woman to be awarded the prestigious Premio Quinto Sol (Fifth Sun Prize) by the germinally influential periodical *El Grito* (The Shout/Cry) in 1972 for her play *The Day of the Swallows* (1971), Trambley left a public legacy of writing, storytelling, and classroom teaching that influenced several generations of readers and students. Her body of work consists of a significant number of acclaimed short stories (including the celebrated tale of feminist coming of age, "Paris Gown" [1973]); several full-length dramas (including the lesbian-themed *Day of the Swallows* and the biographical homage *Sor Juana* [1983]), as well as the novel *Trini* (1986). She is also credited as the first Mexican American woman to have published a collection of short fiction and to write a musical comedy.

Trambley attended schools in her hometown, including the University of Texas at El Paso, from which she received her B.A. and M.A. in English in 1956 and 1978, respectively. From 1979 to the late 1980s, Trambley held various teaching posts in the Department of Special Services in El Paso's public school system. During this period she chaired the English Department at El Paso Technical Institute and taught for five years at El Paso Community College, where she served as drama instructor and produced and directed numerous plays. Her vibrant creative career also included hosting a television program, *Cumbres* (Summits), devoted to cultural topics for the Latino-themed TV station KROD in El Paso.

Although scholars agree that Trambley's intellectual impact was partly sociological and historical as the first celebrated woman writer of the *Chicano Renaissance, her major contributions to Latina and Latino popular culture were primarily literary. She created memorable fictional representations of *gender, sexuality, and ethnicity interlocked with the material issues of social class and economic power. Whether in the violence of her tragic drama *Day of the Swallows* or the stories in the first edition of *Rain of Scorpions and Other Writings* (1975), Trambley presents the social practices associated with love, courtship, and sexuality as a contest of conflicting desires taking place in a *frontera* (border zone) of culture and psychology. Several of her stories are set on geographical borders to capture the liminal challenges of these conflicts (e.g., the México/Paris zone of "The Paris Gown" and the U.S.-México industrial border in "Rain of Scorpions" and "La Yonfantayn"). These and other of her writings also expose the damages and social costs to individuals and *families caused by machismo (hypermasculinity). Similarly in the novel *Trini* and the completely revised second edition of *Rain of Scor-*

pions and Other Writings (1993), Trambley continues her career-long interest in examining and raising consciousness about the personal human relations that lie at the core of authentic community.

Typically the action of Trambley's fiction and drama generate a bilingual, bicultural zone of language and behaviors outside the codes of traditional conventions and beliefs. Clotilde in "Paris Gown" and Beatriz in "If It Weren't for the Honeysuckle" (both revised 1993) personify the heroics of Trambley's protagonists contesting the constricting norms around them, for example. Her work also voices intense concern for representing the full texture of *mestizaje to reflect the potential power of Chicana/o and Mexican experience, as in Refugio's tragicomic relationship with Chucho in "Pay the Criers" and the *telenovela* (soap opera) love story of "La Yonfantayn." Capturing distinctly Latina/o forms of human connectedness, her fictions contain a keen awareness of Mexican-Texan biculturality, Spanish-English bilingualism, and a Chicana feminist resistance to the lasting effects of conquest and colonialism. Her representations thus offer another *Tejano perspective alongside that of Rolando *Hinojosa and anticipate the later borderlands writing of Gloria *Anzaldúa, Benjamin Saenz, and Alicia *Gaspar de Alba.

Further Reading

Candelaria, Cordelia. "Engendering Re/Solutions: The (Feminist) Legacy of Estela Portillo Trambley." In *Decolonial Voices: Chicana/o Cultural Studies in the 21st Century*, edited by Arturo J. Aldama and Naomi Quiñonez. Bloomington: Indiana University Press, 2002.

Candelaria, Cordelia. "Latina Women Writers: Chicana, Cuban American, and Puerto Rican Voices." In *Handbook of Hispanic Cultures in the United States: Literature and Art*, edited by Francisco Lomelí et al. Houston, TX: Arte Público Press, 1993.

González, Laverne. "Portillo Trambley, Estela." In *Chicano Literature, a Reference Guide*. Westport, CT: Greenwood Press, 1984.

Cordelia Chávez Candelaria

Posadas, Las. Las Posadas (The Inns) refers to a popular Christmas tradition and pageant that is performed throughout Latin America, México, and Spain and in most Mexican communities throughout the Southwest borderlands. Celebrated from December 16 through December 24 (Christmas Eve), the pageant is in the form of a *novena (Catholic nine-day devotion), based on the New Testament depiction of Joseph and Mary in their search for a place to stay in Belen (Bethlehem). Often, children dressed as angels carry small figurines of the holy family, or they dress as Joseph and Mary (sometimes on horseback or on mule), visiting a different home each night, reenacting the search for *la posada* (the inn) in the form of a procession. Musicians follow along, playing and singing special *posada* songs. *Los peregrinos* (the pilgrims) consist of friends, neighbors, and family carrying candles with them as they are refused lodging by *los mesoneros* (innkeepers). At each door in the folk ritual, they sing "Tienes alojamiento?"—"Do you have room?" The owner or master of the house will respond, "Leave! Get out of here. This is no *posada*." More verses are then sung by the choir of singers, convincing the owner of the importance of their stay. In the end the owner will let them into his house, where there will be music, dance, fireworks, and candy for the children.

Las Posadas have become a community affair with friends, relatives, and neighbors gathering together to share in a tradition that has come down through the years. Once the religious portion of Las Posadas is complete, the musicians sing *aguinaldos* (carols) and **alabanzas* and give bags of cookies, candies, and toys to the children. There is traditionally a Mexican **piñata*, made into the shape of a star, to represent the mysterious star that guided the three wise men to the Christ child. Traditional **foods* with ritual overtones, including tamales, *pozole* (hominy soup with pork meat and lime), **menudo*, and *bizcochitos* (anise seed cookies), are typically served to all participants. The whole *novena* ritual lasts for nine days, which represents the nine months that Mary was pregnant with the Christ child.

The use of Las Posadas can be traced to the earliest christianization of the Aztecs by Augustine priests in the sixteenth century. In 1519 Hernán Cortés led an expeditionary army to conquer the Aztec empire and capture its gold. Along with the conquistador came the Catholic missionaries, who tried every tactic possible to make the Aztecs believe as they did. One coincidence in particular made it easier for the Augustine priests to teach the new religion to the Aztecs. During the last days of December, around the time of Christmas, the Aztecs celebrated the birth of their god Huitzilopochtli for one night, and celebrations were held the following day in homes. This festival celebrating the birth of Huitzilopochtli was one of the most important festivals of the year for the Aztecs. The missionaries noted the similarities between the two celebrations, inasmuch as the Christmas Masses, as they were called, were originally celebrated in convents and churches but were later performed at haciendas, farms, ranches, and eventually neighborhoods (**barrios*).

The first Christmas celebrated in old México was in 1538 by Fray Pedro de Gant, when he called on all the Indians from twenty leagues around Mexico City to attend. They adopted it and added their own colorful festivities of flowers and feathers. Today in cities across the Southwest, Las Posadas are held annually and continue to blend a variety of cultural influences.

Further Reading

Castro, Rafaela G. *Chicano Folklore: A Guide to the Folktales, Traditions, Rituals and Religious Practices of Mexican Americans.* Oxford: Oxford University Press, 2000.

Flores, Richard. *Los Pastores: History and Performance in the Mexican Shephard's Play of South Texas.* Washington, DC: Smithsonian Institution Press, 1995.

Seth Nolan

Pozo, Chano (1915–1948). Renowned primarily as a *conguero* (conga player), Luciano "Chano" Pozo y González is also famous as a singer, composer, and dancer. He was one of the founding fathers of Afro-Cuban jazz, introducing the conga drum to the genre and almost single-handedly revolutionizing the rhythmic and percussive concepts of bebop. Born in Havana, Cuba, in 1915, Pozo gained notoriety in his *barrio (neighborhood) at an early age for his singing, conga playing, and *rumba dancing. He learned singing and drumming through his membership in the Abakuá sect of the Afro-Cuban religion Lucumí, a sacred ritual practice of spiritual possession (aka *santería*) that would inform his music throughout his life.

By the late 1930s he was a member of the carnival band Los Dandy's, for which he wrote several prize-winning songs. In 1940 he worked in the *Conga Pantera* (Panther Conga) show at the outdoor Havana cabaret Sans Souci, as both a conga player and a choreographer. Although the club catered mainly to American tourists, Pozo also caught the attention of other musicians with his frenzied, flamboyant solos. During the next few years he gained fame and fortune as a composer, his songs being recorded and played in New York by such artists as Orquesta Casino de la Playa (Casino of the Beach Orchestra); Xavier *Cugat; and *Machito, who had also performed with Pozo and Miguelito Valdés, a childhood friend who would in 1946 convince him to move to New York.

While Pozo had little initial success in New York, Valdés was continually looking for work for the non-English-speaking immigrant. In February and March 1947 Valdés arranged for three Pozo-led recording dates featuring Arsenio Rodríguez on *tres* (a small Cuban guitar), vocals by Tito *Rodríguez, and members of Machito's orchestra, whose musical director, fellow Cuban Mario *Bauzá, had met Pozo when touring in Havana two years before. That same year, when Dizzy Gillespie was looking for a conga player to add to his bebop orchestra to explore Afro-Cuban rhythms within the genre, Bauzá suggested Pozo.

On September 29, 1947, Gillespie's orchestra, including Pozo, played a Carnegie Hall concert that has gone on to achieve mythic status as the seminal event in the history of cubop (a term coined by Gillespie and later replaced by Afro-Cuban jazz and even later *Latin jazz). Also during the latter half of 1947, Pozo recorded eight songs in two recording sessions with Gillespie, including their classic co-composition "Manteca" (Lard), as well as "Cubana Be" and "Cubana Bop." Although these sessions were his only work with the band, their impact was enormous and far-reaching in that these were the first recordings mixing the two genres that was meant specifically for listening rather than for dancing, despite the fact that *mambo bands had been around for years, playing jazz-tinged Afro-Cuban music.

During the following year, Pozo toured extensively throughout the United States and Europe with Gillespie's orchestra, his conga solos and fragments of Abakuá chants becoming a featured part of the group's performances. He also recorded with a quartet featuring Gillespie band members Milt Jackson on vibes and James Moody on tenor sax. Pozo's career was abruptly cut short in December 1948, just shy of his thirty-fourth birthday, when, a few hours after beating up a Cuban drug dealer for selling him weak marijuana and then refusing to refund his money, the man found Pozo at the Rio Café and shot him; the *conguero* died on the floor of the Harlem bar while, as legend has it, "Manteca" played on the jukebox.

Further Reading

Roberts, John Storm. *Latin Jazz: The First of the Fusions, 1880s to Today*. New York: Schirmer Books, 1999.

Steward, Sue. *¡Música! Salsa, Rumba, Merengue, and More*. San Francisco, CA: Chronicle Books, 1999.

Yanow, Scott. *Afro-Cuban Jazz*. San Francisco, CA: Miller Freeman Books, 2000.

Ramón Versage

Pregones. *See* Teatro Pregones.

Price of Glory. This 2000 feature-length debut by Carlos *Ávila centers on the lives of a boxing *family called the "Fighting Ortegas" headed by Arturo Ortega, played by Jimmy *Smits in his first starring role after leaving the prime-time television series *NYPD Blue*. The film explores the relationships between fathers and sons and how Arturo Ortega tries to live out his own failed boxing career through his sons as he pushes them relentlessly from the Pee Wee, Silver, and Golden Gloves toward the ultimate goal of winning a title bout and turning professional. The screenplay is an adaptation of a stage play written by Philip Berger, a boxing columnist for the *New York Times*.

The film is also notable in its depiction of boxing as an important community-building activity in the Latina/o culture. In most working-class Latina/o *barrios and in African American communities, boxing clubs and gyms are common. These clubs and gyms become more than just a place to train and work out; they can serve as a type of cultural center that draws the family and community to support its youth as they move up in the ranks. Also, professional Latina/o boxers in many cases become revered role models for youth. As a *sport for youth, boxing provides discipline, structure, and goals that will help the disenfranchised live better lives. In more recent times it is common to see young women entering into the rings to achieve the goals of becoming professional fighters in their own right, as shown in the film *Girlfight* (2000).

Further Reading

http://www.austinchronicle.com/issues/dispatch/2000-03-24/screens_roundup24.html.

http://www.inmotionmagazine.com/cavila.html.

http://www.popmatters.com/film/interviews/price-of-glory.html.
http://www.priceofglory.com.

Arturo J. Aldama

Prinze, Freddie (1954–1977). Born of a Puerto Rican mother and a Hungarian father in New York City, Freddie Prinze attended the New York School for Performing Arts and became a well-known stand-up comic and then lead in a television situation comedy that broke racial barriers, *Chico and the Man* (1974–1978). Set in a garage in a Los Angeles *barrio, the show introduced a multicultural cast to mainstream television, including Scatman Crothers and Della Reese as residents in the diverse neighborhood. Prinze portrayed a *Chicano mechanic who befriended cranky garage owner Ed Brown, played by veteran actor Jack Albertson (1907–1981), who constantly lamented about how East Los Angeles was becoming more Chicano identified. Every week, viewers were summoned to the television by the theme song, written and performed by José *Feliciano. The show became an overnight success and quickly ranked in the top three, slightly behind *Sanford and Son*, the African American classic starring Redd Foxx, and *All in the Family*, with its infamous ideological sparring between the arch-conservative and bigoted Archie Bunker, played by Carroll O'Connor, and his liberal son-in-law Mike, played by Rob Reiner.

In many ways, *Chico and the Man* initiated a tendency in Latino *film and popular culture to have Puerto Rican and other U.S. Latinas/os play Chicanas and Chicanos. More recent examples include Jennifer *López, and her star role as famed Chicana Texan singer *Selena in *Selena* (1997), and Jimmy *Smits and Esai *Morales (both Puerto Rican), who play Chicano Pachucos in the Chicano film classic *Mi Familia/My Family* (1995). Due to Prinze's success in *Chico and the Man* and his reputation as the "Hungarican" stand-up comic who, like other more contemporary comics such as John *Leguizamo and Marga Gómez, satirized his unique ethnic heritage, he achieved a significant amount of crossover success and attention and appeared on several popular talk and entertainment shows. His appearances included the *Dinah Shore Show*, the *Tonight Show* with Johnny Carson, and the *Dean Martin Comedy Roast*. He also achieved a male heartthrob status and was the feature of several teen and college-age magazines, including *Tiger Beat*, *Rolling Stone*, and *Sixteen*. In terms of his comedic style, Prinze idolized Lenny Bruce, wrote all of his own material, and based his stand-up monologues and routines on his upbringing in the working-class borough of Washington Heights.

In addition to his top-rated television comedy and his stand-up appearances, an album, *Looking Good*, featuring his routines "Hungarican," "Survival," and "Crime," among others, was originally released in 1975 by Collectables Records and rereleased in 2000 by the same label. His observations about his own cultural identity and those of his friends are biting and satirical but never cruel, bigoted, or full of profanity or obscenities. His life was cut short when he committed suicide at the young age of twenty-two. In 1976, one year before his death, he became the father of Freddie Prinze, Jr., who has now achieved television and film fame.

Further Reading

Keller, Gary A. *A Biographical Handbook of Hispanics and United States Film.* Tempe, AZ: Bilingual Press, 1997.
http://www.bbc.co.uk/comedy/guide/articles/c/chicoandtheman_7771350.shtml.
http://www.tvland.com/shows/chico/actor1.jhtml.

Arturo J. Aldama

PRLDEF. *See* Puerto Rican Legal Defense and Education Fund.

Puente, Tito (1923–2000). Remembered as "the King of the Mambo," Ernest Anthony Puente, Jr., was born on April 20, 1923, in East Harlem's "El Barrio" neighborhood to parents who had recently arrived from their native Puerto Rico. "Tito," a shortened version of Ernestito, was a childhood nickname bestowed by his mother, who encouraged her children's pursuit of music and dance. Besides studying piano, saxophone, and drums as a child, Puente won prizes for song and dance routines that he performed with his sister Anna at community events, and he harmonized with other boys on the street corners of East Harlem. At age sixteen, Puente left high school to pursue music full-time, playing drums and later timbales with a series of bands. His style was influenced both by the *boleros and *rumbas of his neighborhood and by the big band jazz of Stan Kenton and Gene Krupa. After playing behind José Curbello and Johnny Rodríguez, Puente's big break came when he joined the famous Latin orchestra of *Machito, where he was the first drummer to be featured as a timbal soloist at the front of the band.

Drafted into the navy during World War II, Puente continued his musical pursuits by playing drums and saxophone with the ship's band aboard the USS *Santee* and picking up tips from other musicians who had been drafted into the service. Following the war, Puente returned to New York and worked again with Curbello, as well as with Fernando Álvarez, Charlie Palmieri, and Pupi Campo, before forming his first band, the Picadilly Brothers. Under the GI Bill, Puente attended Juilliard, taking classes in orchestration and arranging, and added vibes to the many instruments he had already mastered. Within a few years Puente had become one of the leading innovators of the new dance craze *mambo, a merging of the Afro-Cuban sound with big band jazz orchestrations for sections of trumpets, trombones, and saxophones. Along with Tito *Rodríguez, Puente became a "mambo king" of the Palladium ballroom. In 1950, Puente was the first Latin musician to play vibes in a mambo orchestra, and his playing was so flashy that he inspired Cal Tjader, Dizzy Gillespie, and other jazz musicians to record in the mambo style with percussionists such as Mongo Santamaría and Chano *Pozo. By the late

Tito Puente. *Courtesy of Photofest.*

1950s, Puente helped create the Cuban-influenced bebop or "Cubop" typified by songs such as "Ran Kan Kan" and "Mambo Inn." His 1958 album *Dance Mania* was the number-one Latin record for several years after its release and was later recognized by the *New York Times* as one of the twenty-five most influential albums of the twentieth century.

With the closing of the Palladium in 1966, and particularly with the rise of rock and roll, it became clear that the mambo craze was over. However, Puente's flexibility and willingness to invent or adapt to new styles ensured his longevity as a performer. When the *pachanga took over from the mambo, Puente mastered that style, as well as continuing with his experiments in *Latin jazz. When rock and roll came along, Puente and his colleagues answered with the *cha cha cha and the boogaloo. Carlos *Santana introduced Puente's musical legacy to the rock generation by recording "Oye cómo va" (Hey, How Is It Going) and "Para los rumberos" (For the Rumba

Musicians) on his album *Abraxas* (1970). By the 1970s, the Latin music community was most closely identified with *salsa, but Puente refused to adopt this term to describe his music. As Puente said in public many times, "Salsa is a sauce, something to eat, you don't dance to it." In other words, the term *salsa* meant many different dance rhythms, and he refused to limit his artistry to any particular genre. It also helped Puente endure the fickleness of the Latin music market and helped him attain a large crossover appeal, particularly with his Latin jazz recordings.

Puente's output during the sixty years of his career was prestigious, recording 120 albums and writing 450 songs and over 2,000 musical arrangements. In the process, Puente worked with nearly every famous figure in Latin music and introduced many future stars including Celia *Cruz, Willie Bobo, Chano Pozo, Mongo Santamaría, Cachao, and Oscar D' León. He was awarded five Grammy Awards during the period 1979–2000, for *Homenaje a Beny* (a tribute to Beny Moré), *On Broadway*, *Mambo Diablo*, *Goza mi timbal* (My Timbales Rejoice), and *Mambo Birdland*. Puente's visibility to a U.S. audience was enhanced by his appearances on television programs such as the *Bill Cosby Show* and the *Simpsons* and by his role as musical director (and a cameo appearance) for the 1992 movie *Mambo Kings*. Other honors included receiving a star on the Hollywood Walk of Fame in 1990 and a National Medal of Arts awarded by President Bill Clinton in 1997. In April 2000, the Library of Congress recognized Puente as a Living Legend only one month before the legend passed away from complications of open-heart surgery. Puente is remembered both for his musical legacy and for his bringing together musicians and audiences of a diverse spectrum in their enjoyment of Latin-based music.

Further Reading

Clarke, Donald, ed. *The Penguin Encyclopedia of Popular Music*. 2nd ed. New York: Penguin, 1999.

Loza, Steven. *Tito Puente and the Making of Latin Music*. Urbana: University of Illinois Press, 1999.

Roberts, John Storm. *The Latin Tinge: The Impact of Latin American Music on the United States*. 2nd ed. New York: Oxford University Press, 1999.

Hope Munro Smith

Puerto Rican Legal Defense and Education Fund (PRLDEF).

The Puerto Rican Legal Defense and Education Fund (PRLDEF) was established in 1972 and is dedicated to securing, promoting, and protecting civil and human rights of the Puerto Rican and wider Latino community through litigation, policy analysis, and education. In addition to protecting civil rights, the goals of PRLDEF (pronounced "pearl-deaf") include civic participation, engagement, and empowerment, preserving a healthy and vibrant Latino culture, participation in community, access to legal and other professions, educational excellence, and being a recognized and respected leader. These goals are accomplished through one of three arms in the organization: the Litigation Division, the Pro Bono Cooperating Counsel Program, and the Education Division.

The Litigation Division has been taking on cases that impact the Latino community since 1972 and constantly has active cases on the dockets. Some of the areas the Division litigates are voting rights, housing rights, immigrants' rights, education rights, environmental rights, and employment rights. The Pro Bono Cooperating Counsel Program solicits assistance from private law firms who provide legal services to the Latino community. The Education Division works with Latino students to encourage careers in law and the legal profession. Some of the services provided in this division include preadmission counseling, financial aid workshops, LSAT (Law School Admissions Test) preparation courses, scholarships, internships, and a mentoring program.

In 1998, PRLDEF merged with the Institute for Puerto Rican Policy (IPR) to form the PRLDEF Institute for Puerto Rican Policy, an arm of PRLDEF, which focuses on policy analysis and advocacy, civic participation, and policy networking and communications. In each of these areas, numerous projects are constantly under way, such as work on bilingual education, the census, voting rights, and election reform. In addition, the institute hosts the IPR Publication Library, making publications, reports, and white papers about key Latino issues available to the public. PRLDEF is a privately funded, nonprofit, and nonpartisan organization with headquarters in New York.

Further Reading

http://www.prldef.org.

Alma Alvarez-Smith

Puerto Rican Traveling Theatre. *See* Theater.

Quebradita. *Quebradita*, meaning "little break," is a modern Mexican American dance as well as a type of music that became popular in Los Angeles and across the southwestern United States during the early 1990s. The dance's name has a dual meaning, referring both to the deep back bends of the female dancer and the "breaking" of a wild horse. Recognizable by the western clothing style of the dancers, energetic music, hat tricks, and daring flips, the *quebradita*'s combination of Mexican, Anglo, and African American influences attracted thousands of young people to participate in dance groups in their schools or communities. Although its popularity as a competition and performance dance has declined significantly, *quebradita* is still danced socially at parties, concerts, and nightclubs in the border region.

Quebradita is most often performed to *banda, or Mexican brass band music. Brass bands in México date to the early nineteenth century, around the time of Mexican independence. Emperor Maximilian of Austria introduced European military bands to the country during his reign in México from 1864 to 1867; in subsequent years, both rural and urban band traditions emerged. Rural, mainly indigenous musicians who played *música de viento* (wind music) at bullfights and community celebrations were known for their facility with improvisation, while urban military and municipal bands mainly performed a European concert repertoire. Strong regional *banda* traditions developed in Sinaloa, Jalisco, Morelos, Guanajuato, and neighboring states, and *bandas* are still an important part of small-town life in the area.

Modern, commercial *banda* music is based largely on the *banda sinaloense*, or Sinaloan band, also known as a *tamborazo* because of its use of a strong drum or tambor sound. But while the original Sinaloan ensembles—which numbered twenty musicians or more—played trombones, trumpets, clarinets, and tubas, popular groups today have replaced many of these instruments with synthesizers and electric guitars. This new style called *technobanda* was developed by music producers in Guadalajara, Jalisco, during the 1980s; in Los Angeles in the mid-1990s its popularity made *banda*-format KLAX the city's top radio station. *Quebradita* songs were popularized by such *technobandas*, though they are commonly played by norteño (northern Mexican accordion–based music) groups as well. The bouncy, fast *quebradita* rhythm is actually an accelerated *cumbia (a dance that, though originally from Colombia, has been popular in México and the border region since the 1970s).

As with many popular dances, the *quebradita*'s history is somewhat hazy. Some believe that it originated in Jalisco or Sinaloa, where *banda* music began, while others believe it came from the U.S.-México border region, since the trend seems to have begun in Los Angeles earlier than in other cities. The steps of the dance may offer some clues, as it combines the *zapateo*, or fast, stomping footwork of traditional *folklórico* dances, with moves from *hip-hop, country line dancing, *salsa, cumbia, *corriditas* (a norteño dance), and even swing. However, even though it is a recently created style, the *quebradita* can be seen as part of a Mexican artistic tradition whose history stretches back for well over a hundred years. Just as in *quebradita*, popular norteña music, traditional *mariachi music, and many of the *folklórico* dances of Jalisco and northern México reflect the rural, ranch life through their use of *vaquero*, or cowboy, clothing; *gritos*, or stylized musical shouts that may have descended from cattle calls; and dance steps that recall country life. Some *quebradita* steps were given names that further tie the dance to the *ranchero* aesthetic: *el toro*, the bull; *el vaquero*, the cowboy; *la piolita*, the little rope.

Although many *quebradita* steps were nationally disseminated through TV music programs and theme movies, regional stylistic variations also exist. California dancers give different names to different styles: *Quebradita* is the style that involves more acrobatics, while *caballito* or *brinquito* is the less athletic, trotting step. In other places, the terms *caballito* and *quebradita* are used interchangeably. California dancers seem to favor hip-hop-based steps, while in Arizona border-style cumbia dancing exerts more influence. Improvisation and innovation are always encouraged, and individual dancers frequently invent and name new steps.

Some of the *quebradita*'s distinctive characteristics include a jumping motion with legs lifted high; a windmilling motion of the lower leg conducted behind the body; a close partner hold, with the woman's left arm wrapped around the man's shoulders, his right arm low on her back, and the woman's right leg sandwiched between the man's (a position common in dances of the Arizona-Sonora region); and of course the death-defying flips and quick back bends performed by the female partner. In addition, the held hands of the partners, instead of remaining at a constant height as they would in

European-style partner dances, are moved around in a rhythmic, improvisational manner. *Quebradita* can be danced individually, in which case the *zapateo* plays a bigger role, but it is best known and most popular as a partner dance. The sensual yet highly athletic nature of the partner's moves increased its appeal among teenagers.

Quebradita dancers wear western-style clothing like jeans, fringed shirts, cowboy boots, and Stetson hats, sometimes accessorized with *cuartas* (small horsewhips), *correas* (leather straps), or bandanas embroidered with the name of the wearer's Mexican state of origin. Dancer's nicknames are often stitched onto a pant leg, and fringe can be added to any part of the costume to enhance the impact of leg, arm, or shoulder movements. Such outfits not only augment the dance's "macho" Mexican image but are necessary for the performance of certain steps: Men perform tricks with their hats, spinning and tossing them between hands, feet, and head (women do the same, though less often); hard-soled boots make possible the distinctive, percussive sound of a *zapateado*. This flashy yet masculine clothing was another factor that contributed to the dance's great popularity.

During the 1990s, *quebradita* dance groups formed in many southwestern cities. In some places these groups were school-sponsored organizations; in others they tended to be more informal and founded by community members. Club members gathered on a regular basis to practice steps and choreograph routines. Most then participated in competitions sponsored by local businesses or radio stations, where they were judged on criteria such as steps performed, synchronization of group members, and dress. Although most dancers in the United States did not wear western clothes in everyday life, hats and boots were nearly always used at such events and were essential for competition. *Quebradita* groups also performed on stage at festivals and live concerts.

Quebradita made an impact on the American Southwest in several ways. First, individual dancers and school officials alike reported increased class attendance, decreased involvement with drugs, and a greater understanding of Mexican-American culture and language from *quebradita* club members. Los Angeles–area *police officers even reported that *quebradita* clubs seemed to help steer youth away from criminal *gangs. Second, the blending of elements of many cultural backgrounds into one distinctively Mexican American art represents a new way youth have found to deal with the competing influences of popular youth culture and *family cultural traditions. Finally, the *quebradita* dance craze made the country take notice of Mexican American popular culture and focused attention for perhaps the first time on the creativity and positive activities of Mexican American youth.

Further Reading

Burr, Ramiro. *The Billboard Guide to Tejano and Regional Mexican Music*. New York: Billboard Books, 1999.

Haro, Carlos Manuel, and Steven Loza. "The Evolution of Banda Music and the

Current Banda Movement in Los Angeles." In *Selected Reports in Ethnomusicology X: Musical Aesthetics and Multiculturalism in Los Angeles*, edited by Steven Loza. Los Angeles: University of California Press, 1994. 59–71.

Hutchinson, Sydney. "Quebradita: The Story of a Modern Mexican-American Dance in the Arizona-Sonora Border Region." Master's thesis, Bloomington: Indiana University, 2002.

Simonett, Helena. *Banda: Mexican Musical Life Across Borders*. Middletown, CT: Wesleyan University Press, 2001.

Sydney Hutchinson

Quinceañera. The term *quinceañera* refers to the common practice among many Latina and Latino families of celebrating the fifteenth birthday of their daughters with a special coming-of-age ceremony. The name *quinceañera* derives from the Spanish words *quince*, meaning "fifteen," and *años*, meaning "years," and may refer either to the girl or the ceremony. In either case, it marks the rite of passage from adolescence to womanhood and is a major event among *families and communities who celebrate it.

Scholars agree that the origins of the contemporary forms of *quinceañera* can be traced to earlier roots. Some believe the origins lie primarily in the ancient Aztec civilization, while others trace them to Spain. The first argument dates the *quinceañera* to pre-Columbian Mayan and Toltec customs in which fifteen-year-olds of both sexes were presented to their tribal communities in festive religious rituals and suggests that the rite honored the young woman's childbearing capacity, thereby enhancing her importance in the community. In Aztec society, at the age of twelve or thirteen a girl could attend two types of preparatory schools, the *calmacac* or the *telpucucali*. Girls who entered the *calmacac* were expected to commit their lives primarily to religious service, while those attending the *telpucucali* were primed for marriage. By the age of fifteen Aztec girls normally were prepared to enter adult life either as wives or in spiritual roles. The second argument, that the *quinceañera* is of Spanish origin, emphasizes the ritual's coming of age into marriageability aspects. After the Spanish colonization of the Americas, scholars note that the rite shifted from marking the onset of physical puberty to a more religious orientation with stronger patriarchal features. Most researchers agree that after the Conquest the native rites of passage adapted to the religious customs of the conquerors and began incorporating Roman Catholic elements into the native ceremonies. *Quinceañera* practices thus appear to have evolved out of the nexus of ancient indigenous customs, Spanish Catholic traditions, and North American influences integrated later.

Today, most traditional *quinceañera* celebrations have two distinct components, the religious ceremony and the secular celebration. Depending on the girl's religious affiliation, a Protestant minister or a Catholic priest conducts the religious service, and the honoree participates usually wearing an elaborate dress (*el vestido*) comparable to a bride's or debutante's gown. She is accompanied throughout the ceremony by an honor court that includes godparents (*padrino y madrina*), friends and their escorts (*damas y chambelanes*), and other family and friends. The religious ceremony, whether Catholic Mass or Protestant service, generally concludes when the young woman reaffirms her faith by reading from a Bible and/or catechism and makes an oath to conduct her new adult responsibilities in keeping with religious teachings. The ceremony typically features symbolic objects (e.g., a medal cross necklace, a finger ring, crown, holy books, flowers, etc.) representing the young woman's faith and her responsibility to God, community, and family.

The secular part of the event usually includes a reception and dance (*la fiesta*) to conclude the celebration. The dance may include a highly choreographed procession with formal introductions of the honoree, her parents, godparents, her court of honor and their escorts, family, and friends. In most secular fiestas specified moments are reserved for the honoree to dance with her father, her escort, and other significant members of her entourage. The great variety of music and food provided at *quinceañeras* depends on the family's ethnicity, social class, geographical region, and financial resources. Among Mexican Americans, traditional foods like beans, tamales, chicken mole, flour or corn tortillas, enchiladas, and *bizcochitos* (cookies) are customary. Food preparation is one of the most significant changes in the *quinceañera* in its shift from the formerly required traditional home-cooked foods to catered foods, including nontraditional convenience trays of cold platters, finger foods, and buffet dishes. However, many contemporary festivities combine both traditional and convenience menus, and some mark *la quinceañera* with a simple birthday party. Elaborate *quinceañera* celebrations that feature formal attire, grand decorations, fancy receptions, professional photographers, special gifts, and a musical band are usually very expensive affairs. As a result, commercial marketing has taken advantage of the *quinceañera* tradition, and specialty stores geared toward providing the material trappings for the celebration are commonplace in Latina/o communities. In whatever form it is observed, following the event the young woman typically gains new privileges in her family, including the first opportunity to begin dating.

Some recent commentary has criticized the traditional *quinceañera* as wrongly emphasizing a girl's sexuality at a time when unmarried teenage pregnancies are a national social crisis in the United States. Some priests have condemned the celebration as advertising a young woman's sexual availability and promoting a *stereotype that Hispanic girls are sexually permissive. Other scholars point out that religious officials traditionally have constructed a limiting view for young women and encourage female subservience to the needs of family and church. Many Catholic officials contend that the rite helps preserve Catholic traditions through its public expression of religious devotion and commitment to virtue. Some literary and cultural studies scholars believe that the coming-of-age rituals reinforce orthodox female identity and social position. Others see the *quinceañera* tradition as serving as an inspiration for Latina/o cultural preservation through new life-cycle ceremonies like *quinceañeros* (male coming-of-age rituals) and *cinquentañeras* (birthday celebrations of life achievements at the age of fifty). At the dawn of the twenty-first century, for many Latinos the *quinceañera* is a hybrid relic of Aztec and Spanish ritual traditions that connect modern young women to their Latina cultural roots, thereby helping to preserve important links to history and heritage.

Further Reading

Cantú, Norma. "La Quinceañera: Towards an Ethnographic Analysis of a Life-Cycle Ritual." *Southern Folklore* 56.1 (1999): 73–101.

Dávalos, Karen Mary. "La Quinceañera: Making Gender and Ethnic Identities." *Frontiers* 16.2–3 (1996): 101–127.

Erevia, Sister Angela. *A Religious Celebration for the Quinceañera*. Austin, TX: Mexican American Cultural Center, 1980.

King, Elizabeth. *Quinceañera: Celebrating Fifteen*. New York: Dutton, 1998.

Salcedo, Michele. *Quinceañera! The Essential Guide to Planning the Perfect Sweet Fifteen Celebration*. New York: Holt, 1997.

Cecilia Aragón

Quinn, Anthony (1915–2001). Born Antonio Rodolfo Quiñones Oaxaca on April 21, 1915, in Chihuahua, México, of Irish and Mexican descent, actor Anthony Quinn occupies a central place in the history of American cinema. Quinn immigrated to the United States with his family in the early 1920s and lived in East Los Angeles as a child, where, before becoming an actor, he earned a living holding a variety of odd jobs, including drawing portraits of movie stars. Quinn, whose film appearances started in 1930, appeared in over 150 films during his lifetime. His appearance in 1952, next to Marlon Brando, in Elia Kazan's *Viva Zapata!* earned him an Oscar for his supporting role as Emiliano *Zapáta's brother. His second Oscar was for his portrayal of the French artist Gauguin in Vincente Minelli's *Lust for Life* in 1956. Other films include Federico Fellini's *La Strada* (1954) and David Lean's *Lawrence of Arabia* (1962). Quinn played the lead role of a Greek peasant who inspires a writer in *Zorba the Greek* (1965). In many ways, Quinn is defined by his versatility as an ethnic-defined thespian who, because of his non-Anglo features, played an Eskimo, a Bedouin, an Italian, and even an Arab prince.

Quinn made appearances for television and theatrical projects during the 1960s and the 1970s. As his cinematographic career slowed down, he became more involved with artistic production. A self-trained artist (as a teenager he had won a scholarship to study architecture under the tutelage of Frank Lloyd Wright), Quinn dedicated his time to create sculptures, to paint, to design jewelry, and to acquire a large number of works of art. He also wrote his memoirs, *Original Sin* (1972) and *One Man Tango* (1997). Quinn's personal life was always considered volatile and passionate like his characters. Married three times, he is the father of thirteen children, including a son, Aidan Quinn, who has developed a successful acting career in film. Quinn died at the age of eighty-six, leaving behind an extraordinary career in film that has placed him in the pantheon of great stars.

Further Reading

Marrill, Alvin H. *The Films of Anthony Quinn*. Secaucus, NJ: Citadel Press, 1975.

Quinn, Anthony. *Lovers and Other Strangers: Paintings by Jack Vetriano*. London: Pavilion, 2000.

Quinn, Anthony. *The Original Sin: A Self-Portrait*. Boston: Little, Brown, 1972.

Gabriella Sánchez

Quintanilla Pérez, Selena. *See* Selena.

Quinto Sol. The epoch of the fifth sun is an Aztec belief that has been embraced by *Chicanos and has been integrated into Chicana/o culture across the Southwest borderlands. According to Aztec culture and mythology, time is partitioned into a fifty-two-year calendar that is then separated into five ages known as the suns. Presently, we are in the fifth and final age, or El Quinto Sol (The Fifth Sun), which falls under the rein of Tonatiuh and is the age of earthquakes. The sun is a prominent symbol in Aztec mythology, typically portrayed as a great warrior with solar rays functioning as darts. The first publisher of contemporary Chicano literature, Quinto Sol Publications has been based out of Berkeley, California, since the 1960s. The Quinto Sol Prize for Chicano literature has been awarded to individuals such as Tomás Rivera and Estela *Portillo Trambley. Artist Frederico M. Vigil of New Mexico produced the 1992 mural *El Quinto Sol*, depicting a woman pregnant with the future, and it can be found in Venice, California, outside the Social and Public Art Resource Center.

Further Reading

Bierhorst, John. *The Mythology of Mexico and Central America*. New York: William Morrow, 1990.

Brundage, Burr Cartwright. *The Fifth Sun: Aztec Gods, Aztec World*. Austin: University of Texas Press, 1979.

Florescano, Enrique. *The Myth of Quetzalcoatl*. Translated by Raul Velasquez. Baltimore, MD: John Hopkins University Press, 1999.

Griffith, James S. "Quetzalcoatl on the Border? Mestizo Water Serpent Beliefs of the Pimeria Alta." *Western Folklore* 49 (October 1990): 391–400.

Armando Quintero, Jr.

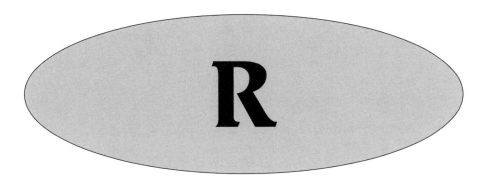

Race and Ethnicity. Referring to ways of categorizing people and populations, the terms *race*, *ethnicity*, and *culture* are widely used and frequently confused. Traditionally, *race* has been used to designate genetically related human groups whose physical characteristics are inherited and transmitted physiologically, whereas *ethnicity* has been applied to shared cultural practices and customs that are learned and acquired socially among people living in identifiable human groups. Also learned and acquired through human interaction, *culture* refers to such learned and socially constructed systems as language, religion, food and cooking, clothing, arts and crafts, sports, and myriad other shared characteristics that unite people into recognizable categories of societal identity.

Because interracial mixture has occurred from the earliest recorded history and appears to be fundamental to the survival of the human species, most anthropologists and other scholars of human populations reject the very concept of race as an accurate or reliable indicator of human grouping. That is, the fundamental need for exogamy (i.e., breeding outside a single pool of blood-related individuals) combined with the ancient and widespread transmigration and trade networking among people over the ages have lessened the importance of racial differences to the process of cultural learning. Consequently, while genetic inheritance, recessive genes, and physical appearance may be of variable significance within particular social groups and political viewpoints, by themselves they normally are not solely determinative of social practices and customs. On the other hand, social practices, beliefs, and customs are determinative of ethnicity and culture. Both terms refer to shared human activities, customary values, and human traits that describe, as well as define, a given population's distinctiveness.

In the Latina and Latino context, the prevalence of *mestizaje (Indian and Spanish mixture, or any hybrid mix) fundamentally serves as the central fact of the racial, ethnic, and cultural inheritance of the Americas, just as other hybrids fundamentally describe the ethnoracial cultures of other geographies (e.g., Europe, the Middle East, the Far East, the South Pacific). The widespread development of *mestizaje* in the Western Hemisphere effectively blurs and overturns the notion of hard, unchanging boundaries between social classifications. The Spanish word for racial mixture, *mestizaje* specifically describes the hybrid mixture of Spanish, Jewish, Native American, African, and Asian heritage that identifies Latina and Latino peoples and cultures in the Americas.

This variability, along with the continuing growth of Latina/o populations in the United States, explains both the cultural similarities and the differences among Latina/o subgroups, which is why ethnic labels vary from one to another or even within a particular group. In this regard, it is important to note that Latinas/os comprise all racial backgrounds and physical features (European, Jewish, Natives of the Americas, African, and Asian, as seen in the case of Chinese Mexicans and Japanese Peruvians, etc.). The predominant language of most of the peoples of Latin America is Spanish, and Spanish helps define aspects of *immigration and Latina/o communities in the United States. However, millions of Latinas/os are fluent in a variety of other languages and dialects. Some of the living tribal languages that predate the arrival of Christopher *Columbus and the Europeans include Quechúa (Peru), Zápotec (México), Mapuche (Chile), Apache, and Navajo (United States), and hundreds of others. Thousands of other indigenous tongues have disappeared in the twenty-first century, unable to survive the hordes of Europeans to the "New World." This is also true for the African and Asian mestizos of the Americas whose linguistic roots and ties to their original cultures have been lost, although scholarly research and current ethnography indicate that many elements of Yoruba, Bantu, Mandarin, and other imported languages have survived as fragments in words for foods, spirituality, names, sayings, and similar forms of cultural and linguistic identity. For Latinas and Latinos in the United States the dominance of the English language expands and complexifies the prevalent *mestizaje* as Spanish and English intertwine, compete, and mutually influence each other and multiple spinoff dialects.

The term *Latina/o* (singular) and *Latinas/Latinos* and *Latinas/os* (plural) are often used interchangeably with *Hispanic* and *Hispanics* to refer to the population subgroups of Mexican Americans, Puerto Ricans, *Cuban Americans, and others. The prevalence of the various forms of "Latina/o" mirrors the usage of many scholars and other specialist researchers who want to underscore the inclusion of women, which is overlooked in the traditional linguistic form "Latino," which is a masculine inflected term in the Spanish language. Similarly, the preference for *Latinas/os* over *Hispanics* parallels specialist usage to underscore the specific racial inclusion of mestizos (i.e.,

American Indian and Spanish hybrids of people and cultures) that is deemphasized in the English-language term *Hispanic*, which focuses on the European Spain and Spanish.

Sociologists and cultural historians agree that the labels minority groups use to identify themselves and their national origin are seldom static. They change over time according to social pressures from families and local communities, political factors, media and advertising fashion, and personal temperament. That pattern of changing self- and group identification continues with Hispanics. Concern for adopting one panethnic label, in fact, led to the emergence of *Hispanic* in the 1980s as a largely political and bureaucratic term to simplify the identity of the fastest-growing population in North America. The rise of *Latino* as a preferred term appears to have emerged from the grassroots population itself, as well as through widespread use of the term by scholars, artists, and other intellectuals. Many scholars and other observers view *Hispanic* as connoting an assimilationist desire to be a part of America's "melting pot" with emphasis on economic security, whereas *Latino* is associated with concern for the preservation of language and culture traditions as well as for issues of social justice and equality. Still, the diversity of the Latina/o population produces many variations and exceptions from these categories.

One example of the shifts and changes in ethnic group terminology is the use of *Mexican*. It was widely used for descendants of both the original Spanish pioneers of the present-day United States and for mestizo immigrants from México after the 1848 signing of the *Treaty of Guadalupe Hidalgo. The group label by others and also in-group identification underwent numerous changes in the twentieth century from *Mexican American*, *Spanish American*, *Spanish-speaking*, and *Spanish-surnamed* to *Chicano, Xicano, Hispanic*, and *Latino*. Although common, changes in ethnic labeling and self-identification are challenges to journalists, educators, and members of the general public who desire to refer to America's ethnic and racial mix accurately. For the most part *Latino* and its more gender-precise derivatives, *Latina/Latino* or *Latina/o*, is the panethnic term of choice in the bicoastal New York and California areas, while *Hispanic* is more common as a panethnic identifyer in the *barrios and borderlands of the Southwest, particularly in Texas and Arizona. In general, these terms and their name shifting over time indicate that they represent people who have been marginalized by historical and institutional racism and may continue to be stigmatized socially due to personal and cultural perceptions that unfairly and erroneously perceive Latinas and Latinos as un-American. Thus, demographic researchers expect that these labels will continue to change as marginalized groups cast off negative *stereotypes.

In addition, many Latinas/os avoid using *Hispanic* because of its emergence in the 1980s among politicians and agencies of the U.S. federal government as a preferred monolithic label to lump all groups together for political expedience. Sociologists and demographers confirm that *Hispanic* was promoted by the U.S. Census Bureau as a means of simplifying its ethnic categories. This occurred despite the continuing self-identification by specific ethnicity and/or race by the actual people being counted. Generally, when asked their ethnicity, most Latinas and Latinos do not specifically refer to themselves as either Latinas or Latinos or Hispanics. Rather, the responses are more precise, often in Spanish, depending on the speaker's origin and native region, for example, Chicano, Mexican, Boricúa, Island Puertorican, Cuban American, and mestiza. For these reasons *Latina/o* is frequently preferred over *Hispanic* as the generic label because the latter emphasizes Spain and Spanish identities, which are significantly less descriptive of the Western Hemisphere's Latin American cultural hybridity, *mestizaje*, and immigrant diversity.

Whether in Spanish or in English, however, the speaker's self-identification will be explicitly gendered by linguistic inflection or by appearance (Chica*na* or Chica*no*, Cuba*na* or Cuba*no*, etc.). This concern for ethnic, racial, and gender precision and inclusivity explains the widespread usage among specialists and other researchers of both *Latina* and *Latino*, often abbreviated as *Latina/o*. This is analogous to specialist and technical precision in other fields that alternate between scientific and lay terminology, depending on the context.

Also of linguistic importance to race, ethnicity, and culture in the Latina and Latino context is the concept of binguality and biculturality due to class stratification and the interracial hybridity of *mestizaje*. Multiple languages are commonly employed by or are part of the background of Mexican Americans, Mexican nationals, Puerto Ricans, Nuyoricans, Cuban Americans, Cubans, and others of the diverse ethnic groups comprising the U.S. Latina and Latino population. This multilinguality includes primarily a variety of Standard Spanish, English, and American Indian idioms, along with their combination in vernacular dialects (e.g., *caló*, creole, Spanglish). Consciously writing from a Latina/o point of view in Standard Edited American English demands a heightened regard for accurate, culturally based translations. Consequently, to comprehend the dynamic vitality of popular cultures requires understanding the linguistic challenges of Latina/o communities. Many believe that the future harmony requires appreciation of and respect for the reality of an evolved *mestizaje* with its treasury of cultural achievement and its potential for innovative genius and human synthesis for a postcolonialist vision of shared humanity and community.

Further Reading

Aldama, Arturo, and Naomi Quiñonez, eds. *Decolonial Voices: Chicana/o Cultural Studies in the 21st Century*. Bloomington: Indiana University Press, 2002.

Bernal, Martha E., and George P. Knight, eds. *Ethnic Identity: Formation and Transmission among Hispanics and Other Minorities*. Albany: State University of New York Press, 1993.

Brock, Lisa, and Digna Casteñeda Fuertes, eds. *Between Race and Empire: African-Americans and Cubans before the Cuban Revolution*. Philadelphia, PA: Temple University Press, 1998.

Oboler, Suzanne. *Ethnic Labels, Latino Lives: Identity and the Politics of (Re)presentation in the United States*. Minneapolis: University of Minnesota Press, 1995.

Cordelia Chávez Candelaria

Radio. *See* Spanish-Language Radio.

Ramona. One of the most famous literary texts relating to California history, Mexican Americans, and American Indians, the novel *Ramona, a Story* was written by American social reformer Helen Hunt Jackson (1830–1885) in 1884. Usually cited by its short title, *Ramona* was inspired by Harriet Beecher Stowe's *Uncle Tom's Cabin* (1852), which Jackson and others believed had helped raise popular support for the abolition of slavery. Jackson stated that she would "be thankful" if she could accomplish "one hundredth part for the Indian" in reforming U.S. government policy what "Mrs. Stowe did for the Negro." She originally titled her romance of social reform *In the Name of the Law*, emphasizing her concern for Indian social justice, but the book was renamed for publication, forever memorializing the title character's name as a quintessential American female legend. Combining the heroic survivor qualities of the captivity narrative tradition and the tragic, romantic mulatta, Jackson's Scottish Indian halfbreed is raised as a California mestiza, thereby adding an American cultural overlay that persists in literary legend, film, popular song, and community drama. Although Jackson wrote *Ramona* in hopes of ending the persecution of Native Americans and peasant workers and although her book aroused a measure of political sentiment against the U.S. government's Indian policy, *Ramona* was most successful in portraying a romantic picture of the California of old México and of the haughty grandeur of the *hacendados* (Mexican ranchers), of the Roman Catholic mission system, of the suffering Cahuilla and Temecula Indians as "noble savages," and of the mestiza hero of the title.

Ramona's creator was born Helen Maria Fiske in Amherst, Massachusetts, in 1830. The future novelist and social reformer was a contemporary and friend of the poet Emily Dickinson. Fiske married a captain of the U.S. Army, Edward Hunt, and experienced the itinerant life of an army wife, moving from post to post with her husband and sons until their tragic deaths in 1863. She began writing in her widowhood, sometimes publishing under the pseudonym Saxe Holm. After marrying her second husband, William Jackson, in 1875, the writer moved to Colorado. Jackson is best known today for *Ramona*, but in her lifetime the prolific Hunt Jackson was equally renowned for another of her writings, the well-researched treatise *A Century of Dishonor* (1881), which laid out the persecution and destruction that defined

U.S. government Indian policy. She was subsequently appointed to a federal commission on the plight of Indians living in the missions of the Southwest. This investigation provided much of the material included in *Ramona*, first published in 1884. The author died in 1885 in San Francisco.

The plot of *Ramona* centers on the romance of the handsome and noble Indian Alessandro and the beautiful and brave mestiza (later revealed to be actually half Indian, half Scottish) Ramona. The action takes place in a pastoral southern California landscape in the 1850s at the height of the Gold Rush and shortly after California had become the thirty-first state. Because Ramona thinks of herself as the orphan niece of Doña Moreno, an affluent Mexican descendant of Spaniards, she bears the ideal fictive picaro breeding of both a privileged lady and a humble servant. When the picaresque maiden falls in love with Doña Moreno's proud Indian worker Alessandro, the couple must elope to escape Moreno's wrath. Forced to leave her affluent hacienda life, Ramona and her husband endure a steady stream of hardship and abuses that allow Jackson to shed light on the theft, deterritorialization, and broken treaties inflicted on Native Americans by European immigrants of every ethnic and national origin. As a literary work, the novel is challenged by the author's failure to seamlessly braid its social reform message with the literary conventions of the romance genre. Nevertheless, the intensity of Jackson's compassionate interest in protecting and preserving the true natives of the Americas, along with the novel's compelling plot convolutions, has kept the book in print for over a century. One important supporter of the author's intense concern for social justice was the Cuban poet and martyr José *Martí (1853–1895), who was so inspired by the novel that he wrote a Spanish translation published in 1929 as *Ramona: (novela americana)*.

The story also spawned an industry of by-products of the same name: at least a dozen movies and documentaries, a familiar popular ballad waltz, several plays including a recent original by Guillermo *Reyes, and an annual outdoor festival staging in Riverside County, California. Some of the most well known portrayals of Ramona include Dolores *del Río's and Loretta Young's screen performances and Raquel *Welch's in an annual festival, *Ramona* Outdoor Play. The *Ramona* Outdoor Play was first staged in 1923, and its organizers advertise it as the oldest continuously running play in the country. Its annual run took place in April and May 2004 in Riverside County, California, just south of Hemet. The waltz song and music entitled "Ramona" was written in 1927 by Mabel Wayne and L. Wolfe Gilbert and dedicated to Dolores del Río for her memorable cinema portrayal of the now-legendary Ramona role. The significance of that legend to Latina/o pop culture is demonstrated by its persistent popularity in addressing the complex intercultural, interethnic, and multilingual aspects of America's fundamental hybrid identity. Significantly, what has elevated many popular culture works such as the novel, film, and song *Ramona*; the films *Salt of the Earth* and

High Noon; the play and film *Zoot Suit*, and documentaries like *The Lemon Grove Incident* and *Los Mineros* (The Miners) produced and directed by Paul *Espinosa to the level of contempory classics is their complex critique of that very status quo.

Further Reading

Dillaye, Ina. *Ramona: A Play in Five Acts*. Syracuse, NY: Dillaye Associates, 1887.

Hufford, David A. *The Real Ramona of Helen Hunt Jackson's Famous Novel*. Los Angeles: Hufford, 1900.

Jackson, Helen Hunt. *Ramona*. New York: Signet, 2002.

Jackson, Helen Hunt. *Ramona*. Electronic Text Center, University of Virginia Library, Charlottesville, 2000. http://etext.lib.virginia.edu/modeng/modeng#J.browse.html.

Johnston, Moira. *Spectral Evidence: The Ramona Case: Incest, Memory, and Truth on Trial in Napa Valley*. Boston: Houghton Mifflin, 1997.

Martí, José, trans. *Ramona (novela americana)*. 2nd ed. Madrid, Spain: Biblioteca Libertad, 1929.

May, Antoinette. *The Annotated Ramona*. San Carlos, CA: Wide World Publishing/Tetra, 1989.

Cordelia Chávez Candelaria

Ranchera. Derived from *rancho*, meaning cattle ranch, farm, or rural settlement, the *ranchera* (country song) refers primarily to a Mexican country song that is very popular among Mexicans and Chicanas/os in the United States. Following the Mexican Revolution of 1910, *rancheras* began to appeal to the urban middle classes; imbued with cultural nationalism and nostalgia, they romanticized the disappearing country lifestyle. The modern *canción ranchera* was popularized by José Alfredo *Jiménez, known as the son of México, who composed over 500 songs during the 1950s and 1960s in Mexico City. The poetic structure is simple and straightforward, but the emotional core and impact are intense and dynamic. The themes are typically about love and unrequited love and express the passions, heartaches, pain, and sensibilities of the urban and rural masses. *Rancheras* are symbolic, expressing the epitome of *lo Mexicano* (ideal Mexicanness). Jiménez performed and recorded many of his original *canciónes*, and many are now regarded as classic, including "Ella" (Her), "Camino de Guanajuato" (Road to Guanajuato), "El Rey" (The King), and "La Vida No Vale Nada" (Life Has No Value), which continue to appeal to younger generations of Chicanas/os. Typically performed by *mariachis, *rancheras* are often performed in other styles including *conjunto* or Norteño (Tex-Mex), *banda de viento* (wind bands), and trios, and may be sung at celebrations, secular rituals, or social gatherings as dance or dinner music or in concert. Even though the *ranchera* is a male-dominated genre, there are several Mexicanas and Chicanas that have become famous *ranchera* singers such as Lola Beltrán, Lucha

Villa, Amalia Mendoza, Lydia Mendoza, Chela Sylva, and *Selena from Texas, Luisa Espinel and Linda *Ronstadt from Arizona, and Gloria Pohl, Angel Espinoza, and El Grupo Sparx from New Mexico.

Further Reading

Gradante, William. "Mexican Popular Music at Mid-Century: The Role of José Alfredo Jiménez and the Canción Ranchera." *Studies in Latin American Popular Culture* 1 (1982): 36–59.

Peña, Manuel. "From Rancero to Jaitón: Ethnicity and Class in Texas-Mexican Music (Two Styles in the Form of a Pair)." *Ethnomusicology* 29 (Winter 1985): 29–55.

Peña, Manuel. *The Texas-Mexican Conjunto: History of a Working Class Music.* Austin: University of Texas Press, 1985.

Peter J. García

RCAF. *See* Royal Chicano Air Force (RCAF).

Real Women Have Curves. *Real Women Have Curves* (2002) was originally written as a play by Josefina *López when she was nineteen years old; it premiered at the Mission Cultural Center in San Francisco in 1990 as an El Teatro de la Esperanza production. Since its premiere, the play has been performed across the United States, including a Spanish-language version produced in New York. A script version was published in 1996 by Dramatic Publishing. As both stage performance and film, *Real Women* has been instrumental in challenging the *stereotypes traditionally associated with Chicana/Latina women, both within and outside *Chicano/Latino culture. The story, a bilingual, semiautobiographical account of a period in López's life, tells of five Mexican/Chicana women who are racing to meet production deadlines to keep their small factory garment business from failure. Working in the tiny sewing factory, the immigrant women discuss intimate aspects of their lives, as well as share their dreams with one another. The story is told from the point of view of Ana (América Ferrera), the youngest among them, who has dreams of going away to college and becoming a writer. A recent high school graduate, Ana must first overcome many obstacles, such as her traditional Mexican *family structure, repressive *gender roles, and the economic impoverishment that requires her to work in the garment industry, historically one of the most difficult, low-paying employment areas for immigrant women in the world. Equally important is the manner in which Ana and the other full-figured women address the pressure they feel to conform to the socially prescribed "ideal" thin body images that surround them in their daily lives.

The movie version of *Real Women Have Curves* was directed by Patricia Cordoso, produced by George LaVoo, and distributed by New Market Films. After seeing the play in 1998, LaVoo approached López with the idea of adapting it to film. Together they wrote the screenplay, which was produced in Los Angeles in 2001 by HBO Films on a budget of $3 million. After its favorable reception at its January 13, 2002, premiere at the Sundance Film Festival, the film, which was originally intended for release on HBO, was instead opened in theaters. Released as a limited-run film on October 18, 2002, *Real Women Have Curves* expanded in less than a month to approximately 150 theaters nationwide. Despite its limited film distribution, the film grossed over $3 million in its first six weeks. The film won the prestigious Audience Award for Best Dramatic Feature at the 2002 Sundance Film Festival, and cast members Ferrera and Lupe *Ontiveros received a Special Jury Prize for Acting. The cast also includes Ingrid Oliu, George *López, Soledad St. Hilaire, Brian Sites, Sandie Torres, Lourdes Pérez, and Jorge Cervera, Jr.

Daniel Enríque Pérez

Rechy, John (1934–   ). John Rechy is an important *Chicano writer who has helped shape the development of postwar American literature. Touted in the late twentieth century as the first openly gay writer to publish an overtly gay American novel (*City of Night*, published by Grove Press in 1963) in the United States, he is recognized nationally and internationally for the pioneering contributions he has made to gay American literature. Even though he identified himself throughout his life as both gay and Mexican American, book reviewers and literary scholars tended to focus on only his sexual identity or, on occasion, his ethnicity but rarely on both as integrated parts of his reality. His unflinching attention to marginalized people in nearly all his writings deserves recognition within Chicana and Chicano literature. Indeed, he used a Spanish-language title for his very first publication, "El Paso del Norte" (El Paso of the North, 1958), an essay on his hometown that was published in the national English-language magazine *Evergreen* and addressed racism against Latinas/os in another essay, "Jim Crow Wears a Sombrero," published in *The Nation* in 1959.

Born in El Paso, Texas, to Guadalupe Flores de Rechy and Roberto Sixto Rechy, he grew up on the border and spoke Spanish as his native language, acquiring English only after he started school. His parents were Mexican, and his father was of Scottish descent. Both fled their respective homes in separate parts of México with their families during different stages of the Mexican Revolution (1910–1916). They established their lives across the border from their homeland in El Paso, where they eventually met, married, and reared John. Rechy wanted to be a writer since boyhood, and he began his first novel at age eight. By the age of thirteen, he had discovered two of his later themes, the painful underside of high school for adolescents who don't fit in and the concept and process of confession. The future author obtained his B.A. from Texas Western College in El Paso and then joined the army, where he served briefly. After being released from the army, he attended the New School for Social Research in New York City, where the hard-edged urban perspective seen in his fictions was further sharpened.

Rechy's first publication, "Mardi Gras," began as a letter and ended up a short story published in the then highly prestigious *Evergreen Review* (1958). His second published story, "The Fabulous Wedding of Miss Destiny," received the Longview Foundation Fiction Prize in 1961 and also attracted favorable notice from reviewers. Its strong reception led him to include it nearly intact in his first and most successful novel, *City of Night* (1963), whose huge success was unexpected. A national and international bestseller, *City of Night* has been acclaimed as one of the most important gay novels of its time and Rechy's greatest achievement. The novel's sensational appeal was international and led to its being translated into over twenty different languages. Concerned with the hip, fast-lane life of male prostitution, *City of Night* is narrated in the first person by a Chicano protagonist and presents a bold account of the mid-twentieth century's urban erotic underworld throughout the United States.

Rechy went on to publish twelve novels, other articles and essays, and a couple of plays. Centering on gay themes, the majority of his novels remained in print for decades and include such titles as *Numbers* (1967), *This Day's Death* (1970), *The Sexual Outlaw: A Documentary* (1977), *Rushes* (1979), *Our Lady of Babylon* (1996), and *The Coming of the Night* (1999). Novels written by Rechy on other topics include *The Vampires* (1971), *The Fourth Angel* (1972), *Bodies and Souls* (1983), *Marilyn's Daughter* (1988), and *The Miraculous Day of Amalia Gómez* (1991). Except for *Numbers* and *The Sexual Outlaw*, which were bestsellers, none of his novels has achieved the remarkable commercial and critical renown of *City of Night*. Virtually all his novels include gay and Chicano characters—a fact often overlooked by many readers. Subjected to harsh criticism and neglect for his graphic depiction of homoerotic themes, Rechy was finally given serious literary respect by Chicano scholars in 1979 reassessment essays by Charles Tatum, Carlos Zamora, and Juan Bruce-Novoa in the journal *Minority Voices*. These writers rejected strict definitions of what constitutes Chicano literature and opened the door to acknowledgment and appreciation of his contributions to the popular culture genre of gay and Chicano fiction in the Chicano literary canon of the late 1980s and early 1990s.

Despite the controversy regarding Rechy's contributions to American literature, his writing's impact on creating and influencing gay male identities cannot be ignored. His work represents a paradigm shift in gay American literature during the 1960s through its representation of an array of unique images of gay men, bisexuals, transvestites, transsexuals, hustlers, and related images of homoerotica. For this important form-shaping role to several generations of gay men, he has become a major gay icon, receiving numerous prizes for his writing. In 1997 he became the first novelist to receive the PEN-USA West's Lifetime Achievement Award, and in 1999 he received the Publishing Triangle's William Whitehead Lifetime Achievement Award.

His most recent project, *Mysteries and Desire: Searching the Worlds of John Rechy*, is an interactive CD-ROM he coproduced in 2000. The CD-ROM is a collection of memoirs, family documents, photographs, taped interviews, video, and other things related to Rechy's life and Chicano and gay culture in general. He also continues to work on his long-awaited autobiography titled *Autobiography, a Novel*. Despite his success and many homages received, his writing continues to generate controversy, especially regarding issues of ethnicity, race, and sexuality. In between the publications of his books, Rechy has taught film and creative writing at Occidental College, the University of Southern California, and the University of California, Los Angeles. He currently resides in Los Angeles, where he continues to teach writing workshops privately and through the University of Southern California.

Further Reading

Bredbeck, Gregory. "John Rechy." In *Contemporary Gay American Novelists: A Bio-Bibliographical Critical Sourcebook*, edited by Emmanuel Nelson. Westport, CT: Greenwood Press, 1993.

Bruce-Novoa, Juan. "In Search of the Honest Outlaw: John Rechy." *Minority Voices* 3.1 (Fall 1979): 37–45.

Castillo, Debra. "Outlaw Aesthetics: John Rechy Interview." *Diacritics* 25.1 (1995): 113–125.

Chávez, John. "Rechy, John Francisco." In *Chicano Literature: A Reference Guide*, edited by Julio A. Martínez and Francisco A. Lomelí. Westport, CT: Greenwood Press, 1985.

Jaén, Didier. "John Rechy." In *Chicano Writers Second Series*, edited by Francisco Lomelí and Carl Shirley. Detroit, MI: Gale Research, 1992.

Rechy, John. "Autobiography: A Novel." *Diacritics* 25.1 (1995): 126–130.

Rechy, John. "On Being a 'Grove Press Author.'" *Review of Contemporary Fiction* 10.3 (1990): 137–142.

Daniel Enríque Pérez

Recording Industry and Studios in the Southwest Borderlands.

The *Chicano music industry, from its inception in the 1940s until the present, has been and continues to be vital to the Latina/o music scene in the United States, yet little has been written on the subject. The focus here is on record companies that were Chicano owned and/or operated and produced music by primarily Chicano musicians for Chicano audiences. Until the 1950s very little music fit into this category. In the 1920s and 1930s only a few Chicano artists recorded for major labels, including Lydia Mendoza, Narciso Martínez, and Santiago Jiménez; during World War II very little music was recorded. Few, if any, musicians recorded for Chicano-owned companies until the late 1940s when a number of Chicano pioneers established independent record labels, first in Texas and later in other border states. They shaped the course of Chicano music in the post–World War II era. For example, Armando Marroquín, owner of Ideal Records and other companies, owned a jukebox business in Alice, Texas, but was frustrated by the unavailability of Chicano records. He started a record company out of his home that developed into one of the largest companies in Texas and helped establish the *Tejano music industry. The signing of many Tejano artists to major labels beginning in the mid-1980s would not have been possible if the independent Chicano-owned record companies had never existed.

Small independent companies came into being in the 1940s because the major record companies ignored most Chicano musicians. These entrepreneurs produced music that was regionally popular and sometimes reached audiences throughout the Southwest United States and México and at times acted as a "feeder" of talent for major record companies. The popular Tejana singer *Selena is a good example. She recorded for a number of independent Texas labels before signing with EMI in 1989 and reaching international popularity. The same is to some extent true for numerous other artists in both Texas and California, including *Little Joe, Mazz, La Mafia, *Los Lobos, *Los Tigres del Norte, and Flaco *Jiménez.

Many of the companies targeted their record releases to specific audiences. Thus, the intended audience for a record might be second- and third-generation Chicano teenagers who liked rock and roll and soul (e.g., Sunny and the Sunliners on Teardrop; Thee Midniters on Whittier), rural Tejanos who enjoyed accordion-based *conjunto* music (e.g., Narciso Martínez on Ideal), first-generation Mexicano immigrants who wanted *rancheras and *boleros (e.g., Lydia Mendoza and Chelo Silva on Falcon), middle-class Mexican Americans who danced to *orquesta* music (e.g., Beto Villa on Ideal), New Mexico residents who wanted homegrown *música norteña* and *cumbias (e.g., Al Hurricane and his brothers on Hurricane), and many other categories of music, including gospel, country, and *banda*, that illustrate the diversity of the Chicano community.

There have been literally hundreds of companies that released 78s, 45s, long-playing albums, 8-track and cassette tapes, and compact discs. Only a few of the larger and more important labels are mentioned here. The focus is on companies that were influential in a particular geographical area or time period in the Chicano community. Musicians have owned a number of recording companies, both large and small. For example, Freddie Records (owned by the singer Freddie Martínez) of Corpus Christi has developed into a profitable enterprise since its founding in the late 1960s. Many other musicians and other local entrepreneurs produced one or a few records on their own, but few reached the longevity of Freddie Records, Falcon Records in McAllen, Texas, Joey Records in San Antonio, or Hurricane and Alta Vista Records in Albuquerque. While most companies have been in the Southwest, there are exceptions. For example, Nestor Gómez recorded an album with a *mariachi band on Tepeyac Records in Chicago where he lived for many years.

A serious problem for independent companies, especially the smaller ones, has been getting their music played on the radio, artist exposure on television, booking live performances and tours, and distribution to retail outlets, particularly in regions outside their local area. While Mexican-owned radio stations on the border began playing Lydia Mendoza and a few other Chicano artists in the 1930s, there was only limited Spanish-language programming in the United States. The first radio station wholly owned by a Chicano did not exist until the 1940s, and while the number of stations with Spanish-language programming continued to steadily increase in the following decades, especially with the advent of both AM and FM programming, it was only in the 1980s and 1990s that there have been huge profits and a substantial market share for stations playing music sung in Spanish.

In sum, the genesis of today's multimillion-dollar radio industry had its beginning in the Spanish-language programs that were only heard a few hours per day or week in a small number of locales. The story is similar for television. In the 1950s and 1960s there were few Spanish-language broadcasts in the United States, and it was common for English-language stations to sell time for part-time Spanish-language shows, often during off-peak hours. Popular early television shows included the *Fandango* program on KNXT in Los Angeles and the *Fiesta Méxicana* show hosted by Johnny Gonzáles, the owner of El Zarape Records, on KTVT in Dallas/Fort Worth. Typical for the 1960s, the latter show was on Sundays for one hour. In the first decade of the twenty-first century the situation is very different. There is extensive Spanish-language programming on numerous channels, and giant networks such as Univision and Telemundo, not to mention Spanish-language stations available on cable from other countries. The changes in radio and television have meant much more exposure for Chicano artists, but this has benefited artists signed to major labels much more than artists on independent labels.

The venues have also changed. While many artists continue to play the halls, clubs, and bars of the Southwest, other artists, especially with the larger independent companies such as Freddie or Joey in Texas, and artists signed to major record labels play in huge nightclubs, major concert halls, and arenas, sometimes to tens of thousands of people. Gone are the days when there was often only one major venue in a city, such as the Million Dollar Theatre in Los Angeles or the Calderon Ballroom in Phoenix, where touring musicians could play. While distribution remains a problem, especially for the smaller companies, the larger independents are now able to place their product in the major retail chains, not to mention distribution in México and other Spanish-speaking countries.

Until the 1950s there were few record stores per se, and records were sold in a wide variety of locations. An example of an early store in the 1950s was the Rio Record Shop in San Antonio. Today, a popular store in San Antonio is Janie's. For many years in Albuquerque there has been Cristy Records, and there is also Alta Vista Records in Albuquerque and Merlin's in Santa Fe. Independent companies still find it difficult to get their records distributed, and the Chicano community often must rely on small Chicano-owned stores or the artists themselves to purchase the music. Thus, as in the past, independent companies are dependent on local record stores to stock their product. The same goes for radio and television where, as in the 1950s and 1960s, label owners and artists have to make personal contacts to get their music played on Spanish-language programs. The changes and growth of the Chicano music industry can also be seen in *Billboard*, the industry's major magazine, which devotes substantial attention to Chicano/Latino music and has published a book on Tejano and regional Mexican music. There is also the *Latin Grammys, the Tejano Music Award, and the Conjunto Festival held in San Antonio each year.

From the 1940s through the 1990s, many labels came and went. In addition, many singers and groups recorded for multiple labels both in the United States and in México. The following paragraphs list some of the most influential record companies and a few selected artists associated with that label.

Influential companies in San Antonio included Sunglow Records (Sunglows, Los Aguilares); Tear Drop (Sunny and the Sunliners, Charlie and the Jives, Rudy Gonzáles y sus Reno Bops, Rocky Gil and the Bishops); Key-Loc (Sunny and the Sunliners); Disco Grande (Gilbert and the Blue Notes); Magda/Marsal Productions (Los Pavos Reales, Ramón Ayala, Los Tremendos Gavilanes); GCP (owned by well-known producer Manny Guerra—Latin Breed, Jimmy Edward), Cara (owned by Bob Grever, the most powerful record company owner in Texas during the 1980s—La Mafia, Mazz); Joey International and Dina (Nick Villarreal, Lisa López, Los Hermanos García); Sombrero/Norteño (Lydia Mendoza).

Outside San Antonio, prominent Texas record labels include Falcon and ARV (Lydia Mendoza, Freddy *Fender, Rene and Rene, Tortilla Factory, Los Alegres de Terán, and many other artists); Ideal (Beto Villa, Isidro Lopez); Bernal and Bego (owned by influential accordionist Paulino Bernal—Conjunto Bernal, Los Dinos, Pedro Ayala, Tony De La Rosa, Los Relampagos del Norte); El Zarape (Little Joe and the Latinaires, Augustine Ramírez, Alfonso Ramos); Buena Suerte (Little Joe and the Latinaires, Little Joe y La Familia, Bobby "El Charro Negro" Butler); Freddie (Freddie Martinez, Ramón Ayala, Roberto Pulido, Joe Bravo, Jaime y Los Chamacos); and Hacienda (Isidro Lopez, Valerio Longoria, Steve Jordan, Romance, Lisa López, Ruben Vela).

Important companies from Albuquerque, New Mexico, include Hurricane (Al Hurricane, Baby Gaby, and Tiny Morrie Sánchez); MORE—Minority Owned Records (Debbie "La Chicanita" Martínez, Lorenzo Martínez); Cristy (Eddie Dimas, Freddie Brown); Alta Vista (Purple Haze, Pablo Gallegos); M.B. Norteño (Max Baca). There were at least a couple of small companies in Arizona that produced records by Mariachi Cobre and Los Changitos Feos.

There were/are many record companies in California, especially in the Los Angeles area. Music was produced for both the U.S. and Mexican markets, and many records have been aimed at the huge Mexican and Central American immigrant communities. Companies include Fama (Los Tigres del

Norte, Brown Express); Ambiente (Lalo *Guerrero—the "godfather" of Chicano music in California), New Vista (Los Lobos—their first album in 1978), Billionaire (Jonny Chingas); Whittier (Thee Midniters); Rampart (The Village Callers, Eastside Connection); Thump (albums of oldies music for *Lowrider* magazine). The Fresno-based bandleader Ray Camacho owned California Artists Corporation, which produced albums by Ray Camacho and the Teardrops, and the Tucson-based Love LTD. There were also records produced for the Farm Workers Union and the *Chicano Movement. Companies include Thunderbird (Viva La Causa: songs and sounds from the Delano Strike); El Centro Campesino Cultural (Huelga en General! Songs of the United Farmworkers by El *Teatro Campesino); Bilingual Media Productions (José-Luis Orozco); Xalman (Alma Chicana de Aztlán). In the 1990s there was a proliferation of *narcocorridos* (songs about drug smuggling), and *banda/technobanda* music. While much of this music has been on major labels, there continues to be a proliferation of artists on independent labels, often owned by the artists.

Although large corporate-owned major record companies have dominated Chicano music since the 1980s, independent record companies continue to exist and sometimes thrive, although often for a short period of time. As in the past, it is difficult to get distribution, radio and television airplay, and extensive bookings unless you are one of the "majors." Factors that explain why Chicano-owned independent companies continue to exist include regional differences in musical tastes, changing musical tastes that are initially or permanently overlooked by larger companies, and economy of scale (a local band may only be able to sell 500 to 1,000 of their CDs at their shows or in local outlets).

Further Reading

Burr, Ramiro. *The Billboard Guide to Tejano and Regional Mexican Music*. New York: Billboard Books, 1999.

Fowler, Gene, and Bill Crawford. *Border Radio*. Austin: University of Texas Press, 2002.

Loza, Steven. *Barrio Rhythm: Mexican American Music in Los Angeles*. Urbana: University of Illinois Press, 1993.

Peña, Manuel. *The Mexican American Orquesta*. Austin: University of Texas Press, 1999.

Peña, Manuel. *Música Tejana*. College Station: Texas A&M Press, 1999.

Reyes, David, and Tom Waldman. *Land of a Thousand Dances: Chicano Rock 'n' Roll from Southern California*. Albuquerque: University of New Mexico Press, 1998.

Tatum, Charles. *Chicano Popular Culture*. Tucson: University of Arizona Press, 2001.

Louis M. Holscher

Relajo. A common phrase used by Chicana/os, *relajo* can be defined as causing disorder or having a lack of seriousness, is derived from the verb *relajar* (to relax), and is similar to the slang "slacker." *Relajo* can be perceived as a behavior consisting of a series of actions, such as gesticulations, laughter, and unarticulated noises. This behavior is mostly observable among friends and family where a bond of unity is created inside the group. In Mexican society, *relajo* is a form of criticizing the political corruption occurring in its government but is also a way to ridicule the differences and separation between the social classes. It is also a way of joking or mocking serious issues that may be seen as socially unacceptable in other circumstances. Through *relajo* one is temporarily relieved of social constraints and the creation of a low-tension environment is established, thus allowing one to feel more at ease.

Further Reading

Gran Diccionario Enciclopedico Ilustrado. Vol. 10. Mexico City: Reader's Digest México, 1979.

Portilla, Jorge. *Fenomenología del Relajo*. Mexico City: Ediciones Era, 1996.

Mónica Saldaña

Resolana. *Resolana* refers to the practice of New Mexico grassroots village dialogue that often produces folk wisdom and usually fosters tight social networks, especially among Mexican American men. The word derives from *resol*, the glare or reflection of the sun that in common speech refers to the sunny side of buildings where villagers in northern New Mexico gather to talk, protected from the elements in the warm sunshine. Coined and popularized by Tomás Atencio, a New Mexico–born *Chicano philosopher, *resolana* is used as a metaphor for enlightenment and social engagement through the stories, gossip, politics, brotherhood, and reflection it encourages. The metaphor is thus one of countless Latina and Latino practices at the grassroots community level that underlie the lasting *folklore and vibrant popular culture of the United States.

Many Chicana and Chicano intellectuals have noted a disharmony between majority Anglo values and behaviors and those of Chicano values. They describe the majority Caucasian side as primarily instrumental or goal oriented, legitimized by dominant society, and systematic in operation. Conversely, they see the other Chicana/o side as primarily moral or value centered, nonlegitimized by the larger society, and operationally unsystematic. This viewpoint explains Chicano values as linked to myth—a world picture told through stories that ascribe meaning to the universe. The *resolana* occurs as individuals gather to talk, and a spiral of thought and action evolves and shifts back and forth from the individual to the group. This give and take of ideas leads to a body of knowledge developed from everyday experience that is documented, objectified, and shared to provide a basis for action. For example, one of the earliest published uses of the *resolana* concept is documented in the first publication of *Agenda: A Journal of Hispanic Issues*, published by the *National Council of La Raza in the 1970s. It is also reflected in *El Cuaderno*, a journal occasionally published in Dixon, New Mexico, by *La Académica de la Nuevo Raza* (New Race Academy) at the height of the *Chicano Movement. The concept has also been used in projects investigating issues of family, culture, community, organizations, leaders and followers, the generation gap, and men and women, as well as on an environmental project in Albuquerque, New Mexico, and on an exploration of Hispanic issues in American universities.

The *resolana* reinforces the notion of dialogue as a flowing stream of meaning. Its key is the willingness to divulge and share assumptions and opinions about the world, and its importance is that it facilitates coherent thought as well as the ability for people to engage and work together in authentic ways. The responsibility of the participants is to be open and free of prejudices and suspend judgment while stories are shared. The responsibility of the group leader is to document and share the stories, thus continuing the spiral of thought and action. As a result, individuals are stronger when they work collectively toward a common vision and achieve consensual validation. The *resolana* thereby derives its thought and actions from its evolved knowledge and folk wisdom, that is, *el oro del barrio* (the gold of the community).

Further Reading

Atencio, T. "Resolana: A Chicano Pathway to Knowledge." Ernesto Galarza Commemorative Lecture: 3rd Annual Lecture. Stanford Center for Chicano Research, Stanford, CA, 1988.

Bohm, David. *On Dialogue*. Cambridge, MA: Pegasus Communications, 1990.

Padilla, Raymond, and Miguel Montiel. *Debatable Diversity: Critical Dialogues on Change in American Universities*. Lanham, MD: Rowman & Littlefield, 1998.

Suazo, Mark. "Mobilizing in Defense of Community: A Case Study of the Sawmill Advisory Council." Master's thesis, University of New Mexico, 2002.

Miguel Montiel

Resurrection Blvd. Premiering on Showtime in June 2000, *Resurrection Blvd.* was a pioneering Latino-themed drama that balanced comedy with tragedy and depictions of violent street life with everyday *family life. The show ran three consecutive seasons and played a total of fifty-three episodes before ending in September 2002. To its credit, *Resurrection Blvd.* featured primarily Latino actors and actresses and employed mainly Latino writers, costume designers, directors, and crew members.

The series follows the lives of the Santiagos, a multigeneration middle-class family trying to live out their dreams in contemporary East Los Angeles under the watchful eye of the patriarch, Roberto Santiago. The dramatic action revolves around family conflicts, including that of son and father, and the way each character copes with the mishaps of life. For example, there is Carlos Santiago's hope of realizing his dream of becoming a champion boxer—largely to help realize his father's dreams, which were dashed by

Roberto's stint in Vietnam. In another episode, a character named Tommy Corrales (Douglas Spain), the son of Paco (Esai *Morales) and Bibi Corrales (Elizabeth *Peña) tells his macho, ex-convict father that he is gay, an announcement that leads to violence and eventually to reconciliation. There is also the struggle of the new-generation Chicana characters as they face sexism in school and work while seeking to move up career ladders. Yolanda studies law and is preparing to get married when her fiancé is killed by hoodlums in a store robbery. Her younger sister Victoria finds a job at a Beverly Hills boutique and falls for a record producer, who makes love to her and then tires of her after a few weeks. And then there is their Aunt Bibi, who goes through financial difficulties and is forced to close her beauty shop because the building has been sold; but her perseverance and endurance lead her first to cut hair from her home and later to manage the club Máscaras (Masks), a Latin music restaurant and nightclub. She typifies the three main female characters in this series, who stand for intelligence, compassion, care, fortitude, empathy, and endurance.

The Latino drama series was directed by Jesús Salvador Treviño and produced by series creator Dennis E. Leoni. The cast includes Tony Plana (as Roberto Santiago), Daniel Zacapa (as Rubén Santiago), Mauricio Mendoza (as Miguel Santiago), Esai Morales (as Paco Corrales), Elizabeth Peña (as Aunt Bibi), Michael DeLorenzo (as Carlos Santiago), Ruth Livier (as Yolanda Santiago), Marisol Nichols (as Victoria Santiago), Nicholás González (as Alex Santiago), Cheech *Marín (as Héctor Archuletta), and Louis Gossett, Jr. (as Ezekiel "Zeke" Grant).

Luis Aldama

Retablos. *Retablos* (religious paintings) are two-dimensional paintings, usually on tin or copper, depicting religious figures such as *santos* (saints) or biblical scenes, a tradition that dates from at least the middle eighteenth centuries in the Southwest borderlands. Made by trained artists, the *retablos* gained a widespread popularity in central México and were later brought north to what is now the Southwest, including New Mexico, Texas, and California. When tin became available in the 1800s, the art prospered and works were occasionally painted by anonymous *retablo* artisans, many of whom employed the baroque style popular in Mexico City. *Retablos* were also purchased from artists and peddlers, who presented them on a door-to-door basis, as well as by selling them in stands that were in place near the church.

From the 1600s to the 1900s, *retablos* were painted on pine wood or animal hides smoothed on one side and covered with gesso and ground with bright colors. Many dyes and pigments were made from plants and dirt, as well as colors imported from México. Often the *retablos* are painted for a specific saint in gratitude for a favor granted, or praising the saint's powers, especially following the survival or restored health following an illness, operation, imprisonment, or human struggle. Many *retablos* depict the survivor praying to the saint and often include expressions of gratitude for requests granted, such as "Doy Gracias" (I Give Thanks), with a brief explanation why the *retablo* was painted and the date and location where it was created. A *retablo ex-voto* (Latin "from a vow") is created to fulfill a vow made to a saint. A brief message, commonly at the bottom of the *retablo*, explains the event portrayed and includes the name of the person expressing gratitude and the date.

Most recently, there has been an upsurge of *retablos* that reflect the immigrant and border-crossing experiences and the miracles involved with having a safe passage to the United States. Arguably one of the most important books on *retablos* was written in 1974 and titled *Mexican Folk Retablos* by author and painting conservator Gloria Fraser Giffords.

Further Reading

Giffords, Gloria Fraser. *Mexican Folk Retablos*. 1974. Albuquerque: University of New Mexico Press, 1998.
"Retablos." *Nuevo Santander Gallery*. http://www.nuevosantander.com/retablo.htm.
"Retablos." *Saints & Martyrs*. http://www.saints-martyrs.com/retablos.

Armando Quintero, Jr.

Reyes, Guillermo (1962–). A prolific and accomplished U.S. Latino playwright, Guillermo Reyes also has made significant contributions to Latina/o popular culture as a director, as a professor of *theater at Arizona State University, where he currently heads the playwriting program, and as the cofounder and artistic director of Phoenix's Teatro Bravo theater company. Well known for his plays centering on *gender and sexuality within *Chicano/Latino culture, among his best-known titles are *Men on the Verge of a His-Panic Breakdown* (1994), *The Hispanick Zone* (1998), and *Places to Touch Him* (2002). His awards include the Emerging Playwright Award from Urban Stages (1996) and the Bay Area Drama-Logue Award (1996) for playwriting.

Reyes was born on February 20, 1962, in Mulchén, Chile, to María Graciela Cáceres. Growing up in Chile, he lived next to a movie theater, which he frequented, and the movies he saw then played an important role in his artistic development, producing his keen admiration for the art of storytelling and for using the screen as a stage. In 1971, he immigrated with his mother to the United States, where they made their home in the Hollywood area. Upon completing high school, Reyes attended the University of California at Los Angeles, where he obtained a Bachelor of Arts in Italian; he later earned a Master of Fine Arts in playwriting from the University of California at San Diego.

Reyes's numerous plays have been well received by both critics and general audiences. Many of them have been widely anthologized and produced throughout the United States. These include *Deporting the Divas* (1996) and *Men on the Verge of a His-Panic Breakdown* (1994). His other titles include

Chilean playwright Guillermo Reyes is also cofounder of Teatro Bravo, one of the few bilingual repertory companies in the country. *Courtesy of Guillermo Reyes.*

The Seductions of Johnny Diego (1990), *The West Hollywood Affair* (1991), *Chilean Holiday* (1996), *Miss Consuelo* (1997), *The Hispanick Zone* (1998), *A Southern Christmas* (1999), *Mother Lolita* (2000), *Sirena, Queen of the Tango* (2001), *Places to Touch Him* (2002), and the Spanish-language *Amores ajenos* (Someone Else's Love, 2003). Reyes has won several awards for his works including the Ovation Award for Best World Premiere Play, in 1994, and the Emerging Playwright Award from Urban Stages, the New York Outer Critics' Circle Award for Best Solo Performance in New York, and the Bay Area Drama-Logue for Playwriting for *Deporting the Divas*. In 1997 he won the National Hispanic Playwrights Contest for *A Southern Christmas*, and in 1998 he received the NOSOTROS (WE) Theater of Los Angeles Playwriting Award for *The Hispanick Zone*. He was awarded an AriZoni in Phoenix in 2000 for directing *Men on the Verge* and another in 2002 for writing *Miss Consuelo*. In 2000, Reyes cofounded and became the artistic director of Teatro Bravo, a Phoenix-based commercial company, dedicated to producing Latino-themed plays and to fostering the professional and creative development of emerging Latino theater professionals.

Further Reading

http://www.getoutaz.com/arts/places0915.shtml.
http://www.ptnj.org/Bios/playwrights.htm.
http://www.tucsonweekly.com/tw/1999-07-15/review2.html.

Daniel Enríque Pérez

Richardson, Bill (1947–   ). Elected governor of New Mexico in 2002, William Blaine Richardson has held the greatest number of significant political and public offices of any Latino in U.S. history. In this light, he represents an important part of the legacy of previous Latina and Latino political and historical leaders and civic servants, and he inhabits America's popular culture domain of media celebrity as a spokesperson for Latina/o and other public issues. Prior to his current governorship, the Mexican Anglo leader held two cabinet-level positions in Bill Clinton's presidential administration (1992–2000)—U.S. ambassador to the United Nations and later Secretary of Energy. Richardson, a Democrat, also was elected to the U.S. Congress as representative from New Mexico's third district. Along with these political distinctions, he is listed in the *Guinness Book of World Records* for the most handshakes made in a day, shaking approximately 8,500 during his first run for Congress. His other honors include receiving the prestigious Aztec Golden Eagle Award, México's highest honor awarded to noncitizens, and being nominated four times for the Nobel Peace Prize for his numerous diplomatic efforts while ambassador to the United Nations, as well as for his special international troubleshooting assignments on behalf of President Clinton and in 2002 for President George W. Bush, a Republican.

Born on November 15, 1947, in Pasadena, California, Richardson grew up in an affluent household in Mexico City with his Mexican socialite mother and his American banker father. He attended Tufts University, where he received his bachelor's degree before continuing to earn a master's degree in 1971 from Tufts' Fletcher School of Law and Diplomacy. Richardson's political career began in 1980 when he ran unsuccessfully for election as New Mexico's representative to the Ninety-seventh Congress of the United States. Charged with being a carpetbagger since he lacked any long-term ties with the state, Richardson said that he moved to New Mexico because of its "Anglo-Latin ethnic stew" and joked that he was a perfect candidate to represent the state because of his Anglo surname, his Spanish/English bilingual ability, and his Indian appearance. He pursued the office again in 1983 and was elected to the Ninety-eighth Congress as a Democrat from New Mexico's third district. Many political scientists have written that his election was especially challenging because New Mexico's third district is considered one of the most diverse in the nation with its triethnic constituency of 44 percent Anglos, 34 percent Hispanics, and 20 percent American Indians.

Richardson was reelected to his congressional seat seven times, each victory occurring with a remarkable 60 percent of the vote total. During his congressional tenure he served as Chief Deputy Democratic Whip and was an active member of the House Commerce, Resources, and Intelligence Committees. Many observers credit his success in elective office and politics as partly due to his energetic interaction with his home constituency, as witnessed by his holding more than 2,000 town hall meetings in New Mexico during his fourteen-year congressional tenure.

On December 13, 1996, President Clinton nominated Representative Richardson to be U.S. Permanent Representative to the United Nations, and he was sworn to office in early 1997. Before, during, and after Richardson's tenure at the United Nations he was asked to address numerous international diplomatic negotiations and to troubleshoot several crises. Ambassador Richardson was credited specifically with freeing hostages and prisoners from

Croatia, Burma, Cuba, Iraq, North Korea, and Sudan. Further, he negotiated the peaceful transfer of power in the former Zaire, known today as the Democratic Republic of the Congo. During his ambassadorship he also helped to build a coalition at the UN Security Council that authorized use of military force against Iraq for its continued defiance of UN sanctions, an accomplishment achieved years prior to the joint U.S. and Great Britain invasion of Iraq in 2003. As a result of Richardson's high-profile diplomacy and relentless efforts to promote peace around the world, he has been nominated for a Nobel Peace Prize on four separate occasions.

On June 18, 1998, President Clinton nominated Ambassador Bill Richardson to be his secretary of the U.S. Department of Energy, and he was unanimously confirmed by the Senate as the new secretary of energy that same year. Secretary Richardson thus became the highest-ranking Latino in the Clinton administration and the first person from New Mexico to serve as Secretary of Energy. In that position, he tackled such problems as environmental protections, gas and oil usage and prices, security breaches at nuclear weapons laboratories, and other pressing issues. He repeatedly emphasized the importance of environmental responsibility and placed it at the forefront of his agenda, which sought the implementation of oil and gas technologies that would allow for the reduction of dependence on foreign resources. As secretary he also championed the concerns of energy industry workers, including asking Congress to provide compensation for the first time to Energy Department employees who fell ill due to their work. In addition, he made it a priority of his administration to make two-thirds of his appointments to women and minorities to redress decades of exclusionary hiring practices.

Shortly after leaving his cabinet position as energy secretary in 2001 Richardson accepted a teaching appointment at the Kennedy School of Government at Harvard University, serving as an adjunct lecturer for two semesters. For his classes he drew from his extensive experience within national and international political and diplomatic realms. Besides teaching at Harvard, Richardson also lectured in his home state at the United World College in Montezuma, New Mexico. During this period he also served as chairman of Freedom House, a private, nonpartisan organization dedicated to promoting democracy around the world, and served on various boards including the Natural Resource Defense Council and United Way International.

Returning to elective politics, Richardson officially announced his candidacy for governor of New Mexico in January 2002. He again demonstrated his energetic personal style of constituency engagement by shaking 13,392 hands in an eight-hour period during his campaign, gaining him another world record that beat that of President Theodore Roosevelt's set on his inauguration day in 1907. On November 5, 2002, he was elected governor of New Mexico by the largest margin of any candidate since 1964. His bipartisan victory was unprecedented in the state, and he took office January 1,

2003. In the escalated post–September 11 tensions associated with U.S. foreign policy, Governor Richardson served the Bush administration by agreeing to open talks with the North Korean government about their nuclear weapons. Richardson's over-two-decades-long political career has enjoyed many successes and shows considerable promise for the future.

Further Reading

http://www.governor.state.nm.us/richardsonbio.html.
http://www.infoplease.com/spot/hhmbio3.html.
http://www.ksg.harvard.edu/press/releases/2001/bill_richardson.htm.

Cristina K. Muñoz

Rinches, Los. *See* Texas Rangers.

Ríos, Alberto (1952–   ). A Regents Professor at Arizona State University in Tempe, Alberto Alvaro Ríos is better known as a poet and short fiction writer of over a dozen books and recipient of numerous literary awards, including being a finalist for the 2003 American Book Award for Poetry for *The Smallest Muscle in the Human Body* (2002). His other celebrated books include *Pig Cookies and Other Stories* (1995), *Teodora Luna's Two Kisses: Poems* (1990), *The Iguana Killer: Twelve Stories of the Heart* (1984), and *Whispering to Fool the Wind: Poems* (1982). Among his numerous prizes are the Academy of Poetry's 1983 Walt Whitman Award for his first volume, *Whispering to Fool the Wind*, and the 1984 Western States Book Award for *Iguana Killer*.

Often mistaken for a Chicano, Ríos is actually the son of Agnes Fogg Ríos and Alberto Alvaro Ríos, an English mother and a Guatemalan father. His mother was a nurse and his father a justice of the peace. The future poet did experience a cultural Mexican American *barrios and borderlands childhood, growing up in Nogales, Arizona, where he was born on September 18, 1952, and where he attended local public schools. Many friends and neighbors thought of him as Mexican American, like the majority of Hispanics in the community. After high school he attended the University of Arizona in nearby Tucson and graduated with a Bachelor of Arts in English literature in 1974. He tried law school for a year (1975–1976), also at the University of Arizona, but shifted course and earned an MFA in Creative Writing in 1979.

Ríos has published his poetry in over 100 journals and magazines, and much of his work has been translated into French, German, Italian, Japanese, and several other languages. His writings have been published in over ninety major literary anthologies, including the prestigious *Norton Anthology of Modern Poetry*. As well, some of his poems have been arranged for musical performance, and two of his compositions have been staged (his story "And Then They Watched Comedies" and his drama *Rossetti's Smile*). Among his subjects and themes are the binational, bicultural experience of

Arizona native Alberto Ríos is an award-winning poet and short fiction writer. *Courtesy of Lupita Barron-Ríos.*

the U.S.-México border and intercultural and intergenerational communication, as well as the Chicana/o adolescent struggle of growing up as an alambrista, a tightrope walker teetering on the border of two cultures in constant interanimation, producing other hybridities. He illuminates the delights, challenges, secrets, and conflicts of the border, always proposing creative and compelling resolutions and compromises for the superficialities that separate people from their true communities.

His other books are *Capirotada: A Nogales Memoir* (1999); *The Curtain of Trees: Stories* (1999); *The Lime Orchard Woman: Poems* (1988); *Five Indiscretions: A Book of Poems* (1985); and the chapbooks *Elk Heads on the Wall* (1979) and *Sleeping on Fists* (1981). He appeared in *Birthwrite: Growing Up Hispanic*, a well-received PBS documentary, and he has written and performed commissioned work for the inauguration of Janet Napolitano, Governor of the State of Arizona, and on the occasion of the visit of President Vicente Fox of México to Arizona. His other awards and recognition include six Pushcart Prizes for poetry and also for fiction, the Arizona Governor's Arts Award, a Guggenheim Fellowship, an NEA Fellowship for the Arts, and the 2002 Western Literature Association's Distinguished Achievement Award. A popular speaker and reader, Ríos is acknowledged to be one of the most outstanding poets in the Americas.

Further Reading

Riggs, Thomas. "Alberto Alvaro Ríos." In *Contemporary Poets*. 7th ed. Detroit, MI: St. James Press, 2001.

Ríos, Alberto Alvaro. *Capirotada: A Nogales Memoir*. Albuquerque: University of New Mexico Press, 1999.

Wild, Peter. *Alberto Ríos*. Boise, ID: Boise State University, 1998.

Wilson, Kathleen, ed. "Alberto (Alvaro) Ríos." In *Contemporary Authors, New Revision Series*, 2nd ed. Detroit, MI: Gale Group, 1999.

Ann Aguirre

Rivera, Alex (1952–   ). A twenty-first-century digital artist and filmmaker, Alex Rivera is considered to be one of the most prolific and effective satirists working in the medium of television at the beginning of the new century. Like performance poets Guillermo *Gómez-Peña and John *Leaños, the Peruvian-born Rivera addresses pressing world social, political, and economic issues from a Latina/o perspective. He conceived and coproduced with

Bernardo Ruiz the antiglobalization documentary *The Sixth Section* (2003), concerning immigrants organizing into mutual aid and nongovernmental organizations across international political borders for the Corporation for Public Broadcasting program *P.O.V.* It explores the multilayered complexities of *globalization and, in his hallmark style, incorporates the techniques of digital animation to present the tale of El Grupo Unicorn, a remarkable transnational grassroots activist group of Mexican immigrants and refugees uniting for common cause in upstate New York, far from their homelands. The inspiring plot describes how the workers combined to raise tens of thousands of dollars to send home for their village near Puebla to improve the infrastructure, such as the installation of electricity, purchase of an ambulance, and the amazing construction of a *béisbol* (baseball) stadium to seat 2,000. By conscious collectivization, will, and hardwork, El Grupo Unicorn succeeded in transforming themselves and their community into a political body with influence in their region and country. By capturing their remarkable story, Rivera's film emphasizes that immigrant workers are both contributing to their adoptive land, as well as radically altering the homelands they leave behind. The documentary thus gives another demonstration of the interanimating, interlocking exchange that constitutes the basis, energy, and power of popular cultural expression.

Rivera directed another production, *PapaPapaPapa* (1995), a short (twenty-eight-minute) experimental satire on the sociocultural and personal effects of *immigration. Playing off the importance of the everyday commonness of the homely *papa*, or potato, the film examines its connection with dietary sustenance and economic power since the time of the Incas, the early cultivators of the lowly staple *food in Peru. Rivera documents *el papa*'s wandering migration north across many borders to become the familiar potato chip of the United States. Extending the satirical metaphor further, the film simultaneously captures a day in the life of another Peruvian, the filmmaker's own father, Augusto Rivera, to underscore the double meaning of *papa*. Their parallel stories weave together and provide a witty and entertaining look at *race and ethnicity and culture, as well as at the ironies of immigration and consumerism. The short feature also examines geographic distance and how, in a highly mobile world of constant diaspora, masses of people cope with its personal and social impacts.

Another Rivera directed-work, *Las papas del Papa* (The Pope's Potato Chips, 1999), is in Spanish and subtitled in English and concerns the 1999 visit of Pope John Paul II to México. Rivera exploits the flexibilities of turn-of-the-millennium digital formats and styles, to record the pope's visit to México, where he is a revered religious figure, and also simultaneously to disclose the merchandizing, product placement, and corporate tie-ins relating to the Roman Catholic Church and hundreds of retailers. The title theme shows the extremes to which entrepreneurial sellers will go in the case of a company selling commercial stickers of the image of the pope (*El Papa*, or holy father) on potato chip bags. Mocking the commerce, the narrative presents the poignant confusion of a boy teetering in the media-hyped world of the late twentieth century as he searches for a shortcut to heaven. *Las papas del Papa* (The Pope's Potato Chips) offers a cleverly amusing parody on *appropriation and authentic faith, as well as on globalization, identity, and power.

The satiric approach to First World appropriation of Third World talents and resources, which is perfected in *Las papas del Papa*, continues in *Animalquiladora* (Beast Factory, 1998), directed by Rivera with animation by Lalo López. Underlying these humorous works is Rivera's keen awareness that a great deal of the behind-the-scenes labor of animation art is done by hand in sweatshop conditions in the globalized factories of the the U.S.-Mexican borderlands, the Philippines, Korea, and most recently, China. The feature *Animalquiladora* shows this reality in a cartoon drawing factory of Tijuana, México. Tongue-in-cheekly presenting the autobiographical sketch of animator Lalo López and Rivera, the animation depicts the artists escaping from the exaggerated hell of drawing logos for the television talk show hosted by celebrities Regis Philbin and Kathie Lee Gifford, co-owner of a garment industry shop outsourced to Asia. Motivated by a conscientized desire to empower the public by raising public awareness of tyranny, injustice, and the need for resistant activism, Rivera's creative digital media art promises to continue digging for information and questioning unregulated authority as he and his collaborators combine the technology of digital imaging and online software with the sharpest of cutting-edge Latina/o satire.

Further Reading

"Netback El Compusino." http://www.alexrivera.com.

Cordelia Chávez Candelaria

Rivera, Chita (1933–). Dolores Conchita Figueroa del Rivero is an award-winning stage and television actress, born on January 23, 1933, in Washington, D.C. She is the daughter of Puerto Rican musician Pedro del Rivero. At the age of sixteen, Rivera won a scholarship to attend George Ballanchine's School of American Ballet in New York City. In 1952, she and a classmate answered a call for dancers for the national touring company of *Call Me Madam*, an Irving Berlin musical choreographed by Jerome Robbins. Rivera won a spot in the chorus line, toured for ten months, and then returned to New York to assume a featured role in *Guys and Dolls*. She followed *Guys and Dolls* with a role in the chorus of *Can-Can*, then had a featured part in *Shoestring Revue*, in which she imitated Marilyn Monroe. For the latter role, Conchita del Rivero changed her name to Chita O'Hara before settling on Chita Rivera. Shortly thereafter, in 1957, Rivera was cast as Anita in *West Side Story*, which again united her with choreographer Jerome Robbins. Her rendition of "America" brought down the house and earned her the first of her seven Antoinette Perry (Tony) Award nominations. She earned Tony nominations for her roles in *Bye Bye Birdie* (1961), *Bajour* (1964), *Chicago* (1975), *Bring Back Birdie* (1981), *Merlin* (1983), and *Jerry's Girls* (1986). In addition to her nominations, she won two Tony Awards. Her first Tony Award was for her portrayal of an Italian American woman who sells her roller rink in *The Rink* (1984), a musical for which Terence McNally was the librettist. McNally adapted Manuel Puig's novel *Kiss of the Spider Woman* (1993) for the stage and, in the process, created what is generally regarded as Rivera's finest role. Rivera takes on two roles in the play: Aurora, the glamorous movie star of the prisoner Molina's fantasies, and the Spider Woman, an embodiment of death. At the age of sixty, Rivera won her second Tony Award for this role, in a profession where most dancers retire by the age of forty. In addition to her work on stage, Rivera has appeared in the film *Sweet Charity*, as the title character's roommate Nickie (although Rivera originated the title role on Broadway) and on television in *The New Dick Van Dyke Show* (1973–1974). She is also considered one of the world's great cabaret performers and has toured as a cabaret artist for over thirty years.

Further Reading

Guthmann, Edward. "A Spider Woman for the Ages." *San Francisco Chronicle*, December 4, 1995, sec. E1.

Richards, David. "Chita Rivera's Webbed Victory." *Washington Post*, March 12, 1995, sec. G1.

"Rivera, Chita." *Current Biography* 45 (1984): 351–355.

William Orchard

Rivera, Diego (1886–1957). Diego Rivera was one of México's greatest social realist muralists whose impact on contemporary public art worldwide and on Chicana/o artists concerned with social issues is monumental. Rivera was born José Diego María Rivera y Barrientos on December 8, 1886, in Guanajuato, México. In 1892, Rivera's *family moved to Mexico City, and in 1897 Rivera began attending the National Preparatory School and the Academia de San Carlos (San Carlos Academy) in Mexico City. One of his teachers was the landscape artist José María Velasco, whose influence was later seen in Rivera's work. In 1906, twenty-six of Rivera's works were included in the Annual Exhibition of the Academia de San Carlos, and that same year, he participated in an exhibition of modern art organized by the magazine *Savia Moderna*.

In 1907, Rivera began a fourteen-year sojourn in Europe and traveled to Spain, France, Italy, Belgium, and England, where he learned about each country's artists and their techniques, leading him to experiment with his own art. During his stay in Europe, Rivera participated in several exhibitions both in Europe and America, (e.g., Academia de San Carlos, 1910; Societé des Artistes Independants, 1910, 1912; 1914 Berheim Jeune, 1913; Berthe Weill

Gallery, 1914; Modern Gallery of New York, 1916). Rivera returned to México in 1921 and met José Vasconcelos, who was the Minister of Education at that time and a dynamic force of the Mexican Muralism movement.

In January 1922 Rivera was commissioned to paint his first mural at the Simón Bolívar Amphitheater of the National Preparatory School in Mexico City, México. His mural *Creation* blended images of indigenous Mexican art with that of a European style called frescoes. In September, Rivera started working on the fresco at the Ministry of Education. In the same year, Rivera married Guadalupe Marín, a painting model he had used in his first mural. Together they had two daughters, Guadalupe and Ruth; they divorced in 1927. In 1922 Rivera also joined the Mexican Communist Party (which would expulse him in 1929, and he would rejoin it in 1954). His work was becoming well known, and requests for his works were increasing.

In 1929, he married the now-world-famous painter and feminist icon Frida *Kahlo, and in 1930, Rivera was commissioned to create a series of murals that reflected México's turbulent history and the struggles of the country's farmers and working-class indigenous peoples in the National Palace in Mexico City, which took him several years to complete.

Also in 1930, Rivera and Kahlo went to the United States for the first time, where Rivera worked on his first two major commissioned projects at the Luncheon Club of the San Francisco Pacific Stock Exchange and at the California School of Fine Arts. His other U.S.-commissioned projects included twenty-seven large-scale fresco murals titled *Detroit Industry* at the Detroit Institute of the Arts, commissioned by Henry Ford in 1932. Rivera's most controversial work in the United States was a giant mural commissioned by the Rockefeller family in 1933 for the lobby of the RCA Building at Rockefeller Center in New York City. Rivera's sixty-seven-foot *Man at the Crossroads* did not please his patrons because it included the image of Vladimir Lenin—Communist premier of the Soviet Union from 1917 to 1924—on a small portion of it. When Rivera refused to change the image, Nelson Rockefeller fired Rivera and had the mural destroyed. 1n 1934 Rivera painted a smaller replica of the destroyed mural in the Palacio de Bellas Artes (Palace of Fine Arts) in Mexico City, where it stands today as an icon of artistic expression.

However, even in México Rivera faced troubles with the content of his works. For example, in 1952 Rivera created the portable mural *Pesadilla de Guerra y Sueño de Paz* (The Nightmare of War and the Dream of Peace), which included portraits of Joseph Stalin and Mao Tse-tung, for the exhibition Twenty Centuries of Mexican Art. José Chávez, director of the National Institute of Fine Arts, refused to include it in the exhibition. Rivera decided to donate his work to the People's Republic of China.

Rivera died of a heart attack in Mexico City on November 24, 1957, at the age of seventy. Rivera's last wishes were to be cremated and to have his ashes mixed with those of Kahlo's. His last wish was not granted. Instead,

Diego Rivera painting *Detroit Industry* at the Detroit Institute of Arts in 1932. *Courtesy of Photofest.*

Rivera's remains were enshrined with great ceremony at the Rotonda de los Hombres Ilustres (Rotunda of Illustrious Persons) at the Dolores municipal cemetery. Rivera is considered one of *Los Tres Grandes* (The Three Greats) among México's mural painters. The other two muralists were David Alfaro Siqueiros and José Clemente Orozco. Rivera's earlier paintings illustrate the classical tradition he learned while studying in Europe. He also experimented with cubism for a short while. However, he found his greatest success in social realist frescoes (mural paintings applied on a surface of wet plaster) in México and the United States. Other select murals include the murals produced at the Autonomous University of Chapingo, 1926; *The History of Cuernavaca and Morelos*, Hernán Cortés Palace, Cuernavaca, México, 1929; *El Agua, Orígen de la Vida* (Water, Origin of Life), Chapultepec, Mexico

City, 1951; and *Sueño de una Tarde en la Alameda* (Dream of an Afternoon in the Alameda), a fresco over transportable panels originally installed at the Hotel del Prado in 1947 and currently in the Museo Mural Diego Rivera, Mexico City. With this mural Rivera faced controversy again; in 1948, after he had finished the mural, Rivera, under pressure, deleted the phrase "God does not exist," which he had included in the mural.

Among his notable paintings are the portraits Rivera made of María *Félix and Silvia Pinal, both Mexican divas of the Golden Age of the Mexican film industry. Other paintings that have been widely reproduced by artists and artisans include *La Molendera* (The Grinder), 1924; *Día de las Flores* (Flower Day), 1935; *Cargador de Flores* (The Flower Carrier), 1935; and *Desnudo con Alcatraces* (Nude with Calla Lilies), 1944. These paintings are now icons that internationally identify Mexican art.

Rivera always worked toward the development of Mexican arts. He was a force and a voice in the intellectual life of México in the twentieth century. His legacy to Mexican people was not just his art, the Anahuacalli museum with his collections of pre-Columbian art, or the houses that became museums after his death. Rather, his concept of public art has impacted artists throughout the Americas.

Further Reading

CONACULTA and the Cleveland Museum of Art. *Diego Rivera: Art and Revolution*. Mexico City: INBA/Landucci Editores, 1999.

Rivera, Diego. *My Art, My Life: An Autobiography*. New York: Citadel Press, 1960.

Rochfort, Desmond. *The Murals of Diego Rivera*. London: Journeyman, 1987.

Tibol, Raquel. *Diego Rivera, Ilustrador*. Mexico City: Secretaría de Educación Pública, 1986.

http://www.arts-history.mx/museos/mu/index.html.

http://www.diegorivera.com.

http://www.pbs.org/wnet/americanmasters/database/rivera_d.html.

Dulce Aldama and Silvia D. Mora

Rivera, Geraldo (1943–   ). Television talk show celebrity Geraldo Rivera is also a writer, a radio host, a reporter, and a producer. Born to a Puerto Rican father (Cruz Rivera) and a Jewish American mother (Lillian, née Friedman) in New York City, he got his Bachelor of Science degree in business administration from the University of Arizona, Tucson, in 1965, studied at the Brooklyn College Law School (New York), and received his law degree from the University of Pennsylvania Law School in 1969. The following year he received a degree in journalism from Columbia University (New York), becoming one of the most scholarly prepared journalists of his generation.

In 1971 he became the first Latino to win the New York State Associated Press Broadcaster Association Award for his investigative series "Drug Crisis in East Harlem." He also became the first Hispanic to be named Broadcaster of the Year in 1972 and 1974. He has received seven Emmy Awards,

Geraldo Rivera sits beside an intravenous drug user in a New York "shooting gallery" as he prepares for a 1987 TV special focusing on the AIDS virus. *Courtesy of Photofest.*

two Robert F. Kennedy Awards, the very prestigious Peabody Award, and the Kennedy Journalism Award, for distinguished broadcast journalism.

From 1970 to 1975 he worked in the television series *Eyewitness News*; from 1975 to 1977 he was a special correspondent for the TV series *Good Morning America*; and then from 1978 to 1985, he was correspondent and senior producer for the prime-time ABC investigative show *20/20*. In September 1987 he began hosting his syndicated sensationalistic television talk show *Geraldo*, which aired during daytime. In 1993 he launched a nightly news talk show under NBC called *Rivera Live*, which followed a more serious and sober journalistic approach. In 1997 he signed a contract with NBC for $5 million a year for six years.

The publication of his autobiography *Exposing Myself* (1991) caused a stir because of the account he gives in it of his many sexual affairs. In more general terms Rivera's name became increasingly synonymous with sensationalistic trash TV talk shows. He was a staunch defender of President Bill Clinton's policies and supported him without fail during the Clinton–Monica Lewinsky scandal in the late 1990s. During the O.J. Simpson trials in 1994, he took the side of the murdered Nicole Brown Simpson and Ron

Goldman. During the 2003 war on Iraq, he was embedded with the 101st Airborne Division and was reprimanded for broadcasting live several of the unit's combat destinations, endangering the lives of the U.S. military men and women. Although Rivera has more recently been associated with sensationalism, his early career proved that he can be a serious journalist. Rivera currently works as a war correspondant for Fox News Channel, where he has been employed since November 2001.

Further Reading

Pendergast, Tom, and Sara Pendergast, eds. *St. James Encyclopedia of Popular Culture*. Detroit, MI: St. James Press, 2000.

Luis Aldama

Rock en Español. From its origins in the 1960s, *rock en español* (rock in Spanish) has developed a large, growing, and international following of eclectic music fans that touches all across Latin America, the Caribbean, and Europe and travels across the U.S.-México border to predominantly Latina and Latino fans with increasing crossover appeal. During the 1960s, Spanish-language rock music was commonly referred to as *rocnrol*, a variation on the American colloquialism "rock and roll." By the 1980s, the music began to acquire a Latin American flair and sophistication and came to be known as *rock en tu idioma* (rock in your language). Then in the 1990s, the term *rock en español* took on broad appeal and an even broader connotation that included a variety of music sung in Spanish, such as rock, rap, rhythm and blues (R&B), punk, heavy metal, fused with traditional folkloric music including *mariachi, *banda, *cumbia, and reggae, to name a few.

The influence of Latino culture on rock music, and vice versa, dates to the early days of rock and roll. A pop rock version of *"La Bamba" was recorded in Spanish by Ritchie *Valens (1941–1959) shortly before his death. It was a megahit. Valens's rendition was based on a centuries-old folk song from the coastal Veracruz region of México. In the 1960s, Carlos *Santana began composing and performing Latin-influenced rock music featuring jazz-inspired Spanish guitar progressions on songs such as the *Brazilian-influenced "Samba Pa Ti" (Samba for you) and Latin- and Caribbean-adorned percussion on songs like "Black Magic Woman" and "Oye, Como Va" (Hey, How Is It Going). Santana's popularity endured. He has had a string of hit albums since the 1960s, and his 1999 recording *Supernatural* won a record eight Grammy Awards. And in the early 1970s the East Los Angeles band *Los Lobos began performing its own brand of rhythm and blues in English, Spanish, and bilingually. Another urban Latin rock fusion band that emerged in Los Angeles is *Ozomatli, who reinvented cumbia, reggae, *salsa, *hip-hop, blues, and rock in service of lyrics that take on overtly political issues and encourage their listeners to engage in nonviolence and social activism on issues such as poverty, racism, globalization, and the Zapatista uprising.

In the meantime, most Latin American rock bands spent their time recording and performing covers of radio hits by American rock musicians. Spanish-language rock music hybrids circulated throughout the hemisphere and Spain for decades. Critics say that it was not until the early 1980s that Latin American songwriters and musicians began composing rock music that reflected and incorporated their personal cultural upbringing and regional musical influences. Only then did *rock en español* start to earn the respect and admiration of music critics and music industry managers. The integration of musical influences on *rock en español* such as salsa, *ranchera*, norteño, ballads, and *boleros helped to dramatically expand the audience base, boosting records sales and legitimizing the status of the genre in the pop and rock music world.

The roots of *rock en español* trace back to México, Argentina, and Spain, though there is some dispute among researchers and musicians as to which of these countries played the most significant role in the genre's early development. In a region of the world where music and nationalist sentiment are often inseparable, the popularity of rock music in Latin America has been interpreted by some in the region as a cultural invasion of sovereignty. The genre's pop rock imitators aside, *los roqueros* (the rockers) assume a rebel's sensibility routinely linked to radical counterculture and leftist political movements. While the nature and popularity of rock music in the United States was shaped in part by the 1960s civil rights era, *rock en español*'s social conscience was largely stifled by the pervasiveness of authoritarian regimes in Latin America. Its recent popularity has been made easier by the steady dismantling over the past three decades of military dictatorships and other repressive governments.

During the 1980s, *rock en español* moved from underground cult music status to widespread commercial success. *Rock en español* groups began selling hundreds of thousands (in some cases, millions) of records to a growing cadre of fans, and record companies in the United States and Latin America began to take notice. More recently, the creation of the Spanish-language cable television networks MTV En Español and MTV Latin America have helped popularize pop and rock music throughout the hemisphere and overseas. The Latin Academy of Recording Arts and Sciences, headquartered in Miami, was created in 1997. The first annual *Latin Grammy Awards were held in 2000 to honor the achievements of the Latin music industry. The show was held in Los Angeles that year and aired on ABC, making it the first Latino-themed, prime-time television awards program broadcast by a major television network in the United States.

In the 1990s, most of the major record producers in the United States created domestic and international Latin music labels. In the meantime, Los Angeles, New York, Miami, Orlando, and other U.S. cities began to develop reputations as meccas for *rock en español* recording artists, producers, and promoters. Unlike their Latin American counterparts, bands originating in the United States often perform bilingual songs, a reflection of the music genre's Americanized fan base in the United States, which may include predominantly English-speaking Latinos or non-Latinos, as well as people who are bilingual or predominantly Spanish speakers.

Rock en español songs cover a gamut of topics from love and sex to politics and personal epiphany, though much of the music lays out a social protest agenda. Observers attribute this to the gradual, if still incomplete, rollback on authoritarianism in Latin America. In Argentina, for instance, a band called Soda Stereo was among the early pioneers of modern-day *rock en español*. In 1984, it emerged with a distinct sound that catapulted it into the ranks of legend, though musicians such as Gustavo Santaolalla, Charly Garcia, and Miguel Mateos are considered major early influences. Soda Stereo is regarded as a groundbreaking band. They produced sixteen albums. Their first album was a self-titled *Soda Stereo* (1984), a blend of punk, new wave, ska, reggae, folk, and electronica. Other Argentinean groups who contributed to the *rock en español* movement include the award-winning Los Fabuloso Cadillacs (1987–) and their politically charged lyrics with a heavy ska-reggae beat; Fito Paez (1977–), a pioneering rock balladeer and now filmmaker and blues-influenced singer and pianist; and the punk-ska band with heavily charged lyrics protesting colonialism and dictatorship, *Todos tus Muertos* (1983). In Chile, there are several early rock groups such as El Congreso and Los Jaivas; in the 2000s one of the most popular crossover pop rock groups from Chile includes the Grammy-winning La Ley.

In México, *rock en español* early roots began with blues rockers El Tri in 1968, who were nominated for Best Album at the 2003 Latin Grammys; their over thirty-year career still has a huge fan base, especially among Mexican immigrants. Another important pioneer Mexican rock group is Los Caifanes (1987–1995). Both El Tri and Los Caifanes are credited with integrating a uniquely Mexican cultural component into their rock music, both in lyric content and, in the case of the Caifanes, in the way they fused rock beats with cumbias and indigenous music to create a new urban rock sound. Some members from Los Caifanes, namely, lead singer Saul Hernández and Alfonso Andre, formed a new band called Los Jaguares (1996–), which is grounded in the indigenous music and philosophies of México and the Americas and whose fusion of folk music with guitar-driven rock has received amazing critical acclaim, including a 2002 Latin Grammy nomination for the album *Cuando la Sangre Galopa* (then the Blood Races, 2002). The other Mexican rock powerhouse whose romantic and politically charged ballads about indigenous struggles and betrayed loves have crossed over to a variety of markets is *Maná, who began in the 1980s, developed a large following in México, the United States, Europe, and Latin America, and have already won four Grammys.

Other pioneering Mexican *rock en español* bands include the Mexico City working-class band Maldita Vecindad (1985–), whose song "Pachuco" about the *zoot suit riots is a now considered a classic among Chicano fans in the United States and working-class youth in México, and the U.S.-México border-based Afro-Latin ska-punk band with songs in support of community and revolutionary struggle in México and Latin America, Tijuana No!, whose recent lead singer Julieta Venegas, and her striking multichord range, was featured in the award-winning film *Amores Perros* (2000). The other major innovator of music forms with their avant-garde jazz-rock eclecticism is the Grammy-winning Café Tacuba (1989–).

Later groups that are having a huge impact on *rock en español* and have huge fan bases in México and among Mexican immigrants include the rap metal band Molotov, whose 2003 video and song "Frijolero" (Beaner) is a direct condemnation of the economic and military policies of the U.S.-México border and the racism that Mexican immigrants face. Their 1997 debut album song, also a bilingual attack on the corruption of Mexican elite, "Gimme Tha Power," had a huge impact on *rock en español* audiences in México and the United States. The Monterrey-based El Gran Silencio is having a huge impact on musical innovations that fuse mariachi and boleros with music from India and from Jamaica in lyrics that reflect the struggles of working-class barrios in Monterrey and along the U.S.-Mexican border.

Groups that have dominated the Grammys in Latin alternative rock from 2001 to 2003 have interestingly originated from Colombia. These include Los Aterciopelados, a punk rock–inspired techno rock pop group spearheaded by Andrea Echeverri; latest Grammy-winning pop rock singer and guitarist Juanes; the award-winning pop rock singer and guitarist *Shakira and the *cumbia vallenato*–based Carlos Vives.

There is an important movement of Latin rock artists that again fused indigenous and mestizo musics with a rock-influenced cadence and politically charged lyrics in Brazil. These artists include some of the pioneering 1970s *tropicalia* performers such as Caetano Veloso, Gilberto Gil, Egberto Gismonti, Roberto Carlos, and Milton Nascimiento and the more jazz-rock *samba fusions of percussionist *Airto and Flora Purim. In the 1990s there appeared heavy metal samba–influenced rock groups, two of the most famous being Mutanta and Sepultura. In 2003 the neo-*tropicalia* Brazilian Los Tribalistas won a Grammy. In Puerto Rico, the pioneering Latin rock group Puya (1992–) fuses speed metal with *mambo and *bomba. From Cuba, there is a rock–hip-hop fusion band, Orishas, that is also very grounded in the Cuban music traditions of the *sones* and *cuartetos*. The band was nominated at the 2003 Grammys but was not able to attend because of visa restrictions.

Spain's Radio Futura's 1984 *La ley del Desierto, La Ley del Mar* (The Law of the Desert, the Law of the Sea) is considered groundbreaking by fusing Arabic, Mediterranean, Indian melodies, and percussion with Spanish rock and pop lyrics and musical overlays. Also, the 1990s Mano Negra, started by Manu Chao—who was born in France but is of Spanish descent—

is credited with fusing Brazilian and Latin music forms with electronica, ska, and punk with a reggae-cumbia beat and lyrics that are both ironic and insightful on a wide variety of political and cultural issues. Chao's *Proxima estación esperanza* (Next Stop, Hope!, 2001), a solo effort, is distinguished by his willingness to incorporate musical forms from every country he visited in Latin America, and here one sees the **corrido* genre taken into a musical cadence informed by electronica.

Despite the growing popularity of the musical genre, *rock en español* stations in the United States remain virtually nonexistent, though that is expected to change as growth among U.S. Latinas and Latinos is expected to continue (an estimated one of every four Americans will be of Latino origin by 2050). The turn of the millennium witnessed a Latin music boom in the United States, with some cities touting more than a dozen Spanish-language stations each by 2003. Most of these station owners, however, focus on ballads, dance, or traditional folk and pop music genres, such as salsa and merengue, and *rock en español* has become part of the regular daily mix of many of these stations. With few *rock en español* stations in the United States, fans must still resort to frequenting specialty or "mom and pop" record shops, alternative music clubs, or the Internet sites of Latin American stations. However, as the fan base continues to grow in the United States, Europe, and Latin America, this vital and inventive musical movement will transcend its underground status along mainstream media outlets, and more and more radio stations and television programs will flourish. In terms of music video programming, there are several cable television sources that have had an impact on promoting the latest *rock en español videos*, as well as some classics from the 1990s. These include *MTV en Español*, *VH-1 Latino*, and *H.TV*. However, these music video stations are only found on Spanish-language programming packages, and in México and Latin America, there is still a huge rift between the type of music that appears on mainstream music video programming and their Latina/o counterparts.

Further Reading

Aparicio, Frances R., and Candida F. Jacquez, eds. *Musical Migrations: Transnationalism and Cultural Hybridity in Latina/o America*. New York: Palgrave, 2002.

Clark, Walter Aaron, ed. *From Tejano to Tango: Essays on Latin American Popular Music*. New York: Routledge, 2002.

Graff, Gary, ed. *MusicHound Rock: The Essential Album Guide*. 2nd ed. New York: Schirmer Books, 2000.

Hernandez, Deborah, Hector Fernández, and Eric Zolov, eds. *Rockin' Las Americas: The Global Politics of Rock in Latina/o America*. Pittsburgh: University of Pittsburgh Press, 2004.

http://members.aol.com/pompanoro/jamcoverstory.html.

http://www.austinchronicle.com/issues/dispatch/1999-11-12/music_feature.html.

http://www.chron.com/cs/CDA/story.hts/features/burr/1778165.

http://www.grita.com/mainfr.htm.
http://www.hispaniconline.com/a&e/tacuba/biography.html.
http://www.pompanoro.indiegroup.com/favorite_links.html.
http://www.Rocketeria.com.

Arturo J. Aldama

Rock en Tu Idioma. *See Rock en Español.*

Rodeo. *See Charreada.*

Rodríguez, Alex (1975–). A son of Dominican immigrants, Alex Rodríguez popularly known as A-Rod, is, at the start of the twenty-first century, one of baseball's biggest superstars and one of its highest-paid players. In February 2004, Rodríguez's trade from the Texas Rangers to the New York Yankees was a major media story, eclipsing even the war in Iraq and the presidential election. Among the elements that made the event so newsworthy were A-Rod's selection as the American League's (AL) Most Valuable Player in 2003, his recognition by many *sports experts as the number-one all-around player in the major leagues, and the suspense that built up when the Yankees' archrivals, the Boston Red Sox, also entered into the bidding for the phenomenal superstar. Another element accounting for the media frenzy was the stratospheric range of his contract, which was reported to be worth nearly a quarter of a billion dollars. The Rangers were required to pay $67 million of their original $179 million acquisition contract for Rodríguez. In accepting the trade, A-Rod agreed to shift positions from short stop to third base, as well as to change jersey numbers from 3 (Babe Ruth's retired number) to 13.

Rodríguez was born on July 27, 1975, in New York City. His family moved to Miami, Florida, where the young Alex attended school. His boyhood was capped by an outstanding experience as a highly successful prep school athlete in Miami's private Westminster Christian High School from which he graduated in 1993. Although he also played football and basketball at Westminster, the future superstar excelled in baseball, a sport he followed avidly as a fan, especially his favorite teams, the nearby Atlanta Braves and the upcoast New York Mets. As a fan, he was inspired by the careers of his most admired professional players—Keith Hernandez, Dale Murphy, and Cal Ripken. The young athlete accumulated stellar statistics in high school, from a .419 batting average with 17 homeruns to 70 runs batted in (RBIs) and 90 steals in 100 games. In his senior year, he hit .505 and safely stole 35 bases out of 35 tries in 33 games, earning him a coveted spot on the 1st Team Prep All-American. He also was honored as the USA Baseball Junior Player of the Year and as Gatorade's National Baseball Student Athlete. He became the only high school finalist in the USA Baseball's Golden

Spikes Award, an honor presented for exceptional amateur competition, and in 1993 became the first high schooler to try out for the U.S. Olympic baseball team. Playing with the U.S. Junior National Squad that same year, Rodríguez suffered a freak injury when he was struck in the cheek by a wild throw while he was sitting in the dugout at an American Olympic Festival in San Antonio, Texas.

His spectacular professional career had a record-breaking start in 1993 when the eighteen-year-old made his major league debut as a shortstop with the Boston Red Sox, after which the six-foot-three-inch and 210-pound right-hander went to the Canadian leagues. The following season in the June free agent draft he was the first player chosen, selected by the Seattle Mariners, where he dazzled the local fans and international aficionados. In December 2000, he signed with the Rangers as a free agent in what was at that time the biggest money deal in the history of professional sports.

What justifies A-Rod's exorbitant yearly salary and long-term contract for some followers of baseball is the consistency of his outstanding performance as a major leaguer, despite playing for two teams, the Mariners and the Rangers, that were not factors in their league's pennant races during his tenure with the clubs. As of 2004, his career batting average is .308, with a high of .318 in 2001, when he also drove in 135 runs. In 2002, he hit 57 homeruns and hit .300. His supporters also point to his other impressive statistics—177 career stolen bases, three consecutive years as AL homerun leader (2001–2003), RBI leader for the AL in 2002, and AL batting champion in 1996 while with the Mariners.

Among A-Rod's many service and charitable activities is his work for the Alex Rodríguez Foundation, which he established in 1998. He also has been an active supporter of the Boys and Girls Clubs of America as one of only three national ambassadors along with U.S. Secretary of State Colin Powell and Academy Award–winning actor Denzel Washington. Another of his efforts is the Alex Rodríguez Education Center, which he recently built in Miami as a scholastic adjunct for Boys and Girls Club programming. His concern for education and economically disadvantaged youth explains his 2002 gift of $3.9 million to the University of Miami for the establishment of a scholarship fund for Boys and Girls Club alumni and the building of a sports training facility. He is married to Cynthia Scurtis Rodríguez, and he recently committed himself to begin study in a degree program at the University of Miami during the off-season. Described as a diamond-quality player on and off the diamond during the media hype over his trade to New York, A-Rod exemplifies the Latino American celebrity as a responsible role model.

Further Reading

The Baseball Encyclopedia: The Complete and Official Record of Major League Baseball. 10th ed. New York: Macmillan, 1996.

Norman, Geoffrey. "A-Rod in Pinstripes." *National Review Online*, February 20, 2004. http://www.nationalreview.com/norman/norman200402201003.asp.

Regalado, Samuel. *Viva Baseball! Latin Major Leaguers and Their Special Hunger.* Urbana: University of Illinois Press, 1998.

Cordelia Chávez Candelaria

Rodríguez, Chi Chi (1935–   ). Part of professional golf's generation of great golfers, Juan "Chi Chi" Rodríguez, an entertainer at heart, is considered a charismatic performer in *sports history, like Muhammad Ali and Joe Namath. His forty-year-plus career has produced twenty-two Senior Professional Golf Association (PGA) Tour victories, eight regular PGA Tour titles, and career winnings of over $7 million. Among his numerous world-class accomplishments are winning four PGA tournaments in each of the 1990–1991 seasons, as well as being the only winner of back-to-back contests in 1991. He also made the record books by becoming the first player on the Senior Tour to win the same event three years in a row, and he set a Senior Tour record with eight consecutive birdies in his victory at the 1987 Silver Pages Classic.

Golf specialists consider the Puerto Rican's major talents to be the power of his swing, his hand-eye coordination, and his creative strategies in overcoming the challenges and obstacles that occur on greens in high-powered competitions. At five feet seven inches tall and weighing less than 130 pounds, the diminutive Latino is considered the longest hitter, pound for pound, in the sport's history. He has been known to drive a golf ball over 350 yards in competition and has consistently hit over 250 yards throughout his incredible career. The popular fan favorite was chosen to represent Puerto Rico on twelve World Cup Teams and was inducted into the PGA's World Golf Hall of Fame in 1992.

Rodríguez was born in Rio Piedras on the island of Puerto Rico on October 23, 1935. Born into a poor working-class family, he toiled with his father in the unforgiving labor of the island's sugar cane fields. He started caddying at the age of six to earn extra money, and he learned to play golf with homemade clubs carved out of guava tree branches and crushed tin cans rounded into golf balls. At the age of twelve he shot an amazing 67 score, thus beginning one of the most successful careers in the game's history.

The celebrity Latino athlete is also admired for extending his reach as a role model beyond the golf links through his commitment and desire to have a positive impact on young people. He founded and has raised over $5 million for the Chi Chi Rodríguez Youth Foundation in Clearwater, Florida, which provides a homelike shelter to troubled and abused youth. His message is powerful in its simplicity: if he could make it with his small physique and boyhood of poverty, then anybody can. For the legendary champion's advocacy and philanthropy on behalf of youth and the Hispanic community, he was awarded the Hispanic Achievement Recognition Award in 1986 and in 1988 won the Replica Hispanic Man of the Year honor. Age and failing health have limited Rodríguez's continued playing, but his standing in professional golf history and as a celebrity in Latino American popular culture is undisputed.

Further Reading

Alliss, Peter. *The Who's Who of Golf.* Englewood Cliffs, NJ: Prentice Hall, 1983.

Seitz, Nick, and Bob Toski. *Superstars of Golf: Swing Studies.* Norwalk, CT: Golf Digest, 1978.

http://www.latinosportslegends.com/chi-chi.htm.

"Juan 'Chi-Chi' Rodríguez." *Latino Legends in Sports.* http://www.latinosports legends.com/chi-chi.htm.

Cordelia Chávez Candelaria

Rodríguez, Luis J. (1954–   ). Luis Rodríguez, one of the most prominent poets, essayists, journalists, and community-based activists around urban Chicana/o and Latina/o youth, was born in Texas on the U.S.-México border and migrated to East Los Angeles, where he grew up and fell into *La Vida Loca of *gang life, then got involved with the *Chicano Movement as a community-based activist, youth rights advocate, and investigative journalist. His most famous and most widely cited autobiography/*testimonio*, *Always Running: La Vida Loca, Gang Days in L.A.* (1993), has had a huge effect on Chicana/o-Latina/o youth, who find inspiration from his life story and afford him the "street respect" of a *veterano* (veteran) in the often violent life of the street. His poetry, essays, and autobiography are also the subject of several academic studies on how youth are criminalized. Although this autobiography received several important awards, including the Carl Sandburg Literary Award, notable mention by the *New York Times*, and a *Chicago Sun Times* Book Award, the book has been censored—because of its graphic depictions of sex, drug abuse, and violence—throughout the United States and has withstood many efforts of removal from public and high school libraries in Illinois, Michigan, and even California, where the book takes place. Ironically, the message of the book is that Chicana/os who feel disempowered should get involved in activities that promote civil rights rather than get involved with the violence of gang life. In addition to his many essays and published interviews, he is the author of eight nationally published books in a variety of genres, poetry, fiction, nonfiction, memoir, and children's literature and, more recently, the author of a spoken-word CD with musical accompaniment titled *My Name's Not Rodriguez* (2002).

His poetry includes *Poems across the Pavement* (1989), *The Concrete River* (1991), and *Trochemoche* (Helter-Skelter, 1998). He is also the author of another nonfiction series of essays on his experiences as a youth counselor in the juvenile corrections system, *Hearts and Hands: Creating Community in Violent Times* (2001). His children's literature includes *America Is Her Name* (1998) and *It Doesn't Have to Be This Way: A Barrio Story* (1999). His most recent collection of semihistorical and semifactual stories of *barrio life is receiving wide acclaim, *The Republic of East L.A.: Stories* (2002).

Rodríguez's notable literary accomplishments have not gone without notice, and he has been the recipient of dozens of important awards that include the 1991 PEN Josephine Miles Award for Literary Excellence; the 1996 Lila Wallace Reader's Digest Award; the 1999 Paterson Prize for Books for Young Adults; the 2001 Premio Fronterizo of the Border Book Festival, Las Cruces, New Mexico; and the 2001 "Unsung Heroes of Compassion" Award, presented by the Dalai Lama. He has also received several important fellowships and grants and has a history of media appearances on the *Oprah Winfrey Show*, *Good Morning America*, the *Jim Lehrer News Hour*, PBS, Univision, Telemundo, and Galavision. In addition to his literary work, Rodríguez keeps a busy schedule as an invited public speaker for urban high schools, universities, book festivals, and community-based organizations dedicated to social change in the Latina/o community.

His most recent interests include further understanding the indigenous roots of Chicano and Mexican cultures and identities and imparting indigenous knowledge to disenfranchised youth.

Further Reading

Brown, Monica. *Gang Nation: Delinquent Citizens in Puerto Rican, Chicano and Chicana Narratives*. Minneapolis: University of Minnesota Press, 2002.

Rodríguez, Luis J. *Always Running: La Vida Loca, Gang Days*. New York: Touchstone Books, Reprint Edition, 1994.

www.luisjrodriguez.com/history.html.

Arturo J. Aldama

Rodríguez, Michelle (1978–   ). Michelle Marie Rodríguez emerged into the national spotlight with her debut *film *Girlfight* (2000), which is important for its depiction of working-class Latinas who enter into professional boxing. Rodríguez was born on July 12, 1978, in Bexar County, Texas, to a Puerto Rican father and a Dominican mother. Rodríguez and her *family lived in Texas until 1986, when they moved first to the Dominican Republic and later to Puerto Rico before finally settling in Jersey City, New Jersey, when she was eleven years old. While in Puerto Rico, her grandmother taught her and her brothers Spanish and instilled in them strict Jehovah Witness morals. Rodríguez felt confined by her family's religious restrictions, and after having been influenced by Jersey City's urban atmosphere, she dropped out of high school at age seventeen.

Exploring the possibility of acting, Rodríguez worked as an extra in 1999 on the sets of *Summer of Sam* and *Cradle Will Rock*. During this time Rodríguez saw the ad that Karyn Kusama put out in *Backstage* magazine for a Latina boxer, and despite her lack of experience in acting and boxing, she auditioned for the part. Rodríguez and three other girls beat 350 girls auditioning for the lead role, and Rodríguez was cast at Diana Guzmán. At five feet six inches tall, Rodríguez trained for five months at Brooklyn's Gleason's Gym. She was so good in the ring that her trainers tried to persuade her to get into professional boxing. She declined the offer, dedicated to her acting ambitions.

Upon release, *Girlfight* and Rodríguez won many awards, such as the Deaxville Festival of American Cinema award for Best Actress, the Las Vegas Film Critics Society for Female Breakthrough Performance, and the Grand Jury Prize at the Sundance Film Festival. By the film's commercial release in September 2000, she was already working on other films. Her film credits include *3 A.M.* (2001), *Resident Evil* (2001), *Fast and the Furious* (2001), and *Blue Crush* (2002). In 2003, Rodríguez appeared in *S.W.A.T.*, based on a 1970s television show.

Further Reading

Parish, James Robert, ed. *The Encyclopedia of Ethnic Groups in Hollywood*. New York: Facts on File, 2003.
http://www.allmovie.com/cg/avg.dll.
http://www.michelle-rodriguez.com/default.htm.
http://www.michelle-rodriguez.net/index.php?view=michelle/bio.php.

Marisol Silva

Rodríguez, Paul (1955–   ). Paul Rodríguez is one of the most recognizable Latino comics on television and in film. Born on January 19, 1955, he is the youngest of five children. When he was three years old, Rodríguez immigrated to California with his family from Mazatlán, México. The family settled in East Los Angeles, where his parents worked in factories until his father suffered an injury, which led him into migrant fieldwork. Rodríguez dropped out of high school and spent a lot of his time on the streets.

Discounting or disbelieving in his ability to be a comedian, Rodríguez recalls his family telling him to concentrate on getting a steady job, not comedy. In the late 1970s, after being released from the U.S. Air Force, Rodríguez received the GED (general educational diploma) and used the G.I. bill to attend college. He graduated from Long Beach City College and enrolled in California State University, Long Beach, with the goal of entering law school; however, an elective theater class changed his life. Murray Becker, his drama professor, recognized Rodríguez's talent and encouraged him to try out at Los Angeles's Comedy Store. Rodríguez was offered a job, and it was there that he captured the admiration and attention of Norman Lear, a television producer who gave him the chance to do the warm-up act for his show *Gloria*. In 1984 Lear developed a show specifically for Rodríguez called *a.k.a. Pablo*. The short-lived show angered the Latino community because of its negative Latin *stereotypes.

Rodríguez made his film debut in the comedy *D.C. Cab* (1984), then appeared in *The Whoopie Boys* (1986) and *Quicksilver* (1986), and gained more fame and notoriety in *Born in East L.A.* (1987) with Cheech *Marín. He also costarred with Whoopi Goldberg and Ted Danson in *Made in America* (1993). In the early 1990s Rodríguez costarred and directed the film

A Million to Juan, released by Samuel Gold-wyn Company. This comedy-drama was an adaptation of Mark Twain's the "Million-Pound Bank Note." Rodríguez described this plot to the *Long Beach Press-Telegram* as the only American-made movie starring a Latino without *gangs, drugs, or cursing.

Rodríguez supports many organizations including Comic Relief and serves on the board of Education First. He hosts the National Leukemia Telethon and has helped raise money for the Hurricane Relief, Project Literacy, the National Hispanic Scholarship Fund, and other organizations. He is also committed to doing outreach to at-risk Latino youth.

Further Reading

Kanellos, Nicolas. *The Hispanic-American Almanac: A Reference Work on Hispanics in the United States*. Detroit, MI: Gale Research, 1993.

Tardiff, Joseph C., and L. Mpho Mabunda. *Dictionary of Hispanic Biography*. Detroit, MI: Gale Research, 1996.

Kim Villarreal

Paul Rodríguez. *Courtesy of Photofest.*

Rodríguez, Tito (1923–1973). Pablo Rodríguez, better known as Tito Rodríguez, is a multitalented *sonero*, ballad singer, and percussionist who formed one of the first *conjuntos* in New York, the Mambo Devils, in 1947. Born in San Juan, Puerto Rico, on January 4, 1923, he began his musical career singing in Latin music bands at the age of sixteen. In 1940 he became the bongo player and vocalist for Enrique Madriguera's *orquesta* in New York, later playing with the Cuarteto Caney and performing very briefly with Xavier *Cugat. Rodríguez became one of the main attractions at dance halls in New York and toured around Las Vegas, Miami, and other major cities around the country in the 1950s and 1960s. Some of his earliest albums from the 1950s include *Latin Jewels* (1959), *Three Loves Have I* (1957), and *Mambos Vol. 2* (1952).

In 1946 Cuban pianist and composer Curbelo recruited Rodríguez and Tito *Puente to his band, which eventually would define the future New York *mambo sound. Longtime friends with Tito Puente, Rodríguez hired him to arrange charts for several songs in 1949, and the two maintained a professional rivalry throughout their careers.

In 1962, Cuban vocalist Miguelito Valdes and *Machito appealed to the feud in the song "Que Pena Me Da" (The Heartache You Bring). His last tune aimed at Puente was "Esa Bomba" on *El Doctor* in 1968. Several of his albums from this era include *Este Es Mi Mundo* (This Is My World, 1968), *In Buenos Aires* (1966), and *Tito Tito Tito* (1964).

Toward the latter part of the 1960s and nearing the eventual end of the mambo era in New York, Rodríguez moved to his native Puerto Rico, where he hosted a television show titled *El Show de Tito Rodríguez*. Major stars such as Sarah Vaughn, Sammy Davis, Jr., and other American entertainers served as guests, making it one of the most popular shows in Puerto Rican television during this time. Rodríguez believed he did not receive an award for his show due to negative anti-Nuyoricans (New York Puerto Ricans), and he felt rejected by his own people. He moved to Coral Gables, Florida, and returned to New York, performing at the Manhattan Center with the title track from his 1968 album "Estoy Como Nunca" (I Am Like Never Before).

Rodríguez, who suffered from leukemia, died in New York City in 1973, less than a month after performing with Machito at Madison Square garden.

Few Rodríguez recordings were released during the 1970s and 1980s; however, since the 1990s to the present, the quantity has increased, and the quality has remained constant, if not better. More recent recordings include *Algo Nuevo* (Something New, 1991), *En La Soledad* (In the Solitude, 1991), *The Best of Tito Rodríguez and His Orquesta* (1992), *Mambo Cha Cha Cha and Rumba* (1993), *The Best of Tito Rodríguez Vol. 3* (1994), *Eclipse* (1994), *Dance Date With . . .* (1994), *Mambo Mona 1949–51* (1995), *Mambo Gee Gee 1950–1951* (1995), *Un Retrato de . . .* (A Picture of . . . , 1997), *Reliquias* (Relics, 1997), *Best of the Best* (1998), *Mucho Cha-Cha* (1999), *Up Tempo* (1999), *RCA Club* (1999), *El Hombre Su Música Su Vida* (The Man, the Music, His Life, 2000), *Tito Dice Separala Tambien* (Tito Says to Separate It, Too, 2000), *Latin Roots* (2000), *Little Bit of Everything* (2001), and *Nosotros* (Us 2003).

Further Reading

Clarke, Donald, ed. *The Penguin Encyclopedia of Popular Music.* 2nd ed. New York: Penguin Books, 1998.

Irene Vega

Rodríguez de Tió, Lola (1843–1924). Known as one of the greatest women in the history of Puerto Rico, political activist Lola Rodríguez de Tió was acclaimed by the educated elites of her time for her high intellectual gifts and was claimed by her compatriots—and, in time, by others, particularly in the Caribbean islands and rim—as a genuine hero. Rodríguez was born in San Germán, Puerto Rico, on September 14, 1843, to a famous father, Don Sebastián Rodríguez de Astudillo, a lawyer and cofounder of the Puerto Rican College of Lawyers, and a high-born mother, Doña Carmen Ponce de León, whose family descended from one of the original Spaniard conquistadors. In addition to her historical importance, Rodríguez is important to contemporary Latina and Latino popular culture as the lyricist of "*La Borin-queña," the official Puerto Rican Commonwealth anthem. In addition, both Cubans and Puerto Ricans acknowledge Rodríguez (whether they know it or not) every time they proclaim the popular refrain that "Cuba and Puerto Rico are the two wings of one bird, receiving flowers and bullets in the same heart," which appeared in her third book, *Mi Libro de Cuba* (My Book of Cuba, 1893).

The future political activist was educated at home by her father, who exposed her to a rich curriculum in the humanities. She is reported to have read eagerly in the Spanish literary classics, history, philosophy, religious studies, and travel and adventure writings. Greatly influenced by the writings of Fray Luis de León, she began to write poetry in his style. She also began declaiming her verses publicly and performed classical and other music on the piano. A major turning point in her life was her marriage in 1863 to Bonocio Tió Segarra, an educated man of progressive ideas who was involved in the political resistance against the Spanish regime. The couple's home soon became a thriving center for liberal reform discussions and political coalition building.

Rodríguez wrote the lyrics for "La Borinqueña" in 1867, altering the original composition by Félix Astol. Its nationalistic, pro–Puerto Rican indigenist and revolutionary lyrics inspired the anticolonial rebels. In 1876 she published her first book of poems, *Mis Cantares* (My Songs). For their political activities, she and her husband were exiled in 1877 to Caracas, Venezuela, but they continued speaking out against the tyrannical governorship in their island homeland. They were able to return to Mayagüez, Puerto Rico, in 1878 and continued their literary and political activities. In 1885 she published her second volume of poetry, *Claros y Nieblas* (Clear Skies and Fogs), which was very favorably received by critics and general readers. In 1889 the couple was again forced to leave the island after an era of horrible political persecutions that resulted in the death, disappearance, and torture of thousands of people seeking democratic reforms and emancipation from Spain's colonial control. She and her husband were forceful in voicing demands for freeing Puerto Rican dissenters and other political patriots jailed at El Morro. Even though they lived outside the island, they continued their campaign for reform and the removal of the governor tyrant. Because of their unabated activism and published support for the independence of Cuba, the couple was again forced into exile in 1895, and they established residence in New York.

In 1898, after the Cuban independence, she returned to Havana, where she was welcomed with great affection and admiration. Many historians write that she and her husband were considered Cubans by the people of that island. Rodríguez published her last book in Cuba in 1893, *Mi Libro de Cuba*. It is in this book where her famous verse appears, one that is still widely known to most Cubans and Puerto Ricans:

Cuba y Puerto Rico son
de un pájaro las dos alas,
reciben flores y balas
en un mismo corazón
(Cuba and Puerto Rico are
the two wings of one bird,
receiving flowers and bullets
in the same heart.)

Finally able to return to her homeland in 1912 and again in 1919, she was honored with a banquet of homage at the Ateneo Puertorriqueño, where the highlight was her recitation of her poem, "Canto a Puerto Rico" (Sing to Puerto Rico). She died on November 10, 1924, in Havana, Cuba, where she is buried.

Further Reading

Herrera, Andrea O'Reilly. *The Pearl of the Antilles.* Tempe, AZ: Bilingual Press/Editorial Bilingüe, 2001.

Martínez-Fernández, Luis. *Torn between Empires: Economy, Society, and Patterns of Political Thought in the Hispanic Caribbean, 1840–1878.* Athens: University of Georgia Press, 1994.

Cordelia Chávez Candelaria

Romero. Directed by John Duigan and starring Raúl *Julia in the lead role, *Romero* (1989) tells the story of the real-life archbishop of El Salvador, Oscar Romero. He is considered a martyr in El Salvador, and his memory holds an almost iconic status among the liberation theology clergy in the Americas and in the popular culture of El Salvador.

During the height of the U.S.-backed civil war in El Salvador, Romero was brutally assassinated by the military on March 24, 1980, while he was conducting Mass. Despite the fact that his personal and *family backgrounds and connections placed him firmly within the right-wing upper-class society of El Salvador, he developed a strong political consciousness as he witnessed widespread human rights abuses by the military against the country's poor and struggling (students and laborers) and the complacency of the Catholic Church toward these unmitigated acts of military violence. Like Oliver Stone's *Salvador* (1986), this feature-length commercial release film attempted to popularize a political message of how the United States backed the "right wing" in Central America in their use of violence and repression.

Further Reading

http://news.bbc.co.uk/1/hi/world/americas/690136.stm.
http://www.lehigh.edu/~ineng/nhl/nhl-Romero.html.

Arturo J. Aldama

Romero, César (1907–1994). Popular stage, *film, and television actor César Romero was born on February 15, 1907, in New York City to Cuban parents, César Julio Romero and María Mantilla, and is the grandson of famed Cuban writer and political figure José *Martí. As a screen star, he played opposite such actresses as Margaret Sullivan, Carol Lombard, Ginger Rogers, Marlene Dietrich, and Betty Grable. Tall and handsome with his signature trim mustache, he was known as Hollywood's most eligible bachelor. Romero studied ballroom dancing and began his career at the age of twenty as a dancer on Broadway in the play *Lady Do* (1927). He acted in numerous other Broadway plays, most notably in the long-running *Dinner at Eight* (1933–1934). Relocating to Hollywood, Romero did a string of comedies between the 1930s and 1950s. He is most remembered for his role as *The Cisco Kid* in a series of films in the late 1930s and early 1940s and as the Joker in the *Batman* television series, which ran in the 1960s. Romero also appeared in other television hit shows such as *Bonanza*, *Zorro*, and *Falcon Crest*. His movies include *The Thin Man* (1934), *Show Them No Mercy!* (1935), *Springtime in the Rockies* (1942), *Captain from Castille* (1947), *Around the World in 80 Days* (1956), *Batman* (1966 and 1967), *Now You See Him, Now You Don't* (1972), and his last film, *Carmen Miranda: Bananas Is My Business* (1993).

Romero received prestigious awards and recognition for his contributions to the film industry and for his impact on and support of the Latino community. In 1984 he was honored at the Hollywood International Celebrity Awards Banquet for his fifty years in the film industry; he received the Nosotros Golden Eagle Award the same year. In 1991 he received the Imagen Hispanic Media Award for Lifetime Achievement, and in 1992, the Beverly Hills Chamber of Commerce recognized him with the Will Rogers Memorial Award. A bachelor all his life, Romero died of a blood clot on January 1, 1994, in Santa Monica, California.

Further Reading

Kanellos, Nicolás, and Cristelia Pérez. *Chronology of Hispanic American History from Pre-Columbian Times to the Present*. Detroit, MI: Gale Research, 1995.

Keller, Gary D. *A Biographical Handbook of Hispanics and United States Film*. Tempe, AZ: Bilingual Press, 1997.

Tardiff, Joseph C., and L. Mpho Mabunda, eds. *Dictionary of Hispanic Biography*. Detroit, MI: Gale Research, 1995.

Alma Alvarez-Smith

Ronstadt, Linda (1946–   ). Linda Marie Ronstadt is one of the most well known singers of *mariachi, rock, country, and American pop music. Ronstadt was born on July 15, 1946, and raised in Tucson, Arizona. Her father is Mexican German, and her mother is of Dutch ancestry. Her *family is

Linda Ronstadt. *Courtesy of Photofest.*

well regarded within the local Tucson community, and her Mexican-born grandfather was himself a musician and conductor of the 1896 Tucson Club Filharmónico.

Ronstadt relocated to Los Angeles in 1964, recording three LPs on Capitol Records with the Stone Ponies between 1966 and 1968 (with Bob Kimmel and Ken Edwards on guitars and vocals). The following solo albums on Capitol labels established her country rock status: *Hand Sown, Home Grown* (1969) and *Silk Purse* (1970), which includes the single hit "Long Long Time," and *Linda Ronstadt* (1972), which includes backing by all four original Eagles. In 1974 she recorded *Heart Like a Wheel* with two hit singles, "You're No Good" and "When Will I Be Loved." By the end of 1982 she had generated five top LPs and a total of eighteen hit singles.

In 1987 Elektra/Asylum Records released *Canciones de mi padre* (Songs of My Father). This album was followed by the sequel *Más canciones* (More Songs) in 1991, also produced by Ronstadt. *Canciones de mi padre* consists of a traditional and popular mariachi repertoire from the golden age of Mexican music.

Ronstadt admits that the most influential figure in her musical development was her aunt, Luisa Ronstadt, a singer, dancer, and actress who called herself Luisa Espinel. *Canciones de Mi Padre* was the title of Luisa's own book of Mexican songs and is a Ronstadt family heirloom. Ronstadt discovered "mariachi music as a way of living." Her biggest challenge was development into a mariachi singer and presenting two album tours by memorizing songs in a language she did not speak with confidence. She faced another challenge in 2004 when rightwing extremists attacked her for recommending the film, *Fahrenheit 9/11*, at the end of a Las Vegas performance.

Further Reading

http://www.divastation.com/linda_ronstadt/ronstadt_bio.html.

Peter J. García

Rosita the Riveter. World War II affected the social and economic status of many American women when a declining workforce, due to the numbers of men going to war and the increased production needs, made it necessary to hire a nontraditional group of workers. Convinced by an aggressive media campaign, women were encouraged to and did take jobs in the defense industry. This era proved to be especially significant for Mexican American women because the labor shortages spurred unprecedented numbers of them into the workforce. Their wage-earning status created a sense of self-sufficiency and intensified issues of self-identity. Although not all women of Mexican heritage joined the workforce during the war, those who did can be viewed as the counterpart to what became known as "Rosie the Riveter." A strong, confident woman who donned work clothes and gripped an acetylene torch while exposing a slightly muscular arm portrayed this image of a national heroine. During the war Mexican American women took their places in defense plants throughout the Southwest and represented "Rosita the Riveter." They received similar benefits to Anglo women, and they endured the same kind of sexual discrimination; but they also dealt with overt racism in the workplace. As a result of their wartime transformations, they questioned and challenged the traditional Mexican roles expected of them as wives and mothers and were determined to live their lives as independent women.

Inherent in responding to the opportunities manifested by the labor shortages, there simmered a desire to fulfill a patriotic duty. The promise of belonging to a nation that had rejected and exploited them caused many to take on their new roles with hopes of change for a better future. Mexican American defense plant worker Margarita Salazar McSweyne recalls being involved in that era when women considered that they were doing something for their country—and at the same time making money. Because of the situation at home, Mexican American men entered the service with no hesitation, and women entered the labor market to discover that, for the first time, they could obtain higher-skilled jobs for much higher wages than they had ever previously earned.

If the war was a temporary boon for white women, for Mexican American women it represented part of a pattern of changes and shifts dependent on the varying needs of the labor market that appeared as an all-too-familiar roller-coaster ride. Nonetheless, the wartime labor shortages created a window of opportunity for ethnic populations historically restricted from achieving economic mobility. Wartime work became the greatest single factor in changing the level of Mexican American employment in the United States.

For Mexican American women the promise of high-skilled labor and good wages pressed them to take advantage of these unprecedented employment opportunities. In her comparative statistical profile of women in the labor market, Vicki Ruiz notes that the number of Mexican American women in clerical and sales positions increased from 10.1 percent in 1930 to 23.9 percent in

1950. These white-collar positions were unattainable by Mexican Americans prior to the war. Wartime employment also gave women the chance to work outside the home and gave them a sense of autonomy and importance. Whereas the traditions of Mexican immigrant women in the 1920s and the 1930s were transformed within a social framework of adjusting to a new culture, and were predicated almost exclusively on the economic survival of the *family, by the 1940s these women and their native-born daughters had become well acquainted with American life. They sought not only economic improvement but also a place in society. Nonetheless, economic necessity remained a major factor in gaining employment. At the onset of the war, Mexican Americans continued to occupy the lower stratum of the economic ladder. In addition, many Mexican and Mexican American women continued to abide by the traditions of their mothers with regard to marriage, family, and customs. And yet the constant exposure to, observation of, and participation in the dominant culture over the preceding two decades set them up, so to speak, to partake in the changes and alterations caused by the war. The new demands of the war on women gave many Mexican American women "cultural permission" to step away from their traditions and take on new customs and expand their experiences and ideas of the world. These new experiences pushed women further into valuing place within and outside the family.

Although scant research has been directed at studying the lives of Mexican-origin women during World War II, the most revealing study in this vein is a collection of the oral histories of defense plant workers compiled by Sherna Gluck. Completed in the 1970s, her important research project, which covers a cultural and ethnic cross section of former workers, sheds light on the lives and experiences of women in the Southern California area. The study includes the stories of nine Mexican-origin women, most of whom were born and raised in the United States. Their experiences as "Rositas" offer some important insights into their lives and the transformations taking place at the time.

Most of the women interviewed were between the ages of eighteen and thirty-five years and had attended public school with little expectation of obtaining good jobs. Consequently they were eager to take advantage of wartime opportunities to obtain higher-skilled work and to earn good wages. Some entered the workforce by interrupting their public education, while others waited until they graduated from high school. The most common response to their work experience is that it took them out of their protected enclave and made them more sophisticated about the world around them. Most of the interviewees are emphatic about how their work experience gave them a sense of heightened self-esteem. It is clear that women took pride in their economic autonomy; and just as important, they gained confidence in their ability to take on the responsibilities of work and family and enjoyed learning new skills, achieving workplace goals, and contributing to the war effort. These experiences are reflected in some of their comments, which are paraphrased here: I felt I was worth something; I expanded my horizons; I felt proud of myself. Many of the interviewees continued to work after the war, no longer content with the traditional role of stay-at-home wife and mother. Several clearly expressed their discontent with the old traditions; they enjoyed their work experiences and had no desire to return to their former traditional roles.

However, several of the women also recall their contempt of the sexual discrimination they experienced in the workplace. For example, interviewee Mary Luna recalls her painful experiences with male hostility and sexism on the job. She endured being yelled at, belittled, and passed over for promotion. In fact, she notes that even though the majority of workers at her plant were female, the men were always promoted over women. She also remembers that some women did manage to make inroads into higher supervisory positions but did so at a price, having to work twice as hard as the men and having to be very aggressive. It appears that most of the female workers were intensely aware of their marginalization.

Perhaps the most compelling consequences of the independence that many "Rositas" gained are revealed in their attitudes about male/female relationships *after* the war. For example, interviewee Beatrice Escheverria-Mulligan expresses her theory for the high postwar divorce rate. She recollects the weariness and uncertainty with which most men returned from the war and how they stood in stark contrast to the women who were cultivating a positive sense of confidence and self-esteem. This caused great conflicts in relationships. María Fierro adds to this by asserting that if she had it to do over again, she would never have gotten married. Her postwar marriage made her intolerant of negative male behavior. She believed she was better off alone, rather than taking on her husband's daily negativity. Many of the interviewees express a similar preference and intolerance of old forms of patriarchal control. Mary Luna also expresses this autonomy.

For "Rosita the Riveter" wartime transformations provided greater freedom and space to cultivate the skills and confidence needed to manage and negotiate personal, social, and economic circumstances. These changes created a *de facto* grassroots feminist consciousness comparable to that which followed the post–Civil War era in the United States and eventually led to the strengthening of the women's suffrage movement that produced the 19th Amendment to the Constitution. The lives of these workingwomen shed light on how they shared common experiences with women of the dominant culture. However, the lives of the "Rositas" also provide insight into the unique cultural dynamics that helped transform a generation of Mexican American women.

Further Reading

Barrera, Mario. *Race and Class in the Southwest.* Notre Dame, IN: University of Notre Dame Press, 1980.

Gluck, Sherna. *Rosie the Riveter Revisited: Women, the War, and Social Change.* Boston: G.K. Hall/Twayne Publishers, 1987.

Ruiz, Vicki L. "And Miles to Go: Mexican Women and Work, 1930–1985." In *Western Women: Their Land, Their Lives*, edited by Lillian Schlissel, Vicki Ruiz, and Janice Monk. Albuquerque: University of New Mexico Press, 1988.

Naomi Helena Quiñónez

Ros-Lehtinen, Ileana (1952–   ). In 1982, when Ileana Ros-Lehtinen began her political career, she made history and began a string of firsts as the first Cuban-born woman elected to the Florida state legislature. Ros-Lehtinen served as a representative from 1982 until 1986, then served as a senator from 1986 until 1989. When she captured a congressional seat in 1989, she claimed the title of first *Cuban American and first Hispanic woman elected to the U.S. Congress. As a Republican member of the U.S. House of Representatives, Ros-Lehtinen represents the Eighteenth Congressional District of Florida and has gained the designation of being the first Hispanic woman to chair a subcommittee.

Ros-Lehtinen was born on July 15, 1952, to Enrique Emilio and Amanda Adato Ros, in Havana, Cuba. At the age of seven, Ros-Lehtinen left Cuba with her parents and brother to escape Fidel *Castro's dictatorship (*see* Cuban Revolution). Although the Ros *family initially thought they would return to Cuba someday, her father eventually came to the realization that the United States would be their permanent home, and he made a commitment to raise his children as patriotic, loyal Americans. He instilled a love for politics in his daughter and encouraged her to pursue a political career.

Ros-Lehtinen earned her Associate of Arts degree from Miami-Dade Community College in 1972, her Bachelor of Arts in 1975, and her Master of Science in educational leadership in 1986, both from Florida International University, then went on to study educational administration as a doctoral candidate at the University of Miami. Ros-Lehtinen founded the Eastern Academy, a private elementary school in southern Florida, where she taught and worked as principal before she began her political career. Understanding firsthand the difficulty of financing an education, once in office one of Ros-Lehtinen's greatest accomplishments has been the creation of the Florida Pre-paid College Tuition Program.

As the first and one of a handful of Latinas who hold political office, Ros-Lehtinen takes her responsibility as a role model seriously. She is concerned about human rights internationally and about issues including education, children, victim's rights, and the environment. She is a visible and vocal opponent to Castro's rule, speaking out against his supporters, while focusing her efforts on *immigration issues and the passage of the Cuban Democracy Act and the Cuban Liberty and Democratic Solidarity Act.

Ros-Lehtinen has been able to help shape foreign policy through her assignments on the Foreign Affairs and Government Operations Committees, as well as the subcommittee on International Operations and Human Rights, assignments of significant importance to her Cuban American constituents.

During the 104th Congress, she was named the chair of the Africa Subcommittee and designated as vice-chair of the Western Hemisphere Subcommittee. Ros-Lehtinen is known for her anticommunist sentiment, her stance on antiabortion and other conservative positions (e.g., the death penalty for convicted organizers of drug rings and flag burners). Much of her work has centered on tax issues such as the prepaid college tuition program, the phasing out of inheritance taxes, tax credits to employers who offer child care, and the Marriage Tax Elimination Act of 1999.

Further Reading

Kamp, Jim, and Diane Telgen. *Latinas: Women of Achievement.* Detroit, MI: Visible Ink Press, 1996.

http://clerk.house.gov/members/inter_mem_list.php?statdis=FL18.

http://www.loc.gov/rr/hispanic/congress/roslehtinen.html.

Cristina K. Muñoz

Royal Chicano Air Force (RCAF). The Royal Chicano Air Force (RCAF) was founded in 1969 as an artists' collective committed to social change in the *Chicano community. The founders, José Montoya and Esteban Villa, were originally part of a group called the Mexican American Liberation Art Front (MALA-F), a group of artists committed to the United Farm Worker struggle. Their philosophy regarding the artist's role to improve and empower the community influenced both men in their roles as activist art cultural workers. MALA-F disbanded in 1969, and Montoya and Villa were hired as professors for the newly created Ethnic Studies Department at California State University, Sacramento (CSUS). Continuing the ideas of MALA-F in their CSUS positions, they formed a new group in support of the movement to organize farmworkers in California. Professors and a group of art, English, and graphic design students became part of this group, including Ricardo Favela, Rudy Cuellar, Juanishi Orosco, Louie González, and Max García. This group chose the name "Rebel Chicano Art Front" as a tribute to MALA-F. Because the acronym RCAF called to mind the Royal Canadian Air Force, the humorous parallel was adopted, and the "Royal Chicano Air Force" was born as a tongue-in-cheek way to avoid confusion with the "Royal Canadian Air Force." They presented their work to the community through murals, print production and distribution, poetry readings, and educational workshops. The RCAF's most notable method of presentation was their murals.

The RCAF membership was the strongest during the early 1970s. Many of those who were members were formers students of Montoya and Villa who wanted to be part of the mobilization of people through their images on murals and print productions. RCAF went beyond using art to educate and help their communities with the creation of the Centro de Artista's Chicanos. This nonprofit organization assisted the cultural and political activism through their traveling projects. The Centro de Artista's Chicanos was also used as an agency to provide the following social services: the low-income Breakfast for Niños program, La Nueva Raza Bookstore, Aeronaves de Aztlán (Automotive Repair Garage), RCAF Danzantes (Cultural Dance Venue), *Barrio Art Program, the Chicano Culture Committee, the Alkali Redevelopment Committee, which worked on housing projects, and the Human Development Unit of Sacramento.

The RCAF is nationally recognized for their work, especially their murals. Their images of cultural empowerment, political involvement, and indigenous heritage remain on many walls today in Sacramento and San Diego as reminders of the long-standing heritage of Chicano peoples and the commitment to social justice in the Chicano community.

Further Reading

http://www.chilipie.com/rcaf.

Silvia D. Mora

Rumba. First documented in the 1850s, *rumba* is the result of colonial trade and the synthesis of the quotidian exchange between the descendants of captive Africans and the dominant Spanish culture. Rumba is an example of Cuba's Afro-European process of transculturation. It has been considered Cuba's first *música criolla* (creole music), a native music characteristic of the Caribbean, and the word is now synonymous with "party" in Latin American and Caribbean countries like Panama, Colombia, and Puerto Rico. Like *tumba* and *makumba*, rumba's general meaning is that of festive celebration and collective social gathering. Rumba's cousins are Brazil's *Samba de (roda)* (*see* Samba), the Colombian *cumbia, the Peruvian *samba cueta*, the Panamanian *tamborito*, and the Jamaican *mento*; all are of secular character in which the male courts or pursues the female through dance. While the word *rumba* originated in Spain, it does not refer to a Spanish dance. Rather, rumba was used as a sexist and classist pejorative to refer to women of "la vida alegre" (the happy life), probably sex workers, "mujeres de rumbo" (lascivious women). In Cuba, rumba became a designation of frivolity and described Afro-descendant fiestas or celebrations organized by the lowest social strata of the time. Thus, the name "rumba" implied and marked its practitioners with prejudice in its very conception in spite of being considered one of the most important cultural manifestations of Cuban origin.

Rumba's ethnic routes trace the Spanish, British, and Portuguese slave trades that brought men, women, and children of different African cultural regions into Cuba. Between 1512 and 1865, people were taken by the slave trade from an area in the West African Coast between the Gulf of Guinea and what is now the Angola Republic. In addition to the 525,828 registered slaves imported during that period, another 200,000 Africans may have been brought to Cuba in the ongoing illegal contraband that continued through 1875, the height of the island's agricultural development. Slavery was abolished in 1880 but it actually ended with passage of the Patronato law on October 7, 1886. The ritual musics of these diverse ethnic groups were characterized by complicated, syncopated rhythmic structures that—in contrast to European convention—emphasized the improvisation of the lower-register instruments. Consequently, higher-pitched instruments passed to a secondary role known as "accompaniment" within the European musical concept.

It is possible that the most direct connection to rumba is the Bantú culture that inhabited the region of the Congo River Delta. Rumba also includes elements from the Ganga culture from Sierra Leone, Ivory Coast, and northern Liberia. In Cuba, however, the ethnic mix and cultural exchange produced a phenomenon of sound fields inversion: the lower-pitched instruments took over the continuous rhythmic patterns, while the higher-pitched became the ones that improvised, thus taking the weight of creating and defining melody. This is why rumba can be understood as a musical form that incorporates African music concepts of interpretation but with an instrumental fusion distributed according to the logic of the European musical discourse. Also, there is an evident influence of Spanish *Cante Jondo* (Deep Song) in rumba's lyrics mixed with onomatopoeic phrases, ideas, and forms of African origin. However, rumba's origins can be located both in Havana's predominantly black, underprivileged urban areas and inner-city zones and within the semirural areas of Mantanzas that surrounded the sugar mills, the *centrales azucareros*.

Rumba's interpretation is based in the percussion of drums or wood boxes, sticks (or claves), and metal spoons. The African contribution is in its rhythm. In most forms of rumba, the singer starts the song with a call sung to the people, known as the *Diana*, which also establishes the keynote for the responding chorus. After the Diana, the singer begins the lyrical portion of the song, based on a ten-lined poetic theme, or *décima, that produces rumba's rhythmic climax. Subsequently, the *capetillo* is the responding chorus, which serves as the cue for dancers to enter the circle. The *capetillo* establishes a call-and-response relationship with the lead singer, who is now free to improvise his lines. During colonial times (known as *tiempo españa*) *rumberos* used two wood boxes of different dimensions, built from the thick wood of catfish boxes—for the larger box—and the fine wood of candle boxes—for the smaller one. The biggest, lowest-pitched box, or *cajon*, maintained the rhythm via repeated patterns and functioned as the *tumbadora*. The smaller box with the highest and brightest pitch, or *quinto*, served to improvise rhythmic fragments based on the musician's individual tastes and skills. Rumba's critical element of improvisation depended on such rustic instruments as the sideboard of a cabinet, an emptied drawer or the catfish and candle light boxes themselves, a *cantina*'s (tavern or other drinking establishment) long bar, glass bottles, frying pans. In short, any sonorous surface. By the 1930s, these rustic elements transformed; the *cajones* were replaced by the popular Cuban *tumbadora*, internationally known as the "conga." Each drum acquired the name of the wood box it replaced, in ascending order of pitch: *tumbadora*, *tres-dos* (or *tres golpes*), and *quinto*.

The variants of rumba that remain in practice are *yambú* (box rumba), *guaguancó* (popular form), and *columbias* (country or rural form). The *yambú* and *guaguancó*'s sources were Havana's *coros de clave* (choruses of clave), and Matanzas' *bandos de calle* (Street Bands). Both took place when the *cabildos*—mutual help associations made up of primarily free men of specific African ethnic groups who performed their music during street processions either celebrating their anniversaries or Christmas festivities. It is likely that the *coros* are as old as the *cabildos* and were music groups dedicated to collective secular singing composed by Afro-descendants, *criollos* (born on the island). While it is possible that the organization of the *coros* indeed maintained or inherited some of the *cabildos*'s structure, the *coros* represented neighborhoods, not African nations as the *cabildos* did. *Cabildos* were self-help institutions and societies primarily concerned with maintaining social cohesion within and between the members of the same nation. They promoted and sustained their culture through secular and religious practices. For instance, Havana's municipality authorized the *cabildos* to use public spaces from 9 A.M. to sunset for their processions and *comparsas* celebrating Día de Reyes (Day of Kings) on January 6.

Some of these *cabildos* were the precursors of famous *coros* such as El Arpa de Oro (The Golden Harp). These choral institutions emphasized the vocal and poetic quality of their compositions to the degree that they had to register them with the "Lapiz Rojo" (Red Pencil) Tribunal, which had the power to approve the quality of the songs and authorize their public performance. They also had a "censor" who corrected the lyrics and the *décimas*'s measurement. The *coros de claves* and *bandos de calle* included as many as 100 voices and held formal competitions. Among the most recognized *clarinas* were Paulina Rivera and La Valenciana; among the *decimistas* were Ignacio Piñeiro and Joseíto Agustín Bonilla. Between 1900 and 1914, some of the most famous claves were "El Paso Franco" (The French Pass) from Havana's Del Pilar (From the Basin), and "Los Roncos" (The Hoarse Ones, founded by Ignacio Piñeiro) from the Pueblo Nuevo neighborhood. Some sources establish these gatherings as what eventually transformed into rumba events. Others separate the *coros de clave* and *bandos de clave* from the subsequent formation of *coros de rumba*. An important group that continues this tradition is Coro Folklórico Cubano, directed by Pedro Pablo "Aspirina" Rodríguez with the cast of Guillermo Triana, Maximino Duquesne, Lazaro Riso, and Zuzana "Beba" Calzado, cofounder in 1953 with Odilio Urfe.

Yambú

The *yambú*, or *rumba de cajón* (box rumba), is the oldest form still in practice, and the Yuka dance is its oldest antecedent. The *yambú* is a dance representation of love, a *canto* (song) of fecundity. The male, with smooth gestures and disguised intentions, symbolically tries to posses the female. But in the *yambú no se vacuna* (there is no vaccination)—the female can dance with careless cadence, unconcerned, as she does not have to protect herself against the known *vacunado*, a male's pelvic gesture typical of the *guaguancó* and symbolic of "possession." While the male's intentions to possess her are the same as in the *guaguancó*, in the *yambú* form, he conceals them. Like the *yambú*, mimetic rumbas also took place during the so-called *tiempo españa*. While *yambú* served as a couple's dance, during the colonial era it also functioned as the rhythm of many known mimetic rumbas that satirized the customs of the period.

Guaguancó

This is rumba's most contemporary modality and internationally the most known form. The *yambú* is the antecedent of the *guaguancó* because the *yambú*'s popularity produced structural modifications in its singing and instrumentation: The singing stretched its compasses, and the original wooden boxes were replaced by cylindrical membranophonic drums made of wood, with goat- or cow-skin heads. These drums were called *tumba*, *llamador*, and *quinto*.

One of *guaguancó*'s most prominent composers was Alberto Zayas Govin, known as "El Melodioso" (The Melodious One). Although a native of Matanzas, he grew up in Havana and became an expert in the field after dedicating himself to extensive research on Afro-Cuban rhythms. During the 1950s, Zayas, in collaboration with Ignacio Piñeiro, Rafael Ortiz, and renowned musicologist Odilio Urfe, invited Carlos Embale to record *guaguancós* with his Grupo Afrocubano. Embale was already a rising star; he was a prizewinner in the Art's Supreme Court, member of the *comparsa* La Jardinera (Garden Party), and singer in Ignacio Piñeiro's Septeto Nacional. Zayas also recorded with other legends such as Alberto Maza, composer of the rumba "El Vive Bien Sopita en Botella" (He Lives Well, Soup in a Bottle), and the great Omo Aña Girardo Rodríguez, teacher of master *rumbero* Pancho Quinto, another important figure.

In the *guaguancó*, the female dancer has to be attentive and protective to avoid being *vacunada* (literally, "vaccinated"). This seduction or fertility dance is the dynamic pursuit of the hen by the cock, a sensuous competition between the female's skilled flirtation and the male's surprising *vacunado* steps, the symbolic gesture of sexual possession. Dancing, he is trying to "win her"; if he fails, another dancer will take the floor with the same intention.

During the 1950s, the rumba took place in city *solares* (working-class living compounds with a central patio) and in *centrales azucareros* (sugar refineries) of the *muelles* (ports). Among the most popular were "El Africa," "Los Barracones," "El Reberbero," and in Matanzas, "El Festejo." *Solares* were, and some still are, places inhabited by *gente sencilla* (common people), where everybody knows each other and rumba is the most appropriated form of entertainment to play and dance to forget their pain—"para olvidar sus penas." Their rumba compositions served as political and social chronicles.

In 1952, a group of friends from the Matanzas neighborhood La Marina used to listen to records at the El Gallo bar until they formalized their spontaneous artistic interaction into the rumba ensemble Guaguancó Matancero. The experienced Florencio Calle Catalino, known as Mulense, directed the group, composed of Esteban Lantri "Saldiguera," Esteban Bacallao, Gregorio Díaz, Pablo and Juan Mesa, Ángel Pellado, and Hortencio Alfonso "Virulilla." They performed in the celebrations of the Marina and Simpson neighborhoods as well as in Havana with important orchestras such as the Orquesta Aragón and Arcano y sus Maravillas. They participated on radio and TV programs with the recording label Puchito in 1953 and 1955; then with Panart in 1954. The contents of their first 78 rpm record in 1954 were the *guaguancó* "Los Beodos" (The Drunks) on one side and "Los Muñequitos" (The Dolls) on the other. "Los Muñequitos" narrated the stories of characters from the weekend comic strips of the *Nation* newspaper. This number, popular through every jukebox in Matanzas and Havana, became such a national hit that people began to identify them as "Los Muñequitos de Matanzas," a name they decided to retain and that gained international recognition. These recordings also established their rumba style, which was eventually generalized as characteristic of the Matanzas region.

In 1947 at a different location in the hemisphere, Luciano Chano *Pozo introduced the *tumbadora* for the first time to the U.S. jazz scene through his collaboration with trumpeter Dizzy Gillespie. Experimenting with the various roots of the African diaspora, they created the intersection between Afro-Cuban rhythmic forms and this U.S. native form. Jazz became the musical location in which other important *rumberos* such as Mongo Santamaría, Candido Camero, Carlos "Patato" Valdès, Julito Collazo, Virgilio Martí, Francisco Aguabella, Daniel "el paisa" Ponce, Orlando "Puntilla" Ríos, and Eugenio "Tótico" Arango eventually met outside Cuba in subsequent decades.

In 1951, Arsenio Rodríguez established himself in New York. He was already internationally known for having revolutionized the music scene in the late 1930s by introducing a piano, three trumpets, *tumbadora*, and a new repertoire to the Cuban form known as *conjunto*. *Conjunto* music eventually became fundamental in the international craze of the Cuban *son period. The *son* soon conflated into rumba's bastardization known then within the cabaret and casino context as "rhumba." Rodríguez's introduction of the *tumbadora* (known as conga) became a trend in the performance of future musical movements such as *guaracha*, *bolero, and *mambo. However, what became his signature was his performance of the *tres*, a stringed instrument that uses three sets of double or triple strings. It is considered a native synthesis of Cuba's Spanish and African cultural heritage. Rodríguez incorporated the rhythms of rumba's *quinto* (the high-pitch solo drum) into his performance of the *tres*. This is not a coincidence; Rodríguez was born in 1911 in Matanzas province, and many of his generation were the grandchildren of slaves, and his grandfather was from the Congo. He became blind at the age of seven, but he learned the secrets of the drum through his *tamborero* uncle Guigo, who was part of the Matanzas genealogy of rumba masters such as Malanga, Tanganica, Mulense, and Andrea Baró. Rodríguez had also learned to play other African-derived bass instruments, such as the *marímbula* (a wooden box fitted with metal prongs), the *botija* (a blown jug), and the *tingo talango* (a stick with a metal string). These instruments were essential in rumba. Some of Rodríguez's rumba-related numbers are "Mulence," which narrated a dispute between the two famous *rumberos*, "Mulence" and "Manana," and many others related to the rumba–rich *barrios (neighborhoods), such as "Buena Vista en Guaguancó" (Nice View in Guaguancó) and "Juventud the Cayo Hueso" (Key West Youth). Rodríguez's virtuosity became a legacy in Cuban music and the world's, embedded in *son*, across jazz, and remaining in *salsa.

One of the reasons that rumba found another home in New York with the *Boricúa people is because Puerto Rico's *bomba music is also of Bantú and Dahomey origin. The Puertorican and Nuyorican community has assimilated the form with their own style and grace. During the mid-1950s, the master Tito *Puente was one of its most important contributors. His Cuban contemporary Mario *Bauzá was another important contributor of the time, along with *Machito and his Afro-Cubans. Since the late 1970s, and at the grassroots level, producer and historian René López has maintained an important connection with Cuba. He traveled there and informally recorded rumbas with the help of Jesús Blanco Aguilar and Odilio Urfé. López recorded his "great heroes," Los Muñequitos de Matanzas. López shared his recordings and experiences with New York musicians of the caliber of Andy and Jerry González, Milton Cardona, Frankie Rodríquez, Gene Golden, and others who eventually became the Grupo Folklórico y Experimental Nuevayorquino. They also had started their New York City rumba journey with figures like Patato Valdes and Julito Collazo. Other younger musicians such as Eddy Bobbe, Eddy Rodríguez, and Felix Sanabria also continued learning from López's tapes and the circulating records of the time—those of Los Muñequitos and Ramon "Mongo" Santamaria's. Mongo arrived in New York in 1950 and recorded the albums *Chango Afro-Cuban Drums* and *Yambú*. The Grupo Folklórico served as an important source for rumba's contemporary movement and *Latin jazz in New York as well as in Havana. Subsequent Nuyorican generations of "becoming *rumberos*" continued practicing in their homes and the public places where they gathered. Patato Valdès—in spite of being a well-established musician—always visited Central Park and played with rumba's up-and-coming generations. Valdés was already known in Cuba for inventing the *tonable tumbadora*, the *tumbadora* with a tuning system based on a metal head rim, hooked bolts, and tensioning legs. The rumbas in Central Park, Prospect Park, and Orchard Beach, as well as on street corners and in local bars of the Bronx, El Barrio (Spanish Harlem), and Loisaida (the Lower East Side and Alphabet City), became trademark of New York City's Afro-Latin diaspora.

By 1962 in Havana, the Ballet Folklórico Nacional, directed by Martha Blanco, opened its doors. The goal of this company was to maintain and sustain the essential African presence in Cuban culture through its artistic practice and oral tradition transmitted through generations from the original sources. The founding consultant was musicologist Rogelio Martínez Furé; Mexican Rodolfo Reyes was the choreographer; and the set designer was Salvador Fernández. They collaborated with many respected musicians and dancers. Of the 400 people who auditioned, a total 56 dancers, singers, and musicians were selected. The ballet's rumba component was interpreted by Luis "Aspirina" Chacón and Justo and Gabriel Pelladito on the *quinto*; Ramiro Hernández, Jesús Pérez, and Felipe Alfonso on *tumbador*; Alfonso Aldama on *tres golpes*; and Emilio O'Farrill on *palitos* or *cata*. The singers were Trinidad Torregrosa and Nieves Fresneda; the dancers were Manuela Alonso, Orlando López, and Zenaida and Ramiro Hernández. The rumba *columbia* dancers were Gabriel Pelladito, Ricardo Gómez, Orlando López, and Luis "Aspirina" Chacón. The *columbia* singer was Mario Dreke Chavalonga, known as the "Tenor of the rumba" and member of the legendary rumba family whose father was "Perico" and whose brothers were "Curvo" and Enrique "Kiki" Chavalonga. In 1980, Kiki arrived in New York City and had become famous by 1981 for his dangerous and acrobatic choreography in the local rumba group Chevere Macunchevere, formed in September 1980.

The Chavalonga family is from the Atarés, a famous neighborhood and mecca of *rumberos* such as Gonzalo Asencio, known as el Tio Tom. Apart from Mulense, Asencio is considered the most prolific rumba composer of his times for his over 200 rumbas, including the controversial "A dónde están los Cubanos?" (Where Are the Cubans?), "Mi Tierra" (My Land), "No Me Culpes A Mi" (Don't Blame Me, sung by Roberto Maza), and his first composition, "Mujer de Cabaret" (Cabaret Woman). The authors and dates of many compositions are unknown because the lyrics are orally transmitted, reorganized in their daily performance, and maintained via collective memory.

From the 1960s on, rumba became the base for the elaboration of different styles and new rhythms, allowing each group to create their particular characteristics. In Havana, Papin and his *rumberos*, later known as Los Papines, presented the duet of Fijo and Alejo interpreting Spanish-style songs. Rumba influenced rhythms such as Pello el Afrokan's "Mozambique," Guanabacoaense Luis "Aspirina" Chacon's "Xicamalé," Tato's rhythm *guapará* from the La Perla neighborhood, and Johnson's *guaguancó* with guitar from the El Cerro neighborhood. In Matanzas in 1957, Francisco "Minini"

Zamora founded Afrocuba de Matanzas, and in the early 1970s Los Muñequitos reappeared with an elaborated work of voices and percussion that they keep renovating to the present.

Rumba in the diaspora, however, marked New York City's music history while it simultaneously revitalized itself with the various Cuban *immigrations, particularly the 1980 "Mariel boatlift" (*see* Marielitos). In addition, there has been an ongoing arrival of already established professional *rumberos* who decided to continue their musical experimentation abroad. The boat lift introduced to New York *rumberos* such as Manuel Martínez Olivera, El Llanero (The Lone Ranger); El Tao la Onda (The Wave of Tao), Daniel Ponce; Orlando "Puntilla" Rios; and Xiomara Rodríguez. El Llanero—Patato Valdès's cousin—contributed to the existing New York City rumba scene with his deep understanding of the strict rules of clave in relationship to singing and the improvisational performance of the *quinto*. Rubén González, known as El Tao la Onda, arrived with his extensive repertoire of original compositions including the popular "La Habana" (interpreted by Yoruba Andabo in the 2002 CD *La Rumba Soy Yo* and awarded the Latin Grammy). Rodríguez has dedicated her life to teaching the dances of rumba and the Cuban religious pantheon. During the late 1950s Patato Valdès and Eugenio "Totico" Arango had already recorded in the United States with Virgilio Martí the rumba classic "Llego Superman Bailando el Guaguancó" (Superman Arrived Dancing the Guaguancó); in 1983, Orlando "Puntilla" Rios recorded with Totico, Abraham Rodríguez, Andy González, and Encarnación Perez another U.S. classic, "What's Your Name?"—a rumba adaptation of the famous 1950s doo-wop by Don & Juan. In 1986 Puntilla also came up with his record *Puntilla from La Habana to New York*, with its classic "Rumba para Elegua." Daniel Ponce, who collaborated with Puntilla, also produced two crucial records for the rumba/Latin jazz collection, "New York Now!" and "Chango Te Llama" (Chango Calls), while introducing rumba into the avant-garde art scene via his collaboration with performance artist Laurie Anderson.

Guarapachanguero

During the late 1970s, the *guaguancó* in Havana took a different direction. A new rumba movement was being created in the La Korea neighborhood, baptized by the same Manuel "El Llanero" Martínez as *guarapachanguero* but invented by his neighbors, the López brothers, "Los Chinitos." One of the brothers, Irian, designed the popular *cajón* (wood box) known as the *raspadura*, a large wood box with a pyramid shape. This new style and instrumentation of complicated syncopation and countertimes became popular only in the early 1980s because of the event that took place in Havana's Peruvian embassy, precipitating the great exodus from the Bay of Mariel. Becoming soon controversial, notorious *rumberos*, such as Jacinto

Scull Castillo "El Chori," Juan de Dios Ramos, the Figueroa brothers, who organized a known *peña* (public gathering place located at Calzada de Luwiano), and others, defied the so-called traditionalists and spread the new rhythm through the city. Indeed, Maximino Duquesne, Marquito Herminio Díaz, and the legendary Francisco Hernández Mora (Pancho Quinto) can be considered *guarapachanguero*'s godfathers. Quinto, founder of the prestigious group Yoruba Andabo, used the sound of the old *cajón* (wood box) as rhythmic base but toned them, respectively, as the *tumbador*, *tres golpes*, and *quinto*, all added to the rest of rumba's original instruments: clave, *catá*, and *chequeré*. Thus Quinto's virtuosity and Chori's flavor conveyed the *guarapachanguero* into the group's rhythmic signature. The original voices of Yoruba Andabo were (the now deceased) composer Calixto Callava, Pedro Fariñas, Guillermo "El Negro" Triana, Juan "Chan" Campos, and Giovanni del Pino, who stayed as the director.

In 1954, Miguel Angel "Aspirina" Mesa Cruz (born in Guanabacoa on June 7, 1926) founded the Conjunto Clave y Guaguancó with the involvement of Argeliers de León and under the direction of Mario Galán. The first singer was Agustin Pina, better known as "Flor de Amor" (Flower of Love), with Rolando, known as "Malanga," and Agustin Gutierrez. "El Pequi" danced with Angelita Valdez, who also was the voice prima. (In rumba, singing duets are performed in voice prima and segunda [prime and second voices].) When Galán passed away, Miguel Chapotin (currently singing with Yoruba Andabo) became the director. Clave y Guaguancó maintained the original format (two wood boxes, one *tumbador* and *quinto*) until Amado de Deus became the director. De Deus incorporated the new *guarapachanguero* current with its original instruments, the *cajones raspaduras*.

The *guarapachanguero* has become a generalized movement among the youngest generations. However, its creators—Los Chinitos—had their own particular style, and in Yoruba Andabo, Quinto added to the form three *batá* drums, while El Chori (from the same group) mixed the base of the *tres golpes* drum with open movements in a separate drum. In other words, in the *guarapachanguero*, the rumba movement traditionally performed in one *tres-dos* drum was split into two drums: The base wood box drum was used for the base part of the phrase, while a *tres-dos* drum was used for the open sounds. This combination resulted in the enrichment of the full *tres-dos* movement. Orlando Lage "Palito" from the same group would play simultaneously two *quintos*, one, a wood box, and the other, a membraphonic *quinto*. All these sounds fall into Quinto's left-hand rhythm using a *cuchara* (spoon) and creating a complicated polyrhythmic dynamic. Indeed, the *guarapachanguero* had revolted into the African logic of reemphazising the lower drum base interpreted within this context in its wood box version. This dynamic had been, and remains, a controversy among *rumberos* because it does not prioritize the *quinto* drum as the unique *solo* drum. The *guarapachanguero* emphasizes the base sound, the *tumbadora* box improvisation—but maintaining its dialogue with the *quinto*. Furthermore, the role of each instrument is performed in two percussive versions, the membraphoic drum and the wood box of both: the *quinto* and the *tumbador*. Within the *guarapachanguero quinto-tumbador* conversation, there exists an influence from the conversation between the *batás*—Itotele, Iya, and Okonkolo—because Quinto's virtuoso polyrhythmic style is founded on his deep knowledge about improvisation with the batá drums. Maximino's style, on the other hand, is based on his experience and deep knowledge of the *caja*; the *tumbadora* drum is dedicated to improvising in *bembes* (Cuban rhythm used in Santería) or guiros. This particular drum is also called a *caja* in other Cuban religious genres such as Palo and Makumba. It is the conversation between the *quinto* and the *tumbadora* or *caja* and the *cajón* that creates *guarapachanguero*'s jazz atmosphere based on improvisation over the same melody; in this context the singer provides the melody. The *tres-dos* (or *tres-golpes*) drum and music phrase (or movement) has historically identified the *guaguancó*. In the *guarapachanguero*, the *tres-dos* can be performed in different places within the clave's phrase. The musician's individual knowledge and control of the *tres-dos* is what helps his/her improvisation and his/her ability of execution in the different sounds of the drum: the low, the open, the slap called *tapado*, and the pressured moff called the *presionado* sound. In the *guarapachanguero*, the function of the *tres-dos* is internalized: *el tres-dos puede no verse pero siempre sentirse* (the three-two may not be seen, but it is always felt).

Columbia

According to tradition, *columbia* is a style born in the countryside, the rural areas located in the Matanzas and surrounding provinces such as Union de Reyes, Jovellanos, and Colón. Oral history has it that in 1880 the first *columbia* songs were performed in a *caserío* (village) named Columbia located between Sabanilla and Union de Reyes. However, it is in 1917 that the so-called *invación de los rumberos* (the *rumberos*' invasion) took place during the sugar season in these regions when famous *rumberos* from all over the country—such as the great Malanga from Sabanilla de Comendador, in Union de Reyes—traveled the island in search of employment. After their arduous labor, they competed among themselves, elaborating complicated dance steps that demonstrated their ability as *columbia* dancers. The dancer uses his steps to communicate with the *quinto* drum percussionist, who is equally improvising in relationship to the dancer's steps—"el baile es sacar chispa del suelo" (the dance is to make the floor spark). This communication between the *columbiano* and the *quinto* soloist is also prevalent in Cuban ceremonial African practices such as the Abakuá's with its Ireme dancing to the Bonko Echemiya drum. The *columbianos*' figures range from the playful mimetic gesture of playing *pelota* (baseball) to highly acrobatic jumps and splits. Older dance traditions such as that of Bantú roots *Mani* were quite famous among slave owners, who originally organized these galas. It is possible that this context served as a model to the male-dance competitive tradition. According to the recognized *columbia dancer*, Mr. Machaco, a member of the group Columbia del Puerto de Cardenas, there were famous female *columbia* dancers who knew the necessary "treaties" to achieve this explosive dance, faster than the *guaguancó* and the *yambú*. The most famous of them was Andrea Baró.

Other women achieved great fame through singing on the rumba scene, such as the *cantadora* Celeste Mendoza, better known as the "Queen of Guaguancó." She was a stylish woman known for her unique way of singing and her beautiful dresses. Her stage presence was such that the audience formed the impression that all the men were dancing with her! Maria Carballo was the recognized director of the *comparsa* La Guarachera de Pueblo Nuevo, where the figure Manuela Alonso, mother of one of the three great *columbia* dancers—Orlando el Bailarín—danced and sang. These *comparsas* included rumba choreographies performed in the Carnival's Presidential Tribune, where famous *rumberas* from all the provinces congregated. Carnival's judges analyze the parade from this tribune.

One of the most representative families in the tradition has been the Aspirina dynasty. They are *rumberos completos* (completely rumberos). As they say, "Lo mismo te la cantan, que te la bailan, que te la tocan!" (likewise we sing, dance, and play). The Aspirinas have become an academia in rumba and the various Cuban religious practices such as Regla de Ocha, Palo Mayombe, and Abakuá. For instance, Pedro Pablo Rodríguez Valdés is the current director of the prestigious Coro Folklórico Cubano. Luis Chacón has his own dance academy and is known for having invented the style of *columbia* danced with knives. In batá drumming and *quinto* percussion, Mario Jauregui is already a legend. As a singer, Miguel Angel Mesa Cruz, "el caballero de la rumba" (rumba cowboy), is the *columbiano mayor* (the best at the highest rank). His elegance fills the stage; his gifts are his high-pitched voice and his ability to improvise elastic *columbia décimas* in Spanish, combined with Congo and Abakuá languages. Controversy is the motor force of rumba *columbia*, a back-and-forth dialogue between the opening and forthcoming singers who have to maintain the topic once it has been established while responding to each other with rhyming verses and/or *décimas*.

In 1992 Los Muñequitos de Matanzas had their first nine-week U.S. tour, the longest ever by Cuban musicians in the United States to date. They recorded *Vacunao* in Boston, produced by Ned Sublette on the Qbdisc label. In 1996, Quinto, with Guillermo "El Negro" [the black one] Triana, Lazaro Riso, Octavio Rodríguez, Juan "Chan" Campos, and Omar Sosa, among others, recorded in Havana and produced in San Francisco Quinto's experimental sounds in *En el Solar de la Cueva del Humo* (In the space of the smoky cave, 1996) produced by Greg Landau on the Round World Music label. Notable is the work of John Santos, Michael Spiro, Jesús Díaz, and the deceased Jerry Shilgi from the Bay Area in developing a West Coast rumba scene with diverse projects and collaborations with Cuban musicians from the island (like Regino Jiménez and Lazaro Ross) and those in the diaspora like Roberto Borrel. Another classic for the record is *Rapsodia Rumbera* (Rumba Rhapsody), produced by Gregorio "Goyo" Hernández under the Cuban label Egrem. Also, under Goyo's musical direction and production (with Helio Orovio's supervision under Unicornio's Cuban label), the CD *La Rumba es Cubana Su Historia* (The Rumba Is Cuban History) includes a broad range of rumba generations such as the great Mario Alfonso Dreke "Chavalonga" and Abreu, the Chinitos' *guarapachanguero*, and female legends Guillermina Z. Armenteros and Zuzana "Beba" Calzado.

Peñas

During the late 1980s and on, the *peñas* became popular public places in Havana to dance and hear rumba performed by recognized groups. *Peñas* in Cuba (related but not the same as those historical ones from the 1960s in Chile, Uruguay, and Argentina) are usually cultural events that take place during the early part of the evening, mostly during the weekend and within small cabarets and houses of culture. The Conjunto Folklórico Nacional has an important role in this history since it organized the known Sabado de la Rumba (Saturday's Rumba) in its Vedado locale. This *peña* generated energy for one on Tuesdays at El Liceo de la Habana Vieja, under the direction of Andres Bayoya, whose commitment to rumba and the organization of street musical events made the carnival's commission classify as "Bayoya" the percussion orchestra that parades with the traditional *comparsas* in Havana's carnival. While in Cuba, Daniel Ponce was a member of El Liceo de la Habanera Vieja (The School of Old Havana). These events open the space to what we now know as rumba *peñas*. The *casas de la cultura* (neighborhood cultural associations or houses) collaborated on the organization of rumba festivals in centro Havana and la Habana vieja, where the legendary *rumbero* Julio Cesar "Wuasamba" (inventor of the wuasamba rhythm) also assimilated the *guarapachanguero* rhythm. His friend, another prestigious *rumbero*, Evaristo Aparicio, known as "El Picaro," was the founder of the group Papa Kun Kun and the composer of musical numbers such as "Si a una mamita," interpreted by classic Puertorican bands such as Batacumbele.

Yoruba Andabo's *peña* came with Eloy Machado, the rumba poet known as "El ambia" who during the 1988–1989 carnivals made the event "El solar del ambia." After the carnival his event was institutionalized in the Jardines de la UNIAC (the garden of the Unión Nacional de Artistas Cubanos), becoming a point of departure for various prestigious and young groups. Another fighter against prejudice is Salvador González, responsible for the *peña* and gallery Callejon de Hamel located in Cayo Hueso's neighborhood and inaugurated by Merceditas Valdez and Yoruba Andabo on April 21, 1990. But the rumba *peña* concept has traveled, its most representative U.S. destination being Union City, New Jersey. La Esquina Habanera has become the meeting place par excellence for *rumberos* and *rumberas* touring, arriving, and living in the United States. Its hosting group, Raices Habaneras, was nominated for the 2003 Latin Grammy. The owner of La Esquina is Tony Sequeira, and he founded the group on March 23, 1996, with David Oquendo as music director. The Esquina Habanera keeps reenergizing itself with the arrival and integration of more professional *rumberos/as* from Cuba such as Frank Bell, Pedro Pablo Martínez, Roman Díaz, and many more.

Rumba is an everyday practice, a secular but spiritual collective experience, a happening. Rumba rejuvenates itself in its own performance; it changes and transforms as it fuses with other rhythms. It is a genre that remains attractive not only to Cubans of all ages but Latinos in general—whose native rhythms, in one way or another, imply African influences. Europeans and Asians also travel yearly to Cuba to collaborate and learn with the Conjunto Folklórico Nacional and the Escuela Nacional de Arte. Rumba's many living legends are committed to sharing their deep knowledge with the musicians, dancers, and academics of the world.

Further Reading

Acosta, Leonardo. *Del Tambor al Sintetizador*. Havana, Cuba: Letras Cubanas, 1983.

Acosta, Leonardo. "The Problem of Music and Its Dissemination in Cuba." In *Essays on Cuban Music*, edited by Peter Manuel. New York: University Press of America, 1991.

Acosta, Leonardo. "The Rumba, the Guaguancó, and Tío Tom." In *Essays on Cuban Music*, edited by Peter Manuel. New York: University Press of America, 1991.

Carpentier, Alejo. *La Música en Cuba*. Mexico City: Fondo de Cultura Económica, 1993.

Castellanos, Isabel, and Jorge Castellanos. *Letras, Música, Arte*. Vol. 4 of *Cultura Afro-Cubana*. Miami, FL: Ediciones Universal, 1994.

Crook, Larry. "A Musical Analysis of the Cuban Rumba." *Latin American Music Review (Austin)* 3.1 (1982): 92–123.

Daniel, Yvonne. *Rumba: Dance and Social Change in Contemporary Cuba*. Bloomington: Indiana University Press, 1995.

Diaz-Ayala, Cristobal. *Música Cubana del Areyto a la Nueva Trova*. 2nd ed. San Juan, Puerto Rico: Editoria Cubanacan, 1981.

Fraginals, Manuel Moreno. *Aportes Culturales y Deculturación: Africa en America Latina*. Mexico City: Siglo Veintiuno Editores, 1977.

Fraginals, Manuel Moreno. *El Ingenio*. Havana, Cuba: Editorial de Ciencias Sociales, 1978.

León, Argeliers. *Del Canto y el Tiempo*. 4th ed. Havana, Cuba: Ed. Pueblo y Educación, 1989.

León, Argeliers. *Música Folklórica Cubana*. Havana, Cuba: Ediciones del Departamento de música de la Biblioteca Nacional "José Marti," 1964.

Linares, María Teresa. "Hoy la rumba." *Revista de Salsa Cubana* 17 (2002).

Manuel, Peter. *Caribbean Currents: Caribbean Music from Rumba to Reggae*. Philadelphia, PA: Temple University Press, 1995.

Martínez Furé, Rogelio. *Conjunto Folklórico Nacional* (first catalogue). Havana, Cuba: Ed. Consejo Nacional de Cultura, 1963.

Mauleón, Rebecca. *Salsa Guidebook for Piano and Ensemble*. Petaluma, CA: Sher Music Co., 1993.

Méndez, Alina. "Arsenio Rodríguez, ¿Dónde Están Tus Maravillas?" *La Gaceta de Cuba 5* (September–October 1998).

Moore, Robin. "The Commercial Rumba: Afrocuban Arts as International Popular Culture." *Latin American Music Review* 16.2 (Fall–Winter 1995): 164–198.

Orovio, Helio. *Diccionario de la Música Cubana: Biográfico y Técnico*. Havana, Cuba: Editorial Letras Cubanas, 1981.

Ortiz, Fernando. *La Africania de la Música Folklórica de Cuba*. Havana, Cuba: Letras Cubanas, 1993.

Ortiz, Fernando. *Los Bailes y el Teatro de los Negros en el Folklore de Cuba*. Havana, Cuba: Letras Cubanas, 1981.

Peñalver Moral, Reinaldo. "Rumba Contra el Sedentarismo." *Bohemia* 40 (October 1, 1974).

Roberts, John Storm. *The Latin Tinge: the Impact of Latin American Music on the United States, 2nd ed*. New York: Oxford University Press, 1999.

Roman Díaz and Berta Palenzuela Jottar

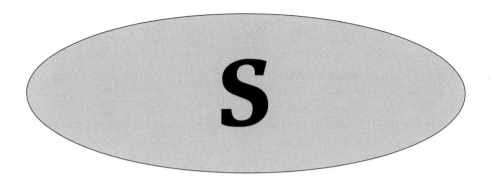

Sábado Gigante. *Sábado Gigante* (Gigantic Saturday) is the oldest-running television series in the history of the Americas without a single repeat episode and conducted by the same host, Don Francisco. The show features family-style entertainment with music, dance, comedy, and significant interaction with the audience that includes quizzes, talent shows, contests, and prizes. *Sábado Gigante* was created by Mario Kreutzberger (Don Francisco) and began its run in 1962 in Santiago, Chile. Kreutzberger, the first child of a Jewish family that emigrated from Germany, was born in 1940 in Talca, a town near Santiago. His reasons for choosing the name of Francisco come from the fact that many Chileans of German Jewish descent are called Francisco.

In 1973 the military coup eliminated television programs related to participation by or representation of the masses because they were considered political or subversive. *Sábado Gigante* was an exception because the content was not considered antagonistic to the new regime. Currently *Sábado Gigante*'s weekly broadcast reaches 90 percent of the Hispanic homes in the United States through nine television stations owned by Univision, thirty-five affiliates, and forty-six cable systems. *Sábado Gigante* is transmitted to all of Latin America and the United States by open channels, except Brazil and Argentina, which receive the program via cable. The program is transmitted to the rest of the world via Galavisión. Half of its Latin American audience is in México.

As the most popular show on the two largest Spanish-language networks in the world—Univision and Televisa—*Sábado Gigante* is a powerful instrument in the homogenization of popular culture. *Sábado Gigante* capitalizes on superficial similarities among vast numbers of people to create a market for its advertiser base. It thus contributes to the creation of a new community made of Spanish-speaking people who are united by purchasing habits and consumerism more than by regional similarities and other cultural unifiers. *Sábado Gigante* is an element of homogenization of Spanish-speaking people because it addresses its audience not in terms of national communities with plural identities but as a market segment of purchasers for the world conglomerate's goods.

Sábado Gigante has worked on building a large audience to reach the largest number of people and to absorb cultural differences. The *globalization of the economy and the media corporations' expansion of their markets are associated with certain cultural changes. The profit base of these industries demands that media industries provide an audience that shares similar habits, tastes, language, age, or background to fuel an economy largely based on economies of scale. Thus, the main trends of multi-national corporations are toward concentration, consolidation, and oligarchy. Some scholars have noted this tendency in U.S. Spanish-language media, a strategy termed "panethnic marketing." This consumer identity is also bought at the expense of broader political discourse and engagement.

Martha Idalia Chew

Latina journalist María Elena Salinas founded the National Association of Hispanic Journalists. *Photo courtesy of* Latino Leaders Magazine.

Salinas, María Elena (1954–). A daughter of Mexican immigrants, María Elena Salinas has become one of the most highly respected and influential Latina television journalists in the United States and Latin America, with over twenty years of experience. She began her career as a broadcast journalist on radio in Los Angeles, California. In 1981 she became a television news reporter for KMEX, an affiliate of the *Spanish-language television broadcast conglomerate Univision affiliate. Her first job as a local news anchor was with KMEX-TV, but in 1987 she moved on to coanchor *Noticiero*, a national news program produced by Univision. Salinas has cohosted *Aquí y Ahora*, a prime-time newsmagazine program for Univision, and she also works on other journalism projects outside of television. She writes a weekly column for Univision.com; provides commentary for

Radio Única, a Spanish-language news radio network; and is a syndicated columnist for King Features.

Salinas has covered important world events and has done exclusive interviews with important political figures such as former U.S. President Bill Clinton, President George W. Bush, the Zapatista commander known as Subcomandante Marcos, and President Vicente Fox of México. She continues to report on stories of importance in the Latino community and supports the education of future Latinas and Latinos. She was honored with two Emmys in 1998 for her coverage of Hurricane Mitch in Central America and has received many other prestigious awards. She is a founder of the National Association of Hispanic Journalists (NAHJ) and has also established a scholarship in her name for journalism students.

Karen Rosales de Wells

Salsa. *See* Food and Cookery.

Salsa. Like other words in Latin music (*rumba, *tango, *mambo), the word *salsa* has meant different things at different times. It is the generic name for a style of Cuban-derived dance music using horns, piano, bass, a percussion section typically containing congas (originally from the rumba), bongo (from the *son*), and timbales (from the *danzón*), with a lead singer (*sonero*) who is able to improvise and a *coro* (chorus) of two or more voices. Drawing heavily on the Cuban genres of *son, son montuno*, and *guaracha*, "salsa" is an industry term rather than a specific rhythm, though by the 1990s it had become so formulaic that an arranger might write "salsa" on a percussion part and the musicians would know what to play.

The origin of the term is culinary: it means "sauce." But North Americans commonly misunderstand because the salsa that is sold in jars in U.S. supermarkets is Mexican-style and a chile-based condiment that makes *food more *picante* (hot). People of the Spanish-speaking Caribbean, however, abhor chile in their food. Their salsa is an oil-based sauce with garlic, onions, meat drippings, and so on, in which the flavor of the dish is highly concentrated and which is used to moisten meat, rice, or other food. It is not optional; it is an essence, central to the dish.

The word *salsa* seems to have first come into Cuban music as a flavor word shouted by musicians, just as they might shout "¡Sabor!" (Flavor), "¡Qué rico!" (How delicious), "¡Vaya!" (Go with it), "Azúcar!" (Sweet), and so forth. It was in that tradition that Ignacio Piñeiro, who modernized the *son* by creating a large repertoire of original compositions for his Septeto Nacional, composed the classic "Échale salsita" (Pour a little salsa on it) in 1932. The first use of the word *salsa* to refer to a style of music seems to have been in Venezuela in the early 1960s, but it was not until around 1974 that the term came into common use to refer to the music being marketed by Fania Records, an independent label in New York run by Jerry Masucci with music director Johnny *Pacheco.

The need for such a term stemmed from two factors. First was the necessity of labeling a new musical movement to be able to identify its audience, just as it had been necessary previously to create such labels as "rock 'n' roll," "rhythm and blues" (R&B), and "country and western." The names of previous major Latin trends—the mambo, the *cha cha cha, the *pachanga—no longer applied, since those referred to specific styles that were no longer current. Second was the need to dis-identify the music as Cuban. By the time "salsa" came into common use, Cuba had been a pariah state for fifteen years, and new music from Cuba was no longer being heard in the American mass media. Meanwhile, though the musical forms of salsa came from Cuba, only a few of the people who were playing this style of music were Cuban, or had ever been to Cuba. The locus of the 1970s salsa boom was the melting pot of New York, where many musicians were Puerto Rican. The Puerto Rican way of playing the Cuban forms was quite distinct from the Cuban way and was instantly identifiable. Meanwhile, there were salsa musicians from all over Latin America, including Dominicans, Venezuelans, Colombians, Panamanians, and others, as well as non-Latinos (often in the horn sections, occasionally on piano, rarely on percussion).

The label "salsa" was a broadly applicable, big-tent kind of idea. But it never applied to all Latin music. There were relatively few Mexicans in New York in the 1970s, and the broad Mexican-American public, which forms the largest component of the fragmented "Latin" music market, never became part of the world of salsa. Nor did "salsa" apply to Dominican *merengue, Colombian *cumbia, or *Latin jazz. It never really applied to the music of the *charangas, the flute-and-violins dance orchestras that had been a staple of Cuban musical life throughout the twentieth century and enjoyed a vogue in New York in the 1960s but never caught on much in Puerto Rico. Some might argue that the term salsa could apply to horn-and-piano band arrangements of Puerto Rican *bomba and *plena, but the main practitioner of that style, Cortijo y su Combo (led by Rafael Cortijo, with Ismael Rivera singing), disbanded before salsa became popular. Mostly the word implies Cuban forms built around a polyrhythmic rhythm section held together by a rhythmic key called the clave.

Among its other accomplishments, the salsa revolution amounted to a declaration of empowerment on the part of the Puerto Rican community in New York. Puerto Ricans had been U.S. citizens since the Jones Act of 1917, and unlike citizens of any independent Latin country, they could enter, leave, and work in the continental United States whenever they wanted, without a passport. As Puerto Rico had historically been a place of great poverty, Puerto Ricans came to New York in large numbers looking for work; by 1930 or so they had become the most numerous Latino group in New York City; and as the century progressed, their earning power and social status improved.

In New York, one rarely encountered a purely Puerto Rican, Cuban, or Do-minican band. Puerto Ricans were an essential part of any Latin music that happened, and they participated as well in every form of African American music in New York, from the start of the jazz era through *hip-hop and be-yond.

New trends in Latin music had traditionally come to New York directly or indirectly from Cuba, but after the break in relations following the *Cuban Revolution of 1959, Cuban music stopped entering the United States, and the Puerto Ricans in New York found themselves thrust front and center. The younger Puerto Ricans responded with the homegrown small-combo style called *bugalú*, a very tasty mix of *barrio-style Latin music with R&B, often sung in English; the genre did not survive the 1960s. But what-ever the reigning style, there was not a moment when New York was not full of high-quality Latin groups, far too many to list here. These artists played in a relatively low-budget world to a relatively small circuit of fans, compared to the marketing universe that English-language music could ad-dress; but those fans were enough to fill clubs and even major concert halls in various parts of the Americas, and they remained fans for life. Salsa ca-reers were long ones; and once released, the albums stayed in print.

Most of the stars of the salsa boom were bandleaders who paid their dues playing Cuban-style music long before it was called salsa. Percussionist Tito *Puente, who was a leader of the mambo boom of the early 1950s, and pi-anist Eddie *Palmieri, who began playing in the mambo era, disclaimed the term, though both would have to be ranked among the most important cre-ators of what came to be called salsa. In Puerto Rico, where the term was universally adopted, prominent groups were relabeled as salsa bands with-out altering their music in the slightest, most visibly Sonora Ponceña (founded in 1954) and El Gran Combo (founded in 1962 from the mem-bership of Cortijo y su Combo; their fortieth anniversary concert in 2002 sold out Madison Square Garden).

Musically, salsa was a largely traditionalist movement marketed as a new trend. Salsa musicians (most of whom were also skilled jazz musicians, in the Latin style) eschewed the new sonic tendencies of American pop music, preferring the fretless electric upright Ampeg "baby bass" to the electric bass guitar that had become universal in rock and R&B. Puerto Rico's long tra-dition of military and municipal bands, a legacy of the Spanish colonial oc-cupation, which had lasted until 1898 and which it shared with Cuba, meant that there was a large supply of skilled, literate horn players. The horn sec-tions that were elsewhere disappearing were of central importance to the salsa band. The electric guitar, which had become ubiquitous in Euro-American popular music, barely appears in the salsa discography; neither did the bands use a trap set (a multidrum configuration including, but not lim-ited to, bass, snare, tom-toms, and cymbals, played by a single drummer, often used in jazz groups and dance bands). Instrumental proficiency was important (unlike in rock and roll, where a cult of amateurism developed that was at times mind-boggling in its extremism), as was ensemble cohesion and professional arrangement of the music. The combination of improvisational stretching out and tight, through-composed (songs in which new melody is provided for each stanza) arrangements gave the music great expressive versatility. Meanwhile, the modest recording budgets available for even the biggest stars were sufficient to make good recordings in adequate studios but did not allow for extravagant superproductions. The engineers (most importantly Jon Fausty) generally stayed away from special effects and emphasized capturing performances simply, cleanly, and fast, with the high-quality equipment that was by then a given, even in the more modest New York studios. The net result is that many salsa records from the 1970s through the early 1980s have a timeless, classic sound, which has dated little. This extensive discography, of excellent quality, remains largely unexplored by, and unknown to, American critics and musicologists.

Salsa bass lines are in countertime, often deemphasizing the "1" of the measure, hitting on the second half of "2," and anticipating chord changes by landing hard on the "4" (as contrasted, for example, with the heavy "1-2-3-4" bass downbeats of merengue). The most common song form, inherited from the Cuban *son montuno*, divides the tune into two main parts: In the first part, a composed lyric states the argument of the song; in the second part (the *montuno*), a phrase by the *coro*—thematically related to the lyric—is repeated hypnotically over a rhythmic piano loop (called *guajeo*). This gives the singer a platform for improvising, commenting on the subject of the song and exhorting the crowd to dance, in a continuation of a lyrical tradition that can be traced back to pre-Islamic Arabic poetry, and which in live performance can extend for a very long time. The piano style derives from the *tres* of the Cuban *son*, which in turn derives from the *sanza* playing of Central Africa; the bongo style in part derives from the age-old African tradition of the talking drum. Horn interludes (called mambo and *moña*, which have different functions) serve as gearshifts between subsections. The entire structure is a foolproof scheme for ratcheting up the dancer's excitement in a controlled manner.

The main stylistic stream of salsa is derived from the *conjuntos* and jazz bands of what is often referred to as the golden age of Cuban music, whose starting point could be the formation of the group Casino de la Playa in 1937 and which continued through approximately 1957. Arsenio Rodríguez was evoked by *salseros*, most explicitly in the 1970s in the group led by Brooklyn-born pianist Larry Harlow, with singer Ismael Miranda. Arsenio's repertoire also provided Puerto Rico's Sonora Ponceña (whose name overtly echoes that of Cuba's Sonora Matancera) with their first two big hits, 1969's "Hachero pa' un palo" (Woodcutter to the Tree) and its follow-up "Fuego en el 23" (Fire on the 23). The style of Sonora Matancera was retooled with great success by the Dominican-born flutist-bandleader Johnny Pacheco, most spectacularly in recordings featuring Sonora Matancera's ex-vocalist Celia *Cruz (based in New Jersey and the only Cuban in the first rank of 1970s salsa stars) and Pete "El Conde" Rodríguez, originally from Ponce, Puerto Rico. Under the name Fania All-Stars, Pacheco led an elite group of singers and players cherry-picked from various orchestras.

Another stream was represented by the work of Nuyorican trombonist-bandleader Willie *Colón, who first surfaced during the *bugalú* era and incorporated newer, more eclectic tendencies. Colón's band, featuring the brilliant but troubled singer Hector Lavoe (who had come to New York from Ponce), was massively popular, at first in New York and then throughout the Latin world. Colón also collaborated with Panamanian singer-composer Rubén *Blades (who had briefly sung with *conguero*-bandleader Ray Barretto, another major figure of the boom) on albums that made Blades into a superstar. Colón and Blades's second collaboration, the 1978 *Siembra* (SOW), with its street-reality lyrics, imaginative arrangements, and swinging band, was the biggest hit of the era.

The success of Lavoe and Blades—and Óscar d'León, Cheo Feliciano, Andy Montáñez, and many others—pointed up a developing trend: The singers were becoming more popular than the bands. Most of the first generation of salsa bandleaders were not singers; *timbalero* Willie Rosario's band in the first half of the 1980s included, at the same time, future solo stars Gilberto Santa Rosa and Tony Vega. It became harder for nonsingers, who were generally better bandleaders, to keep a popular singer. As more singers went solo, they fronted ever more faceless bands. Meanwhile, in the early 1980s the growing Dominican community in New York fostered an upsurge of the simpler, more easily danceable merengue, directly competing with salsa for airtime and dancehall space.

As Latin radio in New York underwent a transformation from small community-oriented AM stations to corporate FM outlets, radio continually pushed salsa in a more pop direction, leading to the ascendancy in the second half of the 1980s of the style known as *salsa romántica* (or *salsa erótica*, or more pejoratively, *salsa monga*). Though romantic lyrics had always been a part of salsa, the new style focused almost entirely on sexy songs addressed to women, sung by high-voiced young males, almost all of whom were white. (The significant exception was the skillful Dominican-born former Típica '73 vocalist José "El Canario" Alberto, whose "Sueño contigo" [I Dream with You] in 1987 was the first major hit for impresario Ralph Mercado's fledgling RMM label, but Canario did not stay in the *romántica* vein, returning to a "rootsier" style.) Some were highly competent *soneros*; others were not. As radio criteria became more rigid, and productions focused more on singers with an interchangeable cast of studio musicians instead of identifiable bands with individual sonic signatures, the records began to sound more alike. The increasing importance of videos led to a greater emphasis on image, and by the late 1980s "salsa" had come to mean something less vital than ten years previously. The romantic style remained dominant in the marketplace as a new generation of artists appeared, most prominently Marc *Anthony, a vocalist of phenomenal talent (and lung power) who started out singing freestyle (Latin disco) before becoming possibly the most popular salsa star ever, then transitioning to platinum-level mainstream pop in English. By the end of the 1990s artists who played nonromantic salsa had begun to call their music *salsa dura*, or *salsa brava*, to differentiate it.

Conspicuously absent from this movement were Miami-based artists, who never fielded a world-shaking Latin dance band. Miami, dominated by Cuban exiles with only a small Puerto Rican population, became a major center for Spanish-language broadcasting, but it was not an important live-music town. The roots of this are perhaps in the demographics of the Cuban Revolution; Miami's large Cuban population was almost entirely white in 1970, as New York was exploding with music; in fact, black people formed under 3 percent of the Cuban community in Miami. Despite the presence of many talented individual musicians in Miami, a critical mass of Cuban music's most vigorous performers—and dancers to patronize them—was lacking. Miami's energies turned more toward studio-created Latin pop.

Meanwhile, Cuba had focused inward since the beginning of the 1960s; the closing by the revolutionary government of the popular dance venues, together with the international isolation of, and sense of emergency in, the country took a serious toll from which Cuban music took a long time to recover. By the end of the 1960s, a new wave of dance music for domestic consumption was developing in Cuba, rooted in Cuban tradition. At the same time, the emerging popularity of salsa was increasing interest in older Cuban styles outside the island and provided a wake-up call for Cuban music, musicians, and recording artists.

In 1983, the Venezuelan *salsero* Óscar d'León performed in four cities in Cuba. Singing in a style deriving in no small part from the Cuban idol Beny Moré and dressing stylishly, he was received as a superstar, appearing before vast crowds, drawing earthquake-level attention from the Cuban media, and reintroducing to a new generation of Cubans the importance of their own music. (Though it was perhaps the high point of his career, he was bitterly denounced for it in the Miami media and has not performed in Cuba since.) Meanwhile, the use of the word *salsa* in Cuba provoked a fierce polemic since, it was argued, salsa was nothing more than Cuban music. By the beginning of the 1990s, however, the term was in general use in Cuba, though the number-one dance band, Los Van Van (founded in 1969), avoided it, preferring to call their music *songo*. The fierce, complicated, percussive music of Van Van and other Cuban dance bands (most notably NG La Banda, founded in 1988) sounded so different from the salsa style heard on the radio in New York that the term *salsa* as applied to these bands concealed more than it explained. An old word, *timba* (which had been more or less synonymous with *rumba*), became the new street term to differentiate the Havana style from salsa; the word surfaced aboveground in 1997, which was arguably the year the style peaked.

There was no chance for Cuban artists to compete with *salseros* in the

U.S. marketplace. Besides governmental obstacles to commerce and travel, Latin radio and television in the United States maintained a total boycott of artists living in Cuba; moreover, even without the political barrier, since the Cuban bands had noticeably more black faces, they would have been less likely to appear on Spanish-language television, which is heavily dominated by white performers. However, Cuban bands frequently shared bills with *salseros* at international festivals, and in the 1990s many American musicians traveled to Cuba, hearing Cuban bands and befriending the musicians. Between 1996 and 2001, as visas began to be granted to Cuban dance bands, their music developed cults along a U.S. touring circuit. With all this activity, elements of the new Cuban style made their way into the music that was still called salsa, covertly helping to rejuvenate it.

Further Reading

Aparicio, Frances. *Listening to Salsa: Gender, Latin Popular Music, and Puerto Rican Cultures*. Middletown, CT: Wesleyan University Press, 1998.

Duany, Jorge. "Popular Music in Puerto Rico: Toward an Anthropology of *Salsa*." *Latin American Music Review* 5.2 (1984): 187–216.

Loza, Steve. *Tito Puente: The Making of Latin Music*. Urbana: University of Illinois Press, 1999.

Manuel, Peter, Kenneth Bilby, and Michael Largey. *Caribbean Currents: Caribbean Music from Rumba to Reggae*. Philadelphia: Temple University Press, 1995.

Robbins, James. "The Cuban *Son* as Form, Genre, and Symbol." *Latin American Music Review* 11.2 (December 1990): 182–200.

Rodríguez, Olavo Alén. "Cuba." In *South America, Mexico, Central America, Central America and the Caribbean*. Vol. 2 of *The Garland Encyclopedia of World Music*, edited by Dale Olsen and Daniel Sheehy. New York: Garland, 1998.

Rondón, Cesar Miguel. *El Libro de la Salsa*. Caracas, Venezuela: Editorial Arte, 1980.

Steward, Sue. *¡Musica! Salsa, Rumba, Merengue, and More*. San Francisco, CA: Chronicle Books, 1999.

Waxer, Lise, ed. *Situating Salsa: Global Markets and Local Meanings in Latin Popular Music*. New York: Routledge, 2002.

Ned Sublette

Salt of the Earth. *Salt of the the Earth* (1954), a historically significant docudrama on a mainly *Chicano-led mining strike in New Mexico, was directed by Herbert Biberman, produced by Paul Jarrico, and distributed by Independent Productions/International Union of Mine, Mill & Smelter Workers. The cast includes Will Geer, Rosaura Revueltas, Juan Chacón, David Wolfe, Mervin Williams, Ángela Sánchez, Clorinda Aldrette, and Ernest Velásquez. Biberman was victimized as one of the "Hollywood Ten" in 1947 and was sentenced to a six-month jail term for contempt of Congress. Along with producer Paul Jarrico, screenplay writer Michael Wilson, and actor Will Geer (of television's *The Waltons* fame), director Biberman was blacklisted during the McCarthy communist witch-hunt, stopping him and the others from finding work in Hollywood.

Biberman's *Salt of the Earth* follows the lives of Latino miners on strike in a small New Mexico mining town. With the exception of a few professional actors and actresses, Biberman chose to use real-life figures to dramatically reenact and give a fully human dimension to this strike in the 1950s that sought to improve working conditions in the mines. By giving a docudramatic style to the mine workers' long, difficult, and extremely dangerous strike, Biberman did not depict the women as passive recipients or mere frightened observers in a struggle led by men in a male-dominated community; on the contrary, he shows them as active participants in the struggle, as organizers who develop their political consciousness and stand up not only to the bosses and the strikebreakers but also to their macho husbands, thus showing in their action a different relational possibility: that men and women can and must act in solidarity if they are to resist exploitation and eventually bring down capitalism. Now considered a classic in the United States, particularly in college classrooms where it is frequently shown, *Salt of the Earth* earned high and enduring critical acclaim in Europe before being allowed release in the United States in 1965.

Further Reading

Keller, Gary D. *A Biographical Handbook of Hispanics and United States Film.* Tempe, AZ: Bilingual Press, 1997.

Luis Aldama

Samba. *Samba* refers to the rhythm that became the foundation for most popular *Brazilian music by the 1940s and, like many other Brazilian rhythms, dances, and musical forms, fused with American jazz and other popular music genres. The term itself most likely comes from the word *semba*, which means to touch navels as an invitation to dance the lundu, an African drum music. According to ethnomusicologist Oneida Alvarenga, "The European polka gave it its movement, the Cuban habanera its rhythm, and Afro-Brazilian music added its syncopations." There are several varieties of samba rhythms including the earliest *maxixe*, which is also known as the Brazilian *tango, combining polka with the lundu, hence regarded as indecent.

The earliest references to samba date to the 1880s. Pianist/composer Francisca "Chiquinha" Hedviges Gonzaga do Amaral (1847–1935) was one of the first musicians to combine European elements with syncopated African rhythms. This new style was soon introduced to middle-class audiences. The first samba composed in 1917 is believed to be "Pelo Telephone," by Ernesto dos Santos (aka Donga). Samba lyrics and dance styles became associated with annual Carnivals in Rio de Janiero. At least one big hit number would emerge each season, typically performed by the dancers with percussion accompaniment. Gonzaga and José Barbosa da Silva (aka Sinho, 1888–1903) composed many of the earliest and most famous Carnival pieces. Bandleader and flautist Pixinguinha also contributed to the samba repertoire—an elegant, sophisticated, and graceful form, which later became *samba-canção*, used in ballad performance.

Samba remained popular in Brazil until the *bossa nova in the 1950s. The Bando du Lua, well known for their accompaniment of Carmen *Miranda, was one of the popular performing groups. She introduced the United States to samba through American films. Her best-known hit was "Mamãe Eu Quero" (I Want My Mama), which was a Carnival samba with a march rhythm, and her recording of "Rebola a Bola" (Rolling Ball) was an *embolada*—a fast samba that gathers speed. Noel Rosa is credited as extending the samba's range with his complex, witty lyrics. In Brazil samba groups developed into "schools," and the form became more commercialized and stylized. The better-known schools such as Mangueira and Portela attracted their own composers. Samba is a dynamic and sexy national symbol for Brazil, with most contemporary composers finding themselves forced to reckon with it.

Several samba types exist, including the following: *Batuque* is a slow samba; *battucada* is a Carnival rhythm; *sambaião* is a hybrid between samba and *baião*; there are several other variations, too numerous to discuss here. Bossa nova borrowed elements of samba with "cool jazz" but was a self-conscious creation rather than an urban folk expression like street dancing.

Further Reading

Clarke, Donald, ed. *The Penguin Encyclopedia of Popular Music*. 2nd ed. New York: Penguin, 1999.

Dunn, Christopher, and Charles Perrone. *Brazilian Popular Music & Globalization*. Miami: University Press of Florida, 2001.

Fryer, Peter. *Rhythms of Resistance: African Musical Heritage in Brazil*. London: Pluto Press, 2000.

Perrone, Charles. *Masters of Contemporary Brazilian Song*. Austin: University of Texas Press, 1989.

Vivianna, Hermano. *The Mystery of Samba: Popular Music and National Identity in Brazil*. Chapel Hill: University of North Carolina Press, 1999.

Peter J. García

Sánchez, Linda (1969–   ). Linda T. and Loretta *Sánchez made history in 2003 as the first sisters ever to serve in the U.S. Congress at the same time. Although Loretta was the first to be elected when she won her congressional district seat in 1996, Linda joined her sister only six years later when she was elected as representative of California's 39th Congressional District in 2002. Their dual elections became a highly publicized political event and constitute a high-profile example of the major impact of America's grassroots politics on the nation's popular culture with its relentless media attention and public representation of Latina and Latino issues. The mediagenic congresswomen also are beneficiaries of the expanding numbers of twentieth- and twenty-first-century Latina/o populations throughout the United States but

Linda Sánchez, with her sister Loretta, made history in 2003 when they became the first pair of sisters to serve simultaneously in the United States Congress. *Courtesy of Linda Sánchez.*

especially in the pacesetter state of California, where the Hispanic demographics have shifted the state's ethnic balance of power.

Sánchez's very large constituency is dispersed throughout a vast area of California. Her district includes the cities of Artesia, Cerritos, Hawaiian Gardens, Lakewood, La Mirada, Lynwood, Paramount, and South Gate. In addition, her district encompasses a large portion of the town of Whittier, small sections of both Long Beach and Los Angeles, as well as parts of unincorporated Los Angeles County—East La Mirada, Florence-Graham, Los Nietos, West Whittier, and Willowbrook. When addressing the needs of her constituency, the rookie congresswoman has prioritized crime prevention, education, health care, unemployment, and creating economic and employment opportunities as her concerns. Sánchez has been named to several important House bodies including the influential Judiciary Committee, along with the Government Reform and Small Business Committees.

Representative Sánchez is the sixth of seven children born to Mexican immigrant parents, and she was born on January 28, 1969, in Lynwood, California. Before her election to Congress, she graduated from the University of California, Berkeley, in 1991, where she earned a Bachelor of Arts in Spanish literature with an emphasis in bilingual education. She continued her postbaccalaureate studies at the University of California, Los Angeles (UCLA), and in 1995 graduated from UCLA's Law School and passed the difficult California bar exam that same year. Practicing law immediately after graduation, she gained invaluable experience as an attorney focusing on labor, employment, and civil rights law. She also worked as legal counsel to the International Brotherhood of Electrical Workers Local 441 from 1998 to 2002 and as executive secretary-treasurer of the Orange County Central Labor Council of the AFL-CIO. As campaign manager she is credited as well with playing a crucial role in helping her sister Loretta get reelected to Congress in 1998.

Further Reading

http://www.house.gov/lindasanchez.

Cristina K. Muñoz

Sánchez, Loretta (1960–   ). Born on January 7, 1960, in Lynwood, California, Congresswoman Loretta Sánchez began her formal education in Southern California before attending American University in Washington, D.C. She received her bachelor's degree in economics in 1982 and went on to earn a Master's in Business Administration in 1984 from American University. She also attended Chapman University in Orange, California, where she was invited to serve as the university's first Latina member of the board of trustees in 2002.

Sánchez's congressional district encompasses the Southern California cities of Anaheim, Garden Grove, Santa Ana, and Fullerton in the economically affluent and politically conservative Orange County. As her district's representative in the nation's capital, she has made a serious commitment to undertake bipartisan projects that return significant funding (more than $300 million in federal tax monies) back to her district for a variety of community projects. Focused on improving Orange County's quality of life, her efforts have supported transportation, crime prevention, education, and environmental protection projects. Representative Sánchez is applauded by her constituents for her Community Office Hours, which she instituted to allow her to be a hands-on, accessible representative who involves constituents in the pertinent issues concerning her district.

As a proponent of establishing peace worldwide, she has been committed to establishing and ensuring human rights not only in her district but among nations throughout the world. Throughout her congressional tenure she has taken special interest in ensuring that a Democratic and peaceful process is established in the Middle East nations. So it is no surprise that Representative Sánchez serves on the House Armed

Loretta Sánchez, one of the small but growing number of Latinas in politics, represents the 47th Congressional District in California. *Courtesy of Loretta Sánchez.*

Services Committee, of which she is the ranking woman. In 2003, she was selected by Democratic Leader Nancy Pelosi to serve as the third-ranking Democrat of the Select Committee for Homeland Security. As part of her duties on this committee, Sánchez was named as the Ranking Minority Member of the Infrastructure and Border Security Subcommittee. In addition, she will also serve on the Committee's Cybersecurity, Science, and Research & Development Subcommittee. During her tenure on the Committee for Homeland Security, she took a leave of absence form the House Committee on Education and the Workforce. Sánchez is a member of various political organizations and groups including the Hispanic Caucus, the Blue Dog Democrats, the New Democratic Coalition, and the Congressional Human Rights Caucus. She also is a member of the Women's Congressional Caucus, Older Americans Caucus, Law Enforcement Caucus, and the Congressional Sportsman's Caucus.

Further Reading

http://www.house.gov/sanchez.
http://www.loretta.org.

Cristina K. Muñoz

Sandoval, Arturo (1949–　). Trumpeter Arturo Sandoval was born on November 6, 1949, in Artemisa, Cuba, a small town near Havana. He began studying classical trumpet at the age of twelve. While growing up in Cuba he would play *sones (a style native to Cuba) with groups of older men in their sixties. At a very young age he expressed his desire to become a professional musician, but his family highly discouraged it, as they thought there was no future in it for him. They felt he did not have the natural talent required to do it.

Sandoval defied his family's wishes and worked diligently to acquire the skills necessary to live out his dreams. At the age of fifteen Sandoval was given a music scholarship to study at the classical music conservatory in Havana. At the age of seventeen he was able to earn a position in the top big band in Cuba, quickly climbing from sixth chair to lead trumpet. In 1973, Sandoval joined in creating the band Irakere. The group combined jazz, rock, and classical music with a Latin percussion section. The group became legendary over only a couple years of existence, earning Grammys for Best Latin Album in both 1978 and 1980.

In 1981, Sandoval left Irakere to form his own group. While playing in his new group he earned Best Instrumentalist in Cuba consecutively between 1982 and 1984. Sandoval was able to reach notes on the trumpet that few other professional trumpet players could play. He began to develop a worldwide reputation for his mind-blowing technique and range on the trumpet.

At this time Sandoval got to meet his longtime hero, trumpeter Dizzy Gillespie, while traveling to Cuba with his UN orchestra. Gillespie had a tremendous influence on Sandoval's playing and later as a person. Gillespie was so impressed with Sandoval's ability on the trumpet that he offered him a position in his orchestra.

After spending time with Gillespie and touring around the world, Sandoval decided to leave Cuba for America. In 1990 he finally defected with his family while touring in Rome. Gillespie was instrumental in helping him seek asylum. After arriving in the United States, Sandoval was given a recording contract with jazz giant Grusin and Rosin Productions (GRP). In 1991, Sandoval recorded "Flight to Freedom" with jazz greats Chick *Corea and Dave Weckl.

Sandoval's versatility has given him the opportunity to record seven records including one all-classical record. In 1994, he recorded his first classical album with the London Symphony Orchestra, directed by Luis Haza. In this album he performs many difficult standard trumpet concertos along with a trumpet concerto he composed. His other records for GRP include Latin styles as well as straight-ahead jazz. Sandoval also appeared on the 1995 Super Bowl halftime show in which he performed with Gloria *Estefan. He also recorded with Estefan on her album *Mi Tierra* (1993) and with the late Tito *Puente. Sandoval also recorded "Colors of the Wind" for the Walt Disney picture *Pocahontas* (1995). He stretched the limits and did what no other trumpeter had done before him, and he recorded a solo piano album titled *My Passion for the Piano* (2002).

In 2000, actor Andy *García helped produce an HBO special movie based on Sandoval's life, titled *For Love or Country: The Arturo Sandoval Story* and played the part of Sandoval in the movie. Sandoval won an Emmy for the sound track of the movie. Sandoval has won a total of three Grammys and has been nominated seven times.

After defecting from Cuba, Sandoval was given a full-time teaching position at Florida International University. He is also in great demand to give clinics throughout the country. His live performances entail much more than just playing the trumpet; he sings, raps, and plays percussion and piano. Sandoval spends half the year on the road performing and giving clinics.

Further Reading

Mandel, Howard. "Arturo Sandoval Comes Out Swingin'." *DownBeat* (October 1996): 18–23.

http://www.arturosandoval.com/home.asp.

George Yáñez

Santaliz, Pedro (1938–). Born in Isabela, Puerto Rico, in 1938, Pedro Santaliz is an actor, director, playwright, and theorist of contemporary Puerto Rican *theater. Since boyhood, he has belonged to La Comedieta Universitaria, a children's theater group in Río Piedras, Puerto Rico. Santaliz earned a bachelor's degree in drama from the University of Puerto Rico, Río Piedras. Pedro moved to New York City and founded El *Nuevo Teatro

Pobre de América in 1963, a troupe of popular theater performing in the streets and in marginalized communities in Puerto Rico and New York City. The troupe's plays portray the social and political issues of the lower and middle classes in Puerto Rico and New York, including drug and alcohol abuse, high unemployment, identity problems, and political corruption in Puerto Rico.

Further Reading

Rivera, Carlos Manuel. "El Esperpento Puertorriqueño: El Nuevo Teatro Pobre de América de Pedro Santaliz." Ph.D. dissertation, Arizona State University, 2000.

Santaliz, Pedro. "Diversiones y Condiciones del Teatro Popular de los Barrios de Puerto Rico: Acercamiento de El Nuevo Teatro Pobre de América." In *Imágenes e Identidades del Puertorriqueño en la Literatura*, edited by Asela Rodríguez de Laguna. Río Piedras, Puerto Rico: Huracán, 1985.

Carlos M. Rivera

Santana. *See* Santana, Carlos.

Santana, Carlos (1947–   ). Carlos Santana, a renowned guitarist and performer of rock and jazz, was born on July 20, 1947, in Autlán de Novarra, México. At the age of five, his father, an accomplished *mariachi violinist, introduced him to traditional Mexican music and basic music theory. His family settled in Tijuana in 1955, where Carlos learned to play guitar, imitating the style of black blues singers like B.B. King, T-Bone Walker, and John Lee Hooker. He played in local rock and roll bands in Tijuana and San Diego during the 1950s. In 1960, his family moved to San Francisco, while Carlos stayed in Tijuana honing his musical skills in the local club scene. After learning English, he enrolled in school in San Francisco a year later. His musical style developed into the signature Afro-Latin rock sound first heard in the 1960s.

In 1966 Santana formed the Santana Blues Band, which became immediately popular throughout the Bay Area, a mecca for American counterculture and alternative music. The band performed at the Filmore West, one of the most important music venues for rock and roll on the West Coast. They shortened their name to Santana before they performed at the New York Woodstock Festival in 1969, where they introduced the East Coast to the band's Latin-style acid rock.

They recorded eight gold and seven platinum albums over the next twenty years, including *Abraxas* (1970), which delivered such favorites as "Black Magic Woman/Gypsy Queen" and "Oye Como Va." Santana and his band have won numerous awards, including the *Billboard* Century Award (1996), Chicano Lifetime Achievement Award (1997), induction into the Rock and Roll Hall of Fame (1998), and Medallion of Excellence Award for community service, presented by the *Congressional Hispanic Caucus. They won a Best Rock Instrumental Performance Grammy in 1988. In 2000, Santana and

Carlos Santana. *Courtesy of Photofest.*

the band won a total of eight Grammy Awards, including Album of the Year for the album *Supernatural*. In 2002 they followed with the album *Shaman*, which featured guest artists like Michele Branch, *Ozomatli, Plácido Domingo, Seal, and Macy Gray. Santana and his band have sold more than 40 million albums and performed for over 20 million fans in over fifty coun-

Rolando Santos is Executive Vice President and General Manager of CNN Headline News. *Photo by Hispanic Business Inc./Kyle Christy/CNN.*

tries and at the 1987 Rock 'n' Roll Summit, the first joint U.S.-Soviet rock concert. They perform for various charities and fund-raisers including Blues for Salvador, San Francisco earthquake relief, Tijuana orphans, the rights of indigenous peoples, and education for Latino youth (in association with the Hispanic Media and Education Group).

Further Reading

http://www.santana.com.

Peter J. García

Santos, Rolando (c. 1957–). Bilingual Texan-Mexican Rolando Santos is one of the most high profile mainstream media executives found in the industry today. In 2002, Santos became the executive vice president and general manager of CNN Headline News, he recently served as the president of CNN en Español, and he oversees CNN's 24-hour Spanish-language news network as well as the operations of CNN Radio *Noticias.* Born in Eagle Pass, Texas, Santos is fluent in English and Spanish and received a Bachelor of Arts in journalism from Texas A&M University. Before joining CNN in 1993, Santos served as the executive producer for the network news for the Telemundo network and as the news director for KVEA Channel 52 in Los Angeles, where he oversaw international news coverage for the Telemundo affiliate. During his tenure, the station won the 1992 Emmy Award for Best Newscast, a first for a Spanish-language newscast. In the summer of 2002, the magazine *Hispanic Business* named Santos as one of the most influential Hispanics in the United States.

Further Reading

http://saber.colstate.edu/issues99/110199/110199cnn.htm.
http://www.hispanicbusiness.com/magazine/?issue=2002m07.

Elizabeth (Lisa) Flores

Saralegui, Cristina (1948–). Cristina Saralegui, the host and producer of one of the most popular television talk shows in the United States and Latin America, was born in Havana, Cuba, on January 29, 1948. Her journalism background is partly attributed to her grandfather, who was known in Cuba as the "Paper Czar." She lived in Havana until the age of twelve, when she moved with her family to Miami, Florida. She attended the University of Miami, where she majored in both mass communications and creative writing. While in college she took an internship with *Vanidades*, the Spanish-language version of the famous women's fashion magazine *Vanity*.

In 1976, Saralegui became the entertainment director for the *Miami Herald*. In 1977 she became editor in chief for *Intimidades* magazine, and in 1979 she assumed the position of editor in chief for *Cosmopolitan en Español*. She enjoyed immense success in the Latin fashion magazine industry before moving into live television and becoming the executive producer and host of her talk show *El Show de Cristina*, for which she received an Emmy Award in 1991 and has drawn over 100 million viewers worldwide in its peak.

Saralegui is considered the Oprah Winfrey of *Spanish-language television in the United States, Latin America, and Europe. In addition to the Emmy Award, she has won several prestigious awards and recognition by major professional, civic, and religious organizations such as the National Organization of Women in Communications, *ALMA, American Cancer Society, the Hollywood Chamber of Commerce, and the National Association of Catholic Communicators. In 1996 she founded, with her husband, the Arriba la Vida/ Up with Life Foundation, dedicated to AIDS awareness and education among Latinas/os.

Further Reading

http://www.cristinaonline.com.

Arturo J. Aldama

Sarape. *Sarape* refers to a type of wool covering or shawl generally made of bright colors and commonly used by indigenous and *mestizos (mixed-race people) of central México and the Southwest. The precise history of the origin of the sarape is not known, but what is known is that it is not indigenous to México; rather, it is a blend of native and Spanish elements.

During México's struggle for independence, the sarape was associated with the native American revolutionaries, becoming a symbol of *Mexicanismo* ("Mexicanness"). It was especially after México's independence from Spain in 1821 that the sarape obtained a stronger bond and symbolism of Mexican patriotism. One of the main users of the sarape was the *charro (horseman), who made it part of his outfit.

The sarape has three basic components: the outside or framing border, the field, and the center. There are a variety of designs used for the border, with the most popular being crisscrossing diagonal lines, repeating parallel diagonal lines, a diamond pattern, or zigzags. Vertical mosaic, diagonal grid, spot repeat, and plain field are the four predominant styles used for the field. The vertical mosaic field is thought to be the earliest style, which is composed of

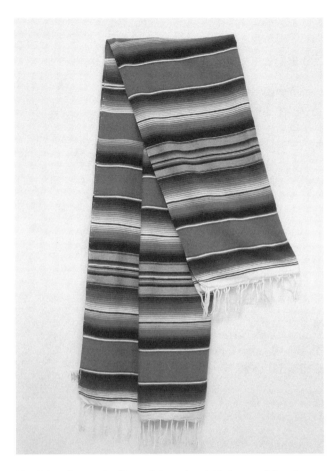

Traditional wear in Central America, México, and Southwest borderlands, the sarape is used much like a sweater or coat, to protect the wearer from the elements. *Photo by Emmanuel Sánchez Carballo.*

narrow stripes throughout the length of the sarape. The diagonal grid field is formed by small feathering design elements in diagonal rows of alternating colors. The spot repeat field evolved from the diagonal grid field, and it is made up of simple design elements. The plain field is entirely woven in one solid color of either natural white or brown color.

Further Reading

Gran Diccionario Enciclopedico Ilustrado. Vol 10. Mexico City: Reader's Digest México, 1979.

Jeter, James, and Paula Marie Juelke. *The Saltillo Sarape.* Santa Barbara, CA: New World Arts, 1978.

Mónica Saldaña

Schifrin, Lalo (1932–). Boris Claudio "Lalo" Schifrin has etched a place in history for himself as a versatile composer and piano player who has written in all major idioms of music. He has been commissioned to compose and perform with the widest range of virtuoso musicians in all major styles of music more than any other composer alive today. Schifrin's credits as a composer include more than 100 scores for film and television, including compositions that have won him four out of twelve Grammy nominations. In addition to his Grammys, Schifrin has a Cable ACE award and six Oscar nominations.

Schifrin was born in Argentina and studied classical music at a very young age under the tutelage of his father, Luis Schifrin, the concertmaster of the Orchestra of the Teatro Colon in Buenos Aires. In 1953, while studying music at the Paris Conservatoire, Schifrin grew interested in and became a jazz musician, performing at night or on weekends with many of the best jazz musicians in Europe.

After returning to Buenos Aires, while leading his own big band, he caught the attention of legendary American jazz musician Dizzy Gillespie, who immediately invited Schifrin to New York to be his arranger and pianist. Schifrin accepted the job offer and moved to New York in 1958, where for the next three years, he worked closely with Gillespie, playing piano for the legend and composing arrangements that would bring them both acclaim. His resumé reads like a list of Who's Who, having performed with such jazz greats as Stan Getz, Sarah Vaughn, Ella Fitzgerald, and Count Basie. In addition to his credits as a jazz musician, he is also a great composer and arranger, generating music for many popular movies such as *Mission Impossible* (1988–1990), *Cool Hand Luke* (1967), *The Competition* (1980), *Dirty Harry* (1971), *The Fox* (2000), *Bullitt* (1968), *Rush Hour* (1998), *Tango* (1998), *Rush Hour 2* (2001), and *Bringing Down the House* (2003).

Schifrin is also known for his classical or "legitimate" compositions. Some of his most well known compositions include "Cantos Aztecas" (Aztec Songs, 1988), which was recorded by Placido Domingo; *Piano Concerto No. 2* (1992), which was commissioned by the Steinway Foundation and later performed by Mstislav Rostropovich and Cristina Ortiz; *Dances Concertantes* (1988) for clarinet and orchestra, which was performed by David Schifrin; and *Concerto for Double Bass and Orchestra* (1988), which was recorded by Gary Karr and the Paris Philharmonic.

Schifrin was commissioned to arrange the music for the Grand Finale concert celebrating the World Soccer Championships in Italy in 1990. His major contribution was to arrange the medleys that would feature the three tenors José Carreras, Placido Domingo, and Luciano Pavarotti, coming together for the first time and singing in harmony. With Zubin Mehta conducting the orchestras of the Rome and France opera companies, the recordings of this performance have proven to be the biggest sellers in the history of classical music. Schifrin was commissioned to arrange the music for subsequent World Soccer Championships in Los Angeles in 1994, Paris in 1998, and Japan in 2002.

In 1993, Schifrin was one of the major composers to bring jazz to orchestra halls with his renditions of jazz classics arranged for orchestra. He has been featured as composer, pianist, and conductor for his ongoing series of "Jazz Meets the Symphony" recordings, bringing together such greats as Ray Brown, Grady Tate, Jon Faddis, Paquito D'Rivera, James Morrision, and Jeff Hamilton to perform his pieces with the London Symphony Orchestra. Schifrin's most recent popular recording is his *Latin Jazz Suite*, which features jazz soloists Jon Faddis, David Sánchez, Ignacio Berroa, Alex Acuña, and the WDR Big Band of Cologne, Germany. This selection received a Grammy nomination.

Schifrin was honored with the BMI Life Achievement Award in 1988 and received his star on the Hollywood Walk of Fame the same year. He has received honorary doctorates from the Rhode Island School of Design and the University of La Plata, Argentina. In 1998, he was presented with the Distinguished Artist Award by the Los Angeles Music Center. Schifrin has been married to his wife Donna for thirty years, and they have three children who all work in the entertainment industry.

Further Reading

Schifrin, Lalo. "Biography." http://www.schifrin.com.
http://www.dougpayne.com/schifrin.htm.

George Yáñez and Alma Alvarez-Smith

Schomburg, Arturo Alfonso (1874–1938). The cornerstone of Arturo Alfonso Schomburg's legacy to the world is the Schomburg Center for Research in Black Culture, once part of a world-famous building, the New York Public Library. The center houses his internationally acclaimed collection of slave narratives, manuscripts, rare books, journals, artwork, and other remnants of African history, which Schomburg gathered over two centuries. Schomburg spent his entire adult life seeking out information about people of African descent as a means of providing respect, understanding, and proof of the many contributions made to world history by people of his multicultural heritage.

Schomburg, born on January 24, 1874, in Puerto Rico, described himself as an "Afroborinqueño" (black Puerto Rican). His mother, María Josefa, was a freeborn black from St. Croix, and his father, Carlos Féderico Schomburg, was a mestizo merchant of German heritage. When Schomburg was in the fifth grade, his teacher made the comment that people of color had no history, no heroes, and no notable accomplishments. This glib comment became the impetus for his lifelong search for knowledge, materials, and artifacts about the heroic lives of people in the Caribbean and Latin America.

Schomburg immigrated to New York on April 17, 1891, and settled on the Lower East Side, where he continued amassing books, pictures, and documents about his heritage and the history of his ancestors. In 1911, his collecting took a rigorous and systematic turn when he met John Edward Bruce (aka Bruce Grit). Grit was a lay historian and journalist who, together with Schomburg, cofounded the Negro Society for Historical Research, an archival institute that influenced black book collecting and published papers with African American themes.

Over the years, Schomburg traveled the world, collecting books and documents where he could find them, and he often employed friends and family to bring back items found in their travels as well. He especially relished finding documentation and learning of the accomplishments of Afro-Latinos such as Puerto Rican artist José Campeche, Haitian liberator Toussaint L'Ouverture, and Afro-Cuban general Antonio Maceo. Schomburg became a formidable debater and prominent figure in the legendary Harlem Renaissance.

In 1926, Schomburg's world-renowned collection was presented to the New York Public Library's Division of Negro History, a move made possible through a $10,000 grant from the Carnegie Foundation. His collection, consisting of thousands of slave narratives, manuscripts, rare books, journals, artwork, and other remnants of African history, won national acclaim and became a global resource. Now renamed the Schomburg Center for Research in Black Culture, the collection has evolved into the most comprehensive compilation of black history, containing nearly 6 million items, including photographs, films, audio recordings, and institutional archives. Upon celebrating its seventy-fifth anniversary, the center underwent technological upgrades, allowing the extensive bibliographic records to be cataloged on CD-ROM, making it easier to research and extending its influence beyond the center's halls.

Further Reading

Knight, Robert. "Arthur 'Afroborinqueño' Schomburg." *Civil Rights Journal* 1.1 (Fall 1995): 3–4.

Cordelia Chávez Candelaria

Secada, Jon (1962–   ). Jon Secada, who was born in Havana, Cuba, on October 4, 1962, has recorded several popular Latin hits and boasts a successful international musical career as a singer and songwriter. At the age of nine, he left Cuba with his family and headed for Miami, Florida, where his parents opened a coffee shop. Secada did not have his musical aspirations at a young age but only discovered them when he was in his teens. He sought to further develop his singing abilities by attending a music conservatory, and during that training, he became a jazz musician. At the same time, he attended the University of Miami and pursued a bachelor's degree in music and a master's degree in jazz vocal performance. His desire to help others led him to later create a music scholarship at the University of Miami. In addition, Secada has been a supporter of the "Keeping Music in the Schools" campaign sponsored by the National Academy of Recording Arts and Sciences. It was during his years in college that Secada developed his ability to write songs. His talents did not go unnoticed by executives of SBK/ERG Records; soon after, they signed a record deal with Secada and launched his singing career.

His debut album *Jon Secada* sold over 6 million copies worldwide. The single title "Just Another Day" emerged as one of the bestselling singles of 1992. The single's success was so great it spent eleven consecutive weeks in the Top 10 of *Billboard*'s Pop Singles chart and topped charts around the world. He released other singles titled "Do You Believe in Us," "Angel," and "I'm Free." Secada firmly secured his place as a pop artist in the English-speaking world and infiltrated the Latino music culture with the release of his Spanish-language album *Otro Día Más Sin Verte* (Another Day Without Seeing You, 1992). This album earned him four consecutive number-one singles on *Billboard*'s Latin charts and awarded him the Grammy for 1992's Best Latin Pop album.

Secada received a Grammy Award for Best Latin Pop Album, which included "Otro Día Más Sin Verte" (Another Day Without Seeing You) in 1992. He also received a Grammy Award for Best New Artist Nominee in 1992. BMI Latin Music Awards recognized Secada's hits including the Most

Performed Latin Songs of 1993 for "Otro Día Más Sin Verte," "Sentir" (I'm Free), and "Cree en Nuestro Amor" (Do You Believe in Us). He received the Bar Latin Music Award for the Most Performed Latin Song of 1993 for "Otro Día Más Sin Verte." He received a World Music Award for Best-Selling Latin American Recording Artist in 1993. He also won a Caribbean Music Award for Best New Latin Pop Album and a *Billboard* Latin Music award for Best Latin-Pop Album of the Year also for "Otro Día Más Sin Verte," as well as the Best Latin-Pop Artist and Best New Latin-Pop Artist of the Year.

Un Año de Rock Awards (Spain's Grammy Award) nominated Secada for Best New Artist of the Year and Best Song of the Year for "Otra Día Más Sin Verte." He was also an American Music Award Nominee for Best New Adult Contemporary Artist. *Billboard* magazine recognized Secada as only the second artist to have two singles on the Hot 100 for thirty weeks or more. "Just Another Day" logged thirty-eight weeks on the chart; while the second single "Do You Believe in Us" racked up thirty weeks. *Billboard* magazine named Secada as the only artist ever to have four consecutive number-one singles from a debut album on *Billboard*'s Latin Singles chart. He was awarded a Hit Radio Award (Hong Kong) for Best Male Artist of the Year in 1993. *Rolling Stone* magazine named Secada Best Male Vocalist 1992–1993 /Readers Poll.

Throughout his career, Secada has worked with Emilio and Gloria *Estefan on numerous musical projects, whether cowriting the lyrics to Gloria's songs or helping Emilio in the recording studio. In his support of other Latin pop stars, Secada has cowritten songs for Ricky *Martin and Jennifer *López. He helped cowrite "She's All I Ever Had" ("Bella" in Spanish) for Martin and his multiplatinum 1999 album *Ricky Martin*. He also cowrote and coproduced López's song "Baila" (She Dances) and her multiplatinum 1999 album *On the Six*.

Further Reading

http://www.jon-secada.com.

Cristina K. Muñoz

Segovia, Josefa (c. 1830–1855). A Mexican woman who lived in Downieville, California, during the era of the Gold Rush, Josefa Segovia was the only female ever executed by hanging in the state of California. She was seized by an angry mob and hanged because she killed an Anglo man who she claimed assaulted and tried to rape her. Her importance to Latina and Latino popular culture in the United States relates primarily to two factors—her reflection of the thorny intersection of *race and ethnicity with *gender issues and her tragedy's echoing of other legends of Mexican history, notably the *La Llorona folk legend and the story of Pancho *Villa's revenge against a wealthy *haciendado* (rancher) who had assaulted his sister. As a poor Mexican woman Segovia inhabited a precarious social position in the male-dominant nineteenth-century world. A subject of both attraction and repulsion, she thus broke several social codes when she killed an empowered Caucasian male, paralleling the Llorona tale and the case that caused future revolutionary Villa to become an outcast in his own homeland.

Although there is limited historical information about her actual person, Segovia has become a significant figure in Gold Rush lore, where responses to her execution ranged from outright protest and resistance at the lack of social justice in the face of mob vigilantism to scornful blame-the-victim attacks on Segovia's moral character. Literary scholars conceive of Segovia as both an ancestor to and an archetypal figure of the literary female characters created by twentieth-century Chicana writers who have responded to millennia of patriarchal privilege and antiwoman violence with sexually transgressive figures. Documents of the period such as newspapers, personal diaries, and unpublished manuscripts suggest that observers linked questions about Segovia's culpability to remarks over her appearance, sexual behavior, ethnic background, and class. In most cases the writers of these accounts were young white males whose imaginations were closely tied to their own experiences as frontiersmen. In particular, while feelings of racial distrust and discrimination ran high due to greed over gold and land claims, they were also in tandem with the intense sexual frustration that men felt because of the scarcity of women in the area.

The events of her lethal retaliation against her assaulter and her lynching occurred in 1855 shortly after California celebrated its first Fourth of July as an official state. Her actions in not only killing her assailant but also publicly admitting that she rightfully defended her honor cast Segovia as an active agent capable of redefining her role as a human being even if her Mexican woman status was demeaned in the often violent environment of the Gold Rush. Her execution and its subsequent retellings cast light on the gendered politics of race and class in early California and in turn strengthen the feminist resistance in her story and the experiences of other Chicanas and women who have voiced similar rejections of the prevailing systems of power and control.

Further Reading

"Josefa Segovia." In *Latinas in the United States: An Historical Encyclopedia*, edited by Virginia Sánchez Korrol and Vicki Ruiz. New York: Routledge, forthcoming.

Maythee Rojas

Segura, Pancho (1921–   ). An Ecuadorian by birth, Francisco Olegario "Pancho" Segura achieved world-class status as a tennis player in the 1940s and 1950s, and he was elected into the Tennis Hall of Fame in 1984. Born and reared in Guayaquil, Ecuador, the future *sports star had rickets as a child that resulted in permanently skinny, bowed legs. When he began playing tennis as a youngster, he had to grip and swing the racquet with both hands to offset his disability. His unorthodox style continued throughout his career, and he is credited as the originator of the two-handed forehand that is commonplace in contemporary tennis. Another of his unchallenged credits is his winning three consecutive intercollegiate men's singles titles in 1943, 1944, and 1945, which has not been repeated since.

Segura arrived on the U.S. tennis scene in the 1940s and was ranked fourth among all U.S. amateurs in 1942 and third in 1943, 1944, and again in 1945. While attending the University of Miami on a tennis scholarship, he won his three intercollegiate men's singles titles, an unprecedented feat. He turned pro in 1947 and barnstormed throughout the country, eventually winning the U.S. Pro Championship Tournament in 1950, 1951, and 1952. He defeated fellow Latino tennis great Pancho *Gonzalez in the finals in 1951 and 1952. A fan favorite throughout his career for his good-natured and pleasant professionalism on the court, Segura competed actively into his forties. He then became a teaching pro in Southern California and coached Jimmy Connors in the early 1970s.

Further Reading

Collins, Bud, and Zander Hollander, eds. *Bud Collins' Tennis Encyclopedia*. Detroit, MI: Visible Ink Press, 1997.

Clifford Candelaria

Selena (1971–1995). Selena Quintanilla Pérez (stage name "Selena") was born in Lake Jackson, Texas, on April 16, 1971, to Abraham and Marcella Pérez and gained national attention following her untimely death. Although Selena was representative of the legacy of Tejana (Texas-Mexican) women solo singers that came before her such as Lydia Mendoza, Chelo Silva, Laura Canales, and Patsy Torres and Tejana duets such as Carmen y Laura, Las Hermanas Cantú, Las Hermanas Gongora, and numerous others, she made the most significant strides in transforming the sound of *Tejano music and Tejano popular culture.

Selena's educational background included attending Oran M. Roberts Elementary in Lake Jackson and West Oso Junior High in Corpus Christi. Although her music travel schedule did not permit her to attend school on a regular basis, Selena completed her high school education in 1989 through the American School, a correspondence high school completion program for artists. Selena also took a few correspondence courses in business through the Pacific Western University.

Selena began singing at the age of eight when her father discovered her strong vocal capabilities. Abraham was the major musical influence in the *family, having been a member of the doo-wop band Los Dinos as a young man. Selena's father quickly engaged the rest of Selena's older siblings; brother A.B. would become lead guitarist and producer of most of her music, and sister Suzette would become the only Tejana drummer in the contemporary surge in Tejano music. Originally, the group was country western–influenced and went by the name of Southern Pearl. Selena's early musical experiences were singing in the family Tex-Mex restaurant business, Papagallo's. Selena made one of her first live television appearances on the Johnny Canales Show in Corpus Christi, Texas. Despite the fact that *Hispanic Magazine* estimated her worth in 1994 at $5 million, throughout her career, Selena continued to make her home in the working-class district of Molina in Corpus Christi, living next to her parents.

Selena's influences included country western, English-language pop, old-school, and especially African American music, including R&B, funk, and disco. Among the influential artists in Selena's young life were Donna Summer and Janet Jackson. Despite the attention paid to her beauty, sexuality, and youthful impact on the Tejano music scene, Selena y Los Dinos made significant contributions to the Texas-Mexican music scene. With their interpretation of songs such as "La Carcacha," "Bibi Bidi Bom Bom," and "Techno Cumbia," Tejano *cumbias would never be the same. In Selena's songs, young Tejanas/Latinas found a cultural site for articulating movement along with sound and for the gendered particularities of expressing love and pain, as well as strength and passion.

Among Selena's biggest accomplishments was the success she attained within the Tejano music genre itself. Not only did she break open the space for young women of her generation to follow in her footsteps, but Selena took Tejano music to locations it had never been before. Although Tejano groups such as La Mafia and Mazz had established fans of the music in northern México and Mexico City, Selena y Los Dinos translocated the unique cultural production of Tejano music to Puerto Rico, Central America, and throughout México. At the time of her death Selena y Los Dinos had scheduled tours for Chile, Brazil, and Venezuela. Selena, unlike any other Tejano music artist before, both transformed and translocated the regionally based music.

Selena y Los Dinos began their recording career in the mid-1980s with Tejano Record labels GP, Cara, Manny, and Freddie Records. Their albums included *Alpha* (1986), *Dulce Amor* (Sweet Love, 1988), *Preciosa* (Precious, 1988), *Selena y Los Dinos* (1990), *Ven Conmigo* (Come with Me, 1991), *Entre a Mi Mundo* (Come into My World, 1992), *Selena Live* (1993), *Amor Prohibido* (Prohibited Love, 1994), and *Dreaming of You* (released posthumously in 1995). In 1987 Selena won the Tejano Music Award for Female Entertainer of the Year, her first of many Tejano Music Awards in the years to come. With her performance at the Tejano Music Awards in 1989, Selena y Los Dinos began a steady flow of Tejano music artists to sign with EMI Latin Records. With their 1991 release *Ven Conmigo* Selena y Los Dinos established its dominance in the Tejano music industry and never relinquished their top position. With the 1992 release of *Entre a Mi Mundo* Selena be-

This famous photo of Tejana singer Selena depicts her as a "Santa Selena" icon. *Associated Research Collection, Tempe, Arizona.*

came the first Tejana to sell more than 300,000 albums. Selena's significance in contemporary U.S. popular music was recognized in 1994 when she won the Grammy for Best Mexican-American Album for *Selena Live*.

Moreover, Selena's creative talents were vast, particularly in the arena of material aesthetic production. As a young woman Selena worked diligently at her talents in clothing design, designing and sewing most of her costumes. A number of drawings and sketches exist representing her early goal to develop a clothing line of her own. Selena originally named the clothing line "Moonchild" (the Greek translation for Selena). In 1992, her dream became reality, when she started her own clothing line and opened the first Selena Etc. Boutique-Salon in Corpus Christi, Texas. The Corpus Christi salon was followed by a second boutique in San Antonio. That same year she married the lead guitarist of her band, Chris Pérez.

Selena's tragic death on March 31, 1995, at the hands of fan club manager Yolanda Saldívar, became one of the most significant historical markers in the public memory of Latinas/os in the United States during the decade of the 1990s. The magnitude of media coverage in the death of this contemporary Mexican American music artist was unprecedented. The *New York Times* covered her death in a front-page story along with brief coverage on nationwide news programs such as *Dateline NBC*. *People* magazine ran a commemorative issue on her life that sold out in a number of hours. In fact, it was this mostly Latina/o consumer response to the *People* commemorative issue that spawned the creation of *People En Español*. Musicians also honored her life in music. Familia RMM, a compilation of Caribbean artists including Celia *Cruz, Manny Manuel, Yolanda Duke, and Tito Nieves, produced the CD *Recordando a Selena* (Remembering Selena, 1996), a collection of some of

Selena's most popular songs reproduced as *salsa and *merengue tunes. The all-female *mariachi Mariachi Reyna de Los Angeles also included in their CD *Solo Tuya* (Yours Alone, 1998) a song tribute titled "Homenaje a Selena" (Homage to Selena). Within five years after her death Selena had been remembered through music television tributes by Johnny Canales, VH-I, and "El Show de Cristina." Her life has also been captured in the Hollywood production titled *Selena the Movie*, starring Jennifer *López as Selena, and in the Broadway musical *Siempre Selena* (Always Selena). The acclaimed Chicana filmmaker Lourdes Portillo also produced and directed the video documentary *Corpus: A Home Movie for Selena* (1999). Today Corpus Christi, Texas, entertains a steady flow of fans and her still very captivated public to her gravesite, monument by the ocean, Selena Boutique, and the museum established in her honor at Q Productions, the family recording studios.

Further Reading

Calderón, Roberto. "All Over the Map: La Onda Tejana and the Making of Selena." In *Chicano Renaissance: Contemporary Cultural Trends*, edited by David Maciel, Isidro Ortiz, and María Herrera-Sobek. Tucson: University of Arizona Press, 2000.

Coronado, Raúl, Jr. "Selena's Good Buy: Texas Mexicans, History, and Selena Meet Transnational Capitalism." *Aztlán* 26 (Spring 2001): 59–100.

Patoski, Joe Nick. *Selena: Como La Flor*. Boston, MA: Little, Brown, 1996.

Vargas, Deborah. "Bidi Bidi Bom Bom: Selena and Tejano Music in the 'Making of Tejas.'" In *Latino/a Popular Culture*, edited by Michelle Habell-Pállan and Mary Romero. New York: New York University Press, 2002.

Vargas, Deborah. "*Cruzando Fronteras*: Remapping Selena's Tejano Music Crossover." In *Chicana Traditions: Continuity and Change*, edited by Norma Cantú and Olga Nájera-Ramírez. Urbana: University of Illinois Press, 2002.

Deborah Vargas

Selena. Directed by Gregory *Nava and produced by Moctesuma Esparza and Robert Katz, *Selena* (1997) chronicles the life of *Tejano music star *Selena Quintanilla Pérez, who is frequently described as the most important and popular Tejano star of all time. The movie begins with Selena (Jennifer *López) and her siblings resisting the musical instruction of their father, Abraham Quintanilla (Edward James *Olmos), himself a musician hoping to recreate Los Dinos, a band he had organized in his youth. The *film, shot entirely on location in Texas, focuses on Selena's meteoric rise to fame during the early 1990s, and its evocative concert scenes capture effectively the immense popular following and devotion of her Mexican American and Mexican audiences. The movie avoids the sensationalism of many superstar bio-pics and instead focuses on Selena's intimate *family relationships, which include her closest friends and extended relatives. Abraham Quintanilla, depicted as an overbearing father who is relentless in his drive to turn his children into musical stars, is shown as controlling every aspect of Selena's career and life.

While Selena loves her father, she questions his strict discipline and dominant control. In spite of her father's attempt to protect her from the influence of Chris Pérez (Jon Seda), a rock guitarist who joins the band, Selena falls in love with Pérez, and they eventually marry.

The other major relationship explored in the movie is that between Selena and Yolanda Saldivar (Lupe *Ontiveros), the president of Selena's fan club and manager of her boutique. The film's ending reveals the drama and poignancy of the young singer's murder and Saldivar's betrayal of Selena's friendship. Sticking to the well-publicized facts of the case, the movie depicts Saldivar's embezzling of her employer's money from the boutique. Faced with the prospect of being exposed, she arranges to meet Selena at a hotel, where Saldivar shoots and kills Selena. The movie's popularity and its engaging sound track reflect the crossover mass appeal Selena had on music audiences in the United States and México. Further testament to her impact are the thousands of fans who make pilgrimages to Selena's hometown of Corpus Christi, Texas, to visit her gravesite and childhood community in solemn remembrance of her music, life, and tragic death. The film, which is distributed by Warner Brothers, also stars Constance Marie, Jacob Vargas, and Jackie Guerra.

Further Reading

http://www.selena-themovie.warnerbros.com.

Louis "Pancho" McFarland

Semana Santa. Semana Santa (Holy Week, or the seven days prior to Easter Sunday) is widely observed in Spain, México, and Latin America and throughout Latina/o communities in the United States. The celebration usually involves multiday processions, the stations of the cross (*via cruces*), dramatic reenactments of *la Pasión* (The Passion), recitation of the rosary, fasting, and other ritual observations held in various neighborhoods, *moradas* (spiritual lodges), and parish churches. The services promote an ethnic and spiritual cohesiveness of the larger Latina/o community.

Further Reading

Montaño, Mary. *Tradiciones nuevomexicanas: Hispano Arts and Culture of New Mexico*. Albuquerque: University of New Mexico Press, 2001.

Peter J. García

Sesame Street. *Sesame Street*, the award-winning children's television show, featuring Bert, Ernie, Big Bird, Oscar the Grouch, and many other lovable muppets, was one of the first television shows to carry bilingual education to mainstream America. Broadcast by more than 300 PBS stations in over 140 countries, children who watch *Sesame Street* can learn numbers, the alphabet, relationship concepts, and basic Spanish words through tried-and-true techniques of fast-paced, highly visual, repetitive skits that entertain while they educate.

First broadcast on November 10, 1969, *Sesame Street* was developed by Joan Ganz Clooney, then executive producer of the Children's Television Network, after years of research and testing. Originally designed to attract inner-city, pre-school-aged children, the show has faithfully drawn audiences of all ages for over thirty years and continues to teach new generations of children the academic and social skills necessary to transition from home to school. Using an educational approach that educates children through entertainment, children learn by observing the daily interaction of muppet characters created by master puppeteer Jim Henson and a human cast, including Sonia Manzano, who played the role of mother and shopkeeper Maria for over twenty-six years, and Roscoe Orman, who adopted the role of science teacher Gordon in 1973.

In addition to the Cookie Monster, Count Von Count, Grover, and the other muppet characters, who have been around since the inception of the show, new characters are added periodically to help round out the cast and continuously emphasize new cultures. In 1989, with input from Carmen Osbahr, Rosita, La Monstrua de Las Cuevas, (The Monster of the Caves), was created and added to the cast of characters who live on *Sesame Street*. Osbahr, the voice of Rosita, wanted the first Latina muppet to be a warm, loving, and colorful character, so the creators designed a fluffy turquoise muppet with big arms for hugging. Rosita speaks English and Spanish, often jumps back and forth between the two, and thinks it is a blessing to be able to communicate in two different languages. In 2001, celebrating its thirty-third anniversary, *Sesame Street* introduced the audience to a new Spanish Word of the Day segment, which is hosted by Rosita and a cast of bilingual children and teaches viewers second-language skills while fostering multiculturalism.

The highly acclaimed *Sesame Street*, now produced by Sesame Workshop (formerly Children's Television Network), has won the Action for Children's Television Special Achievement Award, along with over 100 other awards, including seventy Emmys, two Peabodys, eight Grammys, and four Parent's Choice Awards. It continues to charm audiences with its broad-based curriculum, colorful, creative, and animated vignettes, as well as a steady stream of celebrity guests, such as Gloria *Estefan, John Denver, Faith Hill, Rita *Moreno, Burt Reynolds, Sandy Duncan, Raquel *Welch, Harry Belafonte, the Dixie Chicks, Gene Kelly, Ellen Degeneres, Linda *Ronstadt, and a host of other celebrities.

Further Reading

http://www.sesameworkshop.org.

http://www.tvtome.com/tvtome/servlet/ShowMainServlet/showid~887/.

Alma Alvarez-Smith

Shakira (1977–). Shakira is regarded as a child prodigy who is also an up-and-coming Latina pop star with international appeal, style, fame, and genuine musical talent. She was born Isabel Mebarak Ripoll on February 9,

1977, in Barranquilla, Colombia. Her father was of Lebanese descent and introduced Arabic music and culture to his children. At a very young age Shakira was introduced to Latin popular music and composed her first song at age eight. She speaks three languages, and by age thirteen, she signed her first recording contract with Sony Music Columbia and released her debut album *Magia* (Magic) in 1991. Following her high school graduation, Shakira devoted all of her time and talents to music recordings, including *Peligro* (Danger) and *Pies Descalzos* (Barefeet) in 1996, and spreading her musical popularity throughout Latin America, Brazil, and Spain. *¿Donde Están Los Ladrones?* (Where Are the Thieves?), produced in 1998 by Shakira and Emilio Estefan, helped forge her place in Latin pop rock. The album went multiplatinum in the United States, Argentina, Colombia, Chile, Central America, and México and platinum in Spain.

She has earned a Grammy and two Latin Grammys but admits that her musical interests are not exclusively Latin based. She listens to bands like Led Zeppelin, the Cure, the Police, the Beatles, and Nirvana. Her original songs are fusions of her own unique musical predilection, popular style, and eclectic taste. Her musical interests culminated in the recording of several albums that led to her crossover success in the popular musical mainstream in the United States. Her first album that included English tunes was *Laundry Service* (2002), and it includes "Objection (Tango)," a Middle Eastern–sounding tune; "Eyes Like Yours," a lyrical song; "Underneath Your Clothes"; and the pop rock tune "Whenever Wherever." This recent English album did very well and has given credibility to her as a pop singer. Her Latina style consists of mostly dance music with many eclectic influences present. *Laundry Service* brings a Latin American sound to English popular music, which Shakira admits has been challenging for her to translate. It also is a recording that reflects her unique attempt at a rock sound independent of too many dazzling electronic sound effects. She uses recording engineer Terry Manning, whose work is familiar to heavy metal fans of ACDC and Led Zeppelin and hard rocker Lenny Kravitz.

Shakira. *Courtesy of Photofest.*

She was encouraged to cross over into the English market by Emilio and Gloria *Estefan, so she established a portable recording studio in rural Uruguay and began reading poetry and authors like Leonard Cohen and Walt Whitman for inspiration. Most of her recent songs express her own individual feelings and actual life experiences. She is regarded as one of the most poetic songwriters of her generation and is one of the best female lyricists in Latin America. Her fellow Colombian Nobel Prize–winning author Gabriel García Márquez stated the following about her: "Shakira's music has a personal stamp that doesn't look like anyone else's and no one can sing or dance like her, at whatever age, with such an innocent sensuality, one that seems to be of her own invention."

Further Reading

http://www.shakira.com.

Robert Chew

Sheen, Charlie (1965–   ). Charlie Sheen (born Carlos Irwin Estévez) is the son of actor Martin *Sheen. Born on September 3, 1965, in New York, he grew up in the Hollywood scene and made his acting debut at nine years of age in the movie *The Execution of Private Slovik* (1974). His first starring role came in *Red Dawn* (1984), an anticommunist film about a Soviet invasion of the United States. He gained national prominence in Oliver Stone's Vietnam-based *Platoon* (1986). He has played dramatic, action, and comedy parts in more than forty films and several television series and television movies. Sheen has had roles in popular movies such as *Ferris Bueller's Day Off* (1986), *Wall Street* (1987), *Eight Men Out* (1988), *Young Guns* (1988), *Major League* (1989), *The Three Musketeers* (1993), and *Being John Malkovich* (1999). In 2002 he received a Golden Globe Award for Best Actor in a television series for his work on *Spin City*. Sheen currently stars opposite Jon Cryer in *Two and a Half Men*, a sitcom that premiered on CBS in September 2003 and has been renewed through 2004–2005. In June 2002, Sheen married actress Denise Richards (b. 1971) and on March 9, 2004, they welcomed daughter Sam into the world. Sheen has another daughter, Cassandra (b. 1985), from a previous relationship.

Further Reading

Press, Skip. *Charlie Sheen, Emilio Estévez and Martin Sheen.* Parsippany, NJ: Crestwood House, 1996.

Louis "Pancho" McFarland

Charlie Sheen in *The Rookie. Courtesy of Photofest.*

Martin Sheen. *Courtesy of Photofest.*

Sheen, Martin (1940–). One of the most recognizable figures in prime-time television and in film, Martin Sheen was born Ramón Estévez on August 3, 1940, in Dayton, Ohio, to a Spanish immigrant father and Irish immigrant mother. His passion for acting made him purposefully fail his college entrance exam, and six months later, at the age of eighteen, he moved to New York. Soon he secured television roles in *East Side West Side* (1963) and *As the World Turns.* His first feature film was *The Incident* (1967). Sheen's acting career spans four decades and includes more than sixty films and fifty television series and shows. He has directed and produced movies including *Judgment in Berlin* (1988), *Da* (1988), and *Cadence* (1990). He has narrated more than forty documentary films ranging from the *Eyewitness* science series to historical biographies.

Sheen has received several awards for acting including Daytime Emmys in 1981 and 1986, an Emmy in 1994, a Golden Globe Award in 2001, Screen Actor's Guild Awards in 2001 and 2002, and a Tony Nomination in 1965. His children Charlie *Sheen, Emilio *Estévez, Ramon Estévez, and Renee Estévez all work in the film industry. Sheen has given many outstanding performances including his roles in the movies *Catch-22* (1970), *Badlands* (1973), *Apocalypse Now* (1979), *Gandhi* (1982), *Wall Street* (1987), and *Truth or Consequences, N.M.* (1997). Currently he is cast as President Bartlett on the Emmy-winning television series *The West Wing* (1999–).

Even though Sheen has achieved major success, he has not forgotten his working-class immigrant background and is a committed social justice activist. Over the years Sheen has been involved in farmworker and other workers' rights campaigns, antiwar actions, antipoverty campaigns, protesting the School of the Americas, and antinuclear power and weapons demonstrations. As a result, he has been arrested on dozens of occasions for acts of civil protest.

Further Reading

Press, Skip. *Charlie Sheen, Emilio Estévez and Martin Sheen*. Parsippany, NJ: Crestwood House, 1996.

Sheen, Martin. "Martin Sheen." In *What I Believe*, edited by Mark Booth. New York: Crossroad Publishing Company, 1984.

Silverman, Stephen, and Carly Bashkin. "Sarandon Leads D.C. Anti-War Protest." *People Daily News*, October 28, 2002.

Louis "Pancho" McFarland

Sheila E. (1957–   ). Born on December 12, 1957, musician Sheila Escovedo is a native of Oakland, California, and was the firstborn daughter of Pete and Juanita Escovedo. Her musical record and numerous accomplishments illustrate a vital career and huge contribution to popular culture by a prominent Latina from the United States. At an early age, Sheila was musically influenced by her father's band Azteca. Her debut performance was at age five at the Sands Ballroom in Oakland with an audience of 3,000. Young Sheila was invited to solo with her father during a concert and realized her destiny at this very early age. Intent on becoming a percussionist, by age seventeen she was already recording and touring with popular artists like George Duke, Billy Cobham, Herbie Hancock, Lionel Richie, Diana Ross, Marvin Gaye, Patti LaBelle, Natalie Cole, Stevie Nicks, Don Was, and many international pop musicians and singers.

Released in 1984, Sheila E. composed, performed, and directed *The Glamorous Life* (hit single and video), which was nominated for a multiple Grammy, an American Music Award, and winning MTV's Best Video Award. Following several successful concerts in Europe and the United States, Sheila toured as the opening act for Prince's 1984–1985 Purple Rain tour and soon after began plans for her next album, *Romance 1600*, released in August 1985. The album produced yet another smash hit, "Love Bizarre." Her next tour lasted only three months, opening for Lionel Richie's SRO World Tour in 1986. She returned home to begin her third album, *Sheila E.*, which included the hit single "Hold Me," reaching number one on the *Billboard* chart and gaining further international popularity and acclaim.

Sheila E.'s humanitarian record includes several benefit concerts and performances with Barbra Streisand, Patti LaBelle, Natalie Cole, Shirley McClain, and Liza Minelli for the Aids Project Los Angeles. Sheila also performed on Gloria *Estefan's popular hit album *Mi Tierra* (My Land, 1993) and at the 1996 Summer Games in Atlanta. She performed with popular opera tenor Placido Domingo at the thirty-fifth Annual Academy Awards, and she was featured in the all-girl Grammy production number with lesbian comedian Ellen DeGeneres. One of the highlights of her musical career was the Concert of the Americas (1994), with a vast international and domestic audience.

Her jazz resumé is equally as impressive and includes "A Celebration of

America's Music," a benefit concert for the Thelonious Monk Institute of Jazz hosted by Bill Cosby. Sheila performed with George Benson, Arturo *Sandoval, Herbie Hancock, James Moody, and Jimmy Heath in a special tribute to Dizzy Gillespie. She has also appeared on *MTV Unplugged* with Kenny "Babyface" Edmonds and on Magic Johnson's late-night talk show and has the distinction of being the first female bandleader on late-night television. A talented and ambitious musician, Sheila E. is an international celebrity, performer, composer, and humanitarian.

Further Reading

http://www.vicfirth.com/artists/sheilae.html.

Peter J. García

Smits, Jimmy (1955–). Actor Jimmy Smits was born to a Puerto Rican mother and a Surinam father in Brooklyn, New York, on July 9, 1955. He graduated from Brooklyn College in 1980 with his Bachelor of Arts degree and from Cornell University in 1982 with a Masters in Fine Arts degree. His acting career began in the New York Shakespeare festival Public Theater. Smits is part of a group of Hispanic actors called the "Lat Pack" whose presence in *film became notable during the 1980s. Smits has contributed to bringing political consciousness of Hispanic cultures and their histories to the wider American viewing population through such roles as a passionate Mexican revolutionary in a film adaptation of Carlos Fuentes novel *Old Gringo* (1989), as a Cuban freedom fighter in *Fires Within* (1991), and as the son of a Mexican immigrant living in Los Angeles in *My Family* (also known as *Mi Familia*, 1995). He won the Imagen Award from the Hispanic Media Image Task Force in 1987 because of the way he has been able to break through the common stereotypes of Hispanics promoted by the U.S. entertainment industry.

Although he had previously appeared on *Miami Vice* (as "Eddie Rivera" in episode 1.1, "Brother's Keeper," September 16, 1984), the first role to bring him widespread public acclaim was as the lawyer Victor Sifuentes, whom he played from 1986 to 1991 on the television series *L.A. Law*. His acting in this series won him an Emmy in 1990 for Outstanding Supporting Actor in a Drama Series. His next major television role, from 1994 to 1998, as Detective Bobby Simon on the television series *NYPD Blue*, won him a Golden Globe Award in 1995 for Best Actor in a Television Series (drama). These two roles were important because they showcased the talent of a Hispanic actor in nontypecast roles. Smits's other major television appearances include his roles as Richard Braden in *Stamp of a Killer* (1987), Bo Ziker in *The Highwayman* (1987), David Norwell in *The Broken Cord* (1992), Jim Gardner in *The Tommyknockers* (1993), the title role in *The Cisco Kid* (1994), King Solomon in *Solomon and Sheba* (1995), and Vincent Marra on *Glitz* (1998).

During the time of his first major television role on *L.A. Law*, Smits also landed many film roles: as Julio Gonzalez in *Running Scared* (with Billy Crys-

Jimmy Smits. *Courtesy of Photofest.*

tal, 1986); as Tom López in *The Believers* (with Martin *Sheen, 1987); as General Tomás Arroyo in the *Old Gringo* (with Jane Fonda and Gregory Peck, 1989); as Dr. David Redding in *Vital Signs* (1990); as Nestor in *Fires Within* (1991); and as Walter Stone in *Switch* (1991). More recent film credits include *Gross Misconduct* (1993), *My Family/Mi Familia* (1995), *Lesser Prophets* (1997), *Murder in Mind* (1997), *Bless the Child* (2000), *Die* (2000) (Germany), *Price of Glory* (2000), *The Million Dollar Hotel* (2000), *Angel* (2002), and *Star Wars: Episode II—Attack of the Clones* (2002). Besides his work as an actor, Smits is also a partner (with Jennifer *López, Paul *Rodríguez, and Brad Gluckstein) in The Conga Room club in Los Angeles.

Further Reading

Cole, Melanie. *Jimmy Smits: A Real-Life Reader Biography.* Bear, DE: Mitchell Lane Publishers, 1997.

http://www.eonline.com/Facts/People/Bio/0,128,14656,00.html.
http://www.galegroup.com/free_resources/chh/bio/smits_j.htm.
http://www.imdb.com/Name?Smits,+Jimmy.

Lynn Marie Houston

Soccer. Acknowledged as the world's most popular team *sport, soccer is known outside the United States simply as *football*—or in Spanish, *fútbol*. The National Football League (NFL) sport identified by that name and played in the United States is called "American football" or "NFL football" by the rest of the world. The sport's governing body, the Fédération Internationale de Football Association (FIFA), reports in its 2000 census that a total of 30 million players are registered with FIFA at all age and competency levels in over 200 countries across the globe. Millions more nonregistered amateur and informal participants play pickup games on streets, parking lots, school grounds, beaches, parks, and, mostly in the United States, indoor courts. World football, that is, soccer, has grown increasingly popular in the United States primarily for two reasons: its widespread promotion in the schools as a healthy physical activity for youth and its avid following by millions of immigrants, a great majority from Central and South America, who have retained their participation and team loyalties after settling in North America.

Latin American teams and athletes have long been recognized as world-class participants in the international *fútbol* universe. According to 2004 FIFA statistics, Brazil retains number-one ranking in the world, with Argentina ranked number four and Uruguay number nine. Similarly, some would argue that the most celebrated icon of the game in the twentieth century was Pelé, nickname of Brazilian Edson Arantes do Nascimento, who is still prominent as a legendary role model and ambassador for FIFA in the twenty-first century. Honored with the 1978 International Peace Award, Pelé was selected by sports reporters as Athlete of the Century in 1980. Other highly rated international soccer stars from Latin America include retired Diego Armando Maradona of Argentina and contemporary star Ronaldinho de Assis Moreira of Brazil, now playing for the Spanish team Barcelona FC.

Similarly, the World Cup games, a truly *world* championship established by FIFA in 1930, takes place every four years. The first World Cup champion was a Latin American team, Uruguay, and another, Brazil, has been a dominant force on the World Cup stage since then. In fact, Brazil's domination of the global competition led to its being permanently awarded in 1970 the original trophy cup, the Jules Rimet Trophy, named after the originator of the idea of an international football tournament. After that the Fédération introduced a new world championship award christened the FIFA World Cup.

Despite the worldwide robustness of men's soccer, it historically has not enjoyed overwhelming success as a professional and financially profitable enterprise in the United States. As a result the U.S. men's national team does not have a solid or deep pool of players from which to build a World Cup competitive team. In April 2004, the U.S. team ranked number eleven in its preliminary round group, trailing 118 points behind number-one Brazil, with neighbor México placing a very respectable number four. For this reason many top American soccer players emigrate to other countries to play at the sport at its highest level. Among the very tiny crop of American *fútbol* émigrés playing for the prestigious English Premier League, for example, are Casey Keller (Tottenham Hotspur), Brad Friedel (Blackburn Rovers), and Latino American Claudio Reyna, who plays for Manchester City. The New Jersey–schooled Reyna, dubbed "Captain America" by the British media, previously played for the Glasgow Rangers. Another current world-class sensation, albeit not from the United States, is Mexican Hugo Sánchez, who impressed international audiences in the 1980s while playing in Europe and later with his team and World Cup play.

Other significant U.S. Latino American players have been drafted into professional play in the Major League Soccer conferences. Among these are former Colombian star Carlos Valderrama, who has played for Tampa Bay, Miami, and Colorado; Nelson Vargas (Tampa Bay and Miami); Alex Piñeda Chacón and Diego Serna (Miami); Adolfo Valencia (Miami and MetroStars); Tab Ramos (MetroStars); Mauricio Ramos (Tampa Bay and New England); Carlos Ruiz (Los Angeles); Ryan Suarez (Los Angeles); Dwayne De Rosario (San Jose); Diego Walsh (Kansas City); Jaime Moreno (DC United); and many others.

In contrast to men's play U.S. women's soccer has been relatively successful in international competition, winning two World Cup titles (in 1991 and in 1999). In April 2004 the U.S. women's team held a number-two world ranking after Germany in preliminary rounds. Unfortunately, WUSA, the Women's United Soccer Association, could not maintain its corporate sponsors despite a strong fan base for its professional club. WUSA was established as a base for top-notch players to remain honed for global matches. Interestingly, Latinas as yet have not been major factors in women's soccer at any level.

The thriving practice of world football is inherited from the ancient past, with the earliest known record of it a fourth-century Chinese drawing showing a round ball being foot dribbled on a field. After Marco Polo's thirteenth-century travel to China, India, and parts of Southeast Asia, the game was spread throughout the Roman world as far north as Great Britain, and it took hold. Like other traditional forms of popular culture, soccer was played for centuries in Europe without formal rules and with competitions following local or regional conventions. The English attempted the first major codification of the sport in 1863 with the formation of the Football Association (FA) in London. The FA's unified rules were highly influential and led other countries to do the same. As the game's commercial prospects attracted the interest and participation of business investors, its loose grassroots street-level style was pushed toward uniformity and became the form recognized today. To regulate the sport and maximize its multinational business profitability, FIFA was created in 1913 to set the rules and standards and to coordinate international competitions of all participating football associations, including national teams from countries throughout the globe.

Sports experts describe soccer as a ball and goal game played in an outdoor field (aka "pitch," or *campo* in Spanish). Played by eleven team members on each side, the players consist of forwards, midfielders, defenders, and a single goalkeeper. The object of the game is to control the usually black-and-white ball with any part of the body except hands and arms and, ultimately, to score points or goals (i.e., *goles*) by hitting the ball into the opponent's goal area. The length of a soccer match is ninety minutes split into uninterrupted forty-five-minute halves, with variable minutes of playing time added to compensate for referee stoppages during regulation play. Both avid fans and casual spectators support the entertaining sport by following professional teams and every four years by passionately supporting the national teams that compete globally in the World Cup. As with other sports, vigorous betting and gambling accompany soccer, as does an incredibly lucrative merchandising industry of team product marketing.

Due to world football's being overshadowed in the United States by NFL football, major league baseball, and the National Basketball Association, there as yet have been few Latina and Latino American soccer players to reach the top tier of global athletics. Except for "Captain America" Claudio Reyna, the twenty-first century has yet to see any other *futbolistas* of the caliber of such stars as baseball's Fernando Valenzuela, boxing's Oscar *De La Hoya, golf's Lee Treviño and Nancy Lopez, and horse racing's Angel *Cordero. Many aficionados think that paucity of representation will be remedied within the decade as professional clubs tap into the deeply rooted popularity of soccer among Latin American immigrants and the sport captures the interest of young people in the United States.

Further Reading

Beveridge, Ronald (Milwaukee Bavarian FC, Phoenix OB FC, Scottsdale SWL FC). Interview with author, Tempe, AZ, March 17, 2004.

Fédération Internationale de Football Association. http://www.fifa.com/en/game /laws.html.

Galeano, Eduardo. *El fútbol a sol y sombra*. Montevideo, Uruguay: Ediciones Del Chanchito, 1995.

Soccer Times. http://www.soccertimes.com/index.htm.

Walvin, James. *The People's Game: The History of Football Revisited*. Edinburgh, Scotland: Mainstream, 2000.

Cordelia Chávez Candelaria

Son. *Son* refers to a musical form usually identified with a particular regional sound or music. *Son* is performed either as instrumental dance or vocal song. *Son abajeño*, a *son* from *abajo*, or below, generally referring to the Tierra Caliente region south of Jalisco, has meter and forms similar to that of the *son jaliscience*.

Son huasteca is in 6/8 meter, a compound duple meter with complex hemiola or cross-rhythm patterns. The *son huasteco* is indigenous to the Huasteca region just north of Veracruz on the Gulf of Mexico. *Conjuntos* (ensembles) from this region consist of a violin, small regional guitars called *jarana*, and a *huapanguera* (or *quinta*). Apart from the instrumentation, another characteristic of the *son huasteco* is the falsetto jumps, like wails in the vocal technique. *Mariachis have appropriated *sones huastecas*, which are also called *huapangos*, to their repertory.

Son jaliscience is in 12/8 meter, a compound quadruple meter with a complex rhythmic pattern called *sesquialtera*, which alternates 2 groups of 3 beats (compound duple or 6/8 meter) with 3 groups of 2 beats (simple triple or 3/4 meter). The alternating meters render a rhythmic effect called a hemiola, also called *contratiempo*, in the melody and the harmony. The *son jaliscience* is from the western state of Jalisco and is very much a standard part of the traditional repertory of the mariachi. It is also danced to the *zapateado* (shoe dance), performed on a wooden platform called a *tarima*. The dance represents a courtship between *el gallo* (rooster) and the hen. Musically the composition is organized into an *entrada* (instrumental introduction), *verso* (solo verse), *coro* (chorus, either responsorial or with a separate refrain), a third section of music, new verses, and a shortened version of the *entrada* at the end. The final cadence is a cliché called "the Jalisco tag." Not all *sones jalisciences* fit the above *sesquialtera* rhythm, but they are some of the oldest *sones* in the Mexican repertory.

Son jarocho refers to a regional dance in simple quadruple meter with an ostinato from the region near Veracruz. Performed in the Coliseo, a national theater in Mexico City, as early as 1790, *son jarocho* was performed in Veracruz throughout the nineteenth and twentieth centuries and popularized in California by the 1830s. *Jarocho* means brusque, which also describes the style of the music and dance tradition. The *conjunto* typically consists of the folk harp (*arpa*) from Veracruz, which differs from the *arpa* from Jalisco, and small Mexican guitars called the *jarana jarocha* and the *requinto*. The *décima form is an important part of the *son jarocho* tradition. The vocal timbre is high but does not use the falsetto technique of the Huasteca area, although because both areas are nearby geographically, the two tend to borrow and exchange repertory. The best-known example of a *son jarocho* is *"La Bamba."

Further Reading

Stanford, Thomas. "The Mexican Son." In *The Yearbook of the International Folk Music Council*. New York: n.p., 1972.

Peter J. García

Son Cubano. Because of its deep penetration into nearly every aspect of musical culture within Cuba, its vast international dissemination and popularization, and its immense impact on Latino popular dance music, *son cubano* is the most important of the many popular music genres that originated and developed in Cuba during the twentieth century. The genre, which gave birth to or heavily influenced a multitude of genres, including *mambo, *rumba, *charanga, bugalú, *salsa, songo, timba,* and *Latin jazz, is often described as the first invented by Cubans and as the common denominator in almost all of Cuban music. Emerging from the rural areas of el Oriente, Cuba's eastern provinces, particularly around Santiago de Cuba and Guantánamo, during the late nineteenth century, the original manifestations of *son* (the qualifier *cubano* is added only to distinguish the genre from Mexican *sones,* such as *son jalisciense* or *son huasteco*) consisted of a constant alternation between the improvisations of a solo singer and a short composed refrain sung by a small group. As the genre became increasingly urbanized, an additional structural element, an initial closed "song" section, was added, thereby solidifying the binary form that it retains to this day, the *tema* or *son,* a thirty-two bar song—usually in AABA form—followed by the *montuno,* which is usually much longer than the *tema* and consists of extended instrumental solos (called the *descarga*) and short precomposed horn sections (the mambo or *yambú*) as well as call-and-response vocals (called the *guajeo* and the *coro* or *estribillo,* respectively).

This binary structure is an example of the *son*'s representing a mix of European- and African-derived elements, the *tema* being derived from the European song tradition, while the call-and-response *montuno* has strong African antecedents. This combination exhibits itself in other elements of the genre, including the instrumental ensemble, where European-based plucked stringed instruments, such as the guitar and the *tres* (a Cuban invention consisting of three sets of double strings), play alongside African-based percussion, such as the *bongó* (also a Cuban-invented instrument), and the *marimbula,* a bass instrument derived from the African thumb piano, the *mbira.* The singing, predominantly black and mulatto musicians singing about Afro-Cuban *barrio life in a smooth European-based bel canto style, and the dance, a combination of a European-derived couples dance with African-derived rhythmic steps and movements, also exemplify this mixture of influences.

The Afro-Cuban *son montuno,* a musical genre that combines a Cuban *son* with an improvised *montuno* section, resulting in an intense, almost relentless quality, is fundamentally at the root of today's Latina/o popular music, including salsa. Admired by the peasant or working classes, a *son* is a genre of dance music that combines Spanish and African elements. The *montuno* is usually, but not exclusively, cued in by a break in music with the piano playing rhythmically. This section of the *son* is open and features a *coró* with an individual solo from the horn section. A *coró* is an improvised call-and-response section between a member of the horn section and the lead vocalist. It usually consists of two eight-bar phrases, during which the horn takes a full solo after trading sections with the lead vocalist. A *son montuno* is not fast paced but rather performed at a medium tempo, usually in a reverse clave (2/3) form.

A *sonero* is literally the individual in a salsa group that sings or plays the Afro-Cuban *son*, one of the most popular Afro-Caribbean musical forms. Moreover, a *sonero* is the individual lead singer that usually improvises, rhythmically, melodically, and verbally, against the refrain of the *coró* in the modern salsa ensemble. The word *guarachero* is also used to define the person's role in the salsa ensemble. A *sonero* usually does his or her improvising over the *son montuno* section of a salsa piece. In this part of the piece the vocalist will trade improvised sections with a member of the horn section, which consists of saxophone, trombones, and trumpets.

The confluence of cultures embodied by *son* would lead to its adoption as an important marker of an emerging Cuban national identity that began developing in the decades following Cuba's independence from Spain in 1902 and that sought to unite the entire country—black, white, and mulatto. This process began with the genre's introduction in the capital city of Havana around 1909, brought by immigrants from el Oriente serving obligatory terms as soldiers of the permanent army, a practice that led to mass urbanization during this time. The early *son* ensembles were *tríos*, consisting of guitar, *tres*, and maracas, with at least two of the musicians singing, exemplified by Trío Matamoros, which was founded in Santiago in 1912 by Miguel Matamoros and would reach its height of popularity in the 1920s and 1930s, and Trío Oriente, a group formed within the army before 1910, which would, once its members moved to Havana, add a *bongocero*, effectively transforming itself into a *cuarteto*. While the practice of *tríos* and *cuartetos* performing at dances and parties was brought from el Oriente, others emerged in Havana after *son*'s introduction. These include the publication, in the form of sheet music, and recording and *sones* and the development of *coros de son*, choral groups of eighteen to twenty singers, in Havana barrios, the groups often being associated with a particular barrio.

The development of *son* as a marker of national identity continued in the early 1920s when the genre became popular throughout Cuba, spurred in part by the increasing availability of record players, more affordable records, and the introduction of regular radio broadcasts on the island in 1922. *Tríos* and *cuartetos* were playing at parties thrown by some of the richest white families in Santiago by around 1920, but the elite in Havana was slower to embrace the genre. With the exception of their hugely popular "El son de la loma" (Son of the Hill), Trío Matamoros was playing exclusively *danzones in their performances in the capital. The genre's general acceptance by Havana's largely white upper class would not be solidified until the 1926 appearance of Sexteto Habanero, a *son* group consisting of black musicians, at the Presidential Palace in Havana at the invitation of mulatto president Gerardo Machado.

Son's continued popularity in Havana in the 1920s also led to increased urbanization and sophistication within the genre to accommodate for larger, more cosmopolitan audiences. The *son cuarteto* was soon eclipsed by the *sexteto*—which added claves and *marimbula* (later replaced by the stringed bass)—and the *septeto de son*—which added a trumpet. Recordings by the leading exemplar of this format, Ignacio Piñeiro's Septeto Nacional, and Sexteto Habanera became popular throughout Cuba and abroad. This international dissemination eventually led to the emergence of New York and Paris as important centers for performance and recording by Cuban musicians and to contact between *son* and jazz musicians, which would affect both genres greatly over the ensuing decades. The immediate effect on *son* was the integration of more complex, jazz-influenced harmonies, faster tempos, and the development of a more percussive, rhythmic sound.

The event that served as a catalyst for the popularity of Cuban music worldwide was the 1931 release of Don *Azpiazu's groundbreaking recording of "The Peanut Vendor," a somewhat sanitized arrangement of the Moisés Simón–penned *son-pregón* (literally son cry) "El manisero" (derived from the calls of street vendors in Havana), which, while it had no connection or similarity to the Cuban genre rumba, was given the name *rhumba*. The record was a nationwide hit in the United States and triggered a *rhumba* craze in Tin Pan Alley, on Broadway, and in Hollywood, where in the hands of American songwriters and musicians it became diluted and Americanized, even though its exoticism was one of the main reasons for its popularity. The most prominent figure in popularizing *rhumba* was the Spanish-born and Cuban-bred Xavier *Cugat. Cugat, who, in addition to recording and touring, appeared in a number of Hollywood films, made no claims to the authenticity of the music he was playing, preferring to point to it as a way of introducing Americans to Latin music.

In Cuba, *son* continued to develop and exert great influence throughout the 1930s and 1940s. Its capacity for hybridization led to the development of genres such as *bolero-son*, *son-guaguancó*, and even *blue-son*, and its popularity and influence permeated Cuban music to the extent that *charanga* bands—flute and violin orchestras that had, to that point, mainly been playing danzónes and *boleros—began including *sones* in their repertoire and, in accordance, incorporating more rhythmic elements into their music. The *son* ensemble continued to grow, with *tres* player, arranger, and composer Arsenio Rodríguez adding congas to his band in 1938. Rodríguez, along with his Conjunto Casino, would be a guiding force in the development of the genre. The inclusion of congas was followed by the addition of piano and a second trumpet, forming a new ensemble, dubbed a *conjunto sonero*. In addition to, and perhaps because of, the expanded format, arrangements became increasingly regulated, including the incorporation of precomposed trumpet parts and a standardization of the accompaniment patterns played by the rhythm section. In the process, the *son* gave up some of its informal, collective looseness.

The 1940s also saw the development of mambo, a combination of Afro-Cuban rhythms and big band jazz, the development of which is alternately attributed to Rodríguez in Cuba, Dámaso *Pérez Prado in México and the West Coast of the United States, and *Machito and Mario *Bauzá in New York. The genre began as an expansion of the mambo section, the horn-driven section of the *montuno* in *son*, and incorporated elements of *son*, including the common use of *ostinato* (repeated melodic and rhythmic patterns) patterns in the saxophones adapted from the *tres* patterns of *son*. The subsequent mambo craze in the United States during the early 1950s was paralleled in Cuba by *conjunto sonero*'s period of greatest popularity, attributable in part to the introduction of television to the island. This popularity was led by artists such as Beny Moré—a singer who, after working with many groups including Trío Matamoros and Prado's orchestra, led his own group, Banda Gigante, which incorporated mambo elements into *son*—and La Sonora Matancera, which featured a four-trumpet horn line and a succession of singers that included Daniel Santos and a young Celia *Cruz.

Son fell out of official favor after the 1959 revolution, being derided by the Castro government as a vestige of the decadent Batista regime. However, variants on the genre, including the *changüí* from Guantánamo, remained popular in the rural areas of the Oriente. Meanwhile, in New York, bands that had been playing *charanga* and *bugalú*—a mix of Afro-Cuban rhythms with rock and roll that served as a survival technique for mambo groups in the wake of the latter genre's vast popularity—turned to the *conjunto sonero*, spurring what was called a *típico* revival in the mid-1960s. This revival was partially the result of the influence that Arsenio Rodríguez, who had relocated there from Cuba in 1950, was having on the local music scene and of appearances in the city by La Sonora Matancera.

Around this same time, a brasher, rawer version of *son*, dubbed salsa to obscure its Cuban origins, was being embraced by Nuyoricans as a musical expression of their ethnic identity in light of the new social consciousness that was seizing the racially volatile urban areas of the United States. This new style was exemplified by Willie *Colón, a Nuyorican teenager who led a band featuring a trombone section in the place of the standard trumpets and represented himself as *el malo* (the bad boy), the image reflecting the alienated energy of the barrio. Salsa would go on to attain popularity in many parts of Latin America and to be seen by many as the foremost expression of Latino music in the 1970s, becoming a symbol of pan-Latino identity in the process.

During the 1970s, the dual trends of experimentalism and traditionalism typified *son* in Cuba. The decade's experimental movement was preceded by the formation of Los Van Van in 1969, led by Juan Formell, bass player and former musical director of Orquesta Revé, a *charanga* that specialized in *changüí* and incorporated experimental elements, such as the inclusion of an expanded set of timbales, trombones, and batá drums. Los Van Van, also a *charanga*, infused *son* with elements from rock, rhythm and blues, jazz, and Brazilian music, including the addition of electric guitars, synthesizers, and a drum set, and abandoned traditional standardized rhythmic patterns in the bass and piano, naming the new hybrid *songo*. Following in this same vein was singer/songwriter Adalberto Álvarez's group Son 14. The leaders of the movement toward traditionalism were *tres* player and former rock guitarist Juan de Marcos González, who formed Sierra Maestra along with future ¡Cubanismo! founder Jesús Alemañy in 1976 with the goal of keeping the torch of the great *septetos* alive for a younger generation, and guitarist and singer Eliades Ochoa, who took over the leadership of Cuarteto Patria, a group that had existed since the 1940s, in 1978.

In 1988, former Los Van Van and Irakere flautist José Luis "El Tosco" Cortés formed NG (Nueva Generación) La Banda, a group that combined *songo* with funk and rap influences, spawning the new genre *timba*. With NG La Banda, El Tosco's aim was to combine the flavor of Los Van Van with the musical aggressiveness of the Latin jazz giants Irakere. *Timba* continued its popularity into the mid-1990s, when the *son* of the *conjuntos soneros* of the 1950s was given unexpected and unprecedented exposure and popularity at an international level with the 1997 release of *Buena Vista Social Club. Begun by musical director and organizer Juan de Marcos González and producer Ry Cooder, the American guitarist, as a tribute to the artists of the past, the album went on to sell 4 million copies, win a Grammy Award, and spawn international tours, a host of solo albums by musicians featured on the original recording, and an Academy Award–nominated documentary.

While Ry Cooder insists in his liner notes to *Buena Vista Social Club* that "this music is alive in Cuba, not some remnant in a museum that we stumbled into," director Wim Wenders's documentary *Buena Vista Social Club* posits the endeavor as a salvation project, not merely of the careers of singer Ibrahim Ferrer and pianist Rubén González, both of whom had retired from performing, but of the genre. Wenders focused the attention of the film on the older musicians, such as Ferrer, González, Pío Leyva, and Compay Segundo (whose participation was secured only after he returned to Cuba from an international tour), and gave much screen time to the white American Cooder—who has always downplayed his role in the recordings—while almost completely ignoring the original impetus of the project, the black Cuban Juan de Marcos González. *Buena Vista Social Club* and its many offspring served to fuel a roots movement among musicians in Cuba and nostalgia for an imagined pre-Castro Cuba in the United States that dovetailed with the retro-lounge trend of the late 1990s and with a more sympathetic and open attitude toward Cuba on the part of both the Clinton government and a good portion of the American public.

Further Reading

Cooder, Ry. Liner notes from *Buena Vista Social Club*. Nonesuch Records 79478-2, 1997. Compact Disc.

Manuel, Peter, Kenneth Bilby, and Michael Largely. *Caribbean Currents: Caribbean Music from Rumba to Reggae*. Philadelphia: Temple University Press, 1995.

Mauleón, Rebecca. *Salsa Guide for Piano and Ensemble*. Petaluma, CA: Sher Music, 1993.

"PBS Presents Buena Vista Social Club." *Public Broadcasting System*. http://www.pbs.org/buenavista.

Robbins, James. "The Cuban *Son* as Form, Genre, and Symbol." *Latin American Music Review* 11.2 (December 1990): 182–200.

Rodríguez, Olavo Alén. "Cuba." In *South America, Mexico, Central America, and the Caribbean*. Vol. 2 of *The Garland Encyclopedia of World Music*, edited by Dale Olsen and Daniel Sheehy. New York: Garland, 1998.

Rondon, César Miguel. *El Libro de la Salsa*. Caracas: Impreso por Editorial Arte, 1980.

Steward, Sue. *¡Musica! Salsa, Rumba, Merengue, and More*. San Francisco, CA: Chronicle Books, 1999.

Ramón Versage

Son Montuna. *See Son Cubano.*

Sonero. *See Son Cubano.*

Sor Juana Inés de la Cruz (1648–1695). Born in Nepantla, México, in the second century after the Spanish Conquest, Juana de Asbaje was a child prodigy who in the eighteenth century became known as the preeminent Spanish poet of the colonial era throughout New Spain in the Americas, as well as in Spain and other European countries. She was acclaimed as the "New World Muse" for her prolific sacred poetry and religious dramas, many written before she was twenty. In the late twentieth century, she was reclaimed by Chicanas and other contemporary Latinas as a native-born feminist precursor who, like *La Malinche, provided the oldest documented American source for the principles of *gender equality and the importance of America's bilingual biculturality.

The known facts of her life include that she was born to an unmarried mother and was reared by her grandparents, learning to read her grandfather's books when she was only three. She began writing verse soon thereafter and composed her first lyric play for a church procession when she was eight. Despite her acknowledged brilliance, because of her female sex she was denied access to formal education and eventually chose the convent and the life of a nun as a means of gaining access to literary and scientific knowledge through church libraries. She entered the convent of San Jerónimo in 1669 and remained there until her death. Other than her extensive poetry, her most famous writings are the essays "Athenagoric Letter" (1690) and "Response to Sor Fílotéa" (1691),

Sor Juana Inés de la Cruz, the celebrated Spanish Mexican prodigy, poet, and precursor feminist, is called the "Phoenix of America." This 1750 painting by Miguel Cabrera shows her at study in the convent. *Courtesy of the Cordelia Candelaria Private Collection.*

both arguing passionately and with methodical logic for women's rights to formal schooling. These two writings explain Sor Juana's status as a feminist precursor who, although acknowledged by traditional scholars as a major colonial poet, was slighted as a political thinker until rediscovered in the late twentieth century by women throughout the world. Her amazing intelligence, creativity, curiosity, and courage in challenging the patriarchal status quo, even at the cost of personal freedom, provide a predecessor voice for such other feminist trailblazers as Mary Wollstonecraft (1759–1797) and John Stuart Mill (1806–1873). Twentieth-century writers as diverse as Estela *Portillo Trambley,

Octavio *Paz, and Alicia *Gaspar de Alba, among others, have written major treatments of Sor Juana's remarkable and enigmatic life.

Further Reading

Gaspar de Alba, Alicia. *Sor Juana's Second Dream*. Albuquerque: University of New Mexico Press, 1999.

Paz, Octavio. *Sor Juana Inés de la Cruz, o, Las Trampas de la Fe*. 2nd ed. Mexico City: Fondo de Cultura Económica, 1994.

Paz, Octavio. *Sor Juana: Or, The Traps of Faith*. Translated by Margaret Sayers Peden. Cambridge, MA: Belknap Press, 1988.

Peden, Margaret Sayers. *A Woman of Genius: The Intellectual Autobiography of Sor Juana Inés de la Cruz* 2nd ed. Salisbury, CT: Lime Rock Press, 1987. (Includes translation by Peden of *Respuesta a Sor Filotéa de la Cruz*.)

Portillo Trambley, Estela. *Sor Juana and Other Plays*. Ypsilanti, MI: Bilingual Press/Editorial Bilingüe, 1983.

Cordelia Chávez Candelaria

Sosa, Sammy (1968–   ). Baseball great Samuel Sosa Peralta was born in 1968 in Consuelo, Dominican Republic, the fifth of seven children. His father, Juan Bautista Montero, operated a tractor in the sugar cane fields. His mother, Lucrecia "Mineya" Sosa, had to quit school and begin working as a youth. When Sosa, nicknamed Mikey, was six years old, his father died, leaving his family in extreme poverty and forcing all the children to work. Sosa shined shoes, washed cars, and later worked at a shoe factory in San Pedro de Macoris, after the family moved there in 1981. Despite the hardships, Mineya helped instill honest, hardworking, and humble values in Sosa.

His older brother, Luis, introduced Sosa to organized baseball at about the age of fourteen. In July 1985, Omar Minaya, a scout for the Texas Rangers, signed Sosa to a $3,500 contract. Sosa gave most of the money to his mother. He played his first major league game as a right fielder for the Rangers in 1989. He was traded to the Chicago White Sox later that season, then to the Chicago Cubs before the 1992 season. When he joined the Cubs, he requested and began to wear uniform number 21, in honor of Roberto *Clemente. In 1993, he hit thirty home runs and stole thirty-six bases, becoming the first Cub to achieve the "30-30" milestone. He then signed a $2.95 million, one-year contract in 1994, which increased to over $4 million in 1995. At this point he was the highest-paid player on the team. In 1998, Sosa's performance elevated him to superstar status, when he hit twenty home runs in June, a major league record for most home runs in a single month. He finished with sixty-six for the season, surpassing Roger Maris's major league record of sixty-one, but behind Mark McGuire's new standard of seventy (Barry Bonds would break this new record in 2001). During the last few months of the 1998 season, the historic home run duel between Sosa and McGuire received massive media coverage. The sight of Sosa blowing kisses to his mother after every home run, a ritual begun in 1997, became a familiar sight on television. He batted .308, led the league in runs batted in (RBIs) with 158, and scored with 134, helped the Cubs make the playoffs, and won the National League Most Valuable Player Award (NL MVP).

Later that year, Hurricane George hit the Dominican Republic and caused severe damage. Sosa started a foundation to provide relief and was awarded the Roberto Clemente Man of the Year Award by major league baseball for his humanitarian efforts. He became the first player to hit at least sixty home runs in three different seasons by hitting sixty-three in 1999 and sixty-four in 2001. He led the league in home runs in 2000 with fifty and in 2002 with forty-nine. In 2001 he batted a career best .328, led the league in RBIs with 160, and runs scored with 146, and was runner-up for the NL MVP.

Further Reading

Gutman, Bill. *Sammy Sosa: A Biography*. New York: Pocket Books, 1998.

Sosa, Sammy, and Marcos Breton. *Sosa: An Autobiography*. New York: Warner Books, 2000.

Clifford Candelaria

Soto, Gary (1952–). Renowned *Chicano poet and fiction writer Gary Soto is one of the most lauded and popular Chicano authors currently publishing. Along with Rudolfo *Anaya and Sandra *Cisneros, Soto enjoys commercial success and publishes to a vast international audience. He has received numerous literary prizes throughout his career, including being a 1995 finalist for both the *Los Angeles Times* Book Award and the National Book Award for his *New and Selected Poems*. Twenty years earlier his first poetry publications received similar national recognition, winning the 1975 Academy of American Poets Prize and the *Discovery*-Nation Award. Both major awards led directly to publication of his first two collections, *The Elements of San Joaquin* (1977) and *Tales of Sunlight* (1978), by the University of Pittsburgh Press, a prestigious poetry venue for young talents. As prolific a writer as he is critically acclaimed, he has published dozens of books and is one of the youngest poets ever to appear in the canon-setting anthologies produced by the New York publishing firm W.W. Norton, including in the widely used high school and college textbooks *The Norton Anthology of Modern Poetry* and *The Norton Anthology of American Literature*.

The son of Manuel and Angie Treviño Soto, a working-class Mexican American couple who were both born in the United States, Soto was born on April 12, 1952, in Fresno, California. His father was killed in a work-related accident when the future poet was five years old, a trauma that partly explains the haunting sense of loss and painful solitude threading most of his writings. After graduating from high school, Soto enrolled in Fresno City College, originally intending to study geography. He shifted majors to creative writing and earned his Bachelor of Arts in 1974 from California State

University in Fresno, where he studied with poet Philip Levine whose mentorship and patronage had a singular impact on Soto's future success. Going on to earn a Master's in Fine Arts (1976) from the rigorous University of California at Irvine creative writing program, during graduate study he married Carolyn Sadako Oda (in 1975). They are the parents of one daughter, Mariko Heidi. He taught at the University of California at Berkeley from 1979 to 1991 and since 1992 has been a full-time writer.

In his writing Soto strives to balance a strongly felt and vivid ethnicity with an equally strong desire to transcend ethnic boundaries and allegiances. Literary scholars credit him with masterful craftsmanship, consistent precision, and keen sensitivity to the authenticity of his subject matter. This artistic blend of social awareness with literary style helps explain the extent and high caliber of his acclaim. Throughout his work, he has addressed American racial tensions, often based on incidents from his own childhood experience, as in the collections of fiction *Living Up the Street: Narrative Recollections* (1985; which received a Before Columbus Foundation Award) and *Small Faces* (1986). Besides writing books of poetry and fiction for adults, his work has appeared in major literary and cultural magazines like the *Iowa Review*, *Ontario Review*, *Plouqhshares*, *The Nation*, and the eminent *Poetry*, which has honored him with the Bess Hoskin Prize and the Levinson Award and also by featuring him in *Poets in Person*.

Other major honors include the United States Award of the International Poetry Forum, the California Library Association's John and Patricia Beatty Award (received twice), a Recognition of Merit from the Claremont Graduate School for *Baseball in April* (1990), the Silver Medal from the Commonwealth Club of California, the Tomás Rivera Prize, and others. In addition, he has received writing fellowships from the Guggenheim Foundation, the National Endowment for the Arts (twice), and the California Arts Council.

Branching out to children's and youth literature, as well as to film and music productions, Soto's film *The Pool Party* produced for the Independent Television Service received the 1993 Andrew Carnegie Medal. He also wrote the libretto for a contemporary-themed opera titled *Nerd-landia* for the Los Angeles Opera Company. In 1999 he received the Literature Award from the Hispanic Heritage Foundation, the Author-Illustrator Civil Rights Award from the National Education Association, and the PEN Center West Book Award for *Petty Crimes* (1998). He serves as Young People's Ambassador for the California Rural Legal Assistance agency and for the United Farm Workers of America (UFW), founded by César Chávez. Readers and critics generally agree that the large body of Soto's work of poetry, fiction, plays, children's stories, and films—over twenty-five major titles published between 1990 and 2003—have secured him an indisputable place of achievement in American and Chicano literature.

Further Reading

Bruce-Novoa, Juan. *Chicano Poetry: A Response to Chaos.* Austin: University of Texas Press, 1982.

Candelaria, Cordelia. *Chicano Poetry: A Critical Introduction.* Westport, CT: Greenwood Press, 1986.

Contemporary Authors Online. Gale Group. http://galenet.gale.com.

Torres, Héctor. "Gary Soto." In *Chicano Writers.* Vol. 82 of *Dictionary of Literary Biography*, edited by Francisco A. Lomeli and Carl R. Shirley. Detroit: Gale, 1989.

BJ Manríquez

Soto, Talisa (1967–). Born Miriam Soto on March 27, 1967, in Brooklyn, New York, Talisa Soto, of Puerto Rican heritage, is an internationally known model with covers on *Vogue, Glamour,* and *Mademoiselle* fashion magazines. She is also an actress in drama, action, and science fiction films, having appeared in films such as *Facing Fear* (2000), where she starred as single mom Mercedes, and the sci-fi thriller based on the popular video game *Mortal Kombat* (1995 and 1997), in the role of Kitana. She appeared alongside Benjamin *Bratt in *Piñero* (2001) and was nominated for Best Supporting Actress by the 2002 *ALMA Awards. In 2003 Soto appeared in the latest installment of the *Mortal Kombat* series.

In April 2002, Soto married Bratt, and the following December they announced the arrival of their daughter, Sophia Rosalinda.

Further Reading

http://movies.yahoo.com/shop?d=hc&cf=gen&id=1800023502&intl=us.

http://www.cinema.com/search/person_detail.phtml?ID=15354.

http://www.fulllatin.com/talisa_soto_bio.htm.

Arturo J. Aldama

Soul. During the revolutionary period of the late 1960s came a new style of popular music that combined both *salsa and rhythm and blues (R&B) that was called *Latin soul. Latin soul was most popular among East Harlem and Bronx teenagers, who sang both English and Spanish lyrics over a music that was more Latin than African American.

Ray Barretto was considered one of the pioneers in Latin soul with his album *Acid* in 1967. This album generously blended Latin styles with jazz and R&B ingredients. Cuban-born conga player Ramón "Mongo" Santamaría was also equally influential in the popularity of Latin soul. Santamaría also had a remarkable eye for future trends and up-and-coming musicians. Santamaría made a long line of Latin soul albums for both Atlantic and Columbia. The legendary *Machito also jumped on the bandwagon and recorded a Latin soul album titled *Machito Goes to Memphis* (1967). The influence of R&B on Latin music, and visa versa, continued throughout the late 1960s and well into the 1970s.

George Yáñez

South American Music in the United States. For nearly a century, South American music and music making have had an important impact in the United States. Although perhaps less prominent than their Caribbean and Mexican counterparts, a variety of South American popular music genres, performers, and more recently immigrant communities from Argentina, Bolivia, Brazil, Chile, Colombia, Ecuador, Paraguay, Peru, Uruguay, and Venezuela have also left their mark on the world of American music making. Despite the fact that most Latin American musical influences in the United States since the 1930s are generally associated with the Spanish-speaking Caribbean or México, the first widespread wave of interest in Latin American sounds by American audiences took place nearly two decades earlier with the successful introduction of the Argentinean *tango.

Originally having developed in the working-class sectors of the city of Buenos Aires during the late nineteenth century, the tango arrived in the United States not directly from Argentina. In 1913 the dance duo of Vernon and Irene Castle introduced the dance on Broadway after learning it in Paris, where the genre had been enjoying popularity for some time. Very quickly thereafter, and largely under the guiding hand of the Castles, the tango would become all the rage on the American social dance scene and quickly transcended its novelty status and became an important constituent of standard ballroom dancing repertoire. Similarly, and perhaps due to its initial introduction through the Broadway stage, in later decades the tango became one of the favorite genres to be used for the ubiquitous "Latin number" that was a feature of so many musicals throughout the 1940s and 1950s, perhaps the most notable among these being "Hernando's Hideaway" from *The Pajama Game*. The initial fascination with the dance in the United States led to a variety of tango and tangolike compositions during the 1910s and 1920s, although many of them bore little stylistic resemblance to the Argentinean tango, given the lack of contact with Argentinean practitioners of the genre. Nevertheless, a few South American compositions such as "El Choclo" by Argentinean composer Angel Villoldo and "La Cumparsita" by Uruguayan composer Gerardo Matos Rodríguez did manage to find their way to the United States in sheet music form. At the same time, the early hybridization of the tango with other popular music forms of the time would lay the foundation for what in later decades would become a favorite way of combining Latin American genres with jazz—that is, the use of an introductory section set in a Latin American rhythm, followed by a section set in jazz swing time. The prototype for this was W.C. Handy's tango-influenced "St. Louis Blues," and the practice would later be applied to the combination of jazz with other genres or "exotic" melodies, as is the case with Dizzy Gillespie's "Night in Tunisia," Duke Ellington's "Caravan," or Chick *Corea's "Armando's Rumba," among many others.

The lack of direct contact with Argentinean performers appears to account for why later stylistic developments in the genre, such as its further refinement as a vocal genre in the 1940s, did not make as significant an impact in the United States as the aforementioned dance craze of the early part of the twentieth century. In spite of this, tango did not disappear completely from the American imagination. Since the 1980s the genre has made a return. There have been a number of productions that have featured the tango in recent years (e.g., "Cell Block Tango" from *Chicago* [2003]) and entire reviews devoted to the dance. Avant-garde jazz and twentieth-century art music enthusiasts came to rediscover the tango through the "new tango" compositions of Astor Piazzolla, some of which have become part of the standard repertoires of American and European chamber music groups. At the same time, tango has returned to the social dance scene, as is evidenced by the proliferation of dance clubs that specialize in the tango. These new incarnations, however, oftentimes go beyond the ballroom dance style that managed to develop and attain permanence in the United States. The more recent immigration of Argentinean nationals to the United States has resulted in the introduction and cultivation of other variants of the tango and related genres, such as the *milonga*, that were not as widely known during the earlier part of the twentieth century.

Since the 1950s, American audiences have also become well acquainted with a collection of genres and melodies from the highland regions of South American that are generally identified as Andean. The first significant introduction of Andean music in the United States was by Peruvian singer Zoila Augusta Emperatriz Chavarri del Castillo, better known to her public as Yma Sumac. Sumac got her start in Peru in the 1940s singing what at the time was identified as Inca music—stylized, "semiclassical" renditions of Andean folk melodies and original compositions that emulated the folk repertoire. After a brief recording career in Argentina, Sumac and her husband, composer/arranger Moisés Vivanco, moved to New York. Promoting herself as an Inca princess and direct descendant of the last Inca ruler Atahualpa, she sought to capitalize on her background, previous musical experience, and versatile four-and-a-half-octave vocal range by recording a number of albums for Capitol records (between 1950 and 1959) that fell into what at the time was identified as the exotica music vein. The music of these albums featured arrangements by Vivanco that mainly combined jazz, mambo, and lounge music as a means of transforming the South American folk and traditional repertoire into something that appealed to American audiences' desire for foreign, strange, and remote "native" sounds from other parts of the world. While Sumac's notoriety diminished in subsequent decades, she remained an underground cult figure and has recently been rediscovered due to the renewed interest in 1950s and 1960s lounge music. In recent years, most of her records have been reissued on CD, and some tracks have been included in feature film sound tracks and television commercials.

Perhaps more widely known than Yma Sumac are the Andean panpipe, *charango*, *quena*, guitar, and bombo ensembles that became popular in the

late 1960s and early 1970s throughout Latin America, Europe, and the
United States. Although often promoted as music from indigenous communities in the Andes, this ensemble format and its featured arrangements were
developed largely in major urban centers in Bolivia and Chile, and to a lesser
extent Argentina, Ecuador, and Peru, and provided the template for what
has become a pan-Andean musical style and repertoire. American audiences
became acquainted with this sound from a variety of sources. While in Paris
in the mid-1960s, singer-songwriter Paul Simon became familiar with this
repertoire after meeting and sharing the stage with a group of Argentinean
performers based in Paris that called themselves Los Incas. In later years,
Simon would record a version of the song "Condor pasa" by Peruvian composer Daniel Alomia Robles. He also featured the members of Los Incas, performing under the name Urubamba, in his first solo album, produced an
album for the group, and further promoted their music by inviting them to
accompany him on his 1973 tour. At the same time, changing political situ-
ations, particularly in Chile as a result of the onset of the Pinochet regime
and the persecution of many artists associated with the nueva *cancíon
protest movement, forced a number of well-known groups to live in exile for
over a decade. While most of these groups relocated to Europe rather than
the United States, their geographical displacement made the music more accessible to American audiences. The impact of Andean music in European
pop culture was also felt in the United States, the best example of which is
the Andean-tinged song "Fernando" (1976) recorded by the Swedish pop
group Abba. In some cases, Andean music has had a subtle influence on
American popular culture. One such example is the song "Llorando se fue"
(Crying She Left, 1982) a Bolivian saga popularized in South America by the
Bolivian group Los Kjarkas and whose melody was subsequently appropriated and rearranged in a Brazilian folk style with the intent of introducing
it in the United States as a new Latin dance craze in the early 1990s, the
lambada.

Since the 1980s, political and economic hardships in the various Andean
countries have produced an increasingly large population of immigrants from
these nations in the United States. The pan-Andean character of the popular
music that developed during the 1960s and 1970s and the interest by American and European audiences for this repertoire have provided a number of
performing opportunities and sources of income for members of this immigrant community. Today, most major cities in the United States count many
active performers of Andean music. Most of the members are originally from
Argentina, Bolivia, Chile, Colombia, Ecuador, or Peru, and although likely
to not have performed with each other before arriving in the United States,
they are all quite familiar with the repertoire and style. After all, these individuals have a common familiarity with the music of groups like Inti-Illimani,
Quilapayún, Illapu, Los Kjarkas, and others, and use their renditions of
South American folk and traditional music as templates with which to de-

vise their own sounds. Recent years have also seen the establishment of music and dance academies in major cities in the United States where second- and third-generation aspiring performers can learn the folkloric traditions of their respective countries. The pan-Andean repertoire and performance style has also become a favorite among Latin American music performing ensembles at the university level and can be found in places such as the University of California at Santa Cruz, the University of Texas at Austin, Florida State University, and the University of Illinois at Champaign-Urbana.

Since the 1990s, the most significant contribution of South American music to the Latino and *Chicano community in the United States has been the Colombian *cumbia. Originally, a folkloric music and dance genre from the Atlantic coast of Colombia, cumbia's popular music incarnations of the late 1960s and 1970s became quite influential throughout South America. A predilection for the genre also took root in the area of Monterrey, México, during this time, giving rise to a number of Mexican performers of cumbia. From Monterrey, cumbia quickly disseminated through the northern part of México and to Spanish-speaking communities of the southwestern United States, particularly Texas. Soon the cumbia became an integral part of the accordion-based *conjunto*/norteño style and by the 1980s had developed its own locally based style, which, according to many purists on both sides of the debate, differed greatly from its Colombian progenitor. In the early 1990s this style of cumbia would cross over into the American as well as Mexican, and by extension Latin American, mainstream, thanks to the highly successful but tragically short-lived career of Corpus Christi, Texas, native *Selena Quintanilla. In recent years cumbia in the United States has continued the process of musical hybridization that has been a hallmark of Chicano, Latino, and *Tejano music making for generations. Fusions and adaptations of cumbia with jazz, rock, *hip-hop, reggae, *salsa, Brazilian *samba, techno, trance, and others, have become quite common on both sides of the U.S.-México border and reflect a wide variety of approaches, as is exemplified by the contrasting interpretations of the genre by groups like Quintanilla siblings' The Kumbia Kings and Grupo Fantasma (Texas), *Los Lobos, Los Super Seven, and *Ozomatli (Los Angeles), El Gran Silencio, and Celso Piña (Monterrey). This interest in cumbia has also led to the "rediscovery" of Colombian cumbia by American audiences, not only because some local bands have attempted to reference elements of that style in their own recordings (e.g., the Los Super Seven rendition of the Colombian cumbia "El pescador" [The Fisherman, 2000]) but also by the introduction of Colombian artists like Lisandro Meza and Roberto Torres (best known for his salsa-influenced cumbia "Caballo viejo" [Old Horse, 1981]).

South American performers have also made a number of notable contributions to a variety of other musical genres in the United States. The salsa and *Latin jazz communities have counted with significant contributions from Venezuelan singer Oscar d' León, Colombian groups like Grupo Niche and Orquesta Guayacán, Peruvian percussionist Alex Acuña, and Argentinean saxophonist Leandro "Gato" Barbieri. Argentinean singer-songwriters Atahualpa Yupanqui and Mercedez Soza, and their Chilean precursors Violeta Parra and Victor Jara, have been quite influential with those interested in Latin American protest music. Paraguayan folk harp music, although not widely known with the general American public, has influenced the Mexican *son jarocho ensembles in both México and the United States, as is evidenced by the inclusion of the traditional song "Pájaro campana" (Bell Bird, n.d.) as part of their repertoire. Recent interest in world music, particularly folk traditions belonging to the African diaspora, has brought attention to a number of lesser known musical genres such as the Venezuelan *joropos*, and *quitiplás*, Colombian *vallenatos* and *porros*, Ecuadorian marimba traditions, Peruvian *landós* and *festejos*, and Bolivian *sagas*. Two artists have been particularly notable in this area, thanks to the exposure they have received on American and European record labels: Afroperuvian singer Susana Baca and Colombian folkloric singer Totó la Momposina. There have also been contemporary art music composers and performers, most recently among them Peruvian tenor Juan Diego Flórez, who is currently performing in Europe and the United States to wide critical acclaim. Most recently, the increased awareness by American audiences of Latin American rock and pop bands has received a number of important contributions from Latin America. Among them are Los Fabulosos Cadillacs, Soda Stereo, and Fito Paez from Argentina; Los Prisioneros and La Ley from Chile; *Shakira, Carlos Vives, Juanes, and Los Aterciopelados from Colombia; Tania Libertad, Gian Marco, and Pedro Suárez-Vértiz from Peru; and Desorden Público and Los Amigos Invisibles from Venezuela.

Further Reading

Roberts, John Storm. *The Latin Tinge: The Impact of Latin American Music on the United States*. 2nd ed. New York: Oxford University Press, 1999.

Javier F. León

Spanish Caribbean Music. The Caribbean region is a geographical area of great historical, social, and cultural complexity. It was there that Christopher *Columbus first landed, and it is the region that became Spain's first colonial acquisition. One of the most contested regions in the entire world, the islands of the Caribbean (*see* Antilles) and the countries of the Caribbean rim were inhabited by a number of tribal peoples when they were settled by a variety of immigrants from various European countries. Eventually the European conquest and colonization resulted in four Caribbean language/culture areas: Spanish, English, Dutch, and French. Spanish colonization decimated most of the Caribbean's aboriginal peoples through disease, warfare, and forced relocation. As with the rest of the New World, the Caribbean became a destination for Europeans seeking economic opportunity as well as religious and political freedom (*see* History entries). The new colonists developed the islands by enslaving thousands of Africans for plantation agriculture, cultivating sugar, coffee, cocoa, and other commodities for the European market. Following emancipation in the nineteenth century, other ethnic groups were enticed to fill the gaps in the workforce left by the former slaves, including East Indians, Chinese, southern Europeans, Syrians, and Lebanese. By the mid-nineteenth century, the Caribbean had become the most culturally and ethnically heterogeneous region in the world.

As a result of this complex multinational, multilingual, and multicultural history, Caribbean music contains considerable shaping influences from European and African sources and their hybrid foundations of *mestizaje*. The most African-influenced music in the New World is that which accompanies traditional religions such as Santería in Cuba and Orisa in Trinidad. As in their West African counterparts, these religious ceremonies feature an instrumental ensemble of drums and other percussion that provide rhythmic ostinati (repeated patterns) to accompany dancing and singing. These patterns are the basis of improvisation by a lead drummer, who also guides the choreography of the dancers. In Cuba the drums are called batá, and this drumming tradition made its way to urban centers such as New York City and Miami, where Cuban immigrants settled in great numbers. Americans first heard batá drumming performed by Cuban drummers Francisco Aguabella and Julio Collazo to accompany Katherine Dunham's dance company in 1957. Over time, separate regional styles of batá drumming have developed in the United States to accommodate a growing Santería religious community of Latinos of Cuban, Puerto Rican, and Dominican heritage, as well as a fair number of Anglos and African Americans.

When translated from Spanish to English, the word *toque* literally means "touch," but in the context of Latin percussion, the word *toque* means "beat." Specifically, *toque* means an organized set or phrase of beats for percussion, which originally came from African religious drumming. Each of these *toques* was used to summon a specific God in African ceremonial rituals. The individual players of these *toques* were not particularly judged on their enthusiasm or energy level but rather on their knowledge of all the varying types of *toques*. The individual was also judged on his/her abilities to improvise using the repertoire of the standard *toques* and their overall support of the ensemble performing.

The styles of Caribbean popular music that have gained the widest popularity in the United States have fused in various ways African rhythmic organization and musical texture with European melodic and harmonic structures. Cuba has been the most prolific of expressive sources, beginning with the 1930s North American craze identified as *rumba but actually reflecting characteristics of the *son, a descendant of the *contradanza*, or European "country dance," found throughout the New World. Marked by a variety of spellings, rumba itself is defined by a wide variety of complex music forms and dance styles that are often misunderstood or mistaken for other Latin genres. The 1930s craze, occasionally spelled "rhumba," was not the same genre recognized by Cubans who generally understood Cuban rumba as a vocal genre accompanied by percussion only and associated with lower-class Afro-Cubans. In Cuba it took on African-derived elements, particularly the rhythmic foundation known as clave, a two-measure timeline, which can be felt by musicians and dancers as either a 3/2 or 2/3 pattern that organizes many Latin popular music genres. This pattern is played using a pair of thick wooden sticks, also known as claves, that are struck together. The earliest *son* ensembles were probably voice and percussion only, but as musicians moved from the countryside to Havana, the ensemble often expanded to six members. These included a six-stringed guitar usually played by the singer, a nine-stringed guitar called a *tres*, a bass instrument called a *marímbula* (a relative of the African thumb piano), maracas, claves, and bongo. In the 1920s, bandleaders such as Ignacio Piñero and Ernest Lecuona added one or two trumpet players to the ensemble, and it was this *septeto* (six-member band) style that first gained popularity in the United States.

During the 1930s and 1940s composers began to include more complex harmonic progressions and faster tempos adopted from the authentic Afro-Cuban rumba and the Cuban carnival bands called *comparsa*. The instrumental ensemble further expanded to a format called *conjunto*, adding conga, piano, and more horns to the sound. More innovations took place when the music traveled to New York City, where many Cubans and Puerto Ricans moved during the Great Depression. Latino musicians worked in the same clubs as African American jazz artists and sometimes the same band. For example, Mario *Bauzá played trumpet with the Cab Calloway band before forming a Latin orchestra with his brother-in-law *Machito. Eventually, Machito and other bandleaders such as Dámaso *Pérez Prado and Beny Moré merged the Afro-Cuban sound with the big band jazz practice of arranging contrasting instrumental lines for sections of trumpets, trombones, and saxophones. The new sound was called *mambo, and during the 1940s it completely overtook big band jazz in popularity. The musical influences were interanimating and reciprocal, moving back and forth among musicians and resulting in progressive hybrid sounds. Dizzy Gillespie, for instance, made a number of classic recordings with Cuban drummer Chano *Pozo, thus creating new directions in modern jazz. Mambo orchestras were featured at the Apollo Theater and Savoy Ballroom in Harlem, and eventually this led to an influx of Latin rhythms into rhythm and blues (R&B) and doo-wop.

The *guajira* is a style of music of the working class of Cuba, most popular among Cuban farmers. A simple music, *guajira* utilizes a *décima, a ten-lined verse from seventeenth-century Spain, and instrumentation composed of a small guitar called the *tres* (twelve-stringed guitar), guitar, and varied percussion. The lyrics are usually about issues of the *guajiros* (working people).

The *guajira* is similar to the *son montuno* but lacks the faster driving pace and is more delicate. It is comparable to the country music of Cuba. The emergence of the Buena Vista Social Club (*see Buena Vista Social Club*) brought old *guajira* legends into the limelight, including artists such as Compay Segunda, Eliades Ochoa, and Pio Leyva. The most popular *guajira* ever written is based on the Cuban revolutionary poem "Guantanamera" by José Martí, a piece that has been redone repeatedly and remains popular today.

The famous poem "Dos alas" (Two Wings) by Lola Rodríguez del Tió describes Cuba and Puerto Rico as "two wings of the same bird." However, Puerto Rico did develop its own separate musical genres: These include the *plena, a type of musical commentary accompanied by guitars and a percussion instrument called a *pandero*, and the *bomba, an African-based song genre analogous to the Cuban rumba. Cuban music was enormously successful in Puerto Rico as well as the surrounding Caribbean. Puerto Ricans have always outnumbered Cubans in New York, so it is understandable that "Nuyorican" musicians and audiences would come to dominate the Latin music scene in the city. By the 1950s, a number of Puerto Rican musicians adopted the mambo style, chief among them Tito *Puente and Tito *Rodríguez, who with Machito formed the "big three" bandleaders of New York's famous Palladium nightclub.

During the 1960s greater public awareness of and respect for Puerto Rican and Latina/Latino identity in general paralleled an increasing political activism relating to ethnic heritage and related cultural imperatives. This heightened political consciousness demanded a vibrant musical vehicle that would be exciting to a younger generation yet also distinctively Latin American in origin. Nuyorican musicians responded to the challenge by creating *salsa, essentially a rebirth of the *son*/mambo that incorporated aspects of rock and jazz. The structure of the *son* underlies salsa music, particularly the repeating rhythmic-harmonic patterns carried by the percussion, piano, and bass. In essence, salsa musicians play the same musical forms as before, but the hard-driving arrangements and the addition of trombones to the horn section and timbales to the percussion create a more aggressive sound than the mambo orchestras of the 1950s. Johnny *Pacheco, the founder of the first salsa label, Fania Records, envisioned salsa as an alternative to rock music, an energetic, danceable style that barrio youth could relate to their own experience. Some performers borrowed heavily from rock and R&B, as in the "boogaloo" style pioneered by Joe Cuba, Ray Barretto, and Pacheco. Other performers, such as Eddie *Palmieri and Mongo Santamaría, cross-pollinated their music with the improvisational style of modern jazz. Salsa at its emergence was thus often politically charged, protesting the injustices of barrio life, as in the music of Rubén *Blades and Willie *Colon. Salsa musicians also advocated a pan-Latino solidarity, partly explaining why the music spread in popularity from its origins in New York City throughout the United States, the Caribbean, and parts of South America. Today, there are distinctive salsa styles in Colombia and Venezuela, and this now international music has made inroads in Europe and Japan as well.

Dominicans are among the most recent wave of Latinos to arrive in New York and other large U.S. cities, and central to their life in their new surroundings has been *merengue since the 1980s. Officially the national music of the Dominican Republic, merengue is another descendant of the European social dance music blended with Afro-Caribbean elements. Unlike the Cuban *son*, the main melodic instrument in merengue was the button accordion, brought to the island by German immigrants. During the 1960s, merengue bandleaders such as Johnny Ventura and Wilfrido Vargas fused merengue with rock and salsa to create a new style that was faster in tempo and flashier in presentation. Their new *orquesta merengue* featured a salsa-style horn section that reinforced or replaced altogether the accordion and used the rhythm section typically found in salsa bands. The idea was to compete with imported salsa records, and it worked, creating a self-sustaining record industry within the Dominican Republic. As Dominicans immigrated to New York City during the 1970s and 1980s, merengue became an important link to the island. However, it also became enormously popular with other Latinos, and that success propelled it along the same path as salsa, making merengue an international music.

Although not typically thought of as Latinos, citizens of the West Indies have made significant contributions to Latino culture in the United States. As with other ethnic and racial groups, West Indians from Trinidad and Jamaica moved to North America in great numbers during the second half of the twentieth century. Likewise, their music assumed great significance in retaining their sense of self-worth and pride in their countries of origin. Trinidad is best known for a type of social commentary called *calypso, which is rooted in the West African tradition of verbal challenge and boasting. Throughout each era of popular music in Trinidad, calypso has adapted to current tastes. When the *son* became popular throughout the Caribbean, calypso musicians made their sound more Latin by using a similar instrumentation as accompaniment. In the 1970s, calypso took a turn similar to salsa and, through the innovations of performers such as Ras Shorty I (Garfield Blackman) and Lord Kitchener (Aldwin Roberts), became an internationally oriented dance music called *soca*. While the social commentary form of calypso still exists in Trinidad, *soca* has been more rapidly accepted abroad, particularly among audiences who better understand the more party-oriented lyrics of *soca*. Jamaican reggae emerged as an antedote to North American R&B, beginning life as an upbeat dance music called *ska*. During the 1970s, Jamaican musicians turned to their African roots and produced reggae, addressing in their song lyrics the themes of social injustice and black redemption. Despite the language barrier, the music of Bob Marley in particular crossed international barriers to become a voice for the oppressed worldwide. "Reggae en español" has become popular throughout the Caribbean and Latin America. In the United States the leaders are a generation of young musicians such as New York's King Chango, who are trying yet again to expand the vocabulary of Latin dance music.

Clearly, the contributions of Spanish Caribbean music to U.S. popular culture have been considerable as a grassroots social bond among immigrants and as an art form crossing over ethnic, linguistic, and national experiences. Moreover, music from this region has become an important unifier for Americans of Caribbean heritage and is an important signifier of their unique cultural heritage, even as the music itself appeals to peoples across borders.

Further Reading

Allen, Ray, and Lois Wilcken, eds. *Island Sounds in the Global City Caribbean Popular Music and Identity in New York*. Chicago: University of Illinois Press, 2001.

Amira, John. *The Music of Santería: Traditional Rhythms of the Bata Drums*. Crown Point, IN: White Cliffs Media, 1992.

Aparicio, Frances. *Listening to Salsa: Gender, Latin Popular Music and Puerto Rican Cultures*. Hanover, NH: University Press of New England, 1998.

Boggs, Vernon. *Salsiology: Afro-Cuban Music and the Evolution of Salsa in New York City*. Westport, CT: Greenwood Press, 1992.

Glasser, Ruth. *My Music Is My Flag: Puerto Rican Musicians and Their New York Communities, 1917–1940*. Berkeley: University of California Press, 1995.

Manuel, Peter. *Caribbean Currents: Caribbean Music from Rumba to Reggae*. Philadelphia, PA: Temple University Press, 1995.

Mauleón, Rebecca. *Salsa Guidebook for Piano and Ensemble*. Petaluma, CA: Sher Music Co., 1993.

Roberts, John Storm. *The Latin Tinge: The Impact of Latin American Music on the United States*. 2nd ed. New York: Oxford University Press, 1999.

Waxer, Lise, ed. *Situating Salsa: Global Markets and Local Meanings in Latin Music*. New York: Routledge, 2002.

Hope Munro Smith

Spanish-Language Radio. Spanish-language radio, which continues to reach millions of households on a daily basis, also known as Latino radio, first gained widespread acceptance in the southwestern United States. It was established through a radio brokerage system with Anglo-owned radio stations in the 1920s and 1930s. The system allowed Latino broadcasters, many of whom were trained in México, to purchase blocks of radio airtime for Spanish-language programs.

In 1939, the International Broadcasting Company of El Paso began developing Spanish-language programs to sell to stations nationwide. Seven years later, Raoul Cortez of San Antonio, Texas, received approval from the Federal Communications Commission to operate KCOR-AM, the first Spanish-language radio station owned and operated by a Mexican American in the United States. Cortez opened the nation's first *Spanish-language television station, KCOR-TV, in 1955. His radio station earned national acclaim for creating radio *theater dramas with Mexican American actors that were broadcast around the country.

Spanish-language radio programming continued to grow throughout the 1950s and 1960s. But it was not until the 1970s and the implementation of federal affirmative action rules that the number of Latino-owned radio stations began to grow significantly. Spanish-language radio in the United States has focused on one of three traditional musical formats—Mexican regional, tropical/Caribbean, and a variety of contemporary pop music and ballads. Despite the increasing popularity of *rock en español (rock in Spanish) or Latin *hip-hop in the United States, as well as internationally, there were few stations dedicated to those formats in 2002. In Los Angeles, the top Spanish-language radio market in the country, three of the city's twenty Spanish-language stations play varieties of regional Mexican music, but none focus on rock en español even though Latin American rock bands routinely sell out large local venues. Industry experts, nevertheless, predict that the diversity of music provided by Spanish-language radio stations will grow steadily as the audience for alternative music formats increases. One of the nation's most popular English-language hip-hop stations, KPRW in Los Angeles, reports that 60 percent of its audience is Latino. Latino radio also includes a growing number of bilingual formats. Along the U.S.-México border on stations from California to Texas, deejays mix Spanish-language Mexican and Mexican American music with pop tunes by Latina artists like Christina *Aguilera and Jennifer *López. On-air personalities at these stations routinely speak in "Spanglish," a mix of English and Spanish, as they spin records and converse with listeners.

While Spanish-language radio broadcasters have favored musical programming, especially regional music, they also routinely air shows that provide listeners with information on a wide array of community activities and public services. Radio Campesina (Farmworkers Radio), owned and operated by the United Farmworkers of America, airs regional and international Latin music and serves as a one-stop shop for information about *immigration and other public welfare and social justice issues.

Radio Única (Unique Radio), headquartered in Florida, is a national Spanish-language talk radio network. Founded in 1998, it was the nation's first twenty-four-hour Spanish-language talk and news radio network. In Phoenix, Radio Única announcers helped organize opposition to the state's decision to eliminate bilingual education programs. Labor unions use Latino radio to communicate with members, the presidents of México and the United States have appealed to constituents through weekly radio addresses, and political exile groups in Florida use it to criticize the regime of Cuban President Fidel *Castro. Stations affiliated with the Hispanic Radio Network provide information to Hispanics about health, environment, education, and social justice, as well as information about how to get help in their community (examples of requests include how to get a Social Security card or a driver's license, how to hire a lawyer), according to Poncho Fernández, president of WREV, 1220 AM, in Greensboro, North Carolina.

The Latino radio format also includes *Latino USA*, an English-language news and issues program that airs on National Public Radio stations nationwide. In 2002, *Latino USA* aired its 500th episode. The program is produced at KUT 90.5 in Austin, Texas, and is heard on more than 240 stations in the United States. Latino radio programming is also being distributed through the World Wide Web. *Latino USA*, for instance, archives its programs and offers them free to listeners via the Internet. Web sites such as Salsapower.com, MixLatino.com, and ZonaLatina.com offer listeners a variety of musical formats. Furthermore, hundreds of radio stations throughout Latin America now provide live Webcasts on the Internet.

Latino radio has also become an increasingly important medium for corporate America to sell its products. Industry officials report a 70 percent increase in the number of Latino-oriented radio stations in the United States since 1992. By 2002, there were more than 600 Latino stations nationwide. Meanwhile, the overall commercial radio industry grew by only 10 percent during the same period.

Several demographic trends bode well for the Spanish-language radio market in the United States. The U.S. Latino population totaled 35 million in 2000, accounting for nearly $600 billion in purchasing power. In 2002, Latinos became the largest minority group in the country, growing to 37 million people. If current population trends continue, consumer spending among Latinos is expected to grow to nearly $1 trillion by 2010. In 2050, more than 106 million Latinos will live in the United States. The Spanish-language radio audience also is younger than the general population, (eighteen to thirty-four compared with thirty-four to fifty-five), they have more children (three to four instead of two to three), and Latinos have a steadily growing income basis.

Although Spanish-language radio stations represented less than 6 percent of all stations nationwide in 2001, in communities where Latinos are a major segment of the population, Latino stations attract major audiences. In some cities it is the number-one station. In Los Angeles, New York, Miami, and Chicago, among others, Latino radio stations are among the top five competitors for the broadcast market. In New York 12 percent of the population listened to Spanish-language radio in 2001, according to the Arbitron rating system, with four Spanish-language stations ranked among the twenty-five most popular in the city. A station owned by the Hispanic Broadcasting Corporation, 105.9 FM, bills itself as the largest Spanish-language radio broadcaster in the United States. The station offers listeners a blend of *salsa, *merengue, ballads, and pop music selections. In Chicago, where large Mexican American and Puerto Rican populations coexist, three of the largest Spanish-language radio stations include WIND 560 AM, WLXX Tropical

1200 AM, and WOJO, Que Buena 105.1 FM. Nationwide, the Spanish-language format shows up among the "top 5" ranked stations in all leading Hispanic metro markets. About 12 million people nationwide listened to Latino radio in 2001.

Despite the growing popularity of Latino radio nationwide, advertising spending has not kept pace. While the Latino population in the United States nearly doubled between 1980 and 2000, the amount of money spent on advertising on the Latino radio market was only 3.3 percent, or $607 million, of the $18.4 billion spent in 2001. Researchers found that many advertisers wrongly assumed that Latino consumers could not afford their products, even though U.S. Census figures showed that Latino buying power grew at almost twice the rate of non-Latinos during the 1990s. A report by the Civil Rights Forum on Communications Policy also found that racial discrimination played a role. They found that some advertisers believed that targeting Latinos would erode brand status. Companies also paid less in 2001 to advertise on Spanish-language radio stations. In Los Angeles, number-one rated KSCA 101.9 FM ranks eighteenth in advertising revenue, according to BIA Financial Network, which tracks advertising revenue.

Latinos working for Spanish-language media also complain of receiving lower pay, as compared to their counterparts in the mainstream media outlets. A 2002 report by the Center for the Study of Urban Poverty at the University of California, Los Angeles, found that the median annual salary for Spanish-language radio broadcasters was $41,000; in contrast, on-air talent at English-language stations earned about $90,000 per year.

As in other segments of the commercial radio industry, Latino radio is undergoing growing consolidation as independent stations are sold to radio networks and corporate mergers produce huge media consortiums. For instance, the Univision television network purchased the Hispanic Broadcasting Corporation for $3.5 billion in 2001, merging the nation's largest Spanish-language television network with the country's largest Spanish-language radio network. Critics of this trend complain that corporate conglomeration results in fewer programming choices for Spanish-language radio listeners.

Further Reading

Gutiérrez, Félix, and Jorge Reina. *Spanish-Language Radio in the Southwestern United States*. Austin: Center for Mexican American Studies, University of Texas at Austin, 1979.

Palazzo, Anthony. "Radio: Another Spanish Conquest." *Los Angeles Business Journal*, October 6, 2003, 20.

Veciana-Suárez, Ana. *Hispanic Media, USA: A Narrative Guide to Print and Electronic Hispanic News Media in the United States*. Washington, DC: Media Institute, 1987.

http://www.eradioresource.com/images_pdf/2000_vol6n2/v6n2_hispanic_radio.pdf.
http://www.tsha.utexas.edu/handbook/online/articles/view/SS/ebs1.html.

James E. García

Spanish-Language Television. Spanish-language television has an almost fifty-year history in the United States and has played a key role in informing, entertaining, and engaging the U.S. Latina/o Spanish-speaking audience across generations and across diverse sectors of the community, from new arrivals to original residents whose primary language is still Spanish. The first Spanish-language television station was founded in the United States in 1955. KCOR-TV in San Antonio was owned and operated by Raoul Cortez, who had launched the nation's first *Spanish-language radio station in 1946. Cortez's groundbreaking television station featured live dramas, variety shows, classic Mexican films, and news.

In 1962, San Antonio became home to the Spanish International Network (SIN), the first Spanish-language television network in the country. The network's first station was KWEX (formerly KCOR). Over the next several years, SIN purchased stations in New Jersey, California, and elsewhere. In 1972, SIN's stations were merged into the Spanish International Broadcasting Company, and in 1987 the company was sold to the Hallmark Corporation and First Chicago Venture. Shortly thereafter, the company changed its name to Univision and in 1992 was sold to A. Jerrold Perenchio and a consortium of Latin American investors. Some Hispanic leaders at the time criticized the fact that the network had become foreign-owned. There have been few U.S. Latinos who have owned full-power television stations in the United States.

In 2002, three broadcasting companies dominated the Spanish-language television market in the United States: Univision Communications, Telemundo Inc., and Azteca América. Univision, by far the largest of the three companies, is headquartered in Los Angeles and owns more than fifty television stations and extensive radio and record label interests. Univision also owns the Galavisión cable network and Telefutura, a broadcast network launched in 2001 and originally aimed at younger viewers. Univision officials claim that their programs reached about 97 percent of U.S. Hispanic households, and their audience accounts for approximately 80 to 85 percent of the total Spanish-language television viewers in 2003. All of the top twenty programs in Spanish-speaking U.S. households are broadcast by Univision. Among its most popular programs is *Sábado Gigante*, which celebrated forty years on the air in 2002.

In 2003, Univision was the fifth largest television network in the country. The company's stations air in every major city in the nation. In 2002, Univision announced that it would merge with the Hispanic Broadcasting Radio Network, paying more than $2 billion for the company. Critics of the announced merger complained that if the merger were to occur, too much Spanish-language broadcasting would be concentrated in the holdings of one company.

Telemundo, the next leading competitor in the Spanish-language television market, is headquartered in Hialeah, Florida. Founded in 1987, the company was purchased by NBC in 2002 for $2.7 billion, and since that time Telemundo has begun closing its ratings gap with Univision. The network reaches about 80 percent of U.S. Hispanic households in more than fifty markets, as well as nineteen countries in Latin America. Nevertheless, Telemundo audiences account for about 15 percent of the Spanish-language television viewing public in the United States. In 1992, Joaquín F. Blaya took over as president and chief executive officer, and under his leadership, Telemundo, Univision, and Nielsen Media Research created the first nationwide ratings service focused on the viewing habits of Hispanic television audiences. Telemundo has also aired dubbed versions of English-language television hits like *Dawson's Creek* and *Beverly Hills 90210*. After the

Some of the most popular Spanish-language television stations are readily recognizable from their logos. *Courtesy of Emmanuel Sánchez Carballo.*

purchase of Telemundo by NBC, bilingual journalists began appearing on the company's English- and Spanish-language networks.

The newest arrival on the Spanish-language broadcasting scene is Azteca América. The network is owned by México's TV Azteca broadcast network founded in 1968. TV Azteca is the second largest television broadcasting company in México. Like Univision in the United States, Televisa controls the overwhelming majority of broadcasting in México. Televisa is part owner of the Univision network. Azteca America launched its first U.S. television station in Los Angeles in 2001 but achieved its major expansion of stations in the U.S. market in 2002. The network's programming reached about 30 percent of U.S. Hispanic households in January 2003. Azteca America's programming features *telenovelas* (soap opera–type series) and variety shows, though its program schedule features more *sports and reality programs than rivals Univision and Telemundo.

All three major Spanish-language networks depend heavily on *telenovelas* to fill their program schedule. The programs are extremely popular among Spanish-language television viewers in the United States and throughout Latin America; and Latin American production companies produce many of the *telenovelas* viewed in the United States. Televisa in México and Venevisión in Venezuela are the leading providers of such programming to Univision, though the company also produces its own shows. Some U.S. Hispanics have criticized the Spanish-language networks for providing viewers with few choices besides *telenovelas*, entertainment variety shows, and sports, to the exclusion of public service programs, documentaries, or serious dramas. The popularity of Spanish-language television is directly related to the population growth rate of U.S. Hispanics in the United States, as well as the community's growing middle class. Between 1990 and 2000, the U.S. Hispanic population grew 58 percent to more than 35 million people. In 2002, Latinos became the nation's largest minority group, surpassing African Americans and totaling 37 million people, or about 13 percent of the U.S. population. Predictions about the population growth rate among Hispanics suggest that Spanish-language television audiences will continue to grow dramatically in the coming years. By 2005, census experts estimate the U.S. Hispanic population will reach 44 million people. If the current growth trends continue, there will be more than 100 million Hispanics in the United States in 2050.

Research by Initiative Media in Los Angeles concludes that U.S. Hispanics are avid television fans. In 2002, Hispanics watched about 58.6 hours of television per week, 4.4 hours more per week than typical non-Hispanic viewers. The company's research also found that 49 percent of Hispanics who watched television during prime time watched Spanish-language programming. Notably, the number of prime-time viewers watching Univision alone was greater than the number of Hispanics watching all six English-language broadcast networks combined. Another trend that bodes well for the future of Spanish-language television in the United States is the fact that the greatest percentage increase in television viewership in the United States in 2002 occurred among Hispanic adults eighteen to forty-nine years of age— a coveted demographic for advertisers.

In addition to Spanish-language programming by the three major networks, smaller companies, as well as major cable and satellite providers, are entering the Spanish-language television market. In Indianapolis, WISH, a CBS affiliate, took to the airwaves in February 2003. In North Charleston, South Carolina, WJEA, an English-language station, began airing a Spanish-language newscast with English-language subtitles in 2003. In New York City, Time Warner Cable, one of the nation's largest cable television providers, recently launched a new programming package that included nineteen Spanish-language channels. About one-third of the television-viewing households among Time Warner's New York subscribers are Hispanic. The channels offer these viewers Spanish-language versions of CNN, Discovery, and the Cartoon and Toon Disney networks. Time Warner Cable also plans to launch a twenty-four-hour Spanish-language news channel aimed at New York viewers, and officials say that the number of channels offered its viewers is expected to grow.

Viacom's MTV en Español and VHuno offer younger viewers Spanish-language and English-language music videos. ESPN, the cable sports channel, announced that it would launch a Spanish-language version of the network. Other companies planning investments in the U.S. Spanish-language television market include Plural Entertainment of New York; Nostromo Américas, a joint venture formed by Miami's Venevisión International and Spain's Nostromo network. The nation's leading "video-on-demand" company, iN Demand, offers Spanish-language movies, including English-language films dubbed in Spanish and Spanish-language films with English subtitles.

Despite the creation of new Spanish-language projects, the programming available for Spanish-language viewers remains limited when compared to the offerings for the English-language market. In Brownsville, Texas, in 2002, cable subscribers could receive eleven Spanish-language channels but fifty-eight channels in English as part of a basic service package. The rapid growth of the U.S. Hispanic population has captured the attention of major advertisers. Latinos represented about $600 billion in consumer spending in 2002, and that figure could jump to $1 trillion in 2010. Yet only 3 percent of the money spent on advertising nationwide was spent in the Hispanic market in 2002. Telemundo earned about $559.4 million in revenue during the first nine months of 2002. During the same period, Univision generated about $1.1 billion in revenues. Spanish-language television executives complain that advertisers are unwilling to pay them the kind of money they spend in the English-language market. Experts say that the amount of money spent to advertise on Spanish-language television is expected to grow by about 15 percent annually in the coming years.

Spanish-language television executives blame the disparity in advertising rates for a marked disparity in pay scales among Spanish-language broadcasters and other employers and their counterparts at English-language networks. For instance, Spanish-language television broadcasters in Los Angeles earned about 70 percent less than those at English-language stations in 2002, according to a study by University of California–Los Angeles's (UCLA) Chicano Studies Research Center. Spanish-language broadcasters also offer less in health and retirement benefits than their English-language counterparts. The UCLA study found that the median income for on-air talent at English-language stations in Los Angeles was about $200,000 but $60,000 for Spanish-language television on-air talent; and efforts are under way to unionize more Spanish-language television employees. Meanwhile, Spanish-language television networks in the United States continue to make record profits. Spanish-language television is playing an increasingly important role in U.S. elections. In 2002, a record $16 million in paid political advertising appeared on Spanish-language television channels, according to research conducted by the Hispanic Voter Project at Johns Hopkins University. Most of the 16,000 Spanish-language ads appeared on Univision and Telemundo. While that figure represents only a fraction of the $1 billion spent on political advertising overall that year, spending on Spanish-language campaign ads is expected to rise sharply in coming elections.

Research by Initiative Media has found major differences between the viewing habits of Spanish-language television audiences and Hispanics who watch English-language television. For instance, *telenovelas* are the most watched programs on Spanish-language television, while animated programs, "reality" programs, and *police dramas draw the greatest numbers of Hispanic viewers on English-language programs. Television networks now are developing specific programming aimed at English-dominant U.S. Hispanics because of such viewing differences. The *George López Show*, a sitcom, began airing on ABC in 2002, and the first prime-time Hispanic-oriented television drama, *American Family*, aired on PBS in 2002. Univision's Galavisión cable network began offering a limited amount of bilingual programming in the late 1990s. In 2003, SíTV announced it would begin a cable network on the Dish Satellite network.

Further Reading

"Growing Hispanic Communities Challenge Traditional Media." Associated Press, 2 February 2003.

Terry-Azios, Diana. " 'Tuned In' Coral Gables." *Hispanic Magazine* (October 2000).

Veciana-Suárez, Ana. *Hispanic Media, USA: A Narrative Guide to Print and Electronic Hispanic News Media in the United States.* Washington, D.C.: Media Institute, 1987.

Wright, Christopher. "Despierta ("Wake Up") America! Hispanic Media Comes of Age." http://www.bcfm.com/financial_manager/AprMay03/Despierta.pdf.

http://www.esmas.com/televisahome.

http://www.telemundo.com.

http://www.tvazteca.com.

http://www.univision.com.

http://www.venevision.net.

James E. García

Spanish Market. In México and the Southwest, the Spanish market is better known as *mercado* or *tianguis*, which is a place where people can find a little bit of everything. It is most common for people to go to the Spanish market to buy groceries, but it is not unusual to find stands selling shoes, clothes, and household objects. The products sold in a Spanish market, much like flea markets and swapmeets, are priced by the merchant, making it easier for the merchant and customer to negotiate or bargain.

In Santa Fe, New Mexico, the term *Spanish Market* is applied to an arts and crafts festival celebrated annually during the month of either July or August since 1951 and sponsored by the Spanish Colonial Arts Society as a way to maintain Spanish colonial art forms. To participate in the Santa Fe Spanish Market, artists must be from New Mexico or Colorado and of Hispanic descent. In producing the *santos* (saints), *retablos (religious paintings), *colchas* (quilts), and other arts and crafts for the festival, artists must use skills, materials, and techniques similar to the ones used during the Spanish colonial period.

Further Reading

Gran Diccionario Enciclopedico Ilustrado. Vol. 7. Mexico City: Reader's Digest México, 1979.

Mónica Saldaña

Sparx. Hailed as the Latina equivalent of Abba, Sparx has entertained audiences in the United States, México, and South America with their original style of *grupera*, a type of regional Mexican music; *Tejano (Tex-Mex), *mariachi, and *Nuevomejicano* (New Mexican) popular music and neatly choreographed dance. Members of a larger, extended musical *family from northern New Mexico, the quartet Sparx includes members Carolina, Rosamaría, Verónica, and Kristyna Sanchez-Pohl. With deep family roots in northern New Mexico, Sparx is managed by their father, Mauricio Sanchez. A local and international pop singer himself during the 1950s and 1960s who performed under the stage name of Tiny Morrie, Sanchez also had a couple of crossover English and Spanish hit recordings that topped the charts in México and the United States. The Sanchez-Pohl musical family also touts brother Lorenzo Antonio, an international pop music idol who has several commercial hits and has recorded and toured throughout México, Latin America, and the United States. Likewise, mother Gloria Pohl is also a local *Nuevomejicana* celebrity who was a popular singer during the Chicano era. Pohl continues to travel with the group during their concerts and tours and assists and encourages her daughters with their musical careers.

Their tour and concert circuit has taken them to Argentina and Paraguay, yet they perform regularly throughout the United States, while they continue developing their international pop music career based out of their hometown—Albuquerque. In 1982 during junior high school, they performed in seventy different locations throughout México and the United States. Following the release of several early recordings, their 1994 hit "Te Amo, Te Amo, Te Amo" (I Love You, I Love You, I Love You) topped the charts. Other original hits, like "El Corrido de Juanito" (Johnny's Ballad), released in 1996, was composed by their father and brother and is heard on *Sparx y Lorenzo Antonio Cantan Corridos* (Sparx and Lorenzo Antonio Sing Corridos). From 1983 to 1989, Sparx put their musical careers on hold to finish high school, but by 1991, they produced a new album and returned to the concert scene in a series of antidrug performances aimed at Latina/o youth. They have also supported the Muscular Dystrophy Association and performed benefit concerts to assist the Albuquerque Public Schools.

In 1995, Sparx paid their dues to mariachi and produced a fine recording called *Sparx con Mariachi*, which was followed by a second *Mariachi* recording (2001). By 1995 they were releasing hits that were topping the national *Billboard* charts in México and received their first gold and platinum records from Fonovisa, for selling their first 100,000 copies. They have produced two successful *corrido* recordings (1996 and 1998) with their brother Lorenzo Antonio. In 1997, they released *Tiene que ser Amor* (It Has to Be Love), which includes a traditional Mexican nursery song, or *relacíon*, called "La Rana" (The Frog). They have appeared on Spanish-language television (Univision and Telemundo), in interviews, and at various performances, and although they are virtually unknown among Anglo-Americans in the United States, they remain a Latina pop music sensation well known among Latinas/os in the United States.

Besides their *corrido* and mariachi recordings, they also recorded a Christmas CD titled *Navidad* (1999) with many traditional seasonal tunes like "Noche de Paz" (Silent Night) set to a more upbeat Latin sound. Other recordings include *No Hay Otro Amor* (There Is No Other Love), released in 2000, *Para Las Madrecitas* (For the Mothers), released in 2001, and their 2003 release *Lo Dice Mi Corazón* (My Heart Tells Me), to name a few of their musical accomplishments. Committed to staying together and maintaining a wholesome and positive image, Sparx's popularity seems to hinge on their musical versatility and ability to perform traditional corridos (ballads), mariachi, nursery rhymes, boleros, cumbia, *hip-hop, and pop, which are innovative in arrangement and creative in many of their four-part harmonies.

Further Reading

http://www.sparxonline.com.

Peter J. García

Speedy Gonzalez (1953–1996). Speedy Gonzalez is an enduring and dynamic icon in animation. The sombrero-wearing animated mouse, the fastest in all México, debuted in "Cat Tails for Two" (1953), an episode in Warner Brothers' *Looney Tunes* series. Speedy, who evolved from a ratlike figure with protruding bucked teeth to the version seen today, was, after Bugs Bunny and Daffy Duck, the most popular cartoon character in the Warner Brothers lineup. The cartoon *Speedy Gonzalez* (1955), won an Academy Award, while other cartoons featuring Speedy Gonzalez, "Tabasco Road" (1957), "Mexicali Schmoes" (1959), and "The Pied Piper of Guadalupe" (1961), were also nominated for the Academy Award. Before the dismantling of the Warner Brothers' cartoon studio in 1965, there were three principal directors responsible for the Speedy Gonzalez cartoons: Fritz "Friz" Freleng, Robert McKimson, and Rudy Larriva. Freleng and McKimson's Speedy Gonzalez cartoons were produced at the same time, while the Larriva shorts appeared later in a cheaper animation format and usually also featured the Roadrunner. The Speedy Gonzalez cartoons also featured a colorful array of secondary characters: Speedy's cousin, Slowpoke Rodriguez, the slowest mouse in México; El Vulturo, the Bandito Bird; and the Mexicali Crows. Most often, Speedy was paired with the "greengo" pussycat Sylvester or with Daffy Duck. In "The Wild Chase" (1965), Speedy races the Roadrunner, but both suffer a rare loss to Sylvester and Wile E. Coyote. Speedy continues to be popular, appearing in the recent film *Space Jam* (1996) and in video games. Since the late 1990s, the Cartoon Network, which owns exclusive rights to the cartoon, has opted to remove Speedy Gonzalez from its lineup to avoid offending Mexican Americans. While the cartoon certainly traffics in some *stereotypes, invoking images of laziness, drinking, and womanizing, Speedy has also been positively accepted by the Latino community because he counters many of these by being intelligent, hardworking, and fast.

Further Reading

Cueto, Virginia. "Speedy Gonzalez: Banned in the USA." *Hispanic Online.* http://www.hispaniconline.com/a&e/people/speedy.html.
Hunter, Matthew. "Here Today, Gone Tamale: A Tribute History of Speedy Gonzalez." http://toolooney.toonzonenet/speedy.htm.

William Orchard

Sports. In the minds of many, *sport* is synonymous with popular culture in that its recreational aspects are often perceived as so commonplace and playful that they lie outside the serious activities of business, politics, policy-making, and all the other compelling sectors of society. Yet, like the entertainment and other popular culture industries, *sports*, in the plural form, are very big business and of major relevance to most every other area of American life, including Latina and Latino popular culture. Some scholars and commentators even argue that at the turn of the century the United States suffers from an overabundance and overcommercialization of sports throughout its public culture. To address this widespread, pervasive growth academe has responded with sport studies programs, scholarly research, and classes to systematically examine the nature and organization of sport (i.e., everyday games as playful recreation) and sports (organized games played competitively for gain) as personal pastimes and public cultural phenomena.

Both everyday playful sport and organized sports competitions are, thus, critically important to an understanding of Latina and Latino popular culture. As direct participants, as spectators, and as part of peripheral support systems and services, Latinas and Latinos in the United States have a considerable tradition of participation. According to the adjusted 2000 census report and "Economic Census Data," Hispanics contribute hundreds of millions of dollars and billions of hours to sporting activities, sport-related employment, and spectator sports recreation. The twentieth- and twenty-first-century prominence of such athletic stars as baseball's Fernando Valenzuela, boxing's Oscar *De La Hoya, golf's Lee Treviño and Nancy Lopez, world football's "Captain America" Arena, horse racing's Angel *Cordero, and scores of others illustrates the deep-rooted popularity of sports among Latinas/os.

Historically, athletic talent has been one of the few avenues to socioeconomic success open to American people of color, especially to men. Perhaps the most touted example is the case of Jackie Robinson, the baseball legend and celebrated breaker of the sport's color line segregation. Some researchers date the start of the civil rights era with his 1947 entrance into the professional major leagues in a New York Dodgers uniform. Less well known is the fact that before Robinson's entrance into the big leagues several African American and Latino players and teams had competed in major league baseball (e.g., brothers Welday and Moses Walker played in the Caucasian American major leagues in Toledo, Ohio, 1884). Another step toward the racial integration of baseball occurred in 1885 when the first professional black team, the Cuban Giants of Long Island, New York, was organized and, eventually joined by other black teams, began competing against white teams, including major league clubs and also against major league players freelancing in the off-season. This sporadic integration of the professional diamond continued in the early twentieth century, usually with press references to "Latin" and "Cuban" players instead of "Negro" because in the Jim Crow period of overt antiblack racism, passing as Latinos was slightly more tolerable to the majority of white team owners and fans. This point underscores the fluidity of *race, ethnicity, and culture as social categories, as well as the way that race- and ethnic-based *stereotypes reflect society's political, economic, and pop culture promoters and leaders. Public acceptance of the early instances of integration in sports was short-lived and did not spread widely until after Robinson's initiation into the white major leagues.

Ironically, despite the acceptance of some African Americans passing as Latinos in professional baseball, Latino American athletes were themselves victims of the racist segregation of the time. Research on sports in the scholarly fields of history, sociology, literature, psychology, cultural and sports studies, and others has shown that league owners and players enforced a *de facto* quota to keep the number of Cuban, Mexican, Puerto Rican, and other Latinos low to not offend the fans and hurt the box office revenues. Nevertheless, Latinos participated in America's major leagues in a variety of capacities. One example was Puerto Rican José Sada, who was hired by the Brooklyn Dodgers in the 1940s to scout the Puerto Rican and Mexican baseball leagues for competitive talent to recruit into the white majors in the United States. Sada identified a pool of talent, but they were not hired because of the owners' fear of a Jim Crow backlash from the press and fans.

Another example of Latino participation was the luring of players from the Negro American teams to play in Cuba, México, the Dominican Republic, and elsewhere in the baseball-loving countries of the Americas. Players from the championship Pittsburgh Crawfords, for instance, were paid to play on the Dominican Republic's team in the 1930s, and some went on to be inducted into the Baseball Hall of Fame (e.g., Josh Gibson, James "Cool Papa" Bell, William Julius "Judy" Johnson, and Satchel Paige). Eventually, the Dominican Republic, where baseball continues as a national passion in the twenty-first century, contributed several world-class players to the American major leagues including Juan Marichal, the *Alou brothers (Felípe, Matéo, and Jesús), and Sammy *Sosa. Their numbers were joined by such other future Latino stars as Cuban left fielder Minnie *Minoso, Mexican American pitcher Mike "Big Bear" García, Puerto Rican outfielder Roberto *Clemente, Cuban fielder and slugger José *Canseco, and many others like Venezuelan-born shortstop Luis Aparicio (b. 1934), who, when he retired, held the all-time leader record by a shortstop in most games, assists, and double plays. For nine years he led the American League in stolen bases (1956–1964) and finished his career with a remarkable 506 steals.

Other professional sports that were accessible to Latinos in the twentieth century after many obstructionist efforts to keep them all white were boxing, horse racing, basketball, and especially south of the border, football (i.e., soccer). Other sport betting activities like *cockfighting and dog racing remain popular spectator sports among Latinas and Latinos, even though they are banned or discouraged in many areas.

The heralded achievers mentioned and countless others have proven that the previously monolithic institutions of sports marked by historically sanctioned exclusions of minorities and women can be changed by proactive assaults on invalid racist and sexist social arrangements. They have been active agents in constructing their local circumstances in ways that led to the reconstruction of wider social and political circles. As a result, they helped demythologize sports from narrow, rigid conceptions of an unchanging status quo to broaden access and participation to better reflect the wide-ranging dynamism of the American imagination.

Further Reading

Eitzen, Stanley. *Fair and Foul: Beyond the Myths and Paradoxes of Sport.* 2nd ed. Lanham, MD: Rowman and Littlefield, 2002.

"1997 Economic Census—Arts, Entertainment and Recreation, Sector 71." U.S. Census Bureau. http://www.census.gov/svsd/www/97arts.html.

Cordelia Chávez Candelaria

This early-twentieth-century Cuban figurine depicts a baseball player of the period. *Courtesy of the Associated Research Collection, Tempe, Arizona.*

Sports, Cuban American. Cubans in the United States have a considerable tradition of successful participation in athletics and sports spectatorship to match that of their island compatriots. The twentieth-century and twenty-first-century prominence of such professional

stars as baseball's José *Canseco and scores of other recent island Cuban re-
cruits to America's reputed "national pastime" illustrates the deep-rooted
popularity of sports among Cubans and *Cuban Americans. The deep roots
extend back to such crossover pioneers in professional boxing as *Kid Gavilán and *Kid Chocolate, the professional names of Gerardo Gonzáles and
Eligio Sardinias-Montalbo, respectively. Cubans and Cuban Americans have
been exceptionally successful as well in amateur competition from the Pan
American games to the Olympics.

Both everyday sport—that is, common amateur games enjoyed for playful recreation—and sports, in the plural form as organized commercial competitions sponsored for financial gain, hold a significant place in Cuban
American popular culture. Sporting recreational activities and professional
sports engage the direct participation of millions of Cuban American athletes, spectators, promoters, and the extended and extensive support systems
and services they generate.

Cuban and Cuban American athletes in all professional sports increased
rapidly after Jackie Robinson's introduction into the major leagues in 1947
(see Sports) and in the twenty-first century includes a significant number of
superstars. For instance, joining Canseco on baseball's roster of stars are out-
fielders Tony Oliva and Minnie *Minoso, third baseman Tony Pérez, pitch-
ers Luis Tiant and Adolfo Luque, slugger Rafael Palmeiro, and others with
stellar records, many of whom were imported or self-exiled from major teams
in Cuba. These teams include such powerhouses as Club Almendares, Club
Cienfuegos, Club Habana, and Club Marianao. Similarly, along with Gavilán in prizefighting are four other Cuban boxers in the International Boxing Hall of Fame in Canastota, New York: *Kid Chocolate, Luis *Rodríguez,
Ultiminio Ramos, and Jose Napoles. Boxing experts usually rank Chocolate,
Gavilán, and Rodríguez as the best of the Hall of Fame legends. In amateur
competition, Cuba also has enjoyed several decades of domination in international venues. Some of the most important victories for Cuba's national
boxing teams have included middleweight Rolando Garbey's three Olympic
wins starting in 1968, middleweight Angel Espinosa's World Championship
title in 1986, heavyweight Teofilo Stevenson's win at the 1976 Olympics,
heavyweight Roberto Balado's Olympic gold in 1992, heavyweight Felix
Savon's 1998 Goodwill Games win, and many others.

Cubans have also excelled in other areas of athletics. In 1964 Enrique
Figuerola won the Olympic silver medal in the 100-meter race, and Alberto
Juantorena won gold medals in two fields, 800 and 400 meters. Another
track and field star, Alejandro Casaña, won the 110-meter world record in
the hurdles in 1977. In high jumping Javier Sotomayor competed successfully against his own records in the Barcelona Olympics in 1992 and is a
four-time world champion. Iván Pedroso in the open air long jump has also
won four world titles and competed successfully in the indoor arena long
jump title. Women have joined the male rosters with impressive work, most

notably Ana Fidelia Quirot won the gold medal in Barcelona in 1992 and the silver in Atlanta in 1996 and was the World Cup champion for the 400- and 800-meter races in 1997. These and countless other marquee athletes of Cuban origin have made indelible entries on the international sports record books.

Further Reading

The Baseball Encyclopedia: The Complete and Official Record of Major League Baseball. 10th ed. New York: Macmillan, 1996.

"Cuban Athleticism." http://www.cubasports.com/english/atlet.htm.

Regalado, Samuel. *Viva Baseball: Latin Major Leaguers and Their Special Hunger.* Urbana: University of Illinois Press, 1998.

Sugden, John. *Boxing and Society: An International Analysis.* New York: St. Martin's Press, 1996.

Cordelia Chávez Candlaria

Stage Performers and Film Actors. Broadway stage actor and dancer Chita *Rivera tells a story about arriving one day in 1957 to rehearse a new Broadway musical called **West Side Story* (1957–1959). Upon entering the *theater, she found the front page of the *New York Daily News* tacked prominently on a wall near the stage door. One of the newspaper's lead articles featured a photograph of a young Puerto Rican man charged with murder. Above the photograph the musical's director had scrawled the words: "This is your life." The note presumably was intended to inspire the cast to meet the challenge of performing the production's scenes depicting *gang warfare and the violent aspects of life in the city's Puerto Rican *barrios. Her role as Anita in *West Side Story* helped launch Rivera's long and illustrious career, though she later explained that the world described in the newspaper article had virtually nothing to do with her own upbringing in a quiet working-class neighborhood in the Bronx.

The anecdote underscores how mainstream American theater and *film producers have rarely managed to convey the breadth and complexity of the U.S. Latina/o experience accurately. As a result, the legacy of Latina/o performers in American and other English-language professional theater and film is replete with anecdotes of exclusion, discrimination, and stereotyping at the hands of the almost exclusively Euro-American-run theaters and movie studios.

While opportunities for Latina/o performers have steadily improved over the years, a survey of Latina/o actors by the Tomás Rivera Policy Institute in 2000 found old *stereotypes persist. The think tank based in California surveyed more than 4,000 Latina/o members of the Screen Actors Guild. According to the survey, nearly 75 percent said that having a Latina/o name was still considered a disadvantage in Hollywood. About 50 percent said Latinos are still expected to conform to a limited number of stereotypes to get roles. For instance, one-third of the respondents said they were expected to speak poor English or with a Spanish accent.

Despite such obstacles, there have also been noteworthy accounts of productions and performers who have persevered. *West Side Story* exemplifies these tensions between the integrity and drive for Latina/o actors against a backdrop of Anglo dominance and ethnic minstrelsy. For instance, María, the Puerto Rican lead role in the original stage production of *West Side Story*, was played not by a Latina but by actress Carol Lawrence. For the movie version produced four years later Natalie Wood was cast in the lead role. It is interesting to note that *West Side Story* initially was conceived as an East Side story about Italian and Jewish rivalries, but a rash of news reports about Puerto Rican juvenile delinquents convinced the writers to capitalize on the media attention and the public's fear and fascination with the Puerto Rican community in New York by shifting the ethnic identities.

Although *West Side Story* was a huge theatrical and box office success, it did not inspire a wave of productions featuring Latinas and Latinos as central characters. Instead, in the decades to come only a trickle of opportunities opened up, and even when Latina/o characters were in the script, non-Latinas/os often were picked to play the parts. In the musical *Evita* (September 1979–June 1983), Eva Perón was played by Patti LuPone, Juan Perón by Bob Gunton, and Che *Guevara by Mandy Patinkin. One New York critic charged that the 1979 musical was "about as Latin as a steak-and-kidney pie."

Earlier in 1979, *Chicano playwright and director Luis *Valdez, a founder of California's El *Teatro Campesino, staged *Zoot Suit* (March 1979–April 1979) at the Winter Garden Theatre on Broadway. Unlike *Evita*, Valdez's play featured Mexican Americans in the key Latina/o roles, including actors Edward James *Olmos, Rose Portillo, and Daniel *Valdez in Broadway's first Chicano musical. Based on the infamous 1943 Sleepy Lagoon murder trial in Los Angeles, Valdez's play failed to attract large audiences and closed in less than a month. The 1981 movie version was more successful and helped build the careers of Valdez, Olmos, and others. Valdez went on to direct the hit feature film *La Bamba* (1987). The stage version of *Zoot Suit* was successfully revived by El Teatro Campesino at The Playhouse in San Juan Bautista, California, and toured nationally in 2004.

One of the most recent attempts to produce a major Latina/o-themed Broadway production was *Capeman* (January 1998–March 1998) by songwriter-composer Paul Simon. To the credit of its producers, the musical featured Latina/o actors in the central roles, but the production closed after only three months. Coincidentally, the plot of *Capeman* tells the story of the very same murder featured in the newspaper story that Chita Rivera had read tacked on a backstage wall some forty years before.

Hollywood films have included Latina/o characters since the era of silent movies. As with the theatrical stage, however, Latina/o actors have been largely relegated to undignified roles. In the early days of cinema, Latinas/os were almost exclusively cast as one of several stereotypical archetypes: greaser, bandido, buffoon, Latin lover, dancer, or seductress. Latina/o movie characters typically represented the entire ethnic minority group as un-scrupulous, victimized, violent, libidinal, fatalistic, and accepting of suffering.

Nevertheless, as the movie industry grew, a small group of Latina and Latino actors made a significant impact. The Golden Age of Hollywood, for instance, saw the rise of American and Latin American screen stars such as Rita *Hayworth, Anthony *Quinn, Carmen *Miranda, Dolores *del Río, Ricardo *Montalbán, Gilbert Roland, Ramon Navarro, César *Romero, and José *Ferrer. Hayworth's films include *Gilda* (1946) and *The Lady from Shanghai* (1948). Quinn's long list of credits include *Guns of Navarone* (1961), *Zorba the Greek* (1964), *Viva Zapata* (1952), and *Lawrence of Arabia* (1962). Montalban played opposite Marlon Brando in *Sayonara* (1957) and numerous American and Mexican films, though he may be best known for his role on the long-running television series *Fantasy Island* (1978–1984). Singer-dancer-actress Carmen Miranda, born in Portugal but raised in Brazil, appeared on Broadway and in many motion pictures, and at the prime of her career in the late 1940s, she was the highest-paid performer in Holly-wood, despite her reputation for playing what many viewed as a stereotyp-ical depiction of Afro-Latinas, with her signature tutti-frutti hat. Her film credits include *Scared Stiff* (1953), *A Date with Judy* (1948), and *Copacabana* (1947). Lupe *Vélez made about fifty films, including eight known as the *Mexican Spitfire* series between 1939 and 1943. Puerto Rican–born José Ferrer, who had a successful career on Broadway as a writer, producer, and director before working in film, appeared in *Moulin Rouge* (1952) and *Joan of Arc* (1948), which earned him a Best Supporting Actor Oscar nomination. In 1950, Ferrer became the first Latina/o to win an Oscar for his role in *Cyrano de Bergerac*. Gilbert Roland's career in Hollywood spanned several decades. He was best known as the star of *The Cisco Kid* film series. Pro-duced between 1929 and 1950, the series starred Roland in six of the films between 1946 and 1947. César Romero, Duncan Renaldo, and Warner Bax-ter also played the character of Cisco. In 1961, Puerto Rican Rita *Moreno costarred in the film version of *West Side Story* (1961) and received the Best Supporting Oscar for her role in the movie. Moreno still performs in one-woman stage shows, as well as in film and in television. She was nominated for a 2002 *ALMA Award for her role in an HBO series called *OZ*, where she played a humanistic nun and counselor in a maximum security men's prison. Moreno holds the distinction of being the first actor to win an Oscar, an Emmy, a Grammy, and a Tony Award. Actress Katy *Jurado, a Mexican-born actress, is best known for several films she made in the 1950s. Among her roles, Jurado played Spencer Tracy's wife in *Broken Lance* (1954), which garnered her a Best Supporting Actress nomination. Cuban-born Desi *Arnaz appeared in several films for RKO Pictures and MGM. When wife Lucille Ball took her popular radio series to television sit-com, *I Love Lucy* became one of the most widely watched shows. Arnaz played her TV husband, Cuban bandleader Ricky Ricardo.

In terms of independent film productions the roles for Latinas/os are more central and less stereotypical; however, their reception has been limited and polemical. For example, *Salt of the Earth* (1954), based on a zinc miners strike in New Mexico, was the only movie blacklisted for alleged communist participation in the United States during the Cold War; the film tells the story of Mexican miner Ramón Quintero and his wife Esperanza. The film starred Will Geer, a blacklisted actor, and Rosuara Revueltas. In 1969, Luis Valdez released a documentary film that featured his narration of the Rodolfo "Corky" González epic poem *I Am Joaquín*; although it has been critiqued for its male-centered nationalism, the film has served as an inspiration for Chicana and Chicano youth in their struggles for identity and historical pride.

In recent years, top Latina and Latino actors have included Edward James Olmos, *Zoot Suit* (1981), *American Me* (1992) and *Selena* (1997); Cameron *Díaz, *Something about Mary* (1998), *Being John Malkovich* (1999), and *Vanilla Sky* (2001); María Conchita *Alonso, *Moscow on the Hudson* (1984) and *Caught* (1996); Cheech *Marín, *Up in Smoke* (1978) and *Born in East L.A.* (1987); Jimmy *Smits, *Mi Familia* (1995) and *Price of Glory* (2000); Andy *García, *The Untouchables* (1987) and *Godfather III* (1990); Jennifer *López, *Selena* (1997) and *The Wedding Planner* (2001); Salma *Hayek, *54* (1998) and *Frida* (2002); Benicio *Del Toro, *Basquiat* (1996) and *Traffic* (2000); John *Leguizamo, *Romeo and Juliet* (1996) and *Moulin Rouge* (2001); Benjamin *Bratt, *Miss Congeniality* (2000) and *Piñero* (2001); and Rosie *Pérez, *White Men Can't Jump* (1992), *Fearless* (1993), and *The Road to El Dorado* (2000; voice).

Further Reading

Ramírez Berg, Charles. *Latino Images in Film: Stereotypes, Subversion, & Resistance.* Austin: University of Texas Press, 2002.

James E. García

Stand and Deliver. *Stand and Deliver* (1988) is based on the true story of Bolivian-born Jaime Escalante, a math teacher at Garfield High School in East Los Angeles. Cowritten and directed by Ramón Menéndez and produced by Tom Musca, this Warner Brothers–distributed *film was significant as the first Mexican American–themed Hollywood film to be nominated for an Academy Award (for Edward James *Olmos's portrayal of Escalante). Besides Olmos's Best Actor nomination in 1988, the film swept the Independent Spirit Awards in 1989: Best Director, Best Film, Best Actor (for Olmos), Best Supporting Actor (for Lou Diamond Phillips), Best Screenplay, and Best Supporting Actress (for Rosana de Soto).

Stand and Deliver indicts poverty, lack of role models, bankrupt school districts, and especially educational and institutional racism. The film presents a fairly straightforward depiction of Escalante's engagement in community development through teaching. Dismayed by student apathy—caused by the effects of poverty, abuse, addiction, and hopelessness—Escalante decides to leave his lucrative job as an engineer in private industry to devote himself to making a difference in the lives of young people.

As a Garfield teacher, Escalante strives to make his students see education as a way to better themselves. He does this by connecting with their families and by setting a series of challenges and goals for students who are seen as at risk, disposable, and on the fast track for menial jobs, teenage pregnancies, and prison. He instills hope and intellectual pride in his students and spends extra time in preparing them to succeed in an Advanced Placement exam in math to increase their chances of getting admitted with scholarships to higher education. Escalante was thus able to get youth invested in education as a step for their future.

Eighteen of his students passed the advanced placement calculus examination, and six out of the eighteen obtained a perfect score. Given that this broke precedence for the high school, the Educational Testing Services (ETS) was unwilling to believe that Chicano students from a poor neighborhood were able to achieve high scores in math. Without any proof whatsoever, the ETS nullified the results and argued that the students cheated, thus rein-

Edward James Olmos (left) with the unconventional teacher Jaime Escalante, who Olmos played in the movie *Stand and Deliver. Courtesy of Photofest.*

forcing the *stereotypes of criminality and lack of legitimacy imposed on Latinos. After significant outrage and indignation, the students retook the exam and passed. The cast also includes Andy *García.

Further Reading

Keller, Gary D. *A Biographical Handbook of Hispanics and United States Film.* Tempe, AZ: Bilingual Press, 1997.

Kim Villarreal

Star Maps. Written and directed by Miguel Arteta and produced by Matthew Greenfield, *Star Maps* (1997) tells the tale of Carlos (Douglas Spain), an eighteen-year-old Latino youth who, after spending time with relatives in Mexico, returns to his home in Los Angeles with the dream of becoming an actor. Upon his return, his father Pepe (Efraín Figueroa) puts him to work as a hustler ostensibly selling maps to the homes of Hollywood stars, but this is simply a cover for Pepe's male prostitution business. On the surface, the drama in *Star Maps* appears to be the ordeal of a Mexican American *family trying to adjust to life in Los Angeles, but it is really more about surviving in a dysfunctional family, along with racial stereotyping, discrimination, prejudice, poverty, violence, and other limitations imposed by a society that differentiates people according to skin color. Arteta uses this family as an allegory that decries the social gap between East and West Los Angeles and the tragedy in trying to pursue the Hollywood dream for a Latino teenager. The drama portrays the self-destructive struggle experienced by some *Chicano communities in search of their identity in a hostile environment and the price paid for their survival.

Despite the movie's low budget, mostly inexperienced cast, and controversial topic, *Star Maps* represents a bold and important critique of how Hollywood denigrates Latinos and of how families can destroy themselves in their pursuit of the American dream. *Star Maps* was distributed by Fox Searchlight Pictures. The cast also includes Kandeyce Jorden, Martha Vélez, Lysa Flores, Annette Murphy, and Vincent Chandler.

William Calvo

Stereotypes. Originating from a printing term dating to the early centuries after Johan Gutenberg's invention of moveable type, *stereotype* in the early printing industry referred to cast molds of letters and symbols that, when inked, could be repeated over and over again in identical patterns. From this mechanical origin evolved the use of the term to describe social and psychological imaging and patterns that are based on rigid, unchanging perceptions to define a person, groups of people, cultures, or classes of items according to partial or distorted features. Stereotypes of Latinas and Latinos in the United States thus are defined as representations of Latina/o groups and individual Latinas/os as unchanging ethnic types identified by selective qualities or traits based on experiential or imagined features. Examples of stereotypical terms include "Spic," "beaner," and "Latin Lover"—slurs that emphasize, respectively, the selected features of accented speech (e.g., Spanish speakers who might pronounce "spick" instead of "speak"), common foods eaten (e.g., pinto, black, and other bean varieties), and the hypersexuality ascribed to Hispanics usually in the eighteenth and nineteenth centuries by Caucasian Protestant Christians as a contrast to their own perceived superior morality. Although some distinguish between positive and negative stereotypes (e.g., *romantic* Latin Lover versus *ignorant* Spic), contemporary social science and cultural studies literature underscore the invalid and potentially harmful nature of biased images that distort ethnicity, *race, and culture according to incomplete and rigid depictions, whether idealization or demonization.

In twenty-first-century popular culture studies, the term *stereotype* and the process of *stereotyping* have been equated to or altered by such concepts as "the imaginary," "image construction," "thought collective projection," and related ideas of postcolonialist discourse. These ideas share the assumption that social groups (i.e., thought collectives) generally perceive others through filters of their own experience (image construction) and imaginations, and these perceptions are projected on the Other, often in stereotyping ways (the imaginary). Important scholarly investigations since the 1970s have discovered many eighteenth- and nineteenth-century English-language texts that describe Mexicans as, for instance, lazy, dirty, violent, and sexually promiscuous based on the writer's limited exposure to soldiers, traders, and other workers of the Southwest borderlands and western frontier (*see* Barrios and Borderlands). Early examples of these usages, sometimes called defamatory "greaser" iconography of Mexicans, appear in the writings of Boston writer Richard Henry Dana (1787–1879), of historian Hubert Howe Bancroft (1832–1918), U.S. soldier and senator Thomas Hart Benton (1889–1975), and many other travelers and immigrants to New Spain, México, and after 1848 and the *Treaty of Guadalupe Hidalgo, the U.S. Southwest. Many researchers trace a significant subsoil of this racist iconography to *La Leyenda Negra* (The Black Legend), one of the Americas' most widespread and deep-seated cultural stereotypes. The Black Legend was seeded in the foreign policy of Britain, her New England colonies, and her allies to demonize Spain, her allies, and the colonies of New Spain. Strongly anti-Spanish and anti-Roman Catholic, the Black Legend accused Spain's monarchs of such extraordinary brutality and tyranny as rulers and protectors of their lands, especially in their treatment of New World natives and non-Catholics in general, that it justified England's (and later the United States') designs on Spanish holdings in North, Central, and South America. The Black Legend engendered generations of racist attitudes and prejudice against Spain, Spanish, Catholicism, and by extension, the descendants of colonial México and Latin America.

Other Latina/o stereotypes were generated by Spanish racial purists and their conservative *criollo* (i.e., American-born Caucasian) supporters among Mexicans and other Latin Americans. These race-based and ethno-centric views are at their core white supremacist and anti-*mestizaje* and consist of many color-coded stereotypes including such still commonplace pigment identifications as *trigueño* (buckwheat dark skinned), *moreno* (brown skinned or brunette), and *güero* (fair skinned or blonde) by which individuals are lumped and social stratified. Other largely negative stereotypes include *pocho*, used by Mexican natives to refer to U.S.-born Mexican Americans; *Tio Taco*, applied by Chicanos against other Latinos as an equivalent of Uncle Tom–like subservience or *vendidismo* (i.e., selling out); and *macho*, employed to describe the hypermasculine narcissism of adolescent boys. Like the "Black Is Beautiful" grassroots pride movement of the 1960s, however, many Latina/o artists, activists, and researchers have "talked back" to the colonialist past and redefined and reclaimed concepts like mestizo, *mestizaje*, and the indigenous American Indian roots of all the Americas. For these Hispanics the reclamation is proudly multi and hybrid, black and brown and red and white, in an affirmation of *La Raza Bronce* (literally, the Bronze Race; more idiomatically, Bronze People or community).

The ubiquity of media images in print, radio, *film, television, and their contemporary digital spinoffs has played an important role in stereotyping. Besides reflecting and reproducing stereotypes prevalent in society, the media also reinforce distorted images both through repetition and dissemination and through invention. For example, the "greaser" iconography of the nineteenth century was carefully transferred onto silent film screens in the work of D.W. Griffith (e.g., *Birth of the Nation*, 1915), among many other early filmmakers. The successful silent movies presented overtly sexist, racist, and white supremacist views of America to mass audiences, including such defamatory portrayals of Mexicans and Latinos as *Ah Sing and the Greaser* (1910), *The Greaser's Gauntlet* (c. 1914), and *Broncho Billy and the Greaser* (1914). These and many others carried over to the talkies and radio entertainment media to serve as a basis for similar slurs broadcast directly into private homes. As many film scholars (e.g., Gary D. Keller, David Maciel, Clara Rodríguez) and antidefamation advocates (e.g., the National Association for the Advancement of Colored People, the American Civil Liberties Union, the *National Council of La Raza) have pointed out, the widespread circulation of stereotypes by mass media outlets is due in part to the absence of minority representation in the industry itself. This lack of representation extends from the media board rooms and technical crews to the writers and talent seen and heard by mass consumers. Other media and communication specialists argue that while fair representation on the airwaves would help, the presence of barrio exploitation products (e.g., *gang movies and sexist *hip-hop) proves that numerical equity is inadequate to redress the prevalence of stereotypes within society itself.

On national television there have been only a few Latina/o representations to match the popularity of the Ricky Ricardo character acted by Cuban-born musician Desi *Arnaz on the still-aired comedy sitcom *I Love Lucy*. The success and longevity of Arnaz's role, along with his behind-the-camera contributions as a director and producer, effectively balanced the deployment of ethnic stereotypes on *I Love Lucy* by countering them with humor and plot development. More recent performers like Colombian John *Leguizamo, Chicano George *López, and Nuyorican Rosie *Pérez and TV news anchors and executives like Chicano Rolando *Santos, Soledad O'Brien, and Juan Quiñonez represent compelling counterforces to the demeaning superficiality of conventional Latina/o stereotyping in the media.

Contemporary culture studies specialists at the turn of the century emphasized the critical importance of acknowledging collective imaginaries (i.e., shared symbols and fantasies) to stereotype persistence in cultures and to the formation of stereotypic thinking among individuals. That is, the slurring and marginalization of people perceived to be culturally and racially different is an ancient practice that derived from the prehistorical need for tribal security and defense, a by-product of which was the demonization of "enemies" and "strangers" as alien beings worthy of conquest and destruction— for example, terms like *savage*, *bloodthirsty*, *half-breed*, *nigger*, *greaser*, *witch*, *hussy*, and *illegal* applied to classes of people. When the same tactics are used in the modern world, they usually reflect political and economic agendas for exclusionary private power over the promotion of shared inclusive democracy. The rejection of stereotypes is viewed as merely "political correctness" or "PC," which has been disparaged through a systematic campaign to maintain an unequal, exclusionary socioeconomic status quo. Significantly, what has elevated many popular culture works like the novel, film, and song *Ramona*, the films *Salt of the Earth* and *High Noon*, the play and film *Zoot Suit*, and documentaries like *The Lemon Grove Incident* and *Los Mineros* (The Miners) to the level of contemporary classics is their complex critique of that very status quo.

Further Reading

Chávez, Lydia. *The Color Bind: California's Battle to End Affirmative Action*. Berkeley: University of California Press, 1998.

Gibson, Charles, ed. *The Black Legend: Anti-Spanish Attitudes in the Old World and the New*. New York: Knopf, 1971.

Powell, Phillip W. *Tree of Hate: Propaganda and Prejudice Affecting United States Relations with the Hispanic World*. New York: Basic Books, 1971.

Cordelia Chávez Candelaria

Stowe, Madeleine (1958–   ). Madeleine Stowe, a major award-winning film actress, is of Costa Rican and American descent. She was born Madeleine Stowe-Mora on August 18, 1958, in Eagle Rock, California. She attended the University of Southern California and majored in journalism and film with the intention of becoming a film critic. However, while volunteering for the Solari (now Canon) Theatre, she was discovered by Meyer Mishkin, who was Richard Dreyfuss's agent. She was featured in several television series and movies, beginning with a role as the Virgin Mary in *The Nativity* (1978) before she acted in her first big screen feature film *Stakeout* (1987), which was a star vehicle for Dreyfuss. In early films, Stowe played the damsel in distress to such leading men as Kevin Costner and Jack Nicholson. In 1992 and 1993, she became more associated with strong women characters after two noteworthy turns in the films *The Last of the Mohicans* (1992) and *Short Cuts* (1993). The former was a box office success that gave Stowe the clout to garner more appealing roles, while the latter was a critical success. She received a National Film Critics Association Award for Best Supporting Actress for her portrayal of Sherri Shephard, the knowing wife of a philandering policeman, in Robert Altman's *Short Cuts*. Despite such box office disappointments as *Blink* (1994) and *Bad Girls* (1994), Stowe continues to work in high-profile, big-budget dramas like *Twelve Monkeys* (1995), *Playing by Heart* (1998), *The General's Daughter* (1999), and *We Were Soldiers* (2002).

Further Reading

Carr, Jay. "Madeleine Stowe into the Light." *Boston Globe*, January 23, 1994, B35.

Cliff, Nigel. "Remember Madeleine?" *London Times*, September 16, 1999, F1.

Gabrenya, Frank. "Solitude She Endured While Filming 'Bad Girls' Not New for Stowe." *Columbus Dispatch*, April 27, 1994, F10.

William Orchard

Straw Appliqué. Also known as straw inlay, straw appliqué is the technique that uses bits of split and flattened straw or corn husks to decorate the surface of wooden objects (i.e., crosses, picture frames, small boxes) and continues in Chicana/o communities across the Southwest borderlands. The art form was established in sixteenth-century Europe, even though it is argued that the origins suggest northern Africa. Introduced to México by Spanish colonists, the craft has been in practice by Native Americans and residents of New Mexico since the 1700s, becoming popular in the early 1800s but somewhat disappearing thereafter.

Eliseo Rodríguez is credited with reviving the trade in the 1930s in New Mexico, when he taught his wife Paula the technique, and she passed it down to her children and grandchildren. The *Spanish Market of Santa Fe, featuring the work of New Mexicans, hosts straw appliqué artists including Lorrie Aguilar-Sjoberg, Jimmy Trujillo, and Timothy A. Valdez.

Further Reading

Carrillo, Charles M. "Traditional New Mexican Hispanic Crafts Yesterday and Today." *The Collector's Guide Online.* http://www.collectorsguide.com/fa/fa038.shtml.

Rodríguez, Paula. "Straw Appliqué." *Library of Congress.* http://www.loc.gov/bicentennial/propage/NM/nm_s_bingaman4.html.

Armando Quintero, Jr.

Suarez, Ray (1957–   ). Born in Brooklyn, New York, and of Puerto Rican background, Suarez is one of the most visible Latino radio and television journalists in the United States, as well as a published author. In 1999 he joined the *News Hour with Jim Lehrer* as a Washington-based senior correspondent, field reporter, and anchor. Suarez entered his latest post with over twenty years of radio and television journalist experience. He served as the director of the call-in news program *Talk of the Nation* for National Public Radio between 1993 and 1999. Prior to that, he served as a news anchor for NBC affiliate WMAQ-TV in Chicago. He also has served as a Los Angeles correspondent for CNN, a CBS reporter in Rome, and a reporter for news services in London.

In addition to contributing essays to a wide variety of books dealing with Latino and urban issues, Suarez has authored a book on how suburbs destroy ethnic identity, *The Old Neighborhood: What We Lost in the Great Suburban Migration* (1999). He also is recipient of several awards that include the duPont–Columbia Silver Baton Award in 1994–1995 for on-site coverage of race elections in South Africa. He has also been awarded the 1996 Ruben Salazar Award presented by the *National Council of La Raza NCLR (named for the famous *Chicano reporter who was killed during the 1970 Chicano Moratorium, a protest to stop the sending of Chicanos to the frontline of the Vietnam War), and a Chicago Emmy Award.

In addition to his many accolades and commitment to promoting public debate on a wide variety of topics that include the bombing of Vieques, Puerto Rico, apartheid, crime prevention, recidivism, peace talks in Ireland, and the promotion of Latino authors and intellectuals on both NPR and PBS, Suarez is committed to being a role model for Latino youth. He has worked on *gang prevention issues and is an active member of the National Association of Hispanic Journalists. He is also a founding member of the Chicago Association of Hispanic Journalists. Suarez received his Bachelor of Arts in African history from New York University and a Master of Arts in social science and urban studies from the University of Chicago. He currently lives in Washington, D.C., with his wife and three children.

Further Reading

http://www.npr.org/about/people/bios/rsuarez.html.
http://www.kepplerassociates.com/speakers/suarezray.asp?2.
http://www.pbs.org/newshour/ww/suarez.html.

Arturo J. Aldama

Super, El. *See El Super.*

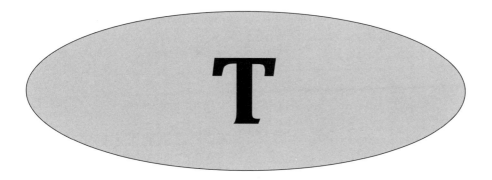

Tale of the Lost Mine. One of the most popular lost treasure tales among Chicana/o communities in the Southwest is the Tale of the Lost Mine, which comes from Cordova, New Mexico, and was originally published in 1932. It refers to a mine that belonged to the Sanchez family of Mora. Spanish colonists who settled near Cordova originally discovered the mine, which at one point was mined by three immigrants (variations of the story list the immigrants as German, French, or Anglo-Americans), although the location of the mine died with them. Many years later, legend has it, a sheepherder from Santa Fe accidentally finds the mine, but before he can divulge the location, he also passes away with the secret. Next, a sheepherder, Juan Mondragon from Cordova, accidentally finds it again and promises to take a man named Romero to it, but Mondragon dies unexpectedly before he can disclose the location of the mine. Romero's grandson, Melaquías Romero, spends the better part of his life attempting to find the mine that eluded his grandfather. The famous Texas folklorist J. Frank Dobie collected other tales of lost mines, many of them out of Texas.

Further Reading

Briggs, Charles, and Julian Josue Vigil. *The Lost Gold Mine of Juan Mondragon: A Legend from New Mexico Performed by Melaquías Romero*. Tucson: University of Arizona Press, 1990.

"Creating a Border: The Cultural Landscape of the Big Bend." National Park Service. http://www.nps.gov/bibe/adhi/adhi1.htm.

Armando Quintero, Jr.

Tango. The dance known as the tango is believed to have originated somewhere in Europe or North Africa, perhaps in Spain or Morocco, and then was brought to the Americas by immigrants. One of the first places that the tango was ever heard was in Argentina, and the first tangos were believed to have been danced in the brothels of Buenos Aires. A conglomeration of rhythms and sounds from places such as Africa and India, with Latin influences involved, many scholars believe the word *tango* comes from the Latin word *tangere* (to touch). Although the precise time of its inception is not known, it is believed that the first piece of music written and published in Argentina labeled a tango piece appeared in 1857 and was called "Toma mate, che." *Mate* is an Argentinean tea, so the title translates to "Drink Tea, Hey."

By the early 1900s the dance had spread throughout Europe and had become immensely popular in Paris. Soon after it gained popularity in North America as well. After 1910–1911 the music could be heard in large urban areas like New York City, and in 1921 Latin actor Rudolph Valentino popularized the tango. Early in the diffusion of tango, mainly working-class people listened to and danced it. Over time the music became more socially acceptable and is now regarded as a staple of ballroom dancing. There are various styles of tango: Argentine, French, Gaucho, romantic, lyrical, international, and American (United States). The international and American versions are thought of as a combination of the best parts of each tango style.

One of the most influential persons in the tango movement is Carlos Gardel, known as El Zorzal Criollo, the songbird of Buenos Aires. He is regarded as a legendary figure in Argentina, in part because Gardel's career coincided with the development of the tango. Born on December 11, 1890, in Toulouse, France, Gardel made the music his own by inventing the tango song with his 1917 hit "Mi noche triste" (My Sad Night), which sold 100,000 copies and was an instant hit throughout Latin America. Gardel toured many South American and European countries and performed in New York. Gardel's career was cut short when he died in a plane crash in Colombia on June 24, 1935. Crowds of people mourned Gardel's death and paid their respects as the singer's body made the journey traveling via Colombia, New York, and Rio de Janeiro to its final resting place in a cemetery in Buenos Aires as they listened to his tango "Silencio" (Silence).

Further Reading

http://www.gardelweb.com.
http://www.history-of-tango.com.

Cristina K. Muñoz

Tanguma, Leo (1941–   ). A product of the 1960s *Chicano Movement, artist Leo Tanguma's work retains the idealism and commitment that motivated him as a young activist. He is well known and respected within Latina and Latino circles of art and activism for his signature murals throughout the Southwest, especially in the greater Denver metropolitan region, which has been his home base for over three decades. His massive acrylic murals are housed in such significant venues as the Denver Arts Museum, the Denver International Airport, the New Mexico Museum of Fine Arts in Santa Fe, the Colorado State Capital, and several sites in Houston, Texas. His 1986 *Rebirth of Our Nationality* commission for the Continental Can Company in Houston was declared an official Texas Historical Landmark. Among his numerous other awards and citations are the 1974 Hispanic Artist of the Year Award from Houston's Institute of Hispanic Culture; the 1989 Best Museum Show from Westword's Annual "Best of Everything in Denver" awards; the 1994 (Denver) Mayor's Award for Excellence in the Arts; and the 1995 Peacemaker Award from the Rocky Mountain Conference of the United Methodist Church.

The future prizewinning muralist was born in Beeville, Texas, on November 5, 1941, to Ramón and Anita Tanguma. In talks and workshops, he has stated that he retains the community values and religious beliefs of his farmworker parents and that they have guided and inspired him in his life and work. He credits his first professional mentor, African American muralist John Biggers, professor of art at Texas Southern University, for guid-

Chicano Movement artist Leo Tanguma is shown here with one of the murals for which he is widely known. *Photo courtesy of Leo Tanguma.*

ing and training him in his vocation as an artist during his student years (1973–1974). Biggers is known for his powerful representations of the black civil rights movement through the lens of social realism. He also acknowledges the good fortune of meeting Mexican mural master David Alfaro Siqueiros, one of his major formative experiences. Paying tribute to these two muralists/teachers, Tanguma attributes their great encouragement to strengthening his understanding of aesthetics as well as his technical abilities. Art scholars have described his style as being both symbolist and realist in that his use of color is stark like that of Spanish surrealist Salvador Dali, but it is also lushly symbolic in the manner of French primitivist Henri Rousseau. The composition of his murals discloses a narrative storytelling shorthand depicting themes of social justice and shows his debt to the school of famous Mexican muralists Diego *Rivera, José Clemente Orozco, and especially Siqueiros.

Committed to public art as a singular tool for social transformation through education, Tanguma describes his efforts to combine art and learning as an unwavering commitment to reflect and to struggle against racism, poverty, chauvinism, war, and other obstructions to authentic human liberation. In the process he has worked to depict what he views as the inherent dignity and beauty of humanity, as in his 1995 sculpturelike mural *The Teacher as Liberator*, commissioned by the North Carolina Center for the Advancement of Teaching. His "sculptural murals" are painted on irregular panels or freestanding structures to evoke the vivid and dynamic form he seeks to enhance his themes. He credits the Chicano Movement for raising his awareness of social justice issues regarding Mexican American history and culture, civil rights, women's issues, youth, working people, the environment, and the many other subjects that still occupy his creativity in Wheat Ridge, Colorado, where he lives.

Further Reading

Goldman, Shifra. "Chicano Art Alive and Well in Texas: A 1981 Update." *Revista Chicanoriqueña* 9.1 (Winter 1981): 34–40.

Valenzuela-Crocker, Elvira. "Tanguma: A Man and His Murals." *Agenda: A Journal of Hispanic Research* 5 (Summer 1974): 14–17.

Cordelia Chávez Candelaria

Tatuaje. *Tatuaje* (tattoo) from the Tahitian *ta tu*, meaning to "to strike" or "to mark," is a popular art form that is an intricate part of Chicana/o and Latina/o subculture often expressing cultural pride and identity. It is prevalent among Chicano youth, *pintos* (prison inmates), and *gang members. Christian symbols and images such as the *Virgin of Guadalupe, Jesus Christ, and the crucifix are some of the most prevalent themes for tattoos among Chicanas/os. Over the past few years, there has been a rise in pre-Columbian symbols and imagery from cultures such as the Aztecs, Incas, and Mayas, such as calendars, gods, and pyramids. This new development has in turn increased the numbers of professional and educated Chicanas/os that are getting tattoos, as they attempt to get in touch with their pre-Columbian ancestry. Gang-affiliated tattoos are done as an initiation rite or to provide a kinship or sense of pride and rebelliousness among the members. Prison inmates, as well as gang members, get tattoos as a tool of empowerment and to increase a sense of individuality. Additionally, the Christian and Chicano tattoos allow prison inmates to feel a sense of connection with their lives prior to incarceration. Although being tattooed is a highly social act, many gang members and ex-prison inmates are beginning to realize that this form of symbolic self-expression can represent oppression and exclusion from the larger-scale social world since many individuals still consider getting tattooed deviant behavior. New Mexico artist Delilah Montoya's print (photograph) *El Guadalupano* (1999) portrays a shackled inmate whose back is covered with a large tattoo portraying La Virgen de Guadalupe.

Further Reading

"La Gráfica Chicana: Three Decades of Chicano Prints 1970–2000." Phoenix Art Museum. http://www.phxart.org/GC_montoya.html.

Nilsen, Richard. "A Mark of Pride." *The Arizona Republic*, March 5, 2003. http://www.azcentral.com/arizonarepublic/arizonaliving/articles/0305tattoos05.html#.

Phillips, Susan. "Gallo's Body: Decoration and Damnation in the Life of a Chicano Gang Member." *Ethnography* 2.3 (September 2001): 357–388.

http://www.sagepub.co.uk/journals/details/issue/abstract/ab018539.html.

Armando Quintero, Jr.

Teatro Campesino. In 1965 El Teatro Campesino (The Farmworkers Theater) paved the way for a radical *theater movement that continues to flourish in the United States today. A central force in the development of the *Chicano Movement, El Teatro Campesino was formed by Luis *Valdez, a former farmworker and later member of the noted San Francisco Mime Troupe. The Teatro Campesino repertory company was founded to address sociopolitical issues affecting the *Chicano community through the performances pieces they created, and Valdez worked closely with union organizer César *Chávez to raise awareness about the farmworkers' plight and to attract funding for *la causa* (the cause of the Chicano Movement). Its celebrated synthesis of forceful politics with excellent dramatic writing and staging contributed to its singular effectiveness as protest and performance in the dynamic decades of the 1960s and 1970s. The first Chicano art to receive international acclaim, Teatro Campesino added performance tours in Germany, France, Italy, and other countries in the early 1970s to its growing college campus and protest rally venues, gaining widespread exposure and spinoff *teatros* along the way.

Using an improvisational style that recaptures the style of the *comedia dell'arte* troupes, which entertained audiences throughout Europe from the six-

This theater program handout promotes El Teatro Campesino's production of *I Don't Have to Show You No Stinking Badges* by founder Luis Valdez (1986). *Courtesy of the Cordelia Candelaria Private Collection.*

teenth to the eighteenth century, El Teatro Campesino developed a critical form of political theater in its use of *actos* (acts) that used simple props, satire, and audience participation to *conscientize* the farmworkers in their struggle to unionize on the back of flatbed trucks. By 1967, the theater troupe began more formal work and took their political agenda beyond the farmworkers' movement. The troupe began addressing issues like the struggle of Chicano soldiers during the Vietnam War in the play *Dark Root of a Scream*. This play, written by Valdez, departed from the style of the *acto* and took the form of the *mito* (myths). Through the *mitos* Valdez and the theater company continued to evolve as artists, exploring their art through the perspective of descendants of the great race that was the Mayan civilization. Their myths and heritage became an integral part of their theater. In 1971 the company moved its operations from Delano, California, where Valdez had started the troupe, to San Juan Bautista, California. Ten years later, in 1981, with funding from the run of Valdez's musical *Zoot Suit, the company renovated an old produce packing warehouse at 705 4th Street into a cultural space that hosts musical artists, comedians, dance troupes, and theater artists from all over the world. For over twenty-five years Teatro Campesino has been staging an evolving series of plays during the Christmas season titled *The Miracle, Mystery, and Historical Cycle of San Juan Bautista*. Every year the company presents either *La Virgen del Tepeyac*, in the style of the classical miracle play, or *La Pastorela*, a traditional shepherd's play, at the Mission San Juan Bautista. El Teatro Campesino has won numerous awards including an Obie Award and several Los Angeles Drama Critics Awards. Three plays written for El Teatro Campesino by Valdez (*Zoot Suit, Bandido,* and *I Don't Have to Show You No Stinking Badges!*) appear in the anthology titled *Zoot Suit and Other Plays* (1992).

The members of El Teatro Campesino have developed their work in the spirit of an ensemble style in which contributing artists play numerous roles and assume various responsibilities for each production. One artist may act, write, direct, stage manage, or produce the plays in a variety of productions. Through ritual, music, theater, and art, the company has built a foundation of important Chicano cultural expression.

Further Reading

Elam, Harry. *Taking It to the Streets: The Social Protest Theater of Luis Valdez and Amiri Baraka (Theater: Theory/Text/Performance)*. Ann Arbor: University of Michigan Press, 2001.

Gonzalez-Broyles, Yolanda. *El Teatro Campesino: Theater in the Chicano Movement*. Austin: University of Texas Press, 1994.

Huerta, Jorge A. *Chicano Theater: Themes and Forms.* Ypsilanti, MI: Bilingual Press, 1982.

Valdez, Luis. *Luis Valdez—Early Works: Actos, Bernabé and Pensamiento Serpentino.* Houston, TX: Arte Público, 1990.

Christina Marín

Teatro Pregones. Teatro Pregones is one of the most important Latina/o *theater companies in the United States. The name of the troupe comes from the typical song of a street vendor in Puerto Rico. This troupe began in 1978 with various artists from New York City including Rosalba Rolón, Luis Meléndez, and David Crommet; in 1980, Alvan Colón-Lespier became the codirector with Rolón. Their dramatic mission includes staging the most important plays in classic Puerto Rican theater. Also, their mission is to create innovative and high-caliber theater grounded in the traditions and artistic expressions of the Puerto Rican and Nuyorican popular culture. The first piece staged was *La colección* (The Collection), an experimental performance that spans over 100 years of the Puerto Rican Theater (1878–1978).

Their play *El abrazo* (The Hug), performed in 1987, was one of the first plays to address the issues of AIDS in the Latina/o community and the issues of homophobia. The way this play educates the audience around the AIDS pandemic and the way it breaks the boundaries between spectators and actors by having members of the audience come on to the stage and provide solutions to the conflicts were influenced by the Brazilian-based Theater of the Oppressed. Other plays include *Tiempo muerto* (Time Death, 1985), *Migrants* (1986), *Medea's Last Rosary* (1991), *Quíntuples* (1993), *Translated Woman* (1995), *El bolero fue mi ruina* (The Bolero Was My Downfall, 1997), *San Miguel amarra tu perro* (Saint Michael, Tie Up Your Dog, 1998), *Fables of the Caribbean* (2000), *En tres actos* (In Three Acts, 2001), *Los Angeles se han fatigado* (The Angels Are Tired, 2001), and *Las viudas alegres* (The Happy Widows, 2002).

Carlos M. Rivera

Tejana Artists. At the close of the twentieth century *Selena represented a significant cultural indentation in Texas-Mexican women's cultural production, marking a historical trajectory of Tejana artists throughout the twentieth century. As the first Mexican American woman to record her music in 1928, Lydia Mendoza transgressed the *gender limitations on women public performers of the time. Known as *la alondra de la frontera* (the lark of the border), she was honored in 1982 with a National Heritage Award from the National Endowment for the Arts. Tejana music artists have been present throughout the varied transformations and stylistic variations of Texas-Mexican music including such early singers as Chelo Silva, Rosita Fernández, Eva Garza, and Rita Vidaurri. Silva, born in Brownsville, Texas, in 1922 and recognized as "la reina Tejana del bolero" (The Tejana Queen of Bolero), recorded her first single in 1954 for Falcón Records and established a strong career in south Texas and México.

Garza and Vidaurri also garnered great notoriety in México and throughout Latin America. Garza, born on May 11, 1917, began on local San Antonio, Texas radio and established a singing career in the *bolero, *son, and *rumba traditions. Vidaurri, born on May 22, 1924, was known as "la belliza morena" (brown beauty) when she toured throughout México, Panama, and Cuba, performing in the bolero and ranchero-bolero tradition. Delia Gutierrez, born on July 5, 1931 in Weslaco, Texas, began singing with her father Eugenio Gutierrez when she was only eight years old. During the 1940s and 1950s she garnered vast popularity as a recording artist with Falcón Records and Discos Ideal. Juanita García learned to sing by imitating singers on the radio. Born in McAllen, Texas, on February 14, 1930, her first recordings in 1951 were with Falcón Records, and she toured with Orquesta Falcón and the Beto Villa Orquesta.

Tejana duets included Carmen y Laura, Las Hermanas Cantú, Las Hermanas Gongora, Las Hermanas Segovia, and Las Hermanas Guerrero. In 1946, Carmen y Laura (Hernández) were the first artists to record with Discos Ideal in Alice, Texas, which is owned by Carmen's husband Armando Marroquín. Las Hermanas Cantu, Nori, Ninfa, and Nellie of Falfurrias, Texas, were born May 8, 1935, March 1, 1937, and October 13, 1943, respectively. Nori and Ninfa were the original duet, followed by Nori and Nellie. They recorded with Ideal, Falcón, and Bego Records and toured extensively throughout the Southwest with groups ranging from Beto Villa's orquesta to Los Tres Reyes. Las Hermanas Gongora, Louisa and Lupe, born in Corpus Christi, Texas, on June 21, 1928, and October 13, 1924, respectively, began their career by singing for radio advertisements in 1939. They toured Texas while in their teens with Stout Jackson's "el teatro carpa" (the tent *theater) and recorded their first single with Falcón records in 1947. Beatriz "la paloma" Llamas, performed during the 1960s and 1970s with many prominent orquestas and conjuntos including Paulino Bernal and recorded on several Mexican regional and *Tejano labels. The 1970s was the decade of Laura Canales. Born August 19, 1954, in Kingsville, Texas, she is recognized as "la reina de la onda Tejana" (the queen of Tejano music). Having consistently recorded over three decades, Laura began singing after high school in 1973 and several years later formed her band.

Patsy Torres, born in San Antonio in 1957, created her own style of Tejano music influenced by women rockers such as Pat Benatar in the 1980s. Thirty-two-year-old Shelly Lares began her career alongside Selena in the mid-1980s and has been a consistent presence in music awards shows. Also in her midthirties, Elida Reyna played in various bands, growing up in Mercedes, Texas, and studied music at Pan American University in Brownsville. Elida y Avante released their first compact disc Atrévete (I Dare You) in 1994.

Master accordionist Eva Ybarra, born in San Antonio in 1945, has been one of the few women to have participated in the tradition of Tejano *conjunto* music. Besides recording and writing her own music Ybarra has passed down this music tradition by teaching the accordion for the Guadalupe Cultural Arts Xicano Music project in San Antonio. Young Tejanas including Victoria Galvan have followed in Ybarra's footsteps. Born in Corpus Christi, Texas, Galvan formed her own group at the age of thirteen and recorded her first compact disc with Hacienda Records at the age of fifteen.

Born in Lake Jackson, Texas, on April 16, 1971, Selena began her recording career as Selena y Los Dinos in the mid-1980s with Tejano Record labels GP, Cara, Manny, and Freddie Records. With the 1992 release of *Entre a Mi Mundo* (Come Into My World), Selena became the first Tejana to sell more than 300,000 albums. In 1994, she won the Grammy for Best Mexican American Album for *Selena Live.*

Tejana artists have also contributed to other music genres. Tish Hinojosa of San Antonio has created her own style of *fronteriza* (border) music, mixing folk, country, and traditional Mexican ballads. Tejanas have also made significant strides in the areas of rockabilly and country western. Besides recording, guitarist Rosie Flores has opened for groups including Jerry Lee Lewis and Asleep at the Wheel. Known as "the cactus flower" in the 1980s, Janie C. Ramirez and her band Cactus Country produced a unique sound blending Tejano and country western.

Further Reading

Acosta, Teresa Paloma. *Las Tejanas: 300 Years of History.* Austin: University of Texas Press, 2003.

Broyles-González, Yolanda. *Lydia Mendoza's Life in Music.* New York: Oxford University Press, 2001.

Patoski, Joe Nick. *Selena: Como La Flor.* Boston: Little, Brown, 1996.

Saldívar, José David. "Frontejas to El Vez." In his *Border Matters: Remapping American Cultural Studies.* Berkeley: University of California Press, 1997.

Vargas, Deborah R. "Las Tracaleras: Texas-Mexican Women, Music, and Place." Ph.D. dissertation, University of California, Santa Cruz, 2003.

Villareal, Maryann. "Cantantes y Cantineras: Mexican American Communities and the Mapping of Public Space." Ph.D. dissertation, University of Arizona, 2003.

Deborah Vargas

Tejano Music. Tejanas/os have a long tradition of religious music and participating in elite Western art music, marching bands, popular U.S. music genres such as country, blues, rock and roll, jazz and hip-hop, and popular Mexican genres such as *música romántica* (romantic music) played by guitar-vocal trios and mariachi music. Nevertheless, their efforts in these areas are not usually what people mean when they speak of Tejano music. The tellingly bilingual label *Tejano music* refers to a relatively specific part of the whole musical life of ethnic Mexicans in Texas. Since the early 1980s, the term has applied in its narrowest sense to a largely secular genre of amplified dance music played by an ensemble that often includes a button accordion, an instrument that rose to prominence during the depression of the 1930s and increased in importance after World War II.

The music incorporates a range of song types and an eclectic array of influences, but for more than fifty years, its core has been a Mexicanized polka rhythm. Fundamentally a product of the San Antonio–Monterrey corridor, Tejano shares its roots with *música norteña* (northern music) or *música regional* (regional music), a very similar accordion-driven music in what is now northeastern México. Musical style, it seems, has responded more to long-standing patterns of migration and trade than it has to political boundaries. Nevertheless, followers and practitioners of Tejano music distinguish it from *música norteña* with a vehemence that smacks of cultural nativism. Since the end of the twentieth century, the rivalry between the two has increased as Tejano music began losing its market share to *norteño* music in many Texas cities, due in part to the growth of new Mexican immigrant communities.

Tejano music represents a fusion of three musical traditions: the *conjunto* (dance band or ensemble), the *orquesta* (literally orchestra but more similar to a big band or swing jazz ensemble), and vocal music. The *conjunto* has traditionally appealed to a working-class audience and centers on the diatonic button accordion, backed up by a *bajo sexto*, an instrument similar to the twelve-string guitar. The typical *conjunto* also includes a bass guitar or *tololoche* (double bass) and a drum set, and some include a saxophone. Although some ensembles use other instruments, the presence of instruments other than these five in the ensemble means one is dealing with something other than a *conjunto*. The *orquesta*, which is much less common today than it was between 1945 and 1980, resembles "big bands" in instrumentation and appeals to a more middle-class audience. Contemporary Tejano groups either augment the basic *conjunto* with a larger horn section and electronic keyboards or dispense with the accordion altogether in favor of the electric guitar-bass-drum-keyboard ensemble common to U.S. popular music. Vocal music, often with guitar accompaniment, was perhaps the most popular Mexicana/o musical genre during the first two decades of the twentieth century, and although it has taken a backseat to the *conjunto* and *orquesta* styles, vocal music has continued to be an important part of the Tejano music tradition. Although some Tejano music is sung in English or a mixture of English and Spanish, songs in Spanish define the genre, and even artists who cannot converse in the language often find themselves forced to memorize song lyrics in it.

Documentation of the musical life in Spanish-dominated and later Mexican communities in what is now Texas before 1920 is sketchy and rare. Nineteenth-century travelers' accounts and other sources describe secular dances called *fandangos and *bailes* at which music was played. Although little information is available about the nature of this music, it is clear that the distinction between fandango and *baile* was related to economic status, with the *baile* being associated with the rural poor and the fandango with the elite. It is also clear that the Central European–derived dances such as the polka, the schottische, and the waltz, which would become important to the formation of Tejano music, were gaining popularity in both México and the U.S. Southwest during the latter half of the nineteenth century, as ethnic Mexican elites sought to imitate European customs and fashions.

This period also saw an influx of European immigrants to Texas, bringing German and Bohemian settlers into contact with ethnic Mexicana/o communities. Not all sources agree about the precise way in which nineteenth-century salon dances reached ethnic Mexicans in Texas. One common view is that Tejanas/os learned the polka and similar dances from Central European immigrants to that state, adapting the dances to their own tastes and creating a distinctly American hybrid. The view of ethnomusicologist Manuel Peña, the foremost expert on Mexican American music in Texas, is that the dances came to Tejanas/os from México, which also saw its share of *immigration from Central Europe, where salon dances, first popular among elites, were later taken up by the common people. Arguing against the "melting pot" idea, Peña maintains that relations between ethnic Mexicans and Central Europeans in Texas were too conflictive for a vigorous musical exchange to have taken place.

Several Mexican American accordionists are known to have played for German and Bohemian dances and learned melodies from musicians in those communities, as evidenced by recordings of Mexican-derived themes by Texas Czech ensembles. Ethnic Mexican musicians were already participating in the international craze for salon dances when Central Europeans reached Texas, and whatever musical exchange may have occurred cannot have been innocent of the era's racial conflict.

The advent of commercial recordings of ethnic Mexican music provides a more detailed documentation of that music's history. Recordings of Mexicana/o music in the United States began to appear in earnest during the 1920s, when the major Anglo-controlled record companies began catering to a wide variety of ethnic and international markets. These companies continued to release music for Mexicana/o audiences until World War II, when the scarcity of raw materials forced them to curtail their activities. Recordings of vocal music appear to have been extremely popular during the 1920s, with the most favored ensemble being the vocal duet with guitar or other string accompaniment. Such music also appears to have been widespread in live performance.

In the luxurious Spanish-language theaters, vocal groups such as the *dueto* Llera sang highly polished versions of popular songs on nationalist themes. Visiting *zarzuela* (Spanish-style operetta) and variety companies also brought singers with them, including *cupletistas*, female singers who performed coquettish songs while interacting with men in the audience. Meanwhile, more marginalized, ambulant singers made their livings outside the theaters in public places singing heroic *corridos and love lyrics for tips. Many of these singers, such as the noteworthy *corridistas* Pedro Rocha and Lupe Martínez of San Antonio, are known today through their recordings. Perhaps the most famous U.S. singer of Mexican descent is Lydia Mendoza, who began her career performing in San Antonio's market square with her family and achieved international fame for her soulful, heartfelt delivery of Mexican country songs. Other notable Tejana singers include Eva Garza, who achieved popularity in Texas before marrying a member of Los Tres Panchos and moving her career to México; Chelo Silva of Brownsville, known for her earthy, impassioned delivery; and Rosita Fernández of San Antonio, whose beauty, poise, and charm have appealed to Anglo and Mexicana/o audiences alike and made her an important part of that city's touristic presentation of its Mexican heritage.

For all the early importance of vocal music, other styles and genres also have deep roots. References to the use of the accordion in Texas go back to the middle of the nineteenth century, and it is clear that by the end of that century ethnic Mexicans in Texas were dancing to the instrument at weddings and at dances called *funciones*. In many cases, the accordion was accompanied by a large drum called the *tambora de rancho* (ranch drum). During the first decades of the twentieth century, *bailes de regalo* (gift dances), in which men offered gifts to women in exchange for a dance, and *bailes de negocio* (business dances), a more stigmatized form in which money changed hands, were common occasions for accordion music. The first ethnic Mexican accordionist to record in the United States was Bruno Villareal. An itinerant musician who made a meager living playing on the street, Villareal was one of a number of similarly situated pioneers of *conjunto* accordion. His contemporary, Narciso Martínez of San Benito, is widely viewed as the "father" of *conjunto*, not so much because he was the first to play it but because he did much to establish the accordion/*bajo sexto* combination as the music's core and because his marcato (strong) articulation and emphasis on the melody side of the accordion decisively influenced the style of later accordionists.

Another important early pioneer was Don Santiago Jiménez of San Antonio, whose style was more legato (smooth) and who is credited with introducing the *tololoche* to the standard ensemble. Both Martínez and Jiménez became well known early on as recording artists, although their fame did not translate into riches, as their audiences were largely poor and record companies provided meager compensation. Jiménez is also known for the work of his sons, Santiago, Jr., who continues very much in a traditional mode set by his father, and *Flaco, who made his name as an experimenter with *conjunto* forms and ambassador of the music to new audiences beginning in the 1960s. Another significant, early pioneer was Pedro Ayala, who was active as a live performer through the 1920s and 1930s but did not record until the late 1940s.

After World War II, in an effort to record music that would appeal to a broader Latin American market, U.S. companies concentrated their efforts abroad, abandoning regional Mexican American genres altogether. In the resulting vacuum, local Mexicana/o entrepreneurs created small record companies to record their music. During this time, *conjunto* underwent a stylistic consolidation of sorts, producing a sound that remains largely unchanged to this day. The public, paid-admission ballroom became the new setting for the performance of *conjunto* music. With their audience increasing its buying power, *conjunto* musicians began to find more opportunities to support themselves full-time through their art. This period also saw a shift in generic focus, in which the polka came to eclipse the waltz, redowa, schottische, and *huapango*, which are seldom heard today.

One of the most important innovators of this era was Valerio Longoria, who made his early career in San Antonio and is widely credited with introducing modern set drums to the *conjunto* ensemble and popularizing the *cancíon corrida and the *bolero as part of its repertoire. He is also among the first *conjunto* accordionists to perform standing up, now a standard practice. However, because he moved away from Texas during the late 1940s, his recording career in that state suffered, and he did not achieve the fame that many felt he deserved until much later. Tony de la Rosa, a native of the small town of Sarita near Corpus Christi, was more fortunate. De la Rosa was widely considered the most popular *conjunto* accordionist in the 1950s and continues drawing crowds to this day. He is usually credited with helping to standardize the role of the drum set in the *conjunto* ensemble and for consolidating the *conjunto*'s electrification by replacing the *tololoche* with the electric bass.

Perhaps the peak of *conjunto*'s stylistic development occurred in the 1960s with the Conjunto Bernal, originally from the Kingsville area, who used dueling chromatic accordions and daring harmonic twists to push the limits of the form. Although the Conjunto Bernal's innovations are widely admired, they are seldom imitated. Perhaps the only well-known accordionist to continue in the direction set by the Conjunto Bernal is San Antonio's Esteban Jordan, whose wildly experimental accordion playing has earned him a cult following among *conjunto* enthusiasts but has not caught on with a broader working-class Mexicana/o audience. For the most part, that audience has remained more or less conservative since the 1960s, although it has proven receptive to the introduction of the ensemble's repertoire of a Mexicanized version of the Colombian *cumbia, an influence of the amplified pop music known in México as *música tropical*. The polka and the cumbia are now *conjunto*'s most popular dance rhythms. Another development of the 1970s was the popularization of *norteño* groups such as Ramón Ayala y sus Bravos del Norte, Los Relámpagos, and the inimitable *Los Tigres del Norte. These groups stick close to the basic ensemble that has been established for *conjunto*, and they enjoy considerable popularity throughout México and parts of the United States where Mexican immigrants live. Although these groups have not introduced many formal musical innovations to the form, they have revitalized the traditional *corrido* through songs about the exploits of antiheroic drug smugglers. As *norteño* music has taken off commercially in both the United States and México, *conjunto*, in the strict sense, has remained a small, regional music in spite of the two forms' similarity.

One of the most important recent developments in *conjunto* music, from an institutional point of view, has been the increasing involvement of culture promoters and folklorists in the form since the 1970s. This intervention has given rise to a new life for the music in festivals sponsored by nonprofit arts organizations, most notably the Guadalupe Cultural Arts Center's Tejano Conjunto Festival, which began in 1982 and continues to this day. Some commercial radio stations, such as San Antonio's KEDA, whose formats emphasize *conjunto*, also stage large festivals during the summer months. The nonprofit festivals have attracted the attention of foreign tourists to south Texas, and some of these tourists have been moved to create their own imitations back home, such as Japan's "Los Gatos" and France's "Los Gallos." The festivals and other work of nonprofit organizations were also largely responsible for restoring Valerio Longoria to prominence in the *conjunto* universe. Almost a forgotten figure at the beginning of the 1980s, Longoria taught accordion at the Guadalupe Cultural Arts Center for many years and may have been the first person to give formal lessons in *conjunto* accordion for a fee in an institutional setting. During this latter part of his career, Longoria was named a National Heritage Fellow and was a regular at festivals and commercial concerts all over southern Texas. Another important recent development in *conjunto* music has been the emergence in the 1980s and 1990s of an unprecedented number of female accordionists in this traditionally male-dominated genre. Eva Ybarra, who fronts her own *conjunto*, is perhaps the most noteworthy of these.

The other important genre that has contributed to the formation of Tejano music is the *orquesta*, a label whose meaning has changed considerably over time. During the 1920s and 1930s, *orquestas típicas* (folk orchestras) and *orquestas de cuerdas* (string orchestras) centered on a mixture of violins, guitars, and other plucked and bowed stringed instruments. These ensembles displayed an eclectic array of instrumentation, and some may have been ad hoc affairs, uniting whatever instruments were available in a given moment. Beginning around the time of World War II, however, ensembles centered more on brass and wind instruments, often with a rhythm section including piano, drums, and bass. These groups became popular at a time when large commercial record companies had lost interest in the ethnic Mexican market in the United States, and for this reason, it was mostly smaller independent local labels that recorded them.

The pioneering figure of the *orquesta tejana* was the Falfurrias-born saxophonist Beto Villa. After initial success with a series of recordings of polkas and other salon dances, Villa assembled a large, professional group that alternated between polkas and waltzes, on the one hand, and boleros, fox trots, swing tunes, and Afro-Caribbean rhythms, on the other. The former genres were seen as homespun and folksy in southern Texas, while the latter were associated with sophistication and cosmopolitanism. This stylistic mixture would set the tone for future *orquestas*, which formed a collective expression of the aspirations and cultural contradictions faced by an emerging Mexican American middle class. After Villa set the standard for such groups, many followed in his footsteps, including Balde González, Isidro López, and Ventura Alonzo, one of *orquesta*'s few female bandleaders. Although these new *orquestas* did acquire a degree of standardization, they were always involved with musical experimentation, and the ensembles seem to have differed from one another in terms of style and repertoire more than *conjuntos* did. The variation seems to be between groups that emphasized the more homespun or *ranchero* genres and those who went for a more sophisticated, cosmopolitan or *jaitón* (high-toned) style.

The *orquesta* is often seen as reaching the pinnacle of its development during the *Chicano Movement of the late 1960s and 1970s, when the music came to be known as *La Onda Chicana* (The Chicana Wave). As ethnic Mexican youth, whose claim to middle-class status was recent and threatened, found themselves enmeshed in a struggle for civil rights, they sought to rediscover their Mexican roots, and the *orquesta* was part of this process. Many of the most popular *orquestas* of this period were fronted by young musicians who had begun their musical careers by aiming for success in mainstream commercial popular music and, finding few opportunities in that market, fell back on the more welcoming Tejano market.

Perhaps the exemplary figure from the *orquesta* movement of the 1960s was José María *Little Joe Hernández, born in Temple, Texas, who led a succession of important *orquestas* and whose performances continue to attract nostalgic fans today. After achieving significant success with a group called the Latinaires, particularly with a recording of Lydia Mendoza's "Amor bonito" (Beautiful Love), Little Joe found himself increasingly drawn toward the Chicano Movement's cultural nationalism and the images and symbols of the growing U.S. counterculture. Recruiting new talent and changing the band's name to "La Familia," Little Joe released a number of albums during the late 1960s and through the 1970s that set a new standard of harmonic and syntactic sophistication in *orquesta* music. These songs were characterized by the careful juxtaposition of simple, homespun *ranchero* singing with highly sophisticated jazzy instrumental breaks with mariachi-like brass accents. Another important figure during this period was Sunny Ozuna, who after making an initial hit on the mainstream Top 40 charts with the romantic "Talk to Me," led a highly sophisticated and well-loved *orquesta* through the end of the 1970s. Other prominent *orquestas* of this time include Jimmy Edward, The Latin Breed, and Tortilla Factory.

Although *conjunto* music settled into a comfortable stylistic groove by 1980, the *orquesta* had effectively died out by that time. As electronic keyboards and studio recording techniques became more and more sophisticated, it became less and less feasible to pay large numbers of musicians when a small group with a small number of instruments could make an even bigger sound. During the 1980s, smaller groups calling themselves Tejano appropriated many of the stylistic innovations of the *orquestas*, centering their performances on a jazzed-up *polquita* (little polka) and often alternating between horn and accordion solos between lyrics. Among the more notable bandleaders who continue this sort of *conjunto/orquesta* mix today are Roberto Pulido, Rubén Ramos, and David Lee Garza, while such artists as Emilio Navaira, Mingo Saldívar (known as "the dancing cowboy" because of his flashy stage moves), and Jaime y los Chamacos continue in what has been called a "progressive *conjunto*" idiom. This term's meaning has always been a little unclear, but it seems to be an analogy to what came to be called "Young Country" music during the same period. Although Tejano music for the most part has represented a retreat from the musical complexity of *La Onda Chicana*, it nevertheless continued to gain popularity.

The early 1990s saw the emergence of a number of groups that were almost completely electronic in their instrumentation and that focused their efforts on the cumbia, sometimes reworking this dance rhythm into a slow, romantic ballad. Such groups as El Grupo MAZZ, La Mafia, and most notably Selena y los Dinos, fronted by the posthumously famous diva *Selena, gained increasing exposure and record sales both in the United States and in México, inspiring dreams of "crossover" success in both markets and attracting the attention of major U.S. record companies. During this time, large U.S. tobacco and beer industries also increased their sponsorship of both the commercial and the ostensible noncommercial sides of Tejano and *conjunto* music.

With the backing of the major labels, the Tejano music industry sought to reinvent itself in the image of the music industry at large. Fan clubs for various musical groups sprouted from Monterrey to San Antonio. Music videos, some highly professional, some awkward and amateurish, made their way to television, while glitzy annual awards ceremonies seemed to show that the music had arrived. Tejano artists during this time began seeking to integrate rap and hip-hop styles into their work, continuing the tradition that the *orquestas* had established of borrowing stylistic elements from African American popular musics. An early successful example was the song "Las hijas de don Simon" (The Daughters of Mr. Simon, 1998) by the group Tierra Tejana, which was later followed by similar efforts by La Sombra and an extremely popular rap/*charanga* by Fandango USA. Although it was widely believed that a fusion of Tejano and rap would take the music world by storm, these early expectations have never completely been fulfilled. Recently, the Kumbia Kings, an electronic group consisting of many former members of the late Selena's backup band, has adopted hip-hop clothing style in an effort to appeal to urban youth.

The 1990s also saw many Tejano artists incorporating country and western elements into their performances. Vocalist Ram Herrera is particularly known for this approach, and many Tejano bands now include country covers in their live performances. A "supergroup" called the Texas Tornados, and consisting of musicians Freddy *Fender, Flaco Jiménez, Augie Meyers, and Doug Sahm, formed during the early 1990s and sought to fuse rootsy *conjunto* elements with a country sensibility. Although the Tornados were popular on Tejano radio stations and appealed to many followers of Austin-based alternative country music, they never achieved commercial success with Anglo country fans nationwide.

In retrospect, it is clear that the major labels' enthusiasm for Tejano music during the middle of the 1990s amounted to a speculative bubble. That bubble burst after the music's sales failed to meet projections and after the death of the industry's most notable star, Selena, in 1995. Since the late 1990s the major labels have continued to do business with a few established performers, but new acts are finding it difficult to achieve exposure and sign recording contracts. Some veteran artists, such as Roberto Pulido and Gary Hobbs, are responding to this situation by attempting to start their own independent labels. Although many of the pioneering local labels of the 1940s, such as Ideal and Falcón, have ceased to exist, small local labels such as Discos Joey and Discos Freddie continue to be a presence in the Tejano music market, particularly for *conjunto* music. Among the more recent important developments in the music has been the growth of what is often called Tejano/*norteño* fusion, a move driven in part by the growing popularity of *norteño* and its increasing dominance of urban *Spanish-language radio markets in the United States. Singer Michael Salgado, whose hoarse, nasal voice echoes such greats as Ramón Ayala, is perhaps the most notable exemplar of this trend. In some ways, it appears that commercial Mexicano dance music in the United States now finds itself in a situation similar to the postwar years in which the disinterest of the major record companies has returned Tejano music to the grassroots.

Further Reading

Broyles-González, Yolanda. *Lydia Mendoza's Life in Music*. New York: Oxford University Press, 2001.

Paredes, Américo. *A Texas-Mexican Cancionero: Folksongs of the Lower Border*, 1976. Austin: University of Texas Press, 1995.

Patoski, Joe Nick. *Selena: Como La Flor*. Boston: Little, Brown, 1996.

Peña, Manuel. *The Mexican American Orquesta: Music, Culture and the Dialectic of Conflict*. Austin: University of Texas Press, 1999.

Peña, Manuel. *Música Tejana: The Cultural Economy of Artistic Transformation*. College Station: Texas A&M Press, 1999.

Peña, Manuel. *The Texas-Mexican Conjunto: History of a Working Class Music.* Austin: University of Texas Press, 1985.

Peter Haney

Telemundo. *See* Spanish-Language Television.

Television. *See* Spanish-Language Television.

Texas Rangers. Better known by Tejanos (Texas Mexicans) as Los Rinches, which is most likely a Spanish mispronunciation of "ranger," the Texas Rangers are well known, loathed, and feared among Chicanas/os for their long history of injustice, brutality, violence, murder, mistreatment, and abuse of Mexican and Indian people as a state militia. Officially organized in 1835 before Texas's Independence from México and the *Treaty of Guadalupe Hidalgo to serve as both lawmen and soldiers, the Texas Rangers' original purpose was to pursue cattle robbers, Indians, and Mexican bandits and institute Anglo-American frontier-style justice in the vast Mexican territory of Texas. The first ten were hired in 1823 to wage war against the Indians, and they remain a legendary institution that today continues to stir fear and distrust among Mexican and Chicana/o communities.

The independence of México in 1821 from Spain had little effect on the frontier communities in New Mexico, Texas, and California. Specifically in the Lower Rio Grande region, settlements remained culturally conservative and regionally isolated, and most Mexican *families were related to one another in any given community. The social organization was typically clannish, and the government was primarily patriarchal with minimal outside influences from the northern *gringo* (foreigner) or *fuereño* (outsider) from the south. North American expansionism and the ideology of Manifest Destiny disrupted the traditional lives of Mexicans in south Texas, introducing cultural conflict and violence. The United States began expanding westward with the purchase of the Louisiana Territory from France in 1803. Soon after, Lieutenant Zebulon M. Pike led an expedition to the Great Plains in 1806 and revealed the intentions of North Americans to steal land and dispossess many original settlers and citizens of New Spain. Pike's descriptions of Texas as a good place to farm fueled the interest of many North Americans.

The "Texians" were the first Anglo-American citizens of the province of Texas arriving in the 1820s, led by Moses Austin. The fifty-nine-year-old Missouri resident was granted permission to settle the northern part of the region by Governor Antonio Martínez of Texas in hopes of creating a buffer between settlers and hostile Indians (primarily Comanche and Apache). Austin returned to Missouri where he died, but his son Stephen continued his father's colonization efforts, and between 1824 and 1827, 300 families took up residence in northern Texas in hopes of gaining free farming land with minimum taxation. Many of these families owned African American slaves and hoped to transform the area into another slave state. Many of the racist attitudes expressed by these Anglo settlers toward the Native Americans and Mexican people were hostile, maintaining the old frontier mentality that "the only good Indian is a dead Indian." Mexicans are a mestizo race and hence regarded as Indians or half Indians.

The Texas colonies expanded quickly, and Austin took the lead in organizing "ranging companies" of men to protect the new settlements from Indian attacks and Mexican bandits. The Texas Rangers were armed with a rifle, knife, and a "Walker Colt," a revolving six-shooter that empowered them and provided an overwhelming military advantage over the Mexican *rancheros*, who rarely owned firearms. Santa Anna disarmed the Mexican militia after 1835, which left the frontier settlements vulnerable to Indian and Texian attacks. The Texas Rangers are credited as being integral to the formation of the Texas Republic, and they continued to play a prominent role in the war against México as members of the U.S. militia following 1848.

Throughout the Lower Rio Grande region, their abuse was never forgotten by the Mexican people, and many stories, tales, and historical accounts about the Texas Rangers passed into Texas Mexican oral history and *folklore through songs and legends like The *Ballad of Gregorio Cortez (El Corrido de Gregorio Cortez). *Corridos (folk ballads) from the region provide detailed historical oral accounts from the late nineteenth century and early twentieth century of bloody and violent border conflicts between Mexicans and the Texas Rangers including Gregorio Cortez, Juan Cortina, and Catarino Garza, who became legendary folk heroes defending their rights and their communities against the dreaded Texas Rangers, as the song goes "con pistola en mano" (with his pistol in his hand).

Throughout the border region of south Texas between 1914 and 1919, the Rangers boasted of killing close to 5,000 Mexicans. Much of the folklore and legends attributed to the Texas Rangers fall under a general heading called *Los Diablos Tejanos* (The Texas Devils). The violence and warfare waged on Mexican and Indian communities produced a heroic image among mainstream Anglo-Americans and Texians depicting the Rangers as a courageous, fearless, and upstanding law enforcement agency. However, according to anthropologist Richard Flores, "the term 'rinche' not only signifies mistrust or deceit, but also the violence and exploitation inflicted upon the *Mexicano* community by the Texas Rangers."

Their one-sided image as heroic protectors of Texas continues to be promoted in popular literature and especially in Hollywood movies and TV shows. More recently Columbia TriStar Television Distribution aired a syndicated action/drama titled *Walker, Texas Ranger* on CBS. The show depicted a fictitious modern-day Texas Ranger, Cordell Walker, whose independent approach to crime solving reaches back to the rugged cowboy frontier tradition of the Old West. In the story, heroes are few and Chuck Norris's character is committed to truth, justice, and Texas constructing a legendary Texas

American hero. Norris and his brother Aaron are the executive producers. The Rangers have evolved over the twentieth century and now serve under the Texas Department of Public Safety as a detective agency. Today they are better trained and educated in high-tech security measures and are still provided with state-of-the-art law enforcement equipment and paid higher salaries. They are regarded as the elite branch of law enforcement in Texas but have a tainted history and jaded reputation that leave much to be desired.

Further Reading

Castro, Rafaela G. *Chicano Folklore: A Guide to the Folktales, Traditions, Rituals and Religious Practices of Mexican-Americans*. New York: Oxford University Press, 2001.

Flores, Richard. "The Corrido and the Emergence of Texas-Mexican Social Identity." *Journal of American Folklore* 105 (1992): 166–182.

Holly Austin, Mary. *Texas: Observations, Historical, Geographical, and Descriptive*, 1833. Austin, TX: Overland Press, 1981.

Paredes, Américo. *With His Pistol in His Hand: A Border Ballad and Its Hero*. Austin: University of Texas Press, 1958.

Paredes, Raymund A. "The Origins of Anti-Mexican Sentiment in the United States." In *New Directions in Chicano Scholarship*, edited by Ricardo Romo and Raymund Paredes. San Diego: Regents of the University of California, 1978.

Prescott Webb, Walter. *The Texas Rangers: A Century of Frontier Defense*. Boston, MA: Houghton Mifflin, 1935.

Tyler, Ron, and Douglas Barnett, eds. *The New Handbook of Texas*. Vol. 6. Austin: Texas State Historical Association, 1996.

Peter J. García

Thalía (1971–   ). A pop singer and actress, Thalía was one of a number of Latino artists who, beginning in the late 1990s, after gaining international fame in Latin America and with Latinos in the United States, sought to expand that fame to mainstream audiences in the United States. Born Adriana Thalía Sodi Miranda in Mexico City, Thalía began her career as a child actor on Mexican television and in theater and as a member of the children's singing group Din-Din, with whom she recorded four albums. Her participation in a 1984 production of the musical *Vaselina*, a Latin version of *Grease*, led to an invitation to join the teen pop group Timbriche. She joined the group in 1986 and recorded three albums with them. During this same time, she accepted small roles in Mexican *telenovelas* (soap operas), the most significant being *Quinceañera* (1988), a Mexican *telenovela* series that for the first time was aimed at adolescents and also firmly established Thalía's screen image in the role of innocent ingénue.

In 1989, Thalía moved to Los Angeles for a year to study English, singing, dancing, and acting. While there, she met Alfredo Díaz Ordaz, who would become her producer and collaborator on three albums, *Thalía* (1989), *Mundo de Cristal* (Crystal World, 1991), and *Love* (1992). The adult image and rock sensibility Thalía displayed on these albums was a departure from what audiences had come to expect from her and were not immediately accepted by all her fans. In 1991, Thalía became the cohost of the Spanish variety show *VIP de Noche*, a role that she filled for six months before returning to México to star in a trilogy of highly rated *telenovelas* that would vault her to international stardom.

The *telenovelas María Mercedes* (1992), *Marimar* (1994), and *María la del barrio* (1995) were international hits, including with Spanish-speaking audiences in the United States. In 1995, Thalía began an association with Miami-based producer and music impresario Emilio Estefan, who, along with wife Gloria *Estefan, created a highly successful Miami crossover effort during the mid- to late 1990s, bringing the music of such Latino singers as Ricky *Martin, Enrique *Iglesias, and *Shakira to mainstream America. Her first album with Estefan, *En éxtasis* (In Ecstasy, 1995), went platinum and featured the hit single "Piel morena" (Brown Skin). Two years later, she released the follow-up to that album, the international hit *Amor a la mexicana* (Love Mexican Style), as well as the album *Nandito Ako*, sung in the native Filipino language of Tagalog. She also contributed three songs to the sound tracks of both the English and Spanish versions of the animated film *Anastasia*. As evidence of her growing popularity among Latinos in the United States, April 25, 1997, was declared "Thalía Day" in Los Angeles.

In 1999, she returned to acting, appearing in the *telenovela Rosalinda* and in her first American feature film, *Mambo Café*. The following year, she released the album *Arrasando* (Razing), for which she did most of the songwriting, and in December she married then Sony Music chairman Tommy Mottola. The album *Thalía con banda: Grandes éxitos* (Thalia with Band: Great Hits), a collection of her previous hits performed with a Mexican *banda*, was released in 2001. In 2002, she released *Thalía*, an album produced mainly by Emilio Estefan, who had previously worked with Enrique Iglesias and popular Latino singer/actor Chayanne, and which included three songs in English. During this time, Thalía became increasingly visible in the American mainstream, appearing in a Dr. Pepper commercial with *salsa queen Celia *Cruz and in 2003 launching the Thalía Sodi Collection, a line of clothing and accessories to be sold at K-Mart stores. Also in 2003, she released *Thalía*, her third album bearing that title, featuring predominantly songs in English, including the first single "I Want You," produced by Corey Rooney, who had previously worked with Jennifer *López, Marc *Anthony, and Destiny's Child, and featuring Bronx-based rapper Fat Joe.

Further Reading

Ciudad Futura. "Thalía-biografía." http//:www.ciudadfutura.com/thalia/bio/index.html.
Fan Fire. "Biography: Thalía 'Arrasando.'" http://www.thalia.com/bio/bio.php?bio=2001.
Fan Fire. "Thalía." http://www.thalia.com/bio/bio.php?bio=2002.

Ramón Versage

Theater. Latino theater in the United States consists of a rich and diverse amalgam of nonprofit and professional companies producing classical, post-modern, and avant-garde theatrical works. However, when indigenous cultures are taken into account, the inspiration for much of the modern genre's stylistic characteristics may be traced back to the hemisphere's precolonial era. Historian Nicolás Kanellos identifies the introduction of "Spanish-language" theater in the hemisphere with the religious "shepherd" plays, known as *las pastorelas*, brought over by Spanish Catholic clerics to proselytize and convert native populations. Kanellos states that the first documented Spanish-language manuscript is thought to have been a Mexican three-act, cloak-and-dagger drama performed in California around the middle of the seventeenth century.

Latino theater today is eclectic and varies according to the multiethnic, multiracial, and multilingual nature of U.S. Latina and Latino artists and their audiences. For instance, Latino theater in the Southwest is often influenced by Mexican, Spanish, and Chicano traditions, or a creative blend of all three. Florida's theater scene features a Cuban or *Cuban American flavor frequently imbued with the politics and aesthetics of its post–Fidel *Castro exile community. New York City's decades-old Puerto Rican theater has begun making room for Mexican American, Mexican, and Dominican influences. Afro-Caribbean influences permeate Latino theater, especially in Cuban and Puerto Rican works. Since the 1960s, California's Latino theater scene has taken its inspiration from the *Chicano Movement, but growing Central American communities have begun to infuse the stage with their own theatrical sensibilities. All the while, Spain's colonial legacy endures in the classic works by Lope de Vega, Tirso de Molina, and other Golden Age (1550s–1650s) dramatists in productions staged by aficionados at theaters across the country. As the Latina/o population continues to grow, the community's expanding economic and political position promises to fuel demands for theatrical forms that challenge cultural traditions even as they maintain a continuity with the past.

Latino theater on the West Coast of the United States took its inspiration from the Chicano civil rights movement. The nation's best-known Chicano theater company, El *Teatro Campesino (The Farmworkers Theater), was created in 1965. It is based in the farming community of San Juan Bautista, California, and was organized by a young playwright named Luis *Valdez. He had quit the activist-oriented San Francisco Mime Troupe to join civil rights leader César *Chávez in Delano, California. Valdez set out to entertain farmworkers while helping to recruit them to Chávez's cause. Five years later, the company began to win awards and establish itself at the vanguard of Chicano theater. Inspired by commedia dell'arte, a popular form of street theater during the Italian Renaissance, El Teatro Campesino mixed humor, Mexican folklore, and techniques of touring tent theater companies known as *carpas*, which traveled the Southwest in the early nineteenth century. El

Teatro Campesino's best-known works include *La Carpa de los Rasquachis* (The Tent of the Underdogs, 1971), which later aired on public television under the title *El Corrido* (The Ballad, 1977), and *Corridos: Tales of Passion and Revolution* (1987), which won the George Peabody Award for Excellence in Television. Valdez also is the author of the musical drama *Zoot Suit*, which premiered at the Mark Taper Forum in Los Angeles in 1979, and he wrote and directed the *film *La Bamba* (1987).

San Francisco's Mission District is home to El Teatro de la Esperanza, which was founded in 1970 by a group of university students. The company focuses on Chicano/Latino culture and often performs the works of its artistic director, Rodrigo Duarte Clarke, who has stated, "Theatre should engage audiences on specific questions, and, in our case, within a Chicano context. I think Theatre is only successful if you can find in it the humanity that we all share." Jorge Huerta, one of the nation's leading experts on Latino theater, is among the company's founders.

In Los Angeles, the Bilingual Foundation of the Arts was founded in 1973 by three Latina artists: Mexican American actress Carmen *Zapata, Cuban-born actress and director Margarita Galbán, and Argentinean-born playwright and set designer Estela Scarlata. The group's seasons typically feature Spanish and English productions. Housed in a former jail, the company produces classic works by Spain's Golden Age playwrights, contemporary popular works, and plays by emerging writers. The organization also sponsors touring educational and children's theater productions under its Theatre for Children and Theatre for Young People programs.

Another Los Angeles troupe, Latino Theatre Company (LTC), was founded in 1985 as the Latino Theatre Lab. Since then, it has produced award-winning productions in theaters such as the Los Angeles Theatre Center, the Mark Taper Forum, and other regional venues. Under the direction of José *Valenzuela, the company earned acclaim for productions such as *Roosters*, *Stone Wedding*, *The Promise*, and *Bandido*. In 1996, the LTC became Los Angeles's first Latino equity theater. The company's season that year included the world premiere of *Luminarias*, written by LTC cofounder Evelina *Fernández. The play was later made into a feature film.

Grupo de Teatro Sinergía in Los Angeles specializes in productions by Mexican playwrights, although it also features works addressing an array of Latino themes. In recent years, the company has staged works by Humberto Leyva and Jesús Alberto Cabrera, as well as original works by the company's artistic director, Rubén Amavizca. Amavizca's plays include *Frida *Kahlo, *Malinche*, and *Macbato*, an adaptation of Shakespeare's *Macbeth* set in East Los Angeles. Grupo de Teatro Sinergía is the resident company of the Frida Kahlo Theatre at the Unity Arts Center.

The vibrant New York theater scene features the internationally renowned Repertorío Español, which specializes in theatrical productions in Spanish. The company was cofounded in 1968 by artistic director René Buch, a graduate of the Yale School of Drama, and executive producer Gilberto Zaldí-var. Four years later, Repertorio Español moved to its permanent home in the Gramercy Arts Theatre on Manhattan's Lower East Side. For English speakers, the theater offers live, simultaneous translations provided by voice actors who watch the play from a soundproof booth. The company's season covers plays from the classics to world premieres of new works by Latin American and U.S.-based Latino playwrights.

New York City is also home to International Arts Relations (INTAR), which calls itself a Hispanic American arts center. Founded in 1966, INTAR is a multidisciplinary facility that presents visual art exhibitions, music, and live theater. The center's founding artistic director is Max Ferrá. Located on "Theatre Row" in Manhattan, INTAR produces plays, musicals, opera, children's theater, and performance art pieces. The productions are staged in English and Spanish. Recent productions have included *Daedalus in the Belly of the Beast*, *Culture Clash Unplugged*, and *The Popol Vuh Project*, a multimedia opera. The Puerto Rican Traveling Theatre is a not-for-profit theater company that has operated under Actor's Equity contracts since its creation in 1969. The company was founded by Puerto Rican actress Miriam *Colón. The company has produced more than a hundred plays in English and Spanish by Latin American, Puerto Rican, and U.S.-based Latino playwrights.

New York City's Queens Borough is home to Thalia Spanish Theatre, a not-for-profit company founded in 1977 by Cuban-born actress and director Silvia Brito. The troupe has produced more than eighty plays and emphasizes new works by writers from Spain. Noted Spanish playwrights Antonio Gala, Jaime Salom, and Jerónimo López Mozo have premiered plays at Thalia Spanish Theatre. The company has won numerous awards including the Encore Awards from the New York Arts and Business Council, a New York State Governor's Arts Award (1997), and the 2002 award for Best Musical Production from the Association of Critics of Entertainment (ACE). The company also produces original dance musicals, *zarzuelas* (Spanish operettas), and shows featuring tango and flamenco. Los Kabayitos Puppet & Children's Theatre in New York presents "family and education-oriented productions," including original new works, and is directed by Manuel Morán. Part of the Society of Educational Arts, Inc., the project includes theater productions, school residency art programs, storytelling, workshops, a traveling museum, and folkloric ballet for youth. Shows are performed in English or Spanish, as well as bilingually. Recent productions have included *La Cucarachita Martina* (Martina, The Little Roach) and *La Caperucita Roja* (Little Red Riding Hood).

The American Southwest is home to several thriving Latino theater companies, most of which are heavily influenced by Mexican and Chicano theater traditions. Teatro Dallas is a nonprofit, professional theater company that stages productions that "reflect the varied cultural experiences of the Latino communities." Founded in 1985 by Jeff Hurst and Cora Cardona, the company produces classical and contemporary works by Latino playwrights. Teatro Dallas also hosts an annual International Theatre Festival, which was initiated in 1993 and has showcased productions from Latin America, Japan, Russia, and other European countries.

Talento Bilingüe de Houston began as a small theater company in 1977. The Houston troupe has since expanded into a multidisciplinary arts organization featuring a year-round schedule of distinguished speakers, poets, as well as live dance and theater performances. Talento Bilingüe de Houston's executive director is Richard Reyes. The company produces original works, as well as productions by national touring companies. In Austin, Texas, Teatro Humanidad declares as its mission the promotion and preservation of *cultura Latina* (Latino culture). The company focuses on new and emerging Latino playwrights and other theater artists, as well as programs aimed at at-risk youth. The award-winning company stages several productions a year. Recent productions have included *Legend of the Poinsettia*, *Luminarias*, *Maricela de la Luz Lights the World*, and *The Wizard of Aztlán*.

Albuquerque, New Mexico, is home to the Southwest Repertory Theatre founded in 1995 by Jennifer Chavez. The company's mission is to become the "foremost producer of Native American and Hispanic Theatre in the United States." The company also hosts a Shakespeare festival and provides classes in acting, musical theater, and dance. Recent productions have included *The Indolent Boys* and *The Tempest*. Closer to the borderlands, Phoenix, Arizona, houses Teatro Bravo, a company founded in 2000. Its artistic director is Guillermo *Reyes, a Chilean American award-winning playwright, who heads the playwriting program at Arizona State University. The nonprofit company produces Reyes's original works, as well as new works by other Latin American and U.S.-based Latino playwrights. Recent productions have included *Entre Mujeres* (Between Women), *Places to Touch Him*, and *Miss Consuelo*. Phoenix's newest Latino theater company is Colores Actors-Writers Workshop, founded by James E. García, a journalist and playwright. García is the author of *American Latino Redux* (2002) and other plays and distinguished as recipient of the First Place Prize for Best Short Drama at the 2003 National Collegiate Competition held at the Kennedy Center in Washington, D.C.

In Denver, Colorado, the creation of El Centro Su Teatro in 1971 was inspired by the nationwide Chicano civil rights movement. The company's original goal was to reacquaint young Chicanos with their heritage because "Mexican Americans had been denied access to their history, language and culture." The company is housed in an old elementary school as part of a multipurpose Chicano arts center, and its artistic director is Anthony García.

The Latino Chicago Theatre Company sponsors plays, musical concerts, and literary readings. The troupe bills itself as the city's first Latino theater company. Its shows are available in English and Spanish, and performances are staged at the Firehouse Theatre on the city's north side. Recent productions have included *Jungle of Cities*, *Parting Gestures*, and *Once Five Years Pass*. Aguijon Theatre Company of Chicago was founded in 1989 by Rosario Vargas. It is a professional, nonprofit theatrical company dedicated to producing Spanish-language productions for "Latino and non-Latino communities interested in the Latin American culture." Teatro Luna was formed by two Latina actresses in Chicago frustrated by the lack of substantive roles for Latinas in theater. The company has produced works on topics such as sexual harassment, eating disorders, body image, interracial dating, and race.

Florida's Latino theater scene includes Teatro Avante in Miami, founded in 1979 by director Mario Ernesto Sánchez to preserve and promote Latino culture. Sánchez created the International Hispanic Theatre Festival in 1986, which hosts Latino theater companies from Latin America and Spain. Miami is also home to the Hispanic Theatre Guild. The company's recent productions have included Spanish-language productions of *P.D. ¡Tu gato ha muerto!*, a translation of the play *P.S. Your Cat Has Died*. The company stages its shows at Teatro Ocho in Little Havana. Miami-Dade Community College is home to Prometeo Community Theatre, which stages Spanish- and English-language plays. Founder and artistic director Teresa María Rojas says the group ventures into all genres, from the classics to street theater.

Further Reading

Kanellos, Nicolás. *A History of Hispanic Theatre in the United States: Origins to 1940*. Austin: University of Texas Press, 1990.

Santaliz, Pedro. "Diversiones y Condiciones del Teatro Popular de los Barrios de Puerto Rico: Acercamiento de El Nuevo Teatro Pobre de América." In *Imágenes e Identidades del Puertorriqueño en la Literatura*, edited by Asela Rodríguez de Laguna. Río Piedras, Puerto Rico: Huracán, 1985.

James E. García

Thomas, Piri (1928–   ). Former ex-con Piri Thomas is best known for the biting autobiographies he began writing while in prison that address the racial *stereotypes he believes society placed on his Puerto Rican, Cuban American, and African American heritage. His most prominent autobiographies include *Down These Mean Streets* (1967), *Savior, Savior, Hold My Hand* (1972), and *Seven Long Times* (1974). Literary critics note that Thomas—using street dialect—raised America's consciousness about social marginalization, everyday life in poverty-stricken and crime-ridden neighborhoods, and the eternal longing for escape.

Thomas was born Juan Pedro Tomás on September 30, 1928, in New York City. His mother Delores was a housewife, and his father Juan, also known as Johnny, was a laborer who immigrated from Cuba to Puerto Rico and then to New York. When Thomas was a youth, he decided to informally change his name to Piri Thomas, the first name taken from the middle letters of the word *spirit*. Growing up in the streets of New York was tough for Thomas. When he was twenty-two years old, he was imprisoned and served seven years for attempted armed robbery and shooting a police officer. Prison motivated Thomas to begin writing about his experiences. Upon release from prison in 1956, Thomas could not find a job and, at the insistence of an aunt, volunteered in prison and drug rehabilitation programs in New York. In 1967, he landed a job at the Center for Urban Education in New York City. He continued to work on his novels until *Down These Mean Streets* was published in 1967.

Thomas is most recognized for *Down These Mean Streets*, which is written in prison lingo and his Spanish Harlem dialect. The book presents a brutally honest recollection of his youth, a dark but lyrical memoir about being Puerto Rican in America, about his family's refusal to accept their African blood, and about life on the street. The book takes readers on a journey through the harrowing accounts of his youth—his downward spiral into drugs, robberies, street fights—concluding with his newfound acceptance, faith, and redemption, all without condemnation or sociological judgments. Literary critics lauded him for creating a new voice—rough-hewn, street smart, and insightful—that maintained a personal connection with readers despite their unfamiliarity with his style of speech. *Down These Mean Streets* was written in four years while Thomas was still in prison, but the manuscript was accidentally destroyed after his release. It took Thomas several years to rewrite the book.

Thomas's second autobiography, *Savior, Savior, Hold My Hand*, is the story of his prison release, his attempt to put his life back together, and the changed world he encounters when he returns to his home. Thomas returns his readers to prison in his next autobiographical novel, *Seven Long Times*, which received more critical acclaim than *Savior*. In *Seven Long Times*, Thomas takes readers through his seven years of imprisonment, first at Bellevue, then Sing Sing, and lastly Great Meadows. Using his signature writing style, Thomas writes of the steel and cement sterility of prison, the brutality of guards and prisoners, and the insanity stemming from both sides of the bars. In addition to his autobiographies, Thomas also has written a young-adult book called *Stories from El Barrio* (1978) and *The Golden Streets*, a two-act play first produced by Puerto Rican Traveling Theatre on September 9, 1970, in New York at Riverside Park. Literary critics praise his collection of novels for their honesty and for bringing the viewpoint of those living on the edge of Spanish Harlem—and inner-city communities in general—into the mainstream of America.

Further Reading

Contemporary Authors Online. Gale Group. http://galenet.gale.com.
Hernández, Carmen Dolores. *Puerto Rican Voices in English: Interviews with Writers*. Westport, CT: Praeger, 1997.
The Official Piri Thomas Website. http://www.cheverote.com/piri.html.

Julie Amparano García

Tigres del Norte, Los. *See* Los Tigres del Norte.

Tin Tan (1915–1973). Tin Tan was the stage name used by Germán Valdés, one of the best character actors to come out of Mexican cinematography to influence Mexicans in the United States. His portrayals of anglicized Mexicans coping with cultural identity and linguistic issues brought the border culture to the movie screen. He is known to have innovated the use of Spanglish, the mixture of Spanish and English, onstage in his performances of Le Pachuco (*see* Pachucos).

Tin Tan was born in Mexico City on September 19, 1915, with the given name of Germán Genaro Cipriano Gómez Valdés Castillo. In his lifetime, Tin Tan had three wives, Magdalena Martínez, Micaela Vargas, and Rosalía Julián, who each bore him two sons.

Tin Tan was an actor of multiple talents who could sing and dance to rumba, swing, cumbia, tango, and *jarabe tapatío*, worked in a circus and a frivolous *theater of varieties, and also worked at a radio station as a spokesman and comedian. In 1943, René Cardona offered Tin Tan a small role in *Hotel de Verano* (Summer Hotel), but it was not until 1945, in the *film *El Hijo Desobediente* (The Disobedient Son) that he became known. Along with Pedro Infante and Jorge Negrete, Tin Tan was part of the Golden Age of Mexican cinematography. He made around 100 movies between the years 1945 and 1972, many in which he performed the role of a stereotypical Pachuco, dressing in a Pachuco manner and speaking Spanglish. He also did work in the Spanish versions of two Disney movies; he was the voice of Baloo in *The Jungle Book* (1967) and of O'Malley the Alley Cat in *The Aristocats* (1969).

Further Reading

"En Breve." *La Opinión, Ethnic NewsWatch.* Arizona State University. July 1, 1998. http://www.asu.edu/lib.

Pastor, Anita. "Los Comediantes: Tin Tan." *Organizaciones Artisticas.* http://famosos .tripod.com.mx/loscomediantes/id21.html.

"Recordando el Cine Mexicano." *Lea Interactivo.* http://www.xsn.net/fravel/ temas.html.

Ríos, Gabriel. "Rafael Aviña le Rinde un Homenaje a 'Tin Tan.'" *Consejo Nacional para la Cultura y la Artes.* http://www.cnca.gob.mx/cnca/nuevo/diarias/ 100299/unabiogr.html.

Mónica Saldaña

Tortilla. A common bread staple of the Americas, tortillas resemble very thin pancakes in their flat, round appearance. Surprising to most Americans is that the first definition for *tortilla* in most Spanish-language dictionaries is an egg dish cooked with potatoes, seafood, and other ingredients and served in pie-wedge slices. Resembling an omelet or quiche, the egg-based tortilla of Spain differs from the thin, flat staple of the Americas made of *harina de maiz* (corn flour) and, since Spanish contact, of *harina de trigo* (wheat flour).

The familiar name of this staple is a perfect example of the cultural *meztizaje*, or hybrid combination of Spanish and Native American Indian customs, for the early Spaniards named what they saw as a flat corn *torta*, a tortilla, when it was filled with other ingredients, and the name became popular. Thus, for over 500 years, native Spanish speakers have defined tortillas by precise ethnicity (i.e., whether Iberian or American) and geography (i.e., whether made in Spain or in the Americas). The last decades of the twentieth century witnessed the growth of this ethnic and geographic impact on the tortilla with the North American/U.S. influence, which has added a method of manufacture to the definition.

Traditionally, the tortillas of México consist of *maza harina* (or corn flour), lard, salt, and water, whereas the tortillas of the U.S. Southwest and borderlands region of Greater México usually are made with wheat flour, lard, salt, and water or milk. Some gourmet appreciators of Mexican cuisines even assert that Mexican *food without corn tortillas would be like Chinese food without rice. In New Mexico the wheat tortillas sometimes also include leavening, either baking powder or soda, which shows further absorption of Spanish and Anglo ingredients by the Mexican and Pueblo cultures. Whatever the basic type, tortillas are all traditionally made by hand, patted or rolled into flat, thin rounds of anywhere from three to twenty-four inches in diameter, depending on the region, and cooked on a hot *comal*, or griddle. North Americans also fry the corn tortillas for making tacos, enchiladas, *chimichangas*, and other filled dishes. Another innovation in the United States is the burrito (literally "little donkey"), a rolled sandwichlike tortilla filled with beans, potatoes, meats, or any ingredient that suits the consumer. Arguably the most notable North American addition to the evolution of this mestizo cultural product is their mass production, resulting in the increased disappearance of home-cooked tortillas as greater numbers of Mexicans and Mexican Americans now buy packaged tortilla products. Another spinoff version of the fried corn tortilla is the *tostada*, a tortilla chip that is sold by the thousands of tons yearly.

Further Reading

Bayless, Rick. *Mexican Kitchen*. New York: Scribner, 1996.

Bayless, Rick. *Mexico One Plate at a Time*. New York: Scribner, 2000.

Gilbert, Fabiola Cabeza de Baca. *We Fed Them Cactus*. Albuquerque: University of New Mexico Press, 1954.

Rebolledo, Tey Diana, Erlinda Gonzales-Berry, and Teresa Márquez, eds. *Las Mujeres Hablan: An Anthology of Nuevo Mexicana Writers*. Albuquerque, NM: El Norte Publications, 1988.

Cordelia Chávez Candelaria

Tortilla Soup. Directed by María Ripoll, and distributed by Samuel Goldwyn Films, the cast includes Héctor *Elizondo, Paul *Rodríguez, Elizabeth *Peña, and Raquel *Welch. *Tortilla Soup* (2001), a U.S. remake of Ang Lee's

1994 Chinese hit *Eat, Drink, Man, Woman*, is a comedy about the power and love of *food. Even more important, though, with its dominantly Latina/o cast, the film is able to immerse its audience into a middle-class Mexican American milieu that is rarely seen in widely distributed films.

This movie, set in Los Angeles, tells the story of a master chef, Martín Naranjo (Elizondo), who prepares exquisite Sunday dinners for his three grown daughters, as he watches their lives change in ways he cannot control. The audience quickly learns that Martín has not been able to taste or smell since the death of his wife and must depend on his best friend, a Cuban chef named Thomas Gómez (Julio Oscar Mechoso), to sample his exquisite dishes. Martín spends most of his time taking care of his daughters; the youngest, Maribel (Tamara Mello), is still in high school; Carmen (Jacqueline Obradors) is a businesswoman; and Leticia (Peña), the eldest daughter, has found religion. Throughout the movie the daughters experience a sudden shift in their lives. Maribel's plans of going to college are suddenly stirred as she meets a handsome Brazilian who entices her to see the world. Despite her father's wishes, Carmen realizes that her heart is actually in the kitchen and not in the successful business career she has made for herself. Finally, Leticia, a repressed schoolteacher, experiences a change when she falls in love with the high school baseball coach. By the film's end, a great shift is even seen in Martín's own life as he falls in love again and accepts the lives his daughters have chosen. The film, centered on the theme of food and *family, shows the culinary richness of Latina/o cuisine and portrays a professional Latina/o family in ways that break the patterns of presenting Latinas/os as lazy, criminal, and violent. It also shows how *gender roles are changing in traditional Latina/o families.

Further Reading

Clark, Mike. " 'Tortilla Soup' a Savory Blend of Romance, Family." *USA Today*, August 24, 2001, E7.

Harrison, Eric. "Tortilla Soup Pleases the Taste Buds." *Houston Chronicle*, August 24, 2001, sec. 1.

Mitchell, Elvis. "Movie Magic: Feasting and Staying Slim." *New York Times*, August 31, 2001, E12.

Erin M. Fitzgibbons-Rascón

Touch of Evil, A. Directed by Orson Welles, this black-and-white classic based on the pulp fiction novel *Badge of Evil* (1956) by Wade Miller is the first and only feature *film in the cinema noir genre that is set on the U.S.-México border. Although it enjoyed moderate success in its initial release, it is now being seen by *Chicano scholars as an important cinematic text that contributes to a popular culture understanding of the U.S.-México border and the surrounding border culture. It also engages such *race-based issues as fears of miscegenation, ethnic minstrelsy, American hostility toward México and Mexicans, and *police corruption.

The main plot centers on two detectives as they work to find the murder suspect of an American border town industrialist. One detective is the obese and overtly racist American Hank Quinlan (played by Orson Welles), and the other is a Mexico City federal drug agent, Miguel Vargas (played by a makeup-darkened, brown-faced, Mexican-accented Charlton Heston). Even though Quinlan frames a young Mexican American mine worker for the murder, Vargas finds out that Quinlan has been framing crimes to cover up his own corruption for several years. This plot of police corruption against Mexicans mirrors the historically real Sleepy Lagoon case of the earlier *zoot suit era, as well as the revelations about Los Angeles Police Department practices of the 1990s.

A Touch of Evil contains notable appearances by Marlene Dietrich, whose skin, like Heston's, is darkened and whose native Swedish accent is meant to be heard as a Mexican accent in her role as a gypsy fortune-teller. Janet Leigh plays Vargas's newlywed American wife who is drugged in a simulated *gang rape scene orchestrated by Quinlan in cahoots with a local Mexican mob boss to throw Vargas off his trail. For a film made in the pre–Chicano civil rights era before 1965, the film's main point about American racism and corruption is progressive for its time. However, the film perpetuates *stereotypes by representing Mexican youth only as members of a crime family involved in the drug trade. Also, the visual language of the film (lighting, mise-en-scène, music) casts the Mexican border town as filthy, dark, and shadow laden, full of strip bars, and driven by criminal activities. In 1958, *Touch of Evil* won the best film at the Brussels International Film Festival where French directors François Truffaut and Jean Luc Godard were the jury chairs. The original director's cut was restored and released in 1998, winning a special award from the New York Film Critics Circle Awards.

Further Reading

Leaming, Barbara. *Orson Welles: A Biography.* New York: Penguin, 1985. http://www.filmsite.org/touc.html (7 October 2003).

Arturo J. Aldama and Bill Nerricio

Traffic. Directed by Steven Soderbergh and produced by Edward Zwick, Laura Bickford, and Marshall Herskovitz, *Traffic* (2000) is an adaptation of the 1990s British miniseries *Traffik*. The film focuses on the vastly important "war on drugs" as a way to explore the failed drug policy of the United States in its relationships with México and Colombia. The original *Traffik* followed a farmer in Pakistan as he sold poppies to be ground into heroin, showed how the heroin traveled into Western Europe, and connected those routes to the high rates of addiction among European youth. The USA Films version of *Traffic* focuses on the drug trade in México, Latin America, and the United States, giving emphasis to the increasing rates of addiction in poor urban areas and among affluent youth. One of the affluent victims of the drug trade is the daughter of the current Drug Czar (Michael Douglas) and head of the Drug Enforcement Agency. Besides the crucial significance of its subject matter, the movie is important for its filmic success. *Traffic* received several Academy Awards in 2001, including Best Director, Best Adapted Screenplay, Best Editing, and Best Supporting Actor for Benicio *Del Toro, who also won Best Supporting Actor at the Golden Globes and Best Actor from the Screen Actors Guild in 2001.

The film uses a nonlinear technique that fuses several story lines that intersect at certain points to attempt to provide an overview of those involved in the drug trade: suppliers, traffickers, dealers, addicts and their *families, law enforcement on both sides of the border (Del Toro as the Mexican detective), and government officials in the United States and México. Although the film was applauded for highlighting the failures of the war on dugs and the consequences of addiction in the United States, many Latinas and Latinos believe that the film perpetuates racist notions of Mexicans and México. Especially criticized is the depiction of Tijuana, a thriving industrial city with a large variety of cultural and intellectual resources, as a place of moral abandon, corruption, violence, and social decay. Camera shots of México and Mexicans are purposefully out of focus and tinged an orange-yellow that distorts the images further. The cinematographic style used to depict México contrasts sharply with the wide angle and extremely clear shots and full use of vibrant color to depict the United States as a place of clarity and moral superiority. The film also perpetuates the Hollywood histories of ethnic minstrelsy, where Euro-American actors play a caricature of ethnic actors, and fears of miscegenation, where a young white rich teenager (Erika Christensen) trades sex for drugs with a young African American dealer in the ghettos of D.C. The cast of *Traffic* also includes Don Cheadle, Luis Guzmán, Dennis Quaid, Catherine Zeta-Jones, Jacob Vargas, Tomás Milian, and Clifton Collins, Jr.

Arturo J. Aldama

Treaty of Guadalupe Hidalgo. Many historians and other scholars date the start of Mexican-*hyphen*-American with the signing of the Treaty of Guadalupe Hidalgo on February 2, 1848, the agreement between the United States and México that ended the Mexican War that began in 1846. If the attacks, revolt, and eventual secession by American Texans against the Mexican homeland were counted, then the war against México started ten years earlier with the famous Battle of the *Alamo in 1836. The Treaty of Guadalupe Hidalgo was signed in a neighborhood known as the Villa de Guadalupe Hidalgo, north of the capital Mexico City by representatives of President James K. Polk's U.S. administration, of the American army leadership under Generals Zachary Taylor and Winfield Scott, of the Mexican government under President Manuel de la Peña y Peña, and Mexican armies under General Santa Anna. One of the most historic watersheds in the history of the Americas and the world, the treaty determined the new political boundary between North America and the United States and Central and South America and México. The parties agreed that the natural carvings of the Rio Grande River and the Gila River were to serve as southern boundaries, and the United States received more than 525,000 square miles (i.e., 1,360,000 square kilometers) of land in exchange for a payment of $15 million. These lands expanded the United States into the Atlantic to Pacific continental country it is today and added Arizona, California, western Colorado, Nevada, New Mexico, Texas, and Utah to the nation's territory. The war and treaty completed American continental expansion until 1853 when the Gadsden Purchase added 55,000 more acres in southern New Mexico and Arizona for railroad development. By the terms of the treaty México also agreed to settle claims made against her by U.S. citizens in the amount of over $3 million.

The Treaty of Guadalupe Hidalgo resulted in cataclysmic changes on both sides of the new border. Many historians concur that the treaty contributed to bloody civil wars in both countries—in México the bloodshed lasted from 1857 until 1910, while in the United States the simmering conflict over slavery was reopened with disputes over whether or not slave owning should be allowed in the newly annexed western states. The U.S. Civil War occurred from 1861 to 1865. The upheavals in México since 1821 and independence from Spain were compounded after 1848 by the uncertainty of the citizenry about their country's future as an independent state, and the ensuing political extremism that followed the signing of the treaty eventually led to violent civil war in 1857.

In human terms, the treaty added approximately 100,000 more people to the U.S. Census, Mexican Americans, who did not immigrate or cross any border to enter the United States but who discovered on February 3, 1848, that the border had crossed them, and they were now part of the incipient population of the United States's largest states. Popular culture representations of the Treaty of Guadalupe Hidalgo appear in a wide range of forms from *corridos and other border ballads to popular folk resistance of the new government through support for border heroes like Joaquín Murrieta, Gregorio Cortez (see Ballad of Gregorio Cortez, The), and Pancho *Villa, who were considered outlaws by the Americans. The war and treaty also produced one of the most distinctive footnotes to popular culture history in the case of the St. Patrick Brigades (known as San Patricios to the Mexicans), a group of seventy-two Irish Catholic defectors from the U.S. Army who chose to fight with the Mexicans with whom they felt greater solidarity. Part of the fascination with the San Patricios is the intercultural, transnational, border-crossing perspectives that they signify as rebels with a cultural cause: the right to uphold their religious beliefs and human identities over their soldierly identifications. In this, they and their allies were visionaries looking ahead to the twenty-first century, once again underscoring the lasting importance of the Treaty of Guadalupe Hidalgo for over 150 years.

Further Reading

King, Rosemary. "Border Crossings in the Mexican American War." In *The Legacy of the Mexican and Spanish-American Wars: Legal, Literacy, and Historical Perspectives*, edited by Gary D. Keller and Cordelia Candelaria. Tempe, AZ: Bilingual Review Press, 2000. 63–85.

Ruíz Cameron, Christopher David. "One Hundred Fifty Years of Solitude: Reflections on the End of the History Academy's Dominance of Scholarship on the Treaty of Guadalupe Hidalgo." In *The Legacy of the Mexican and Spanish-American Wars: Legal, Literacy, and Historical Perspectives*, edited by Gary D. Keller and Cordelia Candelaria. Tempe, AZ: Bilingual Review Press, 2000. 1–22.

Cordelia Chávez Candelaria

Turlington, Christy (1969–   ). Christy Turlington, well-known supermodel of El Salvadoran American descent, was born on January 2, 1969, in Walnut Creek, California, and raised in Coral Gables, Florida, and Danville, California. At age thirteen, Turlington was discovered by a Miami-area photographer and began modeling locally. By age fifteen, she had signed on with Eileen Ford, one of the world's leading modeling agencies. Despite a slow start in the international modeling scene, Turlington joined a cohort of young supermodels in the 1980s that included such figures as Linda Evangelista and Cindy Crawford. Soon she became a spokeswoman for fashion-defining companies Calvin Klein and Maybelline.

In 1999, she earned a bachelor's degree in liberal arts from New York University. Turlington is a committed activist for the antismoking cause (her ten-year smoking habit resulted in early stage emphysema), People for the Ethical Treatment of Animals, and the American Federation for El Salvador. Turlington is a partner in the New York eatery The Fashion Café and has been featured in such films as *Prêt-à-Porter* (1994) and *Unzipped* (1995). She has developed a line of skin care products and has written books on yoga (*Living Yoga*, 2003). In June 2003 she married actor-director Ed Burns, and in October 2003 she gave birth to a baby girl.

Further Reading

Maldonado, Sheila. "Christy Turlington Comes Home." *Latina Magazine* (January 1999).

William Orchard

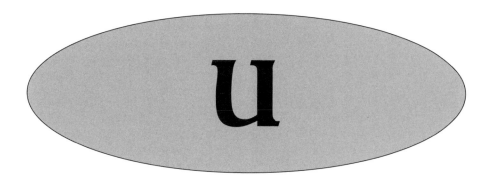

UFW (United Farmworkers Union). *See* Chávez, César *and* Huerta, Dolores.

Ultima, Bless Me. *See* Anaya, Rudolfo Alfonso.

Univision. *See* Spanish-Language Television.

Urista Heredia, Alberto Baltazar. *See* Alurista.

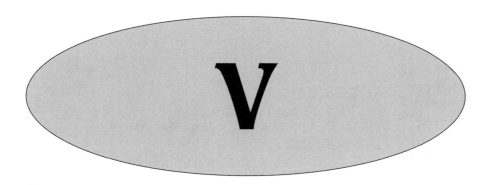

Valdez, Daniel (1939–   ). Daniel Valdez is a composer, musician, singer, and actor with a long list of film and music credits, including *Zoot Suit* (1981), *La Bamba* (1987), *Born in East L.A.* (1987), *Selena Forever* (2000, musical) and *Canciones de mi Padre* (Songs of My Father, 1988, musical). Often seen as competing and collaborating with his well-known brother Luis *Valdez, he holds his own in the world of entertainment as well as in his community, where he works with community-based organizations and schools to serve as a positive role model for Chicana/o youth.

Valdez was born in Delano, California, in 1939 to farmworkers Francisco and Armida Valdez. At the age of seventeen, he joined his brother Luis in the United Farm Workers (UFW) picket lines in Delano, California, protesting the unjust treatment of farmworkers. It was in this environment that he and Luis created the critically significant El *Teatro Campesino, the original *Chicano grassroots *theater, which provided theatrical performances for the farmworkers and helped spread the word about the unjust treatment in the fields. Valdez performed in numerous Teatro Campesino productions and began to incorporate his music to spread the message of the plight of the farmworker to the rest of the world.

In 1973, Valdez released his first solo album *Mestizo*, the first Chicano album recorded by a major label, A&M Records. He quickly fell into the world of concert performing and has performed with greats such as Linda *Ronstadt, Carlos *Santana, Jerry *Garcia, Ruben *Blades, Celia *Cruz, and Tito *Puente. In 1987, Valdez and brother Luis coproduced *La Bamba*, fulfilling Valdez's thirteen-year dream of bringing the life story of Ritchie *Valens to the motion picture screen. He performed in *Zoot Suit* with Edward James *Olmos and starred opposite Ronstadt in her stage produc-

Singer, songwriter, and actor Daniel Valdez. *Photo courtesy of Daniel Valdez.*

tion of *Canciones de mi Padre*. In 1987, he performed some of the featured songs in *Born in East L.A.*, starring Cheech *Marín. In 1996, Valdez was able to spotlight his musical prowess when he wrote the original score for the IMAX film *México*, which traces 3,000 years of Mexican history. In 1997, when the San Diego Repertory Theatre and Southwestern College restaged *Zoot Suit*, Valdez was brought on as musical consultant and historical expert. During this time, he also created his first original musical, *Ollín*, based on one of his original poems in which he describes the conquest of México in song and dance.

In his most recent work, Valdez teamed up with Anthony Garcia as director of Su Teatro in Denver, Colorado, on a musical play titled *El sol que tu eres* (The Sun That You Are), based on the Orpheus myth. The play, set in present-day México, incorporates Aztec and Mayan myths and is a joint venture with Su Teatro, Guadalupe Cultural Center in San Antonio, *Xicanindio Artes in Mesa, Arizona, and La Peña Cultural Center in Berkeley, California. He continues to work with El Teatro Campesino, developing new works and performing as an actor, composer, and director at its ensemble playhouse in San Juan Bautista, California.

Further Reading

http://www.asu.edu/asunews/arts/daniel_valdez_100203.htm.

Cordelia Chávez Candelaria

Valdez, Luis (1940–   ). Known as "The Father of Chicano Theater," Luis Valdez is a screenwriter, director, actor, producer, filmmaker, and playwright. The son of Francisco and Armida Valdez, Luis was born into a *family of migrant workers in Delano, California, on June 26, 1940. Valdez began working the fields at the age of six, and although his schooling was often interrupted, he managed to finish high school and to attend San Jose State College (SJSC), where he earned a B.A. in English. While at SJSC, his playwriting abilities blossomed; he completed *The Theft* in 1961 and *The Shrunken Head of Pancho Villa*, which was produced by the SJSC Drama Department, in 1963. After graduating from SJSC, he moved to San Francisco and became a member of the San Francisco Mime Troupe, where he learned the techniques of "agitation and propaganda" *theater advocated by playwright Bertolt Brecht. These techniques influenced his development of the basic format of Chicano theater, the one-act plays, or *actos*. After about a year with the Mime Troupe, Valdez joined the United Farm Workers Organizational Committee and worked alongside César *Chávez to improve the economic and working conditions of farmworkers.

It was during this time that Valdez founded El *Teatro Campesino, a touring farmworkers' theater troupe. One of the founding principles of El Teatro Campesino is if the *raza* (the people who make up the Latino community) cannot come to the theater, the theater must go to the *raza* community. Based on this principle, the troupe traveled around the countryside, entertaining with *actos* written by Valdez. His *actos* had themes related to the *Chicano Movement and often included folklore and elements of Aztec and Mayan culture. Because the troupe traveled, performances were often done without a script, stage, or props. El Teatro Campesino fostered a sense of pride in Chicanas/os and became the inspiration for over a 100 *teatro* troupes in *barrios and universities throughout the Southwest. Today, Teatro Campesino, the most important and long-standing Chicana/o theater, has a permanent home in San Juan Bautista, California, and continues to dramatize the political and cultural concerns of Hispanics.

As Valdez expanded his work into more conventional theater, he produced one of the earliest Chicano video shorts, *I Am Joaquín*, based on the popular poem by Rodolfo "Corky" Gonzalez. He went on to produce many landmark *films including *Zoot Suit* in 1982, which was based on the Sleepy Lagoon riots in Los Angeles during World War II. *Zoot Suit* was the first play written by a Chicano to be done on Broadway. Another major production for Valdez was *La Bamba* (1987), the story of Ritchie *Valens, a young Chicano who quickly rose to rock and roll fame with his recording of the title song in 1959. *La Bamba* was extremely successful in mainstream and Latina/o markets and was the first major film to be produced and distributed in English as well as in Spanish. Some of Valdez's selected works include *I Don't Have to Show You No Stinking Badges* (1986), *Corridos! Tales of Passion and Revolution* (1987), *La Pastorela: A Shepherd's Play* (1991, a PBS production), and *The Cisco Kid* (1994).

Valdez has won numerous awards for his work, including an Obie, an Emmy, and the Los Angeles Drama Critics Award. He has also received honorary doctorates from San Jose State University and the California Institute of the Arts. His plays, essays, and poems, which are frequently anthologized, continue to be widely read by students, critics, and teaching professionals.

Further Reading

Broyles-González, Yolánda. *El Teatro Campesino: Theater in the Chicano Movement.* Austin: University of Texas Press, 1994.

Valdez, Luis. *Luis Valdez Early Works: Actos, Bernabe and Pensamiento Serpentino.* Houston, TX: Arte Público Press, 1990.

http://www.elteatrocampesino.com/campesin/history/history.html.

Alma Alvarez-Smith

Valens, Ritchie (1941–1959). Born Richard Valenzuela on May 13, 1941, in Pacoima, California, Ritchie Valens was the first Chicano crossover rock star. Raised in a suburb of Los Angeles in the San Fernando Valley, Valens learned

Ritchie Valens. *Courtesy of Photofest.*

to play guitar and sing rhythm and blues and honed his skills by performing at high school dances and at local venues during his teenage years. He was brought to the attention of music promoter Bob Keane, who attended one of Valens's performances in Pacoima. Recognizing the musical talent, Keane signed Valens to record several songs including "Come on Let's Go" (an original song by Valenzuela) at Gold Star Studios in Hollywood on the Del-Fi label. The song was soon on commercial radio stations in Los Angeles and almost made the Top 40 in 1958. Once his musical career was launched, Keane asked Richard to change his name to Ritchie Valens to appeal to a larger Anglo audience. By 1958 Valens began performing in concert and at dances throughout southern California. He recorded * "La Bamba," a well-known folk song from Veracruz, México, and the flipside rock ballad written for his girlfriend, "Donna," on a 45-rpm single. The recording became one of the bestselling 45s of all time. These two hits plus "Come on, Let's Go" form the trilogy of songs for which Valens is best remembered. In 1958 Valens toured the Midwest and East Coast and appeared on *American Bandstand* and on Alan Freed's Christmas show at the Paramount Theater in New York City. His short but successful career ended on February 3, 1959, in a fatal plane crash, along with Buddy Holly and JP "Big Bopper" Richardson, in a snow-covered Iowa cornfield. Members of his band were reluctant to perform his hits following his death, thus avoiding accusations of exploiting Valens's name and reputation. In 1987 the movie *La Bamba* was released, starring Lou Diamond Phillips as Valens. The *film, which revived his music, included original music by Carlos *Santana and Miles Goodman. The performance by *Los Lobos on screen and on the sound track made "La Bamba" a number-one hit. Rhino Records has compiled Valens's short musical career into a three-disc set with booklet.

Peter J. García

Valenzuela, José (c. 1952–). A gifted dramaturge, José Luis Valenzuela is an exceptional influence and presence in Latino pop culture in the United States. As an actor, director, and producer, Valenzuela's chosen mission in drama is to provide a professional artistic forum to express the Latino experience in the United States. Valenzuela participated in the Santa Barbara–based *theater group El Teatro de la Esperanza (The Theater of Hope) for approximately ten years, serving as both an actor and director in the 1970s and 1980s. In 1985, Valenzuela became the director for the Los Angeles Theatre Center's (LATC) Latino Theatre Lab (LTL). Since then he has been involved in various productions ranging from internationally acclaimed theater to mainstream motion pictures. A Ford Foundation grant allowed Valenzuela and the LTL to commission many plays for the LATC until it closed in the early 1990s. In 1991, the LTL moved to the Mark Taper Forum for three years until 1994, when LTL changed its name to Latino Theatre Company (LTC), which Valenzuela still directs, and moved to the Plaza de la Raza for a year in residence. After two years, the LTC was ready for its inaugural season with the debut of *Luminarias, written by Evelina *Fernández, Valenzuela's wife, and directed by Valenzuela. Due to Luminarias's theatrical success, it was made into a feature *film in 2000, directed by Valenzuela, written by Fernández, produced by Sal López, and distributed by New Latin Pictures.

His acting, directing, and film credits include Luminarias (2000); How Else Am I Supposed to Know I'm Still Alive?, for Universal's Hispanic Film Project; Una Vez al Año Para Toda Una Vida, (Once a Year Forever, 1991) for Revlon; A Bowl of Beings (1991), Carpa Clash (1993), S.O.S. (1992), The Mission (1990), and Radio Mambo (1994), for the Miami Light Project, with Chicano theater troupe Culture Clash; Bandido!, with the founder of the *Teatro Campesino, Luis *Valdez; Peer Gynt, by Henrik Ibsen, at the Norland Theatre in Norway; and Manuel Puig's Kiss of the Spider Woman, at the National Theatre of Norway. Awards received by Valenzuela include Drama-logue Awards for directing August 29 and Hijos (Sons), a production for Teatro Jorge Negrete; 1990 Nosotros Golden Eagle Award; and a Berman-Bloch Fellowship for directing. Valenzuela currently resides in East Los Angeles with his wife and is working on his second film, Dementia.

Further Reading

Keller, Gary D. *Hispanics and United States Film: An Overview and Handbook.* Tempe, AZ: Bilingual Press/Editorial Bilingüe, 1994.

http://www.latinotheater.com/history.asp.

Marisol Silva

Vargas, Elizabeth (1962–). Elizabeth Vargas, born in Patterson, New Jersey, on September 6, 1962, has become one of the most prominent Latina journalists in the United States. Vargas was among the first Latinas to be seen on national network news and continues to hold a solid place in television journalism.

Vargas's father Ralf moved to the United States from Puerto Rico and became an Army officer. His assignments around the world allowed Vargas and her siblings to experience a tremendous exposure to countries, cultures, and diversity. She determined at a young age that she wanted a career in journalism and eventually went into broadcasting at the University of Missouri. In the years following college (1986–1989) Vargas worked as a reporter/anchor for the CBS affiliate in Reno, Nevada, and as a lead reporter for KTVK-TV, the ABC affiliate in Phoenix, Arizona. In 1989 Vargas landed a job as a reporter and anchor for WBBM-TV, the CBS affiliate in Chicago, one of the largest local media markets, before being hired by NBC News in 1993, where she served as a correspondent for the NBC News magazine. She also worked as a correspondent and anchor for *Dateline* and the *Today Show* and as a substitute anchor for the weekend editions of *NBC Nightly News*. While working for *Dateline*, Vargas reported on a wide range of issues, including breast cancer research, the People for Ethical Treatment of Animals (PETA) and their war against fur, and the mysterious death of billionaire socialite Doris Duke. In 1996, Vargas switched to the ABC News network, to work as a news anchor for *Good Morning America*. As an ABC News correspondent, Vargas has served as a *20/20* anchor, a *20/20 Downtown* anchor, and as a *World News Tonight Saturday* anchor.

Vargas has covered breaking stories and reported several in-depth investigations throughout her tenure at ABC. In addition, she frequently hosts or gives speeches at galas or symposiums including the National Hispanic Foundation for the Arts benefit and the International Women's Media Foundation. In 2001, she won an Emmy for "Outstanding Instant Coverage of a News Story in the Year 2000," when she anchored the story of the Elián *González case in Miami, Florida. Then in 2002, she was recognized with an *ALMA Award for being an "Outstanding Correspondent or Anchor of a National News Program" for her work with ABC's *20/20*.

In 2002 Vargas married songwriter Marc Cohn, and in 2003 she gave birth to her first child, Zachary Rafael Cohn.

Erin M. Fitzgibbons-Rascón

Further Reading

http://www.PuertoRico-Herald.org.

Vásquez, Richard (1928–). Richard Vásquez is a novelist and award-winning journalist who spent his career writing about the historical and demographic importance of Mexicans and *Chicanos in the U.S. Southwest. Most known for his novel *Chicano* (1970), Vásquez broke ground by being one of the first authors to have a national, mainstream press publish a book about a Chicano *family. In addition, he also is one of the first Hispanic writers to examine issues involving *mestizaje* ancestry, in particular how mestizos define their mixed Mexican ancestry and negotiate their identity. Since then, other writers have taken up the discussion of *mestizaje* in their novels, including Sandra *Cisneros, Richard Rodríguez, and Ana *Castillo.

Vásquez was born on June 11, 1928, in Southgate, California, and raised with his nine siblings in the San Gabriel Valley, outside of Los Angeles. He has worked in various capacities before becoming a writer. Vásquez served a stint in the U.S. Navy, he owned a construction business, and he drove a taxicab until 1959, when he became a reporter for the *Santa Monica Independent* in Santa Monica, California. He was also a reporter for the *San Gabriel Valley Daily Tribune* in San Gabriel, California, and the *Los Angeles Times*, Los Angeles, California, which hired him after the newspaper's reporter Rubén Salazar was killed in 1970 during the Chicano Moratorium protesting the Vietnam War. While working for the *Tribune*, Vásquez won a Sigma Delta Chi award for an investigative article about the city government of Irwindale, where his grandparents were among the first inhabitants. He also held positions as a historian for a book publisher and an account executive for Wilshire Boulevard Public Relations firm.

Vásquez published his first novel *Chicano* in 1970, depicting the epic struggles with the challenges of being mestizo in an Anglo world that is often hostile to those claiming Mexican descent. The story traces patriarch Héctor Sandoval's immigration from México during the Mexican Revolution of 1910 to Los Angeles. *Chicano* spans four generations of the Sandoval family and their attempt to gain acceptance and find happiness in American society. The novel ends on a tragic note, with the quest for assimilation resulting in a son's addiction to heroin and a daughter's death from a botched abortion. Withstanding the test of time, the book remains a popular fixture on high school and college literature syllabi.

Vásquez's next two novels were more optimistic, though not so widely acclaimed or well received. *The Giant Killer* (1977) is an adventure story about a conspiracy to locate different ethnic groups in separate homelands in the United States and a Mexican-American reporter who uncovers the scheme. In *Another Land* (1982), Vásquez creates a romance novel that revolves around two immigrant lovers who are trying to escape from a ruthless criminal. While each novel is different in genre, Vásquez repeats many themes: issue of skin color, assimilation, and the straddling of two cultures.

As a journalist, Vásquez is most noted for his article "Chicano Studies: Sensitivity for Two Cultures," which was reprinted in *The Chicanos: Mexican American Voices* anthology (1971). The essay documents the end of a friendship between two college friends—one of Scandinavian descent and the other of Mexican ancestry—as the two discuss topics from an ethnic studies class. Throughout his newspaper career, Vásquez attempted to explain Mexican American topics to an Anglo audience and explore issues similar in his novels—assimilation and *mestizaje*.

Further Reading

"Contemporary Authors Online." *Gale Group*. http://www.galegroup.com.

Grajeda, Rafael. "José Antonio Villarreal and Richard Vásquez: The Novelist against Himself." In *The Identification and Analysis of Chicano Literature*, edited by Francisco Jiménez. New York: Bilingual Press, 1979.

Rocard, Marcienne. *The Children of the Sun: Mexican Americans in the United States*. Translated by Edward G. Brown, Jr. Tucson, AZ: University of Arizona Press, 1989.

Rodríguez, Joe. "Richard Vásquez." In *Chicano Writers, Third Series*. Vol. 209 of *Dictionary of Literary Biography*, edited by Francisco Lomelí and Carl Shirley. Detroit, MI: Bruccoli Clark Layman Books/Gale Group, 1999.

Serros, Roberto, and Julio A. Martínez. "Richard Vásquez." In *Chicano Literature: A Reference Guide*, edited by Julio A. Martínez and Francisco A. Lomelí. Westport, CT: Greenwood Press, 1985.

Julie Amparano García

Véa, Alfredo, Jr. (1950–   ). A criminal defense lawyer and author of three well-received novels, Alfredo Véa Jr., has been in private practice in San Francisco, California, since 1986. He identifies himself precisely—as a Mexican Yaqui Filipino American—and his novels reflect that same concern for an explicitly named *mestizaje (ethnic hybridity). His first novel, *La Maravilla* (The Marvel or Wonder), published in 1993 by Dutton Press, teems with the multiracial and multicultural reality of Americans in the borderlands of the United States, where it is set in the greater Phoenix, Arizona, area. Likewise, his next two novels, *The Silver Cloud Café* (1996) and *Gods Go Begging* (1999), although set elsewhere, continue Véa's interest in portraying the material actuality of the people and places that surround him. The attorney-author thus follows the creative path of Oscar Zeta Acosta, another Chicano lawyer who authored two of the classic narratives of the *Chicano Renaissance.

Véa was born and grew up in the multiracial and Chicano-identified *barrio area known as Buckeye Road in the Phoenix metropolitan area, a place in the Arizona desert that still exists, although it is greatly changed. Not knowing exactly when he was born, he has chosen June 28, 1950, as his date of birth. His mother, Lorenza, was only thirteen years old when he was born, and she was abandoned by his father after Véa's birth. A mestiza of Yaqui and Spanish ancestry, Lorenza left Buckeye Road when he was six years old, entrusting her son to the care of her parents, Manuel Carvajal and Josephina Castillo de Carvajal, who remained in Arizona. She became a farm laborer in California, migrating from one crop to the next, and eventually giving birth to three other boys and one girl, fathered by different men.

Elements of the future author's autobiography appear in *La Maravilla*, his first novel, with a boy protagonist abandoned by his mother and reared by his *abuelos* (grandparents). Véa writes that the most important influences on his personal growth were his maternal grandparents, who daily exposed him to a rich historical and cultural Mexican/Chicano legacy. They passed their knowledge to him through stories of ancient lore, magic, mysticism, and power that combined the legacy of his grandmother's Iberian Spanish background of Moors and Roma and the history and practices of his grandfather's heritage in the Rio Yaqui Indian tribe with its roots in the ancient Olmecs of México. He states that his Americanization and English language came from listening to the people and voices around him, including the radio and his grandmother's favorite singers (e.g., Sarah Vaughn, the Ink Spots, and Dinah Washington) on the phonograph. The future attorney and novelist's appreciation of American jazz persists, particularly the music of Duke Ellington, Count Basie, and Louis Armstrong. Speaking Yaqui, Spanish, and English languages, Véa's grandfather also learned Gaelic from many years of working as a railroad man with Irish workers. This boyhood within a multilingual, multicultural household instilled him with a strongly felt sense of his Yaqui, Spanish, Mexican, and American mestizo heritage that forms the basis of the global sensitivity and dynamic "marvels" of *La Maravilla*.

As happens to Beto, the boy hero of his first novel, his mother returned to Buckeye Road and reclaimed him from his grandparents when Véa was ten. She took him to California to join his half brothers and half sister and to join her in the fields as a migrant farmworker. During this time Mexican *braceros* (laborers) taught him how to fight in self-defense, and his Filipino friends in Stockton taught him how to read and write. Because of his friendship with French Canadian *braceros* in the northern California fields, Véa studied French in Livermore High School in Alameda County, California. While still in high school, Véa became the sole caretaker of his siblings. He worked, studied, and with the help of his high school teacher Jack Beery, even bought his first house. This Irish German schoolteacher became the *family's friend who mentored him with everything from academics to social and personal etiquette and explains why Véa dedicated his first book to him in 1993.

Decades before that, however, Véa was drafted into the army, and unable to defend his plea as a conscientious objector, he was sent to Vietnam in 1968. Before being drafted, he managed to spend time in some still living Yaqui pueblos in Sonora, México. His grandfather died in 1964 and his grandmother in 1967. After his military service, partly recounted in his third novel, *Gods Go Begging*, he lived for a year in Paris close to the world-famous Louvre Museum, learning to speak French fluently. In 1971 he returned to the University of California at Berkeley, where he earned a dual degree, a Bachelor of Arts in English and a Bachelor of Science in physics. He then entered the law school at Berkeley and received his law degree in 1978.

In 1979 he began working for the Centro Legal de la Raza, and from 1980 to 1986 he served on the staff of the San Francisco Public Defender. Representing poor people in the legal system led directly to his decision to begin his creative writing. While he was working on a death penalty case in a small town in the central California valley in 1989, the presiding judge commented casually that he had not been aware that Mexican lawyers even existed. Fueled by his outrage at the judge's insensitivity and ignorance, Véa began writing his first novel, electing to rent a trailer for the duration of the trial instead of commuting home to the Bay Area so that he could write without interruption. *La Maravilla* was written in a mesmerizing style of *magic realism. The largely autobiographical narrative argues that cultural maintenance and cultural difference, especially in language, are the driving engines of human history and community. The plot covers Beto's education by his *abuelos* and the other inhabitants of Buckeye Road. Like Arturo Islas's *The Rain God* (1984), Sandra *Cisneros's *Caramelo* (2002), and other chronicles of Chicana/o family relationships, *La Maravilla* records a larger cultural and regional history to question the idea of an Anglo, English-only American dream.

Véa's second novel, *The Silver Cloud Café*, published in 1996, continues to raise questions about the Spanish and other Euro-American imperial histories of the Americas. Overflowing with multiple characters and locales, the story about Mexican, Hindu, and Filipino farmworkers combines murder mystery with Gothic horror as a vehicle for the author's historical commentary. The novel is critical of the corrupting effects of unrestricted *globalization and crisscrosses space (with myriad settings in the Philippines, México, and California) and time (with flashbacks to different centuries).

Gods Go Begging, his third novel, extends Véa's fictional memoir to the pain and disillusionment of the Vietnam War. Similar to his first two novels, Véa intertwines the life stories of multiple characters of different *genders, *races, and social classes to follow the Chicano protagonist, Jesse Pasadoble, a criminal defense lawyer, through his posttraumatic stress disorder. The plot is presented through flashbacks to the Vietnamese combat zone and nightmares symbolically linked to three hills: one in Laos, one in Chihuahua, and one in San Francisco. Véa's characterization of a highly motivated advocate, both in law and in literature, affirms his own desire to write for all the poor people he has known and loved because it is important to give voice to who they are and how they came to be.

Further Reading

Bourdreau, John. "In Celebration of All Americans," *Los Angeles Times*, 28 June 1993, E2.

Cantú, Roberto. "Alfredo Véa, Jr." In *Chicano Writers, Third Series*. Vol. 209 of *Dictionary of Literary Biography*, edited by Francisco Lomelí and Carl Shirley. Detroit, MI: Bruccoli Clark Layman Books/Gale Group, 1999.

BJ Manríquez

Velásquez, Nydia (1953–   ). Nydia Margarita Velásquez was the first Puerto Rican woman to be elected to the U.S. Congress, a feat she achieved in 1992.

Velásquez, an outspoken advocate in the areas of voter registration, health care, and family violence, is the Ranking Democrat Member of the Small Business Committee, sits on the Committee on Financial Services, and joins the ranks of Ileana *Ros-Lehtinen, Loretta *Sánchez, and Linda *Sánchez as one of a handful of Latinas exercising their political powers in Congress to address issues that affect the Latino community across the country.

Velásquez was born to Benito and Carmen Luisa Serano in Yabucoa, Puerto Rico. One of nine children, Velásquez inherited a strong social conscience from her father, who was a local political leader when she was growing up. She earned her bachelor's degree at the University of Puerto Rico, then moved to New York, where she earned a master's degree in political science at New York University.

In 1984, she was appointed to the New York City Council. As the first Latina to serve on the council, she became an activist leader of the New York Puerto Rican community. After two years on the council, she was appointed to serve the Commonwealth of Puerto Rico in the United States as national director of the Migration Division and later as head of Community Affairs for Puerto Ricans living in the United States. A Democrat, she went on to represent the twelfth district of New York in the House of Representatives, before joining Congress.

Nydia Velásquez became the first Puerto Rican woman to be elected to the U.S. Congress, in 1992. *Photo by Hispanic Business Inc./Joe Mahoney.*

Further Reading

Vigil, Maurilio. *Hispanics in Congress: A Historical and Political Survey.* New York: University Press of America, 1996.

Alma Alvarez-Smith

Vélez, Lauren (c. 1968–). Actress Lauren Vélez, of Puerto Rican heritage, was born in Brooklyn and raised in Queens, New York. She achieved national attention in her first film, *I Like It Like That* (1994), in which she plays Lisette Linares, a Bronx mother of three who must support her children after her husband is jailed. Prior to her film work, Vélez worked in musical theater, performing with the touring company of *Dreamgirls* and working as Phylicia Rashad's understudy in *Into the Woods*. (Vélez's twin sister Lorraine is a regular performer on Broadway.) Vélez acted in such other films as *I Think I Do* (1997) and *Prince of Central Park* (2000) but is now primarily known for her recurring television roles as Dr. Gloria Nathan on the HBO series *Oz* (1997–2003) and as Detective Nina Moreno on *New York Undercover* (1995–1998).

Arturo J. Aldama

Vélez, Lupe (1908–1944). Lupe Vélez, an early and prolific Latina film actress in the United States and México, was born María Guadalupe Villalobos Vélez on July 18, 1908, in San Luis Potosí, México. Vélez began her acting career on the Mexican stage and quickly immigrated to Hollywood, where she immediately found work in the Laurel and Hardy feature *Sailor Beware!* (1927). Douglas Fairbanks cast her to star opposite him and Mary Pickford in *The Gaucho* (1927) in which, as the mountain girl, she earned rave reviews. She later won roles in such films as *Wolf Song* (1929), *The Cuban Love Song* (1931), *Palooka* (1934), and *Stardust* (1937). The title role in *Hot Pepper* (1933) and her work in *The Girl from Mexico* (1939) earned her the nickname of "The Mexican Spitfire," which was used by the Hollywood gossip columns when chronicling her romances with men like Gary Cooper, Douglas Fairbanks, Charlie Chaplin, Jack Dempsey, director Victor Fleming (*Gone With the Wind, The Wizard of Oz*), Jimmy Durante, and Johnny Weissmuller (Vélez's husband of five years, best known for his portrayal of Tarzan). In the 1940s, less substantial roles were being offered to her, so Vélez, like her countrywoman Dolores *Del Rio, returned to México, where more appealing parts were available. Her portrayal of the title character in the Mexican adaptation of Emile Zola's *Nana* earned Vélez some of the best reviews of her too-short career. At the young age of thirty-six, Vélez died at her home in Beverly Hills, California, on December 12, 1944.

Further Reading

Conner, Floyd. *Lupe Vélez and Her Lovers*. New York: Barricade, 1993.

Rodriguez-Estrada, Alicia. "Dolores Del Rio and Lupe Vélez: Images on and off the Screen, 1925–1944." In *Writing the Range: Race, Class, and Culture in the Women's West*, edited by Susan Armitage and Elizabeth Jameson. Norman: University of Oklahoma Press, 1997.

William Orchard

Vida Loca, La. *See* La Vida Loca.

Vigil, Cipriano (1941–   ). Cipriano Vigil was born in Chamisal, New Mexico, on October 19, 1941, and is regarded as one of the only *Chicano *trovadores* (troubadors) who composes and sings *nueva *cancíon* (new song), a musical and political movement more often associated with Latin America and the Caribbean than with the Mexican borderlands. Vigil's life work has been to preserve the music of the Hispanos (Mexicans of Spanish *criollo* and *mestizo* descent) of New Mexico, and he is regarded as one of the finest folk musicians in the United States. He attended high school until the eleventh grade in Peñasco, New Mexico, and later served in the National Guard for three years. After his tour, Vigil returned to school but dropped out because he felt out of place, being much older than most of the average students. In 1973, he attempted to enroll in the university but was not admitted because he lacked a high school diploma. This did not discourage Vigil, and he finished his GED (general educational diploma). He enrolled in the New Mexico Highlands University in 1974 and obtained a bachelor's degree in music education and later finished his master's degree in bilingual education (1978). He received a five-year scholarship to study in Mexico City (Instituto Nacional de Bellas Artes). He earned another master's degree in *Ethnomusicology and completed his Ph.D. in 1988 from Kennedy Western University.

Since the 1970s, he has worked as a folk musician and storyteller, performing throughout the United States, México, and other counties. Vigil has received many awards for his excellence, promotion, and dissemination of the music of New Mexico. Furthermore, Vigil is a contributing author on a number of books and is a three-time nominee for the National Heritage Award, which recognizes outstanding contributions to U.S. folk music, art, and culture. In 1995, he received the New Mexico's Governor's Award for Excellence in the Arts for his folk music recordings, compositions, and performances. In 2000, his folk music was recognized by the New Mexico Endowment for the Humanities. On four occasions, he presented his music at the Smithsonian Institute in Washington, D.C. (1992, 1994, 1996, 2000).

Vigil and his family are members of the group Los Folkloristas de Nuevo Mexico (The Folklorists of New Mexico); they present educational workshops and perform folk music concerts. Vigil plays seventy-two instruments, and his scholarly interests and political activism attempt to instill pride in New Mexican Hispano culture. He performs in the public schools throughout the Southwest and Northwest. Currently Vigil is on the faculty of the Music Department at a Community College in Espanola, New Mexico, and he holds a strong belief that his students as well as others need to be educated in the Spanish language and culture. Vigil has used his folk music to voice the Hispano rancher's concern over the devastating effects of the takeover and theft of common grazing lands by the U.S. Forest Service and Bureau of Land Management. In his original (1985) composition titled "Se Ve Triste el Hombre" (The Man Looks Sad), he describes how logging has destroyed nature, depleted the water supply, and wrenched communal grazing lands from a colonized and dispossessed people who were once the rightful owners and former ranchers of these lands. Vigil's interests and concerns over nature and folk music have earned him the title of being an American "Living Treasure" by the New Mexico Endowment for the Humanities.

Rose Marie Soto

Villa, Pancho (c. 1878–1923). The given name of the historical figure known as Pancho Villa, one of the folk heroes of the Mexican Revolution of 1910, is Dorotéo Arango, who was born on June 5, 1878, in Hacienda de Río Grande, a ranch in San Juan del Río near Durango in northern México. He grew up working as a peon with his father and siblings on a hacienda; his father died when he was fifteen. He took the name Francisco "Pancho" Villa, at the age of sixteen, when he escaped the area to save his life after shooting one of the wealthy owners of the ranch while defending his sister. Fleeing to the mountains, he spent his teenage years as a fugitive on the run from the rich rancher (*haciendado*) who had violated his sister. He gained a devoted following among local villagers for his generosity and charismatic leadership qualities. Thus at an early age began the still robust "Viva Villa" and "Villa Vive" (Long live Villa and Villa lives) legends.

As a modern legend of history, Villa's life and death are shrouded in mystery. Both his Mexican and North American enemies perceived him as a murdering bandit who thought nothing of slaughtering innocent people and destroying their villages. Conversely, millions of his followers, both north and south of the Mexican border, thought of him as a freedom-fighting Robin Hood figure compelled to oppose the tyranny of President Porfirio Díaz's government to rid the country of centuries of political and economic oppression. His place in history was secured in 1916 when he led a raid on the town of Columbus, New Mexico, a brazen attack that led to his pursuit and eventual assassination in 1923 by operatives of the U.S. Army that had been dispatched to capture him. Villa has been portrayed in American popular culture in both lights: as a ravaging bandit (*bandido*), the early-twentieth-century government label for a Mexican resister, and as a courageous revolutionary (*revolucionario*) Villa, Emiliano *Zapáta, and Che *Guevara were recuperated as icons of resistance by *Chicano Movement activists in the 1960s and 1970s who were seeking historical models for their cause.

The facts of his life are somewhat more contradictory. Many favorable accounts assign Villa an important role as a fighter against injustice in the grassroots resistance known as the Mexican Revolution, but historians have documented that he actually entered the anti-Porfiriato (i.e., Díaz régime) resistance movement relatively late in 1910 after the intense action and violence had already started. He sided with Francisco Madero's forces against the

Pancho Villa was a folk hero of the Mexican Revolution of 1910. *Courtesy of the Cordelia Candelaria Private Collection.*

Porfiriato, but a series of disputes over who would control the northern regions led him to split with Madero's followers in a decision that sealed his fate outside the main civil war action near Mexico City. After the 1913 assassination of Madero, Villa organized a band of several thousand men that gained renown as the famous Division of the North. He joined forces with those of Venustiano Carranza, another revolutionary, and began to rebel against the increasingly dictatorial rule of a former ally, General Victoriano Huerta Ortega, who took over after Madero. Villa became governor of the state of Chihuahua in 1913, and he and Carranza's forces had a decisive victory over Huerta in 1914. They entered Mexico City as triumphant revolutionary saviors, a victory that was shortlived when their mutual rivalry for power split their harmony. With Zapáta and his followers, Villa and his force fled to the northern mountains to try to regain control over the region. To prove his might over that of the Carranza government and to seize needed weaponry and supplies,

Villa decided to raid Columbus in 1916. His pursuit by the American military forced Villa to wage guerrilla activities against both the United States and Carranza's regime until the latter was overthrown in 1920. At that point, he agreed to retire from politics and warfare to his ranch in Parral in the familiar regions of northern México. He was assassinated on June 20, 1923.

Scholars report that Villa did not deny that he was a bandit, but he insisted that he was not a murderer and only used lethal force when he and his followers were attacked or betrayed. U.S. government reports nonetheless contained a vast assortment of anecdotes that were spread in newspaper stories and eventually made their way into the historiography of México and the *folklore of America's *barrios and borderlands. Ultimately, Villa's historical biography, however fascinating, is overshadowed by the paradoxes of his immense legend. Historians generally agree that only a major figure of significant accomplishments can sustain such legendary force over time and across generations. Some argue that even the legendary Pancho Villa could not sustain the demands of myth. As a shrewed, barely literate, and mostly nonpolitical regional strongman, the Villa figure is perhaps most fascinating in the pop culture spinoffs of his legend. For instance, he is forever memorialized as one of the iconic Mexican *revolucionarios* wearing the crisscrossed cartridge belts of resistance *fashion and clothing atop his famous steed, Siete Ligas (Seven Leagues), seen in the 1914 silent movie *The Life of General Villa*, directed by Raoul Walsh with actual film footage of Villa himself. A similar image appears in the 1952 hit *Viva Zapáta*, starring Marlon Brando. The well-publicized made-for-HBO feature-length movie *And Starring Pancho Villa as Himself*, aired in 2003 and starring Antonio Banderas, proves that the strong vitality of the Villa myth continues into the twenty-first century.

Further Reading

Katz, Friedrich. *Imágenes de Pancho Villa*. Mexico City: Ediciones Era/CONACULTA, INAH, 1999.

Katz, Friedrich. *The Life and Times of Pancho Villa*. Stanford, CA: Stanford University Press, 1998.

Meier, Matt S., and Feliciano Ribera. *Mexican Americans, American Mexicans: From Conquistadors to Chicanos*. New York: Hill and Wang, 1993.

Cordelia Chávez Candelaria

Villancicos. *Villancicos* are a popular type of Christmas music that originated in the Middle Ages and remain part of cultural tradition in Latin America, México, and the United States. *Villancicos* are typically anonymous songs with anywhere from two to five verses. Since the Middle Ages these songs have been performed in rural Spanish-speaking regions. *Villancico* comes from *villano* or *campesino*, which means sheepherder or farmer or rancher. The music was mainly used during the festivities at Christmas but was not limited to the holidays. Today *villancicos* are remembered mainly as Christmas songs that are sung to commemorate the birth of Jesus.

Further Reading

"Los Villancicos." www.tema.es/pcrsonal/Tsietes/q@!!Ull4!qi!e.bl!q.

Seth Nolan

Villanueva, Alma (1944–   ). Alma Luz Villanueva is an award-winning poet and novelist, known for eliciting a sense of hope from readers while writing about injustice, suffering, and human weakness. She has been lauded by literary critics for bringing to light issues of female identity within the confines of masculine Chicano culture. Her first novel, *The Ultraviolet Sky* (1988), won the Before Columbus American Book Award in 1989 and was chosen for New American Writing in 1990. Her second novel, *Naked Ladies* (1994), won the PEN Oakland Josephine Miles Award in 1994. Villanueva also has been recognized for her poetry, which has been translated into Spanish, Dutch, French, Italian, German, and Japanese. Her poetry received first prize in the genre in the University of California at Irvine's (UCI) annual Chicano literary competition in 1977, and her poems were published in the UCI *Third Chicano Literary Prize* anthology that same year.

Villanueva was born on October 4, 1944, in Lompoc, California, to a Mexican mother and a German father she never knew. The writer writes that the people who had the greatest impact on her life were her maternal grandparents. Her Spanish-speaking grandfather had a college degree in philosophy, wrote poetry, edited a newspaper in Hermosillo, México, and was a Baptist minister. Her grandmother, a Yaqui Indian from the northern Mexican state of Sonora, reared her in the Mission District of San Francisco, where she taught the future writer about her Mexican and German roots, as well as about the forces of nature. Villanueva's grandmother died when she was eleven years old, leaving her directionless, and at fifteen Villanueva found herself pregnant. She dropped out of school, married, had two more children, and worked odd jobs to maintain her family while her husband was shipped overseas with the U.S. Marines. She has written that her grandmother's influence surfaced to consciousness in her years later, spurring Villanueva to independence and a reawakening of her cultural values. She obtained a divorce, fled city life, and moved to a farm to gain direct contact with nature. Eventually she moved to the Sierra Nevada mountain range in central California, far from any major city, and spent the next four years there. She credits this retreat into nature with giving her writing its strong emphasis on nature.

Villanueva did not start writing until she was in her early thirties and attended City College of San Francisco, and subsequently earned a Master's of Fine Arts in creative writing from Vermont College at Norwich University in 1984. Villanueva was not entirely inexperienced with poetry and writing as her grandmother had exposed her to traditional stories and poems in her childhood. Her first novel, *The Ultraviolet Sky*, received favorable reviews for its portrayal of Rosa, an artist trying to ignore the chaos and uncertainty of her life—including a crumbling marriage, an unplanned pregnancy, and a son quickly coming of age—by painting the perfect sky. Using art as a vehicle for exploring autobiographical memories served her needs as a novelist effectively. Her next novel was also favorably received. In *Naked Ladies*, Villanueva tackles issues ranging from rape, incest, AIDS, and cancer to marital infidelity and racial violence from the viewpoint of four very different women. Both books appear on many college literature syllabi.

In her fiction as in much of her poetry, womanhood and female sexuality are central subjects, as Villanueva examines the ways in which women overcome male dominance and society's entrenched patriarchal conventions. Identifying and celebrating the strengths of womanhood are themes that can be seen in her very first writings. Her first book of poetry, *Bloodroot* (1977), for example, includes forty-seven poems designed for the most part to show that all people belong to the same unity. She maintains that although humans are all interrelated, many men in particular are afraid of accepting this fact, while most women embrace it, thereby producing a major *gender difference that historically leads to misunderstanding and conflict. Villanueva's second book, *Mother, May I?* (1978), is a lengthy, autobiographical poem that recounts her experiences as a woman in a masculine-oriented society. The poem chronicles her early youth, a wonderful time spent with her grandmother, then moves to the violent world of the streets and parks where children are molested, and ends with Villanueva's tough life as a young, single mother living in the worst part of San Francisco. She presents these periods emotionally and vividly with remembered scenes from her girlhood to show that they are reaffirming and demonstrate the perseverance of the female spirit. Her novel *Luna's California Poppies* (2002) has a similar autobiographical theme, with the central character, twelve-year-old Desire, writing an epistolary diary to the *Virgin of Guadalupe. Desire writes about not knowing her father, being abandoned by her mother, her love for her Yaqui grandmother, and her life growing up in a barrio. Villanueva is also the author of other collections of poetry, including *Life Span* (1984); *La Chingada* (1985); *Planet* (1993), which won the Latin American Writers Institute Poetry Award (1994); *Desire* (1998); and *VIDA* (2002). In addition, Villanueva has contributed poems to high school textbooks, published poems and essays in periodicals, and written collections of short fiction. She teaches creative writing at Antioch University in California and is married to Chicano artist Wilfredo Castaño.

Further Reading

Daydí-Tolson, Santiago. *Chicano Writers, 2nd Series*. Vol. 122 of *Dictionary of Literary Biography*, edited by Francisco Lomelí and Carl Shirley. Detroit, MI: Bruccoli Clark Layman Book/Gale Group, 1992.

Sánchez, Marta E. "The Birthing of the Poetic 'I' in Alma Villanueva's *Mother, May I?*: The Search for a Female Identity." In her *Contemporary Chicana Poetry: A Critical Approach to an Emerging Literature*. Berkeley: University of California Press, 1985.

Julie Amparano García

Villaseñor, Victor (1940–   ). Author Victor Villaseñor's writings have helped expose millions of Americans to the racism, brutality, hardships, and the triumphs and nobility of the Mexican immigrant heritage, which comprises part of the historical roots of Mexican Americans dating from 1848 and the *Treaty of Guadalupe Hidalgo. The roots of another large Mexican-American and Chicana/Chicano population precede that period and extend back to the earliest period of New Spain (1540) and the later Mexican era (1810). Although addressing both, Villaseñor began his writing career by shedding light on the issues of *immigration and biculturalism with his first novel *Macho!* (1973). His bestselling novel *Rain of Gold* (1991) emphasized the Mexican American assimilation process through an epic account of his own family's travails as immigrants. Another important Villaseñor credit is for writing the screenplay for the acclaimed made-for-TV *film *The *Ballad of Gregorio Cortez* (1982), with the assistance of a committee of Chicana/o scholars who assisted in adapting the source material from Américo Paredes's folklore scholarship *With His Pistol in His Hand: A Border Ballad and Its Hero* (1958). Originally initiated and sponsored by the *National Council of La Raza, the final script presents turn-of-the-century Mexican-American border history and cultural issues to a broad American audience.

Born on May 11, 1940, in Carlsbad, California, Victor Edmundo Villaseñor was reared by his Mexican immigrant parents, Salvador and Lupe Villaseñor, on a ranch in nearby Oceanside along with his brother and three sisters. The author reports that Spanish was the primary language spoken by the family, and the children attended school with limited English-speaking ability. As a result, neither his parents nor teachers discovered that Villaseñor was dyslexic and having difficulty learning how to read. Struggling with low grades, the demoralized future successful writer, angry and confused, quit high school in his junior year to work on his family's ranch.

A transformation occurred for Villaseñor when he turned nineteen and went to live in México, where he discovered Mexican art, music, literature, and other aspects of a rich cultural heritage about which he knew little. He returned to Southern California the following year, taught himself to read, and began auditing English and creative writing classes at the University of California at Los Angeles; inspired by James Joyce's classic autobiographical novel *Portrait of the Artist as a Young Man* (1916), he resolved himself to writing novels focused on Mexican and Chicano culture. He aimed to convey its bilingual, bicultural achievements and values, as well as the burdens and problems of marginalization. Biographical blurbs on his books note that he wrote nine novels and sixty-five short stories while supporting himself by working at a variety of seasonal labor jobs. He recounts that success did not come easily for him and that he toiled ten years for his first publishing contract, receiving over 250 rejection letters in the process. Eventually *Macho!* was published by Bantam, the largest paperback publisher in the world, and received favorable notices. One *Los Angeles Times* (September 23, 1973) critic compared it to the writing of John Steinbeck in its focus on the Mexican and Chicana/o working poor and in its use of interchapters alternating the fictional plot with journalistic reports. About an undocumented immigrant from Michoácan, the book has sold over 60,000 copies in part because of Villaseñor's active promotion of the book on his own.

Villaseñor's two subsequent books are the nonfiction *Jury: The People vs. Juan Corona* (1977), a chronicle of the infamous Yuba City, California, serial murder case and murder trial, and *Rain of Gold* (1991), an epic saga about his own family's survival of the Mexican Revolution and immigration to the United States. Unable to market it to New York commercial publishers, the author sold it to Arte Público Press, the largest publisher of Hispanic literature in the United States. *Rain of Gold* was greeted with nearly unanimous positive reviews and became a hardcover bestseller in western states markets, particularly for high school and college classes, even though the noncommercial Arte Público Press had very limited resources for marketing and distribution. In 1992 Bantam-Doubleday-Dell published the first paperback edition of *Rain of Gold*, and it became a national bestseller, placing Villaseñor on the map of commercial literary success, including its translation and publication in seven languages.

In national demand for speaking engagements, Villaseñor writes that he is also considering requests for movie rights for his books. Arte Público published Villaseñor's next book, *Walking Stars: Stories of Magic and Power* (1994), a spinoff collection of young-adult stories related to *Rain of Gold*. Other books include *Wild Steps of Heaven* (1996), a chronological prelude to *Rain of Gold*, and *Thirteen Senses: A Memoir* (2001), the sequel to *Rain of Gold* and continuation of the story of the Villaseñor clan. With his wife Barbara Block (whose father Charles Block was an influential Bantam editor for many years), the author still lives on the California ranch where he grew up. An adaptation of Villaseñor's family trilogy for the stage premiered in August 2003 as part of the Steinbeck Festival in Salinas, California, an event he helped organize and for which he served as the John Steinbeck Festival Founding Chair.

Further Reading

Kanellos, Nicolás. "Victor Villaseñor." In *Chicano Writers, 3rd Series*. Vol. 209 of *Dictionary of Literary Biography*, edited by Francisco Lomelí and Carl Shirley. Detroit, MI: Bruccoli Clark Layman/Gale Group, 1999.
Victor Villaseñor Homepage. http://www.victorvillasenor.com.

Julie Amparano García and BJ Manríquez

Viramontes, Helena María   (1954–   ). Author Helena María Viramontes is one of the acclaimed contributors to the flourishing period of Chicana and Latina women writing occurring in the 1980s and continuing in the twenty-first century. Best known for the high literary quality of her books *The Moths and Other Stories* (1985) and *Under the Feet of Jesus* (1995), Viramontes began receiving honors for her work early in her career. She won the *Statement Magazine* first prize for fiction from California State University for her short stories "Requiem for the Poor" and "The Broken Web" in 1977 and 1978, respectively, as well as first prize for short fiction in the prestigious University of California at Irvine Chicano Literary Contest for "Birthday" in 1979. Among her other prestigious awards was receipt of a 1989 fellowship from the National Endowment for the Arts (NEA) and the John Dos Passos Prize in 1995 in recognition of her cumulative achievement as a writer.

Viramontes was born on February 26, 1954, in East Los Angeles, California, to a construction worker father and homemaker mother. She was one of the younger siblings in the *family that consisted of three brothers and five sisters. Among her clearest and dearest recollections, according to her published remarks, is that her parents made their home a welcome haven to members of their extended family and friends from across California's border with México. She graduated from the same Garfield High School that has become one of Latina/o pop culture's icons as a result of the renown it received from the movie *Stand and Deliver* (1988), depicting the inspiring story of math teacher Jaime Escalante. After graduation she went to the scholastically demanding Immaculate Heart College, where she recalls joining only four other Chicanas enrolled at the institution. The future author acknowledges that the experiences of her childhood and elements of her family environment provided her with a rich reservoir for her fiction and outlook as a professor. With her Bachelor of Arts degree from Immaculate Heart, she was admitted into the rigorous and highly selective graduate creative writing program at the University of California at Irvine. Although she left the program before finishing, after she began publishing her work, she managed to complete the remaining requirements of her academic studies, and in 1985 she received a Master's of Fine Arts in creative writing.

Like many other Latina/o writers and artists, Viramontes first published her work in the little magazines of the alternative press that emerged from the *Chicano Movement. Her early work appeared in venues like *XhismArte Magazine*, the journal *Maize* founded by celebrated poet Alurista, and in *Cuentos: Stories by Latinas* (1983), a widely read collection coedited by distinguished writer Cherríe *Moraga. Out of this period of writing and publishing, Viramontes succeeded in contracting her first book, *The Moths and Other Stories* (1985), with the bilingual house Arte Público Press, based in Houston, Texas. During this same period she helped organize at the University of California at Irvine one of the first and among the most respected literary conferences in the United States devoted to Chicana and Latina writers. The proceedings from that conference included writings by Viramontes and were published by Arte Público Press in 1985 as *Beyond Stereotypes: A Critical Analysis of Chicana Literature*. She participated as well in the second Chicana writers conference at Irvine and with distinguished literary scholar María Herrera-Sobek coedited a second important collection of proceedings and other work, *Chicana Creativity and Criticism* (1988).

Continuing her flourishing literary career, Viramontes's application for an NEA Fellowship was successful, and the 1989 award enabled her to attend the Sundance Institute and participate in a workshop presented by Nobel Prize laureate Colombian Gabriel García Márquez. She went on to publish a second collection of her short fiction, *Paris Rats in E.L.A.*, in 1993, and it provided the basis for a screenplay she wrote that was produced by the American Film Institute. That same year her anthology *Chicana (W)rites: On Word and Film*, coedited again with María Herrera Sobek, was published by Third Woman Press. Soon after, she published her first novel, *Under the Feet of Jesus* (1995), which, along with her short fiction, helped establish Viramontes as a critically acclaimed writer and chronicler of contemporary Chicana/o culture in the United States. *Under the Feet of Jesus* is narrated by thirteen-year-old Estrella, a young California migrant worker, who dreams of becoming a geologist. A coming-of-age story, in a California filled with deprivations and hard labor, Estrella relates her rebellious life in the new temporary home with her younger siblings, her mother Petra, and Perfecto, the man who is not her father. Viramontes dedicated this novel to her parents, who met each other while picking cotton, as well as to the memory of César *Chávez, leader of the United Farmworkers.

Her stories and novel are based on her life, her family, and her friends with especially perceptive treatment of the complex lives of women within domestic households and as indispensable contributors to their communities and culture. Many of her themes deal with *gender discrimination against Chicana women and the social issues of racial and sexual restrictions. Throughout her career Viramontes has been concerned with illustrating the often overwhelming tribulations that Chicana mothers, wives, and daughters face. She uses stream-of-consciousness, magic for literary symbols, and multiple narrators showing the thoughts and emotions of the women characters. Other themes in her works include politics, religion, and sexuality. Her influences include Gabriel García Márquez, Ana *Castillo, Sandra *Cisneros, Alice Walker, Ntozake Shange, and Toni Morrison. Her latest novel, *Their Dogs Came with Them*, published in 1996, is about the brutality of the Spanish conquest of the Americas. An assistant professor of English at Cornell University, Viramontes is a consultant for the Michigan Technical University Writing Center Latino Read-In. She also counsels Chicano students at Cornell's Summer College.

Further Reading

Saldivar-Hull, Sonia. "Helen Maria Viramontes." In *Chicano Writers*. Vol. 122 of *Dictionary of Literary Notable Hispanic American Women*, edited by Francisco Lomelí and Carl Shirley. Detroit, MI: Gale Group, 1993. 322–325.

Voices From the Gaps: Women Writers of Color. http://voices.cla.umn.edu/authors/HelenaMariaViramontes.html.

BJ Manríquez

Virgin of Guadalupe. As a symbolic icon, the Virgin of Guadalupe (Virgen de Guadalupe) resides on a lofty pedestal of combined religious, political, and broad cultural meaning among Mexicans and Mexican Americans, regardless of professed sectarian religious beliefs. Known as the patron saint of México, the Virgin of Guadalupe refers to the brown-skinned madonna representation who, according to the Roman Catholic tradition of miracles, appeared before the peasant Indian Juan Diego on December 12, 1531 (also reported as December 9, 1531, in some accounts). This account of her miraculous apparition on Mount Tepeyac, a hill that had formerly been associated with the indigenous worship of the goddess of motherhood and fertility Tonántzin, inextricably linked the Spanish/European Virgin Mary with native beliefs in a transformational example of *mestizaje* (native Mesoamerican and Spaniard hybridity). During the epoch of Spanish conquest and early colonialism, the Church's strategic use of the Virgin of Guadalupe miracle helped convert thousands of the Indians who survived the invaders' violence and diseases that made the conquest possible. The Church built an official structure, La Basílica de Nuestra Señora de Guadalupe (the Basilica of Our Lady of Guadalupe), in a northern neighborhood of Mexico City called Villa de Guadalupe Hidalgo and very near Tepeyac where the two Virgin Mary apparitions reportedly occurred in 1531. Pope Benedict XIV issued a papal bull in 1754 officially canonizing la Virgen de Guadalupe as a saint and decreeing her to be the official patroness and protector of New Spain.

Besides her brown-toned representation, other distinguishing features of the Virgin of Guadalupe are associated with the image believed to have been left as a sign of her appearance to Juan Diego on his *tilma* (cloak), a material relic that still hangs in the Basilica of Our Lady of Guadalupe. Her symbolic features include a spiked aura of light surrounding her image at the base of which lay a large bouquet of roses representing the fresh flowers she presented to Juan Diego in her appearance. Scholars of the Aztec language Nahuátl believe that the native Indians called the Tonántzin-inspired appearance "Tlecuauhtlacupeuh" (pronounced "Guadalupe" by the Spaniards), meaning "la que viene volando de la luz como el águila de fuego" (she who flies from the light like an eagle of fire). This merging of indigenous popular mysticism with the European Catholic tradition of mariolatry (i.e., Virgin Mary worship) had a profound impact on unifying the disparate populations and cultures into a mestizo society.

A cultural icon, the Virgin of Guadalupe is a powerful symbol of the Mexican independence movement, representing feminine strength and compassion. *Photo by Emmanuel Sánchez Carballo.*

The Guadalupe's prominence as a cultural and historical icon intensified in 1810 when the emancipator priest Miguel Hidalgo y Costilla, who was part of the initiators of the Mexican resistance against Spain's dominance, placed her image on his flag of freedom. She thus became a powerful symbol of the Mexican independence movement that has been raised repeatedly in other movements against tyranny. The de facto historical symbolism of the Virgin was further strengthened when the barrio of Villa de Guadalupe Hidalgo itself served as the site where the treaty between the United States and México was signed to end the U.S.-Mexican War on February 2, 1848. The signing of the *Treaty of Guadalupe Hidalgo is imprinted indelibly in the collective Mexican and Chicana/o memory as the end of one cultural identity and the birth of a hyphenated consciousness. After the Mexican Revolution of 1910 the government policy of México became secular, and church and state were officially separated. Nevertheless, the popularity of the Virgin of Guadalupe and the iconography devoted to her in arts and crafts were unaffected by the legal change.

Many contemporary historians, anthropologists, and religious studies scholars identify her as a singularly important master symbol of cultural unity that helped pacify resistance to colonialism and eased the transition to a hybrid mestizo society and eventual nation. Each year, hundreds of thousands of pilgrims from all over the world come to the church, the holiest in México, which was given the status of a basilica by Pope Pius X in 1904. The present church, or Old Basilica, was constructed on the site of an earlier sixteenth-century church and was finished in 1709. When the structure of the Old Basilica became dangerous because of its sinking base foundations, a modern church called the New Basilica was built nearby, and it became the new home of the original *tilma* image of the Virgin of Guadalupe that attracts millions of pilgrims every year. In 2004 masses are still held every hour on the hour in the Basilica to accommodate the capacity crowd of pilgrims who visit the church to pay homage to Nuestra Señora de Guadalupe (Our Lady of Guadalupe).

Among Mexican Americans the Guadalupe symbol was adopted by farmworker organizer César *Chávez as a key banner icon during the United Farmworkers strikes and marches of the late 1960s and 1970s. Her image is prevalent in the artwork produced during and since the *Chicano Movement on murals, picket signs, votive candles, lapel pins, t-shirts, *lowriders, yard shrines, and countless other artifacts. She also is the center of the annual play *La Virgen de Tepeyac* (The Virgin of Tepeyac) performed by El *Teatro Campesino in San Juan Bautista, California, as a tribute to grassroots faith and popular community traditions. In this and millions of other forms, the Guadalupe symbol extends beyond the traditional *jamaicas* (folk fairs or church bazaars) where varieties of her image are staple articles sold to raise money for charity.

In the late twentieth century many Chicana and Mexican feminists began to challenge the idea of the Guadalupe image as having only one unitary, Church-defined meaning. They sought to reclaim her representation for modern twentieth-century advocates of women's rights as an alternative to the patriarchal fundamentalism of the Roman Catholic Church that continues to deny women full participation in its activities. These modern views and reinterpretations have been respectful attempts to capture changed attitudes toward faith and *gender, even though many traditionalists have been offended by their representations. Some of these reinterpretations include such popular culture portrayals of the Guadalupe by Chicana artists Yolanda M. *López, Inez Hernández, and Alma López. Other contemporary renderings appear in the tattoos, *paño* (handkerchief) sketches, and leatherwork of *pinto* artists. Whatever the approach and wherever the imaging occurs, they collectively join the millions of forms that have been made for over 400 years in tribute to the feminine strength and compassion that lies at the core of the Tlecuauhtlacupeuh, or la Virgen de Guadalupe, powers.

Further Reading

Castro, Rafaela G. *Chicano Folklore: A Guide to the Folktales, Traditions, Rituals and Religious Practices of Mexican-Americans*. New York: Oxford University Press, 2001.

McCracken, Ellen. *New Latina Narrative: The Feminist Space of Postmodern Ethnicity*. Tucson: University of Arizona Press, 1999.

Sorell, Víctor A. "Guadalupe's Emblematic Presence Endures in New Mexico: Investing the Body with the Virgin's Miraculous Image." In *Nuevomexicano Cultural Legacy: Forms, Agencies, and Discourse*, edited by Francisco Lomelí, V.A. Sorell, and Genaro M. Padilla. Albuquerque: University of New Mexico Press, 2002.

Wolf, Eric. R. *Sons of the Shaking Earth*. Chicago: University of Chicago Press, 1959.

Cordelia Chávez Candelaria

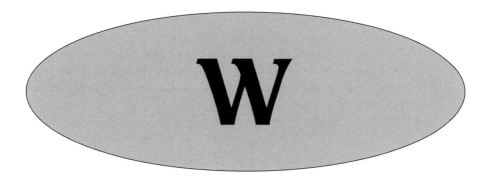

Wedding Customs. Wedding customs in the Latino community are as varied and diverse as the culture itself, with traditions and rituals originating in different regional areas, enmeshed in the cultures of Mexican, Chicana/o, Puerto Rican, and Cuban households. Some customs, often originally connected to social or economic factors, have strayed considerably from tradition and now have only a faint resemblance to the original practice, while others, usually those stemming from religious or spiritual beliefs, have remained virtually intact over the years. In today's popular culture, many couples choose to intertwine old and new customs to celebrate their nuptials in contemporary fashion while expressing pride in their cultural heritage and maintaining a connection to the past.

Courtship, engagement, wedding, and marriage customs in the Latino community are traditionally very formal and demonstrate a high level of respect for all individuals involved. By examining the old customs, traditions, and rituals, we can see how many have carried forward, while others experienced mutations over the years, bringing them to the present versions observed by couples today.

Traditionally, once a young man selects his bride, a series of formal meetings ensue. Out of respect for his bride-to-be, and her parents, the young man does not simply ask the young woman to marry him; rather, he and his parents select two or three *portadores* (bearers) to represent the young man in asking for her hand in marriage. The *portadores* are mature, well-respected men in the community, sometimes an uncle or godfather of the young man, who initially approach the parents of the young lady, to schedule a meeting to discuss the possibility of a marriage. If the parents agree to the meeting, the *portadores* return at a later, specified time and date to present a *petición de mano* (literally translated, it is petition of hand, but it means they are asking for her hand). The parents of the bride-to-be do not respond immediately but are said to *pedir un plazo* (ask for a due date), which allows them time to consider the proposal. When they have reached a decision, the *portadores* are called back to the *family home for the response. If the marriage proposal is accepted, the family puts flowers and candles in front of the Santo (Saint); this is referred to as *puesto de flores* (placing of flowers). The tradition of using *portadores* is practiced today to a lesser degree than in the past, but it is still observed in some areas.

This elaborate and drawn-out process seems cumbersome by today's standards, but at the core of this is an integral key to the culture and Latino community, called *compadrazgo*, a network of kinship that ties people together. The building of this network begins at birth through the identification of godparents for a baby's *bautismo* (baptism), continues through the inclusion of godparents of Communion and/or Confirmation (rites of passage in the Catholic Church), and expands further through wedding rituals. Once a marriage proposal is accepted, a courtship begins that extends beyond the couple and involves both families. It is part of the *compadrazgo*, the extending of the kinship network, that will provide love, guidance, and support for the couple throughout their married life. This courtship, known in today's culture as the engagement period, brings the families together for meals, gift exchanges, celebrations, and activities that will allow them opportunities to get to know each other. One of the first events or meals shared by the families is the engagement dinner, where the families come together and the parents bestow their blessings on the couple.

Shortly after the marriage proposal is accepted, the young man is expected to start supporting his bride-to-be financially, as a way of demonstrating to her parents that he is capable of taking care of their daughter. In addition, he is expected to pay for the wedding and associated feast. After the marriage, he will move his new bride into his parent's home, where they live until they can afford their own home. Like the practice of using *portadores*, some of these practices are observed in varying degrees, while some have undergone transformations to suit more updated perspectives.

The wedding rituals usually begin with a traditional wedding mass. In the past, the tradition was to observe the wedding mass early in the morning, although that is a practice that has been modified so that any time is acceptable in today's society. Tradition and Catholic religion dictate that when a couple gets married, they will be sponsored by *padrinos* (godparents). One of the biggest decisions to be made when planning a wedding in the Latino culture is the selection of the *primero padrinos* (primary godparents). The *primero padrinos* are a mature, married couple who will help the young couple prepare for their wedding, guide them through their marriage, and provide emotional and spiritual support throughout their lives. This is a major, lifelong responsibility that in the Latino culture is a great honor.

When a couple decides to get married, they already have their respective parents and *padrinos de bautismo* (godparents for baptism) in their support network. The *primero padrinos*, also known as *padrinos de boda* (wedding godparents), now become part of a triadic relationship for the bride and the groom. The inclusion of the godparents in the spiritual and emotional nurturing of the couple is akin to an extension of the families in an intimate, close-knit, trusting relationship that lasts a lifetime.

On the day of the wedding, the *primero padrinos* will sign the marriage certificate as witnesses to the marriage, they will help with the church, candles, and flowers, and they will give the *brindes* (wedding toast). In addition to the *primero padrinos*, five other sets of *padrinos* are selected to participate in the wedding rituals. Each set of godparents presents the wedding couple with one of five significant gifts: the *lazo* (lasso), *arras* (gold coins), bouquet, bible/rosary, and *cojines* (cushions). These gifts, based on religious and spiritual values, have withstood the test of time and continue to be observed today by many couples.

The *lazo* resembles a necklace or a rosary and comes in the shape of a figure eight (8), which happens to be the mathematical symbol for infinity. Like a rosary, it has a crucifix hanging from the middle, is often made of beads, and can come in a variety of materials, such as pearls, crystals, satin, or a floral garland. During the wedding ceremony, the *padrinos de lazo* (godparents of the lasso) place one loop of the figure eight over the shoulders of the bride and the other loop over the shoulders of the groom. This ritual physically binds the pair together and symbolizes a lasting union. While in this position, the couple receives a blessing from the priest or person performing the ceremony; then the *padrinos* remove the *lazo* for safe keeping. The *lazo* is a wedding momento that is kept and cherished forever. In a contemporary twist, couples may choose to go a less formal route and not to have *padrinos de lazo* and instead have their parents do the draping of the lasso for the blessing.

Arras are gold coins that are presented to the wedding couple to symbolize financial wealth. In the past, when gold was available, the coins were real gold and represented true monetary value. As gold has become too expensive to have readily available, the coins used in today's wedding ceremonies are facsimiles of gold coins and usually can be purchsed in stores specializing in wedding items. In some cultures, the tradition is to present thirteen coins, while in other cultures or regional areas, they present ten coins. In most Latino celebrations, the groom presents his bride with the coins by letting them run through his fingers, into her hands, symbolizing that he will support her and bring her his wealth. In a more contemporary practice, after the groom presents the coins to his bride, she turns around and lets the coins run through her fingers, back into his hands, symbolizing a common sharing of wealth. In some areas of México and in Colombia, only ten coins are presented, and it is understood that the coins represent the Ten Commandments, which will guide the couple through their marriage. In Puerto Rico, the coins, representing the bride's dowry, are placed in a small basket and left on display during the wedding celebration. After the celebration, the coins are kept by the couple to ensure good fortune and prosperity in their future together, although in some areas, the coins are offered to the Church.

A set of *padrinos* gifts the bride with two bouquets for the wedding day. Traditionally, one bouquet was carried down the aisle during the ceremony, then left for the Virgin Mary in the Church. The second bouquet was tossed to the unmarried female guests during the festivities.

Another set of *padrinos* presents the couple with a rosary and a bible during the wedding ceremony. These significant religious articles are meant to reinforce the importance of religion in the marriage. These godparents are known as *padrinos de libro* (godparents of the bible).

The fifth set of godparents identified for the wedding ceremony are the *padrinos de cojines* (godparents of the cushions). In a traditional Catholic wedding mass, the couple spends much of the ceremony kneeling down before the priest, so godparents gift the couple with a pair of cushions to be used at the wedding.

The traditional Latino wedding is a major production when considering the numbers of people that are involved in the wedding ceremony alone. In addition to the six sets of godparents that are selected to participate in the wedding ceremony, the bride usually selects numerous bridesmaids to attend her. The number of attendants is not set in stone, although traditionally, the tendency was to have many. In today's observances, mostly due to economics, the numbers are fewer, although there still is no set rule or symbolism regarding how many attendants one has. The maid of honor will usually be a sister of the bride, unless she has no sister; then the honor is deferred to a sister of the groom. If neither has a sister, the bride then selects a cousin to be her maid of honor. The wedding ceremony includes a ring bearer and flower girl, dressed as miniature versions of the bride and groom. There is no "best man" in a traditional Latino wedding, although there are as many male "escorts" as there are bridesmaids. The bride is typically walked down the aisle and "given away" by her father. The groom is walked down the aisle and "given away" by both parents. In some observances, the parents stand at the altar with the wedding couple. A variation of this might be for the *primero padrinos* to stand with the couple at the altar. Sometimes the formal procession of getting the wedding participants in and out of the church can take as long as the ceremony itself.

The bride has always traditionally worn a white wedding dress, with a *mantilla* (lace veil) draped on her head, symbolizing virginity. In contemporary celebrations, the white dress has made way for various shades of ecru, off-white, champagne, and other light colors that allow the bride to express herself. In addition, the traditional *mantilla* is often replaced by veils adorned with elaborate head ornaments, tiaras, or simple headbands.

A very important part of the wedding process, most notably practiced in New Mexico and Colorado, is the ritual of the *entrego de novios* (bestowal of the wedding couple). This ritual, often performed to music with special verses written about the wedding couple, may be done during the church ceremony or postponed until the reception. The *entrego de novios* is an opportunity for the parents of the wedding couple, and at times including the grandparents, to pledge or bestow their child to the new partner and their family. In much the same manner as a toast is given in Anglo weddings, the *entrego de novios* is like an extended toast, during which the parents formally acknowledge the couple coming together in this new union as husband and wife, with the extended families pledging their support. After the blessings have been bestowed on the couple, they are presented to the guests as husband and wife. If the ritual is performed at the reception, after being presented to the guests, the wedding couple leads the entire wedding party in a procession called the *marcha* (march). Winding their way among the guests in a serpentlike manner, the wedding party marches to the *Marcha de los novios* (Wedding March), eventually dividing into two lines, holding hands in the air, forming a human canopy. The wedding couple goes under the canopy and emerges at the end to dance their first waltz as husband and wife, while the guests form a circle around them. After allowing the wedding couple to savor their first dance for a while, the wedding guests begin cutting in on the couple. With some variations, this is known as the dollar dance, and it is almost always practiced at Latino weddings, whether Mexican, Cuban, or Puerto Rican. In the dollar dance, men will pin dollar bills on the bride's dress to dance with her, while the female guests pin dollar bills on the groom's jacket to dance with him. This is an opportunity for the guests to further shower the couple with extra gifts of cash, which are typically used for the honeymoon or to help establish their first household. The typical music at a Mexican wedding will be *mariachi music, whereas Colombian wedding celebrations prefer *cumbias or *vallenatos*.

Regardless of the regional area or culture, wedding celebrations will include music, dancing, *food, drinks, and many friends and family. The shared meal during the celebration symbolizes the joining of the two families; therefore, all the favorite foods will be prepared: tamales, fajitas, *carnitas* (little meats), mole, tacos, *paella* (rice), flan, and *sopapillas* (donutlike confections), to name a few (*see* Food and Cookery). In Colombian weddings, guests look forward to sipping a particular drink called *aguardiente*, a sweet liquor made of anise seed. These celebrations are a time for the families to come together and celebrate with all their relatives that have traveled for the wedding, their friends, and neighbors; consequently, they are elaborate and can last for days in some observances.

At the reception, the wedding couple often present the guests with *capias*, small momentos or favors engraved with the couple's names and wedding date. In Latin America and Puerto Rico, *capias* are often pinned to the dress

Capias, momentos with the bride and groom's names and wedding date, are presented to guests at Puerto Rican weddings. *Courtesy of the Alma Alvarez-Smith Private Collection.*

of a doll, which is placed on the table for everyone to admire. Another practice in Puerto Rico is to place a doll on the newlywed's table, as a symbol of fertility. At Cuban receptions, the gifts that are presented to the wedding couple are displayed on a large table for all to see. In addition, in the same spirit as the Puerto Rican *capias*, gifts are given to the guests to thank them for attending. At most Latino receptions, wedding cakes (small, round pastries) are wrapped and given to guests to take home.

It is rare to see a completely traditional wedding celebration today. Most couples tend to pick and choose the traditions, customs, and rituals that make sense for them and bring meaning and value to their special day.

Further Reading

Bautista, Edna. *Viva el Amor: A Latino Wedding Planner.* Albany, NY: Fireside Press, 2001. http://www.members.aol.com/Mjkarl/ethnic.htm.
http://www.muybueno.net/articles/mexicanwedding.htm.

Alma Alvarez-Smith

Welch, Raquel (1940–   ). Raquel Welch, an iconic film actress of Bolivian American heritage, was born Jo-Raquel Tejada on September 5, 1940, in Chicago, Illinois. Her family moved to San Diego, where Welch won a series of beauty contests before graduating high school. She studied acting briefly at San Diego State College but left before completing her degree to raise her two children from her first marriage. After modeling and small film parts in *A House Is Not a Home* (1964) and the Elvis Presley film *Roustabout* (1964), Welch was cast in the science fiction movie *Fantastic Voyage* (1966). The image of Welch clad in a lion-fur bikini to promote her next film, *One Million Years B.C.* (1966), made her an international star. While her films rarely were critical successes, she worked with such impressive talents as John Houston, James Ivory, Frank Sinatra, Gore Vidal, and Mae West. She also took considerable risks, appearing in an interracial love scene with Jim Brown in *100 Rifles* (1969), which was about a 1912 Indian uprising in México. She received a Golden Globe Award for Best Actress in a Musical or Comedy for her work in *The Three Musketeers* (1974). By the end of the 1970s, Welch's film appearances were sporadic and less substantial. Her more recent film appearances include *Naked Gun 33⅓* (1994) and *Legally Blonde* (2001).

In the 1980s, she launched a successful cabaret act and played the lead in *Woman of the Year* on Broadway. She has also appeared regularly in television movies such as *Scandal in a Small Town* (1988) and *Right to Die* (1987), for which she received a Golden Globe nomination, and guest starred in television series like *Mork and Mindy, Spin City,* and *Central Park West.* Also an entrepreneur, Welch has launched a line of wigs, skin care products and a line of yoga and fitness videos.

As an adult, Welch recognized her lack of knowledge about her Bolivian heritage and began writing down her childhood memories in hopes of piecing together her true identity. When she was growing up, her Bolivian father did not allow Spanish to be spoken in their home, nor did he allow them to speak of their Bolivian heritage. She now recognizes that denial as his attempt to ensure that his children were not treated differently in society. The result was a painful emptiness for Welch, which has only recently been alleviated through her reconnection to her roots, aided by a trip to Bolivia in 2002. Although she has played Latinas in her early career, *Bandolero!* (1968) and in *100 Rifles*, Welch now publicly self-identifies as Latina and relishes the opportunity to play Latin roles. Her commitment to her newfound Latina identity is evident in her more recent roles, divorcee Hortensia in **Tortilla Soup* (2001) and Aunt Dora in Gregory **Nava's PBS Latino-themed series *American Family* (2002).

Welch has been married four times, had two children (Damon and Tahnee) with first husband James Welch, and currently lives with her fourth husband, Richard Palmer, a restaurateur.

Further Reading

Mills, Nancy. "Raquel Finds Exciting New Role." *New York Daily News*, 23 August 2001, sec. 40.

Navarro, Mireya. "Raquel Welch Is Reinvented as a Latina: A Familiar Actress Now Boasts Her Heritage." *New York Times*, June 11, 2002, E1.

"Welch, Raquel." *Current Biography* 22 (1971): 436–438.

William Orchard

West Indies. The islands separating the Atlantic Ocean from the Caribbean Sea, the West Indies were the point of "discovery" by Christopher *Columbus in his first voyage in 1492 in search of a shorter route from Europe to the Orient. The region includes all of the islands extending from the southern tip of the Florida Peninsula to the northern coast of South America. Comprising twenty-three separate political entities, the islands are divided into the Greater *Antilles, consisting of Cuba (the largest), Puerto Rico, Jamaica, and Hispaniola (subdivided into the Dominican Republic and Haiti), and the Lesser Antilles, comprising the remaining islands west. The term *Antilles* derives from *Antilia* and refers to the traditional European name prior to Columbus's voyages for the semimythical lands believed to be located somewhere west of the "Old" World across the Atlantic. On medieval maps Antilia was sometimes presented as a continent, large island, or an archipelago. After Columbus's 1493 landings the Spanish term *Antillas* became the most common designation for the new lands, and the Caribbean was called the "Sea of the Antilles" in various European languages. United by geography the West Indies also share a history of colonialism based on the sugar trade and slavery. However, because of their colonial occupation by different European powers (including Spain, France, Great Britain, and the Netherlands), the islands have evolved with distinctly separate political and cultural inheritances, once again demonstrating the wide-ranging diversity within the idea and reality of Latina and Latino experience.

Further Reading

James, Conrad, and John Perivolaris, eds. *The Cultures of the Hispanic Caribbean.* New York: Macmillan, 2000.

Keller, Morton. "Spanish-American War." In *The Reader's Companion to American History*, edited by Eric Foner and John A. Garraty. Boston, MA: Houghton Mifflin, 1991.

Cordelia Chávez Candelaria

West Side Story. Both a major Broadway musical (1957) and award-winning film (1961), *West Side Story* is based on a conception by Jerome Robbins and a book by Arthur Laurents. The composer and music director of the Broadway musical was Leonard Bernstein, with lyrics by Stephen Sondheim and choreography by Jerome Robbins. The select cast of the Broadway musical includes Mickey Calin, Larry Kert, Ken Le Roy, Carol Lawrence, Chita *Rivera, and Art Smith. The award-winning film adaptation was directed and produced by Robert Wise and Jerome Robbins and distributed by United Artists. The cast includes Russ Tamblyn, George Chakiris, Natalie Wood, Richard Brymer, Rita *Moreno, Tony Mordente, Gina Trikonis, Suzie Kaye, Simon Oakland, and Ned Glass.

West Side Story, an adaptation of William Shakespeare's tragic drama of forbidden love *Romeo and Juliet*, is set in the west side of Manhattan in the 1950s in a predominantly Puerto Rican neighborhood. In Shakespeare's

Romeo and Juliet there are two feuding *families, the Montagues and the Capulets; in *West Side Story* there are two rival street *gangs, the native-born The Jets and The Sharks, an immigrant gang from Puerto Rico. María, the Puerto Rican gang leader's (Bernardo's) sister, like Juliet, falls in love with Tony, a Polish American member of the rival Jet gang. As seen with *Romeo and Juliet*, their love, due to the social forces of family and gang feuds, is doomed, and Tony (Romeo) is shot and their love is not allowed to flourish.

When *West Side Story* was finally coming together as a Broadway production in the mid-1950s, there were many doubts as to whether this so-called musical tragedy about American youth would succeed. Its composer and famed conductor Leonard Bernstein feared that the biting satire on contemporary society evinced by *West Side Story* would not find an audience among teenagers—because it shows the underbelly of youth subculture—and would not appeal either to a mainstream thirsty for levity. With some difficulty, including financial and emotional, and notwithstanding its enormous size—it was the first Broadway show with such extensively choreographed dance acts—the show finally opened on September 26, 1957.

The tragic story of Tony and María hit a deep chord in dealing not just with family rivalry but also with racial/ethnic conflicts. (After hearing of the Chicano riots in Los Angeles, Laurents changed the conflict from Italian Jewish to Puerto Rican–Anglo and set it in New York's West Side.) It was a critical and mainstream success. With the exception of reporter Harold Clurman, who called it "phony" in *The Nation*, newspapers such as the *Washington Post* lauded *West Side Story* for its unique vision and artistic commentary on youth and American society. Others considered that as a modern-day adaptation of *Romeo and Juliet* with contemporary youth argot and attitudes, it opened new vistas in the American stage. After its initial success, *West Side Story* ran for nearly two years (772 performances) and continued touring successfully across the nation. In 1961, directors Robert Wise and Jerome Robbins adapted the musical into a film; that year it went on to earn ten Academy Awards, including one for Best Picture, and a special Academy Award was given to Robbins for his choreography. On June 21, 2002, the American Film Institute gave *West Side Story* an award for being one of the greatest love stories of all time.

Further Reading

Garebian, Keith. *The Making of the West Side Story*. New York: Mosaic Press, 1998.
Romeo and Juliet/West Side Story. With an introduction by Norris Houghton. Reissue ed. New York: Laurel Leaf, 1965.
http://www.westsidestory.org.

Luis Aldama

World Football. *See* Soccer.

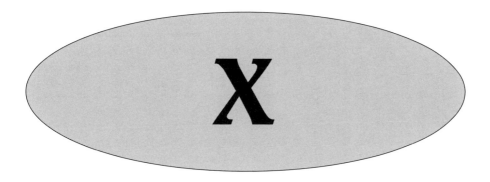

Xicanindio Artes. Founded in September 1976 by Carmen and Zarco *Guerrero, Xicanindio Artes is a collaborative effort among local *Chicano and Native American artists and community organizers in Phoenix, Arizona. Xicanindio was incorporated in February 1977 as a nonprofit, tax-exempt organization that promotes the appreciation of the cultural and spiritual heritage shared by ethnic peoples of the Southwest through the arts. The organization develops grassroots educational and cultural programs directed at youth and working-class communities in the city's *barrios and on the reservations. Xicanindio is a dynamic, creative force in Arizona that provides artistic and cultural services to underserviced and underrepresented populations. The activities of the organization include visual arts exhibitions, printmaking workshops, community-based artist-in-residence programs held in neighborhood centers, summer arts employment programs for high-risk teens, and the presentation of *theater and dance as a primary partner with the national Performance Network. The organization has instituted a community art festival to celebrate *Día de Los Muertos (Day of the Day), held in Mesa, Arizona, on an annual basis in November. It also serves as adviser and fiscal agent of newer arts organizations and assists them in growing artistically and administratively.

Trino Sandoval

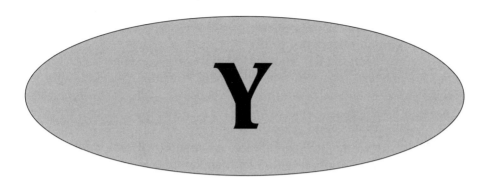

Y

Y Tu Mamá También. This award-winning film contributed greatly to the late 1990s renaissance of Mexican independent film and had a large crossover appeal in the United States. *Y Tu Mamá También* (And Your Mother Too, 2001) is part travelogue and part social commentary on issues of class, sexuality, homoeroticism, death, and contemporary middle-class youth culture in México. Director Alfonso Cuarón depicts the journey of two friends named Tenoch Iturbide (Diego Luna) and Julio Zapata (Gael García Bernal) as they go on a road trip. Tenoch and Julio invent a fictional beach, Boca Del Cielo (Heaven's Mouth), to gain the interest of an older woman, Luisa (Maribel Verdu), in hopes of taking her on a road trip with them. Unexpectedly, Luisa agrees to the trip to escape her unfaithful marriage and her cancer, which is not revealed until the end of the film. Tenoch, Julio, and Luisa share conversations about their friendship, life, passion, and sexual experiences as they drive to a beach on the Pacific coast of Oaxaca. At the end of the film, Tenoch and Julio return to Mexico City in silence, never to discuss the sexual exploration they experienced with Luisa and with each other on their road trip. Tenoch and Julio go their separate ways and with the exception of a chance encounter never talk to each other again. Using voice-over narrative commentary, the director makes comments on the middle-class youth culture of Mexico City and on the disenfranchised rural communities that the central characters encounter as they move toward the coast. Cuarón was recognized for Best Screenplay (2001) by the Berlin Film Festival and nominated for an Academy Award for Best Screenplay (2002), and the film won the Best Foreign Film at the 2003 Independent Spirit Awards. *Y Tu Mamá También* was produced by Amy K. Kaufman and David Linde and distributed by IFC Films.

Silvia D. Mora

Yzaguirre, Raul (c. 1940–   ). Raul Yzaguirre is a lifelong community activist and recognized leader in the Latino community. As president of the *National Council of La Raza (NCLR) (in Washington, DC.), the largest constituency-based Latino advocacy organization in the United States, Yzaguirre is a key national player in the fight for civil rights.

Born in the Rio Grande Valley of South Texas, Yzaguirre began his civil rights activism at the age of fifteen when he organized the American G.I. Forum Juniors, an auxiliary of the Hispanic veterans' organization *American G.I. Forum. He served four years in the U.S. Air Force Medical Corp after his high school graduation in 1958. NCLR came out of a proposal Yzaguirre wrote for NOMAS, the National Organization for Mexican American Services, an organization he founded in 1964. After receiving his Bachelor of Science degree from George Washington University in 1968, Yzaguirre worked for the U.S. Office of Economic Opportunity as a program analyst. In 1969, he founded Interstate Research Associates, which has grown into a multimillion-dollar nonprofit consulting firm.

Yzaguirre has received multiple honorary degrees and was first listed in *Who's Who in America* in 1980. He has received awards from organizations such as the Trustees of Princeton University, the Leadership Conference on Civil Rights, and the National Conference for Community and Justice, just to name a few. He serves on the board of directors for several organizations such as the Enterprise Foundation, the National Democratic Institute, and the National Boards of the Salvation Army and served as chairperson for the Advisory Commission on Educational Excellence for Hispanic Americans, under President Bill Clinton's administration.

Yzaguirre is married to Audrey Yzaguirre; they have six children and three grandchildren.

Further Reading

http://www.nclr.org/president/rybio.html.

Alma Alvarez-Smith

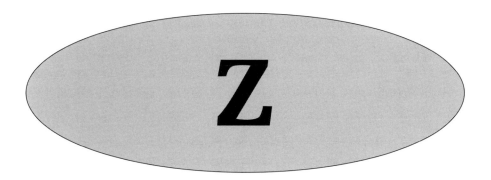

Zapata, Carmen (1927–). Carmen Margarita Zapata, a prolific stage and television actress committed to promoting more positive roles for Latino actors, was born in New York City to Julio Zapata, a Mexican immigrant, and Ramona Roca, an Argentine. It was evident at an early age that Zapata had a knack for entertaining. Although her mother did not approve of Carmen's desire for a career in show business, she did everything she could to provide dancing and music lessons for her. The lessons, coupled with some time at the Actors Studio, studying under Uta Hagen, gave Carmen the head start she needed to achieve success.

Zapata made her debut in the musical *Oklahoma* (1946) and performed the lead role when the show toured. When she returned to Broadway, she took principal roles in numerous productions such as *Bells Are Ringing* (1956), *Guys and Dolls* (1957), and *Stop the World, I Want to Get Off* (1961). Zapata was successful on Broadway but found that it was not "in" to be Hispanic off Broadway. Between plays, she took the name Marge Cameron to get work in nightclubs, singing, dancing, and doing comedy. In 1967 she moved to California to launch a television and film career.

Billed as Marge Cameron, producers claimed she was not "all American" and looked "ethnic." Zapata went back to using her real name but found that she was stereotyped in roles of maids or mothers. Some of her selected films include *Sol Madrid* (1968), *Pete and Tillie* (1972), *Boulevard Nights* (1979), and *Sister Act* (1992). Her extensive television credits include shows such as *Marcus Welby, M.D.*, *Medical Center*, *Mod Squad*, *Owen Marshall*, *Chico and the Man*, *Charlie's Angels*, *Barreta*, and *The Dick Van Dyke Show*. She is most proud of her nine seasons on the PBS bilingual children's show *Villa Alegre* (Happy Home, 1970), where she starred as "Doña Luz." In 1976 she also starred in her own series *Viva Valdez* (Long Live Valdez). With more than 300 television credits to her name, she actually found great success in Hollywood, but she was not pleased with the *stereotyping. This dissatisfaction led her to assist in the formation of the first minority committee of the Screen Actors Guild. She also became one of the original members of NOSOTROS (WE), a Hispanic actors organization founded in 1969 by Ricardo *Montalbán.

Frustration with the type of roles Hollywood was offering Latinas drove Zapata back to Broadway, where she was offered the lead role in a Spanish-language play, *Cada Quien Su Vida* (To Each His Own). Hesitant at first, because she had never done Spanish theater, Zapata eventually agreed to do the production. Although she and her two sisters were raised in Spanish Harlem in a household where the family exclusively spoke Spanish, she did not learn about her Mexican culture as a child. After doing the play, she was compelled to explore her Latina roots, which eventually led her to translations of Hispanic literature. In addition, her desire to create her own stage works led her and her writing partner, Michael Dewell, to the task of translating works by Federico García Lorca, Fernando de Rojas, and J. Humberto Robles Arenas into English.

With her newfound infatuation, Zapata took $5,000 of her own money and, with the help of Margarita Galban and Estela Scarlata, in 1985 founded the Bilingual Foundation of the Arts (BFA), a nonprofit bilingual theater dedicated to bringing Hispanic experience and culture to English- and Spanish-speaking audiences through bilingual theater. As cofounder, president, and managing producer, Zapata has received acclaim from critics and reviewers for her organization's productions. Working closely with the Los Angeles Unified School District to bring works of great Hispanic authors to students, the BFA launched a theater-in-education program, which has served over 1 million elementary students since its inception. Most recently, they have developed a new program called Teen Theatre Project

Carmen Zapata. *Courtesy of Photofest.*

(Teatro para los Jovenes). Modeled after the theater-in-education program, the Teen Theatre Project is designed to meet the needs of junior and high school "at-risk" students. In an effort to deter dropout rates, the program sponsors play productions, which are performed in the schools, followed by open discussions about issues affecting teenagers. Ethnically diverse professional actors who can relate to and communicate with the students perform the plays.

Her extensive community involvement includes numerous board seats for organizations such as the National Conference of Christian Jews, United Way, Boy Scouts of America, and Mexican American Opportunity Foundation. In 1993 she took on the role of commissioner of Los Angeles's Cultural Affairs Department. For her tireless work, she has received a multitude of awards such as Outstanding Woman in Business Award from Women in Film, Boy Scouts of America Community Leadership Award, and Mexican-American Foundation Award. She was recognized as the 1985 Woman of the Year by the Hispanic Women's Council and received the prestigious Governor's Award for the Arts and an honorary doctorate in human services from Sierra University. Of all the awards and recognitions showered on her, her favorite is the Civil Order of Merit (El Lazo de Dama de la Orden del Merito Civil) bestowed on her by King Juan Carlos I of Spain. This is an honor conferred on few and is likened to the bestowal of knighthood by the queen of England.

Further Reading

Keller, Gary D. *A Biographical Handbook of Hispanics and United States Film*. Tempe, AZ: Bilingual Press, 1997.

Tardiff, Joseph C., and L. Mpho Mabunda, eds. *Dictionary of Hispanic Biography*. Detroit, MI: Gale Research, 1995.

Telgen, Diane, and Jim Kamp, eds. *¡Latinas! Women of Achievement*. Detroit, MI: Visible Ink Press, 1996.

Unterburger, Amy L., and Jane L. Delgado, eds. *Who's Who among Hispanic Americans 1994–1995*. Detroit, MI: Gale Research, 1994.

Alma Alvarez-Smith

Zapáta, Emiliano (1879–1919). One of world history's most celebrated revolutionaries and champions of *los de abajo* (i.e., the poor and downtrodden), Emiliano Zapáta was one of the most important grassroots participants in the Mexican Revolution of 1910. He is viewed by many as one of his nation's contributions to the tradition and symbolism of democratic idealism, and his name and ideals are memorialized in México and throughout the Western Hemisphere. In the 1990s, for example, his legendary name was adopted by the indigenous movement for land and civil rights in México's Yucatán peninsula among the rebels of Chiapas who identified their group as the Esfuerzo Zapatista para la Libertad Nacional (EZLN—Zapatista Army of National Liberation). Like other populist resistance movements against economic injustice and political exploitation, the EZLN invoked Zapáta's legend because of his history as a charismatic guerrilla leader, land reform advocate, and martyr for the cause of liberation. Around the world countless posters, flags, books, and movies have been inscribed with Zapáta's image, biography, and slogans for justice and freedom. One of the most famous of these representations is the 1952 movie *Viva Zapáta*, starring Marlon Brando, directed by John Huston, and written by Nobelist John Steinbeck. Another widely distributed icon from the revolutionary's legend is the statement attributed to him—"Es mejor morir de pie que morir arrodillado" (It's better to die on one's feet than on one's knees)—seen on banners, posters, and t-shirts, including silkscreens by the *Royal Chicano Air Force art collective. In Latina/o popular culture, Zapáta with compatriot and ally Pancho *Villa personify the quintessential image of the revolutionary rebel with piercing eyes, bold mustache, sombrero, and cartridge belts.

The historical Zapáta was a mestizo proud of his indigenous blood and cultural roots, who was born in the farm and ranching village of Anenecuilco in the state of Morelos, México, on August 8, 1879. His peasant father trained and bartered horses to support his family. Orphaned in his teenage years, Zapáta helped take care of his siblings and soon became a local village leader in support of his neighbors' rights. By the late 1890s and 1900s, the future rebel against the tyranny of President Porfirio Díaz was taking part in village protests against the *hacendados* (large rancher owners) who were appropriating the smaller family farms and ranches of the peasants (*see* Appropriation and Popular Culture). Arrested in 1897 for his active advocacy for the rights of the people, Zapáta managed to obtain a pardon but refused to curtail his activism. As a result, the government drafted him into military service, where he served briefly until a landowner sponsored Zapáta's release with promise of employment as a horse trainer on his hacienda. Remaining an ardent proponent of agrarian and land reform and equality for the native Méjicano population, he was elected by his neighbors to head the local village defense committee in 1909. Part of his appeal was being a native bilingual Spanish and Náhuatl speaker who was visionary and brave in his sense of social justice. These qualities eventually led him and a large following of villagers to forcibly take back some of the land that had been stolen from them and redistribute it among themselves.

From this grassroots threshold of commitment and action, Zapáta began forming his insurgent revolutionary army even before 1910 and the start of the revolution. He and his followers soon threw their support behind the people's champion, Francisco Madero, and by 1911 his humble force controlled the city of Cuaútla and closed the road to the capital, a victory that helped topple Díaz, who immediately resigned, appointed a provisional government, and escaped to Europe. Buoyed by success, Zapáta became a magnet for supporters and met with the more seasoned politician, Madero, to ask him to support his cause of land reform for the deterritorialized Méji-

Emiliano Zapáta was one of the most important grassroots participants in the Mexican Revolution of 1910. *Courtesy of the Alma Alvarez-Smith Private Collection.*

canos. Madero was cautious in pledging support but forceful in asking Zapáta to disarm and disband his troops. Refusing to oblige, in time Zapáta was able to return to his native state of Morelos with an expanded army estimated at 5,000. The 1911 elections brought Madero into power as president, and Zapáta's hopes for justice through land reform were again blocked by the wary new president. For this reason, Zapáta and his teacher-ally, Otilio Montaño, drafted the Plan of Ayala, a declaration of independence arguing that the provisional president would not carry out the true intent of the revolution and its original supporters, like the landless poor that followed Zapáta. It was at this time that the rebel from Morelos chose "Tierra y Libertad" (Land and Liberty) as his revolutionary campaign theme. Known for his unswerving commitment to return to the poor the meager holdings stolen from them, Zapáta undertook guerrilla tactics and began to seize and redistribute lands from the *hacendados*.

Madero was eventually assassinated in 1913, thus continuing the political turmoil and confusion associated with societies suddenly exposed to freedom after decades of repressive tyranny. The political intrigue brought Zapáta and his army back to Mexico City, where military leaders, politicians, intellectuals, and others met with him, seeking his backing for their visions of what the country needed for harmony. Zapáta maintained his commitment to the Plan of Ayala, as well as his strength as a guerrilla leader even if, as an outsider and uneducated leader, his political influence remained limited in the capital among ambitious and experienced political operatives. Another turning point in the revolution occurred in 1914 when Venustiano Carranza called for all the revolutionary leaders to gather near Mexico City to negotiate new lines of power. Pancho Villa, who led the important northern revolutionary army, rejected Carranza's call on the grounds that the meeting site was not neutral, fair, or safe. The meeting was changed to the state of Aguascalientes in central México, and both Villa and Zapáta attended, bringing their armies to the convention and combining to form an anti-Carranza majority. The coalition voted to appoint General Eulalio Gutiérrez to be the new provisional president, a decision that the ambitious Carranza quickly rejected, reigniting the beleaguered country's hostilities. After war between the Carrancistas and the revolutionary coalition broke out, Zapáta led his army (now known as the Liberation Army of the South and totaling 25,000) into Mexico City. To the surprise of its urban war-weary residents, the rebel peasants occupied the capital politely instead of rampaging destructively as expected. The famous meeting between Zapáta and Villa at the National Palace took place at this time, as the two legends renewed their pledge of alliance in support of the Plan of Ayala. The photograph of them enthroned at former President Díaz's presidential desk is one of the populist triumphs of the revolution.

Although known for his charismatic leadership and shrewd guerrilla strategy, Zapáta also demonstrated abilities as a manager by establishing and carrying out an agrarian plan for land reform. He organized commissions to redistribute appropriated landholdings, and he closely monitored their efforts to ensure fairness and to offset the strong power of the landowners, who worked ceaselessly to maintain their corrupt control of the economy and the government. Among his other accomplishments were the founding of México's first agricultural loan and credit bank and the preliminary reorganization of the sugar industry in his home state into peasant cooperatives. Zapáta even met with U.S. President Woodrow Wilson's personal representative in 1915, an act of diplomacy that underscored the revolutionary's fame and perceived importance in Washington, D.C. Later, after Zapáta gained control of the city of Puebla and his ally Villa was defeated by Carranza, President Wilson's envoy, William Gates, visited Zapáta in Puebla and also toured Mexico City. Gates wrote a number of reports on these travels that presented to the world a stark contrast between the civil order and social harmony of the towns held by Zapáta against the anarchy and upheaval of the capital held by Carranza's generals. When published both in his country and in the north, it is reported that Zapáta expressed a feeling of satisfaction that his lifetime mission for democracy and social justice had been redeemed by the Yankee's favorable reports. Not long after this public praise in the press that helped further his notoriety universally, Zapáta was tricked into an ambush by a Carranza operative in his home state of Morelos. He was shot at a hacienda there and died on April 10, 1919. He is buried in Cuaútla.

Further Reading

Boyd, Lola Elizabeth. "The Image of Emiliano Zapata in the Art and Literature of the Mexican Revolution." Ph.D. dissertation, Columbia University, 1965.

Keller, Gary D. *Zapata Lives!* Colorado Springs, CO: Maize Press, 1994.

Parkinson, Roger. *Zapáta: A Biography.* New York: Stein and Day, 1975.

Steinbeck, John. *Zapáta.* New York: Penguin, 1993.

Womack, John, Jr. *Zapáta and the Mexican Revolution.* New York: Knopf, 1970.

Cordelia Chávez Candelaria

Zarco. *See* Guerrero, Zarco.

Zoot Suit. The zoot suit is one of the major motifs of Mexican American popular culture. It emerged in the early years of World War II, when Mexican American boys and young men in cities such as El Paso and Phoenix, but especially in Los Angeles, began wearing the suit as a youthful symbolic rebellion against the discrimination they faced in daily life. The zoot suit consisted of pants and a coat—very baggy pants that fit high on the waist, with deep "reat" pleats and extremely narrow cuffs, and a coat with wide lapels, shoulder pads that resembled epaulets, and a length sometimes reaching the knees. Accessories to the zoot suit included a wide-rimmed "pancake" hat, long watch chains, and thick-soled shoes. In addition to their unique dress, some Mexican American youth spoke in a special argot called caló. The use of caló, which was a derivative of a fifteenth-century Iberian Roma dialect, not only made their talk incomprehensible to both their Spanish-speaking elders and white English-speaking authority figures, but it also intensified the youths' sense of uniqueness and generational solidarity. In short, "zoot suiters" developed a subculture of their own.

While a majority of Mexican American youth in cities such as Los Angeles wore the zoot suit, individuals' levels of involvement in the youth subculture varied. Many wore only the pants. Others wore traditional fashions during the week and dressed in their zoot suits only on weekends. Others still wore the style on a more continuous basis but did not immerse themselves in the subculture. Only a relatively small number of the most alienated youths, the *Pachucos, fully adopted *La Vida Loca, the crazy life, with its defiant and hostile attitude and antisocial and even pathological tendencies. This group comprised a small proportion of the Mexican American youth population (less than 3 percent by one estimate). Nevertheless, because of their visibility and the publicity they received from the press, the Pachucos defined what it meant to be a zoot suiter both for other Mexican American youths and for the general public.

The reason the Pachuco achieved iconic status was that the whole point of the zoot suit style was to reciprocate the rejection Mexican American youth experienced from white society. The fact that the zoot suit had previously been popular among blacks demonstrates that, at least at some level of consciousness, Mexican American youth were declaring that they understood the racial nature of their subordination. Moreover, such a declaration in the midst of the national crisis of World War II enhanced the message. Especially during the war years when Americans prized conformity to defeat a common foe, Mexican American youth knew that the zoot suit offended whites. Government leaders, including the *police, the press, and the general public, mistook what we now recognize as classic youthful rebellion for the inherent criminality of Mexican American youth. A hysterical fear of Mexican American youth *gangs developed that culminated in the infamous Sleepy Lagoon case and the June 1943 Zoot Suit Riots in Los Angeles.

In subsequent decades, some Mexican Americans have romanticized the figure of the zoot suiter and even the Pachuco. Veterans of the era show off their "drapes," and during the period of the *Chicano Movement, people would show up at parties and dances wearing new zoot suits. In 1976 Luis *Valdez further glorified the phenomenon through his musical play *Zoot Suit*, which played on Broadway and became a feature-length film.

Further Reading

Escobar, Edward. *Race, Police, and the Making of a Political Identity.* Berkeley: University of California Press, 1999.

Mazón, Mauricio. *The Zoot-Suit Riots: The Psychology of Symbolic Annihilation.* Austin: University of Texas Press, 1984.

Edward Escobar

Zoot Suit. Luis *Valdez directed this 1981 film adaptation of his play of the same name, which is based on real-life events related to the Sleepy Lagoon murder trial that shook California in the 1940s. Filmed live during a stage production, this powerful musical drama explores the hostile racial tensions and conflicted social and political backgrounds that characterized Los Angeles during World War II.

At the center of the drama lies the unsolved murder of José Díaz and the biased trial that followed. The trial, combined with sensationalist press coverage, heightened already existing xenophobic sentiments and racial hostility in Los Angeles, which led to the so-called Zoot Suit Riots in June 1943—one of the most dramatic episodes in *Chicano history. *Zoot suits, consisting of baggy pants worn with long, dangling watch chains, broad-shouldered long coats, and topped off by wide-brimmed hats, became the signature outfits of rebellious young Latinos in the 1940s. In the movie, Daniel *Valdez plays Henry Reyna, a character inspired by twenty-year-old, true-to-life zoot suiter Henry Leyvas, who, along with twenty-four other young Latinos, was unjustly charged with Díaz's murder and sentenced to San Quentin prison. Edward James *Olmos, who gave an exceptional performance as El Pachuco (*see* Pachucos), portrays a flamboyant, intelligent, all-seeing figure who is Reyna's zoot-suited alter ego. Tyne Daly plays an activist who attempts to win Reyna's release. At one point during the interrogation, a policeman tells Reyna, "I don't believe you really want to be in the army, you go around dressing [in a zoot suit] like a target." Reyna responds, "I was born a target, right here in L.A."

To explain what happened during the riots, the movie shows the different circumstances affecting the population of Los Angeles at the time, for example, the large number of servicemen in the streets, the arrival of new immigrants, the transformation of the local economy due to the war, and the emergence of a new generation of Mexican Americans who were more affluent, self-confident, and fully aware of their discriminated status. The film draws attention to the struggle that minorities confronted every day, especially in the judicial system and the mass media. *Zoot Suit*, which was distributed by Universal Pictures, represents one of the milestones in Chicano cinema. The cast also includes Abel Franco, Mike Gómez, and Alma Martínez.

Further Reading

Brown, Monica. *Gang Nation: Delinquent Citizens in Puerto Rican, Chicano, and Chicana Narratives*. Minneapolis: University of Minnesota Press, 2001.

Mazón, Mauricio. *The Zoot-Suit Riots: The Psychology of Symbolic Annihilation*. Austin: University of Texas Press, 1984.

Salomon, Larry. *Roots of Justice: Stories of Organizing in Communities of Color*. Berkeley, CA: Chardon Press, 1998.

Villa, Raul. *Barrio-Logos: Space and Place in Urban Chicano Literature and Culture*. Austin: University of Texas Press, 2000.

William Calvo

Zozobra. El Zozobra, from the Spanish word for "gloom," is a large, over-forty-foot-tall, marionette-looking figure, also known as Old Man Gloom, who is set afire in engulfing flames to inaugurate the annual Fiestas de Santa Fe in Santa Fe, New Mexico. Zozobra, who is constructed of precut sticks (for the frame) covered with chicken wire and yards of muslin and stuffed with shredded paper, was the brainchild of local artist William Howard Shuster, Jr. Shuster's inspiration for the figure came from the Holy Week celebrations he witnessed of the Yaqui Indians of México. The name "Zozobra," which is Spanish for "the gloomy one," was originally coined by New Mexican Spanish conquest leader Don Diego de Vargas and later by Shuster and newspaper editor E. Dana Johnson. Shuster introduced the Zozobra in 1926, although the Fiestas de Santa Fe had been celebrated annually since 1712. Shuster signed over control and exclusive copyright of Zozobra to the Kiwanis Club of Santa Fe on June 19, 1964, and they have continued the Zozobra tradition. Spectators who attend the Fiestas de Santa Fe, which occur on the weekend after Labor Day, can be heard chanting, "Burn him" to the figure whose "death" represents the end of gloom and despair and the resurrection of happiness and prosperity.

Further Reading

"The History of the Burning of Will Shuster's Zozobra." Kiwanis Club of Santa Fe. http://www.zozobra.com/zhistory.html.

"Zozobra (Festival)." Library of Congress. http://www.loc.gov/bicentennial/propage/NM/nm_s_domenici3.html.

Armando Quintero, Jr.

Bibliography

ART

Alcantara, Isabel, and Sandra Egnolff. *Frida Kahló and Diego Rivera*. New York: Prestel, 2001.

Barradas, Efraín. *Partes de un todo*. Río Piedras: Editorial de la Universidad de Puerto Rico, 1998.

Barragán, Elisa García, and Luis Mario Schneider. *Diego Rivera y los escritores mexicanos: Antología tributaria*. Mexico City: Universidad Nacional Autónoma de México, 1986.

Cooper, Martha, and Joseph Sciorra. *R.I.P.: Memorial Wall Art*. New York: Henry Holt, 1994.

Flores-Peña, Ysamur, and Roberta J. Evanchuk. *Santería Garments and Altars: Speaking Without a Voice*. Jackson: University Press of Mississippi, 1994.

Gaspar de Alba, Alicia. *Chicano Art Inside/Outside the Master's House: Cultural Politics and the CARA Exhibition*. Austin: University of Texas Press, 1998.

Gaspar de Alba, Alicia. "From Cara to Caca: The Multiple Anatomies of Chicano/a Art at the Turn of the New Century." *Aztlán* 26.1 (Spring 2001): 205–231.

Kitchener, Amy V. *The Holiday Yards of Florencio Morales: "El Hombre de las Banderas."* Jackson: University Press of Mississippi, 1994.

Lindauer, Margaret A. *Devouring Frida*. Middletown, CT: Wesleyan University Press, 1999.

Padilla, Carmella, et al. *Low 'n Slow: Lowriding in New Mexico*. Santa Fe: Museum of New Mexico Press, 1999.

Ramírez, Yasmin, and Henry C. Estrada. *Parallel Expressions in the Graphic Arts of the Chicano and Puerto Rican Movements*. New York: El Museo del Barrio, 1999.

Rodríguez, Antonio. *Guía de los murales de Diego Rivera*. Mexico City: Secretaría de Educación Pública, 1984.

Sorell, Víctor A. "Articulate Signs of Resistance and Affirmation in Chicano Public Art." In *Chicano Art: Resistance and Affirmation, 1965–1985*, edited by Richard Griswold del Castillo, Teresa McKenna, and Yvonne Yarbro-Bejarano. Los Angeles: Wight Art Gallery/UCLA, 1991.

Sorell, Víctor A. "Telling Images Bracket the 'Broken-Promise(d) Land': The Culture of Immigration and the Immigration of Culture across Borders." In *Culture across Borders: Mexican Immigration & Popular Culture*, edited by David R. Maciel and María Herrera-Sobek. Tucson: University of Arizona Press, 1998.

Tibol, Raquel. *Frida Kahló: An Open Life*. Albuquerque: University of New Mexico Press, 1993.

Turner, Kay. *Beautiful Necessity: The Art and Meaning of Women's Altars*. New York: Thames & Hudson, 1999.

Zamora, Martha. *Frida: El pincel de la angustía*. Mexico: n.p., 1987.

Zeitlin, Marilyn A., et al. *South Bronx Hall of Fame: Sculpture by John Ahearn and Rigoberto Torres*. Seattle: University of Washington Press, 1991.

Zuver, Marc, et al. *Cuba-USA: The First Generation*. Washington, DC: Fondo del Sol Visual Arts Center in association with the National Museum of American Art and others, 1991.

http://www.cybrids.com.

http://www.galeriadelaraza.org.

http://www.undo.net/artinpress.

http://www.whitney.org/exhibition/biennial.

BARRIOS AND BORDERLANDS

Antush, John V., ed. *Nuestro New York*. New York: Penguin Group, 1988.

Anzaldúa, Gloria. *Borderlands/La Frontera: The New Mestiza*. 2nd ed. San Francisco: Aunt Lute Books, 1987.

Croucher, Sheila. *Imagining Miami: Ethnic Politics in a Postmodern World*. Charlottesville: University Press of Virginia, 1997.

Didion, Joan. *Miami*. New York: Simon and Schuster, 1987.

García, María Cristina. *Havana USA: Cuban Exiles and Cuban Americans in South Florida, 1959–1994*. Berkeley: University of California Press, 1996.

Levine, Robert M., and Moisés Asis. *Cuban Miami*. New Brunswick, NJ: Rutgers University Press, 2000.

Quiñones, Sam. *Tales from Another México*. Albuquerque: University of New Mexico Press, 2001.

Stepick, Alex, et al. *This Land Is Our Land: Immigrants and Power in Miami*. Berkeley: University of California Press, 2003.

COMICS

Dorfman, Ariel, and Armand Mattelart. *How to Read Donald Duck: Imperialist Ideology in the Disney Comic*. Translated by David Kunzle. New York: International General, 1991.

Hardy, Charles, and Gail F. Stern, eds. *Ethnic Images in the Comics*. Philadelphia: Balch Institute for Ethnic Studies, 1986.

Hinds, Harold, Jr., and Charles Tatum. *Not Just for Children: The Mexican Comic Book in the Late 1960s and 1970s*. Westport, CT: Greenwood Press, 1992.

Nyberg, Amy Kiste. *Seal of Approval: The History of the Comics Code*. Jackson: University of Mississippi Press, 1998.

Rubenstein, Anne. *Bad Language, Naked Ladies, and Other Threats to the Nation: A Political History of Comic Books in México*. Durham, NC: Duke University Press, 1998.

Sabin, Roger. *Comics, Comix, & Graphic Novels: A History of Comic Art*. London: Phaidon, 1996.

Wright, Bradford. *Comic Book Nation: The Transformation of Youth Culture in America*. Baltimore, MD: Johns Hopkins University Press, 2001.

http://www.lacucaracha.com.

CUBAN AMERICANS

Bourn, Peter G. *Fidel: A Biography of Fidel Castro*. New York: Dodd Mead, 1986.

Castro, Fidel. *In Defense of Socialism, 1988–1989*. New York: Pathfinder Press, 1989.

Corbett, Ben. *This Is Cuba: An Outlaw Culture Survives*. Cambridge, MA: Westview Press, 2002.

González-Pardo, Miguel. *The Cuban Americans*. Westport, CT: Greenwood Press, 1998.

Ingalls, Robert P., and Louis A. Pérez, Jr. *Tampa Cigar Workers: A Pictoral History*. Gainesville: University Press of Florida, 2003.

Oppenheimer, Andrés. *Castro's Final Hour: The Secret Story behind the Coming Downfall of Communist Cuba*. New York: Touchstone, 1992.

Pérez, Lisandro. *The Cuban Population of the United States: The Results of the 1980 U.S. Census of Population*. Miami: Latin American and Caribbean Center, Florida International University, 1984.

Torres, María de los Angeles. *In the Land of Mirrors: Cuban Exile Politics in the United States*. Ann Arbor: University of Michigan Press, 1999.

CULTURAL STUDIES

Bakhtin, Mikhail M. *Bakhtin and Cultural Theory*. Edited by Ken Hirschop and David Shepherd. New York: Manchester University Press, 1989.

Bakhtin, Mikhail M. *The Dialogic Imagination*. Edited by Michael Holquist. Translated by Caryl Emerson and Michael Holquist. Austin: University of Texas Press, 1981.

Bakhtin, Mikhail M. *Rabelais and His World*. Bloomington: Indiana University Press, 1984.

Cushing, Frank Howard. *Zuni Folk Tales*. Tucson: University of Arizona Press, 1986.

Erdoes, Richard, and Alfonso Ortiz. *American Indian Myths and Legends*. New York: Pantheon, 1984.

Flexner, Stuart, and Doris Flexner. *Wise Words and Wives' Tales: The Origins, Meanings, and Time-Honored Wisdom of Proverbs and Folk Sayings, Olde and New*. New York: Avon, 1993.

International Encyclopedia of the Social Sciences. New York: Macmillan, 1968.

Jung, Carl G. *Four Archetypes: Mother, Rebirth, Spirit, Trickster*. Princeton, NJ: Princeton University Press, 1959.

Knapp, Bettina Liebowitz. *Music, Archetype and the Writer: A Jungian View*. University Park: Pennsylvania State University Press, 1988.

Walker, Barbara G. *The Woman's Encyclopedia of Myths and Secrets*. San Francisco, CA: Harper & Row, 1983.

FASHION AND CLOTHING

Burns, Leslie Davis, and Nancy O. Bryant. *The Business of Fashion: Designing, Manufacturing, and Marketing*. 2nd ed. New York: Fairchild Publications, 2002.

Cunningham, Patricia A., and Susan Voso Lab, eds. *Dress in American Culture*. Bowling Green, OH: Bowling Green State University Popular Press, 1993.

Eicher, Joanne B., ed. *Dress and Ethnicity: Change across Space and Time*. Washington, DC: Berg, 1995.

Gilbert-Rolfe, Jeremy, with foreword by Marilyn A. Zeitlin. *Art on the Edge of Fashion*. Tempe: Arizona State University Art Museum, Nelson Fine Arts Center, 1997.

Kondo, Dorinne K. *About Face: Performing Race in Fashion and Theater*. New York: Routledge, 1997.

Ríos-Bustamante, Antonio, producer, and Marco Bravo, director. *Latino Hollywood*. Narrator, Hector Ayala. Cinema Guild, 1994–1996. Videorecording.

Scranton, Philip, ed. *Beauty and Business: Commerce, Gender, and Culture in Modern America*. New York: Routledge, 2001.

FILM AND THEATER

Agrasánchez, Rogelio. *Carteles de la época de oro del cine mexicano* (Poster Art from the Golden Age of Mexican Cinema). Guadalajara, Jalisco, México: Universidad de Guadalajara, Instituto Mexicano de Cinematografía, 1997.

Berg, Charles Ramírez. *Latino Images in Film: Stereotypes, Subversion, & Resistance*. Austin: University of Texas Press, 2002.

Bernardi, Daniel. *Star Trek and History: Race-ing toward a White Future*. New Brunswick, NJ; London: Rutgers University Press, 1998.

Bernardi, Daniel, ed. *Classical Hollywood, Classic Whiteness*. Minneapolis, MN; London: University of Minnesota Press, 2001.

Berumen-Garcia, Frank Javier. *The Chicano/Hispanic Image in American Film*. New York: Vantage Press, 1995.

Candelaria, Cordelia. "Social Equity and Film Portrayals of *La mujer hispana*." In *Chicano Cinema: Research, Reviews, and Resources*, edited by Gary Keller. Binghamton, NY: Bilingual Review/Press, 1984.

Dávila López, Grace. "Diversidad y pluralidad en el teatro puertorriqueño contemporáneo: 1965–1985." Ph.D. dissertation, University of California, 1990.

Doane, Mary A., Patricia Mellencamp, and Linda Williams, eds. *Re-vision: Essays in Feminist Film Criticism*. Frederick, MD: University Publications of America, 1984.

Fregoso, Rosalinda. *The Bronze Screen: Chicana and Chicano Film Culture*. Minneapolis: University of Minnesota Press, 1993.

Hadley-Garcia, George. *Hispanic Hollywood: The Latins in Motion Pictures*. New York: Carol Publishing Group, 1993.

Kanellos, Nicolás, and Jorge Huertas. "Introduction." In *Nuevos pasos. Chicano and Puerto Rican Drama.* 2nd ed. Houston, TX: Arte Público Press, 1989.

Keller, Gary D. *A Biographical Handbook of Hispanics and United States Film.* Tempe, AZ: Bilingual Press, 1997.

Limón, José Eduardo. *American Encounters: Greater Mexico, the United States, and the Erotics of Culture.* Boston: Beacon Press, 1998.

Maltin, Leonard. *Leonard Maltin's Movie Encyclopedia: Career Profiles of More Than 2,000 Actors and Filmmakers, Past and Present.* New York: Plume, 1995.

Ramos-Escobar, José Luis. "Factores y funciones del teatro popular en Puerto Rico." *Intermedio de Puerto Rico* 1.1 (1995): 8–10.

Ramos-Perea, Roberto. *Perspectivas de la nueva dramaturgía puertorriqueña. Ensayos sobre el Nuevo Drama Nacional.* San Juan, Puerto Rico: Ateneo Puertorriqueño, 1986.

http://www.communications.uci.edu.

http://www.latinoarts.org/directory/theatdir.htm.

FOLKLORE

Alarcón, Justo. *Los siete hijos de la Llorona: Novela.* Mexico City: Alta Pimería Pro Arte y Cultura, 1986.

Baughman, Ernest. *Type and Motif-Index of the Folktales of England and North America.* The Hague, Netherlands: Mouton, 1966.

Behrens, Laurence, and Leonard J. Rosen. "Fairy Tales: A Closer Look at 'Cinderella.'" In *Writing and Reading across the Curriculum.* 3rd ed. Glenview, IL: Scott, Foresman, 1988.

Bierhorst, John. *The Mythology of Mexico and Central America.* New York: William Morrow, 1990.

Bierlein, J.F. *Parallel Myths.* New York: Ballantine, 1994.

Candelaria, Cordelia Chávez. "Letting La Llorona Go, or Rereading History's 'Tender Mercies.'" *Heresies: A Feminist Publication on Art & Politics* 27 (1993): 111–115.

Castro, Rafaela G. *Chicano Folklore: A Guide to the Folktales, Traditions, Rituals, and Religious Practices of Mexican-Americans.* New York: Oxford University Press, 2001.

De Bouzek, Jeannette, producer/director. *Gathering Up Again: The Fiesta of Santa Fé.* Cinema Guild, 1992. Videocassette.

Garcia Kraul, Edward, and Judith Beatty, eds. *The Weeping Woman: Encounters with la Llorona.* Santa Fe, NM: World Press, 1988.

Gilbert, Fabiola Cabeza de Baca. *We Fed Them Cactus.* Albuquerque: University of New Mexico Press, 1954.

Gleason, Judith, and Elisa Mereghetti, producers/directors. *King Does Not Lie: The Initiation of a Shango Priest.* Filmmakers Library, 1992. 50 min. Videocassette.

Herrera-Sobek, María. *The Bracero Experience: Elitelore vs. Folklore.* Los Angeles: UCLA Latin American Center Publications, University of California, 1979.

Hill, Vicky Trego. *La Llorona: The Weeping Woman.* Audio narrated by Joe Hayes. El Paso, TX: Cinco Puntos Press, 1987.

Limón, José E. *Dancing with the Devil: Society and Cultural Poetics in Mexican-American South Texas.* Madison: University of Wisconsin Press, 1994.

Lomax Hawes, Besse. "La Llorona in Juvenile Hall." *Western Folklore* 27.2 (1968): 155–170.

Lyons, Grant. *Tales the People Tell in México.* Edited by Doris Coburn. New York: J. Messner, 1972.

Mason, Michael Atwood. *Living Santería: Rituals and Experiences in an Afro-Cuban Religion.* Washington, DC: Smithsonian Institution Press, 2002.

Nájera-Ramírez, Olga. "The Racialization of a Debate: The *Charreada* as Tradition or Torture?" *American Anthropologist* 98.3 (1996): 505–511.

Nájera-Ramírez, Olga. "Social and Political Dimensions of Folklórico Dance: The Binational Dialectic of Residual and Emergent Culture." *Western Folklore* 48.1 (1989): 15–32.

Nightingale, Andrea Ramírez. "La Llorona as an Extension of the Great Mother Archetype." Master's thesis, Arizona State University, 1988.

Paredes, Américo. *Folklore and Culture on the Texas-Mexican Border.* Edited by Richard Bauman. Austin: University of Texas Press, 1995.

Pérez, Domino Renee. "Caminando con la Llorona: Traditional and Contemporary Narratives." In *Chicana Traditions: Continuity and Change*, edited by Norma Cantú and Olga Nájera Ramírez. Urbana: University of Illinois Press, 2002.

Rodríguez, Sylvia. *The Matachines Dance: Ritual Symbolism and Interethnic Relations in the Upper Rio Grande Valley.* Albuquerque: University of New Mexico Press, 1996.

Salcedo, Michele. *Quinceañera! The Essential Guide to Planning the Perfect Sweet Fifteen Celebration.* New York: Holt, 1997.

Schoemaker, George, ed. *The Emergence of Folklore in Everyday Life: A Fieldguide and Sourcebook.* Bloomington, IN: Trickster Press, 1990.

Tasca, Jules. *Spirit of Hispania: Hispanic Tales Adapted for the Stage.* Boston, MA: Baker's Plays, 1991.

Vigil, Angel. *Una linda raza: Cultural and Artistic Traditions of the Hispanic Southwest.* Golden, CO: Fulcrum, 1998.

Villanueva, Alma Luz. *Weeping Woman: La Llorona and Other Stories.* Tempe, AZ: Bilingual Press, 1994.

Weigle, Marta. *Brothers of Light, Brothers of Blood: The Penitentes of the Southwest.* Albuquerque: University of New Mexico Press, 1976.

Westerman, William. "Central American Refugee Testimony and Performed Life Histories in the Sanctuary Movement." In *The Oral History Reader*, edited by Robert Perks and Alistair Thomson. New York: Routledge, 1998.

http://www.public.iastate.edu/~rjsalvad/scmfaq/muertos.html.

FOOD AND COOKING

Bayless, Rick. *Mexican Kitchen.* New York: Scribner, 1996.

Bayless, Rick. *Mexico One Plate at a Time.* New York: Scribner, 2000.

De'Angeli, Alicia Gironella, and Jorge De'Angeli. *El gran libro de la cocina mexicana.* Mexico City: Ediciones Larousse, 1980.

Foster, Nelson, and Linda S. Cordell, eds. *Chilies to Chocolate: Food the Americas Gave the World.* Tucson: University of Arizona Press, 1992.

Gilbert, Fabiola Cabeza de Baca. *We Fed Them Cactus*. Albuquerque: University of New Mexico Press, 1954.

Grant, Rosamund. *Caribbean and African Cookery*. Kingston, Jamaica: Ian Randle Publishers, 1988.

MacKie, Cristine. *Life and Food in the Caribbean*. Kingston, Jamaica: Ian Randle Publishers, 1995.

Marcos, Rafael. *Old Havana Cookbook: Cuban Recipes in Spanish and English*. New York: Hippocrene Books, 1999.

Ortiz, Yvonne. *A Taste of Puerto Rico: Traditional and New Dishes from the Puerto Rican Community*. New York: Plume, 1997.

Rexach, Nilda. *Hispanic Cookbook: Traditional and Modern Recipes in English and Spanish*. Secaucus, NJ: Carol Publishing Group, 1995.

Rivera, Oswald. *Puerto Rican Cuisine in America: Nuyorican-and Bodega Recipes*. New York: Four Walls Eight Windows, 2002.

Romano, Dora de. *Rice and Beans and Tasty Things: A Puerto Rican Cookbook*. Translated by Jamie Romano. Hato Rey, Puerto Rico: Ramallo Bros., 1986.

GENDER

Allatson, Paul. " 'Siempre feliz en mi falda': Luis Alfaro's Simulative Challenge." *GLQ: A Journal of Lesbian and Gay Studies* 5.2 (1999): 199–230.

Almaguer, Tomás. "Chicano Men: A Cartography of Homosexual Identity and Behavior." *Differences: A Journal of Feminist Cultural Studies* 3.2 (1991): 75–100.

Bly, Robert. *Iron John: A Book about Male and Female Archetypes*. New York: Random House Audio Cassette, 1990.

Chávez-Silverman, Susana, and Librada Hernández, eds. *Reading and Writing the Ambiente: Queer Sexualities in Latino, Latin America, and Spanish Culture*. Madison: University of Wisconsin Press, 2000.

Christian, Karen. "Will the 'Real Chicano' Please Stand Up?: The Challenge of John Rechy and Sheila Ortiz Taylor to Chicano Essentialism." *America's Review* 20.2 (1992): 89–104.

Cixous, Hélène. "Castration or Decapitation?" In *Contemporary Literary Criticism: Literary and Cultural Studies*, edited by Robert Con Davis and Ronald Schleifer. New York: Longman, 1989.

Gilbert, Sandra. "Life's Empty Pack: Notes toward a Literary Daughteronomy." In *Contemporary Literary Criticism: Literary and Cultural Studies*, edited by Robert Con Davis and Ronald Schleifer. New York: Longman, 1989.

González, Ray, ed. *Muy Macho: Latino Men Confront Their Manhood*. New York: Anchor Books Doubleday, 1996.

hooks, bell. *Feminist Theory: From Margin to Center*. 2nd ed. Cambridge, MA: South End Press, 2000.

Leeming, David, and Jake Page. *Myths of the Female Divine Goddess*. New York: Oxford University Press, 1994.

Logan, Carolyn, ed. *Counterbalance: Gendered Perspectives for Writing and Language*. Peterborough, Canada: Broadview Press, 1997.

Muñoz, José Esteban. *Disidentifications: Queers of Color and the Performance of Politics*. Minneapolis: University of Minnesota Press, 1999.

Quiroga, José. *Tropics of Desire: Interventions from Queer Latin America*. New York: New York University Press, 2000.

Rebolledo, Tey Diana. *Women Singing in the Snow: A Cultural Analysis of Chicana Literature.* Tucson: University of Arizona Press, 1995.

Tannen, Deborah. *You Just Don't Understand: Women and Men in Conversation.* New York: Ballantine, 1991.

Tannen, Deborah, ed. *Gender and Conversational Interaction.* New York: Oxford University Press, 1993.

Walker, Barbara G. *The Woman's Encyclopedia of Myths and Secrets.* San Francisco, CA: Harper & Row, 1983.

GENERAL

Bhabha, Homi K. *The Location of Culture.* New York: Routledge, 1994.

Darder, Antonia, ed. "The Alternative Grain: Theorizing Chicano/a Popular Culture." In *Culture and Difference: Critical Perspectives on the Bicultural Experience in the United States.* Westport, CT: Bergin and Garvey, 1995.

Dorfman, Ariel. *The Empire's Old Clothes.* New York: Random House, 1983.

Guggelberger, George M. *The Real Thing: Testimonial Discourse and Latin America.* Durham, NC: Duke University Press, 1997.

Kanellos, Nicolás, and Claudio Esteva-Fabregat. *Handbook of Hispanic Cultures in the United States: Literature and Art.* Houston, TX: Arte Público Press, 1993.

Katz, Jane. *This Song Remembers: Self-Portraits of Native Americans in the Arts.* Boston: Houghton Mifflin, 1980.

Sandoval, Chela. *Methodology of the Oppressed.* Minneapolis: University of Minnesota Press, 2001.

Shorris, Earl. *Latinos: A Biography of the People.* New York: W.W. Norton, 1992.

Tardiff, Joseph C., and L. Mpho Mabunda, eds. *Dictionary of Hispanic Biography.* Detroit, MI: Gale Research, 1995.

Unterburger, Amy L., and Jane L. Delgado, eds. *Who's Who among Hispanic Americans 1994–1995.* Detroit, MI: Gale Research, 1994.

Wertham, Frederic. *The Circle of Guilt.* New York: Rinehart and Company, 1956.

http://www.museumca.org.

HISTORY, CHICANA/CHICANO

González, Miguel G. *Mexicanos: A History of Mexicans in the United States.* Bloomington: Indiana University Press, 2000.

Gutiérrez, David G. *Walls and Mirrors: Mexican Americans, Mexican Immigrants and the Politics of Ethnicity.* Berkeley: University of California Press, 1995.

McWilliams, Carey. *North from Mexico: The Spanish-Speaking People of the United States.* 1968. Westport, CT: Greenwood Press, 1990.

HISTORY, CUBAN AMERICAN

Belnap, Jeffrey, and Raúl Fernández, eds. *José Martí's "Our America": From National to Hemispheric Cultural Studies.* Durham, NC: Duke University Press, 1998.

Falk, Pamela. *Cuban Foreign Policy: Caribbean Tempest.* Lexington, MA: D.C. Health, 1986.

Herrera, Andrea O'Reilly. *ReMembering Cuba: Legacy of a Diaspora.* Austin: University of Texas Press, 2001.

Johnson, Haynes B., and Manuel Artime. *The Bay of Pigs: The Leaders' Story of Brigade 2506.* New York: W.W. Norton, 1964.

Levine, Robert M. *Secret Missions to Cuba: Fidel Castro, Bernardo Benes, and Cuban Miami.* New York: Palgrave Press, 2001.

Miller, Tom. *Trading with the Enemy: A Yankee Travels through Castro's Cuba.* New York: Maxwell Macmillan International, 1992.

Thomas, Hugh. *Cuba: The Pursuit of Freedom.* New York: Harper and Row, 1971.

HISTORY, GENERAL LATINA/LATINO

Batalla, Guillermo Bonfil. *México Profundo: Reclaiming a Civilization.* Translated by Philip A. Denis. Austin: University of Texas Press, 1996.

Kanellos, Nicolás, and Cristelia Pérez. *Chronology of Hispanic American History from Pre-Columbian Times to the Present.* Detroit, MI: Gale Research, 1995.

Keller, Gary D., and Cordelia Candelaria, eds. *The Legacy of the Mexican and Spanish-American Wars: Legal, Literary, and Historical Perspectives.* Tempe, AZ: Bilingual Review Press, 2000.

Langley, Lester D. *America and the Americas: The United States in the Western Hemisphere.* Athens: University of Georgia Press, 1989.

Langley, Lester D. *The United States and the Caribbean, 1900–1970.* Athens: University of Georgia Press, 1982.

HISTORY, MEXICAN

Castillo, Isidoro. *Indigenistas de México.* Mexico City: Secretaría de Educación Pública Dirección General de Asuntos Indígenas, 1968.

de la Peña, Guillermo. "Nationals and Foreigners in the History of Mexican Anthropology." In *The Conditions of Recripocal Understanding*, edited by James W. Fernández and Milton B. Singer. Chicago, IL: Center for International Studies, University of Chicago, 1992.

Gámio, Manuel. *The Mexican Immigrant: His Life Story.* Chicago, IL: University of Chicago Press, 1931. Reprinted, Salem, NH: Ayer Company Publishers, 1989.

Marshall, C.E. *The Birth of the Mestizo in New Spain.* Vol. 19 of *Hispanic American Historical Review.* Durham, NC: Duke University Press, 1939.

Vasconcelos, José. *The Cosmic Race: La Raza cósmica.* Los Angeles: Centro de Publicaciones, Department of Chicano Studies, California State University, 1979.

HISTORY, PUERTO RICAN

De Jesús, Joy L., ed. *Growing Up Puerto Rican.* New York: William Morrow and Company Inc., 1997.

Duany, Jorge. *The Puerto Rican Nation on the Move.* Chapel Hill: University of North Carolina Press, 2002.

LANGUAGE

Elgin, Suzette Haden.*The Language Imperative.* Cambridge, MA: Perseus Books, 2000.

Lakoff, George. *Women, Fire, and Dangerous Things: What Categories Reveal about the Mind.* Chicago, IL: University of Chicago Press, 1987.

Lakoff, Robin. *Language and Woman's Place.* New York, NY: Harper and Row, 1975.

Moreas, Marcia. *Bilingual Education: A Dialogue with the Bakhtin Circle.* Albany, NY: State University of New York Press, 1996.

Nilsen, Alleen Pace. *Living Language: Reading, Thinking, and Writing.* Needham Heights, MA: Allyn and Bacon, 1999.

Ramos y Duarte, Felix, *Diccionario de Mexicanismos.* n. p., 1895.

Ronowicz, Eddie, and Colin Yallop. *English: One Language, Different Cultures.* New York, NY: Cassell, 1999.

Rosch, Eleanor, and B. B. Lloyd, eds. *Cognition and Categorization* Hillsdale, NJ: Lawrence Erlbaum, 1978.

Santamaría, Francisco J. *Diccionario de Mejicanismos.* México City: Porrúa, 2000.

Scollon, Ron, and Suzanne Wong Scollon. *Intercultural Communication: A Discourse Approach.* Oxford, England: Blackwell, 1995; also London, England: Blackwell, 2001.

Scollon, Ron, and Suzanne B. K. Scollon. *Narrative, Literacy and Face in Interethnic Communication.* Norwood, NJ: Ablex, 1981.

Spears, Richard. *American Idioms Dictionary.* Lincoln, IL: National Textbook Company, 1987.

Stephens, Thomas M. *Dictionary of Latin American Racial and Ethnic Terminology.* 2nd ed. Gainesville: University Press of Florida, 1999.

Whorf, Benjamin Lee. *Language, Thought, and Reality.* Cambridge, MA: MIT Press, 1956.

LITERATURE, CHICANA/CHICANO

Artéaga, Alfred. *Chicano Poetics: Heterotexts and Hybridities.* Cambridge, England: Cambridge University Press, 1997.

Bruce-Novoa, Juan. "Homosexuality and the Chicano Novel." *Confluencia: Revista Hispánica de Cultura y Literatura* 2.1 (1986): 68–77.

Candelaria, Cordelia. *Chicano Poetry, A Critical Introduction.* Westport, CT: Greenwood Press, 1986.

Candelaria, Cordelia. "Engendering Re/Solutions: The (Feminist) Legacy of Estela Portillo Trambley." In *Decolonial Voices: Chicana/o Cultural Studies in the 21st Century,* edited by Arturo J. Aldama and Naomi Quiñonez. Bloomington: Indiana University Press, 2002.

Candelaria, Cordelia. "Letting La Llorona Go, or Rereading Histories 'Tender Mercies.'" In *Literatura chicana, 1965–1995: An Anthology in Spanish, English, and Caló,* edited by Manuel de Jesús Hernández-Gutiérrez and David William Foster. New York: Garland, 1997.

Candelaria, Cordelia, and Ray González. Vol. 84 of *Dictionary of Literary Biography.* Columbia, SC: Bruccoli Clark Layman, 1993: 55–58.

Candelaria, Cordelia, and Ron Arias. Vol. 82 of *Dictionary of Literary Biography.* Columbia, SC: Bruccoli Clark Layman, 1989: 37–44.

Castillo, Ana. *Massacre of the Dreamers: Essays on Xicanisma.* New York: Penguin, 1995.

Gaspar de Alba, Alicia. *The Mystery of Survival and Other Stories.* Tempe: University of Arizona Press, 1993.

Gaspar de Alba, Alicia. *Sor Juana's Second Dream.* Albuquerque: University of New Mexico Press, 1999.

Giles, James R. "An Interview with John Rechy." *Chicago Review* 25 (1973): 19–31.

González, Rodolfo "Corky." *Soy Joaquín/I Am Joaquín. With a Chronology of People and Events in Mexican and Mexican American History*. 1967. New York: Bantam Books, 1972.

Hoobler, D., and T. Hoobler. *The Mexican American Family Album*. New York: Oxford University Press, 1994.

Jaén, Didier T. "John Rechy." In *Chicano Writers Second Series*, edited by Francisco A. Lomelí and Carl R. Shirley. Detroit, MI: Gale Research, 1992.

Martínez, Julio A., and Francisco A. Lomelí, eds. *Chicano Literature: A Reference Guide*. Westport, CT: Greenwood Press, 1985.

Moraga, Cherríe. *The Last Generation: Prose and Poetry*. Boston: South End Press, 1993.

Pérez-Torres, Rafael. "The Ambiguous Outlaw: John Rechy and Complicitous Homotextuality." In *Fictions of Masculinity: Crossing Cultures, Crossing Sexualities*, edited by Peter F. Murphy. New York: New York University Press, 1994.

Pérez-Torres Rafael. *Movements in Chicano Poetry: Against Myths, Against Margins*. Cambridge, England: Cambridge University Press, 1995.

Rebolledo, Tey Diana. *Women Singing in the Snow: A Cultural Analysis of Chicana Literature*. Tucson: University of Arizona Press, 1995.

Rebolledo, Tey Diana, Erlinda Gonzales-Berry, and Teresa Márquez, eds. *Las mujeres hablan: An Anthology of Nuevo Mexicana Writers*. Albuquerque, NM: El Norte Publications, 1988.

Satterfield, Ben. "John Rechy's Tormented World." *Southwest Review* 67.1 (1982): 78–85.

Tatum, Charles M. "The Sexual Underworld of John Rechy." *Minority Voices* 3.1 (1979): 47–52.

Zamora, Carlos. "Odysseus in John Rechy's City of Night." *Minority Voices* 3.1 (1979): 53–62.

LITERATURE, CUBAN AMERICAN

Martí, José. *Our America*. New York: Monthly Review Press, 1981.

Obejas, Achy. *Memory Mambo*. Pittsburgh, PA: Cleis Press, 1996.

Obejas, Achy. *We Came All the Way from Cuba So You Could Dress Like This?* Pittsburgh, PA: Cleis Press, 1994.

LITERATURE, GENERAL LATINA/LATINO

Brogan, Jacqueline V., and Cordelia Candelaria. *Women Poets of the Americas: Toward a Pan-American Gathering*. Notre Dame, IN: University of Notre Dame Press, 1999.

Candelaria, Cordelia. "*Différance* and the Discourse of 'Community' in Writings by and about the Ethnic Other(s)." In *An Other Tongue: Nation and Ethnicity from the Linguistic Borderlands*, edited by Alfred Artéaga. Durham, NC: Duke University Press, 1994.

Candelaria, Cordelia. "Latina Women Writers: Chicana, Cuban American, and Puerto Rican Voices." In *Handbook of Hispanic Cultures in the United States: Literature and Art*, edited by Francisco Lomelí. Houston, TX: Arte Público Press, 1993.

Candelaria, Cordelia, ed. *Multiethnic Literature of the United States: Critical Introductions and Classroom Resources.* Boulder: University of Colorado Press, 1989.

Dale, Doris Cruger. *Bilingual Children's Books in English and Spanish: An Annotated Bibliography, 1942 through 2001/Los libros bilingües para los niños en inglés y en español: una bibliografía con anotaciones, 1942 a 2001.* Jefferson, NC; London: McFarland & Co., 2003.

Díaz-Quiñones, Arcadio. *La memoria rota.* San Juan, PR: Ediciones Huracán, 1996.

Flores, Juan. "Broken English Memories." In *The Places of History: Regionalism Revisited in Latin America,* edited by Doris Sommer. Durham, NC: Duke University Press, 1999.

Foucault, Michel. "What Is an Author?" In *Contemporary Literary Criticism: Literary and Cultural Studies,* edited by Robert Con Davis and Ronald Schleifer. New York: Longman, 1989.

Gusdorf, Georges. "Conditions and Limits of Autobiography." In *Autobiography: Essays Theoretical and Critical,* translated and edited by James Olney. Princeton, NJ: Princeton University Press, 1980.

Holman, C. Hugh, and William Harmon. *A Handbook to Literature.* 6th ed. New York: Macmillan, 1992.

Jameson, Frederic. "The Politics of Theory: Ideological Positions in the Postmodernism Debate." In *Contemporary Literary Criticism: Literary and Cultural Studies,* edited by Robert Con Davis and Ronald Schleifer. New York: Longman, 1989.

Johnson, Barbara. "The Frame of Reference: Poe, Lacan, Derrida." In *Contemporary Literary Criticism: Literary and Cultural Studies,* edited by Robert Con Davis and Ronald Schleifer. New York: Longman, 1989.

Kevane, Bridget A. *Latino Literature in America.* Westport CT; London: Greenwood Press, 2003.

Lyotard, Jean-François. *Toward the Postmodern.* Edited by Robert Harvey and Mark S. Roberts. Atlantic Highlands, NJ: Humanities Press, 1993.

Olney, James. *Autobiography: Essays Theoretical and Critical.* Princeton, NJ: Princeton University Press, 1980.

Riessman, Catherine Kohler. *Narrative Analysis.* Newbury Park, CA: Sage Publications, 1993.

Said, Edward W. "Reflections on American 'Left' Literary Criticism." In *Contemporary Literary Criticism: Literary and Cultural Studies,* edited by Robert Con Davis and Ronald Schleifer. New York: Longman, 1989.

Saldívar, José David. *Border Matters: Remapping American Cultural Studies.* Berkeley: University of California Press, 1997.

Sanjinés, Javier, C. "Beyond Testimonial Discourse: New Popular Trends in Bolivia (1995)." In *The Real Thing: Testimonial Discourse and Latin America,* edited by George M. Gugelberger. Durham, NC: Duke University Press, 1997.

Schiffrin, Deborah. *Approaches to Discourse.* Oxford, England: Blackwell, 1994.

Schwartz, Peter. *The Art of the Long View: Planning for the Future in an Uncertain World.* New York: Currency Doubleday, 1991.

Tannen, Deborah, ed. *Spoken and Written Language: Exploring Orality and Literacy.* Norwood, NJ: Ablex, 1982.

Valentine, Kristin, and Eugene Valentine. *Interlocking Pieces: Twenty Questions for Understanding Literature*. Dubuque, IA: Kendall Hunt, 1991.

Vogler, Christopher. *The Writer's Journey: Mythic Structure for Storytellers and Screenwriters*. Studio City, CA: Michael Wiese, 1992.

LITERATURE, MEXICAN

Foster, David. *Mexican Literature: A Bibliography of Secondary Sources*. Metuchen, NJ: Scarecrow Press, 1992.

Foster, David. *Mexican Literature: A History*. Austin: University of Texas Press, 1994.

Paz, Octavio. *The Labyrinth of Solitude: Life and Thought in Mexico*. New York: Grove Press, 1961.

LITERATURE, PUERTO RICAN

Algarín, Miguel, and Miguel Piñero, eds. *Nuyorican Poetry: An Anthology of Puerto Rican Words and Feelings*. New York: William Morrow, 1975.

Mohr, Nocholasa. "Puerto Rican Writers in the United States, Puerto Rican Writers in Puerto Rico: A Separation Beyond Language." In *Barrios and Borderlands*, edited by Denis Lynn Daly Heyck. New York: Routledge, 1994.

Santiago, Esmeralda. *Cuando era puertorriqueña*. New York: Vintage, 1994.

MUSIC, CARIBBEAN, CUBAN, PUERTO RICAN

Allen, Ray, and Lois Wilcken, eds. *Island Sounds in the Global City: Caribbean Popular Music and Identity in New York*. New York: New York Folklore Society, 1998.

Glasser, Ruth. *My Music Is My Flag: Puerto Rican Musicians and Their New York Communities 1917–1940*. Berkeley: University of California Press, 1995.

Manuel, Peter. *Caribbean Currents: Caribbean Music from Rumba to Reggae*. Philadelphia: Temple University Press, 1995.

Yanow, Scott. *Afro-Cuban Jazz*. San Francisco: Miller Freeman Books, 2000.

MUSIC, CHICANA/CHICANO

Jaquez, Candida. "Meeting La Cantante through Verse, Song, and Performance." In *Chicana Traditions: Continuity and Change*, edited by Norma Cantú and Olga Nájera-Ramírez. Chicago: University of Chicago Press, 2002.

Loza, Steven. *Barrio Rhythm: Mexican American Music in Los Angeles*. Chicago: University of Illinois Press, 1993.

Paredes, Américo. "The Décima on the Texas-Mexican Border: Folksong as an Adjunct to Legend." *Journal of the Folklore Institute* 3 (August 1966): 154–167.

Peña, Manuel. *The Mexican American Orquesta: Music, Culture, and the Dialectic of Conflict*. Austin: University of Texas Press, 1999.

Reyes, David, and Tom Waldman. *Land of a Thousand Dances: Chicano Rock 'n' Roll from Southern California*. Albuquerque: University of New Mexico Press, 1998.

Villarino, José "Pepe," ed. *Mexican and Chicano Music*. New York: McGraw Hill, 1999.

MUSIC, GENERAL

Amira, John. *The Music of Santería: Traditional Rhythms of the Bata Drums*. Crown Point, IN: White Cliffs Media Company, 1992.

Aparicio, Frances. *Listening to Salsa: Gender, Latin Popular Music, and Puerto Rican Cultures*. Hanover, NH: University Press of New England, 1998.

Barz, Gregory, and Timothy Cooley, eds. *Shadows in the Field: New Perspectives for Fieldwork in Ethnomusicology*. New York: Oxford University Press, 1997.

Behágue, Gerard. "Boundaries and Borders in Latin American Musics: A Conceptual Re-Mapping." *Latin American Music Review* 21.1 (2000): 16–30.

Behágue, Gerard. "Latin American Folk Music." In *Folk and Traditional Music of the Western Continents*, edited by Bruno Nettl. 2nd ed. Englewood Cliffs, NJ: Prentice-Hall, 1973.

Behágue, Gerard. *Music and Black Ethnicity: The Caribbean and South America*. New Brunswick, NJ: Transaction Publishers, 1994.

Boggs, Vernon, ed. *Salsiology: Afro-Cuban Music and the Evolution of Salsa in New York City*. Westport, CT: Greenwood Press, 1992.

Cantú, Norma, and Olga Nájera-Ramírez, eds. *Chicana Traditions: Continuity and Change*. Chicago: University of Illinois Press, 2002.

Harpole, Patricia, and Mark Fogelquist. *Los Mariachis!: An Introduction to Mexican Mariachi Music*. Danbury, CT: World Music Press, 1989.

Lipsitz, George. *Time Passages: Collective Memory and American Popular Culture*. Minneapolis: University of Minnesota Press, 1990.

Loza, Steve. "From Veracruz to Los Angeles: The Reinterpretation of the Son Jarocho." *Latin American Music Review* 13.2 (1992): 179–194.

Mauleón, Rebecca. *Salsa Guidebook for Piano and Ensemble*. Petaluma, CA: Sher Music Company, 1993.

Mendoza, Vicente, and Virginia de Mendoza. *Estudio y clasificación de la música tradicional hispánica de Nuevo México*. Mexico City: Universidad Nacional Autónoma de México, 1986.

Myers, Helen. "North America: 3 Hispanic-American Music." In *Ethnomusicology: Historical and Regional Studies*. New York: W.W. Norton, 1993.

Nevin, Jeff. *Virtuoso Mariachi*. New York: University Press of America, 2002.

Paredes, Américo. *A Texas-Mexican Cancionero: Folksongs of the Lower Border*, 1976. Austin: University of Texas Press, 1995.

Peña, Manuel. *The Mexican American Orquesta: Music, Culture and the Dialectic of Conflict*. Austin: University of Texas Press, 1999.

Peña, Manuel. *The Texas-Mexican Conjunto: History of a Working Class Music*. Austin: University of Texas Press, 1985.

Pérez, Leonor Xochitl. "Transgressing the Taboo: A Chicana's Voice in the Mariachi World." In *Chicana Traditions: Continuity and Change*, edited by Norma Cant and Olga Nójera-Ramírez. Chicago: University of Chicago Press, 2002.

Reyes, David, and Tom Waldmann. *Land of a Thousand Dances: Chicano Rock 'n' Roll from Southern California*. Albuquerque: University of New Mexico Press, 1998.

Roberts, John Storm. *Latin Jazz: The First of the Fusions, 1880s to Today*. New York: Schirmer Books, 1999.

Roberts, John Storm. *The Latin Tinge: The Impact of Latin American Music on the United States*. 2nd ed. New York: Oxford University Press, 1999.

Robertson, Carolina, and Gerard Béhague. "Latin America, III, IV." In *New Grove Dictionary of Music and Musicians*, edited by Sadie Stanley. 2nd ed. New York: Grove's Dictionaries, 2001.

Rodríguez, Sylvia. *The Matachines Dance*. Albuquerque: University of New Mexico Press, 1996.

Romero, Brenda. "The Matachines Music and Dance in San Juan Pueblo and Alcalde, New Mexico: Context and Meanings." Ph.D. dissertation, University of California, Los Angeles, 1993.

Schecter, John, ed. *Music in Latin American Culture: Regional Traditions*. New York: Schirmer Books, 1999.

Sheehy, Daniel. "Mexican Music: Made in the U.S.A." In *Musics of Multicultural Americas*, edited by Kip Lornell and Anne Rasmussen. New York: Macmillan, 1997.

Simonett, Helena. "Narcocorridos in Nuevo L.A." *Ethnomusicology* 45.2 (2001): 315–337.

Stevenson, Robert. *Music in Inca and Aztec Territories*. Berkeley: University of California Press, 1968.

Steward, Sue. *¡Musica! Salsa, Rumba, Merengue, and More*. San Francisco: Chronicle Books, 1999.

Wald, Elijah. *Narcocorrido: A Journey into the Music of Drugs, Guns, and Guerrillas*. New York: HarperCollins, 2001.

Waxer, Lise, ed. *Situating Salsa: Global Markets and Local Meanings in Latin Music*. New York: Routledge, 2002.

MUSIC, MEXICAN

Clark, Jonathan. *Mariachi Tapatío de José Marmolejo "el Auténtico."* Arhooli Folklyric, CD 7012, 1993.

Clark, Jonathan. *Mariachi Vargas de Tecalitlan, Their First Recordings, 1937–1947.* Arhooli Folklyric compact disc 7015, 1992.

Clark, Jonathan, and Philip Sonnichsen. *Mariachi Coculense "Rodriguez" de Cirilo Marmolejo, 1926–1936.* Arhooli Folklyric, CD 7011, 1993.

Flores y Escalanate, Jesús, and Pablo Dueñas Herrera. *Cirilo Marmolejo: Historia del mariachi en la ciudad de México*. Mexico City: Asociación Mexicana de Estudios Fonográficos, 1994.

Fogelquist, Mark. "Mariachi Conferences and Festivals in the United States." In *Inheriting and Sharing, Report of the National Endowment for the Arts*. http://www.arts.endow.gov/pub/Report38/Chapter2.pdf.

Gradante, William. "'El Hijo del Pueblo': José Alfredo Jiménez and the Mexican Canción Ranchera." *Latin American Music Review* 3.1 (1982): 36–59.

Hermes, Rafael. *Los primeros mariachis en la ciudad de México: Guía para el investigador*. Mexico City: n.p., 1999.

Loza, Steven. "From Veracruz to Los Angeles: The Reinterpretation of the *Son Jarocho*." *Latin American Music Review* 13.2 (1992): 179–194.

Stanford, Thomas. "The Mexican Son." In *The Yearbook of the International Folk Music Council*. New York: n.p., 1972.

Yañez Chico, Francisco, and Edgar Gabaldón Márquez. *Historias escogidas del mariachi Francisco Yañez Chico*. Mexico City: J.M. Castañon, 1981.

http://www.tucsoncitizen.com/history_culture/mariachi03/festival/4_24_03mariachi.html.

POPULAR CULTURE

Fernandez, James W., ed. *Beyond Metaphor: The Theory of Tropes in Anthropology*. Stanford, CA: Stanford University Press, 1991.

Hinds, Harold E., Jr., and Charles M. Tatum, eds. *Handbook of Latin American Popular Culture*. Westport, CT: Greenwood Press, 1985.

Mintz, Lawrence E., ed. *Humor in America: A Research Guide to Genres and Topics*. Westport, CT: Greenwood Press, 1988.

Mukerji, Chandra, and Michael Schudson, eds. *Rethinking Popular Culture: Contemporary Perspectives in Cultural Studies*. Berkeley: University of California Press, 1991.

Nachmanovitch, Stephen. *Free Play: Improvisation in Life and Art*. Los Angeles: Jeremy P. Tarcher, 1990.

Nilsen, Alleen Pace, and Don L.F. Nilson. *Encyclopedia of 20th-Century American Humor*. Westport, CT: Greenwood Press, 2000.

Smithsonian Institution Task Force on Latino Issues. *Willful Neglect: The Smithsonian Institution and United States Latinos* (Report of the Smithsonian Task Force on Latino Issues), 1988.

Tatum, Charles M. *Chicano Popular Culture: Que hable el pueblo*. Tucson: University of Arizona Press, 2000.

RACE AND ETHNICITY

Acosta-Belén, Edna. "Hemispheric Remappings: Revisiting the Concept of *Nuestra América*." In *Identities on the Move: Transnational Processes in North America and the Caribbean Basin*, edited by Liliana R. Goldin. Austin: University of Texas Press, 1999.

Bernardi, Daniel, ed. *The Birth of Whiteness: Race and the Emergence of U.S. Cinema*. New Brunswick, NJ: Rutgers University Press, 1996.

Brock, Lisa, and Digna Casteñeda Fuertes, eds. *Between Race and Empire: African-Americans and Cubans before the Cuban Revolution*. Philadelphia: Temple University Press, 1998.

Greenbaum, Susan D. *More Than Black: Afro-Cubans in Tampa*. Gainesville: University Press of Florida, 2002.

Hobson, Geary. "The Rise of the White Shaman as a New Version of Cultural Imperialism." In *The Remembered Earth*, edited by Geary Hobson. Albuquerque, NM: Red Earth Press, 1978.

Oboler, Suzanne. *Ethnic Labels, Latino Lives: Identity and the Politics of (Re)Presentation in the United States*. Minneapolis: University of Minnesota Press, 1995.

Sedillo López, Antoinette. *Historical Themes and Identity: Mestizaje and Labels*. New York: Garland, 1995.

Shah, A.A. *The Rule of Impression Formation, Social Cognition, and Priming, and the Development of Stereotypes*. Frankfurt, Germany: Peter Lang, 1987.

Sommers, Laurie Kay. "Inventing Latinismo: The Creation of Hispanic Panethnicity in the United States." *Journal of American Folklore* 104 (1991): 32–53.

RELIGION

Espinosa, Gastón, Virgilio Elizondo and Jesse Miranda. *Hispanic Churches in American Public Life: Summary of Findings/Iglesias Hispanas en la vida pública americana: resumen de los hallazgos.* Notre Dame, IN: Institute for Latino Studies, University of Notre Dame, 2003.

McNally, Michael J. *Catholicism in South Florida, 1898–1968.* Gainesville: University Press of Florida, 1982.

Sikkink, David, and Edwin I. Hernández, eds. *Religion Matters: Predicting Schooling Success among Latino Youth.* Notre Dame, IN: Institute for Latino Studies, University of Notre Dame, 2003.

Stevens-Arroyo, Anthony M. with Segundo Pantoja, eds. *Discovering Latino Religion: A Comprehensive Social Science Bibliography.* New York: Bildner Center for Western Hemisphere Studies, 1995.

SPORTS

"Baseball Almanac." http://www.baseball-almanac.com/players/player.php?p=alouje 01html.

"BIGLEAGUERS.COM." http://bigleaguers.yahoo.com/mlb/players/4/4517/html.

Bunce, Steve, and Bob Mee. *Boxing Greats.* Philadelphia, PA: Courage Books, 1998.

Candelaria, Cordelia. *Seeking the Perfect Game: Baseball in American Literature.* Westport, CT: Greenwood Press, 1989.

Clemens, Breen. *Great Athletes, the Twentieth Century.* Pasadena, CA: Salem Press Series II, 1992.

Gutman, Bill. *Sammy Sosa: A Biography.* New York: Pocket Books, 1998.

Kawakami, Tim. *Golden Boy: The Fame, Money, and Mystery of Oscar de la Hoya.* Kansas City, MO: Andrews McMeel Publishing, 1999.

Le Compte, Mary. "Any Sunday in April: The Rise of Sport in San Antonio and the Hispanic Borderlands." *Journal of Sports History* 13.2 (1986): 128–146.

Light, Jonathan Fraser. *The Cultural Encyclopedia of Baseball.* Jefferson, NC: McFarland, 1997.

Markusen, Bruce. *Roberto Clemente: The Great One.* Champaign, IL: Sports Publishing, 1998.

McGovern, Mike, ed. *The Encyclopedia of Twentieth-Century Athletes.* New York: Facts on File, 2001.

Porter, David L. *Biographical Dictionary of American Sports: Baseball, Revised and Expanded Edition.* Westport, CT: Greenwood Press, 1987.

Sosa, Sammy, with Marcos Breton. *Sosa: An Autobiography.* New York: Warner Books, 2000.

TELEVISION AND RADIO

Gutierrez, Felix. *Spanish-Language Radio in the Southwestern United States.* Austin: University of Texas Press, 1979.

Veciana-Suárez, Ana. *Hispanic Media, USA: A Narrative Guide to Print and Electronic Hispanic News Media in the United States.* Washington, DC: Media Institute, 1987.

http://en.wikipedia.org/wiki/List_of_Spanish_language_television_channels.

http://www.hispanicbroadcasting.com.

http://www.mediachannel.org.

http://www.ryerson.ca/french/spanish/television/index.html.

http://www.tvtome.com.

http://www.univision.com.

WOMEN

Arizón, Alicia. *Latina Performance Traversing the Stage*. Bloomington: Indiana University Press, 1999.

Candelaria, Cordelia Chávez. "Chicana Girlhood." In *ABC-CLIO Girlhood in America Encyclopedia*. Brunell-Formanek, Miriam, ed. Santa Barbara, CA: ABC-CLIO, June 2001.

Candelaria, Cordelia Chávez. "Chicana Poetry"; "La Llorona"; "La Malinche"; and "Latina Writers." In *Oxford Book of Women's Writing in the United States*. Wagner-Martin, Linda, and Cathy N. Davidson, eds. New York: Oxford University Press, 1994.

Candelaria, Cordelia Chávez. "Constructing a Chicana-Identified 'Wild Zone' of Critical Theory." In *Feminisms: An Anthology of Literary Theory and Criticism*. Herndl, Diane P., ed. Piscataway, NJ: Rutgers University Press, 1997.

Candelaria, Cordelia Chávez. "La Malinche, Feminist Prototype." In *Frontiers Classic Edition: Chicana Studies Reader*. Lincoln: University of Nebraska Press, 2002.

Cantú, Norma E. "La Quinceañera: Towards an Ethnographic Analysis of a Life-Cycle Ritual." *Southern Folklore* 56.1 (1999): 73–101.

Dávalos, Karen Mary. "La Quinceañera: Making Gender and Ethnic Identities." *Frontiers* 16.2–3 (1996): 101–127.

Gonzáles, Silvia. "Chicanas in the National Landscape." *Frontiers: A Journal of Women's Studies* 5.2 (Summer 1980): 55–56.

Herrera-Sobek, Maria. "The Discourse of Love and *Despecho*: Representations of Women in the Chicano *Décima*." *Aztlán* 18.1 (1989): 43–55.

Hewitt, Nancy A. *Southern Discomfort: Women's Activism in Tampa, Florida, 1880s–1920s*. Urbana: University of Illinois Press, 2001.

King, Elizabeth. *Quinceañera: Celebrating Fifteen*. New York: Dutton, 1998.

Kristeva, Julia, and Toril Moi. *The Kristeva Reader*. New York: Columbia University Press, 1986.

Lucas, María Elena. *Forged Under the Sun/Forjada Bajo el Sol: The Life of María Elena Lucas*. Edited by Fran Leeper Buss. Ann Arbor: University of Michigan Press, 1993.

Mani, Lata. "Multiple Mediations: Feminist Scholarship in the Age of Multinational Reception." *Feminist Review* 35 (Summer 1990): 25–41.

Pérez, Emma. *The Decolonial Imaginary: Writing Chicanas into History*. Bloomington: Indiana University Press, 1999.

Prieto, Yolanda. *Women, Work, and Change: The Case of Cuban Women in the United States*. Erie, PA: Institute for Latin American Studies, 1979.

Quintana, Alvina E., ed. *Reading U.S. Latina Writers: Remapping American Literature*. New York: Palgrave Macmillan, 2003.

Saldívar-Hull, Sonia. *Feminism on the Border: Chicana Gender Politics and Literature*. Berkeley: University of California Press, 2000.

Trujillo, Carla, ed. *Chicana Lesbians: The Girls Our Mothers Warned Us About*. Berkeley, CA: Third Woman Press, 1991.

Women of Latin America. Produced by Video Spots and Associates, SA, in association with Spanish Television. Directed by Carmen Sarmiento. 13 videocassettes, 60 minutes each. 1997.

Index